W9-BQL-651

Promising Practices for Urban Reading Instruction

PAMELA A. MASON
Tucker School, Milton Public Schools
Milton, Massachusetts, USA

JEANNE SHAY SCHUMM
University of Miami
Coral Gables, Florida, USA

E D I T O R S

INTERNATIONAL
Reading Association
800 BARKSDALE ROAD, PO BOX 8139
NEWARK, DE 19714-8139, USA
www.reading.org

IRA BOARD OF DIRECTORS
Lesley Mandel Morrow, Rutgers University, New Brunswick, New Jersey, President •
MaryEllen Vogt, California State University Long Beach, Long Beach, California,
President-elect • Richard Allington, University of Florida, Gainesville, Florida, Vice
President • Patricia L. Anders, University of Arizona, Tucson, Arizona • Timothy V.
Rasinski, Kent State University, Kent, Ohio • Ann-Sofie Selin, Cygnaeus School, Åbo,
Finland • Cathy Collins Block, Texas Christian University, Fort Worth, Texas • James
Flood, San Diego State University, San Diego, California • Victoria J. Risko, Peabody
College of Vanderbilt University, Nashville, Tennessee • Charline J. Barnes, University
of Northern Iowa, Cedar Falls, Iowa • Rita M. Bean, University of Pittsburgh,
Pittsburgh, Pennsylvania • Carrice L. Cummins, Louisiana Tech University, Ruston,
Louisiana • Alan E. Farstrup, Executive Director

The International Reading Association attempts, through its publications, to provide
a forum for a wide spectrum of opinions on reading. This policy permits divergent
viewpoints without implying the endorsement of the Association.

Director of Publications   Joan M. Irwin
Editorial Director, Books and Special Projects   Matthew W. Baker
Managing Editor   Shannon Benner
Permissions Editor   Janet S. Parrack
Acquisitions and Communications Coordinator   Corinne M. Mooney
Associate Editor, Books and Special Projects   Sara J. Murphy
Assistant Editor   Charlene M. Nichols
Administrative Assistant   Michele Jester
Senior Editorial Assistant   Tyanna L. Collins
Production Department Manager   Iona Muscella
Supervisor, Electronic Publishing   Anette Schütz
Senior Electronic Publishing Specialist   Cheryl J. Strum
Electronic Publishing Specialist   R. Lynn Harrison
Proofreader   Elizabeth C. Hunt

Project Editor   Shannon Benner
Cover Credits   Design: Linda Steere; Background image: Corbis; Student photographs
(from top): Skjold Photographs, PhotoDisc, Skjold Photographs

Copyright 2003 by the International Reading Association, Inc.

All rights reserved. No part of this publication may be reproduced or transmitted in
any form or by any means, electronic or mechanical, including photocopy, or any
information storage and retrieval system, without permission from the publisher.

Web addresses in this book were correct as of the publication date but may have
become inactive or otherwise modified since that time. If you notice a deactivated
or changed Web address, please e-mail books@reading.org with the words "Website
Update" in the subject line. In your message, specify the Web link, the book title, and
the page number on which the link appears.

Library of Congress Cataloging-in-Publication Data
Promising practices for urban reading instruction / Pamela A. Mason,
Jeanne Shay Schumm, editors.
       p. cm.
Includes bibliographical references.
  ISBN 0-87207-518-4
  1. City children--Education--United States. 2. Reading--United
States. 3. City children--Books and reading--United States. 4.
Education, Urban--Social aspects--United States.. I. Mason, Pamela A.
II. Schumm, Jeanne Shay, 1947- III. International Reading Association.
  LC5128.5.P76 2003
  371.4'09173'2--dc21
                                                              2003013528

Contents

Received
MAY 2004
Acquisitions
C. U. Library

RIGHT 1
Children have a right to appropriate early reading instruction based on their individual needs.

RIGHT 2
Children have a right to reading instruction that builds both the skill and the desire to read increasingly complex materials.

Campbell University Library
Buies Creek, NC 27506

RIGHT 3

Children have a right to well-prepared teachers who keep their skills up to date through effective professional development.

RIGHT 4

Children have a right to access a wide variety of books and other reading material in classroom, school, and community libraries.

Campbell University Library
Belas Creek, NC 27506

RIGHT 5

Children have a right to reading assessment that identifies their strengths as well as their needs and involves them in making decisions about their own learning.

RIGHT 6

Children who are struggling with reading have a right to receive intensive instruction from professionals specifically prepared to teach reading.

RIGHT 7

Children have a right to reading instruction that involves parents and communities in their academic lives.

RIGHT 8

Children have a right to reading instruction that makes meaningful use of their first language skills.

RIGHT 9

Children have the right to equal access to the technology used for the improvement of reading instruction.

RIGHT 10
Children have a right to classrooms that optimize learning opportunities.

Preface

Pamela A. Mason and Jeanne Shay Schumm

Tuesday nights seem somewhat empty now. For months, members of the International Reading Association (IRA) Urban Diversity Initiatives Commission held weekly conference calls to discuss our commission "charges," one of which was to recommend and/or create professional development resources to impact urban education and diversity. To respond to this charge, the commission decided to develop a book. Like most IRA commissions and committees, our work is accomplished with the efforts of volunteer IRA members representing different backgrounds and experiences working long distance with short timelines. What united our commission was a common desire to develop a resource that would "feed the hunger" of administrators, teachers, and teacher educators working in urban settings. Administrators and teachers who plan and implement reading programs in urban settings are hungry to know what works—or at least what has promise for working. Teacher educators who plan and implement professional development in reading share this hunger. *Promising Practices for Urban Reading Instruction* represents the Urban Diversity Initiatives Commission's first step in meeting this hunger—an appetizer if you will.

The importance of the work of the Urban Diversity Initiatives Commission is particularly acute as the reading profession faces the challenge of high-stakes testing and standards-based curricula. As Darling-Hammond and Falk (1997) put it,

> Depending on how standards are shaped and used, either they could support more ambitious teaching and greater levels of success for all students or they could serve to create higher rates of failure for those who are already least well served by the education system. (p. 191)

As we pondered our charges and the challenges that face our profession, the commission's weekly conversations led to four major decisions that shaped the design of this volume. The first decision was to take a look at where the International Reading Association is as a professional organization. Nearly two thirds of all children in the United States live in urban settings. Many of these children live in poverty and face the challenge of learning to read in cultural and linguistic environments that are unfamiliar. What has the Association done to meet this need? In recent years, the Association has published increasing numbers of articles related to urban education and cultural and linguistic diversity. We decided that as a starting point our publication would draw primarily from IRA peer-reviewed publications and would provide the reader with a collection of articles that represent promising practices. We also decided to include an annotated bibliography with a larger range of IRA books and articles related to urban issues (see Appendix B).

Now to the second decision: how best to identify and organize potential articles. We decided that the framework for the volume would be the IRA position statement *Making a Difference Means Making It Different: Honoring Children's Rights to Excellent Reading Instruction*. In this publication, the Association declares that it is time to build reading programs on a set of comprehensive principles that honor children's rights to excellent reading instruction and identifies 10 specific principles that are the right of every child.

How to make those rights a reality for children who attend overcrowded urban schools, for children who do not have access to technology, for children of poverty with limited family resources, and for children of cultural and linguistic backgrounds that are different from the mainstream are the challenges for educating students in the new millennium. The United States, its educational system, and its professional organizations have a moral obligation to make those rights a reality for all children in this country and beyond. We decided to make this volume a first step in identifying promising practices for making the 10 literacy rights a reality.

Our third decision was related to the intended audience. After some debate, we decided to make this publication broad based and, like *Making a Difference Means Making It Different*, make it accessible to the profession as a whole including teachers, administrators, and teacher educators. The intent is to "cover the waterfront" and report promising practices across grade levels. We view *Promising Practices for Urban Reading Instruction* as a gateway piece that will pave the way for subsequent publications related to policy and practice and perhaps to more in-depth publications specific to the elementary and secondary level.

Our fourth decision was to have the publication provide some direction about where we as a field need to go. To accomplish this we decided that each right would be prefaced with a "bridge statement" written by an educator with expertise in the topic addressed in that right and in the supporting articles. Each bridge piece provides an overview of the articles and of the issues related to the right, and addresses the need for future research and development in that area.

This collection includes two or three articles for each of the 10 reading rights. A list of the rights with an overview of each bridge piece follows:

1. **Children have a right to appropriate early reading instruction based on their individual needs.** Dolores B. Malcolm reviews articles profiling three programs focused on early reading instruction: a pull-out program for first graders, a literacy walk initiative to develop awareness of community environmental print, and a family book-loan project. She provides provocative questions about how these programs might be replicated in other settings.

2. **Children have a right to reading instruction that builds both the skill and the desire to read increasingly complex materials.** Patricia Ruggiano Schmidt melds her review of two articles with historical roots in the field of reading and her own experience in urban schools to highlight the promise of balanced literacy instruction for diverse learners.

3. **Children have a right to well-prepared teachers who keep their skills up to date through effective professional development.** William T. Hammond's piece focuses on the importance of teaching reading that is respectful of multiple cultures, and it offers some practical suggestions for preservice and inservice professional development in accomplishing this goal.

4. **Children have a right to access a wide variety of books and other reading material in classroom, school, and community libraries.** Barbara J. Diamond's contribution points out the continued paucity of culturally relevant literature for urban students and provides specific suggestions for professional development of teachers to resolve this dilemma.

5. **Children have a right to reading assessment that identifies their strengths as well as their needs and involves them in making decisions about their own learning.** Janette K. Klingner's review of three articles pertaining to the volatile issue of high-stakes testing provides the reader with a promising perspective for thinking about the impact of assessment on children with cultural and linguistic differences.

6. **Children who are struggling with reading have a right to receive intensive instruction from professionals specifically prepared to teach reading.** David Hernandez summarizes two articles:

one a review of the literature on the role of the reading specialist and one a set of case studies of struggling readers.

7. **Children have a right to reading instruction that involves parents and communities in their academic lives.** Patricia A. Edwards's piece challenges the traditional notion of the lack of literacy in the homes of children who are impoverished and/or are new immigrants. She provides suggestions for how teachers can learn about multiple literacy environments and work with parents in more productive and knowledgeable ways.

8. **Children have a right to reading instruction that makes meaningful use of their first language skills.** Robert S. Rueda's review of three articles on students who are English language learners provides a primer for educators on the role of first language in literacy learning. In addition, he offers suggestions for teachers who do not share a common language with their students in their efforts to value and support the students' linguistic background.

9. **Children have the right to equal access to the technology used for the improvement of reading instruction.** Paola Pilonieta and William E. Blanton provide an overview of issues related to access to technology and literacy. They also highlight examples of programs in urban settings that have promise for shrinking the digital divide between affluent and economically challenged schools.

10. **Children have a right to classrooms that optimize learning opportunities.** Jeanne R. Paratore gives an overview of the literature on the following school characteristics that impact the quality of reading instruction: class size, instructional materials, well-prepared teachers, family and community involvement, and well-maintained buildings. She also reviews three articles that address one or more of these factors. Recognizing the complexity of noninstructional factors, Paratore underscores the promise of collaborative efforts so that "no single teacher, administrator, parent, or school board member can 'go it alone.'"

The commission invited two young scholars, Jennifer D. Turner and Youb Kim, to write an afterword to serve as a capstone piece for this collection. We asked Turner and Kim to reflect on the bridge pieces as well as the collection of articles and to provide insights about a vision for future efforts of the commission and the field in general. The authors framed their piece around issues related to key stakeholder ownership of literacy instruction. The issues they posed as well as their challenges for future efforts in literacy instruction and teacher education provide direction for next steps.

Carmelita Kimber Williams and Richard Long provided an overview of the Urban Diversity Initiatives Commission's mission and accomplishments.

Lina Lopez Chiappone summarized more than 70 IRA books and articles in an annotated bibliography of work published since 1990. This collection of resources represents IRA's strong commitment to urban education, which we hope will serve as a springboard for future research.

Finally, William T. Hammond contributed a list of websites that provide additional information about issues and promising practices in urban reading instruction.

We think readers will agree that *Promising Practices for Urban Reading Instruction* is indeed an appetizer. The volume clearly demonstrates IRA's commitment to disseminating research and instructional practices for improving the quality of education for students in urban settings. But we have a long way to go before our hunger can be satisfied. We encourage our colleagues in research to continue seeking answers and to find ways to bring research into practice. We encourage our colleagues in administration and in the classroom to continue sharing what works in your settings. We encourage parents, community leaders, and students to raise their voices and lend their hands to help students grasp the gift of literacy. With these collective efforts, a second edition of this volume can find us closer to making the rights a reality for all.

Acknowledgments

This publication has truly been a collaborative effort, and we have many people to acknowledge. Carmelita Williams first had the vision of founding the International Reading Association's Urban Diversity Initiatives Commission. Carmelita and Donna Ogle have been enormously supportive as we have planned and developed this publication. Rich Long, IRA Director of Government Relations, has served as a catalyst to keep things going and served as a cheerleader along the way. As cochairs of the commission, Bill Hammond and Dave Hernandez have been involved with every step of the book's development. Members of the commission participated in our Tuesday night discussions and many served as authors of bridge pieces; we thank each of the bridge piece authors. Matt Baker, IRA Editorial Director of Books and Special Projects, has provided us with important suggestions for revisions and additions. We would like to thank our editor, Shannon Benner, for making sure that all of the parts of this book fit together well. We are enormously grateful to have had this opportunity to work with our colleagues at IRA, both commission members and staff.

Finally, we would like to reflect a bit about our own collaboration as an editorial team. We met over the telephone and agreed to coedit this book without ever meeting each other face-to-face. We have now have met twice in Boston and several times at IRA meetings and conferences and know that we have a "professional sisterhood" that would never have occurred without this opportunity. We have found this experience to be helpful in our own work as school-based educators and teacher educators. Our hope is that this publication will be helpful to our colleagues who are trying to bring the best of reading instruction to children in urban school settings and that it will provide a road map for future work. Our Tuesday nights now may be somewhat empty, but we hope that this book fills your Tuesday nights and many other days and nights with inspiration, insights, and initiatives that will enhance the literacy instruction in our urban schools.

REFERENCE

Darling-Hammond, L., & Falk, B. (1997). Using standards and assessments to support student learning. *Phi Delta Kappan, 79*(3), 190–199.

Contributors

Pamela A. Mason is the principal of the Tucker School (K–5) in Milton, Massachusetts, USA, where she focuses her attention on her students' developing literacy skills in English, French, and Spanish and on meeting high academic standards. She has held principalships in other urban and suburban school districts, in addition to serving as the reading/language arts coordinator (K–5) in the Boston Public Schools. Mason is also a visiting assistant professor in the Literacy and Language Department of Framingham State College in Massachusetts. Her professional interests are in the student achievement gap and how teacher training can eliminate it. She is cochair of the IRA Urban Diversity Initiatives Commission.

Jeanne Shay Schumm is Professor and Chair of the Department of Teaching and Learning at the University of Miami in Coral Gables, Florida, USA. She teaches graduate courses in reading and serves as Professor in Residence at F.S. Tucker Elementary School, a University of Miami Professional Development School. Her research interests include literacy instruction in urban settings, particularly classrooms that include English language learners and students with reading and learning disabilities. She currently serves as coprincipal investigator on the South Florida Annenberg Challenge Program Evaluation and Project SUCCEED, a teacher quality enhancement project.

William E. Blanton is Professor of Education at the University of Miami, Florida, in the School of Education, Department of Teaching and Learning. He has been a teacher in public and private elementary schools and has been a professor in residence in an urban school in Miami for the past three years. Currently he is a principal investigator of the Fifth Dimension distributed literacy consortium, principal investigator of an in-depth study of the University of Miami Professional Development Schools, and a coordinator of the Fifth Dimension Clearinghouse. His current research is on the application of cultural-historical activity theory to reading comprehension and the preparation of reading teachers.

Lina Lopez Chiappone has taught language arts and reading to culturally and linguistically diverse students in a dropout prevention program in Miami-Dade County Public Schools. She is currently completing a dissertation investigating the use of CD-ROM technology to support reading comprehension for English language learners. As a graduate assistant, she has been a part of several research projects related to preservice teacher education, research-based literacy practices, and program evaluation. She is also an adjunct professor at the University of Miami, teaching several courses in teaching English to speakers of other languages.

Barbara J. Diamond is Professor Emerita of Literacy at Eastern Michigan University, Ypsilanti, Michigan, USA, and also had been a teacher and a reading consultant. Diamond's area of expertise is in issues of multicultural literacy. She has collaborated with three school districts to codirect the multicultural literacy program that received the National Christa McAuliffe Award for Excellence in Applied Research from the American Association of State Colleges and Universities. Diamond has published a book and several articles on multicultural literacy and continues to write and serve as a consultant with the Comer School Development Project in her retirement.

Patricia A. Edwards is Professor of Language and Literacy at Michigan State University in East Lansing, Michigan, USA, where she teaches, writes, and conducts research in the areas of family/intergenerational literacy and connections between home and school literacies. She is the author of two nationally acclaimed family literacy programs: *Parents as Partners in Reading: A Family Literacy Training Program* (1993) and *Talking Your Way to Literacy: A Program to Help Nonreading Parents Prepare Their Children for Reading* (1990). Edwards is a former member of the International Reading Association Board of Directors and currently serves on IRA's Urban Diversity Initiatives Commission and on the Urban Partnership Task Force, a collaboration of IRA and the National Urban Alliance to improve literacy instruction in urban schools.

William T. Hammond is currently a literacy coordinator with the DeKalb County Schools in the state of Georgia, USA. Hammond has been a high school and middle school teacher, a college instructor, and Coordinator of Reading for the Georgia Department of Education. He is an active member of the International Reading Association at the local, state, and national levels, the National Council of Teachers of English, the National Alliance of Black School Educators, and the National Association of Black Reading and Language Arts Educators. He is cochair of the IRA Urban Diversity Initiatives Commission.

David Hernandez III is currently a sixth-grade teacher at Rio Vista Elementary School in Avondale, Arizona, USA. He has taught and been a principal in other urban and rural communities. David also is cochair of the IRA Urban Diversity Initiatives Commission. His professional interests include working with diverse families in helping them to better understand the importance reading, promoting literacy in the community, and helping leaders and educators understand the importance of working in the minority community to promote literacy.

Youb Kim is a Ph.D. candidate in Curriculum, Teaching, and Instruction at Michigan State University, East Lansing, Michigan, USA. She specializes in research on English as a second language literacy, language learning, and assessment. She has taught courses on multiculturalism and on literacy and language learning in the teacher preparation program. She recently accepted an assistant professor position at Vanderbilt University.

Janette K. Klingner is an associate professor at the University of Colorado, Boulder, in the School of Education, Department of Educational Equity and Cultural Diversity. She was a bilingual special education teacher for 10 years before earning a Ph.D. in Reading and Learning Disabilities from the University of Miami in Florida. She was the professor in residence in an urban school in Miami for five years. Currently she is a coprincipal investigator for the National Center for Culturally Responsive Educational Systems.

Richard Long is Director of Government Relations for the International Reading Association. He is based in Washington, D.C., and works on a wide range of national and international literacy issues affecting children and adults. Since IRA created the Urban Diversity Initiatives Commission, he has been the lead staff person on the project. In that roll he has overseen the creation of an Urban Deans' Network, the Urban Academies Program, the Urban Partnership for Literacy, and other projects. He has worked as a national representative for Title I, as well as a counselor in an urban mental health outreach center and at a university reading center.

Dolores B. Malcolm is the Director of Curriculum/Instruction/Professional Development and Programs for the St. Louis Public Schools in St. Louis, Missouri, USA. Her professional interests are in promoting a literacy based curriculum across content areas, and in full implementation of professional development for all staff. As a long-standing member of the International Reading Association she has held many local, state, and national offices and committee positions. She is also a former member of the IRA Board of Directors and is past president (1995–1996) of the Association.

Jeanne R. Paratore is Associate Professor of Education at Boston University in Massachusetts, USA. She has served as a classroom teacher, reading consultant, director of Title I, and university professor. As an integral member of the Boston University/Chelsea, Massachusetts School Partnership, Paratore had many opportunities to collaborate with classroom teachers to improve classroom assessment and instruction of literacy. Paratore founded and now serves as advisor to the Intergenerational Literacy Project, a family literacy program that serves immigrant parents and their children. She is a former member of the Board of Directors of the International Reading

Association and currently serves on both IRA's Urban Diversity Initiatives Commission and Urban Partnership Task Force, a collaboration between IRA and the National Urban Alliance to improve literacy instruction in urban schools.

Paola Pilonieta is currently a first-grade teacher in an urban school and is working on her doctorate at the University of Miami in Florida. She is completing a dissertation exploring the need for a balance between expository and narrative texts in basal readers. While a graduate student at the University of Miami, she supervised preservice teachers assigned to urban elementary schools and has taught language arts and reading methods to undergraduate and graduate students. She also has been a part of several research projects involving professional development, phonological awareness, and other research-based literacy practices.

Robert S. Rueda is a professor in the Rossier School of Education at the University of Southern California in Los Angeles, California, USA. His research interests center on the sociocultural basis of learning as mediated by instruction, with a focus on reading and literacy in English learners, students in at-risk conditions, and students with mild learning handicaps. He is affiliated with two major national research centers—CREDE (Center for Excellence, Diversity, and Education at the University of California at Santa Cruz) and CIERA (Center for the Improvement of Early Reading Achievement at the University of Michigan)—and is currently serving as a member of a U.S. national literacy panel looking at issues in early reading with English language learners.

Patricia Ruggiano Schmidt is Associate Professor of Literacy at Le Moyne College, Syracuse, New York, USA. Her 25 years of teaching in elementary and middle schools and her research interests in urban education give her many insights into literacy learning and instruction. Most of her articles and books revolve around the preparation of teachers for classroom diversity. During the last 10 years, she has designed the ABC's of Cultural Understanding and Communication, a model used for teacher preparation in the United States and Europe. She recently received IRA's Elva Knight Research Grant, which recognizes and encourages the continuance of her literacy research in urban settings.

Jennifer D. Turner is a recent graduate of the Ph.D. program in Educational Psychology at Michigan State University in East Lansing, Michigan, USA, and is a 2001–2002 AERA Minority Dissertation Fellow. Presently, she is an assistant professor in the Department of Curriculum and Instruction at the University of Maryland. She has coauthored several book chapters as well as articles in *The Reading Teacher* and the *National Reading Conference Yearbook*. Her research interests include urban education, multiculturalism and literacy instruction, and teacher education.

Carmelita Kimber Williams is Professor Emerita of Norfolk State University where she served as Chair of the Reading Department, Director of the Children's Reading Partners' Clinic, and more recently as Director of the Center for Excellence in University Teaching. She also served as Campus Coordinator for the Reading Is Fundamental Program for more than 21 years. Williams is a past president of the Norfolk Reading Council, the Virginia State Reading Association, and the International Reading Association. She is presently a member of IRA's Urban Diversity Initiatives Commission. Williams, who began her career as a first-grade teacher, now works as an education consultant and as a speaker to schools and professional organizations focusing on reading and language arts.

International Reading Association
Urban Diversity Initiatives Commission

Note: This commission will serve until May 2006.

William T. Hammond, Cochair
DeKalb County Schools
Decatur, Georgia, USA

David Hernandez, Cochair
Rio Vista Elementary School
Avondale, Arizona, USA

Pamela A. Mason, Cochair
Tucker School
Milton, Massachusetts, USA

Cathy Collins Block, Board Liaison
Texas Christian University
Fort Worth, Texas, USA

Janice F. Almasi
State University of New York
   at Buffalo
Buffalo, New York, USA

Eric J. Cooper
National Urban Alliance
Stamford, Connecticut, USA

Patricia A. Edwards
Michigan State University
East Lansing, Michigan, USA

Darion M. Griffin
American Federation of Teachers
Washington, DC, USA

Abha Gupta
Old Dominion University
Norfolk, Virginia, USA

Etta R. Hollins
University of Southern California
Los Angeles, California, USA

Mary R. Hoover
Howard University
Washington, DC, USA

Sheldon Horowitz
National Center for Learning
   Disabilities
New York, New York, USA

Phyllis C. Hunter
Phyllis C. Hunter Consulting, Inc.
Sugar Land, Texas, USA

Barbara Ann Kapinus
National Education Association
Hyattsville, Maryland, USA

Sarah D. Lang
Norfolk State University
Virginia Beach, Virginia, USA

Dolores B. Malcolm
St. Louis Public Schools
St. Louis, Missouri, USA

Irving P. McPhail
Community Colleges of Baltimore
  County
Baltimore, Maryland, USA

Eileen S. Oboler
Spring Hill College
Mobile, Alabama, USA

Jeanne R. Paratore
Boston University
Boston, Massachusetts, USA

Elizabeth V. Primas
Educational Testing Service
Washington, DC, USA

Robert S. Rueda
University of Southern California
Los Angeles, California, USA

Patricia R. Schmidt
Le Moyne College
Syracuse, New York, USA

Jeanne Shay Schumm
University of Miami
Coral Gables, Florida, USA

Carmelita Kimber Williams
Norfolk State University
Virginia Beach, Virginia, USA

Alan Farstrup, Ex Officio
IRA Executive Director
Newark, Delaware, USA

Richard Long, Ex Officio
IRA Director of Government
  Relations
Washington, DC, USA

Cathy Roller, Ex Officio
IRA Director of Research and Policy
Newark, Delaware, USA

Brenda S. Townsend, Ex Officio
IRA Director of Council and Affiliate
  Services
Newark, Delaware, USA

RIGHT 1

Children have a right to appropriate

early reading instruction based on

their individual needs.

Introduction

Dolores B. Malcolm

n its position statement *Using Multiple Methods of Beginning Reading Instruction* (1999), the International Reading Association states that there is no single method or single combination of methods that can successfully teach all children to read. The summary in the piece further states that because support for various methods has created a "bandwagon" effect, with one or another being embraced as the "one right method," beginning reading instruction has been surrounded by controversy. Earlier research supports the Association's position. For example, in "The Cooperative Research Program in First-Grade Reading Instruction" (Bond & Dykstra, 1967/1997), better known as the First-Grade Studies, data compiled from 27 individual studies of differing approaches to beginning reading found none superior to others. In *Beginning to Read: Thinking and Learning About Print* (Adams, 1990), the author states that it is not just a variety of activities, but many pieces fitting together to support and complement one another based on the needs of the child, that is the key to beginning reading instruction.

The principle expressed in Right 1—children have a right to appropriate early reading instruction based on their individual needs—substantiates these studies and lays the foundation for the focus of the three complementary articles in this section. Common ground among the authors supports the following premises:

♦ Experiences must be integrated with personal meaning.

♦ Explicit (direct) instruction is important for beginning readers.

♦ Early intervention is crucial to success of children throughout school years.

♦ Teachers are critical to addressing individual needs.

♦ Print-rich environments provide a source of literacy learning.

♦ Diversity of age, gender, ethnicity, and social class has implications for literacy learning.

♦ It is important to build on prior knowledge.

♦ Understanding of students' lives is the basis for motivating them to read.

The article by Wanda B. Hedrick and Alice B. Pearish focuses on a successful supplemental pull-out program in which a small group of first graders received intensive, paced, temporary intervention to enhance their regular classroom instruction. Contrary to many unsuccessful pull-out programs, the model combines aspects from various programs—Reading Recovery, balanced literacy, and portfolio documentation—into a daily lesson over a fast-paced period of time. To determine the feasibility of further study of this model for your setting, several questions should be addressed:

- How will students compensate for work missed in their absence from the classroom?
- Is specialized teacher training necessary to prepare teachers to deliver the instruction?
- What resources are available and what additional resources are needed to implement the program?
- What assessments are accessible for placement of students into the literacy group?
- What level of collaboration is necessary between the literacy teacher and the classroom teacher?

Language in the home and the neighborhood community provides the basis for studies in the Orellana and Hernández and Yaden et al. articles.

Marjorie Faulstich Orellana and Arcelia Hernández urge teachers to capitalize on the print-rich environment of the students' community as optimal opportunities for literacy lessons. The words in the immediate home surroundings (e.g., street names, graffiti) generated discussion and writing to motivate learning, with an ever-present caution that not all students were motivated by the same print. The community literacy walk only became meaningful when connections to personal or family experience were present. This allowed the students to integrate literacy across subject areas and mediums. The authors also present questions regarding adaptability to other educational communities:

- How does my classroom interpret the word *community*?
- What environmental print is meaningful for my classroom?
- How does the print build understanding of students' social worlds?
- How does the curriculum connect me to the lives of my students?
- Where in the community can students' print be displayed?

The piece by David B. Yaden and his colleagues features support for an early intervention language literacy and family book-loan program that increased both the behavior and attitude of preschool-age children toward awareness of books, but more important it increased emergent literacy skills. The appropriateness of this intervention speaks to the language and educational barriers of preschoolers when English is not the language in the home and when the parents have less formal education to associate printed resources with literacy development. The combination of a shared reading program, development of writing centers, a book-lending library, and parent workshops served as the components of the program. The results indicated that the program also dually raised the appreciation for books in the home environment and enhanced the knowledge of the parents.

Essential questions to address for replication of this program are,

◆ What language interactions are taking place in the homes of the children you serve?

◆ What are the relationships between the preschool and regular educational programs in the school district?

◆ What resources are available to establish a lending library?

◆ What parent support mechanisms are in place to develop the lending library component?

The first principle in honoring children's right to appropriate early reading instruction stresses the approach of taking each individual from where she is and moving her to where she needs to be. Instruction and classroom resources must be flexible and rich enough to provide for individualization of all student populations—those with special needs, those who are English language learners, as well as those who have advanced skills and knowledge. At the same time this learning must embrace the wider community beyond the schools. IRA's position statement on multiple methods of reading instruction concludes that the beginning reading controversy cannot be settled by prescribing a single method. Because there is no clearly documented best way to teach beginning reading, teachers or reading specialists who are familiar with a wide range of methodologies and who are closest to the children must be the ones to make the decisions about what reading instruction to use. As professionals they also must have the flexibility to modify those methods based on responses to the essential questions that were posed earlier in this piece.

REFERENCES

Adams, M.J. (1990). *Beginning to read: Thinking and learning about print*. Cambridge, MA: MIT Press.

Bond, G.L., & Dykstra, R. (1997). The cooperative research program in first-grade reading instruction. *Reading Research Quarterly, 32*, 348–427. (Original article published 1967)

Hedrick, W., & Pearish, A.B. (1999). Good reading instruction is more important than who provides the instruction or where it takes place. *The Reading Teacher, 52*, 716–726.

Orellana, M.F., & Hernández, A. (1999). Talking the walk: Children reading urban environmental print. *The Reading Teacher, 52*, 612–619.

Yaden, D.B., Tam, A., Madrigal, P., Brassell, D., Massa, J., Altamirano, L.S., et al., (2000). Early literacy for inner-city children: The effects of reading and writing interventions in English and Spanish during the preschool years. *The Reading Teacher, 54*, 186–189.

Good Reading Instruction Is More Important Than Who Provides the Instruction or Where It Takes Place

Wanda B. Hedrick and Alice B. Pearish

"Look out, honey!" Ms. Pearish exclaimed, as she observed a little girl almost running into the wall while walking with a book pulled close to her face. The second grader missed the wall but continued to read as she carried her new library book back to her classroom. The teacher spoke to Joel, a visiting college student, who was walking with her. "She was in my literacy group last year. Many of her classmates were reading independently, but she was one of the ones who could not participate since she couldn't read the simplest text without support." Ms. Pearish explained that literacy group was a small group of first graders who were given supplemental reading instruction.

"So how did you support her in your literacy group?" Joel asked. "In my education classes I've read criticisms of pull-out programs. I'm confused since you're telling me you can pull the children out of class and it helps them. I think one of the criticisms concerns what they may be missing while they're out of the room. Isn't that a problem?"

"The goal of the literacy group is to help them eventually participate in the independent reading in the classroom, so I don't see it as a problem since it is temporary. We use the pull-out group time to give the children quick-paced practice at the things they need but haven't grasped yet. Mainly, they are not able to flexibly use the various cueing systems presented to them in books such as contextual support in text and pictures or letter-symbol relationship." Ms. Pearish continued, "The pull-out group is considered a temporary, early intervention to help them benefit from classroom instruction."

Raising his eyebrows in contemplation, Joel postulated, "So the kind of instruction children receive is really what it's all about as opposed to where or who delivers that instruction."

Ms. Pearish nodded and said, "Don't forget that the main thing is to provide good reading instruction for children." She then gestured good-bye as Joel went into Ms. Salazar's second-grade classroom to observe for his field-

Originally published in *The Reading Teacher* (1999), volume 52, pages 716–726.

based course requirement. Ms. Pearish smiled and briskly walked back down the hall toward her own classroom.

Pull-Out Programs

Traditional pull-out programs have lost favor among educators because they have not produced encouraging results (Spiegel, 1995). Allington and McGill-Franzen (1989) and O'Sullivan, Ysseldyke, Christenson, and Thurlow (1990) contend that these traditional programs focus on lower level skills and give children limited opportunity to read connected text. Moreover, these pull-out programs lack connections with the regular classroom instruction and may even compete with it (Spiegel, 1995). Children in these groups may miss reading and writing opportunities in their classrooms, so these pull-out programs (including Title I and special education) not only provide very little reading experience but also limit children's writing experiences (Allington & Walmsley, 1995). Finally, children may become "trapped" in a pull-out, special program cycle throughout their entire elementary school years (Allington & Cunningham, 1996).

Yet, in recent years, some programs have shown promise. For example, Reading Recovery (RR) has consistently demonstrated success in helping at-risk first graders become independent readers (Pinnell, DeFord, & Lyons, 1994). In RR, first-grade children are pulled out of class for 30 minutes daily over a 10- to 20-week term. In reported studies (Clay, 1990; Lyons, Pinnell, & DeFord, 1993), children in this program have improved enough to be discontinued. In a recent book, Allington and Cunningham (1996) argue that "special programs aren't special enough" (p. 18). Yet, in that same volume they discuss the success of Reading Recovery. They concede that while RR "does remove children from the classroom...it is only for a short time and the goal is rapid return to the classroom with the original problem successfully resolved" (p. 33).

Hiebert (1994) described a small-group design in which Title I teachers and their assistants worked with groups of three first graders each for the first half of first grade and then switched groups for the remainder of the first grade. Although this was not an experimental design, at the end of the first-grade year, teachers documented that more than 50% of the participating children could read at the first-grade level and another 25% could read at the primer level.

An extension of that small-group program was described recently by Taylor, Hanson, Justice-Swanson, and Watts (1997). In that program, second-grade children participated in an intervention program offered as enrichment class twice during the school year. Their program lasted for seven weeks in the fall and another seven weeks in the spring, with daily sessions of 45 minutes each. The building reading coordinator conducted the sessions with the children in the first year, not the regular classroom teacher. In addition to the small-group pull-out portion of the intervention, the second graders in the fall sessions received one-on-one peer tutoring from fourth-grade children. From their results, Taylor et al. demonstrated that the combination of small-group pull-out and one-on-one peer tutoring produced significant differences from the control group that received no enrichment. The following year, the program continued, but regular classroom teachers delivered the instruction while the rest of the class read independently. This variation of the design also produced encouraging results, although not as high as the pull-out program the previous year.

The Reading Recovery model and small-group models such as the ones described by Hiebert (1994) and Taylor et al. (1997) indicate that pulling children out of their regular classroom for instruction can produce positive results. If this is true, then we need to examine the common principles that might guide us in developing successful programs. In addition, we need to see practical applications of these principles and look at the results associated with their implementation.

One of the problems with traditional pull-out programs may simply reflect a greater dilemma within literacy programs in general. The predicament is in the continual pendulum swings back and forth between the four major approaches to beginning reading; that is, "phonics, basal, literature and language experience/writing" (Cunningham, 1991, p. 579). As each approach fails to teach some children how to read, curriculum decision makers tend to change instructional approaches. Unfortunately, as time reveals, the newly adopted approach also demonstrates weakness, and the swing back to a variation of the earlier approach occurs. Adams's (1990) review of beginning reading research and Bond and Dykstra's conclusions from the results of the 1960s First Grade Studies (as cited in Cunningham, 1991) should influence decision makers to design early reading programs that are a mixture of the major reading approaches. Spiegel (1992) specifically called for a blending of whole language with direct instruction.

Acting upon the need for a blending of rival approaches to beginning reading instruction, Cunningham (1991) created a whole-class language arts framework that provided a balance between more traditional reading instruction and the constructivist orientation toward literacy instruction. The traditional component to reading instruction included guided reading with a basal and direct phonics block, while the constructivist component used the writing process and children's literature with a focus on meaning. The design of the small-group pull-out program described here began with the same basic premise as Cunningham's multimethod model. Both programs provide a balance of reading and writing activities with some direct instruction in letter-sound patterns.

Spiegel (1995) proposed 15 guidelines based upon the Reading Recovery model that, if followed, were likely to make traditional remedial programs more successful. Briefly, those guidelines include early intervention, focusing on comprehending of connected text, having children spend time actually reading, promoting children's and teacher's understanding of instructional goals, providing children with opportunity to learn, providing children with reading material at their instructional level, the teaching of strategies and how to use those strategies in new situations, writing as an integral part of the reading instruction, phonemic awareness instruction, congruency with the regular classroom, direct instruction, individualization, monitoring and reinforcing of children's literacy attempts, having the best teachers deliver instruction to the most in need, and accelerating the progress of the children. If pull-out programs follow these guidelines, positive results should occur.

In this article, we describe a pull-out program developed at Schulze Elementary School and evaluate it using the guidelines outlined by Spiegel (1995) and supported by various other reading theorists and practitioners. The article is a description of how the second author taught small groups of children in first grade. The first author observed and documented the program.

The School Context

Schulze, located in San Antonio, Texas, USA, is a pre-K–5 school. The school serves a population that is 98% Hispanic, with more than 85% of the children qualifying for free or reduced-price lunches. Although most of the children speak English, many of their homes are bilingual, with Spanish also spoken.

Each first-grade teacher (including one bilingual classroom) sent a group of children from the classroom each day during the independent reading portion of their 60-minute reading program. Each literacy group met with Ms. Pearish for 30 minutes daily over the course of their first-grade year.

Selection for Group Membership

Intervention began early in the children's reading development as advocated by many reading experts (e.g., Pikulski, 1994; Pinnell, 1989; Snow, Burns, & Griffin, 1998; Spiegel, 1995; Taylor & Hiebert, 1994). At the beginning of the school year, the first-grade teachers composed a list of the children in their classrooms and prioritized them beginning with those most in need in reading. The kindergarten teachers of these children also provided a similar list at the end of the children's kindergarten year. In addition to these lists, the Reading Recovery (RR) teachers tested each child using the Observational Survey (Clay, 1993a). Combining the first-grade and kindergarten teachers' rankings with the testing battery, the teachers assigned the lowest ranking children to be served by a one-on-one program and the next highest rankings to a literacy group setting. Throughout the year, new children were tested upon entering the school to determine their priority level in comparison to the children already attending the school and were placed accordingly. This careful placement of children based on their demonstrated needs supports the principles put forth by Spiegel (1995) calling for programs to individualize and to use the best-prepared teachers to deliver the instruction. A program that matches expert instruction to individual needs is more likely to produce the accelerated progress needed to help children close the gap from where they are to where they need to be.

The Literacy Group Format

The literacy group design took advantage of the most efficient use of the teacher's time (McCormick, 1995). The teacher maintained a brisk pace during the literacy group lessons. In order to accelerate their progress, the groups needed a fast-paced, tightly structured and balanced instructional lesson each day.

Ms. Pearish limited the groups to no more than eight children per 30-minute session. Classroom teachers released the children from their classroom during independent reading time while their higher achieving peers practiced what they had already learned. This provided these children with more opportunity to learn (Spiegel, 1995). Literacy group supplemented the teacher's reading instruction; the classroom teacher continued to maintain the responsibility of providing reading instruction to these children. In the classroom, the children's teachers encouraged the children to practice the strategies taught in literacy group time, thus making the learning congruent with the regular classroom.

Each day, Ms. Pearish selected and conducted activities based upon a combination of support in the literature, her own personal experience as a classroom teacher, and her training as a Reading Recovery teacher. The carefully chosen activities focused on having the children comprehend, analyze, and write about connected text (Clay, 1991) and included direct letter-sound instruction (Adams, 1990). The group time balanced these literacy activities and paced them in order to fit all of them into the limited time frame (see Figure).

The components of each lesson included read-alouds, phonics (specifically letter-names strip, letter-sound cards, Word Wall, and remaking words), shared reading (interactive story chart), guided reading and pocket chart activities, writing aloud/shared writing (specifically sentence structure) and guided writing, and independent or self-selected reading. In the Figure, we show the order of the lesson components and the approximate times required for each. Setting established routines minimized the wasting of valuable instructional time.

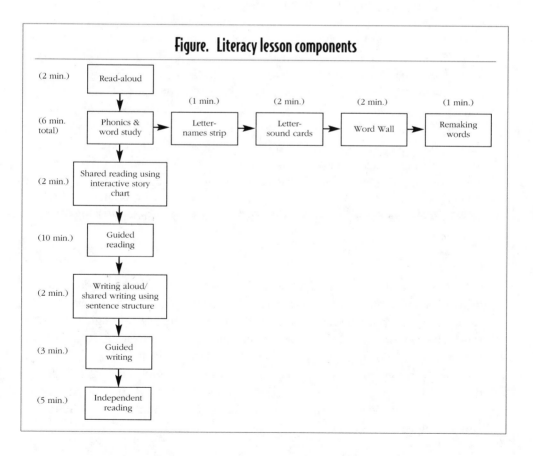

Figure. Literacy lesson components

Read-Alouds

Upon entering the room, the children sat down quickly, and the teacher engaged them in oral language as they interacted while listening to her read a new book. She used short, leveled books with repetitive texts for read-alouds so that the children could easily pick up the language patterns. Providing experience with book language is especially important for children whose experiences with literary language are limited for whatever reason (Heath, 1982). Reading books aloud and discussing these stories with children help them understand about concepts such as plot and characters (Anderson, Hiebert, Scott, & Wilkinson, 1985) as well as enhance their ability to comprehend more complex syntax (Chomsky, 1972). To achieve as readers, however, children must participate in reading themselves rather than only being read to by the teacher (Meyer, Wardrop, Stahl, & Linn, 1994). Therefore, the teacher limited time spent on read-alouds to a brief two minutes and read aloud from books at the children's instructional reading level or easier. While reading the book aloud, she promoted interaction by sitting close to the small groups of children and allowing them to see the text as she read. Sometimes she would purposely slow down and point to a word as she read it aloud to let the children's eyes focus on the letters that composed the word. The teacher encouraged children to join in on the reading as they detected the repetitive language of the text. She also used read-alouds as an occasion to point out to the children that the language found in books differs from the language used in conversations. Afterward, she placed multiple copies of the book read aloud in a basket so the children had the opportunity to select it during the independent reading activity. Formerly read books stayed in the baskets also. This allowed the children to better examine the text directly themselves and to read it independently.

Phonics

Next, to help children understand how words work, the teacher guided them to work with isolated parts of language such as the alphabet and words or word parts. The purpose for these activities is the same as Cunningham and Hall's (1996) word block, the letter identification part of a Reading Recovery lesson (Clay, 1985), and other programs that include direct teaching of phonics (e.g., Bear, Invernizzi, Templeton, & Johnston, 1996; Juel, 1994). Although this portion of the lesson resembled traditional phonics instruction, it differed in intensity. It was minimal and placed a greater emphasis on reading and writing of connected text.

Letter-Names Strip

Even though the letter-names activity took little time, it played a temporary but crucial role in the literacy group time. Being able to identify the names of the letters of the alphabet is a strong predictor of reading achievement (Pikulski, 1996; Snow et al., 1998). Yet, researchers have not established it as a cause of higher reading scores. So how can time spent teaching the letter names be justified? The literacy group activity is justified for two reasons. First, the children in the literacy groups did not initially know the names of many of the letters, so they could not discuss them or use them effectively during literacy activities. For example, if the teacher asked the child to write "c-a-t," the child would need to know the names of the symbols to complete the task. Second, many letter names are good clues for the sound the letter represents, and this knowledge is important for beginning readers as they attempt to figure out new words that they have not previously read.

The letter-names strip activity changed in appearance rapidly and then disappeared when the children mastered the identification of the letters of the alphabet. In the beginning of the year the children chanted in unison the names of the letters of the alphabet as the teacher pointed from A to Z on an alphabet strip located on the wall. Until the children recognized them as separate letters, the teacher moved slowly through "l, m, n, o, p." The teacher based the decision to increase the difficulty of the task by observing the group of children as a whole. Next, the children began to name the letters out loud in unison while the teacher pointed to the alphabet in reverse order from Z to A. After the children could say the names forward and backward fluently, the teacher began to point to the letters out of sequence. After overlearning occurred and the children obtained automaticity (Samuels & Flor, 1997) in naming the letters of the alphabet, the teacher discontinued this component.

Letter-Sound Cards

The letter-sound activity had the same status as the letter-names activity; i.e., it changed in appearance and finally disappeared as it was mastered by all the children. On large cards the teacher printed a capital and lowercase letter and a key word picture that began with that letter. The teacher did not teach every letter-sound variation possible but instead taught the children one sound for each consonant and the short sounds for the vowels. The purpose of this activity was not to teach all potential letter sounds, but to introduce the children to the concept that letters represent sounds and to help them begin to understand that this knowledge can be used as a tool in reading and writing.

This explicit teaching of phonics regularities is supported by several reports that synthesize early reading research (Adams, 1990; Chall, 1967; Snow et al., 1998). Knowledge of letter-sound relationships is necessary to "phonologically recode" or look at the letters of a word and convert it into its appropriate sounds (McCormick, 1995). At first, the teacher presented the cards slowly in alphabetic sequence and required the children to voice in unison the sounds that the letters represented. Later, the teacher presented the cards in random order. When automaticity occurred (Samuels & Flor, 1997), she made and used letter cards without the pictures. After the children mastered this activity, the teacher made and used blend cards containing two letters of the alphabet (e.g., *bl-*, *cl-*). The teacher created a chart for each of the blends as the children recognized them automatically. On each chart, she printed several words beginning with that blend and added to the list as the children encountered new words having the same initial blend.

Word Wall

The Word Wall activity continued throughout the year. When beginning a Word Wall, the teacher selected two or three high-frequency words from the story used for the guided reading (component later in the lesson). Later, she added new common vocabulary words to the wall. Like Cunningham (1995), she organized the Word Walls in sections that contained words that began with each letter of that alphabet. This helps to organize the children's thinking and supports recognition of words. The Word Wall activity became a visual tool to teach the children high-frequency words. Later, when the teacher introduced blends and frequently occurring spelling variations such as *ow* or *igh*, she placed words under cards labeled with the blend or containing the spelling variation in addition to the individual letters system. The children read these words aloud each day in unison as the teacher pointed to them quickly.

Remaking Words

In the remaking words activity the students practiced making two or three new words from the story like *with* or *splash*. Using magnetic letters, each day the teacher had words spelled correctly on a magnetic chart placed in front of the room before the children arrived to group time. The teacher called one child to the magnetic board as the other children watched. To begin the activity the teacher scrambled the magnetic letters of one of the words. As the other children observed, the selected child attempted to reconfigure the word. The teacher supported the particular child as needed. The teacher also asked the group to help if the child had difficulty. She said something like "What sound do you hear first?" The group could contribute information for making the word only after the teacher directed them to do so. This activity showed children how to read words from left to right and focused the children on using sounds, thus enhancing their phonemic awareness (their ability to differentiate and hear sounds in language). Phonemic awareness is considered necessary to reading success (Juel, 1991; Liberman, Shankweiler, Fischer, & Carter, 1974). Although this activity is similar to Cunningham's (1995) "making words," it is different in that other words are not made from these letter combinations and the children see the word before they have to remake it. The teacher pointed out different attributes of letters and words as the activity occurred. The specific level of support offered by the teacher depended on the ability of the selected child.

Shared Reading

The shared reading activity is based on a process described by Holdaway (1979) and promoted by others (e.g., Fountas & Pinnell, 1996; Martinez & Roser, 1985; Pappas & Brown, 1987; Teale & Sulzby, 1986). In shared reading the teacher chose and wrote several key sentences from the story she selected for use in guided reading. The teacher made the chart in advance and used it all week along with the story in the guided reading portion of the lesson. On the first day of the story, the teacher read the sentences out loud to the children as she moved her finger along under the text. She also called upon children to come up and do the pointing and the reading themselves as the class read along with them. This allowed the teacher to see how much support individual children needed in areas of print concept awareness such as reading from left to right, return sweeping at the end of a line of print back to the far left, and one-to-one print matching. Participating in this activity taught the children about these print concepts. Additionally, it gave the children many exposures to the same words in context to encourage automaticity (Samuels & Flor, 1997).

Guided Reading

In the guided reading portion of the lesson, each child had a copy of the book being read. This was a separate story from the one read aloud at the beginning of the lesson and was used all week. The practice of rereading stories for fluency has been advocated for many years (Samuels, 1979). In our version of rereading, the children simply read the story in a variety of ways as the week progressed. On the first day of the week the teacher introduced the book to the children by "walking through the pictures" and spotlighting words she thought the children might have trouble decoding. This helped prepare the children to read the book much like a book introduction in a Reading Recovery lesson (Pinnell, Fried, & Estice, 1991). After introducing the book, the teacher had the children read it out loud or choral read as a group along with her. Choral reading dominated the second day of the reading also. The third through the fifth days' readings of the story varied in format to prevent boredom and to allow the teacher to hear how the various children sounded as they read the story. For example, the teacher might allow half the children to read one page aloud and half to read the next page aloud and so on until the story was completed. Another variation was having the children read the story with a partner, alternating pages as the teacher monitored.

This guided reading is similar to the method described by Cunningham, Hall, and Defee (1998) as the guided reading block in their language arts framework, which also involves a variety of comprehension activities such as story mapping or dramatic reenactments. Because of time constraints, the teacher encouraged comprehension strategy development mostly through guiding questions, discussions about words and their sounds, and opportunities to locate words in text. This helped the children develop a self-extending system of obtaining meaning from print (Smith-Burke & Jaggar, 1994): "A self-extending system means that a child functions like a good reader who approaches text strategically and continues to learn to read by reading" (p. 65). This concept includes the cultivation of the flexible use of cues from print (DeFord, Lyons, & Pinnell, 1991). When children can use the cues from letters in the word, the predictable syntax, the overall content of the story, and all other available cues interchangeably as needed, they are becoming independent in their reading.

The stories selected for this portion of the lesson had controlled vocabulary like that of a basal reader such as the ones found in the Rigby PM (Rigby) book series or the Ready Readers (Modern Curriculum Press) series. These books worked well for two reasons. First, since the vocabulary had some control in the series, the words in one book would be repeated several times in other books at that level. This gave the children practice in identifying the words in a variety of contexts and yet allowed for multiple exposures. Second, because of the leveled nature of the series, the children could benefit from being in their instructional level for longer periods of time if needed.

The teacher discussed the pictures along with book parts and concepts in this activity. She guided the students through the reading as she prompted them to use strategies. This role is similar to the role of the teacher in the Reading Recovery program (Clay, 1985). The teacher gave the children opportunities to become aware of concepts about print as well as use strategies to locate known words, find unfamiliar words, frame words or word parts, and observe grammar. The overriding goal of guided reading was to help children move toward independence.

Writing Aloud/Shared Writing

In this activity, the children worked on sentence structure in an adaptation from an individual Reading Recovery activity (Clay, 1993b). The teacher wrote a sentence taken from the guided reading portion of the session on a sentence strip as the children watched. She modeled and demonstrated her thinking by talking out loud as she wrote. For example, as she wrote the beginning of the sentence she might say, "I'm at the beginning of a sentence so I must remember to begin this with a capital letter." Cognitive modeling taught the children about strategies that they could use as they wrote. Next, the children read the sentence aloud (in unison). Then the teacher cut the sentence into individual words, mixed up the words, and placed them in mixed order into a pocket chart. In the group activity, the teacher randomly called individual students to the front of the group and had them put the sentences back into correct sequence. The teacher discussed capital letters, punctuation, and other concepts about print as well as sentence order and structure.

Guided Writing

In the beginning of the year, the guided writing activity consisted of the children copying the sentence from the pocket chart onto lined paper as the teacher provided support. During the activity, the teacher discussed print concepts and letter formation. Later, as the children became more proficient, this became an independent writing activity as they began to create their own sentences about the story. The teacher provided support as needed. According to Marie Clay (Smith-Burke & Jaggar, 1994) and others (e.g., Pinnell & McCarrier, 1994), writing allows the children to focus on the details of print. They learn how to hear the sounds in the words they are trying to write. Printing out their thoughts on paper is one of the ways some children best learn to read (Cunningham, Hall, & Defee, 1991).

Independent Reading

During the independent reading portion of the lesson, the children read familiar texts. The children selected books from small baskets that included many predictable texts with repeated language patterns and high picture support. Additionally, the teacher selected books to give children practice at applying the common consonant beginnings or onsets and common spelling patterns beginning with a vowel or rimes that they had practiced in the word-level activities. The children's choices increased as the year progressed, and they developed habits of reading independently with the books in their baskets. The teacher actively monitored their reading during this time by listening to children read individually or in pairs and taking running records weekly on each child. The teacher gave prompts and encouraged the children's use of reading strategies by asking questions like, "Does the word make sense in the sentence?" "Do the letters look like they could be said that way?" or "Does the picture give you any clues?"

Portfolios

The teacher documented children's progress weekly by placing work in portfolios. In these portfolios, the teacher placed running records and writing samples. On Fridays, the teacher eliminated several lesson components and extended the independent reading component for the day. This gave her time to take individual running records on all the children as they read from the guided reading story of the week. When the books increased in length, the teacher had the children read only 100 words from the story. These records informed the teacher about the children's individual reading behaviors and allowed her to monitor the progress of the group as a whole. By analyzing the group's running records, the teacher kept the choices for the week's guided reading stories within the group's instructional level. The portfolios also gave the teacher documentation for the regular classroom teachers and parents.

Discussion of First-Year Results

In order to monitor the children's progress, both Reading Recovery teachers at the school tested all children in the first grade at the beginning and ending of the year. On the basis of this testing, the teachers determined the children's instructional reading levels as they corresponded to the appropriate RR book levels. Book levels range from A to 30, with books on level 30 being the most difficult. According to Peterson (1991), level 20 corresponds to the level of a typical end-of-first-grade basal. Askew and Frasier (1997) differ slightly, placing levels 14–18 at a first reader basal level and levels 18–22 as representing a typical second reader. In order to calculate some descriptive statistics we assigned reading levels of a –2 for level A, and a –1 for level B. The mean score for the children in the literacy groups in September was book level 1, and in May, level 12.

Using a *t*-test for significant differences, we analyzed the total set of data for children in literacy groups. The test revealed significant differences in the mean scores of the children (*N* = 31) in May with their earlier scores in September. The mean gain of 11.35 levels was significant. This gain is academically meaningful since the children served in literacy groups scored in the lower third of their class at the beginning of the year. Typically, in this school children would not have acquired reading levels so close to grade level by the end of their first-grade year.

Although the mean score of the pre- and posttesting looked promising, we wanted to look beyond that statistic to see exactly how many children in the literacy group had reached grade-level status by the end of the first grade.

The Table shows 15 of the literacy group children met the local district requirement to be considered at or above grade level for the end of first grade. Of that 15, 11 of the children obtained scores of 14 or higher. This level is similar to those reported as the average text reading level of children at the end of first grade who were discontinued from the statewide RR program in California (Swartz, Hays, Evans-Perry, MacPherson, & DeVeaux, 1996) and Askew and Frasier's (1997) end-of-first-grade levels. Ten of the children scored

Table. Children reaching grade-level status by end of first grade

Number of children	Levels
3	20–26**
8	14–18**
4	12*
10	8–10
6	3–6

Total number = 31

* District's end-of-first-grade average
** Considered on grade level or above for first grade according to Askew & Frasier (1997)

slightly below the first-grade expectancy (levels 8–10). Only 6 out of the 31 children who initially scored so low to be considered at risk for reading failure scored below level 8 at the end of first grade. Prior to using the literacy groups as a means of early intervention, these children would likely have scored much lower at the end of the year.

The numbers, although encouraging, did not tell the full story of the children's reading development. At the beginning of the year, as observed by the literacy group teacher, the children possessed incomplete knowledge of print concepts and did not have the ability to use strategies needed for reading independently. The teacher had to model and instruct the children in the very basic concepts, such as book front and back, where to begin to read, which way to go, and one-to-one matching. She guided them during the lessons to match the text to the spoken word, one-to-one.

Conclusions

In the beginning of the school year, many more children could have benefited from one-on-one tutoring in this low-income school, but the needs were greater than available resources. Having Ms. Pearish work with groups of up to eight children helped address more children's needs than otherwise possible. We suspect several factors are responsible for the children's progress.

First, group placement was carefully based on demonstrated ability to benefit from the group instruction. The children who scored the lowest on the placement assessments received one-on-one lessons and did not participate in the literacy groups. Was the program set up to succeed by only placing the most likely to benefit into the literacy groups? We confess that was the intent exactly. If children needed more intensive one-on-one reading assistance, then that is what they received. We do not suggest that the group program replace individualized tutoring for some children or that the regular classroom instruction be supplanted. We do propose, however, that some children can get extra help in a pull-out group setting.

Second, the design of the program itself contributed to the children's progress. Comparing the program to the guidelines posited by Spiegel (1995), we feel that the most significant contribution to the children's growth lay in providing the children with reading material at their instructional level and then teaching them about strategies they could use independently to gain meaning from print. The teacher provided intensive opportunities for the children to learn as she focused the children on comprehending connected text.

Third, we provided a balanced program by combining activities taken from several reading approaches. The lesson format used direct instruction of the details children need to succeed as independent readers. For example, the children needed to know the sounds of the letters of the alphabet, and therefore the teacher taught that detail directly using the letter-sound card activity.

Finally, Ms. Pearish's training, combined with her ability to devote more preparation time to planning lessons, enabled lessons to be delivered expertly with minimal interruption. Spiegel (1995) calls for the best teachers to instruct those most in need. The best teacher in this case had sharp observational skills combined with a deep understanding of the reading process. These skills enabled her to monitor and reinforce the children's literacy attempts and to adjust her literacy support accordingly.

Could the regular classroom teacher deliver such instruction? Probably. The question, however, becomes an issue of how we use available resources. In many schools, RR teachers, remedial reading teachers, and special education teachers represent a wealth of training and experience for working with small groups of first graders. These teachers have received different kinds of preparation, but all have received extra training designed to help them understand learners who fall behind in literacy. Because of the fast pace of the literacy group lessons, other interruptions by children not in the groups might decrease their effectiveness within the regular classroom. The regular classroom teacher would have 12–17 other children to manage while he or she worked with the 6–8 children in the small group. Under these conditions it would be difficult to sustain the pace of the lesson we described.

Through the use of a small-group, pull-out format, trained teachers can assist many more first graders to achieve grade-level reading by supplying a fast-paced daily lesson in addition to the regular classroom instruction. It is the nature of the instruction, not the location, that is important in pull-out one-on-one and small-group reading programs. Instruction is what really matters!

REFERENCES

Adams, M.J. (1990). *Beginning to read: Thinking and learning about print*. Cambridge, MA: MIT Press.

Allington, R.L., & Cunningham, P.M. (1996). *Schools that work: Where all children read and write*. New York: HarperCollins.

Allington, R.L., & McGill-Franzen, A. (1989). School response to reading failure: Chapter I and special education students in grades 2, 4, & 8. *The Elementary School Journal, 89,* 529–542.

Allington, R.L., & Walmsley S.A. (Eds.). (1995). *No quick fix: Rethinking programs in America's elementary schools.* New York: Teachers College Press; Newark, DE: International Reading Association.

Anderson, R.C., Hiebert, E.H., Scott, J.A., & Wilkinson, I.A. (1985). *Becoming a nation of readers: The report of the Commission on Reading.* Washington, DC: National Institute of Education.

Askew, B.J., & Frasier, D.F. (1997). Sustained effects of Reading Recovery intervention on the cognitive behaviors of second grade children and the perceptions of their teachers. In S. Swartz & A. Klein (Eds.), *Research in Reading Recovery* (pp. 18–38). Portsmouth, NH: Heinemann.

Bear, D.R., Invernizzi, M., Templeton, S., & Johnston, F. (1996). *Words their way: Word study for phonics, vocabulary, and spelling instruction.* Englewood Cliffs, NJ: Prentice-Hall.

Chall, J. (1967). *Learning to read: The great debate.* New York: McGraw-Hill.

Chomsky, C. (1972). Stages in language development and reading exposure. *Harvard Educational Review, 42,* 1–33.

Clay, M.M. (1985). *The early detection of reading difficulties* (2nd ed.). Auckland, New Zealand: Heinemann.

Clay, M.M. (1990). The Reading Recovery programme, 1984–88: Coverage, outcomes and Education Board district figures. *New Zealand Journal of Educational Studies, 25,* 61–70.

Clay, M.M. (1991). *Becoming literate: The construction of inner control.* Portsmouth, NH: Heinemann.

Clay, M.M. (1993a). *An observation survey of early literacy achievement.* Portsmouth, NH: Heinemann.

Clay, M.M. (1993b). *Reading Recovery: A guidebook for teachers in training.* Portsmouth, NH: Heinemann.

Cunningham, P.M. (1991). Research directions: Multimethod, multilevel literacy instruction in first grade. *Language Arts, 68,* 578–584.

Cunningham, P.M. (1995). *Phonics they use: Words for reading and writing* (2nd ed.). New York: HarperCollins.

Cunningham, P., & Hall, D. (1996). Becoming literate in first and second grades: Six years of multimethod, multilevel instruction. In D. Leu, C. Kinzer, & K. Hinchman (Eds.), *Literacies for the 21st century: Research and practice* (45th yearbook of the National Reading Conference; pp. 195–204). Chicago: National Reading Conference.

Cunningham, P.M., Hall, D.P., & Defee, M. (1991). Non-ability grouped, multilevel instruction: A year in a first grade classroom. *The Reading Teacher, 44,* 566–571.

Cunningham, P.M., Hall, D.P., & Defee, M. (1998). Nonability-grouped, multilevel instruction: Eight years later. *The Reading Teacher, 51,* 652–664.

DeFord, D.E., Lyons, C.A., & Pinnell, G.S. (1991). *Bridges to literacy: Learning from Reading Recovery.* Portsmouth, NH: Heinemann.

Fountas, I.C., & Pinnell, G.S. (1996). *Guided reading: Good first teaching for all children.* Portsmouth, NH: Heinemann.

Heath, S.B. (1982). What no bedtime story means: Narrative skills at home and at school. *Language in Society, 11,* 49–76.

Hiebert, E.H. (1994). A small-group literacy intervention with Chapter I students. In E.H. Hiebert & B.M. Taylor (Eds.), *Getting reading right from the start: Effective early literacy interventions* (pp. 85–106). Boston: Allyn & Bacon.

Holdaway, D. (1979). *The foundations of literacy.* Sydney: Ashton Scholastic.

Juel, C. (1991). Beginning reading. In R. Barr, M.L. Kamil, P.B. Mosenthal, & P.D. Pearson (Eds.), *Handbook of reading research* (Vol. 2, pp. 759–788). White Plains, NY: Longman.

Juel, C. (1994). At-risk university students tutoring at-risk elementary school children. In E.H. Hiebert & B.M. Taylor (Eds.), *Getting reading right from the start: Effective early literacy interventions* (pp. 39–61). Boston: Allyn & Bacon.

Liberman, I.Y., Shankweiler, D., Fischer, F.W., & Carter, B. (1974). Explicit syllable and phoneme segmentation in the young child. *Journal of Experimental Child Psychology, 18,* 201–212.

Lyons, C.A., Pinnell, G.S., & DeFord, D. (1993). *Partners in learning: Teachers and children in Reading Recovery.* New York: Teachers College Press.

Martinez, M., & Roser, N. (1985). Read it again: The value of repeated readings during storytime. *The Reading Teacher, 38,* 782–786.

McCormick, S. (1995). *Instructing students who have literacy problems.* Englewood Cliffs, NJ: Merrill.

Meyer, L.A., Wardrop, J.L., Stahl, S.A., & Linn, R.L. (1994). Effects of reading storybooks aloud to children. *Journal of Educational Research, 88,* 69–85.

O'Sullivan, P.J., Ysseldyke, J.E., Christenson, S.L., & Thurlow, M.L. (1990). Mildly handicapped elementary students' opportunity to learn during reading instruction in mainstream and special education settings. *Reading Research Quarterly, 25,* 131–146.

Pappas, C.C., & Brown, E. (1987). Learning to read by reading: Learning how to extend the functional potential of language. *Research in the Teaching of English, 21,* 160–184.

Peterson, B. (1991). Selecting books for beginning readers. In D.E. Deford, C.A. Lyons, & G.S. Pinnell (Eds.), *Bridges to literacy: Learning from Reading Recovery* (pp. 119–147). Portsmouth, NH: Heinemann.

Pikulski, J.J. (1994). Preventing reading failure: A review of five effective programs. *The Reading Teacher, 48,* 30–39.

Pikulski, J.J. (1996). *Preventing reading problems: Factors common to successful early intervention programs* [Online]. Available: http://www.eduplace.com/rdg/res/prevent/index.html

Pinnell, G.S. (1989). Reading Recovery: Helping at-risk children learn to read. *The Elementary School Journal, 90,* 160–183.

Pinnell, G.S., DeFord, D.E., & Lyons, C.A. (1994). Comparing instructional models for the literacy education of high-risk first graders. *Reading Research Quarterly, 29,* 8–39.

Pinnell, G.S., Fried, M.D., & Estice, R.M. (1991). Reading Recovery: Learning how to make a difference. In D.E. DeFord, C.A. Lyons, & G.S. Pinnell (Eds.), *Bridges to literacy: Learning from Reading Recovery* (pp. 11–35). Portsmouth, NH: Heinemann.

Pinnell, G.S., & McCarrier, A. (1994). Interactive writing: A transition tool for assisting children in learning to read and write. In E.H. Hiebert & B.M. Taylor (Eds.), *Getting reading right from the start: Effective early literacy interventions* (pp. 149–170). Boston: Allyn & Bacon.

Samuels, S.J. (1979). The method of repeated readings. *The Reading Teacher, 32,* 403–408.

Samuels, S.J., & Flor, R.F. (1997). Automaticity, expertise, and reading. *Reading & Writing Quarterly: Overcoming Learning Difficulties, 13*, 107–121.

Smith-Burke, M.T., & Jaggar, A.M. (1994). Implementing Reading Recovery in New York: Insights from the first two years. In E.H. Hiebert & B.M. Taylor (Eds.), *Getting reading right from the start: Effective early literacy interventions* (pp. 63–84). Boston: Allyn & Bacon.

Snow, C.E., Burns, M.S., & Griffin, P. (1998). *Preventing reading difficulties in young children.* Washington, DC: National Academy Press.

Spiegel, D.L. (1992). Blending whole language and systematic direct instruction. *The Reading Teacher, 46*, 38–44.

Spiegel, D.L. (1995). A comparison of traditional remedial programs and Reading Recovery: Guidelines for success for all programs. *The Reading Teacher, 49*, 86–96.

Swartz, S.L., Hays, P.A., Evans-Perry, V., MacPherson, A., & DeVeaux, F. (1996). *Reading Recovery in California: 1991–1995.* San Bernardino, CA: California State University.

Taylor, B.M., Hanson, B.E., Justice-Swanson, K., & Watts, S.M. (1997). Helping struggling readers: Linking small-group intervention with cross-age tutoring. *The Reading Teacher, 51*, 196–209.

Taylor, B.M., & Hiebert, E.H. (1994). Early literacy interventions: Aims and issues. In E.H. Hiebert & B.M. Taylor (Eds.), *Getting reading right from the start: Effective early literacy interventions* (pp. 3–11). Boston: Allyn & Bacon.

Teale, W.H., & Sulzby, E. (Eds.). (1986). *Emergent literacy: Writing and reading.* Norwood, NJ: Ablex.

Talking the Walk: Children Reading Urban Environmental Print

Marjorie Faulstich Orellana and Arcelia Hernández

From the window in Camilo's third-floor apartment building in central Los Angeles, California, you can read thousands of words. There are signs for dozens of stores and businesses, posters and advertisements in storefront windows, and handmade ads for services like child care taped on street poles. There are traffic signs, parking signs, and street signs. There is writing on the sidewalks and graffiti on a few walls. There are words on trucks, buses, and cars; on the ambulatory carts of local street vendors; and on the backpacks and T-shirts of hundreds of children who take this route to school. This is an everyday scene alive with print for the taking.

Children and Print-Rich Environments

Literacy researchers have expressed much interest in how children read the print in the world around them (Bissex, 1980; Harste, Woodward, & Burke, 1984; Taylor, 1983; Teale & Sulzby, 1986). Most of this research has focused on homes and classrooms, where a suburban, middle-class bias prevails as to the kind of print that children are exposed to in their daily lives. We need, however, to look beyond suburban homes and schools and recognize that local urban communities offer a rich resource for the teachers of millions of children who attend city schools. Urban environments overflow with print (see Figure 1) in multiple languages and in many different forms, rich with historical, cultural, and contextual meanings that can be plumbed as literacy lessons for children.

As with any instruction, it is important to build on what children already know, as well as their interests. What print do children notice and respond to in the city? How do they read what they see? How do their readings illuminate their understandings of their social worlds? Teachers can use this kind of information to connect urban environmental print with literacy learning at school.

Originally published in *The Reading Teacher* (1999), volume 52, pages 612–619.

Figure 1. Urban environmental print

Photo by Marjorie Faulstich Orellana

Literacy Walks

As part of an ongoing ethnographic study of children's daily life experiences in central Los Angeles, we led children from one first-grade classroom on "literacy walks" through the streets around their school. As researchers, we were interested in children's understandings of the world around them; we wanted to see what the children noticed and what kinds of conversations such walks stimulated. As teachers, we were interested in exploring how the local community could be used to foster literacy experiences and learning at school. Working with a broad notion of literacy, we wanted to use the community as a text to help children read both the word and the world (Freire, 1970).

In this chapter, we share our experiences on two walks with the children. The first took place after school, when we accompanied a group of 6 students to their homes. The second took place during the school day, with 15 students from the first-grade classroom. We describe each walk, how the children participated in each one, and what we learned from them. We then explore implications for teachers' practice: How can we expand children's engagement with the print outside their homes and use this resource in literacy lessons in school? What can we learn about the children we teach from examining their "reading" of the physical world?

The Community and the Children

For our work in the larger ethnographic project, we define *community* as the intake area to an elementary school, which we call Madison (a pseudonym). Madison is one of the largest elementary schools in the United States, with 2,700 children in grades K–5. The children live in apartments within 10 square blocks around the school. They are mostly immigrants or the children of immigrants from Central America and Mexico. A smaller population at the school are from Korean immigrant families; the school borders on an area in which Korean shops can be found. All the students in this first-grade classroom were native speakers of Spanish and used Spanish in most of their interactions with us. There were 32 students in the room at the start of the year, but only 20 at the time of our walks, due to the class size reduction that was implemented in California in 1996–1997.

At the start of our research, we considered the community to be the school's intake area, because the school seemed to be a central meeting ground for families in the area. Throughout the project we also tried to tap children's and families' definitions of community, which was especially important for our study of environmental print. We wanted to walk with the children through their "community," but we needed to understand how children interpreted that word. We met as a group before the classroom walk. We asked the children what they thought the word *community* meant. One student hesitantly offered "El mundo?" (The world?) Someone followed this by naming a local market. Others joined in naming specific landmarks—stores that their families shopped at in the blocks around the school. Because the children mentioned these landmarks, we decided to include these places in our walking route.

Talking the Walk

The first walk took place after school. We accompanied four students from Arcelia's first-grade classroom (Camilo, Cristian, Aldo, and Eva) to their homes. Camilo's older cousins, Yandara and Wanda, also came along. Parents had given their permission for the walk and also to audiotape our conversations along the way. We were excited about studying the urban print environment with the children and eagerly probed for their understanding by asking questions, such as "Who do you think wrote this?" "Why do you think they put this sign here?" and "What do you think they were trying to say?"

We found, however, that the children did not share our enthusiasm for such "conversations." When we asked them to "point out things you see to read," Eva obligingly pointed to the print on an ice cream vendor's cart, Cristian indicated the signs on some stores nearby, and Aldo pointed to some posters on the walls of a gasoline station. But none of the children said much about the meanings or uses of the words they saw.

When we asked what they thought each sign said, the children generally responded by sounding out the words using their knowledge of letter-sound correspondences. The results were sometimes comprehensible, but in general this syllabic approach distorted the words beyond recognition. Sometimes they used Spanish orthography to decode English words, resulting in further distortions of meaning. For example, Camilo sounded out a sign about a "Move-in Special" in which the *m* was missing by saying something like, "o-vay een espay-cee-al." We asked him what he thought it meant, and he simply shrugged.

At one point, Yandara noticed some banners hanging on the streetposts, printed with the words "Recycle motor oil—because the earth can't" in English on one side and Spanish on the back. Looking at the English side, she did not attempt to sound out the words. Instead, she used the graphic—a droplet of water, printed in white on blue—as a cue to the banner's message. She told us the banners were there because a lot of people waste water. "Who put them there?" Marjorie asked. The reply, with a note of boredom, was "Unos señores." This translates as something like "gentlemen" or "misters," a term that indicates greater social distance than other words Yandara might have chosen, such as *hombres* (men) or *gente* (people).

In the next block, we asked Aldo what he thought a sign in front of a church said. His response: "No sé" (I don't know). Arcelia asked the same question of Wanda, who merely shrugged. She asked the group what language they thought the sign was in. No one answered. Marjorie directed a similar query to Yandara, who said, "I don't know." Meanwhile Aldo, Cristian, and Camilo had discovered a series of round stones set in the grass in front of the sign. They counted them and made a game of stepping on the stones without touching the grass. The enthusiasm they showed for their game contrasted sharply with their flat responses to our questions.

When we came to another church with a schedule of services in front, printed in Korean, Marjorie asked Camilo what he thought it said. He shook his head and said "Yo no sé Koreano. Si fuera Korean, sí lo podría hacer" (I don't know Korean. If I were Korean, I'd know how to do it). At another point Aldo "read" a Korean sign as "chung fung shung" and another as "tek tek tek."

Figure 2. Trilingual sign

Photo by Marjorie Faulstich Orellana

When we encountered a set of signs printed in English, Spanish, and Korean (see Figure 2), Marjorie asked the group, "Será que dice lo mismo, o algo diferente en cada idioma?" (Do you suppose it says the same thing, or something different, in each language?) Aldo and Yandara, with barely a glance at the signs, declared that they said different things. Eva seemed excited to find words—*tax services*—that were repeated as the heading for all three signs, and announced "¡Está igual! ¡Está igual!" (It's the same! It's the same!) But for the most part the children resisted our efforts to look closely at the organization of print in different languages.

At this point we started to feel that the literacy walk was a failure. Our talk about the print environment seemed contrived. No matter how natural we tried to make our questions, we came across as adults quizzing children. We realized that we were asking the children to perform a rather strange task—that of analyzing the streets that they walk every day.

Finding Points of Connection

It would have been easy to end the walk and conclude that these children simply weren't interested in the many signs that surrounded them, that they didn't know much about their environmental print around them, and that our idea for a "literacy walk" lacked educational worth. But when we came to a sign bearing the name of the street that Camilo, Yandara, and Wanda lived on, Camilo called for our attention and repeated the name three times. The street sign clearly had meaning for him, and he was excited to show us that he could read it, even out of the context in which he usually encountered it— we were several blocks away from their home. Similarly, when we encountered a video store with posters for children's videos strategically placed at kids' eye level, the children stopped to read the posters and talk about the movies until we insisted that we had to move on.

Another form of print that evoked a great deal of discussion was graffiti (see Figure 3). Although adults, especially community outsiders, may see graffiti as simply ugly writing on walls and make little attempt to make sense of it, these children paid close attention to this print. They deciphered it more readily than we did. When we encountered gang script containing the initials "MS," the following conversation ensued:

Camilo: Teacher! Teachers! Esto es la Mara S. Porque acá está la *S*.
          (Teacher! Teacher! This is the S gang. Because here's the *S*.)

Figure 3. Urban graffiti

Photo by Marjorie Faulstich Orellana

Aldo:	Y aquí la *M*. (And here's the *M*.)
Arcelia:	La *M S*? (The *M S*?)
Camilo:	Sí. (Yes.)
Marjorie:	Mira, y aquí qué dice. (Look, and here what does it say.)
Yandara:	*M S F L S*. Significa Salvatrucha too. (*M S F L S*. That means "Salvatrucha" too.)
Camilo:	Aquí está otra. (Here's another one.)
Marjorie:	Allí está otra, qué dirá? (There's another one. What will that say?)
Arcelia:	Y la *F L S*? (And the *F L S*?)
Yandara:	Son los peores. Más peores. (They're the worst. The most worst.)
Camilo:	Esto es la *C!* Allá está la *C!* (This is the *C!* Over there is the *C!*)

At another point, Aldo pointed out some *rayados* (writing—literally "scratchings") on the sidewalk—graffiti that was scratched in when the cement was wet. He announced, "Por mi casa hay muchas cosas rayadas así." (Near my house there are many things that are written [scratched] like this.) Near these graffiti markings were other, typeset letters etched in the cement. These were city markings for the placement of street lighting. Camilo distinguished between these two forms of writing as follows: "No, porque los cholos rayan mucho, cuando van a escribir, y la gente no raya mucho. Por eso." (No, because the cholos write [scratch] a lot, when they're going to write, and the people don't write [scribble] a lot. That's why.) Waving his hands wildly, Aldo added, "Uhuh. Rayan así, y la rayan grande y fea." (Uhuh. They write like this; they write big and ugly.) Camilo explained why the city print was different: "Es que la gente escribe como con una cosa que es muy dura...." (It's because the people write with something that is very hard....) The kids continued to point out more examples of each kind of print, announcing, "Esto lo hicieron los cholos" (This one was made by cholos), or "Esto lo hizo la gente" (This was made by people).

The children's excitement at encountering these signs renewed our faith in using the urban environment for literacy lessons, but it showed us that we could not do this in a "one sign works for all" manner. Some kinds of environmental print appeared to have more meaning for these children than others. This was a good reminder that we need to understand what is important in our students' lives before making judgments about their motivation to read or their capacity to do so. We realized that the best way of finding out what mattered to the children was to simply listen to them and watch them (in Goodman's [1989] "kid-watching" tradition), rather than to quiz them with our preformulated questions.

Reading the World (Not Just the Words)

We decided to conduct a second walk during the school day, with 15 children from Arcelia's classroom who had permission from their parents to participate. This time we did not focus on the print per se but simply walked with the group, reading the world around us by talking with them about what we saw. We brought a camera, and the children took turns taking pictures. We also took some pictures that purposefully included environmental print to use for more focused discussions in the classroom. We visited a Guatemalan bakery, toured the aisles of a Salvadoran market, and stopped to talk to the family of one of the students who lived en route.

When we focused on reading the world, we found that the children had much to say about many words. They read signs that were personally meaningful: the place where a parent works ("El Querido Pulgarcito Número Dos"); a market where they shop ("Food For Less"); the sign for a preschool they had attended. We spent a long time in the market, a place that is filled with print announcing items that are familiar to the children. Most of the children had been to the store on other occasions with their families, and they had a great deal to say about the things that were sold there, from dried fish and fresh vegetables to machetes and candles.

After returning to school, the children drew pictures and dictated stories about their walk. A few days later, we helped the children write stories to accompany the photographs they had taken. In their pictures about the walk, almost half the class drew the market we had visited and carefully labeled it with its name. Others included signs for other local landmarks.

The photos also prompted children to reveal rich experiential knowledge. For example, Betty dictated a page about helping her parents, who work at the store on the weekends:

Mi mamá y mi papá trabajan en Liborio's. Yo también trabajo allá. En los sábados y los domingos trabajo allí con una blusa así como tiene el señor (en la foto). Hago pupusas y tamales. También hago dulces. Mi mamá y mi papá trabajan conmigo. Yo solita me pongo unas cosas allí adelante de dónde están los pescados. Yo pongo los frijoles. Los pongo allá arriba de las carnes. Solo eso. Me pagan cinco dolares. Y me dejan entrar solita a mí y a mi mami cuando la tienda está cerrada. Hago mucho. La gente paga más y más y más, mucho dinero para la comida.

[My mom and dad work at Liborio's. I also work there. On Saturdays and Sundays I work there, with a shirt like the man (in the photo) is wearing. I make pupusas and tamales. I also make sweets. My mom and dad work with me. I put some things over there where the fish are all by myself. I put the beans there. I put them above the meats. That's all. They pay me five dollars. And they let me and my mom go there when the store is closed. I do a lot. People pay more and more and more, a lot of money for food.]

Cristian wrote about helping an aunt plant trees and flowers and paint the apartment building where she serves as manager. Jasmina told of making tortillas in the restaurant where her mother works. Others used the photographs as a jump-off point for talk about shopping and cooking with their families, or traveling to their countries of origin. The animated conversations contrasted sharply with their shrugs and mumblings of "I don't know" in response to our directed questions during the first walk.

Implications for Literacy Learning

These literacy walks showed us what other researchers and practitioners of holistic approaches to literacy learning have also found (see, for example, Davies, 1989, 1993; Kamler, 1993; Orellana, 1995; Solsken, 1993). It is not enough to simply immerse children with print (in homes, classrooms, or community settings) and expect that they will read and make sense of it. Children engage with some texts more than others; different children are motivated to read different texts. Choices about what to read are shaped by age, gender, ethnicity, social class, and particular life experiences.

The children who accompanied us on our walks seemed to perceive that most official print is written by "señores"—outsiders, adults, men. It is directed at other adults. Much of it is written in languages they do not understand. It is even positioned physically in ways that exclude them; very little official print is posted at children's eye level. We noticed the children craning their necks when we asked them to look at signs placed high on store walls. Most environmental print did not speak to their lives or their interests.

But these children did engage—excitedly—with forms of print that hooked to their experiences: signs for their parents' workplaces, markets where they shop, the names of their own streets. The kids noticed things that were important in peer culture, such as video shop posters. Much of the print that called their attention evoked their experiences as active participants in the work and household activities of their immediate and extended families.

The children in our study also were motivated to read graffiti on the walls that they walked past every day. Graffiti is often positioned closer to their line of view than other print. It is produced by urban youth just a little older than the children in our study, and it has meaning in their lives. Adults, especially outsiders to the community, can drive by these walls with no need to understand what is printed there. But inner-city children's lives and futures depend on their proper reading of gang symbols. They may be quite sophisticated at interpreting graffiti even as they have little say about signs that are placed in their community by outsiders.

Literacy walks can help teachers learn more about their students' worlds outside of school, while using the local environment as a tool to teach about words. We recommend taking such walks because they help us to consider the world from our students' vantage. They also encourage a form of interaction between teachers and students that is not easy to accomplish in a classroom setting.

Teachers can, however, utilize the urban print environment without leaving the school yard. Classes can create journals of different forms of environmental print: signs they see on the way to school, posters on the school walls, words that are visible on the streets outside the classroom window. These ideas can be extended as homework assignments by having the children list all the words they see when they look out their window at home; when they ride on a bus; when they accompany their parents to work; when they go to the market, the laundromat, or church.

Our suggestions may sound familiar to teachers who strive to motivate children's interests and build on their everyday experiences. But the important points are (a) that we build our curriculum on the experiences that children tell us about when we talk with them about their lives and (b) that we get to know their local worlds, rather than make assumptions about what kids do when they are not in school. In addition, we should continuously stretch ourselves to observe the wide range of resources that are available in local communities, especially in urban, inner-city communities, where it may be easier to see problems than resources.

We can also give children the opportunity to create their own public displays of print, finding official channels for them to leave their imprint on the local environment. This seems especially important given that most urban print—except graffiti and some ads that are aimed specifically at children—is positioned above children's eye level. Many schools now encourage students to write the signs that are displayed in the building (including "official" text about school rules), but we can do more to make children's print visible in the environment beyond the school. Children's drawings are often welcomed in public settings; why not seek ways to display their words as well? Our students might paint signs for local markets, bakeries, and restaurants (and include, perhaps, some artwork that helps attract customers). Classroom-produced materials might be displayed in the local library and other such settings. Local stores might be especially interested in displaying the photo essays that children create after visiting these sites during community walks.

Something as simple as sending chalk home also allows children the chance to make their marks on the sidewalks near their homes. One of the children who accompanied us on our walks showed us math problems and written messages that her sister had scribbled in the parking lot beneath her apartment building. He accused her of having "stolen" the scraps of chalk that she used to do this. By sending chalk home as an official homework assignment, we lend legitimacy to this sort of activity.

Conclusion

Community-based literacy walks create an opportunity for children to display knowledge about things that normally find little room for expression in school. They offer a window into the competencies—or "funds of knowledge" (Moll, 1992)—that children develop outside of schools that can be built on in the classroom. And they allow us to utilize valuable local resources: the many forms of print that surround our students (when they walk to and from school every day, go with their families to the market or laundromat, or ride on buses around the city) and the rich experiential worlds that this print names.

Just as teachers and researchers may not pay much attention to urban environmental print or take time to decipher its varied meanings, children may not engage spontaneously with all of the words that they see. But by walking and talking with children, and especially by watching and listening, we can discover the print that attracts each of our students, even as we learn more about their lives, experiences, and interests. We can then use that information to expand their knowledge about print in classroom activities. By linking the reading of *words* to the reading of *worlds* that children know best, we can spark their enthusiasm for literacy learning in school.

This project is part of a comparative case study of children's daily life experiences in three communities in California, USA, funded by the John D. and Catherine T. MacArthur Foundation Research Network on Successful Pathways Through Middle Childhood. The project was also supported by the Institute of Human Development at the University of California, Berkeley. In this project we are looking at resources and opportunities for children, adults' practices that shape children's experiences, and how children see and experience their lives.

REFERENCES

Bissex, G. (1980). *Gnys at wrk: A child learns to read and write.* Cambridge, MA: Harvard University Press.

Davies, B. (1989). *Frogs and snails and feminist tales: Preschool children and gender.* Boston: Allen & Unwin.

Davies, B. (1993). *Shards of glass: Children reading and writing beyond gendered identities.* Cresskill, NJ: Hampton Press.

Freire, P. (1970). *Pedagogy of the oppressed.* New York: Seabury Press.

Goodman, K. (1989). Whole language research foundations and development. *The Elementary School Journal, 90,* 207–221.

Harste, J.C., Woodward, V.A., & Burke, C.L. (1984). *Language stories and literacy lessons.* Portsmouth, NH: Heinemann.

Kamler, B. (1993). No single meaning: Empowering students to construct socially critical readings of the text. *Australian Journal of Language and Literacy, 16,* 307–322.

Moll, L. (1992). Bilingual classroom studies and community analysis. *Educational Researcher, 21,* 20–24.

Orellana, M.F. (1995). Literacy as a gendered social practice: Tasks, texts, talk, and take-up. *Reading Research Quarterly, 30,* 674–708.

Solsken, J. (1993). *Literacy, gender, and work in families and in school.* Norwood, NJ: Ablex.

Taylor, D. (1983). *Family literacy: Young children learning to read and write.* Exeter, NH: Heinemann.

Teale, W.H., & Sulzby, E. (Eds.). (1986). *Emergent literacy: Writing and reading.* Norwood, NJ: Ablex.

Early Literacy for Inner-City Children: The Effects of Reading and Writing Interventions in English and Spanish During the Preschool Years

*David B. Yaden, Jr., Anamarie Tam, Patricia Madrigal,
Danny Brassell, Joan Massa, L.S. Altamirano, and Jorge Armendariz*

The following study is a four-year, longitudinal examination of the effectiveness of a preschool emergent literacy intervention in a "skid row" child-care facility in downtown Los Angeles, California. The primary purpose of the project has been to provide multiple opportunities for Spanish-speaking 4-year-olds to engage in a variety of reading and writing activities within the center, at home, and in the surrounding community. The project is now in its third year of operation, and the results of our study have been very encouraging. Not only are preschool children beginning their kindergarten year at or above grade level in understanding concepts about print, but both preschool teachers and parents have established regular habits of shared book reading and numerous ways for children to write and display their work.

Selected Background Literature

As Goldenberg and Gallimore (1995) have pointed out, the Latino population of school children poses some particular problems for U.S. schools (see also August & Hakuta, 1997; Snow, Burns, & Griffin, 1998). The most recent projected figures (see Population Projections Program, 2000) indicated that by the year 2005 Hispanics will become the largest minority group in the United States, exceeding the number of African Americans (13.3% vs. 13.0%, respectively). Further, in another 15 years, the Hispanic population of school-age children will make up the second largest group behind non-Hispanic whites (21.3% vs. 59.2%; Vernez, Krop, & Rydell, 1999). Compounding the pressure on schools due to rapidly increasing numbers of Spanish-speaking children is the additional fact that many of the parents of these children typically have less formal education than those of both native-born or other non-Latino, foreign-born adults. In the case of Mexican immigrants, slightly less

Originally published in *The Reading Teacher* (2000), volume 54, pages 186–189.

than half (49.7%) have a high school diploma, as compared with 87% of non-Hispanic whites and 60% of other foreign-born adults (Ramirez, 1999). One consequence of this difference in educational level is that many immigrant children come to school unfamiliar with many of the printed resources generally associated with parents' higher levels of schooling.

In a review of studies documenting Latino students' poor achievement in schools relative to other populations, however, Losey (1995) was critical of investigations claiming a "cultural mismatch" between home and school because many do not, in her words, "collect or analyze data from real-life interactions in actual settings" (p. 288). Taking a Vygotskian perspective, Losey stressed that unless studies examine closely the language interactions taking place at home and in school, as well as in the broader social context, conclusions about the success or failure of Mexican American children will be incomplete and narrow. On the positive side, Losey's review singled out research on classroom environments that provide "collaborative learning, lesson plans designed around student interests, a sense of belonging to the classroom community, flexibility in language usage, and a challenging curriculum" (p. 312) as examples of classroom interactions in which improved learning outcomes are most likely to occur.

In designing the present preschool intervention, we have considered Losey's suggestions for creating positive classroom environments for English language learners and built upon the work of other researchers (e.g., Delgado-Gaitan, 1990, 1996; Goldenberg, 1989; Goldenberg, Reese, & Gallimore, 1992; Moll, 1994) who have studied various aspects of learning and parent support within Latino populations in high-poverty areas. This intervention is based upon the premise that positive learning outcomes with immigrant Latino students are most likely to occur when there is an interaction between (a) challenging, meaningful learning tasks; (b) adults who respect children's intellectual ability and their cultural capital; and (c) language activities in which all participants have frequent opportunities to share their ideas and opinions in both their native languages and English. Therefore, some of our guiding research questions are as follows:

◆ What is the influence of exposure to emergent literacy activities in an inner-city, community, child-care setting upon preschool children's Spanish and English literacy learning abilities?

◆ What kinds of English language and literacy support can be provided by parents, extended family members, and child-care center employees in a primarily Spanish-speaking community?

◆ What are the funds of knowledge in these communities from which children can draw, and how can this shared communal knowledge be incorporated into a structured preschool emergent literacy program?

Methodology

Population Description and Setting

Located east of downtown Los Angeles in an area known as "skid row" (Rivera, 1999), Para Los Niños (PLN) is a comprehensive child-care center and family-services support center whose stated mission is "raising children out of poverty into a brighter future." The child-care center houses approximately 136 children, from infants to 4-year-olds. For the most part, the parents of these children work in the nearby garment and toy wholesale districts where the normal working day is about nine hours. In addition, approximately two thirds of the families live in areas of the city where there is a high concentration of gang activity. According to agency figures, over 60% of the families served are single mothers with two to three children, with monthly incomes ranging between US$584 to approximately US$1,050. Further, over 98.7% of families have incomes below U.S. federal poverty guidelines, with 35% of the children prenatally exposed to drugs or alcohol. A substantial number are also considered to be at risk for abuse or neglect. Finally, the great majority of the children in the program are Latino, with usually only one or two African American or Anglo students enrolled per year. Although Spanish is the primary language of communication in the classroom, teachers and paraprofessionals do regularly code-switch into English for the few children who are bilingual or English-speaking only.

The Emergent Literacy Intervention and Procedures

We have drawn upon the research base of best practices for young children (e.g., Bredekamp & Copple, 1997; Hammond & Raphael, 1999; Hiebert & Raphael, 1998) in establishing the principal strategies of the study. Our first goal was to create a two- to three-hour morning language and literacy program at the center for approximately 50 4-year-old preschool children each year by instituting a Big Book shared reading program, installing writing centers, and purchasing over 1,000 children's books. Second, we aimed to provide in-classroom support and ongoing inservices regarding emergent literacy theory, activities, and developmental growth in reading and writing for child-care agency teachers and paraprofessionals. Last, we established a book-lending library for the families and have offered periodic parental workshops on reading at home and other ways to encourage their children's awareness and knowledge of literacy materials and activities. Although the emergent literacy program is primarily being implemented in the two classes of 4-year-olds (55 children), both classes of 3-year-olds (52 children) and the one toddler class (14 children) are allowed to check out books from the parent book-lending library.

Design, Data Collection, and Analysis

The study is quasi-experimental with longitudinal, cross-sectional, and single-subject components as subsequent cohorts of children are being followed into the nearby elementary school for observation and comparison. In addition, various questionnaires have been distributed to both parents and teachers, and interviews are regularly conducted to ascertain teachers', parents', and administrators' ongoing perspectives and feelings about the progress of the program. Further, during the last year, the research team has conducted home visits to capture the literacy activities in which parents engage with their children. In the classroom, data sources include children's writing products, field notes of individual and group literacy behaviors, photographs, and video.

Finally, documentation of growth in concepts about literacy is being measured in at least four ways. First, weekly classroom observations of the children have been described in detailed field notes. Second, pre- and posttesting of all cohorts has been carried out with a Spanish Concepts About Print Test (Escamilla, Andrade, Basurto, Ruiz, & Clay, 1996). Third, we are currently using versions of the Piagetian clinical interviews employed by Ferreiro and Teberosky (1982) as measures to capture children's developmental growth in acquiring written language concepts. Finally, archival records and test scores from the children's elementary experiences are being collected.

Selected Findings Over the First Two Years

The Family Book-Loan Program

Since its inception in July 1998, participation in the book-loan program has grown steadily (see Madrigal, Cubillas, Yaden, Tam, & Brassell, 1999, for complete details). Currently, of the 126 children in the 2-, 3-, and 4-year-old classes eligible to participate, 79% of the 2-year-olds, 44% of the 3-year-olds, and 93% of the 4-year-olds are involved in the program, for an overall percentage of 72%. Even though the book-lending program is open only two days per week, the average number of books checked out per day has risen dramatically from approximately 2 to 24 books over 20 months.

Questionnaires distributed to the families and field notes of conversations with parents at the loan program further underscore both the parents' positive perceptions about the loan program and the ways their children's behavior toward books has changed. For example, in a conversation about her son with a member of the research team, one mother recently said, "Well, now that he is with your program, he has learned a lot...before he didn't even know what to do with a book, he wasn't interested, but now he enjoys taking books home." In addition, over 150 parents have attended the project's three book-loan receptions and literacy workshops on various aspects of book handling and home reading and writing activities. Their appreciation and support of the program have been a constant encouragement to the University of Southern California research team. In the words of another mother, "Es muy importante que hayan programas como este, porque nos enseña a nosotros como padres a tener ideas de como comportarnos con nuestros hijos y poder ayudarlos a ellos. Gracias por todo." (It is very important to have programs such as this one because it shows us as parents ideas of how we can interact with our children and how we can help them. Thanks for everything.)

Concepts About Print

Although the program officially started in January of 1998, due to major renovations in the center that spring, the first cohort of 4-year-old preschool children (1997–1998) experienced only a small portion of the intervention before they left the center at the end of June 1998. They have therefore been designated as one of the comparison groups. At this writing, the second cohort of 4-year-olds (1998–1999) has finished their preschool year, and the children are in kindergarten, while the current cohort of preschoolers is nearly three quarters of the way through their preschool program. It is the performance of the second cohort that we will discuss here.

During their preschool year, this group of 55 children showed a statistically significant average gain of 4.5 points (from 4.2 to 8.7) on the Spanish Concepts About Print Test. This gain reflected increasing knowledge about the directionality of print, awareness that printed words are read instead of pictures, and ability to identify capital and lower-case letters as well as some marks of punctuation. Also, 30% of these children could demonstrate early knowledge of word awareness by being able to track printed words in a sentence while it was being read aloud to them and by isolating written words using space as a boundary. Even more notable is that, at the beginning of their kindergarten year, these children have outscored children from other preschool programs on tests of English in upper- and lowercase letter identification and in vowel and consonant recognition.

Conclusion

The early results of this study show that preschool-age English language learners from high-poverty environments are gaining in their book-handling awareness, letter and word concepts, and understandings of print directionality during an emergent literacy intervention prior to their kindergarten year. In addition, many of the families have established read-aloud routines at home, despite the frequent finding that storybook reading is not a normal practice among Latino families (see Goldenberg et al., 1992). Finally, our study also substantiates the transfer of early language awareness in Spanish to English (cf. Goldenberg, 1994). We anticipate that our longitudinal data for these children as they move through first to third grades will show that emergent literacy activities in either English or Spanish aid in the acquisition of advanced reading and writing skills later in school.

This research was conducted as part of CIERA and supported under the Educational Research and Development Centers Program, PR/Award Number R305R70004, as administered by the Office of Educational Research and Improvement, U.S. Department of Education. The contents of the study described here do not necessarily represent the positions or policies of the National Institute on Student Achievement, Curriculum, and Assessment, or the National Institute on Early Childhood Development, or the U.S. Department of Education, and you should not assume endorsement by the federal government of the United States.

REFERENCES

August, D., & Hakuta, K. (1997). *Improving schooling for language-minority children.* Washington, DC: National Academy Press.

Bredekamp, S., & Copple, C. (1997). *Developmentally appropriate practice in early childhood programs* (Rev. ed.). Washington, DC: National Association for the Education of Young Children.

Delgado-Gaitan, C. (1990). *Literacy for empowerment: The role of parents in children's education.* London: Falmer Press.

Delgado-Gaitan, C. (1996). *Protean literacy: Extending the discourse of empowerment.* London: Falmer Press.

Escamilla, K., Andrade, A.M., Basurto, A.G.M., Ruiz, O.A., & Clay, M.M. (1996). *Instrumento de observacion: De los logros de la lecto-escritura inicial.* Portsmouth, NH: Heinemann.

Ferreiro, E., & Teberosky, A. (1982). *Literacy before schooling.* Exeter, NH: Heinemann.

Goldenberg, C.N. (1989). Parents' effects on academic grouping for reading: Three case studies. *American Educational Research Journal, 26,* 329–352.

Goldenberg, C.N. (1994). Promoting early literacy achievement among Spanish-speaking children: Lessons from two studies. In E.H. Hiebert & B.M. Taylor (Eds.), *Getting reading right from the start: Effective early literacy interventions* (pp. 171–199). Boston: Allyn & Bacon.

Goldenberg, C.N., & Gallimore, R. (1995). Immigrant Latino parents' values and beliefs about their children's education: Continuities and discontinuities across cultures and generations. In M.R. Maehr, P.R. Pintrich, & D.E. Bartz (Eds.), *Advances in motivation and achievement: Culture, motivation, and achievement* (pp. 183–277). Greenwich, CT: Jai Press.

Goldenberg, C.N., Reese, L., & Gallimore, R. (1992). Effects of literacy materials from school on Latino children's home experiences and early reading achievement. *American Journal of Education, 100,* 497–536.

Hammond, W.D., & Raphael, T.E. (Eds.). (1999). *Early literacy instruction for the new millennium.* Grand Rapids, MI: Michigan Reading Association; Ann Arbor, MI: Center for the Improvement of Early Reading Achievement.

Hiebert, E.H., & Raphael, T.E. (1998). *Early literacy instruction.* Fort Worth, TX: Harcourt Brace.

Losey, K.M. (1995). Mexican American students and classroom interaction: An overview and critique. *Review of Educational Research, 65,* 283–318.

Madrigal, P., Cubillas, C., Yaden, D.B., Tam, A., & Brassell, D. (1999). *Creating a book loan program for inner-city Latino families* (CIERA Report No. 2-003). Ann Arbor, MI: Center for the Improvement of Early Reading Achievement.

Moll, L.C. (1994). Literacy research in community and classrooms: A sociocultural approach. In R.B. Ruddell, M.R. Ruddell, & H. Singer (Eds.), *Theoretical models and processes of reading* (4th ed., pp. 179–207). Newark, DE: International Reading Association.

Population Projections Program, Population Division. (2000). *Projections of the resident population by race, Hispanic origin, and nativity: Middle series, 1999 and 2000.* Washington, DC: U.S. Census Bureau.

Ramirez, R.R. (1999). *Current population reports: The Hispanic population in the United States.* Washington, DC: U.S. Census Bureau.

Rivera, C. (1999, May 26). Zoning chief vows action on skid row "crime magnets." *Los Angeles Times,* pp. B1, B3.

Snow, C.E., Burns, M.S., & Griffin, P. (1998). *Preventing reading difficulties in young children.* Washington, DC: National Academy Press.

Vernez, G., Krop, R.A., & Rydell, P. (1999). *Closing the education gap: Benefits and costs.* Santa Monica, CA: Rand Corporation.

RIGHT 2

Children have a right to reading instruction

that builds both the skill and the desire

to read increasingly complex materials.

Introduction

Patricia Ruggiano Schmidt

In spring 1992, just before retirement from his illustrious career in literacy education, Harold L. Herber of Syracuse University—considered the "Father of Reading in the Content Areas"—was asked by a doctoral student why his work had remained credible even while opposing forces raged on about literacy instruction. His reply was simple and powerful: "I was able to dodge the pendulum, the pendulum of educational reform."

Herber's (1978) idea of balanced literacy instruction included motivation for engagement; guided practice for decoding, automaticity, and fluency; and direct instruction of strategies for comprehension. He taught present and future teachers that skills should not be separated from the processes associated with reading to learn in the content areas. Therefore, reading, writing, listening, and speaking were integrated across the curriculum with a necessary emphasis on vocabulary study for concept development, and guided reading and reasoning for higher levels of thinking and questioning. Herber's purpose for such balance was to encourage our democratic citizenry to be critically thinking members of the global society.

Herber's instructional framework (see Herber & Nelson, 1993) included three phases: preparation, guidance, and independence. Each phase relied on direct explicit instruction as well as indirect student-centered instruction. Whole classes, individuals, pairs, and small groups completed assignments, allowing the teacher time to carefully observe and guide. Herber called attention to teacher modeling of literacy behaviors for successful teaching and learning. He emphasized the Zone of Proximal Development, a Vygotskian theory (1934/1978) that urges the teacher to challenge students to reach their potential as the teacher guides, assists, and gradually fades out to facilitate student independence.

Because student needs were a first consideration in his literacy lesson framework, Herber was comfortable teaching at almost any grade level. During the initial phase of the instructional framework, a teacher strives to accommodate the wide range of interests and individual learning differences that increase with each grade level. Furthermore, Herber coined the phrase "connecting the known to the new," meaning that learning to read and reading to learn become relevant to students when the teacher draws from prior knowledge and motivates students for active engagement. These strategies create a learning environment in which pairs and small groups of students work cooperatively, emitting a "healthy hum" (Schmidt, 2001, p. 141). This is a classroom where family backgrounds and experiences are fundamental elements that bring relevance and equity to the teaching and learning of literacy skills and processes.

Herber's balanced approach to literacy development lives on to this day and directly relates to Right 2—children have a right to reading instruction that builds both the skill and the desire to read increasingly complex materials. The two articles in this section emphasize that balanced instruction motivates students to learn how to study words, develop fluency, improve reading comprehension, and promote writing abilities.

Children's Right to Balanced Instruction: Early Childhood

The article by Karin L. Dahl and Penny A. Freppon presents a cross-curricular comparison study that explored literacy learning over two years in a kindergarten and first-grade high-poverty school. The children in the study exhibited an interest in accuracy, phonics growth, and enthusiastic response to literature. A statement from this article summarizes the authors' findings: "When learners see their own experiences as valid knowledge and use reading and writing for their own purposes, the journey toward literate behaviors is soundly underway."

These children were motivated to learn phonics when they were engaged in literacy activities and high-interest materials that encouraged self-expression in speaking and writing and helped children acquire the conventions of language. This, in turn, helped the children think about decoding, spelling, and writing. The children experienced a print-rich environment that included high-interest literature, labels, pictures, language experience charts, and literacy centers. The students were encouraged to interact through reading, writing, listening, and speaking.

Similar to this article, I recently observed a third-grade class in a high-poverty urban setting. Weekly, family and community members visited to share a reading, writing, listening, or speaking activity that coordinated with the curriculum. A mother with her new baby talked about his needs and how she met them. A father took apart a toaster and explained how it worked. A brother talked about finding a job. A minister told about after-school activities in his church. A day-care worker described the games he plays with pre-school children. A sister relayed a story her grandmother told her. An aunt showed how to hem a dress and slacks. A grandmother brought her children's favorite dessert for all to taste. The teacher in this classroom made use of community "funds of knowledge" (Moll, 1992) to motivate and engage so that learning skills and strategies for comprehension made sense. Students listened and recorded key vocabulary from these meetings. From these word lists, the teacher planned explicit instruction of vocabulary and spelling while creating reading, writing, listening, and talking opportunities.

The Dahl and Freppon article supports the balanced instruction witnessed in this third-grade urban classroom environment. The direct explicit instruction of skills was integrated with meaningful literacy activities that motivated students. Home, school, and community literacies were connected to create culturally relevant pedagogy.

Literacy activities that relate to students' lives are not difficult to create for a teacher who is aware of the importance of making literacy learning relevant. For instance, when Moll discusses funds of knowledge in relation to Latino students, he explains that they often demonstrate a greater interest in the mechanics associated with small and large engines used in our daily lives. Similarly, African American community literacies such as oral storytelling, recitation, song, and poetry may be brought into the classroom (Delpit, 1995; Edwards, Danridge, McMillon, & Pleasants, 2001; Walker-Dalhouse & Dalhouse, 2001).

When families from diverse ethnic and cultural backgrounds and lower socioeconomic levels become connected with the school as resources for learning, there is often a narrowing of the academic gap and an increase in positive attitudes toward school (Edwards, Pleasants, & Franklin, 1999; Faltis, 1993; Goldenberg, 1987; Moll, 1992). Teachers who reach out to families and create connections are actually implementing culturally relevant pedagogy. They connect the curriculum to the knowledge and experiences of diverse cultures in their classrooms by validating student family backgrounds and experiences and using the literacies found in the children's cultures. But it is also necessary to explicitly teach students the skills and strategies they need to gain the information and understandings to be successful academically. The second article in this section achieves such balanced instruction.

Children's Right to Balanced Instruction: Adolescence

Alfred W. Tatum's piece makes use of balanced literacy instruction through culturally relevant pedagogy and meaningful literacy skill and strategy activities. The study describes the ways to help struggling readers develop their self-confidence and gain academic achievement through literacy skills and strategies related to reading-writing connections. Additionally, the students were motivated by relevant literature and problem-solving activities.

According to Tatum, the first step required in this process is classroom community building to avoid student embarrassment about sharing work and interests. Therefore, he interviews the students who appear to be the most resistant to sharing in order to discover what they are thinking. He draws from their prior knowledge and experiences in the attempt to begin meeting their classroom needs.

I recently witnessed a ninth-grade global studies class in a high-poverty urban setting. The teachers discovered student television interests in a brief survey at the beginning of the school year and initiated an "Oprah style" interview show. Students knew the television format and questioning behaviors of the hostess, so it was a logical place to start. Each class chose a host who, with a team of classmates who served as writers, created the program for the next day. Part of the half-hour show was a 15-minute interview of the global studies teacher with a performance from two "famous people" in the audience. Through this uncomplicated activity, students immediately became familiar with the teacher and the talents of classmates. This opened the way for personal class interviews and storytelling. The process was then related to text readings on the prehistoric to bronze age of human development. Finally, past human needs were connected to present life in the United States. Vocabulary was introduced and students worked in mixed-ability pairs and triads to complete reading and reasoning guides for key chapter concepts. The teachers also shared printouts of websites and picture books for students to research. The teachers modeled what they expected and gave the students crayons, pencils, and markers necessary to complete tasks in class. Student findings were presented orally with summary drawings and short paragraphs of the past and present. They discussed advantages of life in the past and life in the present. They formed teams to prove their beliefs about the quality of life in the past, present, and future. Presentations of their cases stimulated not only serious debate but also discussion of problem solving for change.

Furthermore, throughout the school year, the teachers connected with leaders of urban centers. They asked for help in gathering resources and support for their course that were thematically connected to the students' communities and world history. From information given to them by urban leaders, neighborhood heroes and "sheroes" were celebrated and invited into class to tell their stories through the interview process. The teachers also highlighted diversity with in-depth weekly coverage of great world leaders of yesterday and today who have left or are leaving their marks on human history.

This successful class directly relates to Tatum's work and gives yet another example of the effectiveness of balanced literacy instruction that connects home and school for relevant, motivational literacy learning and allows for direct explicit instruction of skills and strategies through meaningful content and resources.

Making Balance a Reality

We know that the academic achievement gap between European American and African American and Latino students continues. We know that much of that gap is related to poverty issues and culturally relevant pedagogy. Therefore, we must consider what is working and what could work in urban classrooms (Delpit, 1995; Foster, 1994; Howard, 2001; Ladson-Billings, 1995; Levine, 1994; Lewis, 2001; Nieto, 1999).

Looking back on the work of Herber, thinking about the balance described in the two articles in this section, and visualizing the third-grade and ninth-grade classroom examples help us think about the ways we can make Right 2 a reality in our classrooms and schools. Let us move forward, keeping the following four tenets in mind. First, we know that one method of literacy instruction does not fit all children. Therefore, we must differentiate instruction to meet individual needs and make use of child-centered as well as teacher-directed explicit instruction. Second, we know that connecting with prior knowledge and experiences motivates learning, which increases engagement (Boykin, 1978, 1984). Therefore, we must respect and connect community and family knowledge to school knowledge. Third, we know that students must be able to make sense of the skills and strategies for literacy development. Therefore, we must use relevant, meaningful literature, texts, and materials that motivate and engage students in literacy learning (Stahl, 1998). Finally, we must continue the quest for balance as we attempt to make school a place where collaborative adults empower one another to give our students the best opportunities for learning the most.

REFERENCES

Boykin, A.W. (1978). Psychological/behavioral verve in academic/task performance: Pre-theoretical considerations. *Journal of Negro Education, 47*(4), 343–354.

Boykin, A.W. (1984). Reading achievement and the social-cultural frame of reference of Afro-American children. *Journal of Negro Education, 53*(4), 464–473.

Dahl, K.L., & Freppon, P.A. (1995). A comparison of innercity children's interpretations of reading and writing instruction in the early grades in skills-based and whole language classrooms. *Reading Research Quarterly, 30,* 50–74.

Delpit, L. (1995). *Other people's children: Cultural conflict in the classroom.* New York: The New Press.

Edwards, P.A., Danridge, J., McMillon, G.T., & Pleasants, H.M. (2001). Taking ownership of literacy: Who has the power? In P.R. Schmidt & P.B. Mosenthal (Eds.), *Reconceptualizing literacy in the new age of multiculturalism and pluralism* (Vol. 9, Advances in Reading and Language Research, pp. 111–134). San Francisco: Jossey-Bass.

Edwards, P.A., Pleasants, H.M., & Franklin, S.H. (1999). *A path to follow: Learning to listen to parents.* Portsmouth, NH: Heinemann.

Faltis, C.J. (1993). *Joinfostering: Adapting teaching strategies for the multilingual classroom.* New York: Macmillan.

Foster, M. (1994). Effective black teachers: A literature review. In E.R. Hollins, J.E. King, & W.C. Hayman (Eds.), *Teaching diverse populations: Formulating a knowledge base* (pp. 225–241). New York: SUNY Press.

Goldenberg, C.N. (1987). Low-income Hispanic parents' contributions to their first-grade children's word-recognition skills. *Anthropology and Education Quarterly, 18,* 149–179.

Herber, H.L. (1978). *Teaching reading in content areas* (2nd ed.). Upper Saddle River, NJ: Prentice Hall.

Herber, H.L., & Nelson, J. (1993). *Teaching reading in the content areas* (3rd ed.). Boston: Allyn & Bacon.

Howard, T. (2001). Telling their side of the story: African American students' perceptions of culturally relevant teaching. *The Urban Review, 33*(2), 131–149.

Ladson-Billings, G. (1995). Toward a theory of culturally relevant pedagogy. *American Educational Research Journal, 32,* 465–491.

Levine, D.U. (1994). Instructional approaches and interventions that can improve the academic performance of African American students. *Journal of Negro Education, 63*(1), 46–63.

Lewis, A.E. (2001). There is no "Race" in the schoolyard: Color-blind ideology in an almost all-white school. *American Educational Research Journal, 38*(4), 781–811.

Moll, L.C. (1992). Bilingual classroom studies and community analysis: Some recent trends. *Educational Researcher, 21*(2), 20–24.

Nieto, S. (1999). *The light in their eyes: Creating multicultural learning communities.* New York: Teachers College Press.

Schmidt, P.R. (2001). Inquiry and literacy learning in science: Connecting in a classroom community. In P.R. Schmidt & A. Watts Pailliotet (Eds.), *Exploring values through literature, multimedia, and literacy events* (pp. 125–142). Newark, DE: International Reading Association.

Stahl, S. (1998). Understanding shifts in reading and its instruction. *Peabody Journal of Education, 73*(3 & 4), 31–67.

Tatum, A.W. (2000). Breaking down barriers that disenfranchise African American adolescent readers in low-level tracks. *Journal of Adolescent & Adult Literacy, 44,* 52–64.

Vygotsky, L.S. (1978). *Mind in society: The development of higher psychological processes* (M. Cole, V. John-Steiner, S. Scribner, & E. Souberman, Eds. and Trans.). Cambridge, MA: Harvard University Press. (Original work published 1934)

Walker-Dalhouse, D., & Dalhouse, A.D. (2001). Parent-school relations: Communicating more effectively with African American parents. *Young Children, 56*(4), 75–80.

A Comparison of Innercity Children's Interpretations of Reading and Writing Instruction in the Early Grades in Skills-Based and Whole Language Classrooms

Karin L. Dahl and Penny A. Freppon

This cross-curricular comparison was initiated to shed light on two issues: first, how innercity children in the United States make sense of and interpret their beginning reading and writing instruction in the early grades of school, and second, how learners' interpretations may differ when they experience skills-based or whole language classroom programs. The comparison, therefore, addresses the consequences of differing literacy curricula as they are evident in children's interpretations. We have chosen skills-based and whole language curricula because they are widely used and draw on sharply contrasting notions of teaching and learning. Our focus on innercity children grows from the concern that these children are often particularly vulnerable to the vicissitudes of instruction. We find the research documenting the pervasive failure of this group in literacy learning particularly troubling and see the need for research that explores the effects of curricula as documented from the learner's perspective.

Previous research on innercity children has addressed sociological issues (Ogbu, 1985), family contexts (Taylor & Dorsey-Gaines, 1988), and the influence of instructional factors such as materials, grouping arrangements, and social contexts (Au, 1991; Bloome & Green, 1984). More recent studies have addressed children's sense making within specific curricula (Dahl, 1992; Dahl, Freppon, & McIntyre, 1993; Freppon, 1991, 1993; Oldfather & Dahl, 1994; Purcell-Gates & Dahl, 1991), but have not made extended comparisons across curricula.

While patterns of failure among American innercity children in learning to read and write in the early grades have been well documented (McGill-Franzen & Allington, 1991; Smith-Burke, 1989), few studies have sought children's interpretations of their initial school experiences in reading and writing. Child-centered interpretations of learning to read and write are particularly

Originally published in *Reading Research Quarterly* (1995), volume 30, pages 50–74.

important in the context of current debates about differing instructional approaches. In order to provide productive instructional contexts for beginning readers and writers in innercity schools, educators must know how these children experience skills-based and whole language programs and what consequences may arise.

This cross-curricular comparison was a two-step process; each curriculum was investigated separately, and then the overall comparison was conducted. The two studies involved were an investigation of sense making in skills-based classrooms (Dahl, Purcell-Gates, & McIntyre, 1989) and a study of learner interpretations in whole language classrooms (Dahl & Freppon, 1992). Both studies were designed as ethnographies so that emergent designs and multiple data sources could be used to generate detailed and layered descriptions of children's learning. We wanted to examine the knowledge being acquired by learners (their hypotheses) and to investigate how children's opportunities, interactions, and processes of learning led to the construction of particular models of sense making. The cross-curricular comparison was an ethnology, a comparative analysis of multiple entities (Goetz & LeCompte, 1984). It was conducted by tracing a group of students through a series of comparable data in the skills-based and whole language settings. (See Griffin, Cole, & Newman, 1982, for a discussion of "tracer units.") The thick description, original contexts, and interpretations of each study were preserved in the comparative analysis (Brown, 1990). The focus was on similarities and differences of innercity children's experiences and knowledge, their sense making, across these contrasting literacy curricula.

Theoretical Perspectives

Within each study, children's learning was viewed as transactive. Descriptions of learning events accounted for ways that learner knowledge and patterns of action, social and cultural contexts, and programs of instruction were shaped and transformed in relation to each other. Viewing language learning through a transactional lens meant accounting for the learner's actions and behaviors during instruction as well as accounting for the ways each learner's linguistic-experiential reservoir, background, and stance influenced those actions (Rosenblatt, 1989).

Within this transactive frame, we utilized two main theoretical perspectives. The first of these was the view that classroom reading and writing contexts are socio-psycholinguistic. Learning about reading and writing and engaging in both processes occur in dynamic contexts (Bloome & Green, 1984; Dyson, 1991). The sense learners make depends on social and cultural classroom contexts (Green & Meyer, 1991) and the children's own evolving understandings of written language (Dahl, 1993; Meyers, 1992). Meanings are shaped by transactions among these and other factors (Rosenblatt, 1985). Classroom milieu, the child's individual stance toward literacy (Bussis, Chittenden, Amarel, & Klausner, 1985; Purcell-Gates & Dahl, 1991), development in literacy learning (Clay, 1975; Sulzby, 1985), and the dynamics within specific learning events shape and influence knowledge construction and motivation (Dahl & Freppon, 1991).

The second strand centered on the theoretical differences between the instructional approaches involved in this comparison. The skills-based curriculum is based on the idea that written language is learned through teacher-directed lessons and practiced as discrete skills that are taught sequentially. It uses specific reading and writing tasks as vehicles for skill acquisition and emphasizes a standard of accuracy and neatness as children engage in reading and writing (Knapp & Shields, 1990). Materials, usually in the form of basal readers, worksheets, and writing workbooks, are viewed as instruments for learning specific skills, and the curriculum is centered on the development of reading and writing proficiency (DeFord, 1984). In the skills-based classroom, the role of the student is to learn and integrate specific skills, participate in instruction, and engage in assigned skill practice. The teacher is responsible for structuring learner activities, providing instruction, and monitoring learner progress.

In contrast, the whole language perspective is based on the idea that written language is learned primarily in meaning-centered and functional ways, and reading and writing are learned from whole to part by engagement in the processes themselves (Edelsky, 1991; Goodman, 1986). Whole language classrooms include a variety of printed materials (trade books, catalogs, student-authored works, etc.), and students regularly write about self-selected topics in sustained writing periods. Through daily choices of reading materials and writing topics the student plays a significant role in shaping his or her own learning. The teacher "leads from behind" (Newman, 1985), demonstrating reading and writing behaviors, instructing directly, and supporting children's efforts to learn. Thus, the curriculum is primarily learner centered and driven by a view of children as active language learners (Halliday, 1978; Holdaway, 1979; Wells, 1986).

Review of Related Research

Research in three general areas informed this comparison. The first was a group of studies adopting the situated/sociocultural perspective in the study of children's literacy learning. A second included both emergent literacy explanations of reading and writing development and documentation of sociocultural influences on the success or failure of low socioeconomic status (SES) children in school. The final area of related literature was research exploring instructional dimensions that influence children's literacy learning.

Situated/Sociocultural Perspective

In their British study Edwards and Mercer (1987) investigated ways that knowledge is transmitted and received in elementary classrooms. Their research was based on the premise that human thought, understandings, and knowledge construction are intrinsically social and cultural. In *Common Knowledge* (1987), these researchers describe how the process of education, investigated primarily through the analysis of classroom discourse, imparts different kinds of knowledge. Much of what children learn in classrooms is not the intended aim of instruction but rather other, "hidden agenda" knowledge rooted in the philosophy of instruction itself. Thus, most instruction aimed at transmitting general or decontextualized knowledge inevitably also imparts common knowledge that is embedded in the talk and actions of everyday classroom life.

In the United States, researchers have used ethnographic perspectives to explore routine classroom events that influence young children's sense making (Cochran-Smith, 1984; Dyson, 1989, 1991; Rowe, 1989). Cochran-Smith (1984) documented how contextualized story reading events helped children learn unique language strategies needed to interpret stories. These language strategies were conveyed through teacher/student social interactions during read-alouds. In her investigation of children's writing, Dyson (1991) described how the child's interest, ordinary classroom interactions, and the larger social world influenced writing. Similarly, research analyzing preschool children's social interactions at the writing table (Rowe, 1989) documented the social dimensions of learning and their influence as children posed, tested, and revised their hypotheses about literacy. Children learned the roles of author and audience as they interacted with each other and with their teachers. These investigations demonstrate the importance of understanding the social and cultural milieu of classrooms as contexts shaping literacy development.

In the 1990s, ethnographic investigations continued to explore additional dimensions of children's literacy learning in instructional settings. For example, Kantor, Miller, and Fernie (1992) adopted a situated perspective which acknowledged the importance of classroom social and cultural life. These researchers studied the ways literacy was integral in various classroom contexts. For example, at the art table children focused on merging media and print, while in the block area literacy served to facilitate play and friendship in structuring "rights" and "rules." Results indicated that varying classroom contexts shaped the nature of literacy events and outcomes. A related study by Neuman and Roskos (1992) revealed the influence of classroom environment and documented the effects of literacy objects in the classroom. The presence of books and writing materials merged with and shaped the talk and actions related to literacy in preschoolers' play. The study showed that inclusion of literacy objects in classroom environments increased the quantity and quality of children's literacy activity during play. These studies, in general, underscore the influence of social contexts and classroom structures on early literacy development in schools.

Emergent Literacy Explanations

Research addressing emergent literacy has documented that young learners are aware of written language in their environment and begin their journeys as readers and writers by participating in home literacy events (Holdaway, 1979). The amount and nature of these early experiences affects later success in learning to read and write (Harste, Burke, & Woodward, 1981; Teale, 1986). Events that help children learn that print helps "get things done" (Teale & Sulzby, 1986, p. 28) and early storybook routines shape children's interpretations of literate activity (Gibson, 1989; Harste, Burke, & Woodward, 1983; Heath, 1983; Taylor, 1983; Teale, 1984; Wells, 1986).

Sociocultural mores about literacy permeate these emergent literacy experiences (Ferriero & Teberosky, 1982; Heath, 1982; Schieffelin & Cochran-Smith, 1984). Societal orientations inform children about the ways oral and written language are used in their community and shape interpretations of school-based literacy instruction (Delpit, 1986, 1988). When the expectations of schooling are in conflict with these sociocultural mores, learners experience difficulty and often reject or fail to identify with school-based concepts (Taylor & Dorsey-Gaines, 1988). The literature on at-risk populations indicates that cultural conflicts affect school success (Donmoyer & Kos, 1993; Jordan, Tharp, & Baird-Vogt, 1992; Mitchell, 1992). Intervention programs and attempts to balance schools racially have not reversed the overall pattern that low-SES children often fail to achieve satisfactory progress in reading and writing (Ogbu, 1985; Pelligrini, 1991; Trueba, 1988). Recurring analyses of Chapter 1 programs and special remedial reading efforts often document the failure of such programs to close the gap between these learners and their grade-level counterparts (McGill-Franzen & Allington, 1991). Thus, while this body of research has enriched our understanding of early literacy development, there remains a need to investigate low-SES children's interpretations of beginning reading and writing in school.

Instructional Dimensions

Classic studies of reading instruction have contributed to our understanding of the influence of different kinds of instruction on literacy learning (Bond & Dykstra, 1967; DeLawter, 1970; MacKinnon, 1959). These investigations have focused primarily on the outcomes of reading skills under specific instructional conditions. For example, MacKinnon's (1959) work investigated reading improvement when children read with a tutor and with peers. More recent studies have examined cultural factors and literacy acquisition (Au, 1991) and children's sense making under differing classroom conditions (Freppon, 1991). Freppon's comparative study focused on children's interpretations in skills-based and whole language classrooms but was limited to average readers and their concepts about the purpose and nature of reading. While these studies have described instructional differences and specific outcomes, we have yet to document children's interpretations of instruction in depth and over time in order to more fully understand what learners experience in contrasting curricula.

The current investigation, as a cross-curricular comparison, extends this body of research in a number of ways; it documents learner activity and interpretations of reading and writing across two years of schooling in classes with the same curriculum (skills based or whole language), and it provides a basis for comparison of literacy learning across these years. Thus, this study extends knowledge gained from in-depth classroom studies. It provides a comprehensive account of the learner's perspective, documents and compares learner hypotheses across skills-based and whole language curricula, and draws conclusions about innercity children's success and failure in learning to read and write in these contrasting settings. The focus is on the consequences of each curriculum as seen from the perspective of the children and on the similarities and differences in children's experiences across these two instructional environments.

Method

Sites

The cross-study comparison involved eight classrooms in two Midwest cities. The schools were matched across studies using three socioeconomic indicators. Each school contained a majority of children from urban families with low income levels, most families received public assistance, and the schools' mobility rates were high. Of the three schools involved in the skills-based study (Dahl, Purcell-Gates, & McIntyre, 1989) only two could be matched with comparable whole language sites. Thus, the comparison did not include one skills-based site included in the report of the original study (Purcell-Gates & Dahl, 1991). The elementary school populations in the cross-study comparison were representative of the racial and cultural mix typical of urban low-income populations in the Midwest; that is, they included African American and white Appalachian students. At both the kindergarten and first-grade levels there were two skills-based classrooms and two whole language classrooms.

A critical aspect of the cross-study comparison was whether the skills-based and whole language classrooms selected for the study were reasonable exemplars. Three indicators were used to validate the classroom sites: teacher interviews, classroom observations, and teacher self-report data using the Theoretical Orientations to Reading Profile (DeFord, 1985). Within each study the specific classroom instructional programs were described in terms of their materials, activities, teaching routines, and learner roles.

Skills-based instruction. The skills-based kindergartens included traditional reading readiness programs with extensive emphasis on letter-sound relations; the first-grade programs used a newly adopted traditional basal program with ancillary workbooks and Dittos provided by the central administration. First-grade teachers carried out instruction in small-group sessions, while the remaining students completed seatwork assignments. Learners copied and filled in missing words for sentences written on the chalkboard, and they occasionally wrote in journals and writing workbooks. In first grade, children took part in whole-group choral reading and skill recitation lessons with the teacher. They also participated in small-group round robin reading on a daily basis and had the opportunity to select trade books from a small classroom selection when their work was complete. Teachers followed the skill sequence in the basal program and met deadlines for unit completion established by the district. Storybook reading by the teachers was separate from reading instruction and was often followed by discussion primarily aimed at recall of specific story events or characters.

Whole language instruction. The whole language classrooms utilized extended periods of self-selected independent reading and writing, and teachers worked with individual learners or small groups. The reading materials included a wide variety of children's literature and extensive classroom libraries. Instruction in first grade was carried out with whole-group sessions using extended storybook reading and included teacher demonstrations of reading strategies and skills. The writing program embraced writing workshop routines and used children's literature to suggest story themes and evoke topics. Teachers demonstrated and discussed composing processes and conducted conferences about writing skills with children. Learners engaged in daily writing about self-selected topics and also wrote in journals and shared their writing in whole-class sessions. Most first graders wrote stories that were published within the classroom. Student-authored books and whole-class collaborations were part of the classroom reading materials. Writing and reading share sessions with the whole class were included in the daily schedule.

Informants

In each study a gender-balanced sample of 12 learners in each school site was randomly selected from the classroom pool of kindergarten children who qualified for the federally funded free or reduced lunch program. Since there were two skills-based sites and two whole language sites, this pool provided 24 learners from each study. These 48 children were assessed initially for their knowledge of written language. From this initial sample of learners, the focal learners for each site were randomly selected. Since mobility rates for the schools were relatively high, the initial sample served as a reserve of learners that could be substituted if focal learners moved away early in the study.

Across both studies the focal learners represented similar numbers of urban children who were African American or white Appalachian. Of the eight focal learners in the skills-based study, four were African American children and three were white Appalachian. One white Appalachian learner moved away midstudy. Mobility rates were projected to be particularly high for the whole language study; thus six focal learners were selected in each of the two sites. There were six African American children and six White Appalachian children. All of these focal learners remained to the end of first grade.

Procedures

The process for conducting this investigation involved first executing each study separately and then carrying out the cross-curricular comparison. Step One focused on students' sense making or interpretations within each curriculum and documented their opportunities and processes of learning. Step Two involved data analysis procedures for the cross-case comparison. This comparative analysis entailed tracing the focal learners through their actions and activities over time in order to examine what students learned and how instructional opportunities and patterns influenced this learning. Procedures for this comparative analysis are described in the data analysis section.

Qualitative and quantitative data collection processes in Step One were implemented in similar ways in each investigation to ensure comparability. In each study, one researcher was assigned to each school and engaged in data collection for the two-year period. The initial task was to gain familiarity with students and classroom routines and then begin initial assessment of written language knowledge for the full sample of eligible learners. After the assessment was complete, the focal learners were closely observed across the two-year period and, along with the children in the initial sample, assessed for written language knowledge at the end of first grade. Thus, the weekly observation of focal learners was bounded by pre- and posttests administered at the beginning and end of the study.

Qualitative procedures for documenting learner activity. In each study the researchers generated field notes in twice-weekly classroom visits across the span of two years. One focal learner was followed closely in each observation. That learner wore a remote microphone interfaced with an audiotape recorder so that spontaneous utterances could be captured as the two-hour observation period progressed. Particular attention was paid to learner statements and actions that indicated evolving hypotheses about reading and writing. The emphasis within these research efforts was documentation of the learner's experience as it could be substantiated in talk, reading/writing behaviors, and overt actions. The researchers shadowed focal learners and, where appropriate, probed by asking routine questions such as "What are you doing now?" or, "Tell me about that." The researcher also kept a record of instruction, learner behaviors, and the contexts in which each event occurred. Original field notes were elaborated and typed along with partial transcripts produced from audiotape recordings. Thus, the outcome of each observation was an extended set of field notes in which transcripts of learner talk, oral reading samples, and learner actions were integrated. Copies of all learner papers (writing samples, Ditto sheets) were also included. These elaborated accounts and artifacts were subsequently coded by the research team for learner behaviors and strategies, then analyzed for sense-making patterns.

In both studies, the researchers functioned as participant observers but kept to the observer end of the continuum as nearly as possible, rather than intervening in learning events. The point of these observations was to determine what happens without greatly altering the classroom settings or taking a teaching role during instructional events.

Quantitative assessment of written language knowledge. In each curriculum, learners from the sample of eligible low-SES children (24 in each study) completed an array of six tasks assessing various aspects of written language knowledge. These tasks were administered at the beginning of kindergarten and the end of first grade. Both normed measures and measures unique to this study were used. Our underlying notion was that written language exists as a whole and is composed of various domains that may be examined at different levels. The domains selected were identified as ones related to success in learning to read and write in school (Dahl, Purcell-Gates, & McIntyre, 1989); they formed a picture of each learner's schemata about written language. These assessments included measures of intentionality, alphabetic principle, story structure, concepts about print, written narrative register, and concepts of writing. Table 1 provides a description of each task and describes procedures for task administration.

The six tasks were administered in three sessions spaced over a three-week period. The intentionality task was first for all learners, and subsequent task order was counterbalanced across learners.

Data Analysis

A variety of data analysis procedures were utilized in the two ethnographies and the cross-curricular comparison. Table 2 presents an overview of the two-step process and outlines both qualitative and quantitative data analysis procedures for each major task.

As shown in Table 2, Step One focused on both qualitative and quantitative procedures to determine learner interpretations of reading and writing. Step Two procedures focused on comparisons of data by tracing a group of students through a series of comparable events in the skills-based and whole language settings (Griffin, Cole, & Newman, 1982). In order to understand

Table 1. Summary of written language knowledge assessments

Task	Description	Procedures
Intentionality	Accesses schema for written language as a system with accessible meaning	• Present printed sentence and ask child if there is anything on the paper. Probe to capture child's responses.
Concepts about print	Standardized test (Clay, 1979), taps major book reading and print concepts	• Follow established procedures using the Stones form.
Alphabetic principle	Accesses knowledge of letter-sound relations and alphabetic principle	• Present familiar environmental print in contextualized and decontextualized events. • Ask child to write 10 dictated spelling words. • Ask child to write anything he or she can and to tell about the writing.
Story structure	Accesses schema for the macrostructure of written narratives	• Read a story to the child. Take a short break to prevent rehearsal effects. Ask child to retell story. • Engage the child in puppet play. Prompt the child to "tell me a story" during the course of play.
Written narrative register	Accesses knowledge of syntactic and lexical features found in storybooks using the difference score between an oral language sample and a written language sample	• Ask the child to tell all about an event such as a birthday party or family outing. • Familiarize the child with a wordless picture book. Ask the child to pretend to read the story to a doll. Encourage the child to make it "sound like a real book story."
Concepts of writing	Accesses the child's concepts about writing as a system using the written artifact generated under the "Alphabetic principle" procedure	• Ask child to tell about his or her writing.

Table 2. Summary of data analysis procedures

Step	Task	Data collected	Analyses conducted
Step One. Analysis of data for each study conducted separately	Task #1 (Qualitative): Document evolving learner hypotheses and interpretations of reading/writing in each study.	• Field notes across kindergarten and first grade for each study • Transcripts of learner talk • Written artifacts	• Code data (codes emerge from each data set). • Determine patterns for each focal learner. • Summarize data patterns for half-year periods. • Reduce data narratives to grids for each learner. • Aggregate learner patterns across sites. • Determine major patterns for each study.
	Task #2 (Quantitative): Document change in written language knowledge for focal learners in each study through pre/post comparison.	Pre- and postdata for each focal learner in each study on the following six measures: • Intentionality • Concepts about print • Alphabetic principle • Story structure • Written narrative register • Concepts of writing	• Score pre/post measures and analyze with ANOVA with repeated measures across focal learners within each study.
Step Two: Comparison of data across studies	Task #3 (Qualitative): Compare learner interpretations of reading/writing across skills-based and whole language settings.	• Field notes/transcript accounts of focal learner actions and utterances • Data narratives and grids	• Write global hypotheses and substantiation. • Compare across data sets using tracer units.
	Task #4 (Quantitative): Compare change in written language knowledge scores across skills-based and whole language settings.	• Six tasks measuring pre and post knowledge of written language for learners in each study	• Analyze between-group scores with a 2(Group) × 2(Time) mixed measure ANOVA with repeated measures.
	Task #5 (Combined): Compare reading processes of representative focal learners across studies.	• Reading samples from the midpoint of first grade in two contexts, self-selected trade books and teacher-selected texts	• Compare miscue and strategy patterns across contexts and across studies by proficiency levels.
	Task #6 (Combined): Compare writing events across studies and describe kind of writing produced.	• Kindergarten and first-grade writing data for two time samples (Nov. and Feb.) in both studies—includes all writing samples and related field notes	• Identify kind of writing, amount, and task. Compare across studies.

how children's sense making might differ by instructional contexts, it was necessary to examine the knowledge acquired within each approach. The similarities and differences in measures of written language knowledge for learners in the two curricula were analyzed. Further comparisons were made of learners' reading processes and writing experiences. In these analyses teachers and their actions were not under investigation. Rather, the focus was on comparing children's interpretations of reading and writing as they evolved in the skills-based and whole language classrooms.

Pattern generation across qualitative sources. In each study, coding systems were established that captured categories emerging from field note data. These codes represented both learner behaviors and the context in which they occurred. Coded data were then aggregated to determine patterns of learner behavior and evolving learner hypotheses about reading and writing within each study. Data narratives written for each focal learner further documented learner hypotheses, and grids that summarized learner sense-making patterns were generated to facilitate comparison across learners. The Appendix displays a sample grid prepared for a focal learner in first grade.

When comparisons were made across curricular settings, the grids for each focal learner from each of the sites for each half year were aligned, and successive reviews were made for patterns of behavior across several learners. Specific tracer units were used for comparison: talk and action during reading and writing, interactions during instruction, and patterns of activity during independent work. Researchers' hypotheses about similarities and differences across learners in skills-based and whole language classrooms were written by each member of the research team. Subsequently, the researchers read and reread all of the team members' hypotheses and generated a list of tentative findings for the cross-study comparison. The team reviewed substantiating data in field notes for disputed areas and compiled further documentation when clarification was needed. The tentative findings representing similarities and differences in children's reading and writing patterns were also critiqued by outside consultants in a two-day project review. Attention was paid in this audit to the soundness of research claims and protection against bias.

Analysis of written language knowledge assessments. Scoring procedures for the six written language tasks were drawn from the body of research supporting each task and from the range of children's responses within this study. Table 3 summarizes the scoring procedures and indicates the specific point levels within each task.

Table 3. Analysis and scoring procedures of written language knowledge assessments

Task	Scoring process	Scoring rubric
Intentionality	Range of scores 1–5	1 = No evidence of the concept of intentionality 2 = Response limited to view related to school factors 3 = Child sees purpose of writing as labeling or naming 4 = Child identifies writing as something serving broader purpose 5 = Strong evidence of concept that written language carries meaning
Concepts about print	Scored using Clay's (1979) protocol for Stones	N/A
Alphabetic principle	Scoring scale applied to all three measures with the most frequently occurring level used, range of scores 1–8 points	1 = No evidence of letter-sound knowledge (scribbles, pictures) 2 = Single letter represents word (*P* for "pink," semiphonetic) 3 = Two letters represent a word (*PK* for "pink," semiphonetic) 4 = Maps all sounds heard (*DA* for "day," phonetic) 5 = Maps letter-sounds based on articulation, no nasal articulation (*SG* for "song," phonetic) 6 = Maps letter-sounds based on articulation, includes vowels (*PLEY* for "play," phonetic) 7 = Conventional spelling demonstrated; shows visual, phonetic, and nasal sound strategies 8 = Majority of words spelled conventionally
Story structure	Range of scores 0–8 points, all elements scored	2 pts. = Setting 2 pts. = Reaction involving response of character(s) to formation of a goal 1 pt. = Beginning or precipitating event of an episode 1 pt. = Response of the character to the problem 1 pt. = Outcome or stated success or failure of the attempt 1 pt. = Ending—providing a consequence
Written narrative register	Scored using Purcell-Gates (1988) protocol	N/A
Concepts of writing	Range of scores 1–7, each artifact scored	1 = Drawing: line borders, picturelike marks 2 = Scribbles: writinglike marks, scribbles, shapes 3 = Letter/number forms: scribbles with letters, letterlike, numberlike forms 4 = Letters mixed: pictures with embedded print, letters with numbers 5 = Letters: ungrouped letters, letter strings 6 = Words: pseudowords, words 7 = Words/sentences: extensive word writing, sentences, or stories

As indicated in Table 3, differential weightings were assigned to some items within specific tasks.

In the intentionality task, the salient dimension was the extent of children's understanding of print as meaningful and functional (Harste, Burke, & Woodward, 1983). Thus, the scoring range represented how close each learner came to stating that written language carries meaning. The scale was developed from children's responses in this study as they were questioned about a sentence printed on a piece of paper.

In the story structure task, weighted scores were assigned for various components of the macrostructure of story according to their relative significance among specific story elements (Stein, 1979, 1982; Stein & Glenn, 1975, 1979; Whaley, 1981). *Setting* (character, place, time) and *reaction* (the response of the character to the problem) were assigned 2 points and *beginning, attempt, outcome,* and *ending* were each assigned 1.

The alphabetic principle and concepts of writing scoring represented increments of knowledge and sophistication indicated in children's responses. On the basis of current research, conventional spellings demonstrating visual, phonetic, and nasal sound strategies were scored higher on the scale than use of one letter to represent a word (Gentry, 1982, 1987; Read, 1971). Stories or groups of related sentences were scored higher on the scale than single words or phrases (Clay, 1975, Dyson, 1991; Harste, Burke, & Woodward, 1983; Sulzby, 1992).

Two tasks, written narrative register and concepts about print, were scored according to their prescribed procedures (Clay, 1979; Purcell-Gates, 1988).

Once scoring was complete for all tasks, pre- and posttest results for each study were analyzed for within-group and between-group findings. While the number of students tested in each curriculum was the same at the beginning of kindergarten, patterns of student mobility within these innercity sites reduced the numbers of students tested at the end of first grade. In the skills-based curriculum the initial sample of 24 changed to 15, and in the whole language sample the change was from 24 to 21.

The statistical procedure for cross-curricular comparison was a two-factor hierarchical arrangement augmented by a within-group variable. This one-between/one-within-groups design with provision for unequal Ns (Kennedy & Bush, 1985, pp. 521–531) used a repeated measures analysis. The between-groups variable was the skills-based or whole language treatment, and the within-groups variable was the array of six pre- and posttests (intentionality, story structure, alphabetic principle, concepts about print, written narrative register, and concepts of writing). For each measure, a group (skills-based vs. whole language) × time (pretest, posttest) mixed model analysis of variance (ANOVA) with repeated measures was computed using a $p < .05$ alpha level. Subjects with missing data (due to task refusal) were eliminated from that specific dependent variable only.

This design was chosen because it provided for two specific characteristics of the cross-curricular comparison. First, there was no random assignment of learners to treatments; instead, learners came from intact skills-based or whole language classrooms. Second, teachers differed in spite of careful selection procedures. While teachers were chosen as excellent exemplars of their particular curriculum and had comparable time periods in which to carry out their instruction, there was some variation across teachers. The design we used was appropriate for intact classrooms when they comprised levels of the nested variable (Kennedy & Bush, 1985, p. 522), and it made provision for teacher variation by nesting teachers within the treatment variable.

Analysis of reading processes and writing events. As part of the cross-curricular comparison, analyses were conducted to examine and compare reading processes and writing events across studies. After both studies were concluded, a subsample of six first-grade focal learners, three skills based and three whole language, were selected for a direct comparison of actions during the reading process. These children represented a range of reading experience and ability. The group included a proficient reader, an average reader, and a less-experienced reader from the skills-based and whole language classrooms. Criteria for learner selection were based on triangulated data from field notes, miscue analysis of actual reading samples, and teacher judgment. The sampling of learner reading behaviors was carried out with reading samples from the midpoint of first grade to the end of that year. The classrooms from which these six children were selected included opportunities both to read self-selected trade books and to participate in small-group reading lessons with the teacher. Thus, two contexts, independent reading of self-selected trade books and teacher-directed reading of texts selected by the teacher, were compared across skills-based and whole language first grades. Analysis of reading processes entailed identifying patterns from miscue and strategy data in reading samples across contexts and comparing these patterns across studies by levels of proficiency.

Comparative analysis of writing events that focal learners experienced was also conducted at the conclusion of both studies. The kindergarten and first-grade writing artifacts from November and February, time samples that captured representative periods of instruction and learner activity, were reviewed. The purpose was to describe the writing tasks and generally the kind of writing that focal learners produced during these periods. Field note descriptions of learner behaviors during writing events also were collected for each of the focal learners during these periods. Analysis of writing events entailed tabulating types of writing artifacts for focal learners within the sampled time periods and determining patterns in learner actions and responses to writing activities.

Results

The findings from this cross-curricular comparison spanned three general areas: patterns of learner sense making, written language knowledge measures, and contrasts among reading processes and writing events.

Qualitative Findings: Patterns of Learner Sense Making

The qualitative findings focused on interpretations that learners made of their instructional experiences. In the skills-based and whole language investigations, patterns of behavior were taken as indicators of learner hypotheses about reading and writing. Thus, common patterns across the data grids of the majority of focal learners were taken as learner interpretations of a particular curriculum. Comparison across the two studies revealed five areas in which there were prominent patterns.

Pattern 1: Interest in accuracy. In both studies most focal learners were concerned about accuracy. Comparisons of children's talk and actions across the two groups revealed an interest in "getting it right." In kindergarten, children erased repeatedly when learning to form letters and spell words. They asked each other about letter forms, erased, worked on writing that did not measure up to their standards, and tried again. In first grade they tried to accurately map letters and speech sounds and searched for correctly spelled words by looking through books or using available environmental print. These accuracy-focused behaviors sometimes occurred in whole language groups in spite of the teacher's advice to "get your ideas down" or the direction to spell words as they sounded. In both studies these behaviors were evident in learners with various levels of expertise in reading and writing. It appeared that learners began school with some focus on accuracy and sustained that interest in both curricula.

The concern of focal learners in both studies with accuracy was of particular interest because these two instructional settings differed greatly in their demand for production of correct written language responses. One of the main tenets of the whole language philosophy is acceptance of errors as potentially productive in the learning process. In contrast, the skills-based curriculum is aimed at mastery of specific skills or subskills through practice, and correct responses were highly valued in the skills-based curriculum.

Pattern 2: Phonics growth. While a general progression toward understanding of letter-sound relations occurred among children in both studies, cross-curricular analysis of reading and writing behaviors for January, February, and March of first grade indicated differing strategies for using letter-sound knowledge. Table 4 presents the range of phonics strategies in reading and writing that were recorded in field notes about focal learners during these months. Examples are provided in parentheses to clarify specific strategies. Use of specific strategies is indicated with an x under each focal learner's number. As would be expected, some learners used more than one strategy during this period.

The patterns of strategy use in phonics indicate some areas of similarity. During this period both skills-based and whole language learners used strategies that showed they were gaining awareness of phonics and experimenting with letter-sound relations. The differences were evident in the cluster of whole language learners (8 of the 12 focal learners) using strategies that demonstrated application of their letter-sound knowledge. One skills-based focal learner demonstrated application of letter-sound relations through her conventional reading and use of transitional spellings.

These differences in application of phonics knowledge seemed to reflect the writing experiences in each curriculum and the contexts for phonics practice. Children in whole language classrooms experimented with letter-sound relations during daily writing experiences. These writing periods included individual teacher conferences and frequent peer interactions where coaching on letter-sound relations took place. There also were teacher demonstrations of writing processes in which letter-sound mapping was explained (Freppon & Dahl, 1991).

The letter-sound practice in skills-based classrooms was conducted for the most part as seatwork. There were teacher demonstrations of sounding out with the whole group but rarely were these episodes connected to the reading or writing of connected text. Instead, they were part of separate skill instruction. Learners dependent on the curriculum and learners who were

Table 4. Comparison of phonics strategies in mid–first grade

	Strategy	Whole language learners												Skills-based learners						
		1	2	3	4	5	6	7	8	9	10	11	12	13	14	15	16	17	18	19
Gaining awareness of letter-sound relations	Copies words to complete writing tasks																X	X		X
	Makes series of guesses to identify unknown word in reading (*BL, BLO, BLAY, PLAY, PLOK* for "plate")																	X		X
	Writes single letter for salient sound in a word, context: teacher support (*D* for "these;" *ICP* for "I saw pigs")	X				X	X			X										
	Represents some phonemes with appropriate letter (*GT* for "cheetah")						X		X	X										
Experimentation with letter-sound relations	Sounds out words in reading by exaggerating sounds (*FA LA GUH* for "flag")														X		X			
	Represents some phonemes in word with appropriate letters (*CLSRME* for "classroom;" *WI* for "why")			X					X							X				X
	Produces a nonsense word in reading by using graphophonic cues										X								X	X
	Miscues with matching for the word's beginning sound (*RED* for "rose;" *ME* for "many")							X					X		X	X	X			
Application of letter-sound relations	Uses letter-sound relations to self-correct in reading (*SHIVER* corrected to "shouted")		X					X	X				X							
	Produces transitional spelling for unknown words (*HED UNDR THE HAYSAK* for "hid under the haystack")		X								X	X	X	X						
	Produces conventional spelling				X															
	Reads conventionally using well-organized graphophonemic knowledge				X						X	X		X				X		

Note. Whole language learners: 1 = Addie, 2 = Ann, 3 = Carlie, 4 = Charlie, 5 = Douglas, 6 = Eustice, 7 = Isaac, 8 = Jason, 9 = Maury, 10 = Shemeka, 11 = Tara, 12 = Willie; Skills-based learners: 13 = Audrey, 14 = Ellen, 15 = Eric, 16 = Janice, 17 = Mary Ann, 18 = Maya, 19 = Rodney.

inclined to be more passive approached phonics skill lessons as part of their daily paperwork. Their perspective appeared to be that it needed to be completed to please the teacher. Often these children did not put their phonics skills to use when reading.

Pattern 3: Response to literature. Learners in both studies demonstrated enjoyment of literature. Almost all focal learners were attentive during story-time and listened with rapt attention as stories were read. Storybooks clearly were a source of pleasure and interest within each curriculum.

The cross-study analysis of children's responses to literature, however, revealed considerable differences in hypotheses children held about trade books. These differences were related to two areas: (a) the nature and amount of experience that children had with trade books and (b) the insights that children demonstrated about books.

The role that children's literature played in the skills-based sites was relatively small. Learners in these classrooms listened to storybooks read by their teacher and occasionally explored some trade books after completing their work. For the most part, basal readers and skill worksheets served as the primary reading materials in these classrooms. Even when trade books were available, focal learners tended to stay with their basal materials.

The participation structures during storybook reading were restricted in skills-based classrooms. Teachers preferred that children listen to stories quietly and save their comments until the story's end. Teachers asked children comprehension questions about each story, and children commented about favorite events during story discussions.

A representative storybook lesson occurred when the teacher read *What Mary Jo Shared* (Udry, 1966) while the children listened. This story involved a little girl's quest for something unique to take to school to share. As the story unfolded the little girl considered various animals, such as grasshoppers and even an imaginary pet elephant. At the end of the story the teacher asked if anyone could really have an elephant for a pet. There were several opinions, but Eric was adamant and began vigorously shaking his head yes. He announced, "I keep it outside." The teacher asked, "What would you feed it?" and Eric turned to the page in the book that told what elephants ate. This exchange formed the pattern for successive questions about what children would do and what the book said. Learners, including Eric, were adept at finding information that the book offered and adding their opinions.

The role that children's literature played in the whole language classrooms was somewhat different. Trade books were a central vehicle for literacy instruction. Each day children listened and interacted as several books were read by their teacher. Further, learner-chosen trade books were read by children independently each day in first grade, and many books were incorporated into daily writing experiences. Isaac, for example, was a learner who used familiar books to prompt writing topics. He wrote personal versions of many storybooks, changing the plot or adding a personal twist to the language.

Participation structures during storybook reading with the teacher varied across the two whole language sites, but generally learners in these classrooms were encouraged to participate actively during storybook sessions. Children made predictions, commented on illustrations, asked questions about the story, stated opinions, responded to wordings and letter-sound relations, and acted out story events.

A typical storybook session occurred, for example, when the teacher read a predictable book entitled *Oh No* (Faulkner, 1991). The plot involved a series of mishaps, each resulting in a spot appearing somewhere. The recurring phrase *Oh no* was part of each episode. Children listened and looked at the words and pictures. Midway through the story their comments were particularly revealing.

Teacher:	[reading and pointing to the words] *There's a spot on my skirt. There's a spot on my pants, cause I fell in the dirt.*
Chris:	It looks like mud.
Teacher:	Would it make sense if it says mud?
Children:	Yes.
Isaac:	It's D...dirt.
Terry:	If you don't know what the words say, you can look at the pictures and see if the pictures tell.
Teacher:	Look at the words and the pictures. [nods] That's good. Here's another one. *There's a spot on my sweater.*
Chris:	It doesn't look like a sweater. [pause] It doesn't look like a spot.
Teacher:	Does it look like a shirt?
Children:	[all at once] Yes. Well maybe. No.
Teacher:	So we have to look at the words to figure it out.
Kira:	But sweater and shirt start with the same.
Teacher:	Same letter.
Cindy:	They should put tee shirt because that's what it looks like.

Teacher:	So you don't think this makes sense. But it says—
Terry:	But down there they put sweater.
Teacher:	Shirt starts with *SH*, shhhhh.
Maury:	Just like *The Shrinking Shirt*.
Willie:	And *Jump Frog Jump* [when the protagonist says "shh."]
Teacher:	*There's a spot on my tie. There's a spot on my chin from this blueberry pie. Oh no!*
Willie:	On that page it's just one word, and on the other one it tells where it came from.
Teacher:	That's right. It doesn't tell where the spot on the tie came from.
LaWanda:	It could say, "From the hot dog he ate."
Teacher:	[doubling back] *There's a spot on my chin from this blueberry pie.*
Kira:	Every time I see that it makes me want to eat.
Teacher:	*There's a spot on my shorts* [children all reading along]. *There's a spot on my knee.*
Doug:	That don't look like knee.
Kira:	It sounds like a *E* for knee.
Teacher:	There are *E*s in it.
Sandy:	Two *E*s.
Teacher:	*There's a spot on my dress everybody can see. Oh no!*
Isaac:	Look, it's kind of a pattern with the pattern [Oh no] and the letters too. First it says *S* then *D* then *S*.
Shemeka:	[exasperated] It would make sense if they said where the spot came from and then on the next page tell where it came, before—and then said "Oh no."
Teacher:	So you want "Oh no" on every page? [Shemeka nods in agreement.]
Teacher:	*There's a spot on my spoon—*
Terry:	Probably from not washing good.
Charlie:	From somebody eating with it.
Teacher:	*There's a spot on my bowl. There's a spot on my cup and it looks like a hole. Oh no.*

Sara:	[commenting about the illustration] You know what they should do; they should make water coming out.
Isaac:	It looks like a clock. Turn it [the page] back.

[The teacher turns back so the illustration can be scrutinized, then resumes reading.]

Teacher:	*There's a spot on my hand. There's a spot on my face...*
Chris:	Oh! Oh! I know, I know.
Willie:	I know what that's gonna be.
Maury:	She's got chicken pops.
Teacher:	[reviewing] *There's a spot on my face.*
Tara:	"Oh no" on the next page.
Willie:	That's gonna be spots everywhere 'cause she got the spots off her plate.
Isaac:	Turn it back to the spoon. It looks like a spot.
Maury:	I got the chicken pops right now!

In this segment of storybook interaction, it was clear that learners were engaged in figuring out how the story worked. They attended to pattern and thought about story language, sound-symbol relations, and illustrations. They critiqued the story and related their own experiences to its events. The teacher stopped the story as requested, supported children's efforts to clarify, and listened to volunteered ideas.

When the two representative vignettes about storybook read-alouds were compared, differences in learner opportunities were evident. In the skills-based example, *What Mary Jo Shared*, the learners' responses were elicited at the end of the story only and guided by the teacher's questions. Children participated by using story information to support their opinions. In the whole language example, the discussion took place throughout the story reading event. It was based on learner observations and included teacher responses and questions. The opportunity to construct meaning was present throughout the whole language read-aloud lesson.

Interacting with storybooks in these ways clearly contributed to what these children knew about stories and how they responded to trade books. Data analyses revealed that children in whole language classrooms demonstrated a range of insights from their experiences. These patterns were not evident among learners in skills-based classrooms. Three categories of interpretation were evident: learning storybook language, gathering intertextual knowledge, and adopting a critical stance.

Learning storybook language was evident in children's writing. Their written stories included dedication pages, illustrations, dots to indicate continuing events, and formulaic endings. Patterns of action indicated children were learning about written language from reading and listening to trade books. The following story written in October of first grade by Isaac demonstrated this influence.

The Scary Hairy Spider
When me and Ricky was playing outside, we saw a spider
    and Ricky picked up the spider.
I said, "Ooo gross!"
And I said, "Ricky put that spider down or you will
    get bit and ...
if you get bit, don't come to me!"
And...if you come I will not help you.
And if you ask me twice, I still won't help you.

The End

The story was written in book form, with each line on a separate page. It included illustrations and a title page and was typical of many stories written about daily experiences but shaped by structures and language patterns found in books.

Gathering intertextual knowledge was demonstrated by whole language children in first grade as they spontaneously talked about characters, events, and plot arrangements across stories. Children appeared to be building a story world that included a repertoire of story elements. The following comments were characteristic of this learner pattern:

"Oh that reminds me of the butcher, the baker, and the candlestick maker."

"You have to look for the cat. It's like *Each Peach Pear Plum.*" [Ahlberg & Ahlberg, 1985]

"That looks like a Eric Carle book."

Learners appeared to have a memory for books and used their intertextual knowledge as they participated in story events. In contrast, no pattern of intertextual insights was present in the skills-based study. Learners' attention was directed toward other matters when stories were read by the teacher, and their spontaneous utterances did not include these connections.

Adopting a critical stance was shown as children in whole language class-rooms made suggestions about how professional authors could improve their stories. Children criticized story endings and talked about what would improve the illustrations. In skills-based classrooms children talked about story events and answered comprehension questions. There were few critical comments about stories.

Pattern 4: Coping strategies of learners experiencing difficulty. In both skills-based and whole language classrooms the least proficient readers and writers developed various ways of dealing with teacher expectations and instructional demands. While the patterns of behavior and strategies for coping were similar in some ways for children in the two studies, the cross-study contrasts were significant.

The similarities in behavior patterns were most evident in teacher/student conferences at the individual level. When skills-based teachers gave one-on-one help to learners experiencing difficulty, the children could focus on the lesson and increase their learning efforts. Outcomes of one-on-one interactions in skills-based classrooms often resulted in children getting the correct answer or showing they understood. Similarly, in whole language classrooms, one-on-one teacher/student interactions were productive for learners experiencing difficulty. In this context, learners responded positively and increased their efforts to accomplish the expected task.

The greatest difference in coping behaviors across studies occurred when these same learners worked on their own. Interestingly, passivity appeared to be the most pervasive coping strategy for learners experiencing difficulty in skills-based classrooms. Their strategies also included bluffing their way through reading lessons by reading paralinguistically and copying from others without efforts to produce meaning on their own. Field observations showed that learners sat and stared for periods of time, marked randomly on worksheets just to finish them, and waited for or asked for help. Their behaviors indicated they weren't making sense of what they were doing. One learner acted out somewhat aggressively, but in general the coping behaviors of children experiencing difficulty in the skills-based study seemed aimed at just getting through the assigned reading or writing activity. Rather than "taking on the task" of reading, they tended to avoid it and found ways to get by in the classroom (Purcell-Gates & Dahl, 1991).

One exception to this pattern was a skills-based learner who coped by creating opportunities for individual instruction. Creating a "school for one" (Dahl, Purcell-Gates, & McIntyre, 1989) entailed one of two strategies, either acting out sufficiently to be required to stay after school or interrupting small-group instruction by holding up the workbook, looking baffled, and asking, "What I pose a do?" in a loud voice. Both strategies produced private sessions with the teacher in which personal instruction was given and the learner's questions answered.

The coping behaviors of comparable children from whole language classrooms were shaped by the social contexts in their classrooms. Learners often interacted with their peers when they didn't know what to do. Within the periods of extended independent reading or writing, they tended to tag along with other learners. In doing so they seemed to establish their own support systems. For example, in group reading situations they actively listened to other children and picked up phrases and sentences, saying them along with others. When a struggling learner copied from children's papers during writing, there also was an attempt to write independently by simply adding letters, drawing, or talking about words or letters that could be added. These peer interactions indicated some attempt to carry on the activity meaningfully.

In writing, the least proficient learners in the whole language first grades developed some avoidance behaviors. These children sometimes moved around the room and interacted socially with peers. They also set up elaborate clerical duties such as getting word cards for others, becoming the illustrator in collaborative book writing, sharpening pencils, setting up supplies (paper, pencils, and crayons), and helping or organizing other helpers in writing tasks. They stalled and avoided the act of writing, often altering their behavior only in one-on-one sessions with the teacher.

Pattern 5: Sense of self as reader/writer and persistence. Among the patterns reflecting the learners' interpretations, two trends were particularly prominent in whole language classrooms. Whole language learners demonstrated in nearly every classroom observation a perception of themselves as readers and writers. Further, these learners sustained their attention in literacy episodes and persisted when engaged in reading/writing tasks.

Focal learners in whole language classrooms, particularly in the first-grade year, frequently made impromptu statements about themselves as readers and writers. Rather than focusing primarily on the acts of reading and writing, these children were interested in themselves and their progress. They frequently talked about what they knew how to do, what they were going to do next, and what they saw as a challenge or difficult task. These statements occurred spontaneously within the context of independent reading or writing time. Many remarks about self were made to no one in particular; others were part of the talk among learners as children engaged in reading and writing. The following statements are representative:

"I can read the whole book."

"I got that book at home, I already know it."

"Me and him wrote four books."

"I can read...just not out loud."

"I can spell that without even looking."

"When I was in kindergarten, I couldn't write or spell a thing."

"I'm a gonna write, I'm a gonna draw, I'm a gonna do one more page."

"I'll read it all by myself, I don't need any help."

Within the whole language classrooms this pattern was evident in children who read proficiently as well as in those who struggled with reading and writing, though less proficient readers and writers made more statements about what they were "gonna do" than about what they knew.

Analysis of field notes in whole language classrooms indicated that these statements were often connected with a second pattern of behavior, *persistence*. Consistently, whole language learners moved from reading one book to reading another, sustaining the act of reading across the independent reading period. Learners also read books collaboratively, talking about the pictures, commenting about the story, and reading in turns. These learners appeared to be engrossed in their reading and usually sustained their attention and effort. Sometimes learners kept reading during teachers' signals to put books away, and a few continued reading as the rest of the class began a new activity or lined up for lunch.

The pattern of persistence was evident in writing as some learners worked on the same story day after day or initiated an elaborate writing project and worked on it continuously with the support of friends throughout a given writing period. For example, Eustice, one of the least proficient writers in first grade, began a six-part book about his family. Each separate section addressed a different family member, and the project, spanning three consecutive writing periods with extensive teacher support, was characterized by Eustice excitedly arranging the book's sections in piles on his writing desk, wrestling with what to write about each person, and asking excitedly "Can I publish it?" over and over.

The skills-based classrooms also contained these patterns of sense of self and persistence, but the patterns were restricted to the most proficient readers and writers. Maya, for example, commented "I'm writing without even looking at the board." The pattern was evident in writing events also. For example, Audrey, being assigned to copy a group of sentences from the board and add an illustration, generated an original story. As she added speech bubbles for the characters she elaborated, "There's a red light and there's a stop sign and there's how fast you should be going. And the rain started raining and it come down splash and she said, 'Ha Jan and Pam.'" Audrey persisted with this story well past the lesson. The remote mike picked up Audrey talking through the story again later in the day, this time discussing Jan and Pam with another child (Dahl, Freppon, & McIntyre, 1994).

The frequency of these remarks and episodes differed across studies. Even for the most proficient readers and writers there were only a few scattered utterances captured in the first-grade year in skills-based sites, whereas such utterances were frequent in whole language classrooms, occurring in nearly every classroom visit in the first-grade year. In the skills-based sites the less proficient readers and writers sometimes made spontaneous statements during their work, but the statements were focused on task rather than self.

> "Dag, I wrote this on the wrong one."
>
> "I [know] what I pose to do, but what I pose to do first?"
>
> "I'm pasting my fox next to the *b*, where are you pasting yours?"
>
> (Purcell-Gates & Dahl, 1991)

Learners in skills-based classrooms, for the most part, were engaged in teacher-directed or teacher-assigned tasks and tended to complete them diligently. Their independent reading tended to be brief, and the prevailing pattern was to abandon books after reading a page or two. The most proficient learners, however, did reread basal stories on their own and tended to sustain that activity.

Quantitative Findings: Written Language Knowledge Assessments

The pretest results in both studies showed that these randomly selected children held a very restricted view of written language (Dahl & Freppon, 1991; Purcell-Gates, 1989). When the skills-based pretest results were compared to those of the whole language study, it was clear that children in the two whole language kindergartens scored slightly lower on every measure but one. Learners in both studies tended to view written language as something for school and were generally unfamiliar with print as a way to convey meaning. Learner grasp of print conventions, the alphabetic principle, and concepts of writing indicated little familiarity with written language. Pretest data on story structure and written narrative register showed that learners were unfamiliar with the language of storybooks and the macrostructure of written stories. At the end of the first-grade year learners in both investigations demonstrated considerable improvement.

Of particular interest in this cross-curricular comparison was whether there were significant differences in the quantitative measures when the skills-based and whole language posttest data were compared. A 2 (Group) $\times$ 2 (Time) mixed measures ANOVA with repeated measures was carried out on all six of the written language measures. Tables 5 and 6 present these data.

A significant Group $\times$ Time interaction was obtained for written narrative register only [$F(1,2) = 27.95$, $p <. 05$] with the whole language group scoring higher on the posttest than the skills-based group. The effect size was .07 (Hedges, 1982). Significance was not obtained on any of the other five outcome measures.

Table 5. Means and standard deviations obtained on outcome measures

	Skills-based		Whole language	
	Pretest	Posttest	Pretest	Posttest
Intentionality (1–5)	2.71 (1.68)	4.43 (1.22)	2.29 (1.35)	4.86 (0.65)
Concepts about print (0–24)	7.27 (4.30)	16.60 (4.69)	6.43 (3.88)	18.52 (2.77)
Alphabetic principle (1–8)	1.13 (0.35)	4.60 (1.45)	1.05 (0.22)	4.48 (1.63)
Story structure (1–8)	3.29 (1.59)	4.57 (1.83)	3.62 (1.75)	5.43 (1.33)
Written narrative register* (0–102)	23.92 (18.52)	43.00 (16.95)	19.58 (13.43)	63.42 (18.20)
Concepts of writing (1–7)	3.71 (1.92)	5.93 (1.21)	3.49 (1.88)	6.43 (0.51)

Note. The scores under each measure are the possible range, except for written narrative register, which is the actual range. Standard deviations are in parentheses.
* Significant Group $\times$ Time interaction ($p < .05$) was obtained.

Table 6. ANOVA table for written narrative register

Source	DF	SS	MS	F
Between				
A Group	1	956.47	956.47	3.91
B/A Teachers within Group	2	489.04	244.52	
Within				
C Time	1	15297.07	15297.07	171.93
AC Group × Time	1	2486.88	2486.88	27.95*
BC/A	2	177.94	88.97	

$*p < .05$

Contrasts in Reading Processes and Writing Events Across Studies

The analysis of reading processes involved a proficient reader, an average reader, and a less experienced reader from each curriculum. Each was selected as representative of the given proficiency level within the curriculum. Three findings were evident from the comparison of reading samples for the selected learners at each level of proficiency.

First, the reading behaviors of the selected skills-based learners differed across teacher-directed and independent reading contexts. The skills-based learners used strategies independently that they did not use with the teacher. A finer grained analysis of these patterns is included in McIntyre (1992). In contrast, the selected whole language learners read in similar ways in both contexts.

A second finding was that the whole language learners at each proficiency level demonstrated greater breadth strategically in both teacher-directed and independent contexts. Generally, the strategies of the skills-based learners were to identify known sight words, try to use letter-sound relations, and wait to be told an unknown word. The whole language learners generally used picture clues, skipped unknown words, reread and self-corrected, used letter-sound relations, asked for help, and commented about the story.

Third, the levels of engagement, as shown by patterns of learner persistence, effort, and interest in reading, were different across studies among learners who were average or less experienced readers. In the skills-based study, these two clusters of children did not demonstrate involvement by staying with reading tasks independently. Their whole language counterparts, in contrast, were persistent in their reading and highly active as they read independently.

Descriptions from these comparisons at each proficiency level are presented in the sections that follow. The contrasts include miscue data and evidence of reading strategies from reading samples during the mid and latter part of first grade as documented in teacher-directed and independent contexts.

Proficient readers: Audrey and Charlie. Audrey was the most proficient reader in her skills-based (SB) classroom. She read accurately and fluently in a word-calling manner in teacher-directed contexts, often waiting to be told an unknown word and sometimes sounding words out. Audrey's independent reading involved more strategies. Sometimes she read parts of a story conventionally, then switched to a focus on letter-sound cues. She seemed to experiment or play with the text when reading alone. Consistently, she was actively engaged in reading and performed as a persistent reader in both teacher-directed and independent contexts.

Charlie, in a whole language (WL) classroom, alternated between oral and silent reading. His oral reading substitutions in both teacher-directed and independent contexts indicated that he used all three cuing systems as well as picture clues. Charlie commented while reading and discussed the story line with himself. He worked on unknown words and said occasionally, "I don't know this one." He used letter-sound cues and rereading to figure out words.

Average readers: Mary Jane and Jason. In teacher-directed lessons Mary Jane (SB) simply stopped reading when she came to an unknown word. She read only the words she knew and relied on the teacher to supply unknown words. Teacher encouragement led to the inclusion of some letter-sound cues, though these were rarely employed in independent reading. Working alone, Mary Jane did not tend to remain engaged in reading.

Jason (WL) used a wide range of strategies such as skipping, rereading, and picture clues across contexts. Miscue data indicated that he used story meaning and sentence structure to identify unfamiliar words and that sometimes his substitutions showed an overreliance on phonics. Jason stayed with a story when it was difficult and sometimes commented about what he was reading.

Less experienced readers: Rodney and Ann. Rodney (SB) demonstrated a limited range of skills when reading with the teacher. He guessed at words using his repertoire of sight words (*was? it? is?*) and used picture clues, though often without success. His independent reading often consisted of talking about the story and using picture prompts. By the end of first grade his independent reading had declined, and Rodney tended to avoid reading in any context.

Ann (WL) used several strategies to get unknown words across contexts: rereading, letter-sound mapping, and using picture cues. Miscue analysis indicated an overreliance on phonics using the beginning sound only. Ann often talked about the story, and her independent reading behaviors indicated an active and engaged stance.

Comparison of Writing Tasks Across Studies

Analysis of writing tasks and products indicated that focal learners in skills-based classrooms, for the most part, produced written answers on assigned worksheets as their writing activity in kindergarten. Of these, most tasks involved circling letters that corresponded to beginning sounds of pictured items (e.g., *t* for *tub*) and identifying whole words that corresponded to pictures or color names.

In the whole language kindergartens, writing involved exploration. Learners produced letter strings, usually with accompanying drawings and sometimes with meaning assigned after the work was complete. Children copied environmental print, often adding illustrations, and some writing artifacts included invented spelling.

The contrasts between curricula were more pronounced in first grade. In skills-based classrooms, writing was primarily for sight word and specific skill practice. Children copied sight words from the board, either lists or sentences, and participated in workbook activities that called for copying the correct word or sentence or circling a sight word and its matching picture. Learners worked on making their writing neat and on spelling each word correctly.

While learners routinely completed this writing as "paperwork," there also was some interest in composing. A writing event from the November samples captured this phenomenon. The writing task was to use words written on the board (*rowboat, motorboat,* and *sailboat*) to write a sentence in the *Think and Write* workbook. The workbook page provided places for children to draw and write. The teacher's directions were, "Write a sentence about a boat. You could name the boat. If you need help spelling, raise your hand."

Jamie, a first grader in the skills-based study, began by drawing. After his rowboat picture was complete, he wrote *CAN BOAT* on the lines provided under the picture square. Next, he said "Go" and wrote *GO*. Looking determined, Jamie read his sentence so far under his breath, wrote *TWO* and then reread the sentence again, this time pointing to each word. Continuing the effort, Jamie frowned for a moment, then said "the" and wrote it. He looked at the sentence, sort of scanning it and added an *S* to the word *boat*.

His text read *CAN BOATS GO TWO THE*. Jamie then paused thoughtfully and raised his hand to request the word *river*. The episode ended as Jamie said the word he needed over and over.

Writing in this instance was focused at the sentence level, and the assigned topic was related to a basal story. Jamie was engaged in writing his intended meaning and carefully monitored his work.

A comparable writing event in whole language classrooms occurred in the same time period involving Willie, also a first grader. During the writing workshop period, Willie wrote a spinoff story for the book *The Chocolate Cake*, which he had read earlier. He copied the title and used the book's format. Looking at the book, Willie wrote:

> *DTA SAID M-M-M-M-M.* [Dad]
>
> *GRONDMA SAID M-M-M-M.* [Grandma]
>
> *MYAAT SAID M-M-M-M.* [my aunt]
>
> *BODY SAID M-M-M-M-M.* [baby]

As he slowly said each person's name, Willie looked to the side and listened to the sounds, then he wrote the letters. Next, he copied the repeated phrase from the first page of the book. He arranged one sentence to a page, placing the sentences at the bottom as if illustrations would follow. Willie reread his four pages, then smiled and added the last *WILLIE SAID M-M-M-M*.

In this event there was an effort to map letters and sounds and a supporting text to structure the project. There was no revision after rereading.

In general, when writing tasks and products were compared, the differences reflected the function that writing served in each curriculum. In the skills-based classrooms, the learners completed teacher-assigned writing tasks designed to provide practice in skills. In the whole language classrooms, the writing periods were centered on learner-generated topics and learner exploration of written language. Children often received help from their peers and from the teacher.

The kinds of writing produced differed markedly across curricula. In first grade the children in whole language classrooms primarily produced work at the sentence, paragraph, and story levels. First graders in skills-based classrooms also produced some stories, but for the most part they worked on completing workbook assignments or on text written by the teacher on the board. Many writing tasks included sentence completion, fill in the blanks, and sentence or sight word copying with choices that learners could make among words.

Comparison of Learning Opportunities

While the focus in this cross-curricular comparison was on learner interpretations of beginning reading and writing instruction, contrasts in learning opportunities were evident. In the sections on phonics growth, response to literature, and writing tasks, we described learner patterns of behavior which related to each curriculum. In Table 7 we summarize the learning opportunities in these three areas.

While we recognize that a comprehensive account of differing learning opportunities across curricula is beyond the scope of this article, some distinctions can be drawn from our field note accounts. The two vignettes that follow are representative of reading instruction in skills-based and whole language first-grade classrooms and serve to illustrate differences in learning opportunities during teacher-directed lessons.

Reading vignette—Skills based. In one skills-based classroom, the teacher introduced the basal story "The Yellow Monster," which told about a yellow bulldozer that some children had discovered. She talked briefly to the small group about the author, explained what the word *author* meant, and then read an abstract of the story. She added, "So during the story you should be thinking about...what IS the monster." The children then began to read the story aloud one by one as others followed along, some pointing to the words as they listened. The teacher urged children to focus carefully on words. "Look at the word...what's the word?" she said repeatedly. The children not reading aloud said the word to themselves when the teacher stopped a reader. For example, Shirika read some words incorrectly during her turn. The teacher intervened, "Look at the word, that is not what it says. Put your finger under the sentence *it likes to dig*. The next word is *follow*." Shirika repeated *follow*. During their turns, each of the five children in the group read three or four story sentences. Maya took her turn:

> Maya: *"Here is the monster," said Nina.*
>
> *"Don't go too near it."*
>
> *"Oh, I know what that is," said Linda.*
>
> *"This monster is big and yellow. It's a helping monster," said Tom.*
>
> Teacher: Said who?
>
> Maya: Tim.
>
> Teacher: OK

Table 7. Learning opportunities across curricula

Aspect of literacy	Curriculum	Learning opportunities
Phonics growth	Skills based	Letter-sound relations were addressed in skill lessons. Teachers showed how to sound out words, and learners sounded out words as they read aloud. Worksheets about phonics were required as seatwork. Boardwork asked learners to copy words grouped by letter-sound patterns.
	Whole language	Teachers demonstrated sounding out during whole-group instruction with big books. In reading lessons letter-sound relations were one of the cuing systems that learners used to figure out words. Writing workshops included help for individual learners grappling with what letters to write for their intended meaning. Peers provided letter-sound information during daily writing.
Response to literature	Skills based	Children listened to stories read aloud and responded to the teacher's questions. Children read trade books of their choice when their seatwork was completed or during morning lunch-count routines.
	Whole language	Tradebooks were the primary reading material, and learners read books of their choice independently. Read-alouds with the teacher included children's talk during the story. Information was provided about authors, illustrations, genre, and connections across literary works.
Writing tasks and products	Skills based	Writing tasks were assigned and generally addressed specific skills in the basal program. Learners copied sentences using basal sight words. During boardwork they completed sentences by choosing from word choices that were generated by class members. They worked on specific writing lessons in the *Think and Write* workbook. There were some periods where writing journals were used.
	Whole language	Daily writing workshop periods included sustained writing about self-selected topics. Teachers provided individual conferences during writing workshops. They also demonstrated using letter-sound knowledge to spell words. Learners used trade books to prompt topics and word choices. They copied from books. Peers suggested ideas to one another and worked together on spelling. Learners wrote stories and read them to others.

The story continued with the next reader and the next until it ended with teacher talk about reading carefully rather than rushing and saying the wrong word. "When you come across a word that you don't know, I want you to take the time to figure out what it is. Sound out the word or ask someone," she urged. Learners were then instructed to reread the story, practice the words and think about them on their own.

Reading vignette—Whole language. The whole language teacher and a small group of children looked through their copies of a new paperback, and they talked about what they liked from their initial scanning. They discussed what the story was going to be about after looking at the pictures and noting some of the words. Then one child simply began to read aloud, and others joined in. The teacher moved in and out of the children's parallel oral reading (reading so the children's voices predominated). When children faltered, the teacher asked questions, prompted with the sound that matched the beginning of the word, or asked about the picture. She also asked children to talk about the story, make predictions, and clarify what they thought. The teacher asked, "How do you know?" and "Why do you think that?" as children told their ideas. Midway through the story the teacher asked learners to "read with my finger" and pointed to one particular sentence, encouraging children to reread it with her. Children read the sentence but stumbled on the word *gate*. They talked about how they figured out the word (the various cuing systems they used). The teacher asked children to discuss the developing story in light of its beginning and then invited them to finish on their own. She said, "I'll let you find out what other trouble they get into." After children finished reading on their own, some were asked to do rechecks (rereadings) to clear up parts where they had trouble.

Reflection. In these two vignettes the learning opportunities differed markedly. Learners in the skills-based lesson had the opportunity to focus sharply on words, take their reading turn, listen to others, and practice reading the story on their own. Their attention was directed to the point of the lesson, and they received consistent coaching from their teacher as they read. In contrast, the whole language lesson was more diverse. Learners received various kinds of assistance, they were encouraged to use multiple cuing systems, and each reader read nearly all of the story. There was an opportunity to think about how to read and construct a sense of the story.

When data from Table 7 reporting learning opportunities in phonics, response to literature, and writing tasks are considered along with the reading instructional patterns illustrated in the vignettes, several contrasts are evident. The skills-based curriculum placed children, for the most part, in teacher-directed contexts where they engaged in reading or writing practice and interpreted or made sense of concepts from the instructional program. There was a focus on specific skills and practice opportunities assigned by the teacher. In contrast, the whole language curriculum engaged learners in sustained periods of reading and writing. Planned lessons took place in teacher-directed contexts, there was direct skill instruction focused on strategies, and learner choice was pervasive. Further, individual conferences provided contexts for instruction and support for independent reading and writing efforts.

Conclusions and Discussion

This cross-curricular comparison had two goals: It sought to capture learners' interpretations of beginning reading and writing instruction across the first two years of schooling in skills-based and whole language classrooms, and it structured a comparison across these two contrasting literacy curricula. The point was to make visible the similarities and differences across curricula in the children's interpretations of reading and writing and to extend our understanding of these curricula for innercity children.

The results presented a somewhat paradoxical picture. On the one hand, some findings, particularly those from quantitative measures, indicated a number of similarities in learning outcomes as measured by the tasks assessing written language knowledge. The cross-curricular comparison also documented that children made progress in both approaches. Given the controversy about direct or indirect instruction, especially for minority children (Delpit, 1986, 1988), and the "great debate" about phonics, these findings were of particular interest.

On the other hand, many of the findings demonstrated that learners made different senses of reading and writing in light of their experiences. The significant difference in written narrative register was taken to reflect curricular differences. Whole language learners generated significantly more syntactic and lexical features of story language, and they experienced extended exposure to and interaction with storybooks. In contrast, skills-based classrooms offered less emphasis on literature experiences.

The findings about letter-sound relations suggested that we have been asking the wrong questions. The important issue was not how children were taught in school-based settings, but rather what sense they could make. Unquestionably, phonics learning varied among focal learners in both studies. The essential difference was in the application learners made of their letter-sound knowledge and whether it was meaningful to them in terms of their understanding of written language knowledge. Children in one-on-one conferences with the teacher in both curricula seemed able to focus on letter-sound relations with teacher support. In independent writing contexts in the whole language classrooms children also learned to look twice at letters and sounds and tended to apply letter-sound relations more often during reading and writing episodes.

Finally, the cross-curricular comparison indicated distinctive differences in the affective domain (Turner, 1991). Learners in whole language classrooms expressed extensive interest in themselves as literacy learners. Moreover, their talk and actions revealed an understanding of their strengths and weaknesses as readers and writers. The linked patterns of sense of self as reader/writer and persistence indicated the establishment of a "disposition for learning" and provided evidence of learner ownership and a positive attitude toward literacy. In the skills-based study these two patterns were evident only among the most proficient readers and writers. This learner pattern was considered important in light of the vexing problem of patterns of failure that often characterize innercity learners in public schooling.

The paradox of differing findings from qualitative and quantitative data merits some explanation. In this comparison qualitative and quantitative data sources were considered as multiple perspectives revealing various kinds of information. The qualitative data tapped learner utterances and patterns of action over time and thus yielded data that revealed learner interpretations of reading and writing. The quantitative measures, in contrast, served as pre/post samples and indicated students' written language knowledge in specific domains. Because the sampling and focus differed in some areas across qualitative and quantitative data, the respective findings also differed. For example, data about attitudes toward reading and writing were prominent in the qualitative data but not sampled in the specific quantitative tasks. Similarly, data about accuracy in reading and writing events, responses to literature, and coping strategies of learners were evident in qualitative data, but not assessed in quantitative tasks.

There were three areas where qualitative and quantitative data converged in focus. First, in the area of written narrative register (knowledge of the language of storybooks), the qualitative and quantitative findings were in agreement and favored whole language. Second, in phonics knowledge, the qualitative and quantitative findings were at odds. Qualitative data indicated more application of letter-sound knowledge in daily writing events in whole language classrooms, but this difference was not supported in the quantitative alphabetic principle findings. Third, in writing production there was a difference in qualitative and quantitative findings. The former indicated greater sustained writing experiences for whole language learners, yet the quantitative task assessing writing showed no significant difference in the kinds of writing learners produced.

The disagreement in alphabetic principle findings suggests that, as assessed in these tasks, the two curricula may not differ widely in the phonics knowledge that learners gain. The difference was in what learners in differing curricula did with their phonics knowledge. Finally, in the area of writing production, the differences between qualitative and quantitative findings reflected learner interpretations of the writing task. Whole language learners responded to the writing task as a prompt for knowledge display. They produced lists of words or lists of sentences instead of their usual stories. The testing context and the task prompt appeared to shape learner interpretations about what the task required.

On a more general level, this cross-curricular comparison indicated differences in children's fundamental understandings about what literacy was for. The distinction between literacy skills and literate behaviors is central to understanding the contrasting outcomes documented in this comparison. Literacy skills are the concepts and behaviors that learners use as they read and write. They are elements of proficient reading and writing that are taught and practiced in most school-based settings. Literate behaviors are somewhat broader; they include learners reflecting on their own literate activity and using oral language to interact with written language by reacting to a story, explaining a piece of writing, or describing a favorite book to another person (Heath & Hoffman, 1986). Literate behaviors also include taking on the tasks of reading and writing, valuing one's own experience and personal language and connecting them with written language, and communicating about written language experiences. When learners see their own experience as valid knowledge and use reading and writing for their own purposes, the journey toward literate behaviors is soundly underway.

Children as sense makers in these two studies seemed to exemplify the distinction between literacy skills and literate behaviors. Some of the children in skills-based classrooms did not weave together the "cloth of literacy" (Purcell-Gates & Dahl, 1991, p. 21) nor move beyond their role as answer makers. Generally, they participated in reading and writing events, completed their work and learned literacy skills, but did not get involved personally nor see reading and writing as going beyond something for school. The children in whole language classrooms also learned skills and engaged in literate behaviors. Importantly, some degree of literate behavior was demonstrated by children of all levels of proficiency in these classrooms.

Learners who demonstrated the disposition for learning took on the task of reading and writing for their own purposes. The majority of children in whole language classrooms and the most proficient readers in the skills-based sites demonstrated this pattern of engagement and ownership. Thus, the greatest difference appeared to be not what was being taught, but what children were learning—about themselves, about reading and writing, about school.

Limitations

The comparison of these two studies was restricted to urban, low-SES children learning to read and write in skills-based and whole language kindergarten and first-grade settings. No standardized measure of phonemic awareness was used in the array of quantitative measures that were part of the pre/post comparison. Thus, claims about phonics growth are limited to patterns that were documented in field notes of classroom observations. Comparative studies are generally limited by the extent to which the data being compared are parallel. This current study compared the outcomes of four years of research in eight classrooms in two very different instructional settings. Thus, it is important to clarify some potentially troubling issues that arise in any comparative study and particularly in one of this duration and complexity.

The current research project was guided by some overarching principles. First, children's knowledge construction was identified through patterns of learner talk and action. Researchers focused on the learners' perspectives, and codes and categories emerged from the actual learner behaviors in all eight classrooms. What these learners said and did in consistent ways over time formed the basis of sense-making categories. Second, the instructional contexts of the skills-based and whole language classrooms clearly acted to shape children's behaviors in various ways. Students' talk and actions can only be made manifest within the bounds of behavior considered acceptable in any classroom. The theoretical differences between the skills-based and whole language curricula, subsequent teacher and student reading and writing behaviors, and classroom rules of conduct determined to a large extent the written language interactions that could be observed in these studies. Third, we combined this understanding with careful and rigorous analysis of children's observable actions across both instructional contexts. The reported similarities and differences between skills-based and whole language groups were grounded in what these children, from highly similar low-SES populations and cultural groups, did to make sense of written language in these contrasting curricula.

Implications

The contrasts in learner sense making across studies reinforced the notion that we must consider the learner's perspective and individual differences in reading and writing development in order to understand children's reading and writing behaviors. Beyond documenting classroom curricula and their consequences, we need to know what children believe, what events and contexts shape their thinking, and how instruction can better fit children's evolving knowledge and skills.

In the final analysis, acquiring the disposition for learning may be the most critical occurrence in the early grades. The innercity learners in our study have many years of schooling ahead of them. The prognosis for children who are engrossed in books at the first-grade level and who think of themselves as readers and writers and are mindful of their strengths and weaknesses appears hopeful. It suggests at least the possibility that these children may continue to choose to read in the grades ahead and that they might sustain their roles as writers. In contrast, those who in first grade have already disengaged from literacy instruction appear to have begun the pattern of turning away from school (Dahl, 1992). The contrasts in this cross-curricular comparison tell us that learners are making sense of themselves in terms of their experiences in the early grades and that these early learner perceptions may establish patterns with far-reaching consequences.

Directions for Future Research

Future studies that compare across curricula might focus on some of the issues raised in this investigation. The area of phonemic awareness could be investigated across curricula in terms of instructional interactions and learner interpretations. The contrasting learning opportunities in skills-based and whole language classrooms should be investigated in detail. Finally, cross-curricular comparisons need to extend to the upper grades, where investigations of sustained instruction across two or more years in whole language and/or traditional basal programs have rarely been conducted with primary focus on learner interpretations.

REFERENCES

Ahlberg, J., & Ahlberg, A. (1985). *Each peach pear plum.* New York: Scholastic.

Au, K. (1991). *Cultural responsiveness and the literacy development of minority students.* Paper presented at the annual meeting of the National Reading Conference, Palm Springs, CA.

Bloome, D., & Green, J. (1984). Directions in the sociolinguistic study of reading. In P.D. Pearson (Ed.), *Handbook of reading research* (pp. 395–422). New York: Longman.

Bond, G.L., & Dykstra, R. (1967). The cooperative research program in first-grade reading instruction. *Reading Research Quarterly, 2,* 5–142.

Brown, M.J.M. (1990). *An ethnology of innovative educational projects in Georgia.* Paper presented at the annual meeting of the American Evaluation Association, Washington, DC.

Bussis, A.M., Chittenden, E.A., Amarel, M., & Klausner, E. (1985). *Inquiry into meaning.* Hillsdale, NJ: Erlbaum.

Clay, M.M. (1975). *What did I write?* Portsmouth, NH: Heinemann.

Clay, M.M. (1979). *Stones: The concepts about print test.* Portsmouth, NH: Heinemann.

Cochran-Smith, M. (1984). *The making of a reader.* Norwood, NJ: Ablex.

Dahl, K.L. (1992). Ellen, a deferring learner. In R. Donmoyer & R. Kos (Eds.), *At-risk learners: Policies, programs, and practices* (pp. 89–102). Albany, NY: State University of New York Press.

Dahl, K.L. (1993). Children's spontaneous utterances during reading and writing instruction in whole language first grade classrooms. *Journal of Reading Behavior, 25*(3), 279–294.

Dahl, K.L., & Freppon, P.A. (1991). Literacy learning in whole language classrooms: An analysis of low socioeconomic urban children learning to read and write in kindergarten. In J. Zutell & S. McCormick (Eds.), *Learner factors/teacher factors: Issues in literacy research and instruction* (40th Yearbook of the National Reading Conference, pp. 149–158). Chicago: National Reading Conference.

Dahl, K.L., & Freppon, P.A. (1992). *Literacy learning: An analysis of low-SES urban learners in kindergarten and first grade.* (Grant No. R117E00134). Washington, DC: Office of Educational Research and Improvement, U.S. Department of Education.

Dahl, K.L., Freppon, P.A., & McIntyre, E. (1994). *Composing experiences of low-SES emergent writers in skills-based and whole language urban classrooms.* Unpublished manuscript.

Dahl, K.L., Purcell-Gates, V., & McIntyre, E. (1989). *Ways that inner-city children make sense of traditional reading and writing instruction in the early grades.* (Grant No. G008720229). Washington, DC: Office of Educational Research and Improvement, U.S. Department of Education.

Deford, D.E. (1984). Classroom contexts for literacy learning. In T. Raphael (Ed.), *The contexts of school-based literacy* (pp. 161–180). New York: Random House.

Deford, D.E. (1985). Validating the construct of theoretical orientation in reading instruction. *Reading Research Quarterly, 20,* 351–367.

Delawter, J.A. (1970). *Oral reading errors of second grade children exposed to two different reading approaches.* Unpublished doctoral dissertation, Columbia University, New York.

Delpit, L.D. (1986). Skills and other dilemmas of a progressive black educator. *Harvard Educational Review, 56,* 379–385.

Delpit, L.D. (1988). The silenced dialogue: Power and pedagogy in educating other people's children. *Harvard Educational Review, 58,* 280–298.

Donmoyer, R., & Kos, R. (1993). At-risk students: Insights from/about research. In R. Donmoyer & R. Kos (Eds.), *At-risk students: Portraits, policies, programs, and practices* (pp. 7–36). Albany, NY: SUNY Press.

Dyson, A.H. (1989). *Multiple worlds of child writers: Friends learning to write.* New York: Teachers College Press.

Dyson, A.H. (1991, February). Viewpoints: The word and the world—Reconceptualizing written language development or do rainbows mean a lot to little girls? *Research in the Teaching of English, 25*(1), 97–123.

Edelsky, C. (1991). *With literacy and justice for all: Rethinking the social in language and education.* New York: Falmer Press.

Edwards, E., & Mercer, N. (1987). *Common knowledge.* New York: Methuen.

Faulkner, K. (1991). *Oh no.* New York: Simon & Schuster.

Ferriero, E., & Teberosky, A. (1982). *Literacy before schooling.* Exeter, NH: Heinemann.

Freppon, P.A. (1991). Children's concepts of the nature and purpose of reading and writing in different instructional settings. *Journal of Reading Behavior, 23,* 139–163.

Freppon, P.A. (1993). *Making sense of reading and writing in urban classrooms: Understanding at-risk children's knowledge construction in different curricula* (Grant No. R117E1026191). Washington, DC: Office of Educational Research and Improvement, U.S. Department of Education.

Freppon, P.A., & Dahl, K.L. (1991). Learning about phonics in a whole language classroom. *Language Arts, 69,* 192–200.

Gentry, J.R. (1982). An analysis of developmental spelling in *GYNS AT WRK. The Reading Teacher, 36,* 192–200.

Gentry, J.R. (1987). *Spel is a four-letter word.* Portsmouth, NH: Heinemann.

Gibson, L. (1989). *Literacy learning in the early years through children's eyes.* New York: Teachers College Press.

Goetz, J.P., & LeCompte, M.D. (1984). *Ethnography and qualitative design in educational research.* New York: Academic Press.

Goodman, K. (1986). *What's whole in whole language?* Portsmouth, NH: Heinemann.

Green, J., & Meyer, L. (1991). The embeddedness of reading in classroom life: Reading as a situated process. In C. Baker & A. Luke (Eds.), *The critical sociology of reading pedagogy* (pp. 141–160). The Netherlands: John Benjamins.

Griffin, P., Cole, M., & Newman, D. (1982). Locating tasks in psychology and education. *Discourse Processes, 5,* 111–125.

Halliday, M.A.K. (1978). *Language as a social semiotic: The social interpretation of language and meaning.* Baltimore: University Park Press.

Harste, J., Burke, C., & Woodward, V.A. (1981). *Children, their language and their world: Initial encounters with print* (Grant No. NIE-G-790132). Washington, DC: National Institute of Education.

Harste, J., Burke, C., & Woodward, V.A. (1983). *The young child as writer-reader, and informant* (Grant No. NIE-G-80-0121). Washington, DC: National Institute of Education.

Heath, S.B. (1982). What no bedtime story means: Narrative skills at home and school. *Language in Society, 11,* 49–76.

Heath, S.B. (1983). *Ways with words: Language, life, and work in communities and classrooms.* New York: Cambridge University Press.

Heath, S.B., & Hoffman, D.M. (1986). *Inside learners: Interactive reading in the elementary classroom* [Videotape]. Palo Alto, CA: Stanford University.

Hedges, L.V. (1982). Estimation of effect size from a series of independent experiments. *Psychological Bulletin, 92*(2), 490–499.

Holdaway, D. (1979). *The foundations of literacy*. Portsmouth, NH: Heinemann.

Jordan, C., Tharp, R.G., & Baird-Vogt, L. (1992). Just open the door: Cultural compatibility. In M. Saravia-Shore & S.F. Arvizu (Eds.), *Cross-cultural literacy* (pp. 3–18). New York: Garland.

Kantor, R., Miller, S.M., & Fernie, D.E. (1992). Diverse paths to literacy in a preschool classroom: A sociocultural perspective. *Reading Research Quarterly, 27*, 185–201.

Kennedy, J., & Bush, A.J. (1985). *An introduction to the design and analysis of experiments in behavioral research* (pp. 521–531). Lanham, MD: University Press of America.

Knapp, M.S., & Shields, P.M. (1990). Reconceiving academic instruction for children of poverty. *Phi Delta Kappan, 71*, 752–758.

Mackinnon, A.R. (1959). *How do children learn to read?* Toronto: Coop Clark.

McGill-Franzen, A., & Allington, R.L. (1991). The gridlock of low reading achievement: Perspectives on practice and policy. *Remedial and Special Education, 12*(3), 20–30.

McIntyre, E. (1992). Young children's reading behaviors in various classroom contexts. *Journal of Reading Behavior, 24*(3), 339–391.

Meyers, J. (1992). The social contexts of school and personal literacy. *Reading Research Quarterly, 27*, 297–333.

Mitchell, V. (1992). African-American students in exemplary urban high schools: The interaction of school practices and student actions. In M. Saravia-Shore & S.F. Arvizu (Eds.), *Cross-cultural literacy* (pp. 19–36). New York: Garland.

Neuman, S.B., & Roskos, K. (1992). Literacy objects as cultural tools: Effects on children's literacy behaviors in play. *Reading Research Quarterly, 27*, 203–225.

Newman, J. (1985). Insights from recent reading and writing research and their implications for developing whole language curriculum. In J. Newman (Ed.), *Whole language: Theory in use* (pp. 7–36). Portsmouth, NH: Heinemann.

Ogbu, J.H. (1985, October). *Opportunity structure, cultural boundaries, and literacy*. Paper presented at the Language, Literacy, and Culture: Issues of Society and Schooling seminar, Stanford University, Palo Alto, CA.

Oldfather, P., & Dahl, K. (1994). Toward a social constructivist reconceptualization of intrinsic motivation for literacy learning. *Journal of Reading Behavior, 26*(2), 139–158.

Pellegrini, A. (1991). A critique of the concept of at risk as applied to emergent literacy. *Language Arts, 68*, 380–385.

Purcell-Gates, V. (1988). Lexical and syntactic knowledge of written narrative held by well-read-to kindergartners and second graders. *Research in the Teaching of English, 22*, 128–160.

Purcell-Gates, V. (1989). Written language knowledge held by low-SES, inner-city children entering kindergarten. In S. McCormick & J. Zutell (Eds.), *Cognitive and social perspectives for literacy research and instruction* (39th Yearbook of the National Reading Conference, pp. 95–105). Chicago: National Reading Conference.

Purcell-Gates, V., & Dahl, K. (1991). Low-SES children's success and failure at early literacy in skills-based classrooms. *Journal of Reading Behavior, 23*(1), 1–34.

Read, C. (1971). Pre-school children's knowledge of English phonology. *Harvard Educational Review, 41*, 1–34.

Rosenblatt, L. (1985). Viewpoints: Transaction versus interaction—A terminological rescue operation. *Research in the Teaching of English, 19*, 96–106.

Rosenblatt, L. (1989). Writing and reading: The transactional theory. In J. Mason (Ed.), *Reading and writing connections* (pp. 153–176). Needham Heights, MA: Allyn & Bacon.

Rowe, D.W. (1989). Author/audience interaction in the preschool: The role of social interaction in literacy lessons. *Journal of Reading Behavior, 21*, 311–349.

Schieffelin, B.B., & Cochran-Smith, M. (1984). Learning to read culturally. In H. Goelman, A. Oberg, & F. Smith (Eds.), *Awakening to literacy* (pp. 3–23). London: Heinemann.

Smith-Burke, M.T. (1989). Political and economic dimensions of literacy: Challenges for the 1990's. In S. McCormick & J. Zutell (Eds.), *Cognitive and social perspectives for literacy research and instruction* (39th Yearbook of the National Reading Conference, pp. 19–34). Chicago: National Reading Conference.

Stein, N.L. (1979). *The concept of story: A developmental psycholinguistic analysis.* Paper presented at the annual meeting of the American Educational Research Association. San Francisco, CA.

Stein, N.L. (1982). The definition of a story. *Journal of Pragmatics, 6*, 487–507.

Stein, N.L., & Glenn, C.G. (1975). *A developmental study of children's recall of story material.* Paper presented at the meeting of the Society for Research in Child Development, Denver, CO.

Stein, N.L., & Glenn, C.G. (1979). An analysis of story comprehension in elementary school children. In R.O. Freedle (Ed.), *Discourse processing: Advances in research and theory* (Vol. 2, pp. 53–120). Norwood, NJ: Ablex.

Sulzby, E. (1985). Children's emergent reading of favorite storybooks: A developmental study. *Reading Research Quarterly, 20*, 458–481.

Sulzby, E. (1992). Transitions from emergent to conventional writing. *Language Arts, 69*, 290–297.

Taylor, D. (1983). *Family literacy: Young children learning to read and write.* Portsmouth, NH: Heinemann.

Taylor, D., & Dorsey-Gaines, C. (1988). *Growing up literate: Learning from inner-city families.* Portsmouth, NH: Heinemann.

Teale, W.H. (1984). Reading to young children: Its significance for literacy development. In H. Goelman, A. Oberg, & F. Smith (Eds.), *Awakening to literacy* (pp. 110–121). London: Heinemann.

Teale, W.H. (1986). Home background and young children's literacy development. In W.H. Teale & E. Sulzby (Eds.), *Emergent literacy: Writing and reading.* Norwood, NJ: Ablex.

Teale, W.H., & Sulzby, E. (1986). Introduction: Emergent literacy as a perspective for examining how young children become writers and readers. In W.H. Teale & E. Sulzby (Eds.), *Emergent literacy: Writing and reading.* Norwood, NJ: Ablex.

Trueba, H. (1988). Culturally-based explanations of minority students' academic achievement. *Anthropology and Education Quarterly, 19*, 270–287.

Turner, J. (1991). *First graders' intrinsic motivation for literacy in basal instruction and whole language classrooms.* Paper presented at the annual meeting of the National Reading Conference, Palm Springs, CA.

Udry, J.M. (1966). *What Mary Jo shared.* Chicago: Albert Whitman.

Wells, G. (1986). *The meaning makers: Children learning language and using language to learn.* Portsmouth, NH: Heinemann.

Whaley, J. (1981). Story grammars and reading instruction. *The Reading Teacher, 34*, 762–771.

APPENDIX
Sample grid of learner patterns

Grids summarize learner patterns of activity in reading and writing as documented in field notes. They include notations about activity during instructional periods, information about stance, and dates of important vignettes.

Name: Willie
Time interval: Jan.–May of first grade
Curriculum: Whole language

Reading activity:
Reads whole books with teacher, discusses gist. Frequent near-conventional reading. Miscues show balance of cuing systems, many strategies. Close monitoring of own reading. Self-corrects. Begins to vary strategies in independent reading—sometimes telling a story for pages with extensive text, then reading conventionally pages with a small number of sentences. Often reads collaboratively with friend, alternating pages.

Writing activity:
Writes books with partner, suggests words, writes some sentences, talks about what could come next in story. Sustained writing every period from February on. Writes about personal experience. Composing behavior includes saying words and phrases as he writes them, rereading, asking for spelling, completing the written piece.

Instruction periods (whole group):
Reads along with the teacher. Continually interrupts story reading with comments about patterns or statements connecting prior knowledge with story.

Stance:
Active, interested in reading and writing. Sustains independent work, often deeply engrossed.

Vignettes:

January 16	Sustained reading with teacher, whole book.
March 6	Revision conference with teacher, adds quotation marks.

Breaking Down Barriers That Disenfranchise African American Adolescent Readers in Low-Level Tracks

Alfred W. Tatum

A nationwide thrust in the United States to adopt high-stakes testing for promotion in grades 6, 8, and 11 is forcing many teachers to adopt a test-driven approach to increase the achievement of struggling adolescent readers. District officials assume that high-stakes testing will produce improved learning outcomes. Proponents of high-stakes testing argue that it is students who have done least well in school who will benefit from test-driven instruction. Support for test-driven reform based on standards is not found in analysis of the National Assessment of Educational Progress's 1994 reading assessment (Campbell, Donahue, Reese, & Phillips, 1996). In fact, lower reading achievement is associated with practices that accompany test-driven instruction (Smith, 1991). Evidence suggests that students in states without high-stakes testing perform better than those in states with it (Neill, 1998).

The gap between a comprehensive approach to literacy teaching and the widespread practice of teachers of African American adolescent students with poor reading skills is widening because meeting minimum standards is being emphasized. As an eighth-grade teacher in a low-income African American neighborhood in a large urban area I became concerned about the emphasis being placed on standardized scores as part of a school reform initiative. I wanted to help students nurture their identities so that they would not limit themselves but would seek opportunities not readily available in their community.

Darling-Hammond and Falk (1997) pointed out that

> depending on how standards are shaped and used, either they could support more ambitious teaching and greater levels of success for all students, or they could serve to create higher rates of failure for those who are already least well-served by the education system. (p. 191)

The proliferation of standards and the high rates of retention that result from not meeting these standards indicate that a move toward standards does not always lead to greater levels of success. For example, in Chicago, one of the

Originally published in *Journal of Adolescent & Adult Literacy* (2000), volume 44, pages 52–64.

largest urban school districts in the United States, alternative high schools have been created to accommodate students who repeatedly fail to meet standards. Parents, educators, and members of local school councils have referred to these schools as warehouses for underachieving students of color.

Standards are minimal and do not begin to adequately address the needs of African Americans struggling with reading if the approach to meeting those standards depends on a basic skills orientation. This "goes against the grain of pushing them toward their maximum competency level" (Hillard, 1995, p. 108). As a result, many students will be remanded to the margins of society, never to experience full political, economic, and social participation.

The problem of how to increase the literacy achievement of African Americans is embedded in social, cultural, economic, and historical dynamics. Educational inequities, cultural alienation, and economic deprivation play out in very subtle and pernicious ways in U.S. classrooms. This situation, along with ill-framed misconceptions about African Americans, by both black and white teachers, has a negative impact on literacy achievement for this group.

A closer look at the "good teaching" (Foster, 1993; Foster & Delpit, 1997; Ladson-Billings, 1995a) of African American students has emerged during the past decade. A distinctive educational philosophy and pedagogy along with the aspects of teacher behavior students considered effective have been pointed out. The "good teachers" of African Americans, whose major attributes were revealed by these studies, may be described as follows:

1. They are concerned individuals who command respect, respect pupils, and are strict, although caring, in requiring all students to meet high academic and behavioral standards.

2. They are concerned not only with the students' cognitive development, but also with their affective, social, and emotional development.

3. They use a culturally relevant approach to literacy teaching.

A culturally relevant approach involves talking to black students about the personal value, the collective power, and the political consequences of choosing academic achievement. In such an approach, activities based on African American community norms are incorporated into the classroom, cooperation is emphasized over competition, and learning is structured as a social activity.

Several other requisites have been offered by Ladson-Billings (1995b) for a culturally relevant approach to literacy teaching:

1. Students must experience academic success, develop and maintain cultural competence, and develop a critical consciousness to challenge the status quo.
2. Teachers should attend to students' academic needs, not merely make them feel good.
3. Students' culture should be made a vehicle for learning.
4. Students need help to develop a broader sociopolitical consciousness that allows them to critique the cultural norms, values, mores, and institutions that produce and maintain social inequities.

Using culturally relevant literature is key to a culturally relevant approach. It has been suggested that African American adolescents in low-level reading tracks (particularly those who live in poverty and in politically and socially defunct communities) need to read, write about, and discuss literature that would help them develop cultural competence (Ladson-Billings, 1995b).

There is a fundamental tension between a basic skills approach to meet standards and a culturally relevant approach. Developing cultural competence with culturally relevant literature does not solve the problems of teachers confronted with students who lack reading skills, and increasing reading scores by focusing on skills in isolation will not strengthen cultural competence or nurture students' identities. Economically disadvantaged African American adolescents in low-level tracks need reading instruction that incorporates a culturally relevant framework with explicit strategy and skill development.

Purpose and Description of the Study

An eight-month inquiry into classroom dynamics and instructional practices was conducted to gain insights on ways of integrating explicit strategy and skill development with culturally relevant literature. A literacy framework (Figure 1) was devised for addressing four areas of reading development: word study, fluency, comprehension, and writing. These four areas were integrated in a meaningful way and not addressed as disparate, isolated skills.

Three major strands evolved from the inquiry: barriers that prevented students from reading at their grade level, restructuring the classroom to create a supportive environment, and meshing explicit strategy instruction and culturally relevant literature. In this article I discuss these strands and the

Figure 1. Instructional framework adapted from Timothy Shanahan's (in preparation) Literacy Framework

	Word study	Fluency	Comprehension	Writing
What is included?	• Sight vocabulary • Spelling • Structural analysis • Word meaning	• Reading speed • Oral reading accuracy • Intonation	• Strategies for constructing meaning	• Purposes • Products • Audiences
* How much instructional time?	• 20 minutes daily	• Brief monitoring to as much as 30 minutes daily	• 30 minutes or more daily	• 30 minutes or more daily
How does it change?	• From word recognition to word meaning	• Text difficulty increases • Less repetition to fluency	• Text difficulty increases • Text length increases • Greater individual control	• Text difficulty increases • More distant audiences • Greater individual control
Application	• Individual drill • Provides opportunities to apply knowledge versus teaching rules	• Place emphasis • Silent and oral reading	• Use high-interest materials • Make students responsible • Expand range of responses	• Have authentic purposes for writing • Read student writing

* Adjustments were made based on student's needs and time available for instruction.

instructional approaches used to break down the barriers that prevented students' literate behaviors.

The inquiry was conducted in a class of 29 eighth-grade students (13 boys and 16 girls) who attended a Chicago public school and had reading stanines of 4 or below from the previous year's Iowa Test of Basic Skills. Two students had been retained, and 6 were receiving special education services. The class met for 50 minutes of reading instruction during the first period of the school day.

Half of the students lived in a neighborhood that was recently dubbed the "Second America," one of the United States' darkest places, in *Life and Death on the South Side of Chicago* (Jones, Newman, & Isay, 1997). Living in this neighborhood gave the students a warped perception of their African American identities. Their identities were closely aligned with the racial dehumanizing of inner-city urban youth. They had limited exposure to positive cultural and social experiences.

These students needed literacy instruction to help sustain them for what I have called the four critical years—after elementary school and before college—to avoid the negative trappings of their community. Many students from this school go on to surrounding area high schools that send a relatively small percentage of students to college. Going away to college is an escape from the neighborhood and entry to a new realm of possibilities, and it's something that many students hear discussed as happening to others, not them.

Being disengaged from the reading and writing process put these students at a great disadvantage. They were reluctant to read orally, seldom completed assigned readings, and refused to answer questions when called upon. Students in this class rarely ventured into independent reading. They had become accustomed to worksheets and assessment questions from their basal readers as the primary mode of reading instruction. Dictates for these students were more comprehensive than equipping them with basic skills, "remediating" their shortcomings, or increasing scores on a standardized assessment.

Identifying Barriers

The inquiry was initiated by interviewing four boys during the third week of the school year to determine what prevented their participation in reading. Aaron, Chad, Leroy, and Rufus (pseudonyms are used for all students) were selected because of an observed unwillingness to participate during reading instruction. When asked why they thought students in this class refused to participate in reading and writing activities, Rufus offered, "Students are scared to say something; they talk after school but not in class." Leroy added, "Not just the boys, the girls too." It was at this point that I asked the boys if we should include the girls in our conversations. They thought it was a good idea, and I included the entire class.

As the interviews continued, students blamed derogatory remarks from previous teachers as powerful deterrents to reading. "People think most black people are going to fail, so we don't do the work," stated Rufus. Another student added, "We are not used to reading and writing. It's like we are starting over in eighth grade." They also felt they had limited vocabularies, deficient decoding skills, and poor comprehension strategies. In addition to these reading difficulties, students were reluctant readers because of a fear of embarrassment. To avoid negative comments from a classroom teacher or peers, one student suggested that many of them would rather say nothing than risk opportunities for potential embarrassment. These students were inadvertently pushed away from reading, and barriers had been constructed that prevented their access to highly literate behaviors such as reading, writing about, and discussing literature.

Fear of embarrassment, deficient word-attack strategies, and limited vocabularies were identified as the major barriers to students' success in reading. These "big three" seemed to prevent them from reading materials at their grade level because of the high level of frustration they experienced. Three goals were developed to get all the students involved: reduce fear of embarrassment; decrease the levels of frustration experienced because of their inability to employ word attack strategies; and have students read, understand, discuss, and write about literature.

Creating a Supportive Community

Creating a supportive environment was important for reducing the potential for embarrassment. The classroom was reorganized and instruction was restructured. There were three major goals of these changes. The first was building a classroom community. Openly acknowledging that reading problems existed in the classroom and establishing the goal of helping everyone become better readers were important for letting the students know that there was nothing to be embarrassed about. It was also acknowledged that students did not have to accept all the blame for their problems. By year's end the teacher has to accept some of the responsibility, and I acknowledged that I would accept mine. Also, some of the reading instruction took place as I sat among the students in a circle of chairs that were placed in the center of the class. Placing myself alongside the students gave them the sense that I was on their side.

Involving students in the assessment process was the second goal of creating a supportive environment. Student self-evaluations were included as part of the grading, which gave them some control over the process. They were asked to rate their participation in and contribution to the lesson after each reading session on a scale of 1–5. Students started assessing their own strengths and weaknesses (see Figure 2). They were given the language to communicate their strengths and weaknesses (i.e., "chopped up reading" to assess fluency, "listening to my little critters" to describe comprehension monitoring).

The third goal of creating a supportive environment involved providing space for students to "safely fail" and recover. Before each assessment, students

---

Figure 2. Students' assessments of their participation, contribution, and reading strengths and weaknesses

Lillie: I contributed my picture (visual representation) pretty good, but I did not talk at all. Next time I will contribute what I learn. Today I think I learned a lot but sometimes when I do not talk that do not mean I am not paying attention.

Tisha: We did good as a group today and I think I should get a 3 because everyone in our group did 100% participation. I make up a ideal for my group and they use it but it did not sound right so we chose another topic.

Pam: I spoke on a subject to the class. It felt good to speak on a subject wear everyone want to learn. Now I am not afraid to speak out loud. I did good because I felt the feeling how we really are in life with pain and fear.

Tamara: My attitude is very positive about reading now, but my real attitude in school is bad. I read fluent now that we decode. Now I can read any types of words just calling them out. At home I read a little not a lot, but in school I keep going over those words on the board. Well I'm still not talking wright, but I correct myself a little, that still has a lot of coming together to take place.

Chuck: My vocabulary is getting better by the day. When I learning something new I don't have to be timid. I can be tranquil. Reading is not boring. It is good, excellent. You can feel the breeze. But now I read much better at home or in school by myself. I read fluency.

had the opportunity to practice with a cooperating student. If cooperating teachers could assist student teachers and give them feedback to help them become better teachers, I believed that cooperating students could help one another become better readers. Cooperating students would devise ways to remember new vocabulary, monitor one another's reading miscues (omissions, substitutions, or repetitions), time readings to gauge fluency, or work together to identify textual references when responding to comprehension questions. If the cooperating teams had difficulty figuring out something I would model specific reading strategies to help answer their concerns. The students were given time to practice, fail, and recover in a supportive environment.

Reducing Embarrassment

The voices of young people must be heard and acknowledged in their own way, or they will excuse themselves early from the table of learning (Livdahl et al., 1995). I wanted to give my students a voice. In Livdahl et al., Herbert suggests ways of inviting reluctant readers to respond. One of her practical ideas was the "one-pager," which allows for multiple ways of responding. A one-pager consists of a visual representation (picture or symbol) of a quote that is significant, and a paragraph of the reader's reflection on the reading. This invitation to respond in a variety of ways enhances student participation successfully. The students' confidence grows, thereby supplanting feelings of learned helplessness. Also, using the one-pager is less intimidating because it is an activity that is not teacher centered and makes possible more than one interpretation. Students have to search for what is meaningful to them and not just what the teacher thinks. This had, then, the potential to propel them into more meaning-oriented activities that could foster appreciation for literature.

The visual or picture/drawing aspect was important to students and elicited the following responses:

Martha: Giving a visual representation helped me with what I wanted to say. And then I could explain it.

Tamera: I liked that part it was fun, we got to draw and have fun and all at the same time.

Chad: Well, it was hard because it's very hard for me to draw with no experience at all. I thought it was good because it showed me where I was coming and how I understood it.

Low-ability readers do not spontaneously employ mental imagery as a strategy; they are thereby deprived of full evocation and participation in the story world (Gambrell & Bales, 1986). Also, less proficient readers are at a loss for strategies for stepping into and sustaining "envisionments" (Purcell-Gates, 1991). Thus, the one-pager "nudged" the students to employ this visualizing. Students who had difficulty finding the words to express themselves were given a passageway into classroom activities. Value was placed upon what they had to say. The classroom environment became less threatening as students were assigned to work both collectively and individually on their one-pagers. To eliminate the fear of embarrassment, a supportive classroom environment was created, and the opportunities for failure were reduced.

Attacking the Small Puppies to Get to the Big Dogs

The one-pagers led to increased levels of participation, but the students continued to struggle with decoding. Strategies were needed to break down this barrier without reducing reading to isolated skill and drill. Increasing the students' comprehension was a primary goal, and for this group word knowledge skills were integrally related to such an aim.

When the students had difficulty reading words, their attention was diverted from comprehension and they became preoccupied with decoding individual words. They did not comprehend what they were attempting to read when they focused on individual words. The statement "I do not want to read now" or a deafening silence at my request for a student to read orally became a part of their "refusal to read repertoire."

"Attacking the small puppies to get to the big dogs" was the slogan the class adopted for thinking about decoding. All of the students in the class admitted that they were not afraid of small puppies, and that they would much rather wrestle with a small puppy than a big dog. The small puppies in this analogy were syllables and phonogram patterns. The multisyllable words were the big dogs. This strategy was based on the idea of decoding by analogy where students are taught how to decode words by comparing an unknown word with known "key words" (Gaskins, Gaskins, & Gaskins, 1991).

Students were taught decoding by analogy through direct instruction and by incorporating the strategy into purposeful reading and writing throughout the day. A public display of phonogram patterns was created. Knowledge of phonogram patterns gives students an advantage when determining the pronunciation of words with more than one syllable (May, 1990). Also to assist with decoding, students were taught a shortened version for syllabicating words. They were told that if they could identify the letters *a, e, i, o,* and *u,* and count to 1 and count to 2, that they could decode a large number of multisyllable words. Four rules were given:

1. Split two consonants between vowels (e.g., bal / lad)
2. Move one consonant between vowels to the next syllable (e.g., te / na / cious)
3. Separate neighboring vowels (e.g., jo / vi / al)
4. Do not separate blends or word groupings that needed each other (e.g., ous, qu)

A word-study activity to practice decoding that made a positive impact on the students' self-esteem and supplanted their feelings of learned helplessness while challenging them to perform at a high level of mastery was incorporated. Each morning before the students entered the class five word lists with five words each were placed on the chalkboard. Each student would decode the lists independently in writing. The 25 words were selected from the article, novel, or text the class was required to read. In this manner decoding served as a prereading activity that moved the ensuing substantive reading along at a faster pace. Students were expected to successfully make the transfer to the text. In some cases, those who have trouble with reading do not successfully make this transfer. If strategic decoding is effectively used to break down one of the barriers that inhibit many poor readers the connection is made explicit.

Each word was written using lowercase letters unless a proper noun was used; in that case, the first letter was capitalized (see Figure 3). At the beginning of the year, the students were given five minutes to syllabicate the words. The written portion of this activity was graded daily to assess which students needed more individual attention. After each student decoded the word lists independently, the work was collected and a whole-group activity began.

A visual and an auditory component were added during the whole-group activity. The students, speaking in unison, called out the syllabicated version. The syllabicated version was written on the board. *Indefatigable* would sound like this: Big *I*, little *n*, big *D*, little *e*, big *F*, little *a*, big *T*, little *i*, big *G*, little *a*, big *B*, little *l*, little *e*, and the rewrite above the word would look like *In De Fa Ti Ga Ble*. They would say each syllable independently of the others before attempting the entire word. This activity was kept at a quick rhythmic pace.

Figure 3. Syllabication sheet with lowercase letters used during the first month of the inquiry

Instructions: Capitalize the first letter of each syllable.

Hint: Look for blends   bl, cl, gl, cr, dr,.......
          and digraphs   sh, th, ...

Ex. 1 redundant = Re Dun Dant (3)
Ex. 2 ludicrous = Lu Di Crous

1. resolution _____   6. anonymous (unknown) _____

2. argument _____   7. tyrant_____

3. unanimity _____   8. denunciation _____

4. incredible _____   9. insistence _____

5. independence _____   10. unalterable _____

The class was reading an excerpt from the U.S. Declaration of Independence.

The students stood during the whole-group activity because it removed them from a physical "position of passivity." Seated students use their desks as a barricade to avoid instruction. They slump, fidget, hide behind other students, or pretend to be involved with other tasks not related to the lesson. Students' attention was heightened throughout this activity because they knew their ability to decode one of the word lists individually at a rate of one second per word earned them their seat (an idea set forth by the class). Timing the activity was used to emphasize fluency. The lists were assigned in a nonpredictable manner so that the students focused on all the words.

If a student was having difficulty earning a seat, an echo-reading approach was used. Students became eager to demonstrate their ability to perform. "Can I read all 25 words?" was one question that caused a time management constraint as the year progressed. As these students began to decode successfully, there was a shift from the avoidance techniques used to volunteerism. They became more confident in their abilities to decode words. The time allotted for decoding the words decreased. Five months into the study, two minutes were allotted to decode the 25 words in writing. In a class with 29 students, each child was seated in less than three minutes. The daily syllabication lasted for approximately seven minutes.

Dictation

A paragraph was dictated to the students after the syllabication activity. They were made aware that the same way they attacked the small puppies to get to the big dogs when decoding words, they were to use those same puppies when spelling words. On occasion, the same words from the syllabication lists were used for the dictated exercises to strengthen the connection between the two.

A dictation, usually two to four sentences, that provoked interest, impregnated thought, or gave information pertinent to understanding the reading was given. The students were instructed to write the paragraph verbatim and underline eight preselected words. Words were selected to emphasize common spelling patterns or to bring attention to the essential vocabulary in the literature that was used during instruction. The syllables of these eight words were clearly articulated so that the students could "tune in." Following each dictation, the students exchanged their papers and spelling was assessed. Common mistakes were discussed. The mistakes were highlighted, spelling patterns were discussed, and more opportunities to practice with these spelling patterns were given in subsequent dictated exercises.

Several questions always followed the dictated exercise and were discussed as a prereading activity. Volunteers were called upon to reread the dictated exercise and respond to the questions before the reading selection (see Figure 4).

Figure 4. A sample dictation

People *usually associate* the word *prejudice* with *intolerance* of a *particular* race or *creed*. Prejudice can also exist, however, within a *minority* group that is the victim of *discrimination*.

1. Can you explain why some members of a racial or ethnic group might be given special treatment?

2. What circumstances lead to discrimination?

Dictation was given before reading an article from a local newspaper about cultural diversity.

Vocabulary Development

The students were informed why they were learning to decode and encode words (i.e., to handle the print when reading and writing), yet many of them were failing to construct meaning from the assigned readings because of their small vocabulary base. An ever-growing word wall was created to strengthen their sight and meaning vocabulary. The words selected for study were from the literature assigned to the students. They were told that the words would appear in their readings. Using literature selections to teach students the meaning of words is more effective than assigning vocabulary words at random (Dole, Sloan, & Trathen, 1995).

The word wall was designed to strengthen the relationship between knowing words and reading well. These words were used to address decoding and vocabulary development simultaneously. Students need to see and hear new words repeatedly if they are going to remember them and use them when writing.

The students read the word wall every other day to build their sight vocabulary. Excerpts from songs were associated with the words to enhance their meaning (see Figure 5). Pronouncing the words and singing the excerpts were done every other day during the fourth and fifth month of the study. This approach helped improve new vocabulary retention and gave a sense of music history. It became too time-consuming as the year progressed, so Friday became Word Wall Day. The word wall was also read on occasion when the principal was observing the class and students wanted to show off.

Figure 5. Excerpts from songs selected by the teacher and the students to build meaning vocabulary

retrospect	(excerpt) Looking back on when I was a little nappy-headed boy—Stevie Wonder
deserted	(excerpt) "On My Own"—Patti Labelle
ambitious	(excerpt) And we're moving on up—theme from *The Jeffersons* sitcom
melancholy	(excerpt) All I really want is to be happy—Mary J. Blige
reciprocate	(excerpt) It's the big payback—James Brown
eternal	(excerpt) "Always and Forever"—Heat Wave
cease	(excerpt) "Stop in the Name of Love"—Diana Ross and the Supremes

The power the students received from this new and highly visible word wall was not anticipated. They became excited about learning words.

One morning during tutoring, Charisse said, "It feels good to read and know what it means. I see a lot of our words and know them right away." The students benefited by their "new weapons," as Xavier's comments suggest:

> The words on the wall are easy, but for other students it is hard. The words help me decode better, do fluent reading all the time. I like getting involved in new words because it helps me know them the next time I see them and it helps my comprehension.

They were asked to read these words quickly to facilitate fluency, as Alvin's remarks suggest:

> I think when we decode words it help me know the words better when I read in books and the word be in it and I already know it I don't hesitate to say it, and when you snap your hands it don't scare me or make me nervous. I think it helps me say the words better.

Using a challenging vocabulary wall positively affected the attitudes of many of the students. They began to challenge the advanced reading group from the other eighth-grade class. Words gave them power. Many students added words to the wall that they wanted the other students to learn. They could successfully demonstrate their growth and experience immediate success. Vocabulary tests were given every other Friday to assess the students individually. By the sixth month, a majority of the students consistently earned a score of 90% or better. Using words that they came across in their literature significantly improved their sight-word knowledge. By year's end the word wall had over 450 multisyllabic words that 25 of the 29 students could recognize on sight and consistently spell correctly. They could also attach a meaningful excerpt from a song to approximately 100 of them.

Culturally Relevant Literature

Culturally relevant literature should be used to help African American students understand changes in history, substantiate their existence, and critically examine the present as a mechanism for political, social, and cultural undertakings that may arise in the future. Culturally relevant literature should extend toward empowering students to honor their presence, "a powerful demanding presence not limiting the space in which the self can roam" (Achebe, 1988, p. 53). Racial dehumanizing should not inhibit this space.

Culturally relevant literature was incorporated into the instructional framework to strengthen cultural competence, nurture students' identities, and increase their reading achievement. Literature, articles, essays, and activities were selected to give students the opportunity to use their explicit skill development in meaningful and relevant ways.

Students who struggle with reading often have limited strategies for comprehending text. Strategies were modeled. Self-questioning strategies, constructing graphic organizers, tuning in to the "little critters" in their minds to monitor comprehension, and acknowledging different question and answer relationships were explicitly modeled via "think-alouds." The culturally relevant literature was selected to help the students use deep processing strategies such as applying the information to other contexts, in this case their lives. This also allows them to use their cultural schema as an additional cueing system.

Materials that challenged the students to think about the social and cultural traditions associated with growing up black in the United States were selected. Historical fiction, contemporary fiction, historical nonfiction, and poetry, with emphasis on the ability to survive both physically and psychologically, were used to help the students understand the changes in history and critique their social realities. For example, Booker T. Washington's (1901) *Up From Slavery* was used to examine how tireless perseverance helps to overcome overwhelming odds. Contextualizing Washington's struggle allowed students to examine their lives. Attempts were made to always connect the historical to the contemporary so that the students would not view the information as outdated and irrelevant.

Cooperative Repeated Readings

Although many students were decoding better, increasing their word knowledge, and using the strategies that were modeled three months into the school year, their oral reading was choppy. The transfer from explicit strategy and skill development to the text was not immediate. It was at this point that cooperative repeated readings of literature, appropriate for middle school settings (Dowhower, 1989), were introduced to the class. During the cooperative repeated readings (see Figure 6) each student was given the opportunity to read a selection to a "cooperating student" three times before class discussion. The first reading was used to identify and attack the words that were difficult to decode. This was an extension of the daily syllabication. The second reading was used to eliminate all substitutions, repetitions, and omissions to build

Figure 6. Selections used for cooperative repeated reading

Speeches/letters/documents

* I Have a Dream—Martin Luther King, Jr.
  Appeal to the colored citizens of the world but in particular and very
  expressly to those of the United States of America—David Walker

The Gettysburg Address—Abraham Lincoln

Declaration of Independence—Thomas Jefferson

The Preamble to the United States Constitution

The Preamble to the Illinois Constitution

Poems

* Lift Every Voice and Sing and The Creation—James Weldon Johnson

* If We Must Die—Claude McKay

* Tableau and Incident—Countee Cullen

* For My People and Lineage—Margaret Walker

Short stories/essays

* from Up From Slavery Boyhood Days—
  Booker T. Washington

* from Narrative of the Life of Frederick Douglass—Frederick Douglass

* Reading sources from *African American Literature, Voices in a Tradition,* ©1992 by Holt Rinehart and Winston.

fluency. During the second or third readings, student-initiated questions emerged. The focus of reading shifted from decoding to constructing meaning. The students began to focus on the ideas of the text. They began to incorporate the explicit strategies that were modeled as they moved through the text. This allowed them to participate in class discussions that were anchored by four questions: Which part of the essay was the most meaningful? What was most surprising? What did you disagree with? How is the selection relevant today?

Repeated readings, when discussed and evaluated, gave students a chance to examine their progress and shortcomings. The students became more conscientious in their reading habits and were willing to work toward improvement. As Shaungel wrote, "I noticed that my reading has truly improved because I use to always read chop up reading and now I am *cognizant* that my reading skills are grown up and *mediocre.*" The italicized words are from the word wall used to build meaning vocabulary. This is just one example of how students claimed ownership of their words and used them when writing.

Other students also supported the beneficial effects of repeated readings:

Donella: The changes that I notice in my reading is that I do not become frustrated when I read. I feel that I am picking up speed in my reading.

Kim: I notice that I'm not stumbling over words that I read out of books.

Ashely: I can read some of the words I never knew before and I'm not scared to read in front of the class like I used to be.

Following the classroom discussions the students were asked to address four questions in writing:

◆ How do you believe you would have reacted in a similar situation and why?

◆ What impact does the condition/situation have on you presently?

◆ How will you make an impact to prevent this situation from taking place in the future?

◆ How is the information relevant for future societies?

The students were challenged to debate about ideas and concepts and use the literature to support their arguments. One such debate revolved around whether African Americans should integrate or separate. The students pitted the words of Elijah Muhammad in the *Message to the Black Man* (1965) and work of David Walker (1993) against the ideas of Martin Luther King in *A Testament of Hope* (Washington, 1986), and the writings of Frederick Douglass, in front of the principal, other students, and a local news reporter.

Do the "Write" Thing

Word study, vocabulary development, and confidence in reading became stimuli for writing. I created a bulletin board titled Do the Write Thing. All of the students were familiar with this pun. The movie *Do the Right Thing*, written and directed by an African American, was a favorite among the students. Following class discussions, the students were able to retreat into their "writing zones" and write reflective responses about the readings and discussions. Essays, poems, and short stories were posted on the board. Writing became contagious.

Students responded that they loved to write using the "big words" from the word wall to sound intelligent. I made a big deal of this board, making all the writers feel special. I would ask the students to share their writings orally. Initially I think I might have discouraged some students to add their work. They were willing to place writings on the board, but they did not want to publicly share their personal reflections. Later, students were encouraged to use pseudonyms or sign the writings "anonymous" if they did not want me to bring special attention to the author.

Writing opportunities and literature discussions led to increased usage of new vocabulary. For a sample of one student's writing after reading an article written by Willie Lynch (1712), see Figure 7.

Figure 7. A student's written reflection and attempts to use words (boldface) from the word wall

The Man

I am the black man who ashames his race.
I am the darker brother whom they laugh in my face.
I have many disadvantages that bring me down.
I fight for the power when I know it's not allowed.
Feeling the walls close on to my position in
the center of the earth. Hoping to make peace
inside of the man's world feeling the **dehumanization**
coming from the man who awaits my death.
Making me weak on the inside, taking over my soul,
taking my true love from me, left with nothing to hold.
Lost within myself, this can't be real,
can not stand this **antithesis** of life I feel.
Growing darkness taking dawn I thought I was me,
but now I'm gone.
I have awaited my life too long to let the man pull my arm.
Seeking **chaotic** episodes happening everyday
feeling the critters in my head moaning stay away.
Having my manhood stripped away from me everyday.
Having no respect for society, because I know I must turn away.
Running away from my fears all alone.
There's no way in the world I can be strong, but I must, because it seems
as if my whole race is depending on me. Walking around with
unknown **attributes**. Scared to face the world's **prevaricating**
nations. Hiding from the intimidation that awaits me at home.
Feeling the products of **lethal** weapons growing strong. The
source that kills my brothers an sisters I know its wrong.
I know now I must lend my brothers and sisters a hand, and hope
they learn the true meaning of overcoming
The Man.

A Compelling Change in Attitude

African American students in low-level tracks are often not required to read literature, and they commonly receive limited amounts of reading instruction. Their reading failures are exacerbated by inadequate or poor-quality instruction that focuses solely on improving reading scores. Teachers can increase reading achievement by combining explicit skill and strategy development using a framework to address fluency, word study, comprehension, and writing while using culturally relevant literature to nurture identities and develop cultural competence.

It is difficult to find in the literature a study of African American adolescents in low-level reading tracks that adds to our understanding about the combined use of culturally relevant literature and explicit skill development in reading. This study involved a change in class structure that invited low-achieving adolescent students to learn specific skills and strategies and to read literature. Word study activities, fluency development, and writing in a cooperative environment allowed the students to gain confidence in their reading abilities and to improve reading behaviors. The students in this inquiry did not resist the explicit skills in large part because they were thrust upon them in a very challenging forum, and opportunities to exercise their new knowledge were made available through literature activities.

Culturally relevant literature helped the students develop a broader social consciousness that was observed in their discussions and writings. Students' culture was used as a vehicle to learn new vocabulary. Challenging students to read materials at their grade level and giving them the support to experience academic success contributed to their cognitive development. Restructuring the classroom and engaging the students' voices created a cooperative atmosphere. These goals of a culturally relevant approach for African Americans were meshed with explicit word study, fluency, writing, and comprehension instruction to improve reading skills.

This combination of a culturally relevant approach and explicit strategy and skill instruction resulted in 25 of the 29 students earning promotion to high school under the Chicago Public School System's reform initiative requiring eighth-grade students to achieve a minimum grade-level equivalent of 7.0 on the Iowa Test of Basic Skills. Several students scored well beyond this minimum standard. The quantifiable gains are noteworthy given the fact that all the students were several years below grade level in reading at the beginning of the year.

The shift in attitude that many students experienced from their active involvement in the relevant and meaningful literature experiences was compelling. The reluctance the students exhibited at the onset of the inquiry diminished. The students began to challenge the advanced group of readers and other teachers with ideas and words. They also began to realize that they had the power to break down the barriers that prevented their participation in reading and writing.

> The teaching of reading in the public schools has proceeded as if the content of the text makes no difference. Although schools have been successful in teaching students how to read, they have not been nearly as successful engendering an interest in reading or conveying that reading has some utility outside of the classroom. (Sims, 1990, p. 560)

Using culturally relevant literature helped to engage students and offset much of the resistance and student apathy exercised in low-level reading tracks. It also provided the opportunity to develop deeper processing strategies through reading, writing, questioning, and discussing.

We must rethink the test-driven approach and basic skills indoctrination to bring adolescent students in low-level reading tracks up from the bottom. We also must refine the use of culturally relevant literature. There are limitations with both. But when combined, they make a powerful vehicle for increasing the literate behaviors of African American adolescents. An approach to such instruction has been offered that benefited one group of students, and it has the potential to break down the barriers that disenfranchise other adolescent students assigned to low-level reading tracks.

REFERENCES

Campbell, J., Donahue, P., Reese, C., & Phillips, G. (1996). *National Assessment of Educational Progress 1994 reading report card for the nation and the states.* Washington, DC: National Center for Education Statistics, U.S. Department of Education.

Darling-Hammond, L., & Falk, B. (1997). Using standards and assessments to support student learning. *Phi Delta Kappan, 79*, 190–199.

Dole, J., Sloan, C., & Trathen, W. (1995). Teaching vocabulary within the context of literature. *Journal of Reading, 38*, 452–460.

Dowhower, Sarah L. (1989). Repeated reading: Research into practice. *The Reading Teacher, 42*, 502–507.

Foster, M. (1993). Educating for competence in community and culture: Exploring the views of exemplary African American teachers. *Urban Education, 27*, 370–394.

Foster, M., & Delpit, L. (1997). *Black teachers on teaching.* New York: New Press.

Gambrell, L., & Bales, R.J. (1986). Mental imagery and the comprehension-monitoring performance of fourth and fifth grade readers. *Reading Research Quarterly, 21,* 454–464.

Gaskins, R.W., Gaskins, J.C., & Gaskins, I.W. (1991). A decoding program for poor readers—and the rest of the class, too! *Language Arts, 68,* 213–225.

Jones, L., Newman, L., & Isay, D. (1997). *Our America: Life and death on the South Side of Chicago.* New York: Washington Square Press.

Ladson-Billings, G. (1995a). But that's just good teaching! The case for culturally relevant pedagogy. *Theory Into Practice, 34,* 159–164.

Ladson-Billings, G. (1995b). Toward a theory of culturally relevant pedagogy. *American Educational Research Journal, 32,* 465–491.

Livdahl, B., Smart, K., Wallman, J., Herbert, T.K., Geiger, D.K., & Anderson, J.L. (1995). *Stories from response-centered classrooms: Speaking, questioning, and theorizing from the center of the action.* New York: Teachers College Press

Lynch, W. (1712). *Speech on slave control delivered in Jamestown, Virginia.* Available [online]: www.blackspeak.com/speeches/slavecontrol.htm

May, F. (1990). *Reading as communication—An interactive approach* (3rd ed.). Columbus, OH: Merrill.

Muhammad, E. (1965). *Message to the black man.* Chicago: Muhammad Mosque of Islam No. 2.

Neill, M. (1998). *High-stakes tests do not improve student learning.* FairTest Executive Report. Available [online]: www.fairtest.org/k12/naeprep.htm

Purcell-Gates, V. (1991). On the outside looking in: A study of remedial readers' meaning-making while reading literature. *Journal of Reading Behavior, 23,* 235–254.

Shanahan, T. (in preparation). *Literacy framework.*

Sims, R. (1990). Walk tall in the world: African American literature for today's children. *The Journal of Negro Education, 59,* 556–565.

Smith, M.L. (1991). Put to the test: The effects of external testing on teachers. *Educational Researcher, 20*(5), 8–11.

LITERATURE CITED

Achebe, C. (1988). *Hopes and impediments.* New York: Doubleday.

Hillard, A. (1995). *The maroon within us: Selected essays on African American community socialization.* Baltimore: Black Classic Press.

Walker, D. (1993). *An appeal to the colored citizens of the world but in particular and very expressly to those of the United States of America.* Baltimore: Black Classic Press.

Washington, B.T. (1901). *Up from slavery.* New York: Doubleday.

Washington, J.M. (Ed.). (1986). *A testament of hope: The essential writings of Martin Luther King, Jr.* San Francisco: Harper & Row.

RIGHT

Children have a right to well-prepared teachers

who keep their skills up to date

through effective professional development.

Introduction

William T. Hammond

n 1996, the National Commission on Teaching and America's Future stated, "In a typical classroom of 25 students, today's teachers will serve at least 4 or 5 students with specific educational needs that they have not been prepared to meet" (p. 17). No doubt, by today that number has increased and the ability of teachers to cope with students from diverse backgrounds or with specific educational needs in their classrooms has remained the same or diminished. That fact, combined with the fact that the more than 1,025 teacher education programs in the United States produce scarcely over 100,000 graduates a year but that the nation's schools will need to hire as many as 2 million new teachers within this decade, presents a rather ominous picture for education. The tasks, then, before us are twofold: (1) Recruit more persons into the teaching profession and (2) provide a more informed base of training for potential teachers, making certain to incorporate methods and strategies for teaching the very diverse population of students entering our schools. These best practices should also be shared with the current teaching workforce to make them more effective in meeting the needs of their students.

The guiding philosophy of this section is grounded in Right 3—children have a right to well-prepared teachers who keep their skills up to date through effective professional development.

The articles in this section by Mary Lee Field and Jo Ann Aebersold and by Patricia Ruggiano Schmidt provide keen and thoughtful insight into the cultural and linguistic backgrounds of ESL/bilingual students and directions for teachers to take personal inventory of their professional development and to examine their perspectives on teaching students from cultures other than their own. The primary intent of this discussion is to reinforce the widely held and subscribed-to position that all children can learn and to offer the teacher effective practices to ensure that this belief is realized. Both articles offer clear perspectives on their respective topics and focused directions for meaningful classroom implementation of methodology and pedagogy of literacy instruction. Without advocating specific approaches or commercial programs, the authors seek to guide the reader toward questions for consideration when formulating and selecting appropriate instructional materials and strategies for classroom use. Each article provides the reader with critical data and each suggests implications for instruction of students from other ethnic groups. The thoughtful teacher will ponder the assumptions about students that he or she has made and examine the validity of those assumptions. The resulting examination of beliefs and personal biases in instructional approaches will hopefully produce better-informed and better-prepared classroom teachers.

Some of the questions that may be raised after reading this chapter are as follows:

- How much do I need to know about culture and beliefs of the students I teach?
- How do I apply the new information that I acquire about my students to the classroom?
- As a teacher from a culture different than that of my students, what limitations do I face in reaching them, and how do I overcome those shortcomings?
- How important is it to be culturally sensitive in the classroom? Can it be overdone?
- Should I approach the parents of my students from diverse cultures any differently than I do parents of other students?
- How can I maintain fairness in the classroom?
- Isn't good teaching the same for all students?
- Are there "best practices" for teaching students from other cultures?
- What signs do my students give me to help me know when they understand or don't understand?
- How do assessment practices affect students from other cultures? What are some considerations when selecting assessment/evaluation methods for the classroom or school system?
- What do I know about my students, and how do I incorporate that information into my teaching?
- What concepts do my students have about reading and literacy?
- How do my students "learn"?
- What value do my students place on literacy in their home environment?

Answers gleaned by readers from the aforementioned questions should help provide direction, purpose, and reinforcement of currently held beliefs about teaching and learning styles or insight into new directions to take in the classroom. The answers derived from the self-examinations proposed in these articles, however, may not always prove comforting, even for teachers from the same cultural groups as their students. Because a teacher is from the same ethnic or cultural group as his or her students does not automatically present an advantage in understanding students of a similar background. In teaching, respect must be earned through informed and respectful actions. This will always be a primary key to effective teaching.

One of the lessons to be learned from the two articles in this section is that each teacher still has much to learn about his or her own ethnic group as well as the other groups of children in the classroom. The other lesson to be learned from reading these selections is that ethnic communities are just as diverse within their communities; these communities are not monolithic. There is great variation within the communities: There is variation in the views about themselves and about other communities. This makes it even more compelling for the teachers of these students to learn all they can about their students' communities.

According to an article in *English Update*, a newsletter from the National Research Center on English Learning & Achievement, "While eager to find ways to apply new learning to instruction, teachers make it clear that assistance should be more than technical; it should also provide new ways of looking at what they are already doing" ("Teachers Share Their Views," 2002). Later in that same article the assertion is made that "successful professional development helps teachers to attain their instructional goals, sustain them in their struggles, and above all, inform their professional judgments." The intention of the two articles in this section is to provide teachers, administrators, teacher educators, and staff development directors with new ways of looking at what some teachers already know about teaching students from other cultures, namely that a child's culture does make a significant difference in the approach that a teacher may take in the classroom. To be effective in a culturally diverse classroom, teachers must have knowledge and skill in teaching content as well as the ability to recognize and adapt instruction to the needs of the students.

Once a teacher is culturally aware of and pedagogically sensitive to the instructional needs and preferences of the children, what comes next? How is change or enlightenment of approach incorporated into the instructional program? How might the materials be adapted to the children? How are newly learned behaviors effectively transferred into effective classroom practices? What are the steps to be taken by the dedicated and informed teacher in this area? The Learning First Alliance, in its publication *Every Child Reading: A Professional Development Guide* (2000), offers the following suggestions:

1. Understand the theory and rationale for the new content and instruction.
2. Observe a model in action.
3. Practice the new behavior in a safe context.
4. Try out the behavior with peer support in the classroom. (p. 6)

What is being suggested here, of course, is that it is time for the teacher to practice the newly learned behavior or strategy in a nonthreatening environment. In short, time should be allocated for the teacher to learn the tools of the trade. The other part of this equation for successful implementation of a program or instructional approach is that the change occurs in incremental stages and must be accounted for in the timeline being developed by a school system or an individual. Included in these stages are time for adequate dialogue and interaction for the teacher with others attempting the conversion, time for a reflective analysis of progress, time to understand the flexibility and adaptability of the materials being used, and development of the skills necessary to become proficient in the classroom delivery of instruction. Finally, this implementation process requires adequate time to determine if the change process is going as planned or if modifications in the approach are needed.

So what, in the final analysis, is the message to be obtained from these articles, and how should the lessons set forth here be applied in the classroom? Schmidt urges us to take stock of our professional biases and examine them for strengths and weaknesses in our teaching. Only when we are well informed about ourselves can we hope to inform others. Grant and Wieczorek (2000), in their work on social moorings, express the conviction that

> making connections means looking at the past and present assumption made within what is being written and said about ideas like teacher education. Looking at assumptions means questioning what is stated and what is absent and looking at what those presences and absences produce. (p. 920)

This is the same type of introspection called for by Schmidt. It is thoughtful teaching and creative responding to the demands of an increasingly diverse student population.

A similar message emerges from the Field and Aebersold article. Teaching must always be a respectful activity. Teachers must be knowledgeable about the home conditions and the mindset of their students before effective instruction can occur. Basic assumptions that are commonly made by teachers regarding such items as the value of print and literacy and the appropriateness of praise as a support device are called into question in some school settings with children from other cultures. Failure by the teacher to be adequately informed of these small, but very important, culture variations might well spell disaster in the classroom for the teacher and the student.

In the final analysis, the message is that teachers, regardless of their backgrounds, can become effective teachers of students from widely diverse backgrounds. The voices of research have told us that professional development opportunities are more likely to have the desired positive effects for our students when they are continuous, long-term, and an integral part of the school culture ("Teachers Share Their Views," 2002). As Field and Aebersold conclude, "What is most important is that we remain aware of how culture functions as a cognitive filter for us all, shaping our values and assumptions, the ways we think about reading, and the way we teach reading."

REFERENCES

Field, M.L., & Aebersold, J.A. (1990). Cultural attitudes toward reading: Implications for teachers of ESL/bilingual readers. *Journal of Reading, 33,* 406–410.

Grant, C.A., & Wieczorek, K. (2000). Teacher education and knowledge in "The Knowledge Society": The need for social moorings in our multicultural schools. *Teachers College Record, 102*(5), 913–935.

Learning First Alliance. (2000). *Every child reading: A professional development guide.* Washington DC: First Alliance Publications.

National Commission on Teaching and America's Future. (1996). *What matters most: teaching for America's future: Report of the National Commission on Teaching and America's Future.* New York: Author.

Schmidt, P.R. (1999). Know thyself and understand others. *Language Arts, 76*(4), 332–340.

Teachers share their views about effective professional development. (2002, Winter). *English Update,* p. 6.

Cultural Attitudes Toward Reading: Implications for Teachers of ESL/Bilingual Readers

Mary Lee Field and Jo Ann Aebersold

A substantial body of research in the past 15 years has illustrated how much culture shapes our view of the world, our behavior, and our interpretation of events around us. More specifically, a number of studies focus on how culture shapes children's assumptions about being able to read and the value of reading.

Some of those studies illustrate how different cultures place different emphasis and value on various cognitive activities (Duranti & Ochs, 1986; Fillmore, 1981; Vareene & McDermott, 1986; Wagner, Messick, & Spratt, 1986). That emphasis, in turn, affects the use of these cognitive abilities during reading. Other studies describe the effect of culture on a variety of social factors that influence children's attitudes toward reading and reading instruction (Downing, 1973, 1979; Downing, Ollila, & Oliver, 1975; Heath, 1986; Schieffelin & Cochran-Smith, 1984).

Although this body of research is not always addressed to reading teachers, it enables us to understand better the role of culture in our students' assumptions and behavior. This article highlights some of the most pertinent studies on culturally shaped assumptions about cognition and the nature of reading and explores their implications for reading teachers who work with ESL and bilingual readers.

Because of the variety and complexity of these studies, there are always the dangers of oversimplifying or reinforcing stereotypes, pitfalls that we wish to avoid. We find, for example, some difficulty in presenting studies that come from different research bases; studies of students and their families in their own cultures and native lands are qualitatively different from studies of immigrants to the United States learning ESL in U.S. schools. For the immigrant students in the United States, there are two cultures to deal with: the culture of their parents and the culture of the dominant society.

In addition, while all of the studies cited here concern cognition or literacy, they address them from slightly different viewpoints, including that of mainstream reactions to different cultures, which create other variables. Recognizing these complications, we have selected studies that focus most clearly on the cultural shaping of cognitive abilities and attitudes toward reading.

Originally published in *Journal of Reading* (1990), volume 33, pages 406–410.

Cognitive Activities

Research on the relationship between cognitive activities and reading includes a number of studies about cultural attitudes. A seminal article by Fillmore posits "cross-cultural differences in cognitive style" (1981, p. 26) that provide our framework for synthesizing other recent studies. Culture determines how people interpret and mentally organize the world, functioning like a software program for a computer to shape the way input is manipulated, and to control what is received and processed (Robinson, 1985).

Fillmore itemizes six cognitive activities that appear to vary in different cultures and that have an influence on second language acquisition, including the skill of reading. She emphatically notes that she is not implying a difference in students' abilities or cognitive development but is simply reflecting how these activities are valued and encouraged in different cultures—how much are they practiced, praised, and rewarded.

1. Sustained and systematic attention (both the child's willingness to remain with a given task over a period of time and the child's attitude toward that kind of activity).

2. Verbal memory (how much the child is expected to memorize materials, recite, or repeat texts and narratives).

3. Analyticity (recognizing patterns and generating new material using them).

4. Playfulness (willingness to experiment, to manipulate materials).

5. Mental flexibility (generating guesses, considering alternatives, hypothesizing).

6. Field dependence-independence (proclivity toward being able or unable to see relationships without reference to background).

Of these six, the first five are the ones that appear as discernible factors in the studies that we are presenting. As to the sixth, while Hansen and Stansfield (1981, 1983) have investigated the relationship of field–dependent-independent learning styles on language achievement, and Hansen (1984) has studied the effect of those learning styles on cloze tests, we are unaware of other studies that examine the relationship between field dependence-independence and attitudes toward reading.

Cognitive approaches and patterning differ within societies that are literate, such as the United States. These differences, however, seem less significant than the differences between literate and nonliterate societies, or societies where literacy is emerging. Societies exist in which the ability to read and write one's native language is not important—either because a particular language does not have a writing system or because reading and writing are simply not necessary to conduct one's daily life.

Thus, we do find cultures where lack of literacy is not looked down on; it is simply a way of life. In such cultures, verbal usage and memory are emphasized more than in literate societies. More attention is given to oral language skills and more demands placed on the ability to memorize.

Oral Cultures: Morocco and Samoa

Two separate studies of traditionally nonliterate cultures highlight the distinct but similar oral heritages of Morocco and Western Samoa and the resulting cognitive emphases. These two examples will be compared with U.S. classroom reading activities, using Fillmore's (1981) cognitive framework.

Sustained and systematic attention, the first of Fillmore's cognitive activities, is highly valued in both Moroccan and Western Samoan schools. Although Morocco has had a literate segment in its population for hundreds of years (Wagner et al., 1986), the majority of its population, who speak a colloquial dialect of Arabic or a completely different indigenous language, Berber, have only recently been introduced to literacy. Early education for this segment has generally been provided by Koranic (religious) schools or, more recently, modern schools. Girls are now welcome in school. Curriculum content and teaching methods have changed. Math and writing have been added to instruction in the Koran, and instructional games are now used to some extent.

Even so, rote memorization continues to be a predominant tool both in and out of the classroom—at all levels of education; "memorization has been witnessed throughout the higher levels of modern Moroccan school systems extending into the university, to be a central pedagogical principle and acquisition strategy" (Wagner et al., 1986, p. 253).

Western Samoa has had a similar emphasis on oral-aural skills in its public schools, using choral recitation (Duranti & Ochs, 1986). This is due partially to the unavailability of reading materials in the traditional villages. First literacy skills are usually learned in village pastors' schools, but even there a good amount of time is given to oral reading from the Bible and listening to oral reading.

Verbal memory, Fillmore's second category, is prevalent and valued not only in Moroccan and Western Samoan schools but in those societies as well. Wagner et al. (1986) report on a frequent scene at the bus station where passengers seeking their buses and points of departure commonly ask questions of those sitting around in the station even though they are literate and there are boards with that information posted in various spots.

Another example of the value of sustained attention and verbal memory is taken from Western Samoa, where young children "are expected to notice activities of others and report on it to others" (Duranti & Ochs, 1986, p. 221). Four-year-olds are asked to memorize and can carry lengthy messages to other persons.

In contrast, very little attention is now given to verbal memory or rote acquisition in American society or schools, especially in teaching native English speakers to read.

American schools place great value on analysis in the teaching of reading, Fillmore's third category. They devote a large part of the elementary school curriculum to it. Students are encouraged to look at the parts to see how they contribute to the whole. What relationships exist between the parts? Are there any parts missing? Could the whole be broken down into different parts?

In contrast, neither the Moroccan nor the Western Samoan study described any school or social exchange that indicated the promotion of analytical skills. There, rote memorization and oral memorization constitute reading instruction.

Playfulness, the fourth category, is characterized by an inclination to manipulate language for the sheer joy of doing so—the child who repeats or chants new words or phrases, who inserts them in unlikely places, for instance, calling a friend "a horseshoe." The ethnic studies we cite were socioeducational in nature; therefore, linguistic playfulness was not examined.

However, playfulness accompanies the kind of cognitive activity Fillmore labels as mental flexibility, the fifth category, the ability to generate guesses, "a kind of talent for seeing and entertaining multiple possibilities" (1981, p. 28). "What do you think would happen if...?" "What other choices does X have?" "Why do you think X did such and such?" These are all questions that exemplify the building of cognitive flexibility.

There is no mention of this type of activity in the study on Morocco. There is some evidence that this kind of flexibility is not emphasized in Samoa. Adults who already know the answer to a question will not ask children that question merely to provide them with an opportunity to exercise their language and mental skills (Duranti & Ochs, 1986, p. 230). Heath, citing Schieffelin's and Ochs's work in the South Pacific, states that "labeling and sentence extending practices portrayed as universally common...do not occur in these communities. These groups also do not use the simplifying and attention-focusing strategies (such as the use of 'teaching questions') upon which early reading instruction...usually depends [in U.S. schools]" (1986, p. 215).

In contrast is a study conducted by Vareene and McDermott (1986) on two U.S. students in a U.S. elementary school. Examining the differences between one successful and one unsuccessful student, this study shows that the successful student's mother spent time with her child reviewing her school materials through the use of gamelike activities. For example, the mother might start a sentence stating a fact and the child would finish it. The mother might state an action and the child would state the possible consequences. The cognitive activities that went on in the successful student's home are familiar as activities in U.S. textbooks and schools that promote mental flexibility.

While Moroccans and Samoans are not the major ethnic groups in U.S. schools, we suggest that their cognitive experiences and attitudes regarding reading may be representative of other societies. More research in such cultures is needed to either substantiate or refute the similar emphases in cognitive style and activities that we have noted between Morocco and Western Samoa, two very different societies in similar stages of literacy.

Social Style and Attitudes

Another cluster of recent research centers on social style and the interactive factors crucial to reading. Fillmore notes that the cultural differences for cognitive activities are only suggested by research, but adds that there "is quite clear evidence of such differences related to the social characteristics" (1981, p. 30). Thus far our review of research has considered those cognitive issues as they were observed in the readers' native settings. The following studies focus on sociolinguistic situations both in native and immigrant settings that influence attitudes toward reading. Each one adds elements to our picture of such cultural shaping.

Two studies illustrate how a minority culture's home background influences reading in the language of the majority culture. Downing et al. (1975) examined kindergarten age Indian and non-Indian Canadian children. Both groups spoke English at home, but there were some dialectical differences, and the Indian children's home culture had no tradition of literacy. "On all five measures used the Indian children scored significantly lower. They were less able to recognise literacy activities, less cognisant of their purpose, and had poorer technical knowledge of units of speech and writing" (p. 312). The authors concluded that the Indian children's understanding of the reading process, their "cognitive clarity" regarding literacy skills, was significantly influenced by sociocultural variations.

Indeed, the wealth of ethnographic studies (especially Heath, 1983) that have been completed since Downing et al. have firmly established that children from nonschool-oriented backgrounds do not develop the same literacy orientation as children from school-oriented backgrounds.

Schieffelin and Cochran-Smith (1984) studied three groups: (1) educated, school-oriented parents and their preschool children from a Philadelphia, Pennsylvania, suburb; (2) a Chinese family that had recently left Vietnam, was literate only in Chinese, and had settled in Philadelphia; and (3) a family in a traditionally nonliterate society in Papua New Guinea. The authors concluded that children's interest in print and literacy develops most fully (as in the first case) where there is a cultural orientation toward literacy, but develops with different applications where the children serve as interpreters for their parents, as in the family from Vietnam. Interest in print and literacy generally does not develop in a culture where literacy has limited meaning and function, as in Papua New Guinea.

Downing's 1979 study summarizes and synthesizes the material from his massive earlier study of reading in 14 countries (1973) and identifies numerous social factors that are greatly shaped by culture, including the critical period for learning, the social importance of reading, sex-role stereotypes and standards, educational provisions (facilities), and even class size. In each of these areas, Downing illustrates that decisions that *appear* to be based on fact, scientific evidence, or research are actually shaped by culture and social forces. One compelling example he gives is that cultures determine the best or "critical" age for beginning reading according to social factors rather than physiological ones (1979, p. 122).

Downing also argues that cultural factors create sociolinguistic situations that have an impact on language learning, a conclusion closely linked to his earlier study of Canadian Indian and non-Indian children. He argues that when children's first spoken language is different from the first language they must learn to write (a condition he calls language mismatch), they may become confused and have problems achieving.

Although Downing's main argument is for "cognitive clarity" in the reading-writing process—for children needing to know the exact nature, uses, and value of reading—his discussion of mismatch illustrates that some linguistic situations may be brought about by political decisions or popular emotions about native and second language instruction rather than by educational considerations.

One final example of cultural factors creating a sociolinguistic situation that influences reading ability is described by Lee, Stigler, and Stevenson

(1986). Although they were investigating the "role of orthography in reading" and looking for evidence that the *type* of writing system mediates for or against problems in learning to read, they found no evidence to support that hypothesis (p. 140). However, the study did reveal that cultural differences, the social variable, were the major issues. That the Chinese students in Taiwan had higher reading scores (for L1 reading) than the American students in the United States had (for L1) seemed to be the result of the social-cultural variables: time spent in class, amount of homework, and parental attitudes. They concluded that Chinese students were better L1 readers because they worked harder and were encouraged and supervised more (p. 149).

The weight of evidence from our condensed survey of research on cultural attitudes toward reading may leave the classroom teacher feeling somewhat oppressed. And there are other points we could add, such as cultural differences in the amount of adult praise a child receives in various societies. U.S. culture places great value on praising and rewarding children for their participation and accomplishment, both in school and in society. We feel it is an integral part of children's emotional and mental development. But in Samoan society no praise is given to children who carry out their tasks; they are viewed as having done what they were supposed to do, nothing more (Duranti & Ochs, 1986). It is a sad irony that the caring and supportive American teacher who praises students may be embarrassing those who come from other cultures where praise is not expected, at least until the immigrant student comes to understand the use of praise in American culture.

Implications for Teachers

With all these considerations in mind, what can the teacher do in the reading classroom?

◆ First, investigate your students' cognitive clarity about reading. What concept do they have of reading, of its role in society? What expectations do they have of a reading class?

Johns (1986) lists the following suggestions for reading teachers to help clarify the process for both themselves and their students.

1. Have students share their perceptions about reading.

2. List the assumptions you make while teaching that students may not possess.

3. Write down terms that you use during teaching that students may not understand.

4. Use an audiotape or videotape to record several of your reading lessons. Evaluate the lessons and note terms or assumptions that were not on your original list.

5. Plan strategies to help students develop or refine their perceptions of reading and your instructional language.

6. Determine those reading behaviors you emphasize and reward. Assess the behaviors with respect to helping students form a meaningful concept of reading.

◆ Second, know the home environment of your students (parents, siblings, and present community) and the home culture. Is their native culture literate? Are the relatives literate in their native language? What is the common method of instruction in that culture's schools? Are the relatives living in the present home fluent and literate in English? Is reading in any language a part of their home activities?

To obtain this knowledge, teachers can interview the parents or other relatives, check with other members of the same culture, visit students' homes, or use local reference sources (community groups, libraries, and knowledgeable professionals).

◆ Third, develop a flexible interpretation of reading behavior, one that includes behaviors from other cultures. This information may come from educated informants in that culture. Use a variety of means to check reading comprehension; some of them should be nonprint, such as oral or visual prompts, including pictures, signs, ads, or video clips. Interview the students themselves to determine what they think about reading instruction and what they perceive as relevant and useful. If students think that the teacher values their reasons for reading, then they feel more integrated into the reading process.

◆ Finally, assess the dominant cultural group to which the students respond—their parents or their peers. What advantages and disadvantages does this choice create for them? How might those choices be influencing their progress?

Reading teachers faced with such a diversity of cultural assumptions, both their own and those of each of their students, may feel overwhelmed by the complexity of their task. Our purpose here has been to make teachers conscious of these issues without feeling restricted by them. What is most important is that we remain aware of how culture functions as a cognitive filter for all of us, shaping our values and assumptions, the ways we think about reading, and the ways we teach reading.

REFERENCES

Downing, J. (1973). *Comparative reading.* New York: Macmillan.

Downing, J. (1979). *Reading and reasoning.* New York: Springer-Verlag.

Downing, J., Ollila, L., & Oliver, P. (1975). Cultural differences in children's concepts of reading and writing. *British Journal of Educational Psychology, 45,* 312–316.

Duranti, A., & Ochs, E. (1986). Literacy instruction in a Samoan village. In B.B. Schieffelin & P. Gilmore (Eds.), *The acquisition of literacy: Ethnographic perspectives* (pp. 213–232). Norwood, NJ: Ablex.

Fillmore, L.W. (1981). Cultural perspectives on second language learning. *TESL Reporter, 14,* 23–31.

Hansen, L. (1984). Field dependence-independence and language testing: Evidence from six Pacific island cultures. *TESOL Quarterly, 18,* 311–324.

Hansen, J., & Stansfield, C. (1981). The relationship of field dependent-independent cognitive styles to foreign language achievement. *Language Learning, 31,* 349–367.

Heath, S.B. (1983). *Way with words: Language, life, and work in communities and classrooms.* New York: Cambridge University Press.

Heath, S.B. (1986). Critical factors in literacy development. In S. de Castell, A. Luke, & K. Egan (Eds.), *Literacy, society and schooling: A reader* (pp. 209–229). New York: Cambridge University Press.

Johns, J.L. (1986). Students' perceptions of reading: Thirty years of inquiry. In D.B. Yaden Jr. & S. Templeton (Eds.), *Metalinguistic awareness and beginning literacy* (pp. 31–40). Portsmouth, NH: Heinemann.

Lee, S., Stigler, J.W., & Stevenson, H.W. (1986). Beginning reading in Chinese and English. In B. Foorman & A.W. Siegel (Eds.), *Acquisition of reading skills* (pp. 123–149). Hillsdale, NJ: Erlbaum.

Robinson, G.L. (1985). *Crosscultural understanding: Processes and approaches for foreign language, English as a second language and bilingual educators.* New York: Pergamon.

Schieffelin, B.B., & Cochran-Smith, M. (1984). Learning to read culturally: Literacy before schooling. In H. Goelman, A. Oberg, & F. Smith (Eds.), *Awakening to literacy* (pp. 3–23). Portsmouth, NH: Heinemann.

Stansfield, C., & Hansen, J. (1983). Field dependence-independence as a variable in second language cloze test performance. *TESOL Quarterly, 17,* 29–38.

Vareene, H., & McDermott, R.P. (1986). "Why" Sheila can read: Structure and indeterminacy in the reproduction of familial literacy. In B.B. Schieffelin & P. Gilmore (Eds.), *The acquisition of literacy: Ethnographic perspectives* (pp. 188–210). Norwood, NJ: Ablex.

Wagner, E., Messick, M., & Spratt, J. (1986). Studying literacy in Morocco. In B.B. Schieffelin & P. Gilmore (Eds.), *The acquisition of literacy: Ethnographic perspectives* (pp. 233–259). Norwood, NJ: Ablex.

Know Thyself and Understand Others

Patricia Ruggiano Schmidt

Hey! Teacher! What you know about us?"

Jamel raised this question on the first day of school as Kelly, a second-year teacher, was explaining that this third-grade room would be everyone's home; they would be family. She quickly responded to Jamel and his classmates, "Well, I don't know much about you, but you don't know me either. We'll get to know each other this year."

In spite of her answer, Kelly was uneasy about Jamel's question and about her own response. She decided that Jamel was right. She didn't know much about the families of the children in her classroom.

Throughout her life, Kelly, a white teacher in the United States, had resided in suburban middle-class communities. She had little contact with racially diverse groups of people in educational or social settings. Nor had her preservice teaching experiences prepared her for a K to 6 urban elementary school with 80% African American, 14% Latino, and 6% European American children. Furthermore, differences in socioeconomic status had prevented Kelly from understanding the meaning of the unemployment and poverty that qualified 93% of the children in her school for free or reduced-cost breakfasts and lunches. However, Kelly did realize that there was more to learn about teaching her children from diverse backgrounds, so she enrolled in a graduate-level multicultural literacy course.

"I'm an American; I Don't Have a Culture."

Like many teachers in the multicultural literacy course, Kelly described herself as white, without a culture (Florio-Ruane, 1994; Ladson-Billings, 1994). In fact, this portrait is a typical one for teachers in the United States, since 90.7% describe themselves as white and from the middle socioeconomic levels (Snyder, 1997). Many teachers have not had sustained relationships with people from ethnic and cultural minorities, so their knowledge base has most likely been influenced by mass media (Pattnaik, 1997). Furthermore, preservice experiences often do not prepare teachers for making strong connections between home and school with people from diverse ethnic and cultural backgrounds (Au, 1993; Banks, 1994).

Originally published in *Language Arts* (1999), volume 76, number 4, pages 332-340. Copyright 1999 by the National Council of Teachers of English. Reprinted with permission.

This article focuses on the implementation of a model fostering culturally relevant teaching that Kelly and teachers like her are adapting for their classrooms and schools.

Culturally Relevant Pedagogy:
Knowing Thyself and Understanding Others

Gloria Ladson-Billings (1994, 1995) has given us a clear picture of culturally relevant pedagogy. Her descriptions of successful teachers for African American students tell us about African American and white women educators who have made connections and collaborated with the communities in which their students live and attend school. These teachers build on students' prior knowledge and skills to promote academic excellence and relate learning to the local as well as the global community. They listen to families and ask for help. They are positive, hopeful, and creative in their teaching, using meaningful materials and strategies. They can tell their personal stories and associate their life experiences with their students. Finally, they know about their own teaching and engage in reflective practices with their colleagues.

Irvine and Fraser (1998) reinforce this portrayal of culturally responsive teachers of African American students. The term "warm demanders" summarizes the characteristics of those who use a unique pedagogical style to motivate students for academic achievement by pushing them to the highest levels. Students are actually proud of their teacher's "meanness" and boast of a parental type of relationship.

With the information from these research studies, teacher education programs across the United States are being challenged to prepare similar professionals who are culturally responsive and sensitive to the diverse ethnic and cultural groups of children in their classrooms. These educators would be capable of making culturally compatible and dynamic connections between home and school. However, many programs attempting to develop such teachers fail to consider the emotions and attitudes that present and future teachers possess regarding cultural and ethnic diversity. In light of this information, there is evidence that teacher self-knowledge may be the first and foremost consideration for education programs when attempting to help teachers understand their students (Banks, 1994; Britzman, 1986). For instance, Osborne (1996) states,

> While coming to grips with their own subjectivities which involve classism, sexism, and racism, students in our teacher education program often become angry, disillusioned, and hurt by the process. But without the increased self-awareness,

it is difficult to imagine how teachers can tap into, even recognize, student sub-jectivities. (p. 294)

Fortunately, the descriptions of several promising research interventions (Cochran-Smith, 1995; Florio-Ruane, 1994; Noordhoff & Kleinfield, 1993; Spindler & Spindler, 1987; Tatum, 1992; Willis & Meacham, 1997) suggest new paths toward more meaningful teacher preparation. All incorporate the language arts in order to explore knowledge of self as an important step for understanding and connecting with students and families from diverse backgrounds. As a prerequisite, all emphasize the need for a safe learning environment for the study of self and others, since discussions of cultural and ethnic differences often evoke emotional responses ranging from guilt and shame to anger and despair.

A Safe Learning Environment

Teaching a course on the psychology of racism, Tatum (1992) helped students overcome the resistance to talk and share information about racism by establishing rules for a safe classroom. She urged students to learn classmates' names as a way to begin conversations. She led class discussions about developing mutual respect, trust, and confidentiality. To promote student self-confidence, her initial assignments revolved around small group interchanges. As a result of these activities, an atmosphere of free expression emerged during class dialogue.

Class Dialogue

Willis and Meacham (1997) noted that when a trusting and respectful community had developed in their teacher education classes, dialogue about assigned readings appeared to assist in the discovery of individual student's beliefs. In both classes, about half way through the semester, an interesting phenomenon occurred which they called "break point." Students began relating personal experiences around racism or discrimination and asking for help from the class to understand incidents and beliefs. This was the point at which the class dialogue came together and students recognized the power of racism and its undeniable consequences. They then realized the inequalities that exist in schools and began to discuss future problem-solving approaches.

Similarly, Cochran-Smith (1995) found that opportunities for dialogue about readings directed toward the life experiences of preservice teachers and minority groups increased teacher understanding of racial issues and helped them become allies of students and families of color.

On a cautionary note, dialogue must be carefully monitored. When preservice teachers in Florio-Ruane's Autobiography Club (1994) read about the lives of famous people from minority backgrounds, volatile conversations about equality and education were stimulated. The professor's carefully attentive facilitation provided the means for avoiding serious conflicts that seemed to emerge as individuals promoted personal agendas (Florio-Ruane & deTar, 1995).

Reading and Writing to Understand Self and Others

Class dialogue in a safe setting is often stimulated by the reading and writing assignments. In Cochran-Smith's (1995) study of inquiry and reform in education, preservice teachers first wrote their autobiographies and then discussed reading about race and privilege in society. As they began to relate the readings to their own life stories, white privilege clearly emerged. At that point, the preservice teachers actually rewrote portions of their life stories expressing the pain of learning about the inherent inequities that exist in society and the lack of recognition for Latino, African American, and other minority cultures. They realized how narrow their own formal education had been.

In Florio-Ruane's Future Teacher's Autobiography Club (1994), preservice teachers read autobiographies of individuals from diverse backgrounds, examined their life experiences within a culture and related them to their own life stories. During the process, preservice teachers often become more aware of the elements in their own life stories that revealed cultural identities and were able to scrutinize their own beliefs and attitudes about diversity.

Keeping a reflective journal was another means for promoting self-knowledge and stimulating open dialogue in several studies of preservice teachers. Journal entries and class dialogue illustrated mounting tensions that developed as students read, wrote, listened, and talked about racial issues considered taboo. Reflection and self-analyses brought forth understandings of self and white privilege (Willis & Meacham, 1997).

Equivalent experiences occurred when non-Native preservice teachers prepared for schools in Alaska (Noordhoff & Kleinfield, 1993). They kept journals of their involvement in schools and communities and attempted to analyze the problems associated with cultural similarities and differences during discussions at preservice teacher seminars. Comparing and contrasting their own life experiences with their students' gave them a greater understanding of the teaching and learning process. The journal records of their field work stimulated reflection on their own beliefs about differences and helped them understand others.

Personal Experiences

Present and future teachers who wrote and talked about personal experiences relating to a culture, such as interviewing individuals, visiting neighborhoods, and observing classrooms, not only learned about a new culture, but also learned about themselves and seemed to change attitudes (Cochran-Smith, 1995; Noordhoff & Kleinfield, 1993; Spindler & Spindler, 1987).

In the Teachers for Alaska program (Noordhoff & Kleinfield, 1993), non-Native preservice teachers gathered information about the communities in which they would be teaching, raised their own questions about teaching, and, with the support of colleagues, were encouraged to learn more about their students. They joined local activities to acquire firsthand knowledge of their students' families, customs, and traditions. This allowed these preservice teachers to make connections between home and school for relevant learning/teaching experiences in their classrooms.

Other teachers who have observed culturally different classrooms around the world (Spindler & Spindler, 1987) acquired new perspectives on child development, curriculum goals, teaching, and learning. As these teachers wrote reflections on similarities and differences for cross-cultural analysis, they appeared to increase their understandings of personal and professional practices and develop an appreciation for others who were different. They saw differences as being new perspectives that could be used for problem solving and potential change in their own classrooms.

Language Arts and Knowledge of Self

All of the above studies used the language arts to create consciousness-raising experiences to gain a knowledge of self and others. Knowledge of self and others appeared to emerge through autobiography, reflection on others' autobiographies, reflection about diversity issues, and cross-cultural analysis. Therefore, preservice and inservice programs might consider using these strategies. However, several aspects regarding the efficacy of these strategies need investigation. Does preparation lead to implementation of culturally relevant teaching? Is continued support necessary to maintain changes in attitude that foster home and school connections that are supportive of diversity? These questions stimulated my interest. Therefore, during the last six years, I designed a model focusing upon the development of culturally relevant pedagogy in the context of a multicultural literacy learning course.

ABC's of Cultural Understanding and Communication

The ABC's of Cultural Understanding and Communication (Schmidt, 1998b) was created and developed on the premise of knowing oneself and understanding others. Its components include:

1. An autobiography, written in detail, by each student—to include key life events related to education, family, religious tradition, recreation, victories, and defeats.

2. The biography of a person who is culturally different from the student, written from in-depth, unstructured interviews (Spradley, 1979) that include key life events.

3. A cross-cultural analysis of similarities and differences between the life stories is charted (Spindler & Spindler, 1987).

4. An analysis of cultural differences examined in writing with encouragement for students to explain personal discomforts and identify positive affect.

5. Modifications for classroom practice and communication plans for literacy development and home/school connections based on the preceding process are designed.

The ABC's model is based on a combination of findings from previous research that demonstrates the effectiveness of autobiography, biography, cultural analyses, and home and school connections.

Autobiography: Know Thyself

Research suggests that the first step in developing culturally sensitive pedagogy is to discover one's own cultural identity in order to appreciate the similarities and differences that exist between oneself and others. Noordhoff and Kleinfeld (1993) concluded in their study of teachers preparing for multicultural classrooms, "Prospective teachers need to examine their personal histories and educational biographies for clues to the ways their beliefs, images, and experiences, when unexamined, are likely to limit their effectiveness in educating poor and minority students" (p. 37).

Teachers need to begin with their own knowledge by thinking and writing about memorable life events in their family histories. This will help them become aware of personal beliefs and attitudes that form the traditions and values of cultural autobiographies (Banks, 1994). Since it is well documented that writing is linked to the knowledge of self within a social context (Emig, 1971; Yinger, 1985), writing one's life story seems to construct connections with universal human tenets and serves to lessen negative notions about different groups of people (Progoff, 1975). As a result, teachers acquire an awareness of their own perceptions regarding race, class, gender, and related social issues (Banks, 1994; Sjoberg & Kuhn, 1989). Finally, the process of writing an autobiography sets the stage for learning about another person's life story.

Biographies: Interviewing and Discovering Others

Through the interview process, students can construct the biography of another person from key events in that person's life. Modifications of structured, unstructured, or semi-structured interviews (Bogdan & Biklen, 1994; Spradley, 1979) can be easily taught and the process can be performed in pairs or with the whole group (Edwards, 1996). Recently, research has demonstrated that interviewing people to write their life stories helped teachers as well as their students become more culturally sensitive (Schmidt, 1998b, 1998c; Spindler & Spindler, 1987). After documenting a person's story the discovery of similarities and differences permits interesting cross-cultural analysis.

Cross-Cultural Analysis: Comparing and Contrasting Similarities and Differences

Teachers who have interviewed other teachers from cultures that are different from their own, and who have performed written, cross-cultural self-analyses (Spindler & Spindler, 1987), acquire insights about others and begin to sense their own ethnocentricity. Comparing and contrasting similarities and differences proves to be an interesting way to begin in-depth class discussions that lead to an understanding and appreciation of diversity. Traditionally, similarities among people have been celebrated and differences have been ignored (Cummins, 1986; Trueba, Jacobs, & Kirton, 1990). However, when differences are ignored, a disempowering process occurs as a student's home knowledge is subtracted from the learning community (Cummins, 1986). It is empowering when students' differences, whether physical, academic, or cultural, are recognized. That recognition is part of valuing each individual and his or her family and community in the classroom (Derman-Sparks, 1992; McCaleb, 1994; Paley, 1989).

Communication Between Teachers and Families

Families are children's first teachers and have much to share in a child's literacy development. Teachers must be able to develop collaborative relationships with families in an atmosphere of mutual respect, so that students benefit from their education (Faltis, 1993; Goldenberg, 1987; McCaleb, 1994). However, an imbalance of power exists between highly educated teachers and administrators and less educated, often lower-income parents. Educators may fear saying and doing the wrong things with people who are ethnically and culturally different. But, since teachers are in a power position, they are the logical ones to reach out to the families (Edwards, 1997; Ogbu, 1983).

Research suggests that when present and future teachers meet with people who are different from themselves, the personal is accentuated and internalization of information is fostered. If a teacher has written an autobiography, cultural differences can be examined in a positive manner and can be related to their own personal histories (Banks, 1994; Britzman, 1986; Ladson-Billings, 1994). Therefore, the interview process can serve as a means for sharing life stories and learning about similarities and differences (Spindler & Spindler, 1987).

Edwards (1997), in her work with parent interviews, found that families have a wealth of knowledge to share that can help the teacher motivate and promote the child's reading, writing, listening, and speaking. When a teacher knows the community values, and also values what the community knows, the boundaries between home and school will become blurred in an atmosphere of learning and collaboration.

Children feel pride in knowing their parents are connected to school. When families become actively engaged in the school, trust for the school and the teachers increases (Ladson-Billings, 1994). When communication between teachers and families becomes regular practice, families may decide to join school-wide committees (Faltis, 1993; Reyhner & Garcia, 1989). They may work with the school for the development of curriculum that incorporates family stories (Edwards, 996; Goldenberg, 1987; McCaleb, 1994; Trueba, Jacobs, & Kirton, 1990). They can provide personal perspectives on their culture and offer firsthand learning opportunities, as well as become mentors and tutors before, during, and after school.

Multicultural Literacy Course

The five components of the ABC's of Cultural Understanding and Communication were the major assignments for the preservice and inservice teachers enrolled in a Multicultural Literacy course I designed. The course readings connected with the ABC's model and stimulated class discussions about self-knowledge and how teachers create home and school connections for building classroom community with reading, writing, listening, and talking (Bloome & Green, 1982; Dyson, 1993; Heath, 1983; Schmidt, 1998a; Vygotsky, 1934/1978). Other readings emphasized the need for teachers to develop the cultural and social awareness necessary to help students and their families see the connections between home and school and associate their cultural patterns with the school (Au, 1993; Barrera, 1992; Edwards, 1996; Ladson-Billings, 1994; Nieto, 1996; Schmidt, 1996). Students also responded to case studies (Nieto, 1996; Schmidt, 1998a) and multicultural literature (Diamond & Moore, 1995).

Along with relevant readings, invited guests from the Russian, Chinese, African American, Latino, Native American, and Indian cultures told their personal stories and responded to semistructured interview questions from the class. A cross-cultural analysis was completed for each visitor.

Course instruction was based on constructivist models (Rogoff, 1986; Vygotsky, 1978). In an atmosphere of free and respectful expression, the class worked in pairs and triads, participated in whole class dialogue, and role-played activities. A learning community emerged quickly as I acted as colleague and facilitator in a safe place where conflicts could be openly discussed in relation to knowledge, experience, and reflection (Freire, 1970; Palmer, 1995; Schon, 1987).

At the end of the multicultural literacy course, I asked for volunteers to share their successes in creating home and school connections for classroom communities to develop reading, writing, listening, and talking. Urban, rural, and suburban elementary and secondary teachers opened their classrooms to observation. Several collected data as part of an ongoing study. This article will report on the teachers who work in urban settings only.

ABC's in Practice: Teachers Make Connections

Over the last four years, 14 white female teachers who had taken the multicultural literacy course, built on the ABC's model, volunteered to participate in a study of the classroom implementation of the model. All were teachers who taught in one of five elementary schools situated in high-poverty areas where the majority of their students were from ethnic and cultural minority populations. Through observations, journals, lesson plans, and interviews, the teachers revealed practices for home and school connections that developed classroom and school community through reading, writing, listening, and talking. Their successes also sparked ideas for future plans.

Descriptions of practice in classrooms, communication between home and school, and plans for the future follow, beginning with classroom adaptations of autobiography.

Autobiography and Classroom Practice

At the beginning of the school year, several teachers adapted autobiography exercises for their K–6 elementary classrooms in order to connect home and school for classroom community and promote reading, writing, listening, and speaking across the curriculum. They modeled autobiography by telling personal and family stories, sharing written accounts, and showing personal artifacts. They read excerpts from the autobiographies of famous people from different backgrounds. This stimulated classroom interest and students began to share stories, written and oral, about their families. Students invited their family members to show pictures, explain family objects, and tell family stories. Several families created albums or stories of their lives with photos, illustrations, and written narratives. Some students decided to invite their after-school caregivers or neighborhood friends, not only to share stories, but to act as resource people in content areas. Others even brought pets to school, such as goldfish, hermit crabs, dogs, cats, turtles, rabbits, and even a baby boa constrictor.

Another successful activity was researching family history to discover more about one's origins in the world community. Sharing family stories in class helped students and teachers get to know each other quickly. Students learned about other parts of the world while studying more about themselves.

Simple and complex adaptations of autobiography occurred in classrooms. Simple activities, such as sharing oral and written accounts of personal likes and dislikes, helped students think about their lives. A more complex activity occurred when students wrote their autobiographies through personal, written responses to current events and required literature. Using response journals over a four week period, students wrote 20 to 30 entries. They connected readings to their own lives and then wrote autobiographies. From this experience, they learned about themselves and their own perspectives. Most students volunteered to read aloud portions of their stories. The teachers were amazed at the high quality of writing and sharing.

Throughout the autobiography activities, teachers talked about the uniqueness of each individual and promoted discussions of special talents.

The autobiographies gave teachers information about a student beyond that found in the school's files. They quickly established rapport among students and families at the beginning of the school year. The teachers expressed great satisfaction, "I have never felt this close to a class so early in the year." "I have made informal contact with families in such positive ways." "This was easy; I thought it would be difficult to get the families to come to school and share."

Biography and Classroom Practice

Instead of autobiography as the first student experience, some teachers began with the interview process to develop classroom community through reading, writing, listening, and speaking. K–6 teachers found that interviewing acted as a way to introduce classmates to each other at the beginning of the school year. Students learned to formulate and ask questions about personal interests and family interests at share time and with the "special student" for the day. One-to-one interviews as well as whole-class interviews of a given classmate promoted reading, writing, speaking, and listening in very personal and relevant ways. Students wrote about each other and learned about classmates' talents and interests. Writing another's life story helped them reflect upon their own experiences and begin to think positively about differences.

The interview process was taken into fifth-grade and sixth-grade social studies later in the year as students interviewed primary sources who had experienced some of the major events of the Twentieth Century, like the Great Depression, World War II, and the Vietnam War. This offered students a means of seeing varying perspectives and interpretations of history.

Finally, the interview process not only helped teachers and students connect with families, but also helped them look outside their own perspectives. They acknowledged similarities and differences without fear.

Cross-Cultural Analyses and Classroom Practice

In kindergarten through sixth-grade classrooms, students drew pictures of themselves and others using primary color crayons as well as crayons representing human skin tones. They compared and contrasted physical similarities and differences and displayed their art work. Throughout the year, a lot of positive discussion occurred, based on the portraits.

The Venn diagram served as a clear graphic for studying similarities and differences in the classroom. Self-portraits, photos, discussions of likes and dislikes and autobiographies can all be documented on Venn diagrams. The Figure is a demonstration of their use in a fifth-grade classroom.

Students learned to list similarities and differences in order to compare and contrast themselves with friends and other classmates. Teachers emphasized the differences as special and as a means to celebrate the uniqueness of individuals.

Students from a third-grade classroom composed of European American and African American students became involved in similar exercises as they read multicultural literature. They concentrated on differences, discussing ones that caused discomfort, ones they "admired," and they took the time to explain why. For example, after reading *Saturday and the New You* by Barbara E. Barber (1994), a picture book about an African American girl whose aunt owns a hairstyling salon, Nadji, an African American child, stated, "I wish I had relatives who styled my hair. I want to look good all the time." At the same time, Sherry, a white child, expressed her discomfort concerning the braiding process, "That hair looks good. There's a lot of braids. I'd like mine that way, but I don't like to sit for a long time." Reading literature initiated conversations about similarities and differences and motivated discussions of differences.

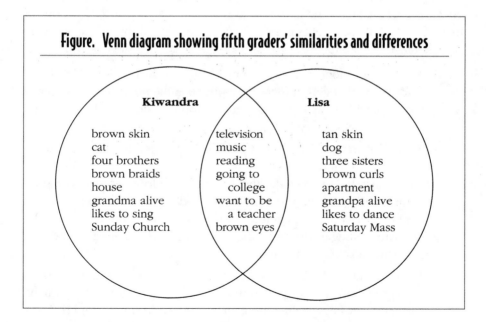

Figure. Venn diagram showing fifth graders' similarities and differences

Kiwandra

brown skin
cat
four brothers
brown braids
house
grandma alive
likes to sing
Sunday Church

television
music
reading
going to
  college
want to be
  a teacher
brown eyes

Lisa

tan skin
dog
three sisters
brown curls
apartment
grandpa alive
likes to dance
Saturday Mass

All of these ideas seemed to strengthen connections between home and school cultures. They also provided opportunities for instruction and practice in reading, writing, listening, and speaking as students talked about, wrote about, read about, listened to, and analyzed each other's stories.

The last step in the ABC's of Cultural Understanding and Communication was often the most difficult and rewarding. The teachers who believed they were becoming successful communicators with families could specifically explain how.

Teachers Connect With Families for Classroom Practice

When the teachers who had written their autobiographies shared portions of their stories with the families of their students, communication between home and school began. The typical role of teachers at conferences is to inform, explain, and question. Instead, the teachers encouraged families to ask them questions. One teacher explained the rationale to families this way, "Knowing about me as a person may help us work together."

At the beginning of the school year, the teachers and parents conferred in school, at a community center, on the phone, or in the homes of the children. At the same time, the families talked about their ideas regarding education, work, play, and religious traditions, and shared their family stories. When teachers took the first step to be interviewed by families and revealed portions of their life stories, those families decided to take the risk and share. Teachers who successfully began communicating with families suggested the following steps:

1. A letter and phone call home to make an introduction is a helpful step before school begins. If there is no phone in the home, then a knock at the door with a small gift, such as an appropriate book for the child, may be a way to begin.

2. A teacher may request a home visit or a personal visit at an agreed-upon location, such as a local community center. Meeting outside the school may be a new and difficult experience for a teacher who does not live in the neighborhood and has not developed relationships with the families. A local community center is neutral ground and may be the place to begin. However, the home is usually where a teacher can learn the most about a family.

3. The time in the home may be only five or ten minutes, but will allow a teacher to gain a better understanding of a given child's environment. Dialogue may begin with a simple hello and explanation: "I am LaToya's

teacher for next year. I am here to give her a small gift and tell you a little bit about me. I hope you and LaToya will ask questions about my life and how I came to your school. I hope you'll ask about what will be going on in class this year. I need your help to make this year the best."

Participating teachers also gave these specific suggestions for what to talk about to strengthen communication:

1. Educational jargon needs to be avoided. Teachers should talk about newsletters, and bring translations or translators if English is a second language. Information about homework hotlines could be provided. Teachers could explain the purpose of future teacher/family phone chats to ask questions and review classwork.

2. Families may be encouraged to provide insights about their children's friends, learning, and discipline.

3. Future visits in the home or school can be discussed for the purpose of sharing student work and/or journals of home and school activities.

4. Families may be encouraged to visit the school with stories, recipes, traditions, or anything else deemed important to them.

5. Families can share their knowledge of the community and access to resources.

6. Families need to be encouraged to call the teacher, visit school, and write letters. The teacher can talk about the culture and structure of the school, so families will know who to contact for questions, comments, and concerns.

All of the above make for topics of talk that promote the development of strong communication links between the home and classroom. If family members cannot come to school to share, they can make costumes, create materials, or make phone calls for the teacher and classroom. Teachers can share materials with them to help support the classroom learning process. The family gets to know the teacher. The teacher gets to know the family while they share lifelong learning skills of reading, writing, listening, and speaking.

Schools Communicate With Families for Classroom Practice

Teachers who have begun to successfully communicate between the classroom and the families of their students have also helped to strengthen school and community projects with their classroom families. One such idea is home/school reading programs where family members learn how to read to their children and encourage reading in the home. In previous years, teachers found that sessions were not well attended, that is until families were asked through notes and phone calls what they wanted to learn and where they wanted to learn it. The program, entitled "How Can I Help My Child With Reading and Writing?" evolved when families and teachers met as a committee, agreed on times and content of the program, and sent out advertisements to school families. As a result, teachers held afternoon and evening hour-long meetings in their classrooms with families and their children. Teachers modeled activities using multicultural literature, flash card games, journals, and worksheets. Then, paired with their children, families participated in read-alouds, and shared reading and writing activities. After several months, an event called "Friday Night Live: Family Reading Time" was launched in the school cafeteria.

The teachers and families who participated in these programs have discovered certain tenets for gaining school-wide participation, and they realize that these must be considered when connecting home and school. First, the school's sincere commitment to family involvement is demonstrated when child-care and transportation are provided. Second, the school solicits ideas from families for school and neighborhood activities and then the two groups plan collaboratively. Third, the school seeks media coverage to promote continued involvement as well as participation by other community members.

Preliminary responses from families have been positive about these steps toward school and community collaboration. Additionally, families have begun to request membership on school decision-making teams, solicit opportunities for participation during staff development workshops, and express an interest in the creation of life-skills and résumé-writing workshops. Last, a school-wide buddy system for families and educators has been suggested to provide person-to-person opportunities for more discussion about new ideas.

Discussion

Present and future teachers often have little knowledge of other cultures because life experiences have isolated them from minority cultures. Consequently, they may lack understanding of minority students in their classrooms (Banks, 1994). Knowledge of one's own cultural identity appears to be a prerequisite for cross-cultural understanding (Osborne, 1996; Zeichner,

1993). Recent research seems to demonstrate that autobiography, biography, and cross-cultural analysis can help teachers and their students and families to develop an understanding of and appreciation for differences in their classrooms and local community (Schmidt, 1998b, 1998c). Teachers who have successfully used the ABC's of Cultural Understanding and Communication have adapted the model and designed plans for connecting with families through reading, writing, listening, and speaking, while simultaneously creating a richer classroom community. It seems that the language arts, as associated with the ABC's, has the potential for promoting plans that strengthen communication between families and school.

REFERENCES

Au, K. (1993). *Literacy instruction in multicultural settings.* New York: Harcourt, Brace, Jovanovich.

Banks, J.A. (1994). *An introduction to multicultural education.* Boston: Allyn & Bacon.

Barrerra, R.B. (1992). The culture gap in literature-based literacy instruction. *Education and Urban Society, 24*(2), 227–243.

Bloome, D., & Green, J. (1982). The social contexts of reading: A multidisciplinary perspective. In B.A. Hutson (Ed.), *Advances in reading language research* (Vol. 1, pp. 309–338). Greenwich, CT: JAI Press.

Bogdan, R.C., & Biklen, S.K. (1994). *Qualitative research for education: An introduction to theory and method.* Boston: Allyn & Bacon.

Britzman, D. (1986). Cultural myths in the making of a teacher: Biography and social structure in teacher education. *Harvard Educational Review, 56,* 442–456.

Cochran-Smith, M. (1995). Uncertain allies: Understanding the boundaries of race and teaching. *Harvard Educational Review, 65*(4), 541–570.

Cummins, J. (1986). Empowering minority students: A framework for intervention. *Harvard Educational Review, 56,* 18–36.

Derman-Sparks, I. (1992). *Anti-bias curriculum: Tools for empowering young children.* Sacramento, CA: California State Department of Education.

Diamond, B., & Moore, M. (1995). *Multicultural literacy: Mirroring the reality of the classroom.* White Plains, NY: Longman.

Dyson, A.H. (1993). *Social worlds of children learning to write in an urban primary school.* New York: Teachers College Press.

Edwards, P. (1996). Creating sharing-time conversations: Parents and teachers work together. *Language Arts, 73,* 344–349.

Edwards, P. (1997, May). *Examining dialogues used in facilitating parental understanding of first graders' reading and writing development.* Paper presented at the annual meeting of the International Reading Association, Atlanta, GA.

Emig, J. (1971). Writing as a mode of learning. *College Composition and Communication, 28,* 122–128.

Faltis, C.J. (1993). *Joinfostering: Adapting teaching strategies for the multilingual classroom.* New York: Macmillan.

Florio-Ruane, S. (1994). The future teachers' autobiography club: Preparing educators to support learning in culturally diverse classrooms. *English Education, 26*(1), 52–56.

Florio-Ruane, S., & deTar, J. (1995). Conflict and consensus in teacher candidates' discussion of ethnic autobiography. *English Education, 27*(1), 11–39.

Freire, P. (1970). *Pedagogy of the oppressed.* New York: Seabury Press.

Goldenberg, C.N. (1987). Low-income Hispanic parents' contributions to their first-grade children's word-recognition skills. *Anthropology and Education Quarterly, 18,* 149–179.

Heath, S.B. (1983). *Ways with words: Language, life, and work in communities and classrooms.* Cambridge, UK: Cambridge University Press.

Irvine, J.J., & Fraser, J.W. (May, 1998). Warm demanders. *Education Week, 17*(35), 56–57.

Ladson-Billings, G. (1994). *The dreamkeepers: Successful teachers of African American children.* San Francisco: Jossey-Bass.

Ladson-Billings, G. (1995). But that's just good teaching: The case for culturally relevant pedagogy. *Theory Into Practice, 34*(3), 159–165.

McCaleb, S.P. (1994). *Building communities of learners.* New York: St. Martin's Press.

Nieto, S. (1996). *Affirming diversity: The sociopolitical context of multicultural education.* White Plains, NY: Longman.

Noordhoff, K., & Kleinfield, J. (1993). Preparing teachers for multicultural classrooms. *Teaching and Teacher Education, 9*(1), 27–39.

Ogbu, J. (1983). Minority status and schooling in plural societies. *Comparative Educational Review, 27*(2), 168–190.

Osborne, A.B. (1996). Practice into theory into practice: Culturally relevant pedagogy for students we have marginalized and normalized. *Anthropology and Education Quarterly, 27*(3), 285–314.

Paley, V.G. (1989). *White teacher.* Cambridge, MA: Harvard University Press.

Palmer, P. (1995, September/October). Community, conflict, and ways of knowing. *Change,* 20–25.

Pattnaik, J. (1997). Cultural stereotypes and preservice education: Moving beyond our biases. *Equity and Excellence in Education, 30*(3), 40–50.

Progoff, I. (1975). *At a journal workshop: The basic text and guide for using the intensive journal.* New York: Dialogue House Library.

Reyhner, J., & Garcia, R.L. (1989). Helping minorities read better: Problems and promises. *Reading Research and Instruction, 28*(3), 84–91.

Schmidt, P.R. (1996). One teacher's reflections: Implementing multicultural literacy learning. *Equity and Excellence in Education, 29*(2), 20–29.

Schmidt, P.R. (1998a). *Cultural conflict and struggle: Literacy learning in a kindergarten program.* New York: Peter Lang.

Schmidt, P.R. (1998b). The ABC's of cultural understanding and communication. *Equity and Excellence in Education, 31*(2), 28–38.

Schmidt, P.R. (1998). *The ABC's Model: Teachers connect home and school.* In T. Shanahan & F.V. Rodriguez-Brown (Eds.), *47th yearbook of the National Reading Conference* (pp. 194–208). Chicago: National Reading Conference.

Schon, D. (1987). *Educating the reflective practitioner.* San Francisco: Jossey-Bass.

Sjoberg, G., & Kuhn, K. (1989). Autobiography and organizations: Theoretical and methodological issues. *The Journal of Applied Behavioral Science, 25*(4), 309–326.

Snyder, T.D., Hoffman, C.M., & Geddes, C.M. (1997). *Digest of education statistics*. Washington, DC: National Center of Education Statistics, Office of Educational Research and Improvement.

Spindler, G., & Spindler, L. (1987). *The interpretive ethnography of education: At home and abroad*. Hillsdale, NJ: Erlbaum.

Spradley J. (1979). *The ethnographic interview*. New York: Holt, Rinehart & Winston.

Trueba, H.T., Jacobs, L., & Kirton, E. (1990). *Cultural conflict and adaptation: The case of the Hmong children in American society*. New York: Falmer Press.

Vygotsky, L.S. (1978). *Mind in society: The development of higher psychological processes* (M. Cole, V. John-Steiner, S. Scribner, & E. Souberman, Eds. and Trans.). Cambridge, MA: Harvard University Press. (Original work published 1934)

Willis, A.I., & Meacham, S.J. (1997). Break point: The challenges of teaching multicultural education courses. *Journal of the Assembly for Expanded Perspectives on Learning, 2*, 40–49.

Yinger, R. (1985). Journal writing as a learning tool. *Volga-Review, 87*(5), 21–33.

Zelchner, K.M. (1993). *Educating teachers for cultural diversity*. East Lansing, MI: National Center on Teacher Learning.

LITERATURE CITED

Barber, B.E. (1994). *Saturday and the new you*. New York: Lee & Low Books.

RIGHT 4

Children have a right to access a wide variety

of books and other reading material in classroom,

school, and community libraries.

Introduction

Barbara J. Diamond

I t is exciting to read the title of Bena R. Hefflin and Mary Alice Barksdale-Ladd's article in this section; the title heralds a discussion of African American children's literature along with guidelines for the authors' literature selection. On the other hand, it is disconcerting that in the year 2001, when the article was written, there was still a paucity of African American literature and that some children, even now, do not find themselves in books they read in the classroom. Similarly, in reading Nell K. Duke's article, it was equally disappointing to find that informational texts in lower SES early elementary classrooms are very scarce indeed. These findings should give educators pause, as well as a sense of resolve to take appropriate actions to address these problems. The question becomes, "How can we support the right of children to access a wide variety of books and other reading material in their classrooms and libraries when such circumstances exist?"

The extensive recommendations and guidelines for high-quality African American children's literature in the Hefflin and Barksdale-Ladd article are a starting point. This list of high-quality books provides teachers with reading material that connects with the lives of their African American students. Although the majority of the books are narrative texts, there are several examples of quality informational books, as well. These books can also be used to help address the problems caused by the lack of informational texts in lower grade urban classrooms.

Strategies to provide access to high-quality informational texts and African American literature to children in urban settings are presented in the following sections.

Introduce Literature to Teachers Through Staff Development

Teachers who want to use informational text and culturally relevant literature in their classrooms must become knowledgeable about children's literature. This is critical as a way of helping children to develop reading and writing skills and reading fluency. The first step in becoming knowledgeable is by reading and interacting with many of the stories and informational books available for children. This is essential, particularly for those teachers who have had limited preparation and exposure to children's literature in preservice college programs. Inservice teachers can take on the task of reading and learning about children's literature themselves if they are motivated and have the time. Generally, however, other classroom demands prevent teachers from reading extensively on their own. Therefore, it is legitimate to include opportunities to identify appropriate literature and read and develop strategies for using informational and narrative books in the classroom through staff development workshops. Indeed, Duke calls for this as one way to inform and motivate teachers. In order to make this happen, however, administrators will need to provide their support. Staff developers can offer guidance and direction, and teachers can be active participants and leaders in the effort.

In workshops conducted with teachers to incorporate a multicultural literacy program in schools with diverse populations, my colleague and I worked with teachers in three school districts. A critical component of the program was to provide teachers with insight and knowledge about the use of multicultural literature, both fiction and informational, in a literacy program (Diamond & Moore, 1995). Teachers learned about the availability of quality literature books and used guidelines that we developed for selection of high-quality, culturally relevant books for their classrooms. After introducing the books, we discussed issues and raised questions about the quality of the books as related to the culture of the characters, events, language, themes, and informational accuracy presented.

During these workshops (held during the school day), teachers often worked in small groups to identify specific strategies for using the literature in their classrooms. Modeling and demonstrations were also a vital part of the workshops. Teachers discovered ways to integrate the informational books about culture into their science, social studies, and math lessons. There were many lively discussions about culture and issues of racism and social justice. Often African American teachers were more passionate about these issues, but the teachers learned from one another and grew to respect and understand one another's opinions.

At the end of the year when the workshops concluded, teachers had developed knowledge of quality literature, both narrative and informational, and its power to help African American, Latino/a students, and students of other backgrounds "authenticate their world" and address and affirm themselves as important individuals.

Implementing staff development through inservice workshops has promising implications for genre development of informational text and culturally and socially relevant literature for children in urban schools. The possibilities for addressing and including the research findings indicating that young children can interact successfully with informational text, for example, should be included in the workshop. Planners also should include students' parents and children's librarians from the school and community as workshop participants. Participants could also continually identify appropriate books for diverse populations of urban students and quality informational text based on the established guidelines. The workshop format provides an opportunity to learn, work together, and discuss and share information.

Use Selected Literature and Strategies That Support a Balanced Literacy Approach

After attending workshops or during the time they are attending the workshops, teachers can implement strategies in the classroom to effectively enhance their students' development of reading, writing, speaking, and listening skills. Duke discusses the rare examples of informational text activities that were observed in the research and suggests that more activities are sorely needed. This is particularly true in low-SES settings, with African American students, Latino/a students, and students speaking other languages.

One way to begin engaging students in the reading of informational text in low-SES classrooms is to use biography, categorized as a subgenre of nonfiction by Goforth (1998) and Tompkins (1997). Duke's classification of informational, narrative-informational, and informational poetic text is a helpful distinction for teachers. Most of the books identified by Hefflin and Barksdale-Ladd in the informational text categories for first grade would fall into the subcategories of narrative-informational or informational poetic.

It is important that African American literature provides students of color and other students in urban settings the opportunity to see themselves in the books they read. Keisha's poignant comments in the Hefflin and Barksdale-Ladd article underscore this point:

> Well, we're black, and it doesn't mean that I don't like white people in stories, but I like seeing people in the book that are my same color. I like seeing black people in books because mostly they have white people in commercials and shows and stuff. And it's like in a book you can see black people.

Students like Keisha, and others, might read several biographies for young readers about Martin Luther King, Jr. individually or in literature circles. Duke's article notes the importance of extensive exposure in one genre: "Children must see, hear, read, and write informational texts before they have any hope of reading and writing them well." In addition to a discussion of the information in the book during and after reading, the teacher could lead the students in a discussion of the features of the biography.

After several experiences with the biographies, the teacher might develop a chart or grid to help the students identify the characteristics of the genre. The grid should have genre characteristics along the horizontal axis and the name of the biography along the vertical axis. As the students check off the characteristics present in each biography, they get a visual representation of the degree to which they meet the identified characteristics. This comparison and contrast activity provides information about the quality of the selected books as biographies and helps students understand that authors vary in the degree and type of information presented. This activity could be used effectively with young primary-grade students, with some modification for kindergartners.

As an extension to reading the biographies, students can use the information gained from a book to write about what they have learned. For example, the book *Dear Dr. King: Letters From Today's Children to Dr. Martin Luther King, Jr.* (Colbert & McMillan Harms, 1998) provides a model for writing letters using information about King. This book grew out of a project in Memphis, Tennessee, USA, the city where King was killed. Parents and school personnel encouraged students to write letters to King about his life and discuss their lives, feelings, and dreams for the future. What evolved were extremely poignant letters written by students ages 6 to 15. A letter by one student reads,

> Dear Dr. King,
> I love you because you made the world
> better because the White and Black
> people couldn't be friends and play together always
> I want to ask you,
> Are there Black and White angels in heaven?
> I think they play together, too.
> Love Morgan, Age 6 (p. 44)

Teachers should read only two or three letters from the book in order to encourage students to generate ideas of their own as they draft their letters. Teachers should review the steps of the writing process before they begin writing. After editing their work, students can publish their letters by sharing them with the class, posting them around the room, or compiling them in a class book.

In *Sky Tree: Seeing Science Through Arts* (Locker, 1995), young readers and writers are presented with another type of informational text. This book focuses on seasonal changes in a single tree. With the text on one page the author records the changes in the tree's world. A picture of a tree adorns the opposite side, highlighting the various changes that occur in the tree during the winter. An example of the text and question follow:

Ice formed on
the river's edge. With its
roots deep in the earth,
the tree stood
ready for winter.

Does this painting make you feel as if something is about to happen?

This text is narrative-informational and provides a model for writing informational text related to science, social studies, and concepts in other content areas. The teacher might point out how other informational texts are not as poetic, but more direct in their language.

There are many informational alphabet books for primary-grade students; these are particularly appropriate for first graders. *Eating the Alphabet: Fruits & Vegetables From A to Z* (Ehlert, 1989) is an example of a colorful book that tells about many types of fruit and vegetables. *A*, for example, is for *artichoke, apricot, avocado, apple*, and *asparagus*. The book could come alive with examples of the fruit brought to the classroom for the students to taste and feel. The book's glossary is a resource for the teacher, giving information about the location and climate where the fruit is grown.

These are a small sampling of the literature and strategies that are appropriate for use by children as they grow in literacy. The possibility is real that reading and writing informational text and text that students can connect to will improve their performance as they continue their school journey.

Engage Parent Support at Home and in School

Parents should be a critical part of the literacy program and can support the use of literature at home and at school. However, outreach efforts between schools and parents are often a challenge. Parents sometime feel alienated from school, and teachers can perceive their absence as a lack of parental concern. These assumptions can result in a divide between home and school that can widen over time (Jenkins, 1981). If parents are to be involved, the school must be perceived as a welcoming place. With a parent as a member of the planning team for the workshops and later the parent's presence at the workshops, some of the problems and misunderstandings can be alleviated.

Several programs have been found to be successful in eliciting and utilizing the support of parents in their child's literacy development. The program Three for the Road (Richgels & Wold, 1998) is one example. The program includes four steps: selecting books, categorizing books, preparing support materials, and scheduling the use of a backpack.

The first step, selection of books, results in books that would give rise to positive parent-child interactions and meet varied parent-child needs. The second step is to sort books according to ease of reading, from the easiest book to a book for independent reading, or a book that was "just right." Books are also categorized by their content (step number three), based on genre. In this program there are six genre-based backpacks, each containing one book for the three levels of reading. The third step involves preparing support materials. In addition to the books, each backpack has a letter to parents, a response journal, writing and drawing materials, hand puppets, a lost-and-found tag, and a checklist of the backpack's contents. The backpacks go home according to schedules worked out by the planners. Demonstrations to discuss the contents and how the backpacks are to be used are conducted and are an integral and important part of the project.

This is just one example of a successful parent-school partnership program that engages parents at home. In order to increase students' reading of high-quality informational texts and culturally relevant literature, a partnership that fosters parent-child reading is critical. Teachers and administrators might examine a program similar to this one and develop modifications that would work in their school and community.

Final Thoughts

Students in early elementary urban classrooms must be readers in order to succeed in school. They must be captivated by literature that speaks to them through characters and events that connect to their lives. When this occurs, students are eager to learn and are excited about reading. At the same time, and equally important, students must hear, read, and write informational text in order to be competitive as they experience the demands of later schooling and of the information age of the 21st century.

Researchers and educators will continue to work to provide greater attention to informational texts in early grades and more opportunities for young readers in urban settings to read quality literature that connects with their lives. Although there are multiple challenges, if we are successful there will be even greater rewards for all children.

REFERENCES

Diamond, B.J., & Moore, M. (1995). *Multicultural literacy: Mirroring the reality of the classroom.* White Plains, NY: Longman.

Duke, N.K. (2000). 3.6 minutes per day: The scarcity of informational texts in first grade. *Reading Research Quarterly, 35,* 202–224.

Goforth, F.S. (1998). *Literature and the learner.* Belmont, CA: Wadsworth.

Hefflin, B.R., & Barksdale-Ladd, M.A. (2001). African American children's literature that helps students find themselves: Selection guidelines for grades K–3. *The Reading Teacher, 54,* 810–819.

Jenkins, P.W. (1981). Building parent participation in urban schools. *Principal, 61*(2), 20–23.

Richgels, D.J., & Wold, S. (1998). Literacy on the road: Backpacking partnerships between school and home. *The Reading Teacher, 52,* 18–29.

Tompkins, G.E. (1997). *Literacy for the 21st century: A balanced approach.* Upper Saddle River, NJ: Prentice Hall.

LITERATURE CITED

Colbert, J., & McMillan Harms, A. (1998). *Dear Dr. King: Letters from today's children to Dr. Martin Luther King, Jr.* New York: Hyperion.

Ehlert, L. (1989). *Eating the alphabet: Fruits & vegetables from A to Z.* Orlando, FL: Harcourt Brace.

Locker, T. (1995). *Sky tree: Seeing science through art.* New York: HarperCollins.

3.6 Minutes per Day:
The Scarcity of Informational Texts in First Grade

Nell K. Duke

n this Information Age the importance of being able to read and write informational texts critically and well cannot be overstated. Informational literacy is central to success, and even survival, in advanced schooling, the workplace, and the community. A primary aim of U.S. education is to develop citizens who can read, write, and critique informational discourse, who can locate and communicate the information they seek.

Despite the clear importance of informational literacy, we fail to develop strong informational reading and writing skills in many students in the United States (e.g., Applebee, Langer, Mullis, Latham, & Gentile, 1994; Daniels, 1990; Langer, Applebee, Mullis, & Foertsch, 1990). Disturbingly, this is particularly true for students from traditionally disenfranchised social groups, a fact of grave concern given the importance of informational texts in U.S. citizenship, higher education, and work.

The failure of schools in the United States to develop adequate informational reading and writing skills in many students has long been recognized. Some scholars have even linked these failures to larger deficiencies in achievement. Chall, Jacobs, and Baldwin (1990) have suggested that difficulties with informational reading may explain the fourth-grade slump in overall literacy achievement and progress. More recently, the work of Bernhardt, Destino, Kamil, and Rodriguez-Munoz (1995) suggested that low levels of achievement in science may be linked, in part, to problems with informational reading and writing, as science achievement is correlated with informational reading ability, but not with the ability to read other forms of discourse examined.

Perhaps the most common and long-standing response to concerns about poor informational reading and writing skills has been to call for providing students with more experience with informational texts, particularly in the early grades (e.g., Christie, 1987a; Freeman & Person, 1992; Hiebert & Fisher, 1990; Lemke, 1994; Littlefair, 1991; Newkirk, 1989; Pappas, 1991a; Sanacore, 1991). Many scholars have suggested that providing more experience with informational texts in the early grades may help to mitigate the substantial difficulty many students have with this form of text in later schooling.

Originally published in *Reading Research Quarterly* (2000), volume 35, pages 202–224.

In recent years, arguments for increasing attention to informational texts in the early grades have gone beyond preparing children for *later* schooling and life. Scholars have pointed out that informational texts can play an important role in motivating children to read in the first place. Some young children find a way into literacy through informational texts that they do not find through narrative and other forms of text (Caswell & Duke, 1998). Informational texts can capitalize on children's interests and curiosities, provide opportunities for children to apply and further develop areas of expertise, and provide valuable links to children's home literacy experiences (Caswell & Duke, 1998; Duthie, 1996; Guthrie & McCann, 1997; Moss, Leone, & DiPillo, 1997; Oyler, 1996; for a related discussion pertaining to secondary and adult readers, see Alexander, 1997). Being more interested in and engaged by text can have a significant impact on learning and development (e.g., Renninger, Hidi, & Krapp, 1992). Thus, even if the early grades are exempt from the responsibility of beginning to develop children's informational literacy for later schooling and life, there are still many reasons to include informational texts early in schooling. Not doing so constitutes a missed opportunity to turn on as many students as possible to literacy.

Although the base of support for greater attention to informational texts in the early grades is wider than ever, there remain few data about the extent to which informational texts are actually included in early-grade classrooms. Examination of basal reading series has shown little presence of informational texts (Hoffman et al., 1994; Moss & Newton, 1998), but more comprehensive data about the inclusion of informational texts in early-grade classrooms have not been available. We simply do not know how much experience students have with informational texts in school, what kinds of experiences are offered, or how this might differ in different schooling contexts.

The purpose of this study is to begin to address the dearth of knowledge about students' experiences with informational texts in the early grades. The study examines the nature and degree of informational text experiences offered to children in 20 first-grade classrooms in two distinct socioeconomic settings in the greater Boston, Massachusetts, metropolitan area in the United States.

Conceptual Framework

This study is built upon the belief that discourse knowledge has a substantial impact on the lives of individuals and groups (Hodge & Kress, 1988; Lemke, 1989). The forms of discourse with which one is and is not fluent affect the way one is viewed by others, one's ability to function in different social contexts, and, ultimately, the opportunities available in one's communities, schooling, and work (Bourdieu, 1991; New London Group, 1996). To be fluent in a type of discourse valued in a particular social setting or group is something of real value—a specific form of cultural capital I term *semiotic capital.* Imparting semiotic capital is an important part of enculturation both within and outside formal schooling.

The ability to read and write informational texts is one form of semiotic capital valued in multiple settings in advanced schooling, community, and work. An important mission of schooling in the United States is to develop this ability in students. Yet, as noted earlier, large numbers of students are unable to read and write informational text critically and well, and this is disproportionately true for students from traditionally disenfranchised social groups. For this reason, this study examines informational text experiences offered to students from two distinct socioeconomic settings to ascertain whether opportunities to acquire informational discourse knowledge differ in these two schooling contexts.

Defining Informational Texts

For the purposes of this study, informational texts are defined as texts and contexts having many or all of the following features: (a) a function to communicate information about the natural or social world, typically from one presumed to be more knowledgeable on the subject to one presumed to be less so; (b) an expectation of durable factual content; (c) timeless verb constructions; (d) generic noun constructions; (e) technical vocabulary; (f) classificatory and definitional material; (g) comparative/contrastive, problem/solution, cause/effect, or like text structures; (h) frequent repetition of the topical theme; and (i) graphical elements such as diagrams, indexes, page numbers, and maps (Christie, 1984, 1987b; Derewianka, 1990; Duke & Kays, 1998; Jan, 1991; Pappas, 1986, 1987).

For the purposes of this study, I divided informational texts into three types: informational, narrative-informational, and informational-poetic. Narrative-informational text is defined as narrative text in which a primary purpose is to convey information about the natural or social world, and in which functional and linguistic features listed above are widely employed. For example, the Magic School Bus (e.g., Cole, 1990) books are narrative-informational. Informational-poetic is defined as poetry in which a primary purpose is to convey information about the natural or social world, and in which linguistic features listed previously are widely employed. For example, the poem *Dogs and Cats and Bears and Bats* (author unknown) about characteristics of mammals is considered informational-poetic ("Mammals are a varied lot; some are furry, some are not..."). Texts coded as informational alone are neither narrative nor poetic in form. Examples of books coded as informational include *The Honeymakers* (Gibbons, 1997) and *Round and Round the Money Goes: What Money Is and How We Use It* (Berger, 1993b).

There are two points of note about my approach to defining informational text: First, in this approach there is attention to both specific linguistic features of text and to functions, audiences, and contexts of the texts. This is congruent with much recent work on genre from a range of scholars (e.g., Cope & Kalantzis, 1993; Freedman & Medway, 1994; Paré & Smart, 1994). Second, in this approach to defining informational texts, no one feature necessarily determines whether or not a text is considered informational. Rather, informational texts are seen as having several among a group of features. In this way, my approach is more akin to that of prototype theory (Rosch, 1976) or feature analysis approaches (e.g., McNeil, 1992), than to a definitional or entailment approach.

The appropriateness of using this approach to genre classification is supported by the very high levels of interrater reliability yielded in this study. As difficult as it may be to define informational text rigidly or absolutely, we know it when we see (and don't see) it—mean interrater reliability estimates for judgments about whether or not a text was informational were 99.6, 97.9, and 99.6 for the three types of data collected in this study. Multiple examples of texts coded as informational are described in the Results section of this article.

Assumptions About Genre Development

Questions about how children develop knowledge of a particular form of discourse, how this development is best facilitated, and even what this knowledge consists of are all areas in need of a great deal more research. There is relatively little empirical guidance, and far less theoretical consensus, on the subject of genre development. That having been said, this study does rest on some assumptions about the development of knowledge of informational text genres and other genres of written language. The reader should be aware of these assumptions, as they have an impact on the ways the data were analyzed and the findings interpreted.

Development Is Genre Specific

I assume that development of genre knowledge proceeds in a genre-specific matter. That is, I assume that one learns how to read or write a genre through experience *with that genre*; experience with other genres may be helpful but will not be sufficient. So, for example, all the experience in the world reading and writing comic books will not by itself render someone able to read or write a cookbook. Similarly, extensive experience with storybooks, while beneficial in many respects, will not alone result in children being able to read and write information books. Learners must have experience with the particular genres in question in order to fully develop the ability to read and write (in) those genres.

Although little research takes up the question of genre specificity in development directly, there is research that speaks indirectly to this issue. One suggestive line of research indicates that children who repeatedly hear particular genres read to them either at home (Harste, Burke, & Woodward, 1984; Purcell-Gates, 1988) or at school (Duke & Kays, 1998; Pappas, 1993; Purcell-Gates, McIntyre, & Freppon, 1995) are able to reproduce those particular genres when pretending to read themselves. Harste et al. (1984) recorded 3- to 6-year-old children's pretend readings of stories, letters, and environmental print embedded in and removed from their contexts. They report many examples in which children as young as 3 offered pretend readings of the written texts with features specific to the particular genre of the text they were pretending to read. Children produced different readings of different genres.

In related work, Purcell-Gates (1988) asked kindergarten-aged children who had been read aloud to at least five times per week from at least two years prior to kindergarten to pretend to read a wordless picture book clearly suggestive of a fictional narrative, fairy tale genre. She found that children produced readings containing many linguistic features of the language of this genre such as a formulaic opening (*Once upon a time...*), use of attributive adjectives (e.g., *the beautiful princess*), and stacking of prepositional phrases (e.g., *at the entrance of the little castle*). Later research (Purcell-Gates et al., 1995) established that, over the two-year (kindergarten and first grade) time period studied, young children who began school with little or no knowledge of written fictional narrative language acquired this knowledge after regular, in-school experience with texts of this type.

Duke and Kays (1998) examined kindergarten-aged children's knowledge of another genre—information books—before and after they had been exposed to a substantial number of texts in this genre. Children's pretend readings of an unfamiliar, wordless information book after three months of exposure to information books reflected greater knowledge of several features characteristic of the information book genre, such as the use of timeless present tense verb constructions and generic noun structures (*Firefighters fight fires* versus *The firefighter is fighting a fire*). With no explicit instruction or guidance, children's response to hearing information books read aloud on a regular basis involved attending to features of that genre and (re)producing those features in a pretend reading context.

In related work, Pappas (1993) asked kindergarten children, on three occasions each, to pretend to read prototypical information books or prototypical storybooks that had been read to them immediately before. Children were not directed toward particular features of any of the books or their genres. Nonetheless, children's readings increasingly approximated the actual texts, with moves toward greater use of characteristic features of each genre, such as coclassification and present tense in the case of information books, and coreferentiality and past tense in the case of fictional storybooks. Children spontaneously attended to these genre-specific features and then distinguished their readings accordingly.

Taken together, work by Duke and Kays (1998), Pappas (1993), Purcell-Gates (1988), and Purcell-Gates et al. (1995) demonstrates children's attention to specific genre features and their ability to (re)produce those features in genre-appropriate contexts. Other studies can be interpreted similarly (e.g., Bissex, 1980; Chapman, 1995; Hidi & Hildyard, 1983; Kroll, 1991; Langer, 1985). At least indirectly, this work suggests that schools must provide students with experience with the specific genres of written language we wish them to acquire.

Genre Development Requires Substantial Experience With the Genre

A second assumption of this study is that substantial experience with a genre is typically necessary for knowledge of that genre to develop, or at least to develop fully. One does not learn to write academic journal articles successfully by reading only one; one is a better reader of how-to books after reading dozens than after reading one's first. Similarly, we must assume that in order to become strong readers and writers of informational texts, a learner would need substantial experience comprehending and producing such text. Children must see, hear, read, and write informational texts before they have any hope of reading and writing them well.

While there is a great deal of agreement about the necessity of substantial or ongoing experience with a genre (e.g., New London Group, 1996), there is currently no empirical research available to speak to the question of how much experience with a given form of written text is necessary for a particular level of acquisition, or how this might differ across individuals, cultures, and circumstances. Some have speculated that there may be a threshold of textual experience beyond which *more* experience will not facilitate acquisition (e.g., Freedman, 1994). Others have suggested that *less* experience with school-valued forms of text at home may be largely to blame for low-socioeconomic status students' relatively weaker grasp of these forms (e.g., Delpit, 1988; Purcell-Gates, 1995). In this study, the amount of textual experience offered to first-grade children in school was examined. Although the study does not determine how much experience is enough, it will provide currently unavailable descriptive information about amounts of experience with informational texts offered in first-grade classrooms, allowing scholars to evaluate current experiential offerings from an empirical basis.

The Nature of Genre Experience Matters Too

It would be naive to think that raw amount of genre experience alone determines one's success at learning to comprehend and produce that genre. Many other aspects of genre experience must also be important. For example, the experience of listening to others read a particular kind of text aloud may contribute differently to genre development than the experience of reading that kind of text oneself. Producing a genre for authentic audiences and purposes may be more educational than practicing such production solely for the teacher for a classroom assignment. Unfortunately, as with the other assumptions about genre development laid out previously, there is currently little research that speaks directly to the relative value and differential contributions of different kinds of genre experiences.

One area that has received a great deal of rhetorical attention, though less actual research, regards the explicit teaching of genre. In both the United States (e.g., Delpit, 1992; Gee, 1992) and, to a greater extent, elsewhere (e.g., Freedman & Medway, 1994; Kaufman & Rodríguez, 1993; Reid, 1987), there has been considerable discussion of, and disagreement about, whether and when to provide children with explicit instruction in the features and functions of particular forms of discourse. Again, this study is not designed to address the question of what kinds of genre experiences best facilitate development (and for what students under what conditions). However, it does provide currently unavailable descriptive information about the nature of experiences with informational texts offered to first-grade children, again allowing researchers to evaluate current experiential offerings from an empirical basis.

Genre Development Is Possible at Young Ages

Finally, I assume that genre development begins early in the lives of children. That is, I assume that even very young children can and do begin to develop knowledge about particular genres they encounter at home, at school, and in their community (e.g., Harste et al., 1984). While the general notion that genre development can and does occur at very young ages has not been particularly controversial, there has been controversy about young children's ability to interact with certain genres of written language. Relevant to the study at hand, there is debate about whether young children are able to handle nonnarrative genres. Some contend that young children are unable to learn from and about texts unless they are in the form of stories, or that, at the very least, their development is *better* facilitated by storied forms (Britton, Burgess, Martin, McLeod, & Rosen, 1975; Egan, 1986, 1993; Moffett, 1968; Sawyer & Watson, 1987). They believe that there exists a developmental progression from story forms to other forms of text, with young children's understanding and interest remaining confined to stories. Moffett (1968) suggested that young children's limited abstracting ability serves to restrict them to understanding only storied forms. Egan (1993) concluded that, for young children, narratives are "the best tools for the educational job" (p. 220).

Increasingly, scholars are drawing into question this notion that narrative is somehow primary in children's development, and that it alone should usher children through their first years of schooling. An emerging body of work suggests that young children *can* learn from and about nonnarrative, informational texts when exposed to them (e.g., Caswell & Duke, 1998; Christie, 1987a, 1987b; Donovan, 1996; Duke & Kays, 1998; Hicks, 1995; Newkirk, 1987; Pappas, 1991b, 1993). Hicks (1995) documented a classroom of first-grade children who were able to interact with expository oral and written texts in impressive ways in a classroom environment rich in such texts. Work by Pappas (1993) and Duke and Kays (1998) described earlier demonstrates that kindergarten-aged children are able to produce pretend readings of information books with several features specific to informational genres after experience with such texts.

Importantly, the literature indicates that young children not only can interact successfully with informational texts, but also enjoy doing so. The literature contains numerous reports of young children deeply engaged with informational texts (e.g., Duthie, 1996; Fisher, 1994; Guillaume, 1998; Kamil & Lane, 1997; Newkirk, 1989; Richgels, 1997). There is evidence that for some children informational texts can even act as a catalyst for overall literacy development (Caswell & Duke, 1998; Duthie, 1996). On the basis of currently available literature on the subject, I assume that inattention to informational texts in the early grades cannot be justified on the basis that young children are unable to work with or enjoy these forms of text.

Given these assumptions—that children can begin to learn and benefit from informational text experiences very early in schooling, and that substantial experience specifically with informational texts is essential for informational genre development to occur—I ask these questions: How much exposure to and experience with informational text is offered to students in their crucial first-grade year, and what kinds of experiences are offered?

Method

Sample

In order to begin to build an empirical base of information about the inclusion of informational texts in early-grade classrooms, I conducted a descriptive, observational study of 20 first-grade classrooms in 10 school districts in the greater Boston metropolitan area. Among the aims of the research project is a comparison of print environments and experiences offered to students in very low- and very high-socioeconomic status (SES) school districts. Thus, districts of study were selected from among over 50 school districts in the area on the basis of measures of levels of education, poverty, and per capita income in the district (Entwisle & Astone, 1994) (see Table 1). Specifically, 10 first-grade classrooms were chosen from among the 6 highest SES school districts in the area, and 10 first-grade classrooms were chosen from among the 4 of the 6 lowest SES districts in the area. The number of classrooms drawn from each district was based upon the number of schools in the district. From among the high-SES districts I chose one classroom each from three districts, two classrooms each from two districts, and three classrooms from one district. From among the low-SES districts I chose two classrooms each from two districts and three classrooms each from two districts.

Being at socioeconomic extremes for the area, the districts are fairly socioeconomically homogeneous—the low-SES districts would have few middle- or high-SES students and the high-SES districts would have few low- or

Table 1. Socioeconomic information about school districts participating in the study, expressed as means

District type	Selection criteria		
	Per capita income	Percentage of families below poverty	Percentage of residents with bachelor's degrees
Low SES	14,400	11.4	17.0
High SES	39,200	1.0	63.9
State average	17,200	6.7	27.2

District type	Other information		
	Elementary per pupil expenditure	MEAP reading scores†	Percentage going on to four-year college
Low SES	3,800	1,245	40.0
High SES	5,600	1,470	87.7
State average	4,100	1,350	52.0

Note. Means are used to obscure the identity of participating districts. Information is based on 1990 census data as reported in the Massachusetts Executive Office of Education's School District Profiles.
† MEAP is the Massachusetts Educational Assessment Program.

middle-SES students. The socioeconomic homogeneity of the districts is bolstered by the fact that the greater Boston metropolitan area is relatively socioeconomically segregated and comprises many relatively small school districts as opposed to a smaller number of larger, and thus likely more diverse, school districts. Although differences between classrooms in low- and high-SES districts are not the primary focus of the study reported here, the composition of this sample does have the benefit of providing information about informational text experiences in two distinct settings.

In 7 of the 10 school districts, participating schools were selected at random from among all district elementary schools. In the other 3 districts, selection procedures were adjusted to help ensure the most purely low- or high-SES population possible: (a) one school in a high-SES district was eliminated because it served a substantially lower SES population through a special arrangement; (b) a subset of schools in a low-SES district were eliminated because they contained a higher SES population according to district administrators' judgments and information such as school lunch data; and (c) schools in one low-SES district were selected at random from within each school zone, as zones constituted a meaningful level of organization in the district. Of 19 elementary schools initially contacted about participating in the study, a total of 18 consented; the declining elementary school was replaced by an alternate selected at random.

Within 17 of the 19 elementary schools, a single first-grade classroom was selected at random for possible participation in the study. In the 18th elementary school *two* classrooms were selected at random for participation in the study due to the lack of availability of a second elementary school in that district (that district was selected at random from among the high-SES districts to be the one with two participating classrooms within a single school). In the 19th elementary school, which had some bilingual first-grade classrooms, the participating classroom was selected at random from among the *nonbilingual* classrooms only, as I believed that the participation of a bilingual classroom could raise confounding issues and diminish generalizability of the study. Seventeen of the 20 classroom teachers initially contacted agreed to participate in the study. The other three classrooms (one high SES, two low SES) were replaced by alternate classrooms chosen at random.

Each teacher who agreed to participate in the study received a letter containing guidelines and information about the study. This letter provided teachers with general information about the study without revealing details, such as hypotheses about the scarcity of informational texts that might affect their instruction in ways detrimental to the validity of study findings. I requested in the letter, as well as verbally, that, as much as possible, teachers go about their activities as though I were not there. The fact that I often seemed to be looking at texts, rather than the teacher or students, may have further discouraged uncharacteristic practices during observation days. Teachers generally characterized observation days as fairly typical: On a scale of 1 to 5 (with 5 being most typical), teachers' mean rating for observation days was 4.40 (low SES: 4.35, $SD = 0.49$; high SES: 4.44, $SD = 0.39$, $t(17) = -0.44$, two-tailed $p = 0.66$; see Data Analysis Procedures section for detail about testing procedures).

Teachers had an average of 18.2 years of teaching experience (low SES: 15.1, high SES: 21.2) and 10.4 years experience teaching first grade (low SES: 8.3, high SES: 12.4). All teachers were female. The racial and ethnic composition of participating classrooms varied. High-SES classrooms were mostly white, with a few minority students in some cases; low-SES classrooms each included some white, some African American, and some Latino students, although in widely varying proportions. Some classes included students from other racial and ethnic groups, but generally in small numbers. This sample was not designed nor is it adequate to make comparisons among schools that serve primarily students of a particular racial or ethnic group.

Data Collection Procedures

Each classroom was visited for four full days over the course of a school year. Observation days were spread throughout the school year and across days of the week in order to decrease the likelihood that a particular unit of study or weekday routine would unduly affect the overall findings for that classroom. The order of observations for the first round of visits was determined at random. Subsequent observation dates were scheduled by maintaining roughly the original order but making small adjustments as needed for pragmatic reasons (such as vacation dates or field trips).

My stance during classroom visits was strictly as observer; I did not attempt to participate in classroom activities or interact with students. Rather I was occupied much or all of the time recording information about the following: (a) print on classroom walls and other surfaces, (b) print materials in the classroom library, and (c) any classroom activities that involved print in any way. This included making descriptive notes about texts and activities as well as conducting preliminary coding of texts and activities (a preliminary coding system had been developed during a pilot of the procedures); coding was completed, checked, and refined following visits to the classrooms. Because much coding did occur on site, coding procedures are discussed in this section of this article.

Displayed print. Text on classroom walls or other surfaces (known hereafter as displayed print) was recorded. This included any text directed at students (as opposed to the teacher or parents), semipermanent in nature (as opposed to notes appearing briefly on the chalkboard as part of a particular classroom activity), and displayed in some way (as opposed to a stack of papers ready to go home). It did not include books that were displayed, as data about those were collected during examination of the classroom libraries (see later discussion). Texts were defined as "the entirety of a linguistic communication" (Harris & Hodges, 1995, p. 255) and thus sometimes had more than one physical piece, as in an alphabet frieze made of 26 pieces of paper but coded as one text. Authorship was considered in determining what constituted a text so that, for example, a set of 20 name tags made by the teacher constituted one text, but if each of 20 students made his or her own name tag, that was coded as 20 texts. Other examples of displayed texts included rules, lunch menus, greeting cards, labels, calendars, model spelling tests, posters identifying the names of different shapes, colors, or sounds, lists of class jobs, and maps.

Each text was coded for text type or genre. The text's function as well as linguistic features was considered. Comparison of a second researcher's coding of displayed print in four classrooms during one visit each yielded a mean interrater reliability estimate of 90.5% for number of texts and 99.6% for whether or not text was informational (although this interrater reliability estimate should be interpreted with some caution, as there were relatively few even arguably informational texts encountered during the reliability check process). None of the items counted by one of us but not by the other had been coded as informational. A total of 6,023 different pieces of displayed print were counted and coded for genre over the course of the study.

Classroom library. Text in the classroom library was recorded. On visit 1, this included all books and magazines presently available to the class. Thus, it did not include any books or magazines the teacher was keeping in storage or otherwise deemed off-limits to students. It also did not include any textbooks, basal readers, school library books, or other materials kept in individual students' desks and available only to that individual student. However, if such materials were shelved as part of the classroom library, and available to the class for reading material, they were recorded. Also recorded were books that were only temporarily stored in individual students' desks (e.g., because a student was saving the book to read during sustained silent reading time) but actually from and soon to return to the classroom library collection available to all students (this sometimes necessitated looking in students' desks or cubbies).

On visits 2, 3, and 4, any books and magazines that I determined (by referencing past notes and teacher input) were *newly* available to students were counted, where availability was defined in the same way as described previously. On all visits, I recorded information about the location of each book including whether it was fully displayed (i.e., had all or almost all of its front cover visible). This allowed me to determine both the number of informational books displayed and how that compared to the rate of display of other kinds of books in the classroom library.

As many books and magazines as possible were coded for text type or genre. In cases in which it was not possible to code all of the materials in a library, due to time limitations, coding was conducted in such a way as to be as representative as possible. If books in different parts of the classroom library seemed to differ in kind, I made sure to code a representative proportion of books from each part of the library, by such means as coding every fifth book encountered. Comparison of a second researcher's coding of four classroom libraries, one visit each, yielded a mean interrater reliability estimate of 97.9% for whether or not the text was informational. A total of 18,393 books and magazines were counted over the course of the study; 12,160 of them were coded for genre. Those that I did not have time to code for genre were coded as miscellaneous.

Written language activities. Information about any activity that occurred during regular class time and involved written language in any way was recorded. Activities that occurred during lunch, recess, and like times were not observed or recorded. Activities that occurred during *specials* (such as gym or art) were observed and recorded, but using different procedures, as explained later in this section. Among regular class time activities, information recorded about each activity included (a) the genre of text included in the activity, (b) what was done with the text (e.g., read, written), and (c) the length of the activity in minutes. Collection of information about the length of the activity allowed for both reporting raw amounts of time spent with informational texts and for reporting time spent with informational texts as a percentage of time spent in school, in class, or in class with any form of written language. The use of time as a base unit of analysis also facilitated comparability across districts, classrooms, and days (Durkin, 1978–1979; 1987).

The length of activities was measured from the time the majority of students were involved in the activity to the time the majority of the students were no longer involved in the activity. For example, if the teacher read aloud to the students, timing was conducted from the beginning to the end of the read-aloud event, and the genre of the book read aloud was coded/counted for that number of minutes. If students were expected to be completing a worksheet at their seats, timing was conducted from the time the majority of students began the worksheet to the time the majority completed the worksheet (or were expected to stop working on the worksheet, such as when it was time for lunch), and the genre of the worksheet text (usually just *worksheet*) was coded/counted for that number of minutes. Other examples of texts used during written language activity times include calendars, biographies, graphs, globes, poems, lists, math word problems, and so on. For the purposes of this article, the important distinction is, of course, between those texts that were coded as informational, narrative-informational, or informational-poetic and those that were not.

During times in which different students were expected to be doing different things, such as when students were divided into reading or math groups, I timed the overall time spent in groups and gathered as much information as possible about each group's print activities—most notably whether print was involved and, if it was, the types of text that were used. However, it was not possible to account for written language activity of each group simultaneously on a minute-by-minute basis. Thus, these situations are analyzed separately, as explained in the following section. Finally, during times when all students were expected to be doing the same thing but the texts used within the sanctioned activity varied, such as when all students were expected to be reading a book silently but what book they were reading was their choice, I recorded the total time of the activity and then coded the genre employed as *various*. In these cases I typically made some descriptive notes about overall impressions of the types of text involved.

Observations were made during a total of 79 school days (I was unable to observe during a fourth visit to one of the high-SES classrooms). These included half or early release days only in cases in which this was a regular part of the district's schedule, such as in one district in which every Wednesday was an early release day. In total, I observed 27,671 minutes of school time, 23.06 hours per classroom on average. Of this, 19,046 minutes were spent in class (not involved in specials such as art or gym, not at recess, and so on) and of the time spent in class 12,790 minutes, or an average of 10.66 hours per classroom, were spent with written language. All minutes spent with written language were coded for the genre(s) employed.

A second researcher coded written language activities during all or part of one visit each to four classrooms (two low SES, two high SES). This amounted to 1,220 minutes of school time, 860 minutes of class time. Our mean interrater agreement for total minutes of whole-class written language activity time was 97.3%. Among whole-class written language activity time that we both coded—492 minutes in total—our mean interrater agreement was 99.6% for whether or not the text was informational (although this interrater reliability estimate should be interpreted with some caution, as there were very few minutes of time spent with even arguably informational texts during the 860 minutes of class time observed for the reliability check).

Specials. When permitted by specials teachers (in all but a few cases), I also observed students during specials. I recorded as much information as possible about any specials activities involving print in any way and, when the special was held outside the regular classroom (in the gym, for example), about print on the walls and other surfaces, and any books or magazines in the room available to students. Given the brevity of specials, it was difficult to record this information as carefully or thoroughly as during regular class time, but the records are certainly sufficient to indicate whether specials constituted a significant source of informational text exposure and experience for students.

Data Analysis Procedures

Coding described above was entered into three databases—one for displayed print data, one for classroom library data, and one for written language activity data. Analyses proceeded from there.

Displayed print. The total number of displayed texts recorded across all visits and classrooms was tallied, counting those that appeared on more than one consecutive visit only once each. The total number of informational displayed texts was also tallied. The number of informational displayed texts was calculated as a percentage of total displayed texts, first at the classroom level, and then across classrooms. Descriptive notes about informational displayed texts observed were reviewed as well for the purpose of identifying common examples of such texts.

Classroom library. The total number of books and magazines coded for genre was tallied. Also tallied was the total number of books and magazines coded as informational. The ratio of texts coded as informational to all texts coded for genre was determined. This ratio was then applied to the total number of books and magazines in the classroom library (including those I was unable to code for genre) to provide an estimate of the number of informational texts per classroom and per child. In the per-child calculations, each classroom's class size (in the case of visit 1), or mean class size (in the case of visits 2 through 4), was divided by the estimated number of informational texts in that classroom. The resulting percentages were then averaged across classrooms within socioeconomic setting (low SES and high SES).

The total number of books that were coded as fully displayed (i.e., with all or nearly all of the front cover of the book visible) was counted, as was the number of informational books that were fully displayed. The percentage of fully displayed books coded as informational was calculated. In addition, descriptive notes about the topic of displayed books (e.g., whether they were related to a theme of study) were reviewed.

Written language activities. The total number of minutes spent in whole-class written language activities was tallied, as was the total number of minutes spent with informational text. Time spent with informational text was then calculated as a percentage of the following: (a) time spent with written language as a whole class, (b) time spent with written language in general (including time in which students were divided into doing different things), (c) time in class, and (d) time in school. Descriptive notes about activities that occurred when students were divided into groups doing different things were examined carefully for any activities involving informational text. The number of these activities was quantified, though their length in minutes was not, for reasons explained previously.

Search and find techniques in the database were used to identify all activities that involved informational texts. Descriptive notes for each of these activities were examined to identify the most common kinds of informational text activities observed. Notes were also examined for any uses of informational texts during group times.

Low- and high-SES comparison. A multivariate F-test through MANOVA comparing low- and high-SES classrooms was conducted for the following variables: (a) number of minutes spent with informational text, (b) number of informational texts in classroom libraries on visit 1, (c) number of informational texts newly available to students in classroom libraries on visits 2 through 4, and (d) number of informational texts among displayed print. This test was conducted at the classroom level (not by days), thus $N = 20$. The test indicated SES differences at a $p < .05$ level of statistical significance, $F(4, 15) = 4.25$, $p < .05$. An F-test of the corresponding variables in percentage form (such as percentage of the classroom library devoted to informational books) was also conducted. This test indicated SES differences at the $p < .10$ level of statistical significance, $F(4, 15) = 2.70$. On the basis of these tests, t-tests for SES differences in individual variables were conducted and are reported throughout the Results section of this article. Because this is a planned comparison study, statistical significance was considered to be reached when two-tailed $p < .10$. Population variances for variables in the study are, of course, unknown. I took a conservative approach in assuming these variances to be unequal and using the Welch-Aspin t-test procedure. For all tests, two-tailed p-values were used.

Results

Results of this study reveal an overall scarcity of informational text in these first-grade classrooms. As detailed in the following sections, there was little informational text among displayed print, in classroom libraries, and in class-room written language activities. The scarcity of informational text was particularly acute in the low-SES classrooms.

Displayed Print

There was little informational text on classroom walls and other surfaces. Indeed, of all texts counted across the four visits, classrooms displayed a mean of only 9.4 informational texts on classroom walls and other surfaces, and four classrooms displayed no informational text at all. In percentage terms, a mean of only 2.6% of texts on walls and other surfaces met the definition of informational text being used in this study. As shown in Figure 1, no more than 10% of any individual classroom's displayed text was informational. For low-SES classrooms the mean percentage of informational text displayed was 1.5%, for high-SES classrooms the mean percentage was 3.6%, $t(14) = 1.80$, $p < .10$. Because low-SES classrooms typically had fewer displayed texts to begin with, this meant that low-SES classrooms had a mean of only 4.3 informational texts displayed across four visits, as compared to a mean of 14.5 informational texts for high-SES classrooms, $t(12) = 1.88$, $p < .10$.

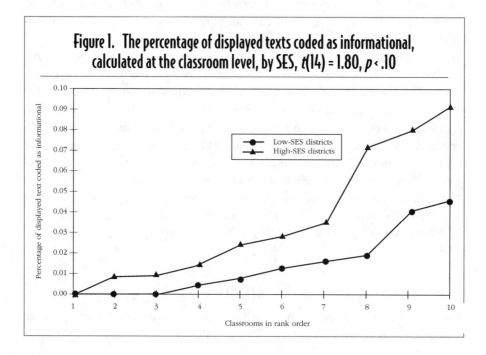

Figure 1. The percentage of displayed texts coded as informational, calculated at the classroom level, by SES, $t(14) = 1.80$, $p < .10$

One rare example of display of informational text occurred in a classroom in which students had written reports on a topic of their choice. Report titles included "How Did the Titanic Sink?" "How Fast Can Cheetahs Run?" and "Slavery." Reports varied in complexity, but all included many features of informational texts. In another classroom a teacher had written and posted informational text related to items in the room that she or students had brought in, such as plants, a piece of bark, and different types of seeds. For example, next to a citron plant the teacher had posted: "Citron/The Citron is a semi-tropical plant. It makes a sharp smelling oil which is used in making perfume, soap, and insect repellent." Later in the year in this same classroom, student-generated informational texts were posted around the classrooms. Related to a unit on whales, every text began "The important thing about whales is..." but from there texts varied in their presentation of information about whale classification, habitat, eating habits, and so on. On the day I observed, several children were seen reading their peers' whale texts and proudly pointing out their own. Commercially produced informational texts about whales were also posted throughout the room.

Classroom Library

Informational texts were also scarce in the classroom libraries of classrooms studied. Informational texts of any kind comprised a mean of only 9.8% of the classroom libraries as recorded on visit 1. In terms of actual books, this constituted a mean of only 59.1 informational texts per classroom available to students on this visit. The vast majority of these books were coded as straight informational (50.2 per classroom), though some were judged narrative-informational (8.2 per classroom), and a few as informational-poetic (0.66 books per room). On several occasions I noted a topic of study in the classroom, such as senses, teeth, or spring, and found few or no informational texts on that topic either displayed or shelved in the classroom library. Typically, relatively easy-to-read information books, such as *On the Go* by Ann Morris (1990), *Make Mine Ice Cream* by Melvin Berger (1993a), or *Spider* by David Hawcock and Lee Montgomery (1994), were especially rare.

The scarcity of informational texts in classroom libraries was relatively more acute in the low-SES classrooms. Several factors contributed to making this the case. First, there were many more books and magazines overall in the high-SES classroom libraries as compared with the low-SES classroom libraries. The high-SES classroom libraries had a mean of 738 books while the low-SES classroom libraries had a mean of nearly 40% less than that, with

449 books and magazines per classroom. With fewer books overall, one would expect fewer information books.

Second, however, there was actually a much smaller proportion of informational text in the low-SES classroom libraries. As shown in Figure 2, while a mean of 12.7% of the books in the high-SES classroom libraries were informational, only slightly more than half that proportion—6.9%—of books in the low-SES classroom libraries were informational in type. Third, mean student enrollment as recorded on visit 1 was nearly 4 students higher for low-SES district classrooms than for classrooms in high-SES districts. Thus, when calculating in terms of mean number of information books per student, as Fractor, Woodruff, Martinez, and Teale (1993) suggested, students in low-SES classrooms have even fewer information books available to them (see Table 2).

Data regarding books newly available to students on visits 2 through 4 presented a similar picture. Relatively few of the books added to classroom libraries over the course of the year were informational. Of books present in the classroom libraries on visits 2, 3, or 4 that were not present in the classroom libraries on visit 1, a mean of only 9.7% were informational. This amounts to a mean of 35.3 information books newly available to students as recorded on all three visits total spread across the school year (29.1 informational, 5.5 narrative-informational, 0.76 poetic-informational). Again, informational texts were particularly scarce in the low-SES classrooms. There were

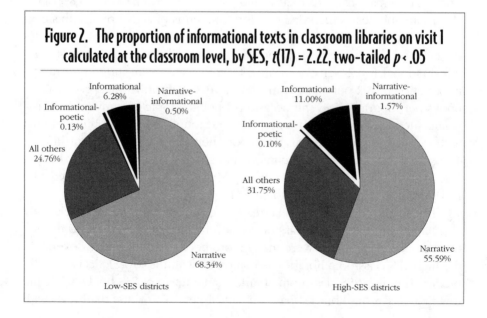

Figure 2. The proportion of informational texts in classroom libraries on visit 1 calculated at the classroom level, by SES, $t(17) = 2.22$, two-tailed $p < .05$

Low-SES districts

Informational 6.28%
Narrative-informational 0.50%
Informational-poetic 0.13%
All others 24.76%
Narrative 68.34%

High-SES districts

Informational 11.00%
Narrative-informational 1.57%
Informational-poetic 0.10%
All others 31.75%
Narrative 55.59%

many more books newly available to students in high-SES settings (a mean of 210 versus 443 newly available books across the three visits); a greater proportion of the newly available books in high-SES classrooms were informational (see Figure 3); and the fact that there were more students in the low-SES classrooms on average meant that the books per students measure was especially low for students in low-SES settings (see Table 2).

Table 2. Mean number of informational books in the classroom library per student, by district SES

Type of text	All books, Visit 1		Newly available books, Visits 2–4†	
	Low-SES districts	High-SES districts	Low-SES districts	High-SES districts
Informational	1.20 (1.17)	3.28 (1.82)***	0.61 (0.77)	1.94 (1.14)***
Informational-poetic	0.01 (0.04)	0.04 (0.08)	0.01 (0.02)	0.07 (0.11)
Narrative-informational	0.11 (0.20)	0.58 (0.80)	0.11 (0.14)	0.35 (0.19)***

Note: Values were calculated at the classroom level. † Figures are for all three visits combined. Two-tailed * $p < .10$ ** $p < .05$ *** $p < .01$

Figure 3. The proportion of informational texts newly available in classroom libraries on visits 2–4 calculated at the classroom level, by SES, $t(17) = 2.96$, two-tailed $p < .01$

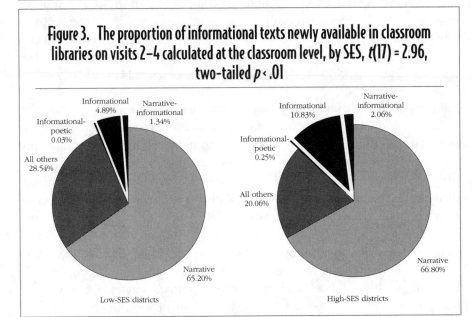

Low-SES districts

Informational 4.89%
Narrative-informational 1.34%
Informational-poetic 0.03%
All others 28.54%
Narrative 65.20%

High-SES districts

Informational 10.83%
Narrative-informational 2.06%
Informational-poetic 0.25%
All others 20.06%
Narrative 66.80%

In the area of classroom libraries there is substantial variation from classroom to classroom in the inclusion of informational texts. On visit 1 the proportion of the classroom library devoted to informational text ranged from a low of 0.6% in one classroom to a high of 25.0% in another. On visits 2 through 4 this ranged from a low of 0.0% to a high of 23.2%. Similarly, the number of informational texts available to students varied from 1.0 to 201.8 per classroom on visit 1 and from 0 to 111.6 per classroom newly available on visits 2 through 4. Thus, children in some classrooms may find few or no informational texts in their classroom libraries, while children in other classrooms may find a considerable number of these texts.

In addition to the informational genres discussed above, the case of what I term *periodical* genres should be noted. With few exceptions, I coded any magazines or newspapers in the classroom library as periodicals. Periodicals were characterized as having a variety of different genres or subgenres within them. In some cases periodicals contain relatively few informational pieces (e.g., most issues of *Cricket* magazine), but in other cases periodicals contain a great deal of informational text (e.g., most issues of *Ranger Rick* magazine). Thus, in some cases, periodicals, while coded as a separate category, could have provided another medium for informational text exposure. Here again, however, low-SES students were provided with less potential exposure to informational texts, as periodicals comprised a much greater proportion of the high-SES classroom libraries—on visit 1: 1.75% (SD = 4.30) in low-SES classrooms versus 10.9% (SD = 12.0) in high-SES classrooms, $t(11)$ = 2.27, $p < .05$; on visits 2 through 4 among newly available texts: 0.34% (SD = 0.82) versus 0.78% (SD = 1.37) in high-SES classrooms, $t(15)$ = 0.876, *ns*.

Display of informational print resources. Interestingly, as shown in Table 3, informational texts from the classroom library were sometimes displayed disproportionately often. That is, for example, although a mean of only 12.7% of the books in the high-SES classroom library on visit 1 were informational, a mean of 25.2% of the books fully displayed on visit 1 were informational in type. In contrast, however, a disproportionately small number of informational texts from the classroom library were fully displayed in low-SES classrooms (4.3% displayed versus 6.9% in library). Among the newly available texts on visits 2 through 4, both low- and high-SES classrooms displayed a disproportionately large number of informational texts. Again as illustrated in Table 3, however, given how few informational texts there were in many of the classrooms to begin with, the disproportionate display of

Table 3. Mean number and percentage of fully displayed books that are informational, by district SES

	District type			
	Low SES		High SES	
Books and magazines	*M* (*SD*) *M*% (*SD*)		*M* (*SD*) *M*% (*SD*)	
All available, Visit 1				
Fully displayed	0.4 (0.7) 4.2 (10.4)		4.3 (5.5)** 25.2 (21.1)**	
Newly available, Visits 2–4				
Fully displayed, mean per visit	0.6 (0.8) 9.9 (14.3)***		3.6 (2.5)*** 22.5 (13.6)*	

Two-tailed * $p < .10$ ** $p < .05$ *** $p < .01$

informational text in the aforementioned cases still often amounted to little informational text displayed in raw terms.

Written Language Activities

Perhaps more important than the extent to which informational texts are available in the classroom environment is the extent to which they are actually used in classroom activities. Here, again, informational texts were scarce.

During whole-class written language activity time. In all 79 days of observation combined, the total time spent with informational texts during whole-class written language activities was 282 minutes or an average of 3.6 minutes per day. As illustrated in Figure 4, this is a very small fraction of the time students spent in school, in class, and with written language. Moreover, 7 of the 20 classrooms spent *no* time with informational texts in any of the 4 days each that they were observed; another 7 classrooms each spent an average of less than 5 minutes per day with informational texts, and the remaining 6 classrooms spent an average of no more than 10 minutes per day with informational forms.

Although instances of informational texts activities were rare, it may be helpful to provide descriptions of some I did observe as examples for readers. The most common activity involving informational text was teacher read-

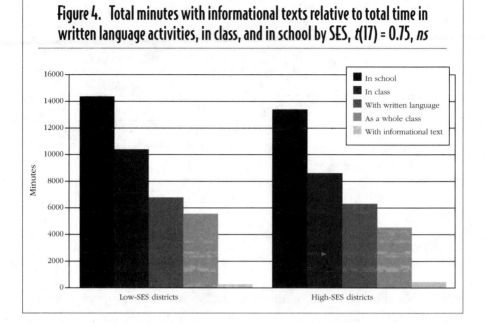

Figure 4. Total minutes with informational texts relative to total time in written language activities, in class, and in school by SES, $t(17) = 0.75$, *ns*

Legend:
- In school
- In class
- With written language
- As a whole class
- With informational text

aloud. A total of 117 minutes, 18 instances (13 high SES, 5 low SES) of teacher read-aloud of informational text were recorded. Some of these episodes were quite brief, as when a teacher read a short passage from an article about turkeys; others were lengthier, as when teachers read aloud entire information books. Often, information books read aloud related to some unit of study. In one classroom, the book *Round and Round the Money Goes: What Money Is and How We Use It* (Berger, 1993b) was read as part of a unit on U.S. currency. In another classroom the teacher read aloud *The Honeymakers* (Gibbons, 1997) as part of a unit on insects. A related set of activities with informational text involved choral reading, in which students, and usually the teacher as well, read aloud together. One class choral-read a narrative-information book *The Seasons of Arnold's Apple Tree* (Gibbons, 1984) as part of a class unit on apples. Another class choral-read an informational poem, *Dogs and Cats and Bears and Bats*, as part of their unit on mammals. Group-reading of informational text accounted for another 36 minutes, 5 instances (2 high SES, 3 low SES) of written language activity time across the school year.

A third common category of informational text activity involved semi-structured writing of informational text, which comprised another 78 minutes during six instances (three high SES, three low SES) of written language activity. For example, students in one classroom made their own version of a popular informational-poetic book: *A House Is a House for Me* (Hoberman, 1978). After having heard the book read aloud to them and having brainstormed a list of different homes (e.g., igloo, nest, drey, cave), each student was provided with a paper reflecting the book's pattern:

A _____ is a house for a _____.

A _____ is a house for a _____.

A _____ is a house for a _____.

And a house is a house for me.

Students' completed pages were compiled to make a class book. In another class, students were assigned to write a book about signs of spring. The teacher provided students with the title of the book and a class-brainstormed list of signs of and facts about spring. Students chose from among items on this list (and anything else they had thought of) to develop their compositions. In another class, students were asked to write three things they had learned about Mary McLeod Bethune from an assembly they had attended a previous day. The three remaining occasions of semistructured informational writing are described in the following paragraphs.

A few of the informational text activities observed did illustrate some of the reasons why scholars have argued that informational text experiences are important. For example, in a classroom in which students had been studying about outer space, the teacher read aloud the information book *Is There Life in Outer Space?* (Branley, 1984) and then the imaginative fictional narrative *Space Case* (Marshall, 1980). Throughout the readings the teacher led discussions about distinguishing what is real from what is not and the use of written material in drawing these distinctions.

Kamil and Lane (1997) identified learning to evaluate the truth value of text as one important reason to involve informational text in early literacy curricula. Kamil and Lane also identified as important learning to read only what is necessary in informational texts. The notion of selective reading was also underscored in a few of the informational text activities observed. For example, in one classroom students were having difficulty solving a word problem about the shape of the moon on a particular day of the month. The teacher led the students to go back to an information book they had looked at on a previous day, find the relevant passage and illustration, and use the information there to solve the problem. In another classroom, the teacher read passages of *The Amazing Dandelion* (Selsam & Wexler, 1977) that were specifically relevant to dandelion reproductive processes, the topic of study. Later, when students were asked to "draw them [pictures of different phases of the dandelion reproductive process] like scientists" a student asked to see one key illustration in the book again to aid in the illustrating, demonstrating the student's understanding of selective use of informational text.

In one classroom both the notions of selective reading and of evaluating the truth value of text were communicated through a series of read-aloud activities. As part of a unit on arctic animals, students had been studying penguins. In one afternoon devoted to penguin study, the teacher read aloud penguin-related passages from the information book *Life in the Polar Regions* (Newbridge Press, 1994), penguin-related passages of informational text downloaded from the World Wide Web, and a list of myths about penguins, also downloaded from the Web. Through these selective readings from multiple sources of informational text and through a discussion contrasting the myths about penguins with the other materials, the teacher highlighted differences in the truth values of texts, commenting about one myth that "They didn't research it. They didn't read books to find out."

Sometimes when informational texts were employed, it was actually in the service of narrative texts. For example, on three occasions the informational writing task was to write, as a group with the teacher as a scribe, facts about an author (the task was indeed to list facts; this was not constructed as biographical writing). In each case the author being written about was known for his or her *narrative* texts.

In a related case, a teacher had been working with her reading group on the topic of spiders, based on a unit from the Houghton Mifflin Invitation to Literacy series (1996). In the most in-depth reading group work with informational text observed in this study, the teacher reminded students of an information book on spiders (*A New True Book of Spiders*, Podendorf, 1982) she had read on a previous day, created a webbing about spiders with students, showed and discussed with students a diagram of the anatomy of a spider and map of where in the United States spiders live, and shared with students a poster showing different types of spiders. Following these activities, the teacher asked students, "Why have we been studying spiders?" Students' responses included such things as because spiders are interesting and because spiders are helpful to humans. After several responses the teacher told students that these were not the reasons they had been studying spiders. Instead, she said, they had been studying spiders because they had been reading *The Itsy Bitsy Spider*, a narrative song book included in their basal reading series

(Houghton Mifflin, 1996). Thus, the value and function of the informational reading were somewhat undermined.

Informational text during non–whole-class times. The spiders unit examples notwithstanding, informational texts were also scarce during reading groups and other non–whole-class times of the school day. Among small groups other than reading groups there were no occasions of informational text use in the 79 full days of observation. In reading groups, I observed informational text being used in any way only seven times (five high SES, two low SES), only five of which involved students themselves reading or writing. Thus, during times most clearly designed to teach children to read, children were typically not taught to read informational text. Rather, learning to read typically meant learning to read fictional stories, or simple descriptive text ("I like apples. I like pears...").

In one exceptional case, a reading group—the highest in the class—was *twice* observed interacting with informational text. On one occasion the group round-robin-read a narrative-informational piece entitled "Little Tugs and Big Boats" from the Macmillan basal reading series (Macmillan Reading Program, 1987). On another occasion the group round-robin-read an informational piece called "Animal Families," also from the Macmillan (1987) basal series. Prior to and throughout this reading the teacher led discussion around the theme that people in families help one another in different ways and that animal families do this too. Students were encouraged to share examples of ways in which people in their own families help one another and to read the text for examples of helping behaviors in animal families.

In another classroom, a less difficult informational text was employed with a reading group. The text, called *Garbage* (Iversen, 1994), had a simple, predictable structure—"Some people burn their garbage/Some people compost their garbage" and so on—which students successfully read as a group. The text linked closely to an ongoing class unit on waste management, particularly recycling strategies; through discussion, the teacher and students in the group made these links explicit. Occasions such as these, however, were rare. Thus, except for a few small groups of students on a few occasions, the 282 minutes of time spent with informational texts cited previously constituted the totality of organized in-class time spent with informational texts in 79 full days of observation across 20 classrooms.

Informational text during time with various genres. Recall that when students were all expected to be doing the same thing, but the texts used within the sanctioned activity varied, the genre was coded as *various*. It is possible that during such times some students may have spent additional time with informational texts not accounted for in the figures previously cited. However, descriptive notes suggest that this did not provide a substantial additional source of informational text experience. During sustained silent reading times, for example, students could choose to read or look at informational books. However, they were constrained by the fact that there were few informational texts in the classroom library, and that few such texts were displayed or even present in the library. Notably, on those limited occasions in which students were observed accessing informational text during reading times, they often seemed to be highly engaged. On several occasions groups of students were observed excitedly discussing and attempting to read informational books on high-interest topics such as snakes and insects. On another occasion a student approached the teacher to point out that two informational books he had been reading about dinosaurs had the same illustration. The teacher took the opportunity to talk with the student about how sometimes authors share information with one another and learn from the books that others have written. Relatedly, there were also occasions in which students brought informational reading material from home to share during sharing time. Students seemed to enjoy communicating their interest in the material to classmates and teachers.

Individual choice during writing times presented a varied picture. In some classrooms, there was little or no writing choice time and thus little or no additional informational text experience for individual students. In other classrooms there was more choice time for writing, but the writing choices were somewhat constrained. In fact, in several classrooms the constraints were that students could write only stories (the teachers' term) or, in some cases, only true stories (again, the teachers' term). In cases of this kind I still coded the genre as *various* because it was not always clear what the teacher included as stories, and in several cases I observed students in these classrooms writing something other than stories, usually some sort of descriptive text.

In only one classroom I observed was the writing of informational texts during writing choice time clearly sanctioned. In this classroom, the front of students' writing folders had a list of "Topics I Know a Lot About." Students were encouraged to write on these topics, which resulted not only in narratives of personal experience but also in informational texts on topics such as Beanie Babies, hockey, and the science museum. In a second classroom one of the students' writing options was an expert story (the teacher's term), which I gathered based on the teacher's explanations was, despite its name, a form of nonnarrative, informational text (see Christie, 1984, for a discussion relevant to this usage of the term *story*).

Finally, there were classrooms in which students could write anything they wanted. I observed little spontaneous informational writing during these times. This contrasts with some reports of spontaneous expository writing among young children (Chapman, 1995; Newkirk, 1989). However, given how little exposure to informational texts was provided to students in these same classrooms, and the important connections between expository reading and writing (e.g., Moss, Leone, & DiPillo, 1997), this is not entirely surprising.

SES differences in written language activities with informational text. As shown in Figure 4, once again there was less inclusion of informational texts in the low-SES districts' classrooms, although differences in this case do not reach a level of statistical significance. Students in low-SES classrooms spent less time with informational text in classroom written language activities even though, in raw terms, they actually spent more time than students in high-SES classrooms in school, in class, and with written language. In percentage terms, in low-SES classrooms a mean of 1.9% of the time spent with written language (as a whole class) involved informational texts; in high-SES classrooms 3.8% of time spent with written language involved informational texts in some way. As shown in Figure 5, half the low-SES classrooms spent no time at all with informational text in the four full days observed, as compared to one fifth of the high-SES classrooms. Similarly, during non–whole-class times, I observed informational text being used five times in high-SES classrooms and only two times in low-SES settings.

Specials

Not surprisingly, specials observed during the course of this study very rarely included informational text in their activities or, in most cases, in their displayed print or print resources.

If not informational texts, what genres were common in classrooms? Among displayed print, the most common genres recorded were word-level items such as labels and children's names. Among extended texts on classroom walls and other surfaces, narrative and descriptive texts were among the most common. In the classroom libraries, as previously illustrated in Figures 1 and 2, the overwhelmingly more common genres were narratives, particularly fictional narrative (as opposed to true stories). In classroom

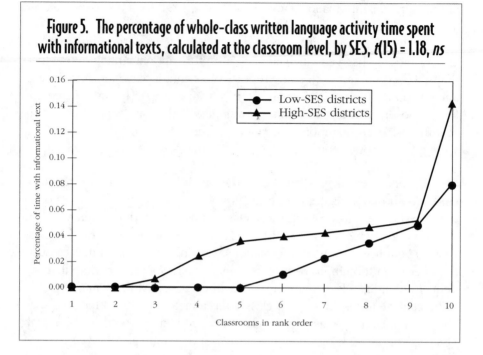

Figure 5. The percentage of whole-class written language activity time spent with informational texts, calculated at the classroom level, by SES, $t(15) = 1.18$, _ns_

Percentage of time with informational text

Classrooms in rank order

- Low-SES districts
- High-SES districts

Table 4. Categories of text commonly used in classroom written language activities, by district SES

District type					
Low SES			High SES		
Text category	_M_ %	_SD_	Text category	_M_ %	_SD_
Worksheets	21.5	10.2	Depends upon student ("various")	14.7	10.5***
Individual letters, words, sentences	17.3	10.8	Narratives	13.1	3.3
Narratives	15.9	7.7	Worksheets	12.6	7.1**
Descriptive text	4.5	4.2	Individual letters, words, sentences	7.0	9.0**

Note. Asterisks indicate differences between low- and high-SES classrooms in use of that text genre.
Two-tailed * _p_ < .10 ** _p_ < .05 *** _p_ < .01

written language activities narrative texts were again among the most commonly used, as shown in Table 4. As the Table indicates, some forms of text were well represented in written language activities of the classrooms observed; informational text, however, was not among them.

Discussion

Summary

Results of this study provide empirical confirmation of the suspected paucity of informational texts in the early grades. Across the 20 classrooms included in this study, there was relatively little informational text in classroom libraries, on classroom walls or other surfaces, and in classroom written language activities. These findings are cause for concern both because of the missed opportunity to prepare students for informational reading and writing they will encounter in later schooling and life and for the missed opportunity to use informational text to motivate more students' interest in literacy in their present lives. Of particular concern is the fact that informational text was particularly scarce in the classrooms in low-SES settings. In this study, students with less socioeconomic capital were offered fewer opportunities to develop this important form of semiotic capital—the ability to read and write informational texts.

Limitations

Four limitations of this study should be noted. First, the design of this study does include some clustering of classrooms within school districts. That is, there are, in some cases, multiple study classrooms located within a single school district. To the extent that the district itself influences the variables studied at the classroom level (e.g., if a reading program mandated at the district level affects the types of text observed at the classroom level), the generalizability of the data is affected. The impact of this limitation is mitigated somewhat, however, by the fact that there were several different school districts involved (four low SES, six high SES) and by the fact that there is little clustering at the school level (only one school had more than one classroom participating in the study). Further, I noticed little commonality among classrooms within a district that seemed attributable to characteristics of that district. For example, I observed no single science text or approach within a district that would result in the use (or nonuse) of a standard amount of informational scientific text across classrooms. Classroom and SES-level variables seemed to have a far greater impact.

A second and more significant limitation of this study is its geographical specificity. All districts observed were located in the state of Massachusetts and within a relatively small geographic area. The districts, schools, and classrooms in this study may have certain things in common because of their geographic and political proximity. For example, average school spending in Massachusetts is lower than in many other states (Morgan, Morgan, & Uhlig, 1998), and, thus, schools in Massachusetts may have fewer books in general, and informational books in particular, than schools in other states. Similarly, socioeconomic differences in the presence of informational text may be more or less pronounced in Massachusetts than they are elsewhere. Research in other geographic regions would have to be conducted to investigate these possibilities.

A third limitation of this study was the limited analysis of informational text use in small-group and individual work times in and outside of the classroom. As explained previously, when different groups of students or individual students were expected to be doing different things, such as when students were divided into reading groups, I tried to record as much information as I could about what each group or individual was doing. This was sometimes difficult, and it is possible that I missed some interactions with informational texts during these times. More important, the interactions with informational texts that I did observe during these times were not included in the overall totals for time spent with informational text, as there was no satisfactory way to account for only a fraction of the class working with informational text at a particular time. Rather, these interactions were analyzed and discussed separately (see Informational text during non–whole-class times). Although there were few interactions with informational text during the small-group and individual work times, at least as far as I was able to observe, this is nonetheless a limitation that should be borne in mind.

Finally, the way in which informational text was defined in this study had a direct impact on the results. A different definition of informational text, broader or more narrow than the one used here, would likely yield different results. Thus, the results of this study should always be read through the definition of informational text used.

Conclusions

Several conclusions can be tentatively drawn from this study. First, those who are calling for substantial attention to informational text in the early grades (e.g., Christie, 1987a; Freeman & Person, 1992; Hiebert & Fisher, 1990; Lemke,

1994; Littlefair, 1991; Newkirk, 1989; Pappas, 1991a; Sanacore, 1991) have apparently not succeeded in sufficiently affecting classroom practice. In the first-grade classrooms studied, informational text was rare and, in some classrooms, almost nonexistent. A stronger, more comprehensive approach to increasing attention to informational text in the early grades is needed (see later discussion).

Second, theories about the primacy of narrative in genre development, though increasingly questionable from an empirical perspective (e.g., Caswell & Duke, 1998; Christie, 1987a, 1987b; Donovan, 1996; Duke & Kays, 1998; Hicks, 1995; Newkirk, 1987; Pappas, 1991b, 1993), still appear to have a hold on early schooling. As reported earlier, narrative text was relatively common among extended text on classroom walls and other surfaces, the majority of texts in the classroom libraries were narrative, and narrative forms were among the most common in classroom written language activities. In contrast, informational text was rarely found on classroom walls and other surfaces, made up only a small portion of classroom libraries, was uncommon in classroom written language activities, and was almost never employed in classroom reading instruction. A growing research base attests to the fact that narrative is not the only form of text from and about which young children can learn. The observed inattention to informational text in first grade cannot be justified on the basis that young children cannot handle informational text forms.

A third conclusion that can be drawn from this study is that content area instruction does not necessarily provide substantial informational text experience in first grade. In the context of schooling, informational texts are largely associated with content area instruction, as in science and social studies. Thus, one might think that neglect of informational genres in early literacy curricula is made up for by inclusion of these forms in science, social studies, and other disciplines. However, this study, unlike many other observational studies in the literacy field, examined literacy experiences offered to students throughout the entire school day, across the curriculum. Still, little use of informational text was observed.

Fourth, this study suggests that continued low levels of achievement in informational reading and writing should not be attributed solely to the difficulty of these forms of text. Rather, there is now greater reason to hypothesize that students perform poorly with informational text at least in part because they have insufficient experience with it. As Newkirk (1989) argued with regard to writing:

> Not unreasonably, then, we might attribute some of the difficulties that students experience with exposition to the virtual exclusion of this writing from the books that they must read. I suspect that, in some studies on report or persuasive

writing, children are being asked to write a kind of discourse *that they have never read.* Little wonder that they have trouble.... [I]t is simplistic—or at least premature—to claim that this difficulty derives from the inherent difficulty of expository or argumentation or in the inherent limitations of students. (p. 29, emphasis in original)

Fifth, even the few informational text activities observed in this study speak to the potential of informational text to be a productive part of early-grade curricula. As many examples described in this article demonstrate, informational text can be a vehicle to gain, work through, and communicate knowledge about the natural and social world, a vehicle to inspire and attract students to literacy.

Finally, to the extent that the findings of this study hold true more widely, children attending school in low-SES districts are provided with even less access to and experience with informational text in school than their high-SES counterparts. This is a very serious finding because of the importance of being able to access and communicate information in our society. The notion that those with more socioeconomic capital are schooled to possess relatively higher levels of this important form of cultural capital is troubling indeed.

The observed SES differences in informational text access and experience merit some additional thinking about the long-noted fourth-grade slump in reading achievement (Chall, Jacobs, & Baldwin, 1990). Traditionally, the fourth-grade slump has been explained as resulting from the increase in demand for expository reading and writing that is thought to occur around fourth grade. Perhaps one reason this slump is reportedly more pronounced among low-SES students is that they have had less pre–fourth-grade school experience with informational text forms. Similarly, perhaps more low-SES students would develop a stronger interest in reading if their first, critical years of schooling offered a less narrow reading diet.

Strategies for Addressing the Scarcity of Informational Text

In the following paragraphs, I suggest several strategies for addressing the scarcity of informational text in many early-grade classrooms beyond simply calling for greater attention to these forms (an approach that has apparently been inadequate). First, we should encourage publishers of literacy programs, basal and otherwise, to incorporate more informational text into their materials. In the first-grade classrooms studied, far more time was devoted to language arts than to any other curriculum domain, and commercial literacy programs were used for part or most of literacy instruction in many classrooms. Because basals, and perhaps other literacy programs, include little informational text (Hoffman et al., 1994; Moss & Newton, 1998), they contribute to the overall scarcity of informational text observed. By exerting influence on basal publishers and publishers of other materials aimed at schools (e.g., The Wright Group), we can have an influence on the types of texts to which students are exposed in school.

Relatedly, curricular mandates and reform projects may provide a mechanism for addressing the scarcity of informational text. For example, including specific calls for informational literacy in state standards for the early grades might influence local reading series adoptions toward series that include more informational text or push local curriculum development projects to include greater attention to informational text forms. We should urge educators and officials at the local and state levels to involve informational literacy in their mandates and reforms.

Teacher training is another avenue through which to address the scarcity of informational text in early-grade classrooms. We should share with preservice and practicing teachers the research demonstrating that young children, including those from low-SES settings (e.g., Caswell & Duke, 1998; Duke & Kays, 1998), can interact successfully with informational text. We should offer teachers some of the extant descriptions of early-grade classrooms that have successfully incorporated informational text into their curricula (e.g., Duthie, 1996; Fisher, 1994; Kamil & Lane, 1997; Richgels, 1997).

Another strategy for increasing attention to informational text in the early grades is to link informational reading and writing to science achievement. As noted earlier, at least one study has shown a relationship between science achievement and informational reading and writing ability specifically (Bernhardt et al., 1995). It may be possible to take advantage of the recent upsurge of concern about science achievement brought about by the release of the Third International Math and Science Survey (TIMSS) report, which shows low levels of science and mathematics achievement among students in the United States as compared with those in other industrialized nations, to increase attention to informational text in inservices, standards, curricula, and other areas. We should investigate the possibility that affording greater attention to informational text in the early grades may improve not only students' later language arts performance, but their performance in later content area work as well.

Parents may provide another avenue for increasing attention to informational text in primary-grade classrooms. Including more informational text in home reading programs, parent workshops, and family literacy programs may influence teachers to include more of such texts in their classrooms, while at the same time increasing children's experience with such texts in their homes. In my experience some parents of young children are not aware of informational text as a possible form of reading material for their children. However, once they begin reading information books and other informational texts with their children, their attitudes toward such text forms are positive. Parents have indicated that they find information books for children interesting, and many have remarked to me that they, as well as their children, learned something from the book or other material they had read. Informational texts may also be congruent with the types of text parents themselves read in their daily lives (see, e.g., Caswell & Duke, 1998). As more parents see informational literacy as important for their children, others in education may follow suit.

Another strategy for increasing inclusion of informational text in the early grades is to work on increasing the budget available for reading materials in the early grades. While this is no small task, bringing about increases in the amount of money districts spend on trade books and other reading materials might well result in greater inclusion of informational texts, particularly if budgetary increases were accompanied by professional development opportunities around building high-quality classroom libraries and working with a variety of genres. The purchase of new books would allow educators to take advantage of the high-quality information books now available for young children. This could be especially important in low-SES settings, where the overall number as well as the proportion of informational texts are smaller. This may be at least in part because of budgetary differences between the low- and high-SES districts. Recall that, among the districts in this study, mean expenditure was US$1,800 more per pupil in high-SES districts than in the low-SES districts. Money should be considered in addressing the scarcity of informational text in early-grade classrooms.

Finally, a strategy for increasing attention to informational text that should be avoided—we should not attempt to increase time spent with informational text solely through decreasing attention to narrative text. This approach of pitting narrative against informational is ultimately self-defeating for those who count themselves as advocates for either type of text. Rather, at least with regard to written language activities, I urge us to look to other commonly used forms of text, for which few scholars are advocates, to replace with informational text forms. For example, recall from Table 4 that worksheets account for 21.51% of written language activity time in low-SES classrooms, 12.62% of time in high-SES classrooms. Individual letters, words, and sentences, unembedded from any larger textual context, use up another 17.28% of time in low-SES classrooms (although much less time in the high-SES settings). I urge scholars to scrutinize the cost-benefit of these kinds of texts before encroaching upon class time spent with narrative texts.

Directions for Future Research

In the Assumptions About Genre Development section earlier in this article, I suggest several areas regarding overall genre development in need of further study. There is also a need for further research looking specifically at the development of informational genre knowledge. Most critically, there is a need to investigate a fundamental premise on which calls for greater attention to informational texts rest—that greater experience with informational texts in the early grades actually does make a difference in children's fluency with these forms of text later in schooling. Relatedly, additional work is needed to test whether the presence of informational text in early-grade classrooms actually does serve to promote literacy early in children's education. Studies in these areas should be conducted in low-SES as well as other settings to ascertain whether the fourth-grade slump and other phenomena are indeed productively addressed through greater attention to informational texts in the early grades.

Another area of research needed would compare different approaches to incorporating informational texts into early-grade classrooms, to determine whether some practices have a more positive approach on students' literacy achievement than others. Some of the more common informational text experiences offered to students in this study, such as teacher read-alouds and semistructured writing, suggest areas for investigation. Also informative would be studies of different techniques for scaffolding informational reading among young learners, such as K–W–L (Know–Want to Know–Learned) (Ogle, 1986) or Questioning the Author (Beck, McKeown, Hamilton, & Kucan, 1997), and the contributions of explicit teaching of informational text features to young readers' and writers' development.

A third area in need of investigation regards the difficult question of *how much* informational text experience *is enough* to prepare students for the demands of later schooling and life and to capture the attention of those students turned on to literacy through informational reading and writing tasks. Since the minutes in the day, books in the library, and print on the walls are all limited, we need to determine which genres should take priority and how much experience, access, and exposure should be devoted to those genres. This presents multiple challenges for research and suggests the need for serious conversation about what kinds of texts we most want students to read, write, use, and critique. We will need clear textual priorities to design schooling that will guide students though the mass of texts in the 21st century.

REFERENCES

Alexander, P.A. (1997, March). *A case for the motivational nature of exposition: Contrasting information-finding with knowledge-seeking.* Paper presented at the annual meeting of the American Educational Research Association, Chicago.

Applebee, A.N., Langer, J.A., Mullis, I.V.S., Latham, A.S., & Gentile, C.A. (1994). *NAEP 1992 writing report card* (Report No. 23-W01). Washington, DC: U.S. Government Printing Office, Education Information Branch, Office of Educational Research and Improvement, U.S. Department of Education.

Beck, I.L., McKeown, M.G., Hamilton, R.L., & Kucan, L. (1997). *Questioning the author: An approach to enhancing student engagement with text.* Newark, DE: International Reading Association.

Bernhardt, E., Destino, T., Kamil, M., & Rodriguez-Munoz, M. (1995). Assessing science knowledge in an English/Spanish bilingual elementary school. *Cognosos, 4,* 4–6.

Bissex, G.L. (1980). *Gnys at work: A child learns to write and read.* Cambridge, MA: Harvard University Press.

Bourdieu, P. (1991). *Language and symbolic power* (G. Raymond & M. Adamson, Trans.). Cambridge, MA: Harvard University Press.

Britton, J., Burgess, T., Martin, N., McLeod, A., & Rosen, H. (1975). *The development of writing abilities.* London: Macmillan.

Caswell, L.J., & Duke, N.K. (1998). Non-narrative as a catalyst for literacy development. *Language Arts, 75,* 108–117.

Chall, J.S., Jacobs, V.A., & Baldwin, L.E. (1990). *The reading crisis: Why poor children fall behind.* Cambridge, MA: Harvard University Press.

Chapman, M.L. (1995). The sociocognitive construction of written genres in first grade. *Research in the Teaching of English, 29,* 164–192.

Christie, F. (1984). Young children's writing development: The relationship of written genres to curriculum genres. In B. Bartlett & J. Carr (Eds.), *Language in education conference: A report of proceedings* (pp. 41–69). Brisbane, QLD, Australia: Mt. Gravatt Campus.

Christie, F. (1987a). Genres as choice. In I. Reid (Ed.), *The place of genre in learning: Current debates* (pp. 22–34). Melbourne and Geelong, Australia: Deakin University, Centre for Studies in Literary Education.

Christie, F. (1987b). Factual writing in the first years of school. *Australian Journal of Reading, 10,* 207–216.

Cope, B., & Kalantzis, M. (1993). Introduction: How a genre approach to literacy can transform the way writing is taught. In B. Cope & M. Kalantzis (Eds.), *The powers of literacy: A genre approach to teaching writing* (pp. 1–21). Pittsburgh, PA: University of Pittsburgh Press.

Daniels, H.A. (1990). Developing a sense of audience. In T. Shanahan (Ed.), *Reading and writing together: New perspectives for the classroom* (pp. 99–125). Norwood, MA: Christopher Gordon.

Delpit, L. (1988). The silenced dialogue: Power and pedagogy in educating other people's children. *Harvard Educational Review, 58,* 280–298.

Delpit, L. (1992). Acquisition of literate discourse: Bowing before the master? *Theory Into Practice, 31,* 296–302.

Derewianka, B. (1990). *Exploring how texts work.* Rozelle, NSW, Australia: Primary English Teaching Association.

Donovan, C.A. (1996). First graders' impressions of genre-specific elements in writing narrative and expository texts. In D.J. Leu, C.K. Kinzer, & K.A. Hinchman (Eds.), *Literacies for the 21st century* (45th yearbook of the National Reading Conference, pp. 183–194). Chicago: National Reading Conference.

Duke, N.K., & Kays, J. (1998). "Can I say 'once upon a time'?" Kindergarten children developing knowledge of information book language. *Early Childhood Research Quarterly, 13,* 295–318.

Durkin, D. (1978–1979). What classroom observations reveal about reading comprehension instruction. *Reading Research Quarterly, 14,* 481–533.

Durkin, D. (1987). A classroom-observation study of reading instruction in kindergarten. *Early Childhood Research Quarterly, 2,* 275–300.

Duthie, C. (1996). *True stories: Nonfiction literacy in the primary classroom.* York, ME: Stenhouse.

Egan, K. (1986). *Teaching as storytelling.* Chicago: University of Chicago Press.

Egan, K. (1993). Narrative and learning: A voyage of implications. *Linguistics and Education, 5,* 119–126.

Entwisle, D.R., & Astone, N.M. (1994). Some practical guidelines for measuring youth's race/ethnicity and socioeconomic status. *Child Development, 65,* 1521–1540.

Fisher, B. (1994). Writing information books in first grade. *Teaching PreK–8, 25*(3), 73–75.

Fractor, J.S., Woodruff, M.C., Martinez, M.G., & Teale, W.H. (1993). Let's not miss opportunities to promote voluntary reading: Classroom libraries in the elementary school. *The Reading Teacher, 46,* 476–484.

Freedman, A. (1994). "Do as I say": The relationship between teaching and learning new genres. In A. Freedman & P. Medway (Eds.), *Genre and the new rhetoric* (pp. 191–210). Bristol, PA: Taylor & Francis.

Freedman, A., & Medway, P. (1994). Locating genre studies: Antecedents and prospects. In A. Freedman & P. Medway (Eds.), *Genre and the new rhetoric* (pp. 1–20). Bristol, PA: Taylor & Francis.

Freeman, E.B., & Person, D.G. (Eds.). (1992). *Using nonfiction trade books in the elementary classroom from ants to zeppelins.* Urbana, IL: National Council of Teachers of English.

Gee, J.P. (1992). *The social mind: Language, ideology, and social practice.* New York: Bergin & Garvey.

Guillaume, A.M. (1998). Learning with text in the primary grades. *The Reading Teacher, 51,* 476–486.

Guthrie, J.T., & McCann, A.D. (1997). Characteristics of classrooms that promote motivations and strategies for learning. In J.T. Guthrie & A. Wigfield (Eds.), *Reading engagement: Motivating readers through integrated instruction* (pp. 128–148). Newark, DE: International Reading Association.

Harris, T.L., & Hodges, R.E. (Eds.). (1995). *The literacy dictionary: The vocabulary of reading and writing.* Newark, DE: International Reading Association.

Harste, J.C., Burke, C.L., & Woodward, V.A. (1984). *Language stories and literacy lessons.* Portsmouth, NH: Heinemann.

Hicks, D. (1995). The social origins of essayist writing. *Bulletin Suisse de Linguistique Appliqué, 61,* 61–82.

Hidi, S.E., & Hildyard, A. (1983). The comparison of oral and written productions in two discourse types. *Discourse Processes, 6,* 91–105.

Hiebert, E.H., & Fisher, C.W. (1990). Whole language: Three themes for the future. *Educational Leadership, 47*(6), 62–64.

Hodge, R.I.V., & Kress, G.R. (1988). *Social semiotics.* Cambridge, England: Polity Press.

Hoffman, J.V., McCarthey, S.J., Abbott, J., Christian, C., Corman, L., & Curry, C., et al. (1994). So what's new in the new basals? A focus on first grade. *Journal of Reading Behavior, 26,* 47–73.

Houghton Mifflin. (1996). *Invitations to literacy* (series). Boston: Author.

Jan, L.W. (1991). *Write ways: Modeling writing forms.* Melbourne, Australia: Oxford University Press.

Kamil, M.L., & Lane, D. (1997, March). *A classroom study of the efficacy of using information text for first-grade reading instruction.* Paper presented at the annual meeting of the American Educational Research Association, Chicago. Available: http://www-leland.stanford.edu/~mkamil/Aera97

Kaufman, A.M., & Rodríguez, M.E. (1993). *La escuela y los textos* [The school and the texts]. Buenos Aires, Argentina: Santillana.

Kroll, L.R. (1991). *Meaning-making: Longitudinal aspects of learning to write.* Paper presented at the annual meeting of the American Psychological Association, San Francisco, CA. (ERIC Document Reproduction Service No. ED340043)

Langer, J. (1985). The child's sense of genre: A study of performance on parallel reading and writing tasks. *Written Communication, 2,* 157–188.

Langer, J.A., Applebee, A.N., Mullis, I.V.S., & Foertsch, M.A. (1990). *Learning to read in our nation's schools: Instruction and achievement in 1988 at grades 4, 8, and 12.* Princeton, NJ: Educational Testing Service.

Lemke, J.L. (1989). Social semiotics: A new model for literacy education. In D. Bloome (Ed.), *Classrooms and literacy* (pp. 289–309). Norwood, NJ: Ablex.

Lemke, J.L. (1994, November). *Genre as a strategic resource.* Paper presented at the annual meeting of the National Council of Teachers of English, Orlando, FL.

Littlefair, A.B. (1991). *Reading all types of writing: The importance of genre and register for reading development.* Philadelphia, PA: Milton Keynes.

Macmillan Reading Program. (1987). *Connections.* Old Tappan, NJ: Macmillan McGraw-Hill School Division.

Massachusetts Executive Office of Education's School District Profiles. (1996). [Online]. Available: http://www.eoe.mass.edu/pic.www/pic.html

McNeil, J.D. (1992). *Reading comprehension: New directions for classroom practice* (3rd ed.). New York: HarperCollins.

Moffett, J. (1968). *Teaching the universe of discourse.* Boston: Houghton Mifflin.

Morgan, K.O., Morgan, S., & Uhlig, M.A. (Eds.). (1998). *State rankings 1998: A statistical view of the 50 United States* (9th ed.). Lawrence, KS: Morgan Quinto Press.

Moss, B., Leone, S., & DiPillo, M.L. (1997). Exploring the literature of fact: Linking reading and writing through information trade books. *Language Arts, 74,* 418–429.

Moss, B., & Newton, E. (1998, December). *An examination of the informational text genre in recent basal readers.* Paper presented at the National Reading Conference, Austin, TX.

New London Group. (1996). A pedagogy of multiliteracies: Designing social futures. *Harvard Educational Review, 66*, 60–92.

Newkirk, T. (1987). The non-narrative writing of young children. *Research in the Teaching of English, 21*, 121–144.

Newkirk, T. (1989). *More than stories: The range of children's writing*. Portsmouth, NH: Heinemann.

Ogle, D.M. (1986). K-W-L: A teaching model that develops active reading of expository text. *The Reading Teacher, 39*, 564–570.

Oyler, C. (1996). Sharing authority: Student initiations during teacher-led read-alouds of information books. *Teaching and Teacher Education, 12*, 149–160.

Pappas, C.C. (1986, December). *Exploring the global structure of "information books."* Paper presented at the annual meeting of the National Reading Conference, Austin, TX. (ERIC Document Reproduction Service No. ED278952)

Pappas, C.C. (1987, August). *Exploring the generic shape of "information books": Applying typicality notions to the process.* Paper presented at the World Conference of Applied Linguistics, Sydney, NSW, Australia. (ERIC Document Reproduction Service No. ED299834)

Pappas, C.C. (1991a). Fostering full access to literacy by including information books. *Language Arts, 68*, 449–462.

Pappas, C.C. (1991b). Young children's strategies in learning the "book language" of information books. *Discourse Processes, 14*, 203–225.

Pappas, C.C. (1993). Is narrative "primary"? Some insights from kindergartners' pretend readings of stories and information books. *Journal of Reading Behavior, 25*, 97–129.

Paré, A., & Smart, G. (1994). Observing genres in action: Towards a research methodology. In A. Freedman & P. Medway (Eds.), *Genre and the new rhetoric* (pp. 146–154). Bristol, PA: Taylor & Francis.

Purcell-Gates, V. (1988). Lexical and syntactic knowledge of written narrative held by well-read-to kindergartners and second graders. *Research in the Teaching of English, 22*, 128–160.

Purcell-Gates, V. (1995). *Other people's words: The cycle of low literacy*. Cambridge, MA: Harvard University Press.

Purcell-Gates, V., McIntyre, E., & Freppon, P. (1995). Learning written storybook language in school: A comparison of low-SES children in skills-based and whole language classrooms. *American Educational Research Journal, 32*, 659–685.

Reid, I. (1987). A generic frame for debates about genre. In I. Reid (Ed.), *The place of genre in learning: Current debates* (pp. 1–8). Deakin University, Centre for Studies in Literary Education.

Renninger, K.A., Hidi, S., & Krapp, A. (Eds.). (1992). *The role of interest in learning and development*. Hillsdale, NJ: Erlbaum.

Richgels, D.J. (1997, December). *Informational texts in kindergarten: Reading and writing to learn*. Paper presented at the annual meeting of the National Reading Conference, Scottsdale, AZ.

Rosch, E. (1976). Classification of real-world objects: Origins and representations in cognition. In P.N. Johnson-Laird & P.C. Wason (Eds.), *Thinking: Readings in cognitive science* (pp. 212–222). Cambridge, England: Cambridge University Press.

Sanacore, J. (1991). Expository and narrative text: Balancing young children's reading experiences. *Childhood Education, 67,* 211–214.

Sawyer, W., & Watson, K. (1987). Questions of genre. In I. Reid (Ed.), *The place of genre in learning: Current debates* (pp. 46–57). Melbourne and Geelong, Australia: Deakin University, Centre of Studies in Literary Education.

LITERATURE CITED

Berger, M. (1993a). *Make mine ice cream.* New York: Macmillan.

Berger, M. (1993b). *Round and round the money goes: What money is and how we use it.* Nashville, TN: Ideals Children's Books.

Branley, F.M. (1984). *Is there life in outer space?* New York: Harper Trophy.

Cole, J. (1990). *The magic school bus inside the human body* (B. Degen, Illus.). New York: Scholastic.

Gibbons, G. (1984). *The seasons of Arnold's apple tree.* New York: Scholastic.

Gibbons, G. (1997). *The honeymakers.* New York: Scholastic.

Hawcock, D., & Montgomery, L. (1994). *Spider.* New York: Random House.

Hoberman, M. (1978). *A house is a house for me.* New York: Scholastic.

Iversen, S. (1994). *Garbage.* Bothell, WA: The Wright Group.

Marshall, E. (1980). *Space case* (J. Marshall, Illus.). New York: Puffin.

Morris, A. (1990). *On the go* (K. Heyman, Illus.). New York: Mulberry.

Newbridge Press. (1994). *Life in the polar regions.* New York: Author.

Podendorf, I. (1982). *A new true book of spiders.* Chicago: Children's Press.

Selsam, M.E., & Wexler, J. (1977). *The amazing dandelion.* New York: Morrow.

African American Children's Literature That Helps Students Find Themselves: Selection Guidelines for Grades K–3

Bena R. Hefflin and Mary Alice Barksdale-Ladd

L iterature is a powerful medium. Through it, children construct messages about their cultures and roles in society. Literature offers them personal stories, a view of their cultural surroundings, and insight on themselves. When children read books that are interesting and meaningful to them, they can find support for the process of defining themselves as individuals and understanding their developing roles within their families and communities.

From the time they enter school, most African American children read literature that seldom offers messages about them, their past, or their future. All too often books used in primary classrooms contain too few African American characters, or they include characters who are African American in appearance only. Many of these stories say little about African American culture, or they present only the history of African Americans as slaves without including any "nonslavery" or modern representations. In short, today's African American children often cannot find themselves in the literature they are given to read.

The purpose of this article is to suggest guidelines for selecting African American children's literature of high literary and artistic quality for grades K–3. To validate the importance of African Americans in society, the guidelines are for all teachers, whether they have African American children in their classrooms or not. We also provide a list of selected recent books with an African American context that meet the same criteria for quality.

What If You Can't Find Yourself?

To read for years and not encounter stories that connect closely with one's own cultural understandings and life experiences is problematic. One primary motivation for reading fiction involves the pleasure that can be taken in relating to characters, their lives, their problems, and their experiences. When readers frequently encounter texts that feature characters with whom they can connect, they will see how others are like them and how reading can play a role in their lives.

Originally published in *The Reading Teacher* (2001), volume 54, pages 810–819.

A love of reading will result. Alternatively, when readers do not encounter characters who are like them, reading is likely to be frustrating rather than pleasurable. For children, repeated frustration is not likely to lead to personal affirmations and the development of a love of reading. If teachers continually present African American children with texts in which the main characters are predominantly animals and white people, it stands to reason that these children may begin to wonder whether they, their families, and their communities fit into the world of reading. Our interviews with African American adults, remembering their early years in school, speak of this type of reading experience as being one of isolation. (All adult and student names are pseudonyms.)

> For the first 15 years of my life, I didn't find myself in books, and I didn't relate to them. Once I discovered books and characters I could relate to, I gained the love of reading. (Tracey)

> The joy of reading is in stepping into the experience of the characters. When the characters look like, talk like, think like, and act like us, it's easy to share in the experience. I think that after we've had that experience a few times, it becomes easier to understand the experiences of people who are less like us. But in becoming a reader, and learning to love reading, experiencing books that mirror our own lives is extremely important—which for me began when I became an adult. (Robin)

> I didn't feel a strong connection between my world and classroom-related literature experiences. My learning experiences did not speak to me because people who looked like me weren't in the literature. I didn't value my experiences with literature in my early years of learning. (Tyrone)

Similarly, the third-grade African American students we interviewed voiced their preferences, needs, and concerns:

> Well, we're black, and it doesn't mean that I don't like white people in stories, but I like seeing people in the book that are my same color. I like seeing black people in books because mostly they have white people in commercials and shows and stuff. And it's like in a book you can see black people. (Keisha)

> It's not that I don't like white people or nothing, but you're glad because you don't see a lot of books that have black people in them. And it's not to be rude to white people, but you can imagine what they're [black people] thinking of...it might give you a better idea. Again, nothing against white people, but you like to see blacks because [white authors] portray black people like they don't got no manners or nothing. And white people, they know everything and they get a good education. But, that's not always true cause the black people, they get a good education too. But they portray us as not having any manners. When you see [black] people like that, [white] people think that we're stupid. (Marisa)

> I like reading about my heritage and I like stories about black people. There isn't anything wrong with white people...they're just a different color. They're

actually people, so they're the same as us, but a different color. But, I would like to see more, you know, black people in stories. (LaVon)

The problem of not finding oneself in books runs deep and wide in the context of schooling in the United States. Historically, the absence of black images in children's literature was birthed from the social structures that slavery imposed. The inaccurate images of African Americans that appeared in literature from 1830 to 1900 were nurtured by stereotypes, a publishing industry that was not invested in authentic portrayals of African Americans, and lack of understanding (MacCann, 1998). There was very little change in characterizations of African Americans or the number of texts featuring authentic African American characters from 1900 until about 1970 (Harris, 1997). As a result, historically, the vast content of children's literature connoted a clear message: African American children are not valued in society, and books have little to offer them that is personal, relevant, and affirming (Harris, 1993; Sims-Bishop, 1987).

Given the absence and misrepresentation that so many African Americans—young and old—feel about the literature of their youth, we searched for African American children's literature of high literary and artistic quality for grades K–3. Our plan was to locate literature that establishes African American children as children, authenticates their own world (Clifton, 1981), and—most important—speaks to these children about themselves and their lives (Harris, 1990; Sims-Bishop, 1993).

But how much of this literature is available? Where do you find it? How do you select high-quality African American literature that will lead to affirming reading experiences in which children will be able to relate to stories and characters?

How Much African American Children's Literature Is Available?

The number of African American children's books steadily increased in the latter part of the 20th century, especially in the 1990s (Harris, 1997; Rand, Parker, & Foster, 1998; Sims-Bishop, 1997). In real terms, however, the increase was very small. For example, in 1998 approximately 4,500 books were published in the United States for children (Horning, Moore-Kruse, & Schliesman, 1999). Only 3% of these books featured African Americans as main characters or focused on African American culture (Rand et al., 1998). Of this 3%, only two thirds of the books were created by African American authors or illustrators (Horning et al., 1999).

Here is the bottom line: Very few books with African American protagonists are published for children. Our bottom line reduces this number even further: How many of these books are high-quality works of literature for African American children?

What Are the Characteristics of "Good" African American Children's Literature?

The answer to this question is complex. "Goodness," as it turns out, depends on a number of factors: How the literature evolved, readability, marketing, and audience appeal are essential considerations (Temple, Martinez, Yokota, & Naylor, 1998). For our purposes, two interrelated layers mark the characteristics of good African American children's literature: those characteristics general to all children's literature and those specific to African American children's literature.

General characteristics. Characteristics of excellence in children's books are a result of the literary and artistic craft of the author and illustrator. The skills with which authors and illustrators use the tools of their medium to tell the tale are the most essential characteristics that distinguish good children's literature from the rest. "To know what 'good books' are for different children requires some intelligent way of talking about goodness and mediocrity in books—an accepted set of terms for looking at the literary features of children's books" (Temple et al., 1998, p. 7). By drawing upon Temple et al.'s framework on the qualities of children's literature, and Huck, Hepler, Hickman, and Kiefer's (2000), Cullinan and Galda's (1994), and Lynch-Brown and Tomlinson's (1999) guidelines for evaluating children's picture books, we outlined the characteristics of an author's and illustrator's craft that mark high-quality children's literature.

In seeking well-developed narratives for primary-grade children, readers should look for works that contain the following characteristics.

1. Books should include memorable, well-portrayed characters; in contemporary stories these characters are usually children the same age as the child reader.

2. Books should present a plot that provides interesting events in an understandable sequence. Plots produce conflict to build excitement and suspense. For primary-grade readers plots should be direct and clear so that children will not have difficulty following the sequence of events, yet plots should be complex enough to capture the attention and lead to predictions, questions, and wonderings. In realistic stories the plot

should deal with problems, events, or issues that children will understand and to which they can relate.

3. Books should incorporate well-crafted language that is concrete and vivid—the language should read smoothly and reflect the mood of the story.

4. Books should contain a worthy and truthful theme. Further, the illustrator's work should catch the attention of the reader, move the story forward, and enhance the meanings and tone presented by the author.

Table 1 outlines these characteristics, along with key questions, so they can be readily used to rate (from 1 to 5) the overall quality of a children's book.

Specific characteristics. In addition to these general considerations for selecting high-quality children's literature, there are specific guidelines to note with regard to the selection of the most appropriate African American children's literature. We have developed a more detailed set of guidelines aimed specifically at African American children's literature, based upon the work of Sims-Bishop (1997), Banks (1991), our own experiences, and those of teachers with whom we have collaborated. There are specific authors and illustrators who have established solid reputations for publishing culturally sensitive literature for children. While we would not recommend that selections of African American literature for children come exclusively from these works, familiarity with these authors, illustrators, and their works is very helpful in becoming accomplished at selecting high-quality texts to share with children.

As general guidelines (in addition to drawing from works by established well-known African American authors and illustrators) we recommend that teachers and parents look for books that have the following characteristics.

1. Books should include characters who are well developed and portrayed in authentic, realistic contexts.

2. Books should use language that is authentic and realistic, particularly dialogue that correctly portrays African American dialect appropriate to the character.

3. Books should incorporate illustrations that portray African American and other characters and settings authentically and realistically.

4. Books should present accurate information.

We have found these guidelines, as outlined in Table 2, to be workable tenets for the selection of high-quality African American children's literature. While all of these story elements may not be found in every good African

Table 1. General characteristics of high-quality primary-grade picture books

Feature	Questions	Rating				
		1 Low	2	3 Medium	4	5 High
Character	• Does the story contain a memorable character who is about the same age as the students?	Low		Medium		High
Plot	• Is the plot direct, clear, and stimulating? • Will students understand the problems, events, and issues? • Will students be able to easily follow the sequence of events? • Will students enjoy the story?	Low		Medium		High
Well-crafted language	• Does the story contain natural, vivid language? • Do the words evoke clear, concrete images of characters and actions? • Does the language reflect the mood of the story?	Low		Medium		High
Worthy, subtle, and truthful theme	• Is the story's theme one that students will find worthy, subtle, and truthful? • Will the theme interest students? • Is the author's intended message understandable without being heavy-handed?	Low		Medium		High
Quality of illustrations	• Does the illustrator use elements of media, design, and style in original and expressive ways?	Low		Medium		High
Function of illustrations	• Do the illustrations establish the mood, theme, and setting as the story unfolds? • Do they add or clarify information? • Do they enrich the story?	Low		Medium		High

Table 2. Specific characteristics of high-quality African American children's literature

Feature	Questions	Rating				
		1 Low	2	3 Medium	4	5 High
Character portrayal	• Does the author identify the characters as African American? • Does the author include current and accurate information about African American beliefs, traditions, shared values, and other cultural referents? • Does the author present realistic and positive images of African Americans?					
Language use	• Does the dialogue correctly portray African American dialect? • Is the language authentic and realistic? • Will students understand, identify with, and accurately reflect upon the characters' language?					
Illustration authenticity	• Do the illustrations reflect reality? • Do they reveal variety in settings and African American physical features and coloring, or are characters merely colored brown? • Do the illustrations present positive images of African Americans in aesthetically pleasing ways?					
Information accuracy	• Does the story contain a motif or an authentic aspect of African American history? • Is the information accurate? • Does the story add a distinctive voice or worldview?					

American children's book, the more elements that are found, the greater the likely appeal for all children. These guidelines also include key questions and a rating scale (from 1 to 5) to evaluate the quality of African American children's literature.

How Do the Characteristics Apply to a Specific Piece of Literature?

To illustrate how these general and specific characteristics work in practice, we applied them to the African American children's biography *Duke Ellington: The Piano Prince and His Orchestra* by Andrea Davis-Pinkney and Brian Pinkney (Hyperion, 1998). Although biography is nonfiction, it can be evaluated similarly to fiction due to its narrative form. However, there is an additional requirement for biography—accuracy.

The story describes the life of legendary Edward Kennedy "Duke" Ellington and provides a glimpse into one of the liveliest eras of American music history. In this tribute to the jazz legend, the music is portrayed through illustrations that represent constant motion with vivid spirals, waves, and colorful swirls. Table 3 illustrates how we applied the general characteristics of children's literature to the story. Our rating for each of the characteristics is noted in Table 3.

Character. The text is realistic and engaging as it introduces a young Duke Ellington who does not enjoy playing the piano because he finds it boring. As the story progresses, Duke becomes a teenager and begins incorporating sounds and rhythms that he finds exciting. Over time, Duke develops a unique style that transforms the music industry.

Plot. The book chronicles Duke Ellington's musical career. The story begins with his childhood—he was born in 1899 in Washington, D.C.—and ends when he became an adult and played at New York City's Carnegie Hall on January 23, 1943. The story is presented chronologically, so it is easy for children to follow; however, it is written so as to keep children wondering about what will happen and where the story will lead.

Students will enjoy the story because it addresses a problem that is common for many children. Duke Ellington was introduced to a new skill, and, although he understood that practice was essential in developing this skill, he found that practice was very boring. Duke addressed the problem in a unique way that involved setting and accomplishing personal goals (facets of a child's life that parents and teachers alike impress upon young children). Duke

Table 3. General characteristics of high-quality primary-grade picture books applied to *Duke Ellington: The Piano Prince and His Orchestra*

Feature	Response	Rating				
Character	• The story begins with a child protagonist (Duke Ellington) and follows him in his adult life through his musical career.	1 Low	2	3 Medium	4	⑤ High
Plot	• A chronological plot follows the challenges and successes of Duke Ellington's life.	1 Low	2	3 Medium	4	⑤ High
Well-crafted language	• The language is used in ways appropriate for understanding jazz.	1 Low	2	3 Medium	4	⑤ High
Worthy, subtle, and truthful theme	• Students will identify with the theme of growing up and finding yourself.	1 Low	2	3 Medium	4	⑤ High
Quality of illustrations	• The illustrator uses the visual elements of line, shape, and color effectively.	1 Low	2	3 Medium	4	⑤ High
Function of illustrations	• The illustrations are integral to the story and extend the text.	1 Low	2	3 Medium	4	⑤ High

Ellington became successful because he was talented and had the resourcefulness and encouragement to build upon his talents.

Well-crafted language. The story contains natural, vivid language used in culturally appropriate, soulful, descriptive ways. For example, one line reads, "Duke's Creole Love Call was spicier than a pot of jambalaya. His Mood Indigo was a musical stream that swelled over the airwaves" (p. 11).

Worthy, subtle, and truthful theme. Students will identify with and remember the theme of the story—growing up and finding yourself—because it is presented in an entirely believable way. In addition, this is an appropriate literary element for young readers to reflect upon as they look at themselves and their own processes of growing up and finding themselves as individuals with unique talents and qualities.

Quality of illustrations. The illustrator uses the elements of shape, color, texture, rhythm, variety, space, paint, expressionism, and representation in divergent, self-expressive, artistic ways.

Function of illustrations. The illustrations are eye catching. The bold, vibrant colors and intricately detailed scenes set the mood and add luster to the story. The dancers leap off the page while the visual interpretations of the music serve as devices that transport the reader to this era of music history.

Table 4 demonstrates how we applied the specific characteristics of African American children's literature to the story. The ratings for the characteristics are noted in Table 4.

Character portrayal. The author identifies the characters as African American and presents a positive, realistic message about Duke Ellington's musical career. Duke Ellington's desire was to celebrate the history of African American culture through his music. He accomplished this goal through songs about "the glories of dark skin, the pride of African heritage, and the triumphs of black people from the days of slavery to years of civil rights struggle" (p. 26).

Language use. The story is a narrative in which African American dialogue true to the characters is used in several parts of the story. For example, a section reads, "Yo, you got the Duke?" "Slide me some King of the Keys, please!" and "Gonna play me that Piano Prince and his band" (p. 23). This dialogue represents African American dialect that is historically accurate for the period of time in which Duke Ellington lived. Had the entire story been written in this way, it might have been difficult for many students to understand. Instead, the author has chosen to intersperse this type of dialect in the text, providing readers with a perspective on African American language use

Table 4. Specific characteristics of high-quality African American children's literature applied to *Duke Ellington: The Piano Prince and His Orchestra*

Feature	Response	Rating				
		1 Low	2	3 Medium	4	(5) High
Character portrayal	• The author presents accurate and positive images of an African American whose outstanding musical career is portrayed.	1 Low	2	3 Medium	4	(5) High
Language use	• The dialogue accurately portrays African American dialect of the time. • The language of the text is rich and flows well.	1 Low	2	3 Medium	4	(5) High
Illustration authenticity	• The illustrations reveal variety in African American physical features and coloring. • The illustrations reveal a variety of settings. • The illustrations present positive images of African Americans.	1 Low	2	3 Medium	4	(5) High
Information accuracy	• The story contains authentic, accurate information about Duke Ellington's musical career.	1 Low	2	3 Medium	4	(5) High

in the world of Duke Ellington and, thus, helping the reader enter the world of Duke Ellington.

Illustration authenticity. The illustrations in the story reveal variety in African American physical features and coloring. For example, Duke is referred to as having "honey-colored fingertips" while other characters appear to be darker in color—a reflection of reality (p. 21). The illustrations also present positive images of African Americans as in the scenes portraying New York City's Carnegie Hall and the Cotton Club in Harlem.

Information accuracy. The book contains authentic information about Duke Ellington's musical career. The story highlights the African American experience by describing how African Americans supported and enjoyed listening to Duke Ellington's music. At the end, the author includes facts about Duke Ellington's life and provides the sources used to obtain the information.

Valuable Book, Valued Readers

The guidelines presented in this article provide a way for teachers and parents to thoughtfully and purposefully evaluate the quality of African American children's literature for the primary grades. Determining quality, in this case, lies in the ability to select literature that is affirming and liberating to children. Historically, African American children did not have literature that reflected their experiences. To find the best of this literature, then, is to help these children find themselves in books. To read literature that mirrors themselves and their lives is to feel valued—to have power.

When African American children encounter literature that offers messages about them, their culture, and their roles in society, they have enhanced opportunities to reflect upon themselves as people and their own development. Culturally sensitive stories, views, and insights can allow children to realize that literature has value for them as individuals. To select a balanced collection of stories, we included in our bibliography (see chapter Appendix on page 216) literature that plays and riffs with everyday events of African American life and literature that represents accurate, authentic accounts of slavery. With repeated exposure to engaging literature in which children find themselves establishing personal connections with characters, the likelihood is great that reading will become an appealing activity. Over time, the love of reading may empower students both as readers and as individuals.

For teachers and parents interested in finding African American children's literature, we have carefully crafted an annotated bibliography of books from

1996 to 2000 that meet our selection guidelines for high-quality African American children's literature. We suggest the bibliography be used as a starting point in selecting literature, and note that the list should be expanded according to individual needs and preferences. The books are recommended for beginning, young, and early intermediate readers (K–3). The title, author, illustrator, year, summary, publisher, and ISBN (International Standard Book Number) are provided for each book. The books are arranged in alphabetical order beginning with the author's last name.

REFERENCES

Banks, J.A. (1991). *Teaching strategies for ethnic studies* (5th ed.). Boston: Allyn & Bacon.

Clifton, L. (1981). Writing for black children. *The Advocate, 1,* 32–37.

Cullinan, B.E., & Galda, L. (1994). *Literature and the child* (3rd ed.). New York: Harcourt Brace.

Harris, V.J. (1990). African American children's literature: The first one hundred years. *Journal of Negro Education, 59,* 540–555.

Harris, V.J. (1993). Contemporary griots: African-American writers of children's literature. In V.J. Harris (Ed.), *Teaching multicultural literature in grades K–8* (pp. 57–108). Norwood, MA: Christopher-Gordon.

Harris, V.J. (1997). Children's literature depicting blacks. In V.J. Harris (Ed.), *Using multiethnic literature in the K–8 classroom* (pp. 21–58). Norwood, MA: Christopher-Gordon.

Horning, K., Moore-Kruse, G., & Schliesman, M. (1999). *Cooperative Children's Book Center choices 1998.* Madison, WI: Friends of the Cooperative Children's Book Center.

Huck, C., Hepler, S., Hickman, J., & Kiefer, B. (2000). *Children's literature in the elementary school* (7th ed.). New York: McGraw-Hill.

Lynch-Brown, C., & Tomlinson, C.M. (1999). *Essentials of children's literature* (3rd ed.). Needham Heights, MA: Allyn & Bacon.

MacCann, D. (1998). *White supremacy in children's literature: Characterizations of African Americans, 1830–1900.* New York: Garland.

Rand, D., Parker, T., & Foster, S. (1998). *Black books galore! Guide to great African American children's books.* New York: John Wiley & Sons.

Sims Bishop, R. (1987). Extending multicultural understanding through children's books. In B. Cullinan (Ed.), *Children's literature in the reading program* (pp. 60–67). Newark, DE: International Reading Association.

Sims Bishop, R. (1993). Multicultural literature for children: Making informed choices. In V.J. Harris (Ed.), *Teaching multicultural literature in grades K–8* (pp. 37–53). Norwood, MA: Christopher-Gordon.

Sims Bishop, R. (1997). Selecting literature for a multicultural curriculum. In V.J. Harris (Ed.), *Using multiethnic literature in the K–8 classroom* (pp. 1–19). Norwood, MA: Christopher-Gordon.

Temple, C., Martinez, M., Yokota, J., & Naylor, A. (1998). *Children's books in children's hands: An introduction to their literature.* Needham Heights, MA: Allyn & Bacon.

Barnwell, Ysaye M. *No mirrors in my Nana's house.* 1998. Ill. Synthia Saint James. Harcourt Brace. ISBN 0152018255.

> There were no mirrors in Nana's house for her granddaughter to look into and judge herself against another culture's definition of beauty. This story about inner beauty teaches how to love yourself just the way you are, and not to compare yourself with other forms of beauty.

Curtis, Gavin. *The bat boy and his violin* (1999 Coretta Scott King Honor Award). 1998. Ill. E.B. Lewis. Simon & Schuster. ISBN 0689800991.

> A young boy loves to play the violin, but his father needs a bat boy for his baseball team, not a violin player. The boy decides to play his violin in the dugout, and he manages to inspire the players.

English, Karen. *Big wind coming!* 1996. Ill. Cedric Lucas. Albert Whitman. ISBN 0807507261.

> Sarah Ann's family prepares for a hurricane by boarding up windows and storing water for the family. During the harsh winds, Sarah Ann realizes that she left her favorite doll outside and runs off to find her. There is considerable damage, but somehow the doll is found safely after the storm.

Gilchrist, Jan Spivey. *Madelia.* 1997. Dial. ISBN 0803720521.

> Madelia can't wait to go home from church to play with her six new jars of watercolors. As Madelia thinks about what she is going to paint, she waits impatiently for the sermon to end. Suddenly, Madelia becomes inspired and knows precisely what she will do.

Holman, Sandy Lynne. *Grandpa, is everything black bad?* 1999. Ill. Lela Kometiani. The Culture Co-op. ISBN 0964465507.

> This picture book describes how a little boy named Montsho looks around his environment and notices that things associated with blackness are bad. Montsho learns to appreciate his dark skin when his grandfather teaches him about his African heritage.

Howard, Elizabeth Fitzgerald. *What's in Aunt Mary's room?* 1996. Ill. Cedric Lucas. Clarion. ISBN 0395698456.

> Susan and Sarah help their aunt locate a key that unlocks the door in Great-Aunt Flossie's house. They are surprised to discover a family Bible in which Susan is given permission to write her own and Sarah's name.

Howard, Elizabeth Fitzgerald. *When will Sarah come?* 1999. Ill. Nina Crews. Greenwillow. ISBN 0688161804.

> While his sister Sarah goes off to school, Jonathan stays at home and plays throughout his busy day. As he anxiously listens and waits for Sarah to come home, he rides his firetruck, watches mail falling through the mail slot, plays with his teddy bear, and listens to the sounds of the tree trimmers. Jonathan finally hears the sound of Sarah's yellow school bus. His sister is finally home!

Hru, Dakari. *The magic moonberry jump ropes*. 1996. Ill. E.B. Lewis. Dial Books for Young Readers. ISBN 0803717547.

April and her sister love to jump Double Dutch. But nobody in the neighborhood wants to jump rope, until Uncle Zambezi arrives with a pair of brightly dyed jump ropes from Africa and claims that they will grant wishes.

Lester, Julius. *Sam and the tigers*. 1996. Ill. Jerry Pinkney. Dial Books for Young Readers. ISBN 0803720289.

This is a retelling of Helen Bannerman's *The Story of Little Black Sambo* (1923, HarperCollins). In this story a little boy named Sam (in fact all of the characters are called Sam) outsmarts a gang of hungry tigers. The tigers turn into a pool of butter, and that night Sam and his family have tigerstriped pancakes for dinner.

McKissack, Patricia C. *The honest-to-goodness truth*. 2000. Ill. Giselle Potter. Atheneum. ISBN 0689826680.

When a young girl is caught in her first lie to her mother, she decides to tell only the truth. Soon, she begins to spread the truth all over town about how Thomas didn't have enough money for lunch and needed to borrow some from the teacher. She learns there's a right and wrong way to tell the truth.

Medearis, Angela Shelf. *Rum-a-tum-tum*. 1997. Ill. James E. Ransome. Holiday House. ISBN 0823411435.

In the late 1800s, a young girl wakes to the festive, celebratory sounds of street vendors busily selling their produce on Market Street in New Orleans, Louisiana. She is mesmerized by Creole women in red bandannas, baskets of richly colored fresh fruits and vegetables, and a jazz parade that lights up the town.

Miller, William. *The piano*. 2000. Ill. Susan Keeter. Lee & Low. ISBN 1880000989.

This story, set in the early 1900s, is about a unique friendship between a little girl named Tia and her employer, an elderly woman named Miss Hartwell. Tia loves music; Miss Hartwell teaches her how to play the piano. In return Miss Hartwell is given a rare and precious gift.

Mollel, Tololwa M. *My rows and piles of coins* (2000 Coretta Scott King Illustrator Honor Award). 1999. Ill. E.B. Lewis. Clarion Books. ISBN 0395751861.

A little boy works very hard and saves his money to buy a new bike, only to discover that he doesn't have enough.

Nolen, Jerdine. *Big Jabe*. 2000. Ill. Kadir Nelson. Lothrop, Lee & Shepard. ISBN 0688136621.

In this modern tall tale, Addy, a house slave on Simon Plenty's plantation, finds a little boy floating down the river in a basket. Addy is taken by the boy's ability to call fish to jump out of the river and into her wagon. In no time at all, the little boy grows into a giant named Jabe, who has the strength of 50 men and the ability to transport slaves away to freedom.

Orgill, Roxanne. *If I only had a horn: Young Louis Armstrong.* 1997. Ill. Leonard Jenkins. Houghton Mifflin. ISBN 0395759196.

> This autobiographical picture book describes how young Louis Armstrong received his first instruments. Before playing the trumpet, he played the bugle and the cornet. His first musical success occurred in the Colored Waifs' Home Band.

Pinkney, Andrea D. *Bill Pickett: Rodeo-ridin' cowboy.* 1996. Ill. Brian Pinkney. Gulliver. ISBN 0152021035.

> This biography describes how Bill Pickett became the most famous black rodeo performer who ever lived and the first African American to be inducted into the National Cowboy Hall of Fame.

Pinkney, Andrea D. *Duke Ellington: The piano prince and his orchestra* (1999 Caldecott Honor Award & 1999 Coretta Scott King Honor Award). 1998. Ill. Brian Pinkney. Hyperion Books for Children. ISBN 0786801786.

> This biographical picture book illustrates the life of the legendary jazz composer Duke Ellington.

Schroeder, Alan. *Minty: A story of young Harriet Tubman* (1997 Coretta Scott King Illustrator Award). 1996. Ill. Jerry Pinkney. Dial Books for Young Readers. ISBN 0803718888.

> This fictionalized account based upon real events profiles the early life of Harriet Tubman and her relationship with her parents. The story describes how she became a conductor on the Underground Railroad.

Siegelson, Kim. *In the time of the drums* (2000 Coretta Scott King Illustrator Award). 1999. Ill. Brian Pinkney. Hyperion Books for Children. ISBN 078680436X.

> This story is based on the Gullah legend of a slave rebellion at Ibo's Landing in South Carolina. Mentu's grandmother Twi was born in Africa and remembers her experiences well. Twi teaches her grandson many things, including how to play ancient rhythms on a goatskin drum. One day, slave ships arrive at Mentu and Twi's island. The slaves refuse to get off the ships because they know they are not home. Twi knows she must take her people back to Africa, so together Twi and the slaves walk into the ocean for home. Mentu is left all alone, but he grows up strong, begins a family of his own, and teaches them all that his grandmother taught him.

Sierra, Judy. *Wiley and the hairy man.* 1996. Ill. Brian Pinkney. Lodestar Books Dutton. ISBN 0525674772.

> This African American folk tale describes how Wiley and his mother outsmart the Hairy Man by tricking him into doing things for them. But Wiley's mother warns him that he must trick the Hairy Man two more times in order for the beast to go away forever.

Steptoe, John. *Creativity.* 1997. Ill. E.B. Lewis. Clarion. ISBN 0395687063.

> An African American child learns to appreciate his similarities and differences with his friend Hector from Puerto Rico. Once Charlie befriends Hector he helps him adjust to the new school and neighborhood. Charlie even tries to help Hector with his English.

Stewart, Dianne. *Gift of the sun: A tale from South Africa.* 1996. Ill. Jude Daly. Farrar, Straus & Giroux. ISBN 0374324255.

This South African tale describes how a farmer named Thulani wants to do no more than lie in the sun all day. After a series of lopsided exchanges with others to make his life easier, he finds that his crop is worth something after all. A pocketful of sunflower seeds proves to be very beneficial.

Tarpley, Natasha. *I love my hair.* 1998. Ill. E.B. Lewis. Little, Brown. ISBN 0316522759.

This picture book celebrates African American identity through hair. Every night before bedtime Keyana sits down with her mother to get her hair combed. It hurts, but her mother gently reminds her of all the different ways that she can wear her hair.

Thomas, Joyce Carol. *I have heard of a land* (1999 Coretta Scott King Illustrator Honor Award). 1998. Ill. Floyd Cooper. HarperCollins. ISBN 0060234776.

Set in the late 1800s, this lyrical tribute describes what it was like for African American pioneers to journey westward to Oklahoma to begin a new life. Newly freed slaves were anxious to receive railroad tickets to travel to a place where all people were promised free land and a new beginning.

Wilkins, Verna Allette. *Dave and the tooth fairy.* (1998). Ill. Paul Hunt. Gareth Stevens. ISBN 0836820894.

Dave's wobbly tooth finally comes out when he sneezes. But he doesn't know where it went. His grandfather and the tooth fairy get a shock when they look under his pillow later that evening.

Woodtor, Dee Parmer. *Big meeting.* Ill. Dolores Johnson. Simon & Schuster. ISBN 0689319339.

During the midsummer heat, families from all over cross the wooden bridge at Pigeon Creek and travel to grandma and grandpa's home for a special reunion. They gather at church for fellowship, to learn about their heritage, and to celebrate the gospel.

RIGHT 5

Children have a right to reading assessment that

identifies their strengths as well as their

needs and involves them in making decisions

about their own learning.

Introduction

Janette K. Klingner

Quick...think of a few kinds of tests frequently administered to children and what they are used for. Chances are that you thought of the classroom tests you administer to determine what your students have learned from a particular unit of study, and that you use the results from these tests to help you determine students' grades and also to evaluate your own teaching. Yet you might also have thought of IQ tests, which are used to determine students' academic potential and place them in programs for students who are gifted or have learning disabilities or some other exceptionality. Or you might have considered the high-stakes tests now implemented by more and more states across the United States as a way to evaluate schools and hold them accountable for student achievement. The two articles in this section focus on these different forms of assessment.

In the first article, Lee Gunderson and Linda S. Siegel argue against the use of IQ tests to define learning disabilities, particularly with English language learners. They point out problems with the assumptions underlying IQ tests, saying that these tests "assess only what a person has learned, not what he or she is capable of doing. An IQ test is not culture free, because background is important; nor is it language free, because it requires knowledge of English." Gunderson and Siegel believe that the use of intelligence tests in general to identify students with learning disabilities is inappropriate, and that to use them with culturally and linguistically diverse students is particularly inappropriate. Yet the use of IQ tests remains widespread as a way to identify children for special education or programs for gifted and talented.

The authors quote Oller (1997), who notes that verbal IQ tests really should be called "measures of **primary** language skills" when used with native English speakers. When IQ tests are administered to English language learners they should be called "measures of **second** (or **nonprimary**) language skills." Oller is further quoted in the Gunderson and Siegel article: "If these changes are made, the absurdity of calling a normal person who has not yet learned a certain dialect of English 'retarded,' 'learning disordered,' 'language impaired,' 'learning disabled,' and the like, will be averted."

In particular, Gunderson and Siegel lament the use of IQ tests to determine eligibility for remediation for reading disabilities. They note that the relationship between IQ scores and reading achievement varies greatly, and that typically only about 20 to 25% of reading scores can be predicted accurately from IQ scores. Many other factors have as much or more predictive power, such as parental income. In other words, a student with an IQ of 80 or 90 might respond just as well to reading instruction or do as well on a reading test as a student with an IQ of 110. IQ does not predict a student's ability to benefit from remediation.

Gunderson and Siegel offer alternatives to IQ testing for determining which students would benefit from remediation. They suggest that a careful analysis of errors in reading, spelling, and writing samples would be more useful. They recommend using informal reading inventories, noting, "Teachers can and should trust their own observations and instincts." Also they state, "What is needed is that teachers be given the time, support, and staff development required to administer and interpret both holistic and standardized measures." This seems to be a common theme running through both articles—and the conclusion of both.

What Do Others Say About Discontinuing the Use of IQ Testing for Determining Eligibility?

There seems to be growing support for this idea. In the recently released report *Minority Students in Special and Gifted Education* by the National Research Council Committee on Minority Representation (Donovan & Cross, 2002), the authors recommend doing away with IQ tests to define learning disabilities and other high-incidence disabilities, citing bias and difficulty interpreting scores.

Actually, concerns about using IQ tests with students from diverse backgrounds have a long history (Laosa, 1977). IQ tests have been criticized because of problematic test development procedures and test uses that create linguistic and cultural bias (Garcia & Pearson, 1994; Samuda, 1989). Researchers have reported that students' test performance is affected by their differential interpretation of questions, lack of familiarity with vocabulary, limited English language proficiency, and issues of language dominance (Garcia & Pearson, 1994). The following list, adapted from Overton (1996), provides an overview of possible sources of bias in evaluation practices:

1. *Inappropriate content.* Students of ethnically diverse backgrounds may not have had adequate exposure to the constructs or concepts tested by an instrument.

2. *Inappropriate standardization samples.* Different ethnic minority groups may not have been well represented in the normative sample used to establish the standards for the test.

3. *Examiner and language.* A test conducted in English or an examiner of a cultural or linguistic background different from that of the student may cause the student to feel intimidated and may not be as clearly understood.

4. *Measurement of different constructs.* Specific constructs in the test may represent a majority culture; tests may only measure the extent to which students have absorbed the mainstream white, middle-class culture.

5. *Different predictive validity.* Tests that are used to predict future educational outcomes may not adequately do so for some students.

6. *Translation of tests in English to other language.* Translating tests into another language may result in a loss of the original meaning and influence test performance. Also, translating tests makes the use of the norms for the instrument invalid.

Recommendations for Alternative Assessment Procedures

Several alternative procedures have been recommended as having potential for conducting linguistically and culturally sensitive assessments, such as portfolios and authentic assessment procedures, dynamic assessment, learning potential assessment, and testing-the-limits approaches (Brown, Campione, Webber, & McGilly, 1992; Figueroa, 1989; Gonzalez, Brusca-Vega, & Yawkey, 1997; Rueda, 1997; Sternberg & Grigorenko, 2000). Moll (1990) suggests looking for the cultural, linguistic, and social resources—what he calls "funds of knowledge"—that students and their families bring to the school setting, and using these as strengths upon which to build problem-solving abilities.

In the second article in this section, Frank Serafini compares and contrasts three assessment paradigms—measurement, procedure, and inquiry—recommending that teachers become more involved in making assessment decisions and establishing criteria for how students will be evaluated.

First, Serafini describes and critiques "assessment as measurement," noting that the primary assessment of this type is the large-scale, norm-referenced standardized test. Serafini explains that this form of testing is based on a belief that knowledge is something that dwells outside of and separate from the learner, as if the learner were an empty vessel or blank slate ready (or not) to be filled. Learning is viewed as the transmission of knowledge from the informed to the uninformed. Yet teachers and others experience learners as being very different from this. Serafini outlines teachers' concerns about standardized tests, noting that the tests do not provide information that is helpful in making day-to-day instructional and curricular decisions and that teachers see relatively little use for their results. Yet because of the high stakes outcomes associated with large-scale tests, such as funding allocations, the tests often become very competitive. It is important to keep in mind that high-stakes tests were not designed to support classroom instruction, but rather were *designed essentially for program evaluation.* As an eighth-grader from New York explained, "It matters for the school, but not for your future individually" (Traub, 2002).

"Assessment as procedure" is closely related to "assessment as measurement" in beliefs about knowledge and learning, but the methods used for collecting data are somewhat different; for example, portfolios are used instead of multiple choice tests. As with measurement, the primary purpose is to report information to external stakeholders rather than to inform classroom instruction. Teachers are still asked to objectively measure students' abilities and report their findings in numerical form to external audiences.

"Assessment as inquiry," on the other hand, is based on constructivist theories of knowledge and learning and is relatively more student centered. In the inquiry process, the teacher uses various techniques to develop a picture of what each child knows and can do. Results from these assessments are used to guide day-to-day instructional decisions. A crucial difference between this and other forms of assessment is that classroom instruction does not stop in order to assess learning (or to prepare for test taking)—rather, assessment is part of the learning process, not separate from it. "The purpose shifts from an external focus on comparison and student ranking to an internal focus on informing classroom practice" (Tierney, 1998). Teachers are no longer simply the "test givers" but are vitally involved with the process, deciding which assessment devices generate the most useful information for their instructional purposes. These new assessments are not accepted blindly, but are judged on the type of information they create, their purpose, and the needs of the audiences involved.

Serafini clearly advocates the "assessment as inquiry" model and believes that teachers should have a say in how they assess their students. He notes, "Teachers and students should have a voice in what is taught, how this knowledge is eventually assessed, and what criteria are used for evaluation." He recommends that teachers get involved in negotiating the criteria used to assess student performance, and that educators should consider "'models of excellence' already available in the outside world that classroom teachers and students can use to judge the quality of the work done in schools." For example, he suggests examining the criteria used for winning the Nobel Prize or Pulitzer Prize. He believes that bringing in multiple voices may create more authentic, ultimately more useful, criteria.

Yet times have changed since Serafini published this article, and the reality is that the emphasis on "assessment as measurement" is growing. On January 8, 2002, U.S. President George Bush signed into law the No Child Left Behind Act, with reformed standards and increased testing at its core (see Traub, 2002, for a discussion of the "test mess"). The law leaves U.S. teachers without a choice—they are required to administer high-stakes tests. Therefore the question about what teachers' role should be must be reframed. High-stakes testing is not going away anytime soon, yet at the same time we know that high-stakes test results are not very useful for guiding classroom practice. This leaves teachers with a dilemma.

What Can Teachers Do?

What can teachers control and what is beyond their influence? Teachers are under a microscope as never before and are feeling increasing pressure to make sure their students perform well on large-scale standardized tests. How can teachers change a challenging situation into an advantage for them and their students? In other words, how can teachers turn lemons into lemonade? Teachers must become well informed about various assessment procedures. If teachers are going to be empowered they need to fully understand the assessment process, how to observe learners, and how to make curricular decisions based on what they observe. There is more at stake than just how to evaluate schools. Bigger issues concern what is valued in education and what place particular content areas and learning processes are to have in the school curriculum. As high-stakes testing takes on a more predominant role, it is the test designers who increasingly are determining the curriculum—teaching to the test is precisely what these companies want. This curriculum is generally "old-fashioned"; schools that have previously prided themselves on their creative, student-centered programs are shifting their focus to memorizing dates and places (Traub, 2002). But must it really be this way? Is this an overreaction? What if schools and teachers let it be OK to just be good enough on the tests used for evaluation purposes, and also used their *own* assessments that measured what they deemed most valuable? Then a challenge becomes how to get the word out about all the different ways students are achieving in addition to those assessed by high-stakes tests.

It is important to remember that there are different purposes for assessment, for different audiences, and that high-stakes testing does not and cannot take the place of other forms of testing, such as assessment as inquiry. So then the question becomes how to fit it all in, how to administer the mandatory high-stakes tests and still have time for meaningful assessment and instruction. And that is where teachers do have some choices. Serafini recommends that teachers and others should reflect on and dialogue about the quality of experiences provided for students and the effectiveness of the decisions they make in their classrooms.

REFERENCES

Brown, A.L., Campione, J.C., Webber, L.S., & McGilly, K. (1992). Interactive learning environments: A new look at assessment and instruction. In B.R. Gifford & M.C. O'Connor (Eds.), *Changing assessments: Alternative views of aptitude, achievement, and instruction* (pp. 121–211). Boston: Kluwer.

Donovan, M.S., & Cross, C.T. (Eds.) (2002). *Minority students in special and gifted education.* Washington, DC: National Academy Press.

Figueroa, R.A. (1989). Psychological testing of linguistic-minority students: Knowledge gaps and regulations. *Exceptional Children, 56*(2), 145–152.

Garcia, G.E., & Pearson, P.D. (1994). Assessment and diversity. In L. Darling-Hammond (Ed.), *Review of research in education* (No. 20, pp. 337–391). Washington, DC: American Educational Research Association.

Gonzalez, V., Brusca-Vega, R., & Yawkey, T. (1997). *Assessment and instruction of culturally and linguistically diverse students with or at-risk of learning problems.* Needham Heights, MA: Allyn & Bacon.

Gunderson, L., & Siegel, L.S. (2001). The evils of the use of IQ tests to define learning disabilities in first- and second-language learners. *The Reading Teacher, 55,* 48–55.

Laosa, L.M. (1977). Nonbiased assessment of children's abilities: Historical antecedents and current issues. In T. Oakland (Ed.), *Psychological and educational assessment of minority children* (pp. 1–20). New York: Brunner/Mazel.

Moll, L.C. (Ed.). (1990). *Vygotsky and education: Instructional implications and applications of sociohistorical psychology.* Cambridge, UK: Cambridge University Press.

Oller, J.M., Jr. (1997). Monoglottosis: What's wrong with the idea of the IQ meritocracy and its racy cousins? *Applied Linguistics, 18*(4), 467–507.

Overton, T. (1996). *Assessment in special education: An applied approach* (2nd ed.). Upper Saddle River, NJ: Merrill.

Rueda, R. (1997). Changing the context of assessment: The move to portfolios and authentic assessment. In A.J. Artiles & G. Zamora-Duran (Eds.), *Reducing the disproportionate representation of culturally diverse students in special and gifted education* (pp. 7–25). Reston, VA: Council for Exceptional Children.

Samuda, R.J. (1989). Psychometric factors in the appraisal of intelligence. In R.J. Samuda & S.L. Kong (Eds.), *Assessment and placement of minority students* (pp. 25–40). Toronto, Canada: Hogrefe & Huber.

Serafini, F. (2001). Three paradigms of assessment: Measurement, procedure, and inquiry. *The Reading Teacher, 54*, 384–393.

Sternberg, R.J., & Grigorenko, E.L. (2000). *Teaching for successful intelligence to increase student learning and achievement.* Arlington Heights, IL: Skylight.

Tierney, R.J. (1998). Literacy assessment reform: Shifting beliefs, principled possibilities, and emerging practices. *The Reading Teacher, 51*, 374–390.

Traub, J. (2002, April 7). The test mess. *The New York Times Magazine*, pp. 46–51.

The Evils of the Use of IQ Tests to Define Learning Disabilities in First- and Second-Language Learners

Lee Gunderson and Linda S. Siegel

Joe Sun (pseudonym) immigrated from Hong Kong with his family when he was 11 years old. He struggled with school and failed nearly all of his classes. He had difficulty learning both English and the material presented in his academic classes. He received some English as a Second Language (ESL) help, but after three years of continued failure he was referred for assessment. It was found that Joe could not define words such as *thief* or *brave*, words that should be easy for most English-speaking students his age. When asked, he was unable to read easy words such as *rug, with, stove, ground*, and *airplane*. He read *even* as *eve, finger* as *fighter, size* as *sat, felt* as *fit*, and *lame* as *lem*. He was asked to read pseudowords, but he did so with great difficulty: *ift* was *ept, Nan* was *ang, Chad* was *chand*, and *ap* was *aip*. When asked, he spelled *correct* as *coright, him* as *her*, and *must* as *mucs*. He had great difficulty repeating two-syllable nonwords and could not delete initial and final phonemes. However, he did have outstanding visual-spatial skills.

The teachers in Joe's school were faced with a difficult and perplexing question, "Was Joe failing to learn because he was learning English as a second language (ESL), or was he learning disabled?" It is often difficult to determine which individuals are learning disabled when they are native speakers of a language. However, the task is considerably more complex when they are second-language (L2) learners.

There are students at all levels, kindergarten to university, who have difficulty learning. Indeed, the number of school-age students identified as learning disabled in the United States rose from 797,000 in 1976–1977 to 2,317,000 in 1993–1994 (Kavale & Forness, 1998). Many individuals find learning difficult or impossible for reasons that are not always clear to teachers. In many cases they may have some type of learning disability. That is, they may have significant difficulty in acquiring reading, spelling, writing, or mathematical skills. The U.S. National Joint Committee on Learning Disabilities (2000) published an expanded definition of learning disabilities first developed in 1994:

Originally published in *The Reading Teacher* (2001), volume 55, pages 48–55.

Learning disabilities...[refer] to a heterogeneous group of disorders manifested by significant difficulties in the acquisition and use of listening, speaking, reading, writing, reasoning, or mathematical abilities. These disorders are intrinsic to the individual, presumed to be due to central nervous system dysfunction, and may occur across the life span. Problems in self-regulatory behaviors, social perception, and social interaction may exist...but do not by themselves constitute a learning disability. Although learning disabilities may occur...with other handicapping conditions (for example, sensory impairment, mental retardation, serious emotional disturbance), or with extrinsic influences (such as cultural differences, inappropriate or insufficient instruction), they are not the result of [them]. (National Joint Committee on Learning Disabilities, 2000)

Learning disabilities are not always outwardly visible; they must often be inferred. To determine whether an individual has a learning disability, school personnel are usually required by policy to administer an intelligence test (e.g., see Kavale & Forness, 1998). A student may be diagnosed as having a reading disability if there is a large and significant discrepancy between an IQ test score and reading achievement. The United States Department of Education (1977) established rules and regulations for detecting learning disabilities.

A specific learning disability may be found if (1) the child does not achieve commensurate with his or her age and ability when provided with appropriate educational experiences, and (2) the child has a severe discrepancy between achievement and intellectual ability in one or more areas relating to communication skills and mathematical abilities. (p. 65083)

There are a number of different discrepancy-based models of disability involving IQ scores in use, and it has been argued for some time that they should be replaced by approaches based on grounded theories of learning (Willson, 1987). However, this discrepancy definition of learning disability continues to shape policy in many jurisdictions, including the United States (cf., Kavale & Forness, 1998), the United Kingdom (cf., United Kingdom Department for Education and Employment, 2000), and Canada (cf., British Columbia Ministry of Education, 1999). We have concerns about the use of intelligence tests to determine who is reading disabled and who is not. We are particularly concerned when the students speak a first (L1) or primary language other than English, are from backgrounds that are culturally different from the mainstream, or are from low socioeconomic backgrounds. We are convinced that these students are penalized because of the use of IQ tests. Indeed, we are certain that some students who should be identified as learning disabled are not, and some who are identified should not be. We believe that the use of IQ testing and the discrepancy concept is invalid and harmful, and is particularly destructive for those students who differ linguistically and culturally from the "norm." We agree with Strickland (1995) that students with a record of school failure, classified with labels ranging from "learning disabled" to "educably mentally retarded," are often deprived of educational opportunities because of those labels. In many cases students are being improperly labeled on the basis of the results of an IQ test.

What Role Does IQ Play in the Assessment of Learning Disabilities?

The intelligence test is one of the primary instruments used in the identification of learning disabilities. In many cases, an individual cannot be identified as learning disabled unless an IQ test has been administered. Federal law in the United States, for instance, indicates that a disability exists if "a child has a severe discrepancy between achievement and intellectual ability" (34 CFR 300.541). The U.S. Head Start program policy stipulates that a disability exists when "the child has a severe discrepancy between achievement milestones and intellectual ability in one or more...[areas]" (45 CFR Part 1308, Section 1308.14 Eligibility criteria: Learning disabilities). As outlined in the U.S. Individuals with Disabilities Education Act (IDEA), a learning disability exists if the student has "an IQ of 70 or higher, and a severe discrepancy between intellectual ability and academic achievement in one or more areas" (1990, Section 1401).

In many jurisdictions, funding is not available for students who have not been administered an IQ test. We are convinced, however, that the presence of a discrepancy is not a necessary part of the definition of a learning disability and, furthermore, that it is not necessary to administer an IQ test to determine whether a learning disability exists.

Measuring Intelligence

The concept of "intelligence" should signify skills in reasoning, problem solving, critical thinking, and adaptation to the environment. Although this notion appears logical, it breaks down when one carefully examines the content of IQ tests. Typically they consist of measures of factual knowledge, definitions of words, memory recall, fine-motor coordination, and fluency of expressive language; they probably do not measure reasoning or problem-solving skills. They assess only what a person has learned, not what he or she is capable of doing.

An IQ test is not culture free, because background is important, nor is it language free, because it requires knowledge of English.

In some subtests on an IQ test extra points are given for responding quickly, thereby putting a premium on speed. An individual with a culturally based slow, deliberate style may not achieve as high a score as an individual who responds more quickly. This is a problem that cannot be overcome by simply translating the test into a student's first language. In essence, IQ tests are based on the notion that scores do not represent a single entity but are a composite of many skills. (For an extended discussion of the content of IQ tests, see Siegel, 1989.)

It is argued that IQ tests are needed to measure the "potential" of an individual. This argument implies that there is some measure that can reliably predict how much an individual can learn and what can be expected of him or her. In this view IQ scores predict the limits of academic performance. A person with a low score is not expected to have high levels of academic skills, while one with a high score is. In other words, an IQ score is thought to estimate reliably how much knowledge an individual can be expected to acquire. However, there is evidence that this putative relationship is neither strong nor reliable. There are individuals who have low scores on IQ tests, less than 80 or 90, who also have average or above average scores on reading tests. Indeed, reading comprehension may be more influenced by background knowledge (e.g., Schneider, Körkel, & Weinert, 1989) or phonological skills (e.g., Siegel, 1993) than IQ scores.

Our perusal of the research for the purpose of writing this article revealed that the relationship between IQ scores and achievement, particularly in reading, varies greatly, but that in the typical case only about 20–25% of reading scores can be predicted accurately from IQ scores. In most cases, there appears to be no reliable relationship between IQ and reading scores. It should also be noted that parental income predicts achievement with the same level of accuracy. Should we decide on educational programs for students based on parental income? We hope the answer is no, and we think that it is equally inappropriate to use IQ in this way.

There is an additional problem with the use of IQ tests for individuals with learning disabilities. Most of these individuals have deficiencies in one or more of the component skills that are part of IQ tests, and, therefore, their scores are an underestimate of their competence. It seems illogical to find that someone has deficient memory or language or fine-motor skills and then say that they are less intelligent because of the deficiency.

There is evidence to suggest that it is unnecessary to use an intelligence measure to define a reading disability. When children with reading disabilities are divided into groups on the basis of their IQ and compared on a variety of reading, language, memory, spelling, and phonological tasks, there are no differences in scores on the reading-related tasks (Siegel, 1988). The reading-disabled group in this study was quite homogeneous in relation to reading-related skills, and administering an IQ test did not provide useful information about performance differences on reading-related tasks.

If individuals are poor readers but show no discrepancy between their IQ and reading scores, then they are not considered reading disabled. If they show this discrepancy they are said to have a reading disability. There are a significant number of studies that find no difference in reading, spelling, phonological, or even reading comprehension skills of learning-disabled individuals with high and low IQ scores. Furthermore, there are no differences between disabled and poor readers on measures of the processes most directly related to reading (e.g., Siegel, 1988, 1992; Stanovich & Siegel, 1994; Toth & Siegel, 1994).

Siegel (1992) compared two groups of children who had low reading scores. One group, the disabled readers, had reading scores that were significantly lower that those that were predicted by their IQ scores, and the other group, the poor readers, also had low reading scores, but these were not significantly lower than would be predicted by their IQ scores. On a variety of reading, spelling, and phonological tasks, there were no significant differences between these two groups in reading comprehension. These results have been replicated in a study of adults with reading disabilities (Siegel, 1998). It seems that there is no need to use IQ scores to predict the differences between the individuals traditionally called learning disabled and those who have equally poor achievement and lower IQ scores. IQ scores do not appear to predict who is able to benefit from remediation (Arnold, Smeltzer, & Barneby, 1981; Kershner, 1990; Lytton, 1967; Van der Wissel & Zegers, 1985; Vellutino et al., 1996). One study (Yule, 1973) found that reading-disabled children with lower IQ scores made more gains than reading-disabled children with higher scores. We agree with Lyon (1995), who stated,

> The assumption that a discrepancy between achievement and aptitude (typically assessed using intelligence tests) is a clear diagnostic marker for learning disabilities or can be considered a pathognomonic sign is at best premature, and at worst invalid. (p. 12)

To this point we have argued that IQ tests are inappropriate for identifying disabilities, but our discussion has focused on their use with native English speakers. We turn now to the case of individuals whose first or primary language is not English.

Intelligence and Language

Researchers have explored the issues related to intelligence for nearly 100 years. Binet and Simon (1905), for instance, created a test they believed measured intelligence. Spearman (1904) developed the notion of "general intelligence," or the "g factor." One argument is that intelligence is innate and testable and that it does not necessarily require language. Unfortunately, intelligence tests are not language-free. They require an understanding of the language of the test and the testing process. Oller (1997) noted the following:

> To reform the use of IQ and other school testing procedures, it is essential to start calling "verbal IQ tests" *measures of **primary** language skills* [emphasis in original]. When they are applied to persons for whom the language of the test is not the primary language, they are *measures of **second** (or **nonprimary**) language skills* [emphasis in original]. If these changes are made, the absurdity of calling a normal person who has not yet learned a certain dialect of English "retarded," "learning disordered," "language impaired," "learning disabled," and the like, will be averted. (pp. 493–494)

Language-free or nonverbal IQ tests also require language (Oller, 1997). Oller argued that such tests "are measures of conceptual skills that are accessible only through proficiency in some particular language, usually the test-taker's primary language" (p. 494). He cautioned, further, that "the results of all 'nonverbal' tasks should be regarded with reasonable skepticism" (p. 494). The use of IQ tests to assess students whose primary language is different from the language of the test is dubious at best because it denies the relationship between language and culture. Indeed, we learn a language as members of particular cultures. We have concluded that

> The cultural factor must be considered in administering and interpreting any standardized tests, especially those that purport to measure intellectual ability. Memory, learning, perceiving, and problem solving cannot be measured except through content. And content is always culturally related. We must accept that intelligence tests measure the degree to which the individual's knowledge and skills enable him or her to function intelligently in a culture, rather than assessing pure intelligence in some way. (Siegel & Gunderson, in press)

English as a Second Language (L2) Students

The number of students for whom English is a second language continues to increase. As this number increases, so does the number of ESL students who have difficulty learning. Some have learning disabilities. The problem is to identify the learning disability when there are complex linguistic and cultural differences that confound the assessment process (Siegel & Gunderson, in press). We have found that

> culturally/linguistically diverse students may be seen as disabled (when, in fact, they are not), and therefore, identification as a student with special needs is inappropriate. Or, the gifts and talents of culturally and linguistically diverse students may be overlooked, which prevents them from receiving the services that would contribute to the development of their potentials. Or, students from linguistically and culturally diverse backgrounds may have genuine learning disabilities and need some special education assistance, but remain unidentified. (Siegel & Gunderson, in press)

We have come to the conclusion that the use of intelligence tests in general to identify learning-disabled students is inappropriate. To use them to identify learning disabilities for students who differ linguistically and culturally from the mainstream is particularly inappropriate. Unfortunately, as we have pointed out, such use of intelligence tests is widespread.

Intelligence Tests and Second Language

Second-language students may not receive access to help with their reading, spelling, writing, or arithmetic problems because of their performance on IQ tests. This is unfortunate, and a result of a failure to acknowledge that there is a serious discrepancy between the language of the test and the language of the student. IQ tests are wholly inappropriate for ESL students for a variety of reasons. ESL students vary in their knowledge of English, and the variance has important consequences for their performance on an IQ test. Language is complex. It includes phonological, syntactic, semantic, pragmatic, and background knowledge. A mature first-language speaker has learned the phonology—how to produce and understand the sounds—of his or her language. He or she can produce and comprehend grammatically acceptable utterances and communicate with other speakers of the same sociolinguistic group. The mature language speaker understands how to be polite, what language is appropriate for different contexts, how to take turns in a conversation, who to talk to and who to defer to, how to switch codes so that the language matches the situation, how to use intonation to produce meaning, who to respect, gender- and age-appropriate roles, who to look at and who not to look at, and how to react appropriately to different situations, including testing sessions. In essence, to do well in a testing situation, an individual must know a great deal about both the second language and the second culture (see Gunderson & Anderson, 2003).

Most ESL students do not possess the complex second-language and second-culture knowledge required to succeed in such situations, and the individual doing the testing may not have the knowledge of the student's first culture or first language to be able to differentiate discrepancies from differences. Translating a test that has cultural biases into different languages does not eliminate the inherent difficulties related to cultural biases or scoring schemes that favor faster response times. IQ tests are simply wrong for identifying learning disabilities for ESL students.

The Matthew Effect

One of the reasons for the inappropriateness of IQ tests is the "Matthew effect." Stanovich (1986, 1988a, 1988b) has conceptualized the Matthew effect as "the tendency of reading itself to cause further development in other related cognitive abilities such as intelligence such that 'the rich get richer and the poor get poorer'" (Stanovich, 1986, p. 361). Certain minimum cognitive capabilities must be present to begin reading; however, once reading begins, the act of reading itself further develops these same cognitive capabilities. This relationship of mutual reinforcement is called the Matthew effect. This reciprocal relationship between reading and other cognitive skills is reflected in performance on IQ tests and, consequently, undermines the validity of using an IQ discrepancy-based criterion because children who read more gain the cognitive skills and information relevant to the IQ test and consequently attain higher IQ scores. Children with reading problems read less and, therefore, fail to gain the skills and information necessary to allow for the development of abilities measured by IQ tests.

As a result of the Matthew effect there will be a decline in IQ scores for disabled readers with increasing age, because vocabulary and knowledge increase as a result of experiences with print through the act of reading. In a cross-sectional study, Siegel and Himel (1998) found that the IQ scores and, in particular, vocabulary scores of older reading-disabled children were significantly lower than those of younger reading-disabled children. Similar declines in IQ and vocabulary were not noted for normally achieving readers, that is, children who showed age-appropriate reading skills. However, reading scores of the children with reading problems compared to chronologically age-matched children remained relatively constant with time so that there was not an overall decline in skills. Younger children were much more likely to be classified as disabled readers (as opposed to poor readers) than older children because of the "decline" in IQ scores that resulted from lack of print exposure.

The Matthew Effect and Second-Language Students

If the Matthew effect exists in English, it is likely that it exists for readers of other languages. A number of second-language researchers have found that immigrants with L1 reading backgrounds develop L2 reading faster than those without reading backgrounds (e.g., Collier, 1987; Cummins, 1979, 1984; Cummins & Swain, 1986). Immigrant students with four to six years of successful L1 literacy backgrounds have higher achievement levels than those who have little or no L1 reading experience (Gunderson & Clarke, 1998). These findings suggest the existence of a second-language Matthew effect. We paraphrase Stanovich by saying "the L1 rich will become the L2 rich."

Negative Consequences of IQ Test Use

The negative consequences of using an IQ test to define learning disability are quite serious. Many learning-disabled children who need help, but do not meet the discrepancy definition, are not getting it. Berninger (1998) noted that only 44% of the children who met the criterion for low reading achievement also met the criterion for the IQ achievement discrepancy. This means that 56% of the children who need it do not get help for their learning problems, because they have low IQ scores. She also noted that only 36% who met the criterion for IQ achievement discrepancy also met the criterion for low achievement. This means that the remaining 64% are eligible for remedial help when they really do not have low achievement scores and do not need remedial help. The consequence of using IQ means that children with lower IQ scores, although not necessarily very low, will not receive the help that they need. Berninger stated that children with low IQ scores and low achievement "would benefit from support services" (1998, p. 535).

The fact that there is no difference in reading skill between children who have a discrepancy and children with the same kind of problems but with no discrepancy should be a clue that the IQ test is not really useful. In other words, IQ does not predict the ability to benefit from remediation. The IQ test is particularly insidious because in the present educational system children must often be administered an IQ test to determine whether they have a learning disability. Resources in most systems are quite limited, and the child must wait a long time although he or she is having difficulties in school. It would make much more sense to recognize these difficulties, whether or not an IQ test is done, and start remediation immediately. Teachers are in the best position to observe whether or not individual students have learning difficulties.

In many places in the world the type of help that children receive for their reading problems depends on their IQ, and children with higher IQ scores are more likely to receive the remediation that they need. The use of IQ to define reading disability seems fatally flawed because it is confounded by socioeconomic status and age. The implications seem clear. If the IQ-achievement discrepancy is used as a part of the definition of reading disability, and if reading-disabled and poor readers are treated differently by the school system, then children with lower IQ scores, even though they have serious reading problems, will not get the help that they need. Therefore, the use of IQ scores systematically discriminates against certain children. To help all children learn to read, teachers should recognize some of the difficulties inherent in making inferences about reading potential based on IQ scores and instead develop detailed analyses of reading, spelling, arithmetic, and writing skills. (See Siegel & Heaven, 1986, for a detailed discussion of these issues.)

The use of IQ tests with ESL or English-dialect students is inappropriate. There is no way that an IQ test can reliably measure intelligence, even if it exists and can be tested, when the student's first or primary language is different from the language of the test. The results are problematical. Indeed, they marginalize ESL students. They fail to identify true reading-disabled students. They are not able to differentiate a first-language learning problem from a second-language learning problem or from a general language learning problem. In summary, use of the IQ test may be harmful to the education of children because it often prevents those who really need help from getting it.

What Teachers Can Do

The IQ test as it is currently given does not provide much information about the child's achievement difficulties. A careful analysis of errors in reading, spelling, arithmetic tests, and in writing samples is more useful. Millions, perhaps billions, of U.S. dollars are spent each year on IQ test administration and scoring. Teachers can and should trust their own observations and instincts. It is relatively easy to identify which children are having significant difficulties with reading, spelling, written work, and math, especially as they function in learning situations independently and in groups with other students. Teachers who believe particular students have learning difficulties can confirm their beliefs by the administration of standardized tests of letter recognition, word identification, and comprehension. Such tests are usually available in schools or school districts. A great deal of information is also available through the administration of an informal reading inventory. Analyses of students' production errors or miscues reveal a great deal about their skills. For example, does the child read the word *have* to rhyme with *gave* or *said* as *sayed* (rhyming with *maid*)? In this case, the child has not yet mastered the complex, often irregular pronunciation of English vowels. Does the child read *father* as *five* or *takes* as *tells*? These kinds of errors indicate that the child is paying attention only to the first letter and then guessing.

Students' spelling errors reveal information about their knowledge of phoneme-grapheme correspondences. Does the child spell *nature* as *nachure* or *education* as *educashun*? The student demonstrates a good knowledge of letter-sound correspondences, but a poor visual memory and a lack of understanding of the structure of English words. No English word ends in -*shun*, although *shun* is an English word. In English the orthography uses -*tion* or -*sion*.

It was concluded that Joe Sun (the student mentioned in the introduction) had a learning disability. The difficulty in making the determination was in separating errors he made related to influences from his first language, Cantonese, from those directly related to difficulties in reading English. Cantonese is an open-syllabic language without final consonant clusters (see Chang, 1987). Typically Cantonese speakers substitute glottal stops for final consonants and consonant clusters in English, such as /faɪ/ for /faɪv/ (*fi* for *five*). These errors were not evident in Joe's reading nor were other second-language features. Indeed, the teacher's analysis of his errors suggested he had a learning disability.

If teachers were given the time and opportunity to administer individual achievement tests and to analyze the results, particularly the errors, students, teachers, and administrators would be helped more than by the administration of an IQ test. What will make the difference for the student is that he or she receives early instruction based on a thoughtful analysis of the student's needs and abilities. We will not recommend a particular method or approach because we agree with Duffy and Hoffman (1999) who noted that "reading instruction effectiveness lies not with a single program or method, but rather, with a teacher who thoughtfully and analytically integrates various programs, materials, and methods as the situation demands" (p. 11). There is also no perfect IQ test or achievement test to determine a child's strengths and weaknesses. What is needed is that teachers be given the time, support, and staff development required to administer and interpret both holistic and standardized measures.

REFERENCES

Arnold, L.E., Smeltzer, D.J., & Barneby, N.S. (1981). Specific perceptual remediation: Effects related to sex, IQ, and parents' occupational status; behavioral change pattern by scale factors; and mechanism of benefit hypothesis tested. *Psychological Reports*, *49*, 198.

Berninger, V.W. (1998). Specific reading and writing disabilities in young children: Assessment, prevention, and intervention. In B. Wong (Ed.), *Learning about learning disabilities* (2nd ed., pp. 529–555). San Diego, CA: Academic Press.

Binet, A., & Simon, T. (1905) New methods for the diagnosis of the intellectual level of subnormals. *L'Annee Psychologique*, *5*, 191–244.

British Columbia Ministry of Education. (1999). *Assessing disabilities* [Online]. Available: http://www.bced.gov.bc.ca/specialed/review/report/id.htm

Chang, J. (1987). Chinese speakers. In M. Sawn & B. Smith (Eds.), *Learner English: A teacher's guide to interference and other problems* (pp. 224–237). Cambridge, England: Cambridge University Press.

Collier, V.P. (1987). Age and rate of acquisition of second language for academic purposes. *TESOL Quarterly*, *21*, 617–641.

Cummins, J. (1979). Cognitive/academic language proficiency, linguistic interdependence, the optimum age question and some other matters. *Working Papers on Bilingualism*, *19*, 197–205.

Cummins, J. (1984). *Bilingualism and special education: Issues in assessment and pedagogy*. Clevedon, England: Multicultural Matters.

Cummins, J., & Swain, M. (1986). Linguistic interdependence: A central principle of bilingual education. In *Bilingualism in education* (pp. 80–95). New York: Longman.

Duffy, G.G., & Hoffman, J.V. (1999). In pursuit of an illusion: The flawed search for a perfect method. *The Reading Teacher*, *53*, 10–16.

Gunderson, L., & Anderson, J. (2003). Multicultural views of literacy learning and teaching. In A. Willis, G.E. Garcia, R. Barrera, & V. Harris (Eds.), *Multicultural issues in literacy research and practice*. Mahwah, NJ: Erlbaum.

Gunderson, L., & Clarke, D.K. (1998). An exploration of the relationship between ESL students' backgrounds and their English and academic achievement. In T. Shanahan & F.V. Rodriguez-Brown (Eds.), *National Reading Conference Yearbook 47* (pp. 264–273). Chicago: National Reading Conference.

Kavale, K.A., & Forness, S.R. (1998). Covariance in learning disability and behavior disorder: An examination of classification and placement issues. In T.E. Scruggs & M.A.

Mastropieri (Eds.), *Advances in learning and behavioral disabilities* (Vol. 12, pp. 1–42). London: JAI Press.

Kershner, J.R. (1990). Self-concept and IQ as predictors of remedial success in children with learning disabilities. *Journal of Learning Disabilities, 23*, 368–374.

Lyon, G.R. (1995). Toward a definition of dyslexia. *Annals of Dyslexia, 45*, 3–27.

Lytton, H. (1967). Follow up of an experiment in selection of remedial education. *British Journal of Educational Psychology, 37*, 1–9.

National Joint Committee on Learning Disabilities. (2000). *Learning disabilities: Issues on definition* (1990, January) [Online]. Available: http://www.ldonline.org/njcld/defn_91.html

Oller, J.W., Jr. (1997). Monoglottosis: What's wrong with the idea of the IQ meritocracy and its racy cousins? *Applied Linguistics, 18*, 467–507.

Schneider, W., Körkel, J., & Weinert, F.E. (1989). Domain-specific knowledge and memory performance: A comparison of high- and low-aptitude children. *Journal of Educational Psychology, 81*, 306–312.

Siegel, L. (1988). Evidence that IQ scores are irrelevant to the definition and analysis of reading disability. *Canadian Journal of Psychology, 42*, 201–215.

Siegel, L. (1989). Why we do not need IQ test scores in the definition and analysis of learning disability. *Journal of Learning Disabilities, 22*, 514–518.

Siegel, L. (1992). An evaluation of the discrepancy definition of dyslexia. *Journal of Learning Disabilities, 25*, 618–629.

Siegel, L. (1993). Phonological processing deficits as the basis of a reading disability. *Developmental Review, 13*, 246–257.

Siegel, L. (1998). The discrepancy formula: Its use and abuse. In B.K. Shapiro, P.J. Accardo, & A.J. Capute (Eds.), *Specific reading disability: A view of the spectrum* (pp. 123–135). Timonium, MD: York.

Siegel, L., & Gunderson, L. (in press). *Assessing the individual learning needs of students with linguistically and culturally diverse backgrounds.* Victoria, BC: British Columbia Ministry of Education.

Siegel, L., & Heaven, R. (1986). Defining and categorizing learning disabilities. In S. Ceci (Ed.), *Handbook of cognitive, social, and neuropsychological aspects of learning disabilities* (Vol. 1, pp. 95–121). Hillsdale, NJ: Erlbaum.

Siegel, L., & Himel, N. (1998). Socioeconomic status, age and the classification of dyslexics and poor readers: The dangers of using IQ scores in the definition of reading disability. *Dyslexia, 4*, 90–104.

Spearman, C.E. (1904). General intelligence: Objectively determined and measured. *American Journal of Psychology, 15*, 201–292.

Stanovich, K.E. (1986). Matthew effects in reading: Some consequences of individual differences in the acquisition of literacy. *Reading Research Quarterly, 21*, 360–407.

Stanovich, K.E. (1988a). Explaining the differences between the dyslexic and garden variety poor reader: The phonological-core variable-difference model. *Journal of Learning Disabilities, 21*, 590–604, 612.

Stanovich, K.E. (1988b). The right and wrong places to look for the cognitive locus of reading disability. *Annals of Dyslexia, 38*, 154–177.

Stanovich, K.E., & Siegel, L. (1994). Phenotypic performance profile of children with reading disabilities: A regression-based test of the phonological-core variable-difference model. *Journal of Educational Psychology, 86*, 24–53.

Strickland, K. (1995). *Literacy, not labels: Celebrating students' strengths through whole language.* Portsmouth, NH: Boynton/Cook.

Toth, G., & Siegel, L. (1994). A critical evaluation of the IQ-achievement discrepancy based definition of dyslexia. In K.P. van den Bos, L.S. Siegel, D.J. Bakker, & D.L. Share (Eds.), *Current directions in dyslexia research* (pp. 45–70). Lisse, the Netherlands: Swets & Zeitlinger.

United Kingdom Department for Education and Employment. (2000). *Special educational needs in England* [Online]. Available: http://www.dfee.org.uk/

United States Department of Education. (1977). Definition and criteria for defining students as learning disabled. *Federal Register, 42:250,* 65083.

Van der Wissel, A., & Zegers, F.E. (1985). Reading retardation revisited. *British Journal of Developmental Psychology, 3,* 3–9.

Vellutino, F.R., Scanlon, D.M., Sipay, E.R., Small, S.G., Pratt, A., Chen, R., et al. (1996). Cognitive profiles of difficult to remediate and readily remediated poor readers: Toward distinguishing between constitutionally and experientially based causes of reading disability. *Journal of Educational Psychology, 59,* 76–123.

Willson, V.L. (1987). Statistical and psychometric issues surrounding severe discrepancy. *Learning Disabilities Research, 3*(1), pp. 24–28.

Yule, W. (1973). Differential prognosis of reading backwardness and specific reading retardation. *British Journal of Educational Psychology, 43,* 244–248.

Three Paradigms of Assessment: Measurement, Procedure, and Inquiry

Frank Serafini

Different assessment frameworks have different intended audiences, are used for different purposes, and use different procedures to collect information (Farr, 1992). However, these are not the only differences. Each of these assessments may also involve different beliefs about the nature of knowledge, the level of teacher and student involvement, the criteria for evaluating student achievement, and the effects of these assessment frameworks on classroom instruction (Garcia & Pearson, 1994).

The differences between standardized, norm-referenced testing programs and classroom-based assessments have been written about extensively (Neill, 1993). However, as one begins to investigate the various assessment frameworks contained in the professional literature, the distinguishing features of these assessment frameworks, commonly referred to as performance-based, authentic, or classroom-based assessment, tend to overlap and blend.

Various assessment frameworks use similar procedures and data collection methodologies, and many of these "alternative" assessments do not adhere to traditional criteria of standardization, reliability, and objectivity (Linn, Baker, & Dunbar, 1991). This article is intended to help teachers and other concerned educators by providing a broader perspective concerning assessment frameworks or "paradigms" and how these assessments affect classroom practice.

Short and Burke (1994b) described three paradigms of curriculum. They suggested that curriculum could be viewed as Fact, as Activity, and as Inquiry. In this description, curriculum as Fact refers to knowledge as a commodity that is "transferable" and exists separately from the "knower," whereas curriculum as Activity is concerned with the actual activities within the classroom, and curriculum as Inquiry is concerned with the process of creating knowledge in the classroom. As teachers begin to move from a teacher-directed curriculum, based on the transmission of "facts," to a student-centered curriculum, based on inquiry processes, the purposes of assessment and the methods used to collect information may need to be revisited.

Originally published in *The Reading Teacher* (2000/2001), volume 54, pages 384–393.

In reference to Short and Burke's work, Heald-Taylor subsequently developed three paradigms for literature instruction (1996) and three paradigms for spelling instruction (1998). Heald-Taylor used Short and Burke's curricular paradigms to analyze literature and spelling instruction to help teachers understand their own perspectives, or paradigms, concerning literacy development and classroom practices. This article will look at the distinctions between these three paradigms and use the structure suggested by Short and Burke to shed light on the differences between the various assessment frameworks that operate in schools today.

Short and Burke originally developed these three paradigms to distinguish between the traditional models of curriculum development and an inquiry model. The traditional model, curriculum as Fact, is based on modernist or positivist perspectives of reality and epistemology (Elkind, 1997). From this perspective, knowledge is viewed as an objective commodity that can be transmitted from teacher to student and subsequently measured through standardized forms of assessment (Bertrand, 1991).

In comparison, from a constructivist perspective—curriculum as Inquiry—knowledge is viewed as socially and cognitively constructed by humans as they interact with their environment (Fosnot, 1996). Knowledge is viewed as a construction and not a commodity that exists separately from the "knower." It is this shift from a positivist perspective to a constructivist perspective that underlies the differences in the assessment paradigms to be described in this article.

The curricular paradigms described by Short and Burke are purported to represent different philosophical views of reality, knowledge, and learning (Short & Burke, 1994a). However, in describing the differences between the three paradigms in assessment, one must also look at the level of student and teacher involvement, the methods used to gather information, the purposes or goals of the assessment framework, and the intended audiences for the results. Paralleling the structure used by Short and Burke, the three paradigms of assessment are entitled (a) assessment as measurement, (b) assessment as procedure, and (c) assessment as inquiry.

In this article, I will describe how the three assessment paradigms are similar and how they are different, using various writing assessments—specifically writing portfolios—to help distinguish between the different paradigms. Next, I will present several factors that I believe support teachers making a "paradigm shift" from assessment as measurement to assessment as inquiry. Finally, I will explain several pedagogical suggestions that teachers in transition are using to change their perspectives on assessment.

Assessment as Measurement

The first paradigm is assessment as measurement. As mentioned previously, this paradigm is closely associated with a positivist or modernist view of reality and knowledge. The primary instrument of this paradigm is the large-scale, norm-referenced standardized test. These standardized tests are designed to objectively measure the amount of knowledge that a student has acquired over a given time (Wineburg, 1997). A major concern for classroom teachers is whether these assessments provide the necessary information required to make day-to-day instructional and curricular decisions (Johnston, 1992).

In the assessment as measurement paradigm, knowledge is believed to exist separately from the learner, and students work to acquire it, not construct it. The student is seen as an empty vessel, a "blank slate," ready to be filled up with knowledge. Learning is viewed as the transmission of knowledge from teacher to student while meaning is believed to reside within the text, and only one interpretation or judgment is accepted in the standardized tests (Short & Burke, 1994b).

In this paradigm, objectivity, standardization, and reliability take priority over concerns of teacher and student involvement. In these tests, the role of the classroom teacher is scripted, scoring is done by computer, and the tests are kept secured to ensure fairness. The student's primary role in these standardized testing programs is that of test taker. In other words, there is little opportunity for self-evaluation or student reflection. The test is given and a score is tabulated. In this externally mandated form of assessment, classroom teachers have little or no input to the decision-making process and relatively little use for the results of these assessments in directing classroom and curricular decisions (Rothman, 1996).

Primarily, standardized tests are designed to compare large-scale educational programs and to provide accountability to public stakeholders (Murphy, 1997). These tests are used by school districts, state or provincial education departments, and other external stakeholders to rank and compare schools and children (Meier, 1994). Because of the high-stakes agenda associated with these standardized tests, such as funding decisions and school appropriations, they may become highly competitive (Kaufhold, 1995). These tests were not designed to support classroom instruction; rather, they were designed for large-scale educational and program evaluation (Taylor & Walton, 1997).

In the assessment as measurement paradigm, decisions about the information to be collected, and the means of evaluating this information, are usually determined by authorities outside the classroom. For example, writing ability is measured on standardized tests by means of multiple choice questions that focus primarily on issues of grammar, word choice, and spelling. The test items are designed to measure the amount of "writing knowledge" students have accumulated over their school experiences. These tests are also concerned with what a child has not learned or understood. In this way, standardized tests are concerned with deficits of knowledge as well as accumulations.

In this paradigm, portfolios or collections of authentic writing samples are not generally used to evaluate students' writing abilities. In fact, rarely will an actual example of student writing even be evaluated in a standardized testing program.

Assessment as Procedure

The assessment as procedure paradigm has elements of the assessment as measurement paradigm as well as the assessment as inquiry paradigm. In this paradigm, the primary focus is on the assessment procedures, not on the underlying purposes of the assessment program or the epistemological stance. Epistemologically, this paradigm is closely related to the assessment as measurement paradigm. Knowledge is still believed to exist independently from the learner; this knowledge can be transmitted to the student and eventually objectively measured.

The main difference between this paradigm and the assessment as measurement paradigm is that the procedures have changed to resemble qualitative data collection methods. However, even though the methods have changed, the underlying beliefs that student achievement can be objectively measured and that knowledge exists independently from the learner have not. In this way this paradigm has elements of the measurement and the inquiry paradigms.

Daly, a social philosopher, referred to a focus on procedures as "methodolatry" (as cited in Noddings, 1992). She described methodolatry as an overemphasis on the correct method of doing things, rather than a focus on the purposes for doing those things. This definition of methodolatry captures the essence of this paradigm very well. The assessment as procedure paradigm is primarily concerned with different methods for collecting data rather than new purposes or audiences for collecting this information.

In this paradigm, like the assessment as measurement paradigm, teachers and students are not directly involved in making decisions concerning the assessment procedures or the purposes for these assessments. The primary concern is with reporting information, albeit information gathered by new methods, to external stakeholders and not with directing classroom instruction (Cizek, 1998).

In Arizona, for example, many portfolio assessment projects were initiated by school district administrations in response to the state-mandated Arizona Student Assessment Program (ASAP). In response to the ASAP, many teachers were directed by their districts to keep portfolios of children's work as part of the state writing assessment. They were required to use a "generic rubric" to score each piece of writing in the student's portfolio and submit a final writing score for each student. This portfolio score would be in lieu of the ASAP performance-based test score. Teachers simply collected the student work, used the rubric to determine a score, and submitted the score to the state department. This was done because an authority outside the classroom directed them to do so.

Because of this situation, these portfolios often become an end in and of themselves. The portfolios were mandated and used to provide scores for the state department. Because of the external mandate, limited teacher input, and little or no staff development, these portfolios became a classroom activity, something teachers were required to administer, rather than a vehicle to promote student or teacher reflection or direct classroom decisions (Smith, 1991).

In this paradigm, the actual procedures for collecting student work, the activities themselves and not the purposes for collecting the student work, have taken priority. As a result of the ASAP, some teachers became more concerned with the type of folders to be used and the procedures for passing these portfolios on to the next grade level than with discussing the various ways these portfolios could be used to promote reflection and self-evaluation.

In the assessment as procedure paradigm, teachers are still being asked to objectively measure students' abilities and report information in numerical form to external audiences. They remain outside the decision-making process, barely involved in determining the purposes for these assessments.

Many of these "assessment as procedure programs" are destined to fail because they become an end in and of themselves. Classroom teachers have not been involved in the creation of these new methods, which are not intended to provide new insights to a child's learning. Teachers are simply burdened with another set of procedures given to them by their administration in order to provide scores for an external authority.

In effect, the procedure or method of collecting information in and of itself does not determine the assessment paradigm. This paradigm is a blend of two other paradigms. It is the purpose and the audience for these assessments, along with the epistemological stance and methods used to gather information, that helps determine the paradigm.

Assessment as Inquiry

In the assessment as inquiry paradigm, assessment is based on constructivist theories of knowledge (Fosnot, 1996), student-centered learning (Altwerger, Edelsky, & Flores, 1987), and the inquiry process (Short, Harste, & Burke, 1995). Here, the teacher uses various qualitative and quantitative assessment techniques to inquire about particular learners and their learning processes. It is a process of inquiry, and a process of interpretation, used to promote reflection concerning students' understandings, attitudes, and literate abilities.

Not only have the procedures changed for collecting information, but so have the levels of teacher and student involvement, the purposes of these assessments, the epistemological perspective, and the audiences for the information created. In the assessment as procedure paradigm, the changes were only at the pedagogical level, concerned with new information-gathering procedures. In comparison, within this paradigm the purpose of the assessments is a deeper understanding of individual learners in their specific learning contexts. The audience has also changed from external authorities to the teachers, parents, and students involved in the classroom.

Assessment, in this paradigm, is viewed as a social, contextually specific, interpretive activity (Crafton & Burke, 1994). Knowledge is believed to be constructed by the individual within the social contexts of the learning event, rather than being acquired solely through transmission or direct instructional techniques. In this paradigm multiple interpretations are encouraged, and each learner transacts with different texts and the world to create meanings (Rosenblatt, 1979).

Using assessment as inquiry, teachers are no longer simply test administrators. Rather, teachers and students are viewed as active creators of knowledge rather than as passive recipients (Wells, 1984). Instead of using tests to measure student abilities and compare children, teachers use these classroom-based assessment procedures to facilitate learning, direct curricular decisions, and communicate more effectively with students and parents (Serafini, 1995).

In this assessment as inquiry paradigm, it is believed there is no simple prescription for each student's ailment or a program that one can administer quickly and relatively effortlessly to eliminate inappropriate behaviors.

Assessment is not viewed as an "objective" measurement process, intended for comparisons and prescriptions; rather, it is seen as a human interaction involving the human as the primary assessment instrument (Johnston, 1997). The differences between this paradigm and the assessment as procedure paradigm are in why teachers implement these procedures, not necessarily how these procedures are carried out. What is done with the information and for whom the assessments are conducted has also changed.

Instead of state or provincial education departments mandating a particular portfolio assessment program such as the ASAP example used earlier, teachers implement their own portfolio assessment process to collect samples of student work in order to make appropriate instructional decisions. These portfolios have become vehicles to promote reflection and student self-evaluation (Tierney, 1998). The methods used to collect information may be similar, but the purposes and the goals of the assessment as inquiry paradigm are quite different.

In this paradigm, portfolios are seen as a vehicle for promoting student and teacher reflection, self-evaluation, and goal setting. These portfolios are an ongoing collection of work used to understand a student's interests, abilities, needs, and values. The artifacts in the portfolios are not usually scored or used to compare children against their same-age cohorts; rather, students reflect upon the contents in order to understand their academic progress and to document their growth. This has been referred to as learner-referenced assessment (Johnston, 1997).

The work included in these portfolios has been created in a more authentic context, rather than in a testing situation (Bergeron, 1996). In this paradigm, classroom instruction does not stop in order to assess learning. Assessment is viewed as part of the learning process, not as separate from it.

Portfolios are noncompetitive and attempt to focus on students' strengths rather than their deficiencies (Murphy, 1997). The portfolios in this paradigm are used to uncover the possibilities for students, to understand each child as a whole, and to attempt to provide a window into a student's conceptual framework and ways of seeing the world.

Educational communities would look radically different if this were the dominant theory of assessment; however, standardized tests will not disappear tomorrow. This shift from assessment as measurement to assessment as inquiry will take time, resources, administrative support, and dialogue among interested educators. Viewing assessment as inquiry would shift the focus of assessment research and practices from the standardized testing programs to the classroom itself, where assessment may be of more service in helping teachers to improve classroom learning experiences (Serafini, 1998).

Supporting Teachers in Transition

The shift toward an inquiry-based assessment paradigm places different demands not only upon classroom teachers but also on school administrations, staff development programs, and teacher education models. Making changes in a teacher's practice or educational belief system demands considerable time, research, and the opportunity for teachers to collaborate (Fullan, 1994). In general, teachers need time, support, and the opportunity to have a dialogue with colleagues. Teachers need time to read professional literature concerning assessment, engage in dialogue with other teachers in transition, and have the chance to try these new procedures in a supportive, collaborative environment.

Time is already at a premium during the school day for classroom teachers. Paperwork, school site committees, staff meetings, large classroom enrollments, and shortened preparation periods all contribute to the inadequate amount of time allotted to professional development. Administrators and staff development specialists need to become more creative and supportive in finding time to help classroom teachers understand these new assessment procedures, read about their implementation, try them out in the classroom, and reflect on their progress.

Change can be threatening. Teachers, like other educators, need peer support when working through new ideas. A trusting environment where teachers can enter into open dialogue with one another is of primary importance. However, when teachers are allowed to voice their concerns and ideas, change may become less threatening.

By looking at the existing school structures and developing alternatives to the traditional school day, administrators may find new ways to create time for teachers to collaborate, research new assessment practices, and take the first step toward making a shift in their assessment beliefs and practices. When teachers and administrators come to value the changes necessary to move toward reflective practice and assessment as inquiry, it becomes easier for these groups to justify the time required to support these changes.

In making this shift, teachers will need to reevaluate not only the procedures used to generate information about their students but also the purposes and audiences for the information collected. In this way it is a "paradigm shift," a new stance toward assessment and knowledge as well as a change in the actual procedures used (Cambourne & Turbill, 1997).

Making the Shift

In order to make this paradigm shift from assessment as measurement to assessment as inquiry, teachers need a supportive environment where administration and staff development programs provide time to collaborate with other educators, time to reflect, and the opportunity to work through the new purposes and procedures in the new assessment framework. The general support mechanism needs to be in place to allow teachers the time, dialogue, and collaboration necessary for change to occur.

Along with these general supports, specific changes in a teacher's practice and thinking may support a transition to this new paradigm. Teachers may want to consider the following ideas: (a) teachers as knowledgeable, reflective participants; (b) meaningful student involvement; and (c) negotiating criteria used to assess student performance. Each of these ideas will now be addressed in more detail, including some practical suggestions for teacher consideration.

Teachers as Knowledgeable, Reflective Participants

The teacher as a knowledgeable, reflective participant is the foundation for the assessment as inquiry paradigm. Rather than relying on testing agencies outside the classroom context to evaluate student progress, teachers in this paradigm assume an active role in the assessment process. This new role involves using observational strategies and other classroom-based assessment procedures to gather information about student achievement.

The information collected is then interpreted by teachers on the basis of their existing knowledge and experiences. Teachers reflect on and interpret classroom experiences and student performances to make decisions about curriculum and instruction, rather than relying solely on the interpretations or scores from an externally mandated test. The more extensive the teacher knowledge base, the more effective the interpretations and subsequent instructional decisions (Fenstermacher, 1994). When teachers assume an active role in the assessment process, the audience and purposes for these assessments shift from an external focus on comparison and student ranking to an internal focus on informing classroom practice (Tierney, 1998).

Traditionally, teachers were perceived as "program operators," and the knowledge they needed to be successful was based on how to implement prepackaged curriculum or present the lessons scripted for them in teacher manuals (Bullough & Gitlin, 1985). Subsequent traditional teacher education programs were developed around methods courses that explained how to deliver the curriculum. These notions of teacher as automated program delivery person become problematic in shifting to an assessment as inquiry paradigm.

Many teacher education programs have attempted to restructure their programs to develop teachers who assume an active, reflective role in curriculum and assessment decisions (Ross, 1989). The teacher as a reflective participant is a different stance than the transmission or direct instruction models still taught in some traditional teacher education programs (Zeichner, 1987). If teachers are going to make the transition from assessment as measurement to assessment as inquiry, they need to know more about observing learners, learn how to make curriculum decisions based on these observations, and increase their knowledge base concerning child development and learning processes.

In the assessment as inquiry paradigm, teacher participation means that not only do teachers administer the assessments, but they also have a voice in the decisions as to how, when, and for what purposes these assessments are being used. Teachers are no longer simply the test givers, but become critically involved, deciding which assessments generate the most useful information for their instructional purposes. These new assessments are not blindly accepted, but are judged on the type of information they create, the purposes for these assessments, and the needs of the audiences involved.

As reflective participants, teachers make a commitment to learn from past experiences. It is an intentional, systematic, and deliberate focus on why things occur and what effects these experiences have on student learning (Dewey, 1933). Reflection has been defined as "systematic enquiry into one's own practice to improve that practice and to deepen one's understanding of it" (Lucas, 1991, p. 85).

Reflective thinking is initiated by the perception of a problem (Dewey, 1933). It is this acknowledgment of uncertainty and "unsettledness" that initiates the inquiry process. In other words, in order to be reflective participants, teachers need to be able to discuss their doubts and inquiry questions without being seen as unknowing or incompetent. Being able to make one's practice "problematic" has been observed as a first step in this process (Valli, 1997). When teachers have no doubts about their practice or the programs they are using, reflection remains of minimal importance.

In working toward becoming knowledgeable, reflective participants in the assessment process, teachers have assumed the role of teacher-researcher to better understand the experiences and interactions in their classrooms (Cochran-Smith & Lytle, 1992). In doing so, teachers have become producers of research and knowledge as well as consumers (Richardson, 1994). By videotaping classroom events (Berg & Smith, 1996), observing peers at work in classrooms, and working in team teaching situations, teachers are opening up new avenues for dialogue and collaboration. This has allowed teachers the opportunity to become more reflective about their practice. Teachers also use journal writing as a way to help understand the perspectives and beliefs they bring to their practice and their effect on classroom events (Hubbard & Power, 1993).

Many teachers have used journal writing to create belief statements or platform statements about their philosophy of education in order to understand the expectations and hidden beliefs they bring to the assessment process (Kottkamp, 1990). In writing these statements, teachers have been able to "unpack" their values and biases and to distance themselves from their practice in order to critique it more effectively. The purpose of these procedures is to help teachers see their practice from a different, more critical perspective (Osterman, 1990).

Another way to help teachers make this shift is to support the development of teacher dialogue groups. When teachers come together to discuss educational issues that are relevant to their practice, change and growth become possible (Ohanian, 1994). Teacher-research groups (Queenan, 1988) and assessment-driven teacher dialogue groups (Stephens et al., 1996) help provide a structure for teachers to support one another through the change process. Through these dialogue groups, teacher-research groups, and journal writing, teachers are inquiring into the quality of the learning experiences provided for their students and the effectiveness of the decisions they make in their classroom.

Meaningful Student Involvement

The assessment as measurement paradigm has historically left students out of the assessment process (Bushweller, 1997). Assessment has been something we do "to" students rather than "with" students. Schools administer standardized tests and send them off to be scored by external testing agencies; eventually the results of the tests are reported back. Through this traditional assessment as measurement paradigm, students and schools have come to rely on external testing agencies to judge their effectiveness and to document their educational progress. This lack of involvement has created passive recipients, not active participants, in the learning as well as the assessment process (Calfee & Perfumo, 1993).

In the assessment as inquiry paradigm, portfolios of student work, student-led conferences, learning response logs, and negotiated reporting procedures include the student in the assessment process (Tierney, Carter, & Desai, 1991). This new level of involvement helps students to accept more responsibility for their learning and to reflect on their own educational progress. Students need to be invited to participate in determining the criteria by which their work will be judged and then play a role in actually judging their work (Kohn, 1993).

Portfolios are used as a vehicle to promote reflection on students' academic progress as well as document their growth in various subject areas (Graves, 1992). Students collect work generated during the school year to evaluate their progress and set goals for their future learning experiences. Many times these portfolios are used in conjunction with student-led conferences where students share their portfolios and reflections with parents and other interested audiences. These portfolios have an authentic purpose and are a primary vehicle for supporting student reflection as well as student involvement in the assessment process.

Another way students are involved in the assessment process is through negotiated reporting configurations (Anthony, Johnson, Mickelson, & Preece, 1991). Students are invited to become intimately involved in the creation of their report cards in a negotiated process with both teachers and parents. This process may begin by allowing students to evaluate their efforts and performances, based on criteria negotiated between the teacher's perspective, the information contained in various standards documents, and the beliefs and values of the community. Opening up the criteria used to evaluate student work and inviting students to participate in the evaluation process help students begin to feel a part of the assessment process, rather than as passive recipients of someone else's evaluation.

Another way of involving students in assessing their progress is through classroom-designed rubrics (Rickards & Cheek, 1999). Rubrics are negotiated forms of criteria explicitly written for particular classroom work and activities. Again, opening up the conversation to include students in the decisions about what criteria are used to evaluate their progress helps students become involved in the assessment process. When students become an active part of the assessment process, assessment becomes a process of inquiry rather than an external measurement reducing student performance and ability to a numerical score for comparative purposes.

Negotiating the Criteria Used to Assess Student Performance

The debate over what children should be taught and what they need to know in order to be successful adults has been going on in the United States for centuries (Bracey, 1995). This debate has been rekindled by many of the standards-based restructuring initiatives across the United States and other countries (Noddings, 1997). The creation of standards documents by state legislatures and federal education agencies, along with the standardized testing that usually accompanies these documents, has tended to restrict programs to the assessment as measurement paradigm, while at the same time supporting agendas tied to gatekeeping and exclusion (Tierney, 1998). These documents are written as general learning statements by people far removed from actual classrooms and students. The negotiation of educational criteria becomes a highly political issue and hence a highly controversial one (Shannon, 1996).

As educators, we just don't know all that students need to know, nor are we able to teach them everything we do know (Wiggins, 1989). The criteria used for assessing student performance should be open for negotiation and revision to adapt to our changing societal demands. Teachers and students should have a voice in what is taught, how this knowledge is eventually assessed, and what criteria are used for evaluation.

With all of these restructuring efforts, teachers have been bombarded with standards created by federal and state agencies, local school boards, and professional organizations like the National Council of Teachers of English and the International Reading Association. Using these documents as guidelines, teachers may open the negotiations by writing detailed belief or platform statements concerning their expectations for student learning and behavior (Kottkamp, 1990). These platform statements provide a place to open up a discussion among parents, teachers, and school officials about the experiences to be provided for students during the school year. By presenting their criteria to be negotiated, teachers open up a space for different voices to be heard concerning what is of value in education and what place particular content areas and learning processes are to have in the school curriculum.

As mentioned before, classroom rubrics designed with student and teacher input are an excellent vehicle for negotiation and involvement in the assessment process. Students and teachers come together to "unpack" their values and beliefs about education in order to expose these to discussion and negotiation. It is this process of negotiation that is of primary importance, not necessarily the actual documents that are created in the process (Boomer, 1991).

The items included on school district report cards and how amenable these cards are to change should also be open to negotiation. School report cards are a written statement about what the community deems valuable in education. If it is on the report card and it gets a grade, it is probably seen as important by that community. Even the amount of space designated for each subject area is a statement concerning how much value is placed upon that topic. The larger the space, it seems the more value is assigned to that particular subject or topic.

In negotiating the criteria used to assess student performance, educators should consider the "models of excellence" already available in the outside world that classroom teachers and students can use to judge the quality of the work done in schools. Possibly educators can look to various awards, such as the Newbery or Pulitzer prize for writing or the Nobel prize for science, in order to find criteria that are authentic and can be incorporated into the negotiation of student evaluation. What are the authentic models of criteria available for assessing student performance? Instead of school districts and education departments being the sole creators of these criteria of student progress, opening up the discussion to bring in multiple voices may create more authentic, more useful criteria.

No Quick Fix

When educators begin to acknowledge the complexity and the interpretive nature of the learning and assessment process, traditional assessment as measurement procedures become problematic. All assessments are interpretive; unfortunately teachers and students rarely become involved in large-scale testing programs' interpretations or dissemination of results. The assessment as inquiry paradigm offers teachers another perspective from which to understand the needs and abilities of their students, using different assessment methods for different purposes and audiences.

Making this shift from assessment as measurement to assessment as inquiry takes time, administrative support, collaboration, and the opportunity to engage in dialogue. Simply mandating new procedures for teachers to administer will not help teachers make this shift in assessment paradigms.

It is my hope that classroom teachers will begin to take an active role in the assessments used in their classroom. Teachers need to involve students in the assessment process in meaningful ways, become knowledgeable, reflective participants in the assessment process themselves, and negotiate the criteria used to evaluate academic performances. As educators, we need to acknowledge the complexity of the learning process and stop trying to find the quick-fix solutions to both educational and assessment issues. When assessment becomes a process of inquiry, an interpretive activity rather than simply the "objective" measure of predetermined behaviors, teachers will be able to use assessment to make informed decisions concerning curriculum and instruction in their classrooms.

REFERENCES

Altwerger, B., Edelsky, C., & Flores, B. (1987). Whole language: What's new? *The Reading Teacher, 41*, 144–154.

Anthony, R., Johnson, T., Mickelson, N., & Preece, A. (1991). *Evaluating literacy: A perspective for change*. Portsmouth, NH: Heinemann.

Berg, M.H., & Smith, J.P. (1996). Using videotapes to improve teaching. *Music Educator's Journal, 22*(5), 31–37.

Bergeron, B. (1996). Seeking authenticity: What is "real" about thematic literacy instruction? *The Reading Teacher, 49*, 544–551.

Bertrand, J. (1991). Student assessment and evaluation. In B. Harp (Ed.), *Assessment and evaluation in whole language programs* (pp. 17–33). Norwood, MA: Christopher-Gordon.

Boomer, G. (Ed.). (1991). *Negotiating the curriculum: A teacher-student partnership*. Sydney, Australia: Ashton-Scholastic.

Bracey, G. (1995). *Final exam: A study of the perpetual scrutiny of American education*. Washington, DC: Technos Press.

Bullough, R.V., Jr., & Gitlin, A. (1985). Schooling and change: A view from the lower rungs. *Teachers College Record, 87*, 219–237.

Bushweller, K. (1997). Teach to the test. *The American School Board Journal, 184*, 20–25.

Calfee, R., & Perfumo, P. (1993). Student portfolios: Opportunities for a revolution in assessment. *Journal of Reading, 36*, 532–537.

Cambourne, B., & Turbill, J. (Eds.). (1997). *Responsive evaluation*. Portsmouth, NH: Heinemann.

Cizek, G. (1998). The assessment revolution's unfinished business. *Kappa Delta Pi Record, 34*, 144–149.

Cochran-Smith, M., & Lytle, S. (Eds.). (1992). *Inside/outside: Teacher research and knowledge*. New York: Teachers College Press.

Crafton, L., & Burke, C. (1994). Inquiry-based evaluation: Teachers and students reflecting together. *Primary Voices, 2*(2), 2–7.

Dewey, J. (1933). *How we think*. Chicago: Henry Regnery.

Elkind, D. (1997). The death of child nature: Education in the postmodern world. *Phi Delta Kappan, 78*, 241–245.

Farr, R. (1992). Putting it all together: Solving the reading assessment puzzle. *The Reading Teacher, 46*, 26–37.

Fenstermacher, G. (1994). The knower and the known: The nature of knowledge in research on teaching. In L. Darling-Hammond (Ed.), *Review of research in education, 20* (pp. 3–56). Washington, DC: American Educational Research Association.

Fosnot, C.T. (1996). Constructivism: A psychological theory of learning. In C.T. Fosnot (Ed.), *Constructivism: Theory, perspectives and practice* (pp. 8–33). New York: Teachers College Press.

Fullan, M. (1994). Why teachers must become change agents. *Educational Leadership, 50,* 12–17.

Garcia, G.E., & Pearson, P.D. (1994). Assessment and diversity. In L. Darling-Hammond (Ed.), *Review of research in education, 20* (pp. 337–391). Washington, DC: American Educational Research Association.

Graves, D. (1992). Portfolios: Keep a good idea growing. In D. Graves & B. Sunstein (Eds.), *Portfolio portraits* (pp. 1–12). Portsmouth, NH: Heinemann.

Heald-Taylor, B.G. (1996). Three paradigms for literature instruction in grades 3 to 6. *The Reading Teacher, 49,* 456–466.

Heald-Taylor, B.G. (1998). Three paradigms of spelling instruction in grades 3 to 6. *The Reading Teacher, 51,* 404–412.

Hubbard, R.S., & Power, B.M. (1993). *The art of classroom inquiry: A handbook for teacher researchers.* Portsmouth, NH: Heinemann.

Johnston, P.H. (1992). Nontechnical assessment. *The Reading Teacher, 46,* 60–62.

Johnston, P.H. (1997). *Knowing literacy: Constructive literacy assessment.* York, ME: Stenhouse.

Kaufhold, J.A. (1995). Testing, testing. *The American School Board Journal, 182,* 41–42.

Kohn, A. (1993). Choices for students: Why and how to let students decide. *Phi Delta Kappan, 75,* 8–20.

Kottkamp, R.B. (1990). Means for facilitating reflection. *Education and Urban Society, 22,* 182–203.

Linn, R., Baker, E., & Dunbar, S. (1991). Complex, performance-based assessment: Expectations and validation criteria. *Educational Researcher, 20*(8), 15–21.

Lucas, P. (1991). Reflection, new practices and the need for flexibility in supervising student teachers. *Journal of Higher Education, 15*(2), 84–93.

Meier, T. (1994). Why standardized tests are bad. In *Rethinking our classrooms: Teaching for equity and social justice* (pp. 171–175). Milwaukee, WI: Rethinking Schools.

Murphy, S. (1997). Literacy assessment and the politics of identity. *Reading and Writing Quarterly, 13,* 261–278.

Neill, M. (1993). A better way to test. *The Executive Educator, 15,* 24–27.

Noddings, N. (1992). *The challenge to care in schools.* New York: Teachers College Press.

Noddings, N. (1997). Thinking about standards. *Phi Delta Kappan, 79,* 184–189.

Ohanian, S. (1994). *Who's in charge? A teacher speaks her mind.* Portsmouth, NH: Heinemann.

Osterman, K. (1990). Reflective practice: A new agenda for education. *Education and Urban Society, 22*(2), 133–152.

Queenan, M. (1988). Impertinent questions about teacher research: A review. *English Journal, 77*(2), 41–46.

Richardson, V. (1994). Conducting research on practice. *Educational Researcher, 23*(5), 5–10.

Rickards, D., & Cheek, E., Jr. (1999). *Designing rubrics for K–6 classroom assessment.* Norwood, MA: Christopher-Gordon.

Rosenblatt, L.M. (1979). *The reader, the text, the poem.* Carbondale, IL: Southern Illinois University Press.

Ross, D. (1989). First steps in developing a reflective approach. *Journal of Teacher Education, 40*(2), 22–30.

Rothman, R. (1996). Taking aim at testing. *The American School Board Journal, 183,* 27–30.

Serafini, F. (1995). Reflective assessment. *Talking Points: Conversations in the Whole Language Community, 6*(4), 10–12.

Serafini, F. (1998). Making the shift. *Talking Points: Conversation in the Whole Language Community, 9*(2), 20–21.

Shannon, P. (1996). Mad as hell. *Language Arts, 73,* 14–18.

Short, K., & Burke, C. (1994a). *Creating curriculum.* Portsmouth, NH: Heinemann.

Short, K., & Burke, C. (1994b). *Curriculum as inquiry.* Paper presented at the Fifth Whole Language Umbrella Conference, San Diego, CA.

Short, K., Harste, J., & Burke, C. (1995). *Creating classrooms for authors and inquirers.* Portsmouth, NH: Heinemann.

Smith, M.L. (1991). Put to the test: The effects of external testing on teachers. *Educational Researcher, 20*(5), 8–11.

Stephens, D., Story, J., Aihara, K., Hisatake, S., Ito, B., Kawamoto, C., et al. (1996). When assessment is inquiry. *Language Arts, 73,* 105–112.

Taylor, K., & Walton, S. (1997). Co-opting standardized tests in the service of learning. *Phi Delta Kappan, 79,* 66–70.

Tierney, R.J. (1998). Literacy assessment reform: Shifting beliefs, principled possibilities, and emerging practices. *The Reading Teacher, 51,* 374–390.

Tierney, R.J., Carter, M.A., & Desai, L.E. (1991). *Portfolio assessment in the reading-writing classroom.* Norwood, MA: Christopher-Gordon.

Valli, L. (1997). Listening to other voices: A description of teacher reflection in the United States. *Peabody Journal of Education, 72*(1), 67–88.

Wells, G. (1984). *The meaning makers.* Portsmouth, NH: Heinemann.

Wiggins, G. (1989). The futility of trying to teach everything of importance. *Educational Leadership, 47,* 14–18.

Wineburg, S. (1997). T.S. Eliot, collaboration, and the quandaries of assessment in a rapidly changing world. *Phi Delta Kappan, 79,* 59–65.

Zeichner, K. (1987). Preparing reflective teachers: An overview of instructional strategies which have been employed in preservice education. *International Journal of Education Research, 11,* 565–575.

RIGHT

Children who are struggling with reading have

a right to receive intensive instruction

from professionals specifically prepared

to teach reading.

Introduction

David Hernandez III

Struggling readers have a small window of time to develop proficiency. It is imperative that children who have difficulty learning to read—for whatever reason—have access to systematic, intensive, and regular instruction. Professionals in classroom and clinical settings who have the knowledge and skills to build on students' strengths, recognize their challenges, and plan appropriate interventions that will move readers toward greater proficiency should have the primary responsibility for planning and implementing this instruction. While the role of parents, paraprofessionals, and volunteers cannot be underestimated, as Wasik (1998) points out, quality tutoring programs need to have supervision from professionally trained reading specialists.

In response to this need for excellence, many states have increased the number of reading courses required for preservice and inservice teachers. Clearly, the general public and policymakers are beginning to realize that reading IS rocket science (see Moats, 1999) and that teacher preparation for meeting the task of teaching struggling readers is of vital importance.

Historically, the International Reading Association (IRA) has taken a strong stance in support of specialized training for reading professionals. In recent years, this stance has been strengthened as indicated by the following four examples. (1) In 1995, the Association formed a commission to examine the role of the reading specialist. Products of this commission include a position statement titled *Teaching All Children to Read: The Roles of the Reading Specialist* (IRA, 2000) that outlines the critical roles of the reading specialist in the areas of instruction, assessment, and leadership. (2) The IRA publication *Making a Difference Means Making It Different: Honoring Children's Rights to Excellent Reading Instruction* underscores the importance of professional preparation in reading. This publication states that a reading specialist should be called on prior to a student beginning to struggle in reading and writing. It also states, "Many of these children need more and different kinds of instruction, and they have a right to instruction that is designed with specific needs in mind. Reading specialists are specifically prepared to supervise and/or provide this instruction" (p. 8). (3) In 1999, IRA convened the National Commission on Excellence in Elementary Teacher Preparation for Reading Instruction to conduct a three-year investigation of reading teacher preparation and to provide leadership for change. The results of the study are available in the publication *Prepared to Make a Difference: Research Evidence on How Some of America's Best College Programs Prepare Teachers of Reading* (IRA, 2003). (4) IRA is currently revising *Standards for Reading Professionals* (1998), which serves as a roadmap for quality teacher preparation in reading at all levels.

The two articles in this section will not only enlighten but also further strengthen the role and importance of a trained reading professional in the schools. The article by Diana J. Quatroche, Rita M. Bean, and Rebecca L. Hamilton reviews the literature related to the reading resources specialist and provides guidelines for practice and future research. The article by Susan Babbitt and Maureen Byrne presents an excellent study profiling the critical role of the reading professional in tutoring urban youths of various social and economic status.

The Role of the Reading Specialist

As previously stated, IRA has taken a strong position on teacher preparation in reading. This is particularly true in the case of the reading specialist. The IRA Commission on the Role of the Reading Specialist defines a reading specialist as "a specially prepared professional who has responsibility (e.g., providing instruction, serving as a resource to teachers) for the literacy performance of readers in general or struggling readers in particular."

The importance of the reading specialist in schools has been under scrutiny, and in some regions the number of reading specialists has declined. In recent years, administrators and public policymakers have raised a variety of questions related to reading specialists. Examples of these questions follow:

- Do we really need reading specialists in our urban schools?
- How vital is the reading specialist in the performance of our students?
- What role has the U.S. federal government taken to address financial equity between urban and rural schools to ensure that students of color have professionals specifically trained to teach reading?
- Does a reading specialist need to be certified?
- Does research prove that students who are serviced by certified personnel show improvement?

◆ Why do educators wait until a student begins to struggle dramatically before calling a reading specialist for assistance in the classroom?

◆ Why are our Title I schools taking the reading specialist out of the classroom and replacing this person with a paraprofessional?

◆ Are educators integrating the reading specialist into classrooms and/or multidisciplinary teams?

Quatroche, Bean, and Hamilton's article in this section represents one aspect of the work of the IRA Commission on the Role of the Reading Specialist. One charge of the commission was to conduct a literature review of research related to the role of the reading specialist to provide answers to critics and to provide guidelines for practitioners, teacher educators, and researchers. Several key ideas emerged from the literature review.

First, the role of the reading specialist is complex and varied. Obviously there is a need for research examining models of reading specialist roles at the school level that have high impact in terms of stakeholder satisfaction and student achievement. In the meantime, professional training for the reading specialist needs to take that complexity and variability into account. In addition, forums for communication among reading specialists need to be provided so that they have an opportunity to share challenges, concerns, and successes.

Second, research indicates that the reading specialist does not work in isolation. The reading specialist has the potential for working with all key stakeholders at a school level. Administrators, classroom teachers, educators, and the reading specialist need to learn how to work together as a team. There needs to be a set of guidelines so that each person understands the importance of his or her role. Each person needs to know and understand the role of support, collaboration, interaction, and opportunities to establish a successful dialogue and network to help in the continued success in reading and writing of each and every student. In addition, the reading specialist needs to learn how to market and articulate his or her role so that all stakeholders are aware of what services can be provided and the limitations of those services (Radencich, Beers, & Schumm, 1993).

Third, this literature review clearly delineated some of the potential stressors that reading specialists face in the midst of the variability and complexity of their roles and in communication with key stakeholders. Potential stressors can also emerge from the pressures of high-stakes tests, alignment with professional standards, and working in high-needs schools. Professional management issues such as exploring careers, setting goals, managing time and stress, and resolving conflicts are areas that need further exploration. Documenting how exemplary reading resource teachers "manage it all" in urban schools is a fertile field for research.

Finally, although more research about the impact of the reading specialist on student achievement is warranted, Quatroche, Bean, and Hamilton conclude that the most important role of the reading specialist is instruction for struggling students. That instruction might be direct through in-class or pullout services or indirect through classroom teacher professional development and in-class support. Nonetheless, Quatroche and her colleagues state, "Professionals with extensive knowledge of reading instruction can and do make a difference. These professionals may not always have a 'certificate,' but they do have the specialized expertise that makes them specialists in reading."

The article presented in this section and other Commission on the Role of the Reading Specialist initiatives provide a launching point for future work in researching and documenting best practice in the role of the reading specialist.

The Trained Reading Specialist's Impact on Student Reading Achievement

The children's rights in *Making a Difference Means Making It Different* acknowledge that students learn how to read and write at different rates and in different ways. The article by Babbitt and Byrne in this section provides data indicating how three 13-year-old urban youths with varying degrees of social and economic status improved their reading and writing scores and skills with nine months of tutoring. The authors went further to structure challenging and relevant instruction that allowed students to succeed and become self-sufficient learners. They also were able to help provide lifelong learning skills and to help in developing resources. The article explains how the authors enabled their students to become self-sufficient learners and the steps it took them to get there.

Babbitt and Byrne found common threads among the age group of three students. One, in particular, was the greatest risk of dropping out of school. The researchers also found that motivation and support were needed by each child to show improvement in their own continued success. The authors show how they were able to bring in other professionals to help the students control their own learning and writing throughout the whole study.

Babbitt and Byrne begin to research the students' background including, but not limited to, their homes, schools, and other outside forces that can either make or break a student. Teachers in the urban setting need this information to help in their continued success to teach decoding, vocabulary, fluency, comprehension, and other strategies.

In short, the researchers discovered that providing tutoring in reading that is part of an overall comprehensive program involving subject matter, teachers, parents, and the community brought great success for students. Included in these successes are the students, educators, and families. The case studies of Diego, Marisol, and Lynette put a face on the issue of teaching reading in urban settings and demonstrate the reasons why collaboration among all key stakeholders is vital. In the truest sense, this study demonstrates that it does take a village to help educate a child.

Final Word

When reading the two articles in this section one is reminded that students' poverty of condition has nothing to do with their poverty of the mind. Educators must focus on the students and their right to receive intensive instruction from professionals specifically prepared to teach reading. Reading professionals do not work in a vacuum. We can provide enormous expertise—but other professionals and community members can provide expertise as well. Collaboration is not a buzzword—it is an absolute necessity for student success. Diego, Marisol, and Lynette deserve the best. As Arlene Ackerman, Superintendent of San Francisco Public Schools, observes,

> We must not tolerate below-average performance any longer. We must do more than give lip service to the belief that "every child can learn...." We must hold ourselves accountable for getting the kinds of results we know our children can produce. We must end the cycle of failure, and we must begin today.

REFERENCES

Babbitt, S., & Byrne, M. (1999/2000). Finding the keys to educational progress in urban youth: Three case studies. *Journal of Adolescent & Adult Literacy, 43,* 368–378.

International Reading Association. (1998). *Standards for reading professionals* (revised). Newark, DE: Author.

International Reading Association. (2000). *Teaching all children to read: The roles of the reading specialist* [position statement]. Available: http://www.reading.org/positions/specialist.html

International Reading Association. (2003). *Prepared to make a difference: Research evidence on how some of America's best college programs prepare teachers of reading* [information packet]. Newark, DE: Author.

Moats, L.C. (1999). *Teaching reading IS rocket science: What expert teachers of reading should know and be able to do.* New York: American Federation of Teachers.

Radencich, M.C., Beers, P.C., & Schumm, J.S. (1993). *A handbook for the K–12 reading resource specialist.* Boston: Allyn & Bacon.

Quatroche, D.J., Bean, R.M., & Hamilton, R.L. (2001). The role of the reading specialist: A review of research. *The Reading Teacher, 55,* 282–294.

Wasik, B. (1998). Using volunteers as reading tutors: Guidelines for successful practice. *The Reading Teacher, 51,* 562–570.

The Role of the Reading Specialist:
A Review of Research

Diana J. Quatroche, Rita M. Bean, and Rebecca L. Hamilton

Schools that lack or have abandoned reading specialist positions need to reexamine their needs for specialists to ensure that well trained staff are available for intervention with children and for ongoing support to classroom teachers. (Snow, Burns, & Griffin, 1998, p. 12)

The report of the National Research Council (Snow, Burns, & Griffin, 1998) focused on the need for improving the quality and effectiveness of reading programs and instruction for young children. The report also stressed the importance of well-prepared teachers of reading in the classroom and recommended that schools have "reading specialists who have specialized training related to addressing reading difficulties and who can give guidance to classroom teachers" (p. 333). The International Reading Association, in 1995, also made several important recommendations in an issue paper titled "Who Is Teaching Our Children? Reading Instruction in the Information Age." Two recommendations in particular underscore the importance of using qualified reading specialists to instruct students having difficulty learning to read:

School boards should evaluate whether or not they have professionals with the strongest background in teaching reading; and

Reading specialists need to be a part of every classroom where there are students needing help to learn how to read. (cited in Long, 1995b, p. 6)

Yet in recent years, many schools in the United States seem to be developing reading programs that employ fewer reading specialists. In fact, they may be hiring more nonprofessional personnel to perform duties traditionally assumed by reading specialists (Long, 1995a). This phenomenon, along with increasing concern about the reading achievement of students, especially those in high-poverty areas, led the International Reading Association to form the Commission on the Role of the Reading Specialist. The commission was charged with several important responsibilities. One of these is addressed here; that is, to develop a literature review that summarizes what we know about the role of the reading specialist and the various roles that reading specialists as-

Originally published in *The Reading Teacher* (2001), volume 55, pages 282–294.

sume. For the purposes of this review, *reading specialist* is defined as a specially prepared professional who has responsibility (e.g., providing instruction, serving as a resource to teachers) for the literacy performance of readers in general or struggling readers in particular. This definition of *reading specialist* was developed by the commission as a means of facilitating its work.

Methods

To conduct this literature review, we examined journals in the field of reading research and instruction, government documents, technical reports, and ERIC documents that related to the role of the reading specialist. The search was limited to the research and literature from 1990 to the present and included journal articles, reports, and papers. The decision to use 1990 as the beginning date for the literature search seemed appropriate because major changes occurred in the role of the specialist in the late 1980s, primarily due to guidelines specified in the reauthorization of Title I in the United States. This is a program supported by the U.S. federal government to improve the literacy and math performance in schools where a large percentage of the students come from low-income families. The review is focused on the literature and research that specifically addressed the roles that reading specialists assumed and some of the changes in Title I that have had an impact on the role of the reading specialist. Of specific interest were documents that provided empirical evidence. In addition, self-reports of reading specialists have been included. Of the literature reported in this review, 18 documents reported on empirical research that was conducted through observations, interviews, and surveys of reading specialists, or of principals, teachers, and others who had direct contact with reading specialists. A list of the research articles reviewed and their focus is provided in the Table.

We analyzed the research using the following steps. An initial reading of each article was done. If the article was a report of research, a summary of basic research methods was written, with attention to sample, methods, and findings. Articles that presented a point of view or review of literature were also summarized, with attention given to findings. After the initial reading, each article was read again and this time the focus was on looking for themes or concepts that were discussed in the articles. As a result of this reading, four prominent themes or areas emerged; each of these is discussed in depth in the following sections.

Table. Studies relating to role of reading specialist

Study	Type	Subjects	Focus
Barclay & Thistlewaite, 1992	Survey	Special reading teachers	Instruction Assessment Communication with teachers and parents Organize/administer school reading program
Barry, 1997	Survey	Secondary principals	Assessment Instruction Specialist/content teacher team teaching
Bean, Cooley, Eichelberger, Lazar, & Zigmond, 1991	Observation	Reading specialists Classroom teachers	Instruction in pullout setting Tutoring in in-class setting
Bean, Grumet, & Bulazo, 1999	Observation	Classroom teachers Reading specialist interns	Major/assist Support to classroom teacher Station teaching Parallel teaching Team teaching
Bean, Knaub, & Swan, 2000	Survey	Principals	Leadership
Bean, Trovato, Armitage, Bryant, & Dugan, 1993	Interview	Reading specialists Federal coordinators Reading teacher-educators	Consult with classroom teachers Staff development Instructional support Instruction

(continued)

Table (continued). Studies relating to role of reading specialist

Study	Type	Subjects	Focus
Bean, Trovato, & Hamilton, 1995	Focus groups	Reading specialists Classroom teachers Principals	Instruction Develop materials Inservice Consultant Student advocate Parent involvement
Davis & Wilson, 1999	Case study	Reading specialist	Effect of setting
Gelzheiser & Meyers, 1991	Observation	Reading specialists Classroom teachers	Instruction
Hamilton, 1993	Observation	Reading specialists	Student advocate
Henwood, 1999/2000	Self-report	Reading specialist	Collaboration
Hoffman, Baumann, Moon, & Duffy, 1997	Survey	Principals	Diagnostic testing Remedial reading Instruction
Jaeger, 1996	Self-report	Reading specialist	Collaborative consultant
Klein, Monti, Mulcahy-Ernt, & Speck, 1997	Survey Interview	Principals Classroom teachers Curriculum leader	Remedial instruction Teacher resource Diagnostic testing Modeling strategies Diagnosis and remediation Collaboration Educational leadership Parent/community link Resource to teachers

(continued)

Table (continued). Studies relating to role of reading specialist

Study	Type	Subjects	Focus
Kletzein, 1996	Self-reports Observation	Reading programs	Team teaching
Maleki & Herman, 1994	Survey	Middle school teachers Secondary teachers	Resource person Consultant Knowledge of English curriculum
Reutzel, Hollingsworth, & Cox, 1996	Survey	U.S. State legislators	Sources of information
Tancock, 1995	Observation Interview	Reading specialists	Resource person Support person

Diversity and Complexity of Roles

Although the qualifications for reading specialists may vary from state to state, according to International Reading Association guidelines (1998) a reading specialist is someone who, in addition to providing assessment and instruction, conducts professional development, helps to set reading program goals, helps other staff members achieve those goals, interprets the reading program to parents and community, demonstrates appropriate reading practices, and keeps staff members aware of current research. However, many reading specialists are funded by Title I. These reading specialists assume roles and responsibilities that are dictated by the requirements of that funding program. As that program has changed, so have the roles of the reading specialist.

Traditionally, students in Title I programs received additional instruction from a reading specialist, who typically served eligible students by pulling them out of regular classroom instruction. In these settings, a reading specialist spent time instructing students in all areas of reading, but essentially focused on remedial instruction. Now, however, federal guidelines promote models that necessitate much more attention to students' classroom performance to enhance their ability to perform high-level skills. Thus, we see more of a focus on in-class programs that require reading specialists to work more closely with classroom teachers. We also see more diversity in how schools choose to spend their Title I funds. Because of rising costs and the objective of teaching as many children as possible, many schools have opted to use Title I funds to support smaller class sizes or instructional aides. Consequently, the funds that previously supported the hiring of reading specialists may now be used for classroom teacher and paraprofessional positions. This is especially true for schools that are eligible for schoolwide projects.

Of the four studies using a survey methodology, only Barclay and Thistlewaite's (1992) surveyed reading specialists themselves to obtain an idea of how they viewed their work. Barclay and Thistlewaite sent a survey to 380 teachers who were either Title I teachers who held a master's degree in reading or were certified to teach reading in grades K–12. These teachers identified instruction as a very important responsibility, while additional responsibilities included conducting formal assessment, communicating with teachers and parents, and organizing and administering school reading programs. The respondents also identified administrative duties, acting as resources to teachers, and conducting teacher inservices as somewhat important responsibilities. When asked to identify their most pressing personal needs, respondents indicated they would like more information on their role as a resource to teachers and ranked the resource role as important. Although these reading specialists ranked instruction as their most important responsibility, the data showed that they also wanted to assume the role of teacher resource through the demonstration of strategies and model lessons, but indicated that they needed inservice education to help them fulfill this role.

Differences in how reading specialists perceive their roles versus how administrators view the specialists' roles are apparent (Barry, 1997; Hoffman, Baumann, Moon, & Duffy, 1997). In responding to surveys regarding reading specialists' roles and estimating the amount of time they spent on various responsibilities, administrators noted that a great deal of the reading specialists' time was spent instructing struggling readers in individual and small-group settings, with little time spent on staff development. Responsibilities such as selection of reading materials, program leadership, and evaluation of the reading program varied among the respondents, with some indicating that the reading specialist spent considerable time fulfilling those roles. High school principals described two roles for the reading specialist: working as a team with content teachers and assuming responsibility for assessment and instruction of struggling readers. What is clear is that from the perspective of building administrators, reading specialists' major responsibilities are diagnostic testing in reading and the provision of remedial reading instruction.

Classroom teachers had very different expectations for reading specialists (Maleki & Herman, 1994; Tancock, 1995). Unlike building administrators, who viewed the reading specialists' major responsibilities as assessment and instruction, middle and secondary teachers expected the reading specialist to function as a specialized resource person or as a consultant, while elementary classroom teachers viewed the reading specialist as a support person. Although these two studies had small sample sizes, they do highlight how expectations for the role differ.

Although remedial instruction was identified as very important in several of the previously mentioned studies, closer observation of actual practice indicates that remedial instruction may not differ much from typical classroom instruction. Gelzheiser and Meyers (1991) observed 48 teachers in six elementary schools. Remedial reading teachers, rather than spending more time on research-based instructional reading practices than classroom teachers, spent the same amount of time on purpose setting, modeling, giving information, and emphasizing how to complete a task or activity. In addition, the classroom teachers and reading specialists put similar emphases on comprehension, phonics, and indirect reading activities. In effect, classroom teachers and reading specialists divided their time equally and in similar ways among nonreading activities, proactive instruction, student participation, and reaction to student work, thus resulting in similar systems of remedial and developmental instruction.

Observation and interviews of three reading specialists revealed that they assumed many tasks beyond instruction (Tancock, 1995). For example, reading specialists joined local reading councils, stayed after school to talk to teachers, served on school committees, wrote grants, taught university classes, read aloud in classrooms, and reinforced skills taught in the regular classroom. In addition, interviews revealed that these specialists all realized they needed to make concessions in order to have good working relationships with the classroom teachers. Classroom teachers and reading specialists viewed the role of the reading specialist differently. The classroom teachers viewed the reading specialist as a support person, while the reading specialists viewed themselves as resource persons who shared information and gave teachers feedback on student progress. Further, all classroom teachers believed that the reading specialist and the classroom teacher needed to coordinate instruction.

In a statewide study conducted to discuss issues concerning Title I reading programs and the elements that made certain programs effective, one of the issues that focus groups addressed was the role of the reading specialist (Bean, Trovato, & Hamilton, 1995). Focus group meetings were held across the state with reading specialists, classroom teachers, and principals. Reading specialists indicated that they had many different roles and responsibilities: instructor, developer of materials, provider of staff development, and consultant. As instructors, they had many responsibilities that went beyond providing specialized instruction to Title I children; specifically, they believed they served as advocates for students and had an important responsibility to enhance student self-esteem and motivate students to learn.

Members of all focus groups agreed that the role of the reading specialist should be determined by student needs. Of concern to all groups was the development of positive collaborative relationships between classroom teachers and reading specialists. Classroom teachers viewed the specialist as someone who could help them plan instruction. Although teaming with classroom teachers was perceived as the most important role for the reading specialist, this was the role the specialists felt least prepared to fulfill (Bean, Trovato, & Hamilton, 1995).

As mentioned previously, one of the contributing factors to the change in the role of reading specialists seems to be the recent change in Title I guidelines, because Title I provides sources of funding for a large percentage of reading specialists in schools. Specifically, the initiation of schoolwide programs in schools in which 75% or more of the students are from low-income families generally requires a change in the role of the reading specialist. Because *all* students in these schools are eligible to receive instruction from the reading specialist, often these programs represent a shift away from pullout programs; yet schools do not appear to be including reading specialists in the classrooms where students need extra help learning to read (Long, 1995a). Although schoolwide program changes seem at first to be more comprehensive and thus potentially a more effective use of Title I funds, problems for students having difficulty learning to read persist. Indeed, in studying the long-term effects of Title I schoolwide projects in 40 elementary schools, researchers compared the achievement levels of first through fifth graders in schoolwide and nonschoolwide settings (Winfield & Hawkins, 1993). The results call into question the effectiveness of schoolwide projects. First graders in all classrooms performed the same regardless of setting. Third graders in schoolwide projects did less well than third graders in nonschoolwide projects, and the differences in the achievement levels of fourth and fifth graders were not statistically significant. The only group that performed better in a schoolwide project was the second graders. In these schoolwide projects there appeared to be a tendency to hire fewer reading specialists and rely more heavily on classroom teachers. Perhaps the core of the problem is that there are varying and frequently minimal state requirements for the amount of preparation in reading instruction for classroom teachers. In fact, Market Data Retrieval (1997) and *Education Week* (Manzo & Sack, 1997) have reported that in most cases classroom teachers need only one or two courses in reading to satisfy elementary teacher certification requirements.

To summarize, the data on the roles and responsibilities of reading specialists indicate that they have traditionally assumed many important responsibilities. The evidence also shows that the roles of reading specialists are perceived differently by different professionals. Reading specialists tend to view themselves as individuals who provide specialized instruction, administer formal assessments, and communicate with teachers and parents. In addition, many specialists organize and administer school reading programs, assume administrative duties, are a resource for teachers, provide formal teacher inservice, and are student advocates. Classroom teachers and administrators, however, tend to view reading specialists as support personnel—there to "lend a hand," so to speak, to the larger, developmental program of reading instruction. Although reading specialists tend to have a broad view of their own potential roles (i.e., instructor, resource person, administrator), classroom teachers seem to be more concerned about responsibilities that have a direct impact on their own classrooms; classroom teachers want to decide the way support is offered. Thus, the reading specialist has a complex position that necessitates juggling many responsibilities, from serving as an instructor of struggling readers to assuming a leadership position in schools.

Influence of Context

The roles that reading specialists assume depend on the context of instruction. Context includes the people with whom the reading specialists work (i.e., classroom teachers and their expectations) and the setting or location of the work (i.e., pullout or in-class settings).

Many Title I reading programs are moving toward in-class models where the reading specialist works in the classroom along with the classroom teacher. In examining data from the years 1985–1992 gathered by the Blue Ribbon School Recognition Program of the U.S. Department of Education, Kletzien (1996) reported that schools were moving toward an in-class model of instruction. Follow-up observations and school self-reports supported this conclusion. Such a change may in and of itself determine the expectations for the reading specialist. Considering Tancock's (1995) findings that reading specialists adapted their roles to individual teacher's expectations when operating in an in-class model, classroom teachers may well be in a powerful position for influencing what the reading specialist does or does not do.

Because settings are so important and diverse, specialists can become unsure of their role. In the previously discussed Bean et al. study (1995), specialists felt that the many changes in Title I guidelines tended to make their role a constantly evolving one. Perhaps even more important, setting changes and mandates may create situations where specialists have little voice in determining their own roles and responsibilities critical to the success of students in need.

Results of a study by Hamilton (1993), which documented the instruction and practices of two exemplary reading specialists in an in-class model, indicated that these specialists were most effective in a student advocate role; that is, relaying important information to classroom teachers about their students. The advocacy role seemed to result from the specialists' sensitivity to, and deep knowledge of, the personal and academic needs of their students. Their philosophies reflected strong convictions about the ability of remedial students to succeed, and they asserted that student advocacy was one of their primary responsibilities.

The classroom teacher's role was viewed as responsibility for comprehensive instruction of the class as a whole. The reading specialist's role, however, was viewed as a combination of advocate for and instructor of individual students, interacting with students in a way that appeared effective in boosting confidence within an instructional context. As such, when reading specialists have both the option and control to choose their own roles, they may well provide an additional or perhaps absent source of encouragement and commitment to the success of individual students in critical need.

Support for specialists assuming a student advocate role is found in previously cited focus group research (Bean et al., 1995) investigating the aspects of effective Title I programs. In that investigation, reading specialists, classroom teachers, and principals were asked to identify some of the most important benefits of Title I programs. All three groups agreed that when specialists assumed a student advocacy role, they were making one of the most important contributions to the potential success of low-achieving students. Professionals in that study indicated that specialists were sometimes able to prevent teachers from penalizing students who could not do assigned work due to reading difficulties, and that they provided insights into the reasons individual students were experiencing difficulty.

In a study on the effects of setting on the remedial reading program, researchers (Bean, Cooley, Eichelberger, Lazar, & Zigmond, 1991) noted the effects on the role of the reading specialist in the pullout and the in-class setting. In the pullout setting, reading specialists assumed the role of instructor. In the in-class setting the reading specialists functioned as monitors or tutors. There were greater amounts of time when the reading specialist had no direct interaction with students in in-class settings. The reading specialists worked with students after the classroom teacher completed group lessons, generally helping students finish assignments. In this in-class setting the reading specialists spent larger amounts of time on skill workbooks and worksheets. In some cases the instructional material was too difficult for the students, and then the specialists would help students complete this work. When performing this function, the reading specialists helped children deal with the difficult material and reinforced what the classroom teacher had taught.

The researchers noted that the reading specialists had to find ways of working with the classroom teachers and had to accommodate their teaching to the approaches of the classroom teachers. The in-class setting was a challenge for the reading specialists because they had to follow the lead of the classroom teacher and because they felt they were not always meeting the instructional needs of students.

In a later study, where training in collaboration was provided, researchers observed the interactions between classroom teachers and reading specialist interns and identified five types of collaborative teaching: major/assisting, supportive, station, parallel instruction, and team teaching (Bean, Grumet, & Bulazo, 1999). In *major/assisting teaching* one teacher is responsible for instruction, while the other teacher serves as an assistant. In *supportive teaching* one teacher is responsible for instruction to the whole class, while the other teacher works with individuals or small groups. In *station teaching* students participate in stations or learning centers where activities have been planned for them. Each teacher assumes responsibility for one or more stations. *Parallel instruction* is described as each teacher teaching the same content to different groups, while *team teaching* has two teachers sharing the teaching of one lesson. During interviews, the interns and the teachers agreed that for collaboration to be effective there needed to be good communication, flexibility, respect, and trust. They also agreed that for two parties to collaborate effectively in the classroom, they needed to have similar philosophies concerning instruction and classroom management.

Constraints on the role of the reading specialist can also come from influences such as state and school policies and from students themselves. In comparing one reading specialist's instruction at the third-grade level and the seventh-grade level, researchers found differences. At the third-grade level the reading specialist found it necessary to prepare students for state and district mandated testing. At the seventh-grade level, student attitudes toward reading tended to influence instruction (Davis & Wilson, 1999).

In summary, the responsibilities assumed by reading specialists differed a great deal depending on context. Reading specialists who pulled students out tended to provide specialized instruction (often remedial), while reading specialists working in the classroom assumed many more responsibilities, from serving as aides or monitors to providing specialized instruction to serving as coteachers.

Do Reading Specialists Make a Difference?

It is difficult to find research that provides a direct link between the existence of reading specialists and reading achievement in the schools, yet researchers looking at effective reading programs and attempting to determine the qualities that ensure program success most often indicate the need for well-prepared professionals in reading. Wasik and Slavin (1993) reviewed five special programs that attempted to prevent early reading failure by providing one-to-one tutoring: Reading Recovery, Success for All, Prevention of Learning Disabilities, Wallach Tutoring Program, and Programmed Tutorial Reading. After reviewing the five programs, the researchers concluded that programs using highly prepared teachers had a more positive impact on student reading achievement than programs that used paraprofessionals. To be even minimally effective, a program must provide for the improvement of instruction. Highly trained professionals in reading have the judgment, flexibility, and knowledge of children's learning to provide for this high-quality instruction.

In a later review of several other effective school-based early intervention programs including Success for All, Winston-Salem Project, Boulder Project, Early Intervention in Reading Project, and Reading Recovery, it was noted that all used experienced, certified teachers. Several of the programs had teachers specially trained in reading instruction, and in the programs where aides were used, those aides were closely supervised by certified teachers. The conclusion of this review was that successful early intervention programs were taught by knowledgeable teachers who had been professionally prepared (Pikulski, 1994).

Spiegel (1995) analyzed the existing observational research in traditional remedial classrooms, specifically Chapter 1 programs, and in the Reading Recovery program. She cited the fact that in many remedial programs the students who need the best instruction often receive the worst instruction. In addition she noted the practice of using aides, who may or may not be trained, to deliver instruction to children who are experiencing difficulty in learning to read. She recommended that "Children most at risk should be taught by the best teachers" (p. 94).

The Connecticut Association for Reading Research (Klein, Monti, Mulcahy-Ernt, & Speck, 1997) surveyed principals who reported that 36% of the personnel providing remedial instruction in Title I programs were not certified in reading/language arts. In the schools without personnel certified in reading/language arts, personnel providing remedial services included volunteers, aides, and peer tutors. One disturbing trend seems to be that instead of reading specialists, persons with the least amount of preparation in reading typically work with the neediest and most challenging children. Also, in this same study, it was found that schools with certified language arts consultants (reading specialists) had higher achievement scores than comparable schools without such personnel.

Indeed, according to the Market Data Retrieval report (1997), states that have above average proficiency scores according to the 1994 National

Assessment of Educational Progress Reading Report are also the states with the highest percentage of reading specialists. However, according to the same report, only 26% of the schools in the United States have certified reading specialists. Although there may be other factors influencing this relationship, these data provide information that raises questions about whether we are providing the well-prepared professionals needed in the schools, and about the need for additional research that links the presence of reading specialists with student achievement.

The importance of reading specialists is underscored by the results of a questionnaire sent to the principals of schools identified as having exemplary reading programs (Bean, Knaub, & Swan, 2000). These principals reported that "the presence of reading specialists was critical to the success of the reading program, with 97.4% of the principals indicating that specialists were important to very important" (p. 1).

In summary, effective programs tend to have personnel well prepared to teach reading, who may or may not be reading specialists. Further, programs that have professionals with the strongest backgrounds in the teaching of reading have the highest success rates. Therefore it appears critical that professionals with extensive knowledge of reading instruction be part of every classroom where there are students who need help learning to read.

How Specialists Should Function

The literature includes recommendations for ways that reading specialists can and should function. Jaeger (1996) and Henwood (1999/2000), both reading specialists, described how the reading specialist can assume the role of a collaborative consultant through her or his impact on curriculum development, instructional problem solving, and parent liaison work. For example, as a collaborative consultant, the reading specialist can offer resources to teachers, give personal suggestions, engage in demonstration teaching, do team teaching, and provide ongoing staff development.

Likewise, Vacca and Padak (1990) recommended that reading specialists develop collaborative relationships with classroom teachers. In addition, reading specialists need to develop good listening skills and pool their expertise with that of classroom teachers. These relationships are necessary, as the classroom teacher and the reading specialist share ownership for each child's success in reading.

Another recommendation (Margolis, Denny, & Hollander, 1994) is that reading specialists be part of multidisciplinary teams so that their assessment expertise can be used in the area of diagnosis and also to devise appropriate instructional strategies. Margolis et al. suggested that because so many of the children referred to the school psychologist have reading problems, reading specialists are the personnel who are most equipped to design and implement focused instruction and to lend support to teachers. They also discuss the fact that reading specialists are the most familiar with formative evaluation procedures and thus able to conduct in-depth comprehensive evaluations of the reading and writing abilities of referred children.

Similarly, reading specialists and federal coordinators (Bean, Trovato, Armitage, Bryant, & Dugan, 1993) highlighted the importance of communication and collaborative skills along with strong leadership skills if individuals are to function successfully as reading specialists. They recommended that programs for preparing reading specialists begin to provide practice in school-based settings, so specialists will be prepared to assume these new roles. Although the clinical practicum usually conducted at the university was thought to be valuable because it provided opportunities for specialists to work intensively with one or two students, reading specialists and federal coordinators both felt that a school-based practicum would provide further experience with activities such as serving as a member of an instructional support team; communicating with parents, teachers, and administrators; and serving as a resource to classroom teachers.

Interestingly, a survey of U.S. state legislators found that 70.5% used their personal contacts with specialists in the field of reading when they wished to be informed about current issues in reading education (Reutzel, Hollingsworth, & Cox, 1996). This survey provided legislators with 15 information sources and asked whether a respondent had or had not used the information source within the last year. Respondents were then asked to rank the usefulness of each source. These legislators indicated that specialists in the field were their most helpful source of information because of the limited time legislators had to accomplish what was expected of them in their role.

Responsibilities

Given the evidence found in the review of research, we conclude that reading specialists' roles may include six major responsibilities: instruction, assessment, leadership, resource/consultant, collaborator, and student advocate. The

Figure is a graphic representation of roles discussed or investigated in the research and literature. It provides a useful tool for reading specialists for thinking about their positions or for teacher educators who are responsible for planning and preparing programs for reading specialists.

When thinking about instruction, the reading specialist must consider where and how much instruction will take place and what the focus of such instruction will be. When considering assessment, the reading specialist must

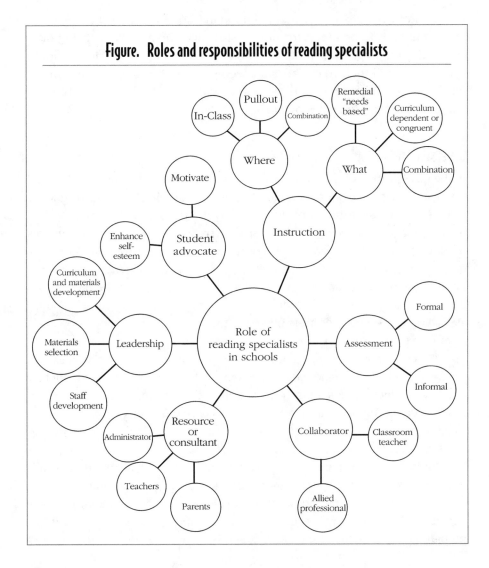

Figure. Roles and responsibilities of reading specialists

decide when to use formal or informal assessment and how to link it to instruction. As a collaborator, the reading specialist must find ways to work effectively with classroom teachers and other professionals. When serving as a resource person, the reading specialist must work with parents, teachers, and administrators. Leadership on the part of the reading specialist can involve staff development, the selection of materials, and curriculum development. As a student advocate, the reading specialist must find ways to motivate and enhance students' self-esteem.

Each of these responsibilities is important; however, the major responsibility continues to be the instruction of students who are experiencing difficulty with reading. Over time, there has been some shift in how reading specialists fulfill their role. This shift seems to be related to changes in the guidelines for Title I funding because the position of reading specialist is often funded by this federal program.

Diversity and Complexity of Roles

In the past, instruction for students experiencing reading difficulties was based upon student needs, often identified through the administration of diagnostic tests. At the present time, instruction is more often focused on helping students manage or succeed in the classroom, based on the belief that students need to experience a congruent, coordinated reading program. More frequently, instruction by reading specialists occurs within the classroom setting rather than in pullout settings, which demands that specialists be more proficient in working with another adult (Bean, Cassidy, Grumet, Shelton, & Wallis, 1999). Thus, reading specialists need communication and collaboration skills to effectively instruct students experiencing difficulties within multiple contexts. In conclusion, it is not that the major role of the reading specialist (assessing and instructing students with reading difficulties) has changed, but that the way in which the role must be accomplished has changed. It is this change that has created tension and anxiety for some reading specialists as well as for classroom teachers who also must deal with changes in their own teaching practices (Bean, Trovato, & Hamilton, 1995).

Furthermore, given the emphasis on congruence and alignment, the reading specialists' role has become more complex. The specialists must adjust to classroom teachers' expectations and demands as well as meet their own expectations for how they should perform. Reading specialists often feel unprepared to assume this responsibility, and in some cases may be unprepared to handle the complexity of working not only with students with difficulties, but also with difficult teachers.

Influence of Context

Because of recommended changes in how reading programs for students at risk are delivered (schoolwide programs, early intervention, inclusion), there have also been changes in the personnel working with these students. In some schools the position of reading specialist has been eliminated, and reading specialists have been asked to assume classroom teacher positions. In other instances, paraprofessionals and other personnel without strong backgrounds in reading have been asked to assist classroom teachers in instructing students. This occurrence, again, has created a tension for individuals who have seen themselves as the primary teachers for students with difficulty reading.

The role of the reading specialist—resource to teachers, administrator or leader of the reading program, supervisor of paraprofessionals—differs depending on the specific job description or context as well as on the competencies of the individual. More respected and competent reading specialists are more likely to find themselves in a leadership or resource role.

Effect of the Reading Specialist

The literature seems clear that instruction, to be effective, must be delivered by well-prepared professionals. Professionals with extensive knowledge of reading instruction can and do make a difference. These professionals may not always have a "certificate," but they do have the specialized expertise that makes them specialists in reading. There is certainly a need for continued research in this area, especially about the effects of reading specialists on students' achievement.

In summary, although reading specialists have many different responsibilities, a major role seems to be the assessment and instruction of students with reading difficulties. The other aspects of their role differ depending on the context in which they find themselves. The new configurations for meeting the needs of at-risk students demand that specialists know more than how to teach students, however. They require reading specialists who are able to collaborate and communicate effectively—who can work effectively with other adults in the school, not only classroom teachers but special educators, parents, and administrators. Well-prepared professionals can make a difference. The quality of that difference rests upon clearly understood and communicated professional roles and instructional practices that are grounded in current research. Thus, reading specialists—not just reading programs—hold enormous potential for effecting the education of students.

Implications

The results of this review of research and literature provide information that may be useful for various constituencies by providing some guidelines and recommendations for how reading specialists, classroom teachers, administrators, and teacher educators might work together.

Reading Specialists

Reading specialists need to become more aware of the complex nature of their positions, which requires that they assume not only an instructional role but also one that demands collaboration with classroom teachers, other allied professionals, and parents. Perhaps reading specialists within a district or even across districts need to establish a network that will enable them to share successful strategies for broadening their roles.

Classroom Teachers

Without the support and cooperation of classroom teachers, the reading specialist will have a difficult job. Thus, any professional development efforts should involve classroom teachers so that they are aware of the various tasks that reading specialists can assume. At the same time, such professional development efforts should reflect the importance of quality classroom teaching and emphasize how classroom teachers and reading specialists can work collaboratively to improve students' literacy performance.

Administrators

District and school administrators will be able to make maximum use of the reading specialist if they have an understanding of the position's multiple roles. Scheduling classes so that reading specialists and classroom teachers have opportunities to plan and interact is a key responsibility of administrators. Reading specialists also need the support of administrators so that they will feel more comfortable in working with teachers in a collaborative manner.

Teacher Educators

Any programs developed for preparing reading specialists must be broad enough to encompass multiple tasks and responsibilities. Initial requirements for teaching experience and good interpersonal skills must be emphasized. Programs need to include experiences that will assure that reading specialists have the necessary knowledge and understanding of literacy; at the same time, experiences that assist reading specialists in building their leadership and consultant skills must be included in the program.

Recommendations for Research

This review of the research and literature also provides helpful information regarding the need for additional research. The paucity of empirical research related to the role of the reading specialist was striking. Although there are data from studies in which reading specialists and others affected by their performance are interviewed, these self-reports provide information about perceptions of these participants only. There seems to be a need for more observational studies that follow reading specialists as they perform their roles. How do effective specialists function in various settings and in different contexts? How do they handle difficult situations when working in in-class settings? To what extent do they assume leadership responsibilities in the school? Moreover, there is certainly a need for more study of the effectiveness of reading specialists. What makes an effective reading specialist? Do specialists make a difference in the reading performance of students and, if so, why? Just as researchers have studied the role of the principal as an important factor in school achievement, so, too, should educational researchers investigate the relationship between the role of the reading specialist and the effectiveness of the school reading program.

REFERENCES

Barclay, K.D., & Thistlewaite, L. (1992). Reading specialists of the 90's: Who are they and what do they want? *Reading Research and Instruction, 32*, 87–96.

Barry, A.L. (1997). High school reading programs revisited. *Journal of Adolescent & Adult Literacy, 40*, 524–531.

Bean, R.M., Cassidy, J., Grumet, J., Shelton, D., & Wallis, S. (1999). *The role of the reading specialist: A national survey.* Unpublished manuscript, University of Pittsburgh, Pittsburgh, PA.

Bean, R.M., Cooley, W.W., Eichelberger, R.T., Lazar, M.K., & Zigmond, N. (1991). Inclass or pullout: Effects of setting on the remedial reading program. *Journal of Reading Behavior, 23*, 445–464.

Bean, R.M., Grumet, J.V., & Bulazo, J. (1999). Learning from each other: Collaboration between classroom teachers and reading specialist interns. *Reading Research and Instruction, 38*, 273–287.

Bean, R.M., Knaub, R., & Swan, A. (2000, April). *Reading specialists in exemplary schools.* Paper presented at the 45th International Reading Association convention, Indianapolis, IN.

Bean, R.M., Trovato, C.A., Armitage, A., Bryant, J., & Dugan, J. (1993). *Preparing reading specialists for Pennsylvania schools—Year 2000* (Tech. Rep.). Pittsburgh, PA: Institute for Practice and Research in Education, University of Pittsburgh.

Bean, R.M., Trovato, C.A., & Hamilton, R. (1995). Focus on Chapter 1 reading programs: Views of reading specialists, classroom teachers, and principals. *Reading Research and Instruction, 34*, 204–221.

Davis, M.M., & Wilson, E.K. (1999). A Title I teacher's beliefs, decision-making, and instruction at the third and seventh grade levels. *Reading Research and Instruction, 38*, 289–300.

Gelzheiser, L.M., & Meyers, J. (1991). Reading instruction by classroom, remedial, and resource room teachers. *Journal of Special Education, 24*, 512–526.

Hamilton, R.L. (1993). *Chapter 1 reading instruction: Exemplary reading specialists in an inclass model.* Unpublished doctoral dissertation, University of Pittsburgh, Pittsburgh, PA.

Henwood, G.F. (1999/2000). A new role for the reading specialist: Contributing toward a high school's collaborative educational culture. *Journal of Adolescent & Adult Literacy, 43*, 316–325.

Hoffman, J.V., Baumann, J.F., Moon, C., & Duffy, G.G. (1997). *U.S. elementary reading instruction survey.* Athens, GA: University of Georgia, National Reading Research Center.

International Reading Association. (1998). *Standards for reading professionals* (revised). Newark, DE: Author.

Jaeger, E.L. (1996). The reading specialist as collaborative consultant. *The Reading Teacher, 49*, 622–629.

Klein, J., Monti, D., Mulcahy-Ernt, P., & Speck, A. (1997). *Reading/language arts programs and personnel in Connecticut schools: Summary report.* Hartford, CT: Connecticut Association for Reading Research Report.

Kletzien, S.B. (1996). Reading programs in nationally recognized elementary schools. *Reading Research and Instruction, 35*, 260–274.

Long, R. (1995a, August/September). Preserving the role of the reading specialist. *Reading Today*, p. 6.

Long, R. (1995b, October/November). New IRA issue paper stresses need for reading professionals. *Reading Today*, p. 6.

Maleki, R.B., & Herman, C.E. (1994). What do rural middle-secondary teachers expect of reading programs and reading specialists? *Reading Improvement, 31*, 101–106.

Manzo, K.K., & Sack, J.L. (1997, February 26). Teacher training seen key to improving reading in early grades. *Education Week*, p. 28.

Margolis, H., Denny, V.H., & Hollander, S.K. (1994). Reading specialists: A valuable resource for serving special education students. *Special Services in the Schools, 9,* 185–206.

Market Data Retrieval. (1997). *Are elementary schools staffed to meet the reading challenge?* Skelton, CT: Author.

Pikulski, J.J. (1994). Preventing reading failure: A review of five effective programs. *The Reading Teacher, 48,* 30–39.

Reutzel, D.R., Hollingsworth, P.M., & Cox, S.A.V. (1996). Issues in reading instruction: U.S. state legislators' perceptions and knowledge. *Reading Research and Instruction, 35,* 343–364.

Snow, C.E., Burns, M.S., & Griffin, P. (Eds.). (1998). *Preventing reading difficulties in young children.* Washington, DC: National Academy Press.

Spiegel, D.L. (1995). A comparison of traditional remedial programs and Reading Recovery: Guidelines for success for all programs. *The Reading Teacher, 49,* 86–96.

Tancock, S.M. (1995). Classroom teachers and reading specialists examine their Chapter 1 reading programs. *Journal of Reading Behavior, 27,* 315–335.

Vacca, J.L., & Padak, N.D. (1990). Reading consultants as classroom collaborators: An emerging role. *Journal of Educational and Psychological Consultation, 1,* 99–107.

Wasik, B.A., & Slavin, R.E. (1993). Preventing early reading failure with one-to-one tutoring: A review of five programs. *Reading Research Quarterly, 28,* 178–200.

Winfield, L.F., & Hawkins, R. (1993). *Longitudinal effects of Chapter 1 schoolwide projects on the achievement of disadvantaged students.* Baltimore: Center for Research on Effective Schooling for Disadvantaged Students. (ERIC Document Reproduction Service No. ED366671)

Finding the Keys to Educational Progress in Urban Youth: Three Case Studies

Susan Babbitt and Maureen Byrne

Teaching 13-year-olds can be difficult, for they live in a precarious world of transition, straddling childhood and adolescence. When these students have reading or academic problems, teaching becomes even more complicated. Working with urban teenagers who have social or emotional issues caused by life stresses as well as learning problems presents a particularly difficult challenge.

What follows are case studies of three different 13-year-olds, clients of an urban multidisciplinary mental health agency, who participated in the agency's after-school individualized reading program. The students have all been given pseudonyms. For these students, emotional stresses have greatly interfered with their learning and educational progress. What will be shown are the successes and failures that occurred with these students during the course of nine months of tutoring, as their life stresses continued to affect their educational lives.

Diego: Man of the Family

Diego was in a self-contained sixth-grade special education class for severely learning-disabled students. He had been in special education since the second grade. He was the oldest boy in a household of five cared for by his mother, a single parent. Charming and sweet, sporting a loopy grin and a diamond stud in his left ear, Diego was earnest and reasonably motivated once engaged. He could generally be counted on to work consistently without interruption for up to 30 minutes. The key was to get him to show up for the sessions.

Marisol: Teenage Sophisticate

Marisol was in a regular seventh-grade class, homogeneously grouped to include all seventh graders in her school who read below the 10th percentile as measured by previous citywide testing. She received special education instruction in the form of daily Resource Room teaching. Marisol was very attractive and

Originally published in *Journal of Adolescent & Adult Literacy* (1999/2000), volume 43, pages 368–378.

looked older than her 13 years. She became depressed as a child, and that depression had been made worse by the death of her young mother in the past year. Marisol lived in a household of nine children held together by a strong maternal grandmother who emigrated from Puerto Rico as a young woman and managed to bring a number of family members to the mainland United States. Marisol came to every session. The key was to get her to do anything.

Lynette: Scholarship Student

Lynette was in the eighth grade at an expensive independent school. On scholarship from the school and the agency, she had attended private school since the third grade. Gaps in her knowledge and certain organizational difficulties had become more apparent in the sixth grade, and Lynette had been receiving tutoring at the agency since the seventh grade. Tall for her age and substantially overweight, Lynette stood out at school for her size, for her socioeconomic level, and for being African American. Lynette had carried adult responsibilities in her family for years. She came to every session and was generally motivated. The key was to give her enough foundation so that her potential was not sapped and depleted by family concerns and crises.

Diverse Students, Common Themes

While these students had very different academic and learning needs, there were, nonetheless, some common themes. All three were at that critical developmental stage that occurs during the middle school years, when adolescents' belief in their own competence may decline (Harter, Whitesell, & Kowlaski, 1992). Indeed, researchers suggest the stakes are even higher for students with multiple problems; they are at the greatest risk of dropping out of school during these years (Caldwell & Ginthier, 1996; Dunn & Griggs, 1988; Hobbs, 1990; Tuma, 1989).

Language was a factor for two of the three students. Diego and Marisol, both born in the United States, grew up in households where Spanish was spoken, although by their own admission they were not fluent in Spanish. More research needs to be done on the impact of this circumstance on literacy acquisition. Despite the growing multiculturalism of the United States, during the past 10 years only 3% of all literacy research has dealt with cultural or linguistic diversity, and less than 1% of the children's literature produced annually features Latino families or communities (Jiménez, Moll, Rodríguez-Brown, & Barrera, 1999).

For each of the three students motivation was an issue, although in different ways. Two of the three students displayed little evidence of what researchers have called "intrinsic" motivation, or motivation internal to the learner (Deci, Vallerand, Pelletier, & Ryan, 1991; Sweet & Guthrie, 1996; Wigfield, 1994). Yet we know from past research that this is necessary in order for children to employ strategies for processing text beyond the literal level (Guthrie, Alao, & Rinehart, 1997).

For Diego and Marisol, motivation was essentially extrinsic; that is, it was imposed on them from someone or for something outside themselves, resulting in *compliance* motivation (Sweet & Guthrie, 1996). For example, Diego was in serious trouble in school, failing all his subjects. His mother, who had an intense concern for Diego's education and learning, insisted with the support of the family social worker that Diego attend the reading sessions (Baumann & Thomas, 1997). Marisol was not failing in school, but her attendance at the agency was mandated by her grandmother, who recognized Marisol's need for multiple services. While Marisol may eventually rebel from this tight control, at this point in her life she had no choice.

In contrast, intrinsic motivation for educational achievement seemed a possible goal for Lynette. She had been rewarded for her own academic potential by being sent to a school where academic achievement was esteemed. However, living in a family with no previous experience with the intensity and competitiveness of a college-preparatory school made it difficult for her to nurture and sustain inner motivation. As will be shown, nurturing that inner motivation became a major objective of her educational plan.

Educational Plan for Diego

At the beginning of the academic year, Diego was assessed as being able to decode and comprehend at the third-grade level, using *Aesop's Stories for Pleasure Reading* (Dolch, Dolch, & Jackson, 1951) as text for an informal reading inventory. On the Surveys of Problem-Solving & Education Skills (SPES, 1986) his decoding score was comparable to that achieved on the informal assessment, but comprehension scores were even lower, presenting the instructor with a student scoring five or more years below grade level in reading.

Writing and spelling were also difficult for him. On a written personal questionnaire that he completed in September, Diego wrote "bih clos" for

"Buy clothes," "becas she nis" for "because she is nice," and "I get in fithet" for "I get in fights." His invented spelling suggests that despite some knowledge of the alphabetic code, Diego had difficulty retrieving commonly used words.

The educational plan for Diego noted his history of erratic attendance at previous educational activities at the agency. However, it was also observed that he seemed to respond well to incentives. That, coupled with his apparent eagerness to please, was to be the linchpin in motivating him to attend regularly.

A clear statement of attendance standards and the firm willingness of the teacher to apply them were critical components of Diego's treatment plan. His family life suffered from a severe lack of order and consistency. Diego had spent several years in foster care as the result of his mother's substance abuse behavior. His father had been incarcerated and subsequently deported to Ecuador. His 21-year-old sister lived in the household but without her four children, all of whom had been placed in foster care. Diego's younger brother was dying of a lung disease. Diego's mother, free of drugs for several years, was struggling to hold the family together.

The tutor determined that Diego would need a structured, skills-based educational approach. He had severe problems at the word level that prevented him from reading connected text and utilizing comprehension strategies. Fast and accurate word recognition is related to proficient reading as well as skillful reading comprehension and was deemed essential for Diego's progress (Adams, 1990; Perfetti, 1985; Stanovich, Cunningham, & Freeman, 1984). Further, despite the fact that 75% of students master the alphabetic code without explicit instruction (Liberman, Shankweiler, & Liberman, 1989), Diego obviously had difficulty automatically applying it to text.

Mastery of specific high-frequency words thus became the criterion for the initial contracts between teacher and student. Diego was to receive prizes for being able to read, write, and spell correctly words in isolation and in sentences. The use of such extrinsic rewards would do little beyond encouraging student compliance, and the instructional methodology was clearly rudimentary, yet the instructor viewed this as a necessary first step in order to motivate Diego to attend the sessions (Sweet & Guthrie, 1996).

The ability to spell the word in a sentence was an important, and more difficult, part of the task. At issue was Diego's ability to process two or more cognitive demands simultaneously. Students with language difficulties present a challenge for the instructor in terms of both the manner and timing in which multiple pieces of verbal information are presented (Bryant, 1980).

As instruction proceeded, certain things became clear. For one thing, the highly structured nature of the task was very appealing to Diego. The predictable nature of the sessions provided a contrast to the unpredictability of his family life, which was dominated by the health problems of the younger brother and the erratic behavior of the oldest sister. Also, he was able to achieve some successes each week, as he made his way through the list of words. For this reason, the goal and the reward seemed reasonable, attainable, and sufficiently challenging (Turner, 1997). Through the end of October, he had missed only one session, and that was an excused absence.

As Diego was making relatively good progress in learning to read and spell the high-frequency words, it was also necessary to ensure that he was reading connected text at his instructional level and given practice applying decoding skills as one of many strategies when encountering difficult material. For a while, he and the teacher read short fables from *Aesop's Stories for Pleasure Reading* (Dolch et al., 1951). Diego was able to comprehend the stories, as measured by his ability to retell them, make accurate predictions, or answer inferential questions. His oral reading, however, remained slow and deliberate, and time limits precluded the application of strategies such as repeated readings (Morris, Ervin, & Conrad, 1996; Samuels, 1979).

During this period, new high-frequency words were being introduced. By the middle of December, Diego seemed less interested in working for specific prizes, but still continued to work diligently at learning his words, a sign that his motivation was becoming more intrinsic. It appeared that this activity managed to advance but not overwhelm Diego's abilities (Turner, 1997). Also, Diego's decreasing need for prizes confirmed our belief that while extrinsic rewards are initially helpful in getting students to do a difficult task, these rewards become less necessary as social interaction and satisfaction with task completion take over (Sweet & Guthrie, 1996).

Unfortunately, Diego's attendance became more problematic at this time. While his absences were usually excused and were occasioned by health problems in the family, they nonetheless interfered with the momentum that had been building. Even worse, Diego received his report card showing he was failing every subject. Ultimately, we agreed upon a system that required Diego to remember his appointments by means of notes he put up in his apartment. The importance of making Diego responsible for getting to sessions and assuming ownership of his own learning was considered integral to a successful outcome (Au, Schen, Kawakami, & Herman, 1990).

For the next several months, Diego's attendance was perfect, and his punctuality, while still somewhat problematic, did improve. During this period, lessons focused less on skills work and more on high-interest, contextual reading (for example, a book about snakes that he chose). The use of such integrated instruction, unifying reading, writing, and science, as well as student-directed material, aided in the gradual development of Diego's intrinsic motivation and his investment in the lessons (Guthrie et al., 1997; Sweet & Guthrie, 1996).

Over the course of the sessions, Diego's tutor noticed that he learned concepts more completely when information was initially presented to him in concrete fashion. Thus, wherever possible, he and the tutor would act out things to understand the content. For example, the notion of comparative sizes of various snakes became more meaningful to Diego when he and the instructor actually paced off together the lengths of a boa, an anaconda, and a python.

By mid-March, Diego was making progress in his tutoring sessions. He was, however, continuing to have difficulties in school, as his brother's medical condition worsened and his sister's problems escalated. In spite of these stressors, for the remaining two months of the school term Diego was reasonably on time and missed only a few sessions, always for legitimate reasons. During that time, the family moved into a new apartment away from the oldest daughter, and Diego's mother worked with her social worker to arrange a lung transplant for her youngest son.

At the start of the year, the biggest concern about Diego had been his willingness to attend after-school reading sessions. Establishing a contract between instructor and student and providing external rewards as an incentive both to come to sessions and to work while there proved to be effective in the beginning, but became increasingly less important as time went on. Rather, successful task completion and the need to connect with a stable and caring adult were proving to be strong motivators for Diego once he established a pattern of coming to his sessions. His overall yearly attendance was 80%.

Not all of the educational goals set for Diego at the beginning of the year were realized, and in some cases work was not even begun. Fortunately, though, slowing down does not mean stopping. In June, Diego again took the SPES test. While he continued to be markedly below grade level, his progress exceeded expectations, as he improved one grade level in decoding and three levels in comprehension.

In our view, a major reason for this improvement involved Diego's commitment to the tutoring and his desire to work to see if he could "get" it. What the nine months of tutoring seemed to have given him were less the specific skills and strategies, although they were certainly important, but more the confidence that he would be able to use those skills and strategies to make some sense out of printed text, which may have represented a shift in self-perception. Diego had, in fact, become "task-involved," assuming greater control over his own learning (Johnson & Winograd, 1985).

Diego's year was deemed a success. He had overcome his attendance problems, demonstrated improvement in his skills, and seemed to have made a commitment to "coming to reading." He graduated from the sixth grade and was accepted at an alternative junior high school with a special education seventh-grade class. He continued with the reading program at the agency for another year.

Educational Plan for Marisol

Marisol was reading at the third-grade level, four years below her grade placement. On the SPES (1987), she passed all sections at the third-grade level, able to process both isolated words and connected text.

Motivation for Marisol was hindered by two factors. For one thing, she perceived text that she was able to decode as much too childish. Also, her fragile emotional situation often interfered with her willingness to cooperate. Unlike Diego, she was moody and temperamental. She suffered from enuresis as well as depression. Although Diego did not have a father in the household, he did have a mother who cared deeply for him even though life stressors sometimes left her unable to carry out effective parenting. Marisol's much-loved mother had died at 27 years of age, after a lingering illness, when Marisol was 12 years old. In two years, Marisol would be the age that her mother had been when Marisol was born.

On the positive side, Marisol demonstrated a flair for fashion and style and expressed interest in pursuing a career as a hair stylist. Like many of her peers, Marisol was beginning to think about her future (Kos, 1991). If anything, her expectations were too low.

Unlike Diego, Marisol was able to write and spell with reasonable accuracy, albeit at a level much lower than her current grade. Her ability to decode unfamiliar words, however, was limited, fitting the profile of many severely disabled readers (Olson, Kliegl, Davidson, & Foltz, 1985; Vellutino, 1979). A psychoeducational evaluation done four years earlier indicated the existence of possible cognitive and memory limitations as well as problems with receptive language and verbal fluency. Such difficulties with language proficiency could be expected to have a negative effect on the acquisition of reading skills (Mather, 1992).

Given the severe delay in Marisol's reading skills, it was felt that, like Diego, she could benefit from at least a measure of structured, skills-based instruction. Research findings suggest, in fact, that severely disabled readers need direct instruction; they do not learn "by osmosis" (Haring & Bateman, 1997, p. 148). Glass analysis (Glass & Glass, 1976), an analytic decoding method, was felt to be one appropriate instructional tool. It was decided to use this method because it provides the older student with the opportunity to decode more sophisticated words sooner, rather than later, in the instructional process. For someone like Marisol, sophisticated in so many other ways, this aspect was important.

The Glass analysis words were also used to expand Marisol's limited vocabulary. She often did not know the meaning of the words she was decoding, such as *shabby, establish, brag, scold, brash, ignore,* and *editor.* While this was certainly not formalized vocabulary study and, in fact, is not consistent with the prescribed Glass methodology, it nonetheless served the purpose of providing discussions about language and increasing her knowledge of more complex vocabulary. Although Marisol often appeared depressed and remote during much of her sessions, she nonetheless responded reasonably well to the Glass analysis approach, meaning that she did not refuse to do the task.

Another goal for Marisol, that of reading a minimum amount of connected text each week, proved to be much more difficult. Over a four-week period several choices were tried from various popular book series, all of which were at her instructional level and would have been theoretically ideal books for teaching both comprehension and word attack skills. However, none were successful, and Marisol continued to essentially disengage herself from any part of the lesson that involved text reading. Possibly Marisol was defending herself from an activity that in the past had been fraught with failure and that she felt might erode her fragile sense of competence (Guthrie et al., 1997; Johnson & Winograd, 1985).

At this juncture the instructor decided to read aloud to Marisol with the goals of exposing her to more language and narrative structure and allowing her to employ many of the comprehension strategies used by good readers (Elley, 1989; Ivey, 1999). For a time, Marisol enjoyed listening to fairy tales from *A Treasury of Stories From H.C. Andersen* (Koralek, 1996). We have found that children referred to our clinic often prefer to work with fairy tales and magical stories. Possibly, these stories are removed from their own stresses yet describe conflict and difficulties that the characters must, and do, overcome (Bettleheim, 1977).

An unexpected benefit of the read-aloud strategy came when Marisol asked to read some of the text herself. Perhaps she was responding to the smaller type and more complex text, which appeared "older" than some of the children's series. Also, Marisol was not being required to read, only to listen. By deciding herself that she wanted to read, she was controlling the situation, rather than having an adult tell her what to do, something very important for young adolescents (Anders & Pritchard, 1993). Present research findings suggest that we can turn over some control to students while maintaining responsibility for flow and content (Pearson, 1996). For children who experience many traumas and uncertainties in life, such as Marisol, being able to control a situation becomes very important. Unfortunately, the success with this genre was short-lived. Marisol's depression made it difficult for her to sustain an interest in almost anything, a situation that had clear implications for her educational progress (Goleman, 1995).

Findings on what makes teachers effective suggest that the failure to adapt or to acknowledge students' feedback is characteristic of poor teaching (Babad, Bernieri, & Rosenthal, 1991; Wubbels, Creton, & Holvast, 1988). As a result of Marisol's resistance, it had become increasingly clear that if there were to be any success, the educational goals must be realistic and decided upon reciprocally. It was hoped that giving Marisol her own choice of reading material would result in increased comprehension and motivation (Andersen, Shirey, Wilson, & Fielding, 1987; Turner, 1997). However, Marisol's motivation remained fragile and volatile.

Ultimately, her teacher realized that her work with Marisol must somehow connect with those things in Marisol's life that were emotionally sustaining to her at the moment, and to which she would pay attention, if the teacher were going to be even moderately effective with her (King, 1985; Rissler & Steinberg, 1991). Remembering that Marisol had mentioned that she wanted to be a hair stylist, her teacher found several hair style magazines directed toward African American and Latina audiences. These magazines were interesting to Marisol and related to her needs (Farnan, 1996; Ivey, 1999). She was willing to try to read from them, even though the text presented certain problems. The language was relatively complex and occasionally metaphoric; the vocabulary sophisticated. However, this meant that short sections of text were filled with educational opportunities that Marisol did not resist.

The principal structured teaching activity that arose from the shared reading was vocabulary acquisition. Researchers have shown that direct instruction informs reading comprehension when new words can be integrated into already existing schema through a natural print environment (Beck &

McKeown, 1991; Harmon, 1998). Contextualized word study has been found to be particularly useful for students with verbal processing difficulties. Because some words recurred in many of the issues, Marisol was able to see them in use and reinforce her learning (Harmon, 1998).

Writing, too, was something Marisol was occasionally interested in. If included intermittently, at appropriate times, it proved to be a powerful instructional vehicle. To be successful, Marisol had to have a story she wanted to tell. During the nine months, this happened only once, but it enabled her teacher to work with her over five sessions, during which Marisol wrote, rewrote, and edited three drafts before completing her final version. Her motivation to tell this story was high. Because Marisol's expressive language was limited, the effort to produce the story was particularly valuable because she had to search, and re-search, her mind to find appropriate words. With each revision, as she would listen to her teacher read her words back to her, she found new things to say.

Unfortunately, this experience could not be duplicated. However, for a short period after this she became interested in writing poetry. Using *Honey, I Love* by Eloise Greenfield (1986) and *Spin a Soft Black Song* by Nikki Giovanni (1988), she wrote several poems modeled after their work. Provided with the structure and basic key words from individual poems by Greenfield and Giovanni, Marisol was able to create her own poems. Using the computer to write them in attractive fonts and with appropriate illustrations gave her a product that she could be proud of.

Ultimately, Marisol presented a major dilemma for the reading staff at the agency. Clearly in need of academic remediation, she had an attendance rate of well over 90% at her twice-weekly reading sessions. However, her engagement in the learning activities was erratic and often minimal. While she was not confrontational and seemed to have developed a reasonable relationship with the teacher, her depression and general neediness were severe enough to interfere greatly with her learning. With a waiting list of other children who needed remediation, what should be done with a student like Marisol on whom so much effort had been expended, with seemingly little result? The situation seemed to demand a sort of educational triage.

From a teaching perspective, the nine months of tutoring appeared relatively unproductive. To continue to work with her the next year seemed problematic. However, in Marisol's case, the benefits of an effective multidisciplinary approach became quite clear. What appeared to be problematic for the educational staff was viewed quite differently by the case psychologist. While the inherent difficulties were acknowledged, the bottom line consideration was whether *any* progress had been made during the nine months and whether Marisol *needed* the educational services. If so, then commitment to the client's well-being demanded ongoing remediation.

As it turned out, there was, indeed, some measure of progress. Marisol did show improvement on the informally administered SPES (1987) assessment, improving one grade level, from the third to the fourth, on one decoding and two comprehension subtests. She remained, however, four years below actual grade placement.

As the direct result of close and frank communication between educators and psychologists, a decision was made to continue Marisol in the reading program for one more year and to work collaboratively to ensure an appropriate high school placement for Marisol.

In what was a possible indication that the psychologists were right and the educators wrong, when Marisol heard the news that she had to "come to reading" again next year, she seemed pleased. Perhaps she realized that the teacher's educational choices for her throughout the year had been thoughtful and caring attempts to meet her inarticulated needs.

Educational Plan for Lynette

Unlike Diego and Marisol, Lynette did not have a reading disability. Instead, she was reading on grade level and attending a respected private school that was associated with a well-regarded graduate school of education. There were multiple goals for this plan: to assist Lynette with organizational skills such that she could successfully meet the high demands of five content areas, to support her unspoken appreciation of learning and knowledge, and to convince her that she had the ability to succeed on her own in a competitive academic environment.

While Lynette's intellectual ability had never been questioned, it had become clear that she needed help using that intellect to produce a consistent body of academic work that reflected it. Her homework was done erratically, usually during free periods at school. Assignments that were completed were often buried in a seemingly bottomless book bag. In general, her approach to the details of producing academic work was disorganized and unsystematic.

Many of these characteristics are familiar to those working with this age group. In some cases, maturation is all that is needed to effect a cure. In other cases, the lack of organization may be a lifelong trait, but not necessarily an impediment to success. In Lynette's case, however, a timely measure of academic success was critical in order to sustain her scholarship.

As a result, the need to teach organizational and study skills and to emphasize the importance of self-monitoring became critical components of Lynette's educational plan. As the year progressed, periodic "book bag checks" were made, and, occasionally, half a session might be devoted to filing material in the proper place in Lynette's binder.

As important as this was, an even more important component of her educational plan was the need to show Lynette how to study, to make her aware that when she did study she could do well. The instructor wanted to instill in Lynette the sense that learning was exciting and liberating, and could be an end in itself, so that she could "feel the flow" (Csikzentmihaly & Csikzentmihaly, 1988).

To that end, Lynette and her teacher continued the pattern that had begun the past year; that is, in each session they identified and worked on the most challenging language arts or social studies homework for the week. This year the task was to do more of the same, but with the added goal of weaning Lynette from her teacher's support, because she would no longer have a tutor as a resource when she reached high school. Lynette needed to know that she could do it on her own; the instructor's task was to "get out of her way" (Pearson, 1996).

Sessions with Lynette were much more straightforward and conventional than those with Diego and Marisol. She was motivated to do her work, she realized that this was the best time she had during the week to work on her homework, and she took an intellectual interest in most of the subjects. In contrast to Diego and Marisol, Lynette had an attention span that allowed the instructor to work with her for an hour or more at a time.

Unlike Marisol and Diego, Lynette lived within a nuclear, working-class family. Although Lynette's mother had the strength to escape from what she herself described as a highly dysfunctional home situation, she had nonetheless brought into her own family many of the same behaviors she had run away from. Her marriage to a much older man was troubled. In addition, she had two younger children who were learning disabled, one severely. Her effective and ongoing intervention in the latter's educational life engaged much of her time and effort, often depleting her of the energy needed for other family issues.

To these tensions in Lynette's life were added the burdens occasioned by being a minority scholarship student in an independent school whose population was essentially white, educated, and middle or upper class. Such a situation may create conflict within the student as he or she daily inhabits two different worlds and has to make adjustments constantly in order to adapt to each world. In addition, there may be conflict within the family because the educational opportunity presented to the child may be perceived as a threat: the more successful the education, the greater the potential distance from the family-socially, economically, and culturally (Ogbu, 1993). Indeed, Lynette's father was at odds with his wife regarding Lynette's schooling and was known to be vocal in his distrust of what Lynette was "becoming."

In addition to these stressors, Lynette's family struggled with how best to support the educational demands being placed on her. While her mother tried to provide quiet places and study times for Lynette, her own inconsistent personality made it difficult for her to be successful. As a result, Lynette had to struggle more than most of her classmates to meet the educational requirements of her school.

The stressors on Lynette affected her academic life somewhat differently than did stressors in the lives of Diego and Marisol. For example, her frequent school lateness kept her from attending important early morning math review sessions or sometimes even first period classes. Occasionally she was not allowed to accompany her class on trips because her harried mother felt that on those days Lynette's time was better spent at home helping in her licensed day-care practice. Also, Lynette had to attend weekly church meetings on school nights and all day on Sundays, which sometimes upset the delicate balance between church and school activities.

Fortunately, Lynette's academic performance showed continuing growth during her eighth-grade year. While her school did not give letter grades on their reports, she showed that she was able to handle the intellectual content of her subjects. Although she continued having problems getting work done on time, she was increasingly able to work on major academic tasks at home, an accomplishment that boded well for high school success.

In addition, she acted the part of the Wizard in her eighth-grade play, *The Wizard of Oz*, participated in the class's study of mythology, and ran as her party's candidate for president pro tempore of the class senate during a unit on the U.S. government. After lengthy intervention on the part of the agency, her mother allowed Lynette to accompany her class on the year-end trip to Washington, D.C.

On Lynette's final exams, she achieved solid Bs in both subjects in which she had been tutored. She felt especially proud that she had studied for the exams on her own.

As she enters high school, Lynette and her family will no longer be clients of the agency. While they are still at risk, after many years at the agency staff felt enough gains had been made for them to attempt to function on their own. Lynette will be attending a small, alternative public high school which is a tier below the city's rigorously selective public high schools but which is nonetheless academically challenging.

At her eighth-grade graduation, Lynette's family repeatedly emphasized that the next milestone for Lynette would be her marriage. Although the agency staff who attended understood their concern, they insisted, with equal emphasis, that they expected to be invited to her college graduation as well.

Finding the Key to Educational Success

In varying degrees, the nine months of tutoring had been positive for each of these students, an outcome we would not necessarily have predicted when we began our case studies. In each situation, several things conspired to make the year a relative success.

First, and possibly foremost, we have found that progress in meeting educational goals for these children in this clinical setting is more often achieved if a relationship develops between student and teacher, a relationship made more possible by what Tharp and Gallimore (1980) term "responsive teaching." Teacher ingenuity becomes critical to the learning process, as educational goals and strategies may have to be radically adjusted or even abandoned in order to find ways to engage the student. The resulting relationship with a stable, caring adult becomes the connector to achieving longer term, more distant educational goals that otherwise seem very removed from their daily lives. Thus, social exchange between individuals, in this case teacher and student, becomes a source of cognitive growth (Gardner, 1983; Rogoff, 1990; Turner, 1997; Vygotsky, 1978).

In our experience, this is the most critical component to success in working with this at-risk population, as we have seen children and young people, described as troublemakers at school, often with multiple suspensions, come with reasonable regularity to their reading sessions at the agency because they appear to have made that all important connection with their teachers. Indeed, educators are becoming increasingly aware of the social aspects of instruction and their influence on cognitive outcomes (Pearson, 1996). Clearly, this connection is much more easily made and sustained in a one-to-one setting.

Second, events in these families' lives in this particular year did not spin out of control. In those instances when this might have happened, the agency's therapeutic staff was there to manage and contain any incipient crises. The importance of that support cannot be underestimated as it once again points to the significance of emotional stresses on the learning process and the importance of recognizing and dealing with them.

If there is any lesson to be drawn from this admittedly qualitative research with a very small sample, it is probably one based essentially on common sense. Educational success for urban youth with learning and emotional stressors is certainly achievable when the teacher finds that key, unique to each child, which allows them together to overcome obstacles that might otherwise be insurmountable. The foundations of that success, however, are best supported when the family has available the resources of educational and mental health professionals who are able to work together for the benefit of both child and family. For most of us, but particularly for these children, the world of the mind does not exist apart from the worlds of the heart and the soul.

REFERENCES

Adams, M.J. (1990). *Beginning to read: Thinking and learning about print.* Cambridge, MA: The MIT Press.

Anders, P.L., & Pritchard, T.G. (1993). Integrated language curriculum and instruction for the middle grades. *The Elementary School Journal, 93,* 611–624.

Anderson, R.C., Shirey, L.L., Wilson, P.T., & Fielding, L.G. (1987). Interestingness of children's reading material. In R.E. Snow & M.J. Farr (Eds.), *Aptitude learning and instruction: Cognitive and affective process analysis* (pp. 287–299). Hillsdale, NJ: Erlbaum.

Au, K.H., Scheu, J.A., Kawakami, A.J., & Herman, P.A. (1990). Assessment and accountability in a whole literacy curriculum. *The Reading Teacher, 43,* 574–578.

Babad, E., Bernieri, F., & Rosenthal, R. (1991). Students as judges of teachers' verbal and nonverbal behavior. *American Educational Journal, 28*(1), 211–234.

Baumann, J.F., & Thomas, D. (1997). If you can pass Momma's tests, then she knows you're getting your education: A case study of support for literacy learning within an African-American family. *The Reading Teacher, 51,* 108–120.

Beck, I., & McKeown, M.G. (1991). Conditions of vocabulary acquisition. In R. Barr, M. Kamil, P. Mosenthal, & P.D. Pearson (Eds.), *Handbook of reading research* (Vol. 2, pp. 789–814). White Plains, NY: Longman.

Bettleheim, B. (1977). *The uses of enchantment: The meaning and importance of fairy tales.* New York: Vintage.

Bryant, N.D. (1980). The effects of some instructional variables on the learning of handicapped and nonhandicapped populations: A review. *Integrative Reviews of Research, 1,* 1–70.

Caldwell, G.P., & Ginthier, D.W. (1996). Differences in learning styles of low socioeconomic status for low and high achievers. *Education, 117,* 141–147.

Csikzentmihalyi, M., & Csikzentmihalyi, I.S. (1988). *Optimal experience: Psychological studies of flow in consciousness.* Cambridge, England: Cambridge University Press.

Deci, E.L., Vallerand, R.J., Pelletier, L.G., & Ryan, E.M. (1991). Motivation and education: The self-determination perspective. *Educational Psychologist, 26,* 325–346.

Dunn, R., & Griggs, S.A. (1988). High school dropouts: Do they learn differently from those who remain in school? *The Principal, 34,* 1–8.

Elley, W.B. (1989). Vocabulary acquisition from listening to stories. *Reading Research Quarterly, 24,* 174–187.

Farnan, N. (1996). Connecting adolescents and reading: Goals at the middle level. *Journal of Adolescent & Adult Literacy, 39,* 436–445.

Gardner, H. (1983). *Frames of mind: The theory of multiple intelligences.* New York: Basic Books.

Glass, G.G., & Glass, E.W. (1976). *Glass analysis for decoding only.* Garden City, NY: Easier-to-Learn.

Goleman, D. (1995). *Emotional intelligence.* New York: Bantam.

Guthrie, J., Alao, S., & Rinehart, J. (1997). Engagement in reading for young adolescents. *Journal of Adolescent & Adult Literacy, 40,* 438–446.

Haring, N.G., & Bateman B. (1997). *Teaching the learning disabled child.* Englewood Cliffs, NJ: Prentice-Hall.

Harmon, J.M. (1998). Vocabulary teaching and learning in a seventh-grade literature-based classroom. *Journal of Adolescent & Adult Literacy, 41,* 518–531.

Harter, S., Whitesell, N., & Kowlaski, P. (1992). Individual differences in the effects of educational transitions on young adolescents' perceptions of competence and motivational orientation. *American Educational Research Journal, 29,* 777–807.

Hobbs, D. (1990). School based community development: Making connections for improved learning. In S. Raferty & D. Mulkey (Eds.), *The role of rural schools in community development* (pp. 57–64). Mississippi State, MS: Southern Rural Development Center.

Ivey, G. (1999). A multicase study in middle-school: Complexities among adolescent readers. *Reading Research Quarterly, 34,* 172–193.

Jiménez, R.T., Moll, L., Rodríquez-Brown, F., & Barrera, R. (1999). Conversations: Latina and Latino researchers interact on issues related to literacy learning. *Reading Research Quarterly, 34,* 217–230.

Johnson, P.H., & Winograd, P.N. (1985). Passive failure in reading. *Journal of Reading Behavior, 17,* 279–301.

King, D.H. (1985). *Writing skills for the adolescent.* Cambridge, MA: Educators Publishing Service.

Kos, R. (1991). Persistence of reading disabilities: The voices of four middle school students. *American Educational Research Journal, 28,* 875–895.

Liberman, I.Y., Shankweiler, D.P., & Liberman, A.M. (1989). The alphabetic principle and learning to read. In D.P. Shankweiler & A.M. Liberman (Eds.), *Phonology and reading disabilities* (pp. 1–35). Ann Arbor, MI: University of Michigan Press.

Mather, N. (1992). Whole language reading instruction for students with learning disabilities: Caught in the crossfire. *Learning Disabilities Research and Practice, 7,* 87–95.

Morris, D., Ervin, C., & Conrad, K. (1996). A case study of middle school reading disability. *The Reading Teacher, 49,* 368–377.

Ogbu, J.U. (1993). Variability in minority school performance: A problem in search of an explanation. In E. Jacob & C. Jordan (Eds.), *Minority education: Anthropological perspectives* (pp. 83–111). Norwood, NJ: Ablex.

Olson, R., Kliegl, R., Davidson, B., & Foltz, G. (1985). Individual and developmental differences in reading disabilities. In T. Waller (Ed.), *Reading research: Advances in theory and practice* (pp. 1–64). London: Academic Press.

Pearson, P.D. (1996). Reclaiming the center. In M. Graves, P. van den Broek, & B.M. Taylor (Eds.), *The first R: Every child's right to read* (pp. 259–274). New York: Teachers College Press; Newark, DE: International Reading Association.

Perfetti, C.A. (1985). *Reading ability.* New York: Oxford University Press.

Rissler, J., & Steinburg, C. (1991). In practice. *Training and Development, 45,* 11–12.

Rogoff, B. (1990). *Apprenticeship in thinking: Cognitive development in social context.* New York: Oxford University Press.

Samuels, S.J. (1979). The method of repeated readings. *The Reading Teacher, 32,* 403–408.

Stanovich, K.E., Cunningham, A.E., & Freeman, D.J. (1984). Intelligence, cognitive skills, and early reading progress. *Reading Research Quarterly, 19,* 278–303.

Sweet, A.P., & Guthrie, J.T. (1996). How children's motivations relate to literacy development and instruction. *The Reading Teacher, 49,* 660–662.

Tharp, R.G., & Gallimore, R. (1993). Teaching mind in society: Teaching schooling and literate discourse. In L.C. Moll (Ed.), *Vygotsky and education: Instructional implications and applications of sociohistorical psychology* (pp. 175–205). Cambridge, England: Cambridge University Press.

Tuma, J.M. (1989). Mental health services for children: The state of the art. *American Psychologist, 44,* 188–189.

Turner, J.C. (1997). Starting right: Strategies for engaging young literacy learners. In J.T. Guthrie & A. Wigfield (Eds.), *Reading engagement: Motivating readers through integrated instruction* (pp. 183–204). Newark, DE: International Reading Association.

Vellutino, F.R. (1979). *Dyslexia: Theory and research.* Cambridge, MA: MIT Press.

Vygotsky, L.S. (1978). *Mind in society: The development of higher psychological processes* (M. Cole, V. John-Steiner, S. Scribner, & E. Souberman, Eds. and Trans.). Cambridge, MA: Harvard University Press. (Original work published 1934)

Wigfield, A. (1994). Expectancy-value theory of achievement motivation: A developmental perspective. *Educational Psychology Review, 6,* 49–78.

Wubbels, T., Creton, H., & Holvast, A. (1988). Undesirable classroom situation: A systems communication perspective. *Interchange, 19,* 25–40.

LITERATURE CITED

Dolch, E.W., Dolch, M.P., & Jackson, B.F. (1951). *Aesop's stories for pleasure reading.* Champaign, IL: Garrard.

Giovanni, N. (1988). *Spin a soft black song.* New York: Farrar, Straus & Giroux.

Greenfield, E. (1986). *Honey, I love.* New York: HarperTrophy.

Koralek, J. (reteller). (1996). *A treasury of stories from H.C. Andersen.* New York: Kingfisher.

RIGHT 7

Children have a right to reading instruction

that involves parents and communities

in their academic lives.

Introduction

Patricia A. Edwards

P arent involvement in education is no passing fad; it is here to stay. It is center stage within policy circles, professional organizations, and the media. There is strong evidence of the benefits of families in the educational lives of their children—research has shown that the more comprehensive and long-lasting the parental involvement, the greater the influence is likely to be, not just on children's achievement but also on the quality of schools as institutions serving the community (Henderson, 1987). Many educators believe that parent involvement holds the greatest promise for meeting the needs of the child (Edwards, 2004; Epstein, 2001). Statements like the ones that follow further attest to the benefits of parent involvement to student learning and academic development.

- Parents are the first teachers children meet. They are also children's teachers for the longest periods. Beginning at birth, children's experiences affect their success in becoming literate individuals. The success of the school literacy program frequently depends on the literacy environment of the home. (Morrow, 1993, p. 40)

- Trying to educate children without the involvement of their family is like trying to play a basketball game without all the players on the court. (Olson, 1990, p. 17)

- Parents act as role models for the literacy behaviors of their children, and the children of those parents who are poor models find that each year they slip farther behind in school. For them school is not the key to opportunity but to failure. (Darling, 1988, p. 3)

- Literacy learning begins in the home, not the school, and...instruction should build on the foundation for literacy learning established in the home. (Au, 1993, p. 35)

- Adults who live and interact regularly with children can profoundly influence the quality and quantity of their literacy experiences. (Snow, Burns, & Griffin, 1998, p. 138)

- It may be that children can learn to become literate on their own without formal instruction, but when experiences with literacy take place in family environments, the emotional reactions of the parents can affect the child's progress significantly. (Leichter, 1984, p. 46)

- Children will have many teachers in their lives, but only one family. It must be the family who help maintain the continuity of the child's education. The parents were the child's first teacher and will remain the most important throughout the child's life. (Potter, 1989, p. 28)

- Although schools may have capable and dedicated teachers, schools are by their nature isolated from the larger world. Children learn from everything they see and do—at home, at school, and everywhere else. (Schickedanz, 1986, p. 128)

- Every aspect of a family—the way it is organized, the way it works, the things it values, the relations that it has with the rest of society—all have some effect on what children learn.... All children are shaped by their families' teacher and the kind of environment their families create for learning. (Weston, 1989, p. 1)

- Families form the non-constructed, spontaneous institution which has principal responsibility for childrearing. (Coleman, 1987, p. 35)

- Since parents are the closest, most intimate, and most persistent teachers that most children have, they teach their youngsters the basic attitudes, efforts, and conceptions of self, and for many—this occurs within the social environment of the household. (Sutherland, 1991, p. 121)

- The family's main contribution to the child's success in school is made through the parents' dispositions and interpersonal relationships with the child in the household. Children receive essential 'survival knowledge' for competent classroom role enactment from their exposure to positive home attitudes and communication encounters. (Clark, 1983, p. 1)

- What parents do to help their children is more important to academic success than how well-off the family is. (U.S. Department of Education, 1986, p. 7)

- [Parents] bear a responsibility to participate actively in [their] child's education. [They] should encourage more diligent study and discourage satisfaction with mediocrity and the attitude that says "let it slide"; monitor [their] child's study; encourage good study habits; encourage [their] child to take more demanding rather than less demanding courses; nurture [their] child's curiosity, creativity, and confidence; and be an active participant in the work of the schools. (National Commission on Excellence in Education, 1983, p. 35)

It is encouraging that *Making a Difference Means Making It Different: Honoring Children's Rights to Excellent Reading Instruction* explicitly states, "Children have a right to reading instruction that involves parents and communities in their academic lives." As the two articles in this section illustrate, research is beginning to emerge that sheds light on promising practices for how to engage parents in meaningful and respectful ways in their child's literacy development. Jennifer C. Dandridge, Patricia A. Edwards, and Heather M. Pleasants report data from two urban elementary schools where administrators "broke the mold" and developed home and school connections that made a difference. Robert J. Nistler and Angela Maiers report outcomes of a program evaluation of a family literacy program. The program organizers built a learning community where parents had a genuine role in their child's reading and writing education and were no longer "silent partners."

Before discussing this right regarding involving parents and communities in children's academic lives in more detail, it is useful to point out that showing parents how to help their children has been a hotly contested issue. Also, it is useful to suggest that there is a need for teachers to employ a multiple consciousness approach in their classrooms. According to Edwards, with Pleasants and Franklin (1999),

> Upon entering the classroom, one can guarantee that all children in any given classroom *do not* have identical racial, ethnic, religious, social, educational, or financial backgrounds to the teacher. Teachers must learn from parents' stories in order to gain a better sense of who the children are and expand their own schema to encompass an increasingly diverse society and classroom. (p. xx)

The Book Reading Controversy: Should Parents Receive Assistance?

Parents reading aloud to their children is assumed to be a prerequisite for success in school. As early as 1908, Huey revealed that "the secret of it all lies in the parents reading aloud to and with their child" (p. 32). In *Becoming a Nation of Readers*, the authors state that "parents play roles of inestimable importance in laying the foundations for learning to read" (Anderson, Hiebert, Scott, & Wilkinson, 1985, p. 57). Mahoney and Wilcox (1985) conclude, "If a child comes from a reading family where books are a shared source of pleasure, he or she will have an understanding of the language of the literacy world and respond to the use of books in a classroom as a natural expansion of pleasant home experiences" (p. ix).

However, the overemphasis on parent-child book reading has caused concern among some researchers (Anderson & Stokes, 1984; Erickson, 1989). For example, some researchers have challenged the validity of the claim that the failure of some children in learning to read may be related to the fact that many of these children come from homes where their parents have never read a book to them (Anderson & Stokes, 1984; Auerbach, 1989; Erickson, 1989; Heath, 1982, 1983). Some researchers have even challenged the notion that the "education" of parents for a specific kind of literacy interaction (the one-on-one middle-class dyadic interaction) should be encouraged and in some cases coerced (Anderson & Stokes, 1984; Auerbach, 1989; Erickson, 1989; Taylor & Dorsey-Gaines, 1988). Based on these concerns, some researchers have raised two serious issues: one the "blaming the victim" syndrome and the other the claim that the homes of poor, minority, and immigrant children are lacking in literacy.

Generally speaking, some researchers do not disagree that one-on-one parent-child interactions are correlated with success in literacy learning, but fear that agreeing that one-on-one parent-child interactions are the way to encourage literacy might stigmatize those who do not readily adapt to this way of interacting (Anderson & Stokes, 1984; Erickson, 1989). For example, Erickson (1989) argues that one should not

> assume that being read aloud to at home is a necessary condition for learning to read and write in school. To believe that is to allow us yet another opportunity to blame low-income parents for their children's school failure. Treating that belief as authoritative truth can be seen as a well-intentioned means of inadvertently putting those children and parents at risk in acquiring literacy. (p. xv)

Similarly, Anderson and Stokes (1984) argue that book reading is not the only way of becoming literate and that nonmainstream children participate in literacy experiences that are unrelated to books. Despite these arguments, Erickson admits that his position may be too extreme and perhaps he should "think twice before condemning all early childhood interventions as coercive and misguided" (p. xv). Anderson and Stokes admit that experiences with books are strongly considered in evaluating children's readiness for school and that nonmainstream children's lack of experience with books could be a contributing source to poor school performance.

Although strong arguments have been posed against book reading, it should be noted that when children enter school, the suggestions most frequently made for parent involvement according to Vukelich (1984) are as follows:

1. Read to your child.

2. Be a good literate role model.

3. Provide books, magazines, etc. for your child to read.

4. Build a reading atmosphere at home (place, time, library area).

5. Talk and listen to your child.

6. Exemplify a positive attitude toward reading.

7. Provide experiences for children that are reading related, e.g., library trips, or that can be used to stimulate interest in reading.

8. Read environmental signs; capture reading opportunities in the environment.

9. Provide contact with paper and pencils.

10. Be aware of your child's interests.

11. Point out similarities and differences in objects in the environment. (p. 473)

All of these are excellent suggestions for bridging the gap between home and school. Among families who routinely read stories to their children, Adams (1990) estimates that children spend from 1,000 to 1,700 hours in one-to-one literacy activities before entering school. Adams suggests that these children experience another 2,000 hours of print "guidance" by watching *Sesame Street* and perhaps another 1,000 or 2,000 hours by playing with magnetic alphabet letters, participating in reading and writing activities in playgroup or preschool, exploring with paper and pencils, and playing alphabet games on a computer. But for children in many families, there are no storybook routines, no magnetic letters on the refrigerator, no easy access to paper or pencils for creating messages, and no literacy games to play on a computer. Perhaps there is not even the opportunity to watch *Sesame Street* on television. Such children will begin first grade without the "thousands of hours of school-like reading experience" (Adams, 1990, p. 90) that other families have the resources to provide. Adams's findings point to the fact that many preschool children enter school each year without having been "marinated" in print.

What I found in my 1989 study titled "Supporting Lower SES Mothers' Attempts to Provide Scaffolding for Book Reading" is that book reading is a very simple teacher directive, but a very complex and difficult task for some parents (see Edwards, 1989). I put forth the argument that to simply inform parents of the importance of reading to their children is not sufficient. Instead we must go beyond *telling* to *showing* lower SES parents how to participate in parent-child book-reading interactions with their children and support their attempts to do so.

Literacy learning begins at birth. In the years before school, parents play a vital role as their children's first literacy teachers (Morrow, 1993), and especially with respect to reading (Taylor & Strickland, 1986). Book reading is the parent-involvement activity most frequently requested by teachers (Vukelich, 1984), and parents need to understand that storybook reading is the cornerstone of reading instruction in the early grades (Edwards & Garcia, 1991; Taylor & Strickland, 1986). "Not only do they have the right to know, they have the right to receive assistance in how to participate in book reading interactions with their young children" (Edwards, 1991, p. 211). This message echoes Darling's (1988) contention that "parents must be assisted in literacy development, and they must be provided with targeted services that help them support the development of their children" (p. 3).

I contend, like Gadsden (1994), that "many parents want assistance in using school-like models for literacy" (p. 14) and book reading is one of those school-like models. For more than three decades, studies have shown that when parents read to and with children, their children's literacy is developed (Anderson et al., 1985; Chomsky, 1972; Laosa, 1982; Teale & Sulzby, 1986).

Why Is There a Need for Teachers to Develop a Multiple Consciousness?

Some researchers get nervous when the homes of poor, minority, and immigrant children are depicted as lacking in literacy. As a way of debunking these claims, a growing number of researchers have been able to demonstrate that the homes of poor, minority, and immigrant families are not lacking in literacy (Anderson & Stokes, 1984; Auerbach, 1989; Chall & Snow, 1982; Delgado-Gaitan, 1987). For example, Auerbach and her colleagues reported that they did not go into their students' homes or communities to examine literacy uses and practices or to collect data, but they listened, read, and talked to students about literacy in their lives. From these interactions with their students, they were able to conclude that their students did not lack literacy. Anderson and Stokes (1984) uncovered a range of reading and writing experiences that young children from poor families participated in or witnessed. Sources of experiences in literacy, in addition to typical school or "literacy-for-literacy's sake" activities, included literacy events for daily living needs (e.g., paying bills or obtaining welfare assistance), entertainment (e.g., solving a crossword puzzle or reading a television guide), and religion (e.g., Bible-reading sessions with children). Similarly, Taylor and Dorsey-Gaines's (1988) in-depth account of the families and lives of black, urban 6-year-olds who were successful in learning to read and write revealed that their parents provided a rich literate environment.

Based on the evidence presented in the studies cited here, few can successfully argue that the homes of poor, minority, and immigrant children lack literacy. However, it should be noted that in all these studies the parents recognized the importance of literacy, and especially the importance of reading to their children. For example, Anderson and Stokes (1984) describe the situation of a mother who could not read well enough to read storybooks aloud to her child; this mother recognized the importance of literacy and was being tutored to learn how to write, and she passed on what she was learning to her child.

We learned from researchers (for example, Anderson & Stokes, 1984; Auerbach, 1989; Taylor & Dorsey-Gaines, 1988) that literacy is not lacking in the homes of poor, minority, and immigrant families, but we did not learn how to help teachers build on the multiple literacy environments from which these student come. Edwards and Garcia (1991) point out,

> Ideally, schools should recognize and incorporate the different interaction patterns and literacy events that characterize non-mainstream and mainstream communities. For this to happen, however, we need considerably more research—documenting the different types of interaction patterns and literacy events common in non-mainstream communities—and more teacher training. (p. 183)

Because the above statement was made more than 10 years ago, several researchers, including myself, have worked hard to respond to it. Two such studies are included in this section. Nistler and Maiers's stance toward the value of home-school connections is consistent with Morrow's (1995) call for studies of family literacy that take a variety of perspectives in order to gain knowledge not only from professionals but from the families as well. The parents know their child and what occurs in their family better than any outsider, and teachers need to respect and learn from the families they serve. It is especially important in listening to parents as they tell their stories to simply collect the information and analyze it to match potential needs with available resources, not to pass moral, political, or personal judgment on what they are saying. Doing so could risk permanently closing off current and future communication efforts. On the other hand, as Nistler and Maiers's data indicate, taking the time to engage parents can yield powerful benefits for children and the community.

DuBois (1990) wrote of the plight of African Americans prior to desegregation. He commented that the white person need only be conscious of what it was like to be white, a life without restrictions based on race. However, black men and women needed to have what he called a "double-consciousness"—to know what it was to be black and know the associated limitations, but also to know the life of white people as different and less limiting than their own. In the 20th-century, broadly diverse U.S. culture, teachers need to employ a multiple consciousness. Danridge, Edwards, and Pleasants argue that teachers must learn from parents' stories in order to gain a better sense of who the children are and expand their own schema to encompass an increasingly diverse society and classroom.

The Dandridge et al. article provides compelling data about the challenges administrators face in urban schools and how two principals faced these challenges by making "a personal investment in students, families, and community." In particular, the article describes how principals used parent stories as a vehicle to promote engagement in school activities and in students' literacy education.

In the book *A Path to Follow: Learning to Listen to Parents* (1999), I, along with Pleasants and Franklin, suggest that collecting parent literacy stories is an excellent vehicle for helping teachers gain a better understanding of families and children and the literacy environments in which they live. The book clearly outlines how to collect, analyze, and react to the parent stories that are collected. We defined parent stories as narratives gained from open-ended interviews. In these interviews, parents responded to questions designed to provide information about traditional and nontraditional early literacy activities and experiences that have happened in the home. We further defined parent stories through their ability to construct home literacy environments. Some examples of the questions used to collect parent stories are as follows:

- ◆ What do you and your child enjoy doing together?
- ◆ All children have potential. Did you notice that _____ had some particular talent or "gift" early on? If so, what was it? What did your child do to make you think that he or she had this potential? Were there specific things you did as a parent to strengthen this talent?
- ◆ Is there something about your child that might not be obvious to the teacher, but might positively or negatively affect his or her performance in school if the teacher knew? If so, what would that something be?
- ◆ What activities or hobbies do you participate in as an individual? With your spouse or friends? As a family?
- ◆ Can you describe "something" about your home learning environment that you would like the school to build on because you feel that this "something" would enhance your child's learning potential at school?

By using stories as a way to express the nature of the home environment, parents can select anecdotes and personal observations from their own individual consciousness to give teachers access to complicated social, emotional, and educational issues that can help to unravel for teachers the mysteries around their students' early literacy beginnings. Still further, we point out that many parents have vivid memories about

- ◆ the kinds of routines they did with their children,
- ◆ specific interactions they had with their children,
- ◆ observations of their children's beginning learning efforts,

- ways in which their children learned simply by watching them,

- perceptions as to whether their occupation determined how they raised their children,

- descriptions of "teachable moments" they had with their children, and

- descriptions of things about their children that may not be obvious to the teacher but would help their children's performance if the teacher knew about them.

Additionally, many parents have scrapbooks, audiocassettes, videotapes, photographs, or other artifacts to share their children's literacy history.

Parent stories can provide teachers with the opportunity to gain a deeper understanding of the "human side" of families and children (i.e., why children behave as they do, children's ways of learning and communicating, problems parents have encountered and how these problems may have impacted their children's views about school and the schooling process). On a final note, we suggest in the book that because teachers' evaluations of students are sometimes based on quick observations, they frequently fail to take into account the experiences that students have brought with them to school. Teachers are thus lacking vital information that can help them better understand and teach their students. Parents can fill in some of the missing pieces by providing stories about their child's early learning experiences at home.

REFERENCES

Adams, M.J. (1990). *Beginning to read: Thinking and learning about print.* Cambridge, MA: MIT Press.

Anderson, A.B., & Stokes, S.J. (1984). Social and institutional influences on the development and practice of literacy. In H. Goelman, A. Oberg, & F. Smith (Eds.), *Awakening to literacy* (pp. 24–37). Exeter, NH: Heinemann.

Anderson, R.C., Hiebert, E.H., Scott, J.A., & Wilkinson, I.A.G. (1985). *Becoming a nation of readers: The report of the Commission on Reading.* Washington, DC: National Institute of Education.

Au, K.H. (1993). *Literacy instruction in multicultural settings.* Fort Worth, TX: Harcourt Brace Jovanovich.

Auerbach, E.R. (1989). Towards a social-contextual approach to family literacy. *Harvard Educational Review, 59*(2), 165–181.

Chall, J.S., & Snow, C. (1982). *Families and literacy: The contributions of out of school experiences to children's acquisition of literacy* (A final report to the National Institute of education). Cambridge, MA: Harvard Graduate School of Education.

Chomsky, C. (1972). Stages in language development and reading exposure. *Harvard Educational Review, 42*(1), 1–33.

Clark, R. (1983). *Family life and school achievement: Why poor black children succeed or fail.* Chicago: University of Chicago Press.

Coleman, J.S. (1987). Families and schools. *Educational Researcher, 16*(6), 32–38.

Danridge, J.C., Edwards, P.A., & Pleasants, H.M. (2000). Making kids winners: New perspectives about literacy from urban elementary school principals. *The Reading Teacher, 53,* 654–662.

Darling, S. (1988). *Family literacy education: Replacing the cycle of failure with the legacy of success.* Washington, DC: Office of Educational Research and Improvement. (ERIC Document Reproduction Service No. ED332749).

Delgado-Gaitan, C. (1987). Mexican adult literacy: New directions for immigrants. In S.R. Goldman & H.T. Trueba (Eds.), *Becoming literate in English as a second language* (pp. 9–32). Norwood, NJ: Ablex.

DuBois, W.E.B. (1990). *The souls of black folk.* New York: Vintage Books/The Library of America.

Edwards, P.A. (1989). Supporting lower SES mothers' attempts to provide scaffolding for book reading. In J. Allen & J.M. Mason (Eds.), *Risk makers, risk takers, risk breakers: Reducing the risks for young literacy learners* (pp. 222–250). Portsmouth, NH: Heinemann.

Edwards, P.A. (1991). Fostering early literacy through parent coaching. In E.H. Hiebert (Ed.), *Literacy for a diverse society: Perspectives, practices, and policies* (pp. 199–213). New York: Teachers College Press.

Edwards, P.A. (2004). *Children's literacy development: Making it happen through school, family and community involvement.* Boston: Allyn & Bacon.

Edwards, P.A., & Garcia, G.E. (1991). Parental involvement in mainstream schools. In M. Foster (Ed.), *Readings on equal education: Qualitative investigations into schools and schooling* (pp. 167–187). New York: AMA Press.

Edwards, P.A., with Pleasants, H.M., & Franklin, S.H. (1999). *A path to follow: Learning to listen to parents.* Portsmouth, NH: Heinemann.

Epstein, J.L. (2001). *School, family, and community partnerships: Preparing educators and improving schools.* Boulder, CO: Westview Press.

Erickson, F. (1989). Foreword: Literacy risks for students, parents, and teachers. In J. Allen & J.M. Mason (Eds.), *Risk makers, risk takers, risk breakers: Reducing the risks for young literacy learners* (pp. xiii–xvi). Portsmouth, NH: Heinemann.

Gadsden, V.L. (1994). Understanding family literacy: Conceptual issues facing the field. *Teachers College Record, 96*(1), 58–86.

Heath, S.B. (1982). What no bedtime story means: Narrative skills at home and school. *Language in Society, 11*(1), 49–76.

Heath, S.B. (1983). *Ways with words: Language, life, and work in communities and classrooms.* Cambridge, MA: Cambridge University Press.

Henderson, A.T. (1987). *The evidence continues to grow: Parent involvement improves student achievement.* Columbia, MD: National Committee for Citizens in Education.

Huey, E.B. (1908). *The psychology and pedagogy of reading.* New York: Macmillan.

Laosa, L.M. (1985). *Indices of the success of Head Start: A critique.* Paper presented at the Research Directions for Minority Scholars Involved With Head Start Programs conference, Howard University, Washington, DC.

Leichter, H.J. (1984). Families as environments for literacy. In H. Goelman, A. Oberg, & F. Smith (Eds.), *Awakening to literacy* (pp. 38–50). Exeter, NH: Heinemann.

Mahoney, E., & Wilcox, L. (1985). *Ready, set, read: Best books to prepare preschoolers.* Metuchen, NJ: Scarecrow Press.

Morrow, L.M. (1993). *Literacy development in the early years* (2nd ed.). Boston: Allyn & Bacon.

Morrow, L.M. (Ed.). (1995). *Family literacy connections in schools and communities.* Newark, DE: International Reading Association.

National Commission on Excellence in Education. (1983). *A nation at risk: The imperative for educational reform.* Washington, DC: Author.

Nistler, R.J., & Maiers, A. (2000). Stopping the silence: Hearing parents' voices in an urban first-grade family literacy program. *The Reading Teacher, 53,* 670–680.

Olson, L. (April, 1990). Parents as partners: Redefining the social contract between parents and schools [Special Issue]. *Education Week, 9*(28), 17–24.

Potter, G. (1989). Parent participation in the language arts program. *Language Arts, 66*(1), 21–28.

Schickedanz, J. (1986). *More than ABCs: The early stages of reading and writing.* Washington, DC: National Association for the Education of Young Children.

Snow, C.E., Burns, M.S., & Griffin, P. (Eds.). (1998). *Preventing reading difficulties in young children.* Washington, DC: National Academy Press.

Sutherland, I.R. (1991). Parent-teacher involvement benefits everyone. *Early Child Development and Care, 73,* 121–131.

Taylor, D., & Dorsey-Gaines, C. (1988). *Growing up literate: Learning from inner-city families.* Portsmouth, NH: Heinemann.

Taylor, D., & Strickland, D.S. (1986). *Family storybook reading.* Portsmouth, NH: Heinemann.

Teale, W.H., & Sulzby, E. (1986). *Emergent literacy: Writing and reading.* Norwood, NJ: Ablex.

U.S. Department of Education. (1986). *What works: Research about teaching and learning.* Washington, DC: Author.

Vukelich, C. (1984). Parents' role in the reading process: A review of practical suggestions and ways to communicate with parents. *The Reading Teacher, 37,* 472–477.

Weston, W.J. (1989). *Education and the American family: A research synthesis.* New York: New York University Press.

Making Kids Winners: New Perspectives About Literacy From Urban Elementary School Principals

Jennifer C. Danridge, Patricia A. Edwards, and Heather M. Pleasants

> Over the years, I've seen it's necessary to work together as a team. It can't be "I am the boss, and the teachers' job is to do whatever I tell them to do." I can't work that way. One of the things that I did in the beginning of the year was to have my parking sign that says "Reserved for the Principal" pulled out from in front of the building and put at the furthest spot [possible] because I am, literally and figuratively, the least important person here. This place could run for two or three years without a principal. It isn't gonna run one day without a secretary, and a custodian, and the teachers who come into the classrooms and work with our students. (Urban elementary principal)

We believe that these words from Mr. Carter (pseudonym) convey the reality of many principals working in today's urban U.S. schools. Drug and alcohol abuse, high crime rates, incessant violence, and extreme poverty are just a few of the negative ecological factors that create challenging educational circumstances for such schools and their surrounding communities. Traditionally, teachers and parents shouldered the blame for students' low test scores and poor academic performance. More recently, principals have become targets; they have found themselves face to face with the daunting task of educating students in an urban community plagued by multiple risks. The purpose of our article is to highlight the urban principal as a stakeholder who is within the midst of the crisis in public education, but whose voice is often marginalized. More specifically, we illuminate the struggles and challenges of two elementary school principals who have become empowered to work proactively with teachers, parents, and students in an effort to enhance culturally diverse students' literacy development.

In most studies of urban schooling (see Anyon, 1997; Goodlad, 1984; Kozol, 1991), the voice of the principal is noticeably absent. We surmised that many researchers and practitioners perceive principals to be disconnected from the complexities of teaching and learning in the classroom. Their administrative positions can be seen as removing them from the day-to-day challenges of managing and instructing students, and of dealing with their families. Consequently, teachers and staff often perceive their principal to be "the boss" who handles the organizational affairs of the school, disciplines

Originally published in *The Reading Teacher* (2000), volume 53, pages 654–662.

students and teachers, distributes resources (i.e., personnel, equipment, and materials), facilitates staff relations, and enforces rules and regulations (Bliss, 1991; Parsons, 1958). For decades, the image of the traditional urban principal has been the organizational manager, whose piles of paperwork in the office emphasize the bureaucratic nature of schooling and the hierarchical nature of authority, responsibility, and control within educational settings (Bliss, 1991; Parsons, 1958; Seashore Louis & Miles, 1991).

Contemporary Urban Principals Get a New Attitude

Mr. Carter's words connote that the role of the urban principal is changing with the times. Recent studies of urban schools, particularly the school reform and effective schools research, have thrust urban principals into the limelight. Because such schools are now viewed as "communities" within these two theoretical frameworks, there has been greater emphasis upon team approaches toward administration, instruction, and home-school connections (Bliss, 1991; Ramirez, Webb, & Guthrie, 1991). As a result, the role of the urban principal has shifted from manager to builder (Polite & McClure, 1997). For example, urban principals encourage teachers and students to buy into their vision for the school by fostering a collegial environment that is inspirational and educational (Sergiovanni, 1994).

Further, urban principals have become responsible for building collaborative partnerships between teachers and parents, implementing programs that connect home and school, and creating inroads with community agencies. Urban principals are responsible for understanding multiple perspectives (i.e., teachers, students, parents, and community leaders) and addressing the competing needs and interests of these groups. This is an essential task because the success of the school is deeply nested within the interdependent relationships of these groups (Enomoto, 1997). Consequently, urban principals can no longer afford to sit in their offices tucked away from the rest of the school; their futures are inextricably connected to that of their school, its constituents, and the surrounding community.

Urban principals are critically aware that this interdependence of school, home, and community also creates a greater sense of accountability for the effectiveness of their schools (Osterman, Crow, & Rosen, 1997). Often, they find themselves in the eye of the storm as pressure for higher test scores and better-educated students mounts from multiple sources—the school district, the parents, the community, businesses, and society at large (Bogotch &

Taylor, 1993). The pressure that urban principals feel is all too real—they are ultimately held responsible for low student achievement and test scores, despite the acute lack of financial resources, personnel, and other educational materials that plague inner-city schools (National Council of Jewish Women, 1999).

Urban principals whose time is largely spent managing these financial struggles are less likely to find time to fulfill their responsibilities as instructional leaders. Yet this is an extremely critical role for urban principals, particularly in elementary schools where teachers often function in isolation (Bliss, 1991; Peterson & Lezotte, 1991). Urban principals can be completely overwhelmed by the prospect of having conversations about curriculum and instruction because the rules about "good" teaching are always changing, and they feel uncomfortable admitting that they don't have all of the answers (Neufeld, 1997). Further, some urban principals are reluctant to discuss instruction because they are uncertain about how to move teachers, particularly those who doubt or are stubborn, toward a unified vision of teaching and learning (Neufeld, 1997).

However, urban principals are finding it difficult *not* to become involved with instructional issues. More often, they are being drawn into heated discussions with teachers around effective instruction. One particularly visible discussion centers on the literacy achievement of urban students. Principals must deal with unresolved debates around whole language and phonics and must still respond to pressures to raise students' reading achievement scores on standardized tests. Consequently, as the instructional leaders, urban principals now find themselves labeled as "incompetent" and "weak" when they do not deliver better results. Thus, urban principals are now finding themselves in the hot seat that teachers traditionally have occupied where issues in literacy instruction are concerned.

In addition, urban principals are given the task of connecting the cultural literacies of home and school. Within schools, principals are responsible for facilitating an environment that (a) emphasizes the interdependence between teaching and learning, (b) sets high expectations for staff and students, (c) establishes guidelines for student and teacher behavior, and (d) expresses a generally positive attitude toward education and young people (Bliss, 1991; Seashore Louis & Miles, 1991; Peterson & Lezotte, 1991). When teachers and students participate in a school culture they perceive as productive, respectful, and supportive, they are likely to coconstruct classroom discourse that facilitates the acquisition of school-based literacy (Corno, 1989). Establishing a collaborative school culture is critical in urban schools, since this environment can be very uninviting for parents. By increasing connections between home and school literacies, urban principals can develop an academic environment that respects the multicultural literacies of students and their families. In sum, successful principals of urban schools are often perceived as miracle workers. However, to label them in this manner is to miss an important opportunity to understand how principals manage their professional lives within schools.

In the remainder of this article, we share the insightful stories of two principals who have worked in the same urban, Midwestern school—we'll call it Baker Elementary. These two men were extremely sensitive to their students, the majority of whom come from culturally and linguistically diverse families and low socioeconomic backgrounds (Michigan School Report, 1998). They worked tirelessly with parents, teachers, and the community in an effort to provide a quality education and have experienced the triumphs and the hardships associated with the urban principalship. We see the narratives of these two principals as creating a new "safe space" for other administrators to enter the conversation about the intersections of urban communities, their schools, and their members.

Mr. Williams's Story:
District Pressure, Low Test Scores, Frustrated Teachers

Mr. Williams (pseudonym) was principal at Baker Elementary from 1989 to 1997. He had been an elementary and middle school teacher for six years, and, as a result, he had a wide range of teaching experiences with students from diverse backgrounds. As an African American, he was deeply concerned about the welfare and the educational experiences of minority students. This focus is desperately needed in many inner-city areas because the minority-student population is typically disenfranchised in urban educational institutions (Anyon, 1997; Kozol, 1991; Reglin, 1995).

Mr. Williams felt that his determination was critical to being an educator and administrator. He also believed it was critical not to allow hearsay and negative publicity to deter him from working in urban schools. This kind of resilience is essential for someone who is walking into the lion's den of an urban school, as Mr. Williams's comments exemplified.

> When I came to the school, I arrived at a place that was totally gone defunct. A certain individual that had stayed there, for I think seven years, had not done anything, and the community was in an uproar, and the teachers went downtown and

complained. The board members ended up forcing him out, so I came under very stressful circumstances. When I got there, a woman that I knew who was an assistant elementary director told me she was glad to finally see me. She also told me, "You don't know what you've got." And she went right out the door without another word. I was like, "Whoa, what is this?" And I knew I was in for something.

Mr. Williams soon discovered that the "something" was a student population whom he described as "very high need." Of the 454 students at the school, 98% were from low-socioeconomic neighborhoods that were violent and drug infested. Further, 67% of his families were mobile, and during the school year these families moved up to four times causing children to relocate to different schools several times per year. Undoubtedly, these factors had severe consequences upon the literacy development of these children who, on average, were reading at least one year below grade level (Michigan School Report, 1998). Although Mr. Williams initially had difficulties with some teachers who constantly blamed students and their families for the school's negative publicity, low achievement, and poor test scores, he did not let this deter him from challenging these negative attitudes.

> When I got to the school, some of the staff members were always blaming the child. The child's poor, the child can't speak English, the child is bad. I said, "You know what? The best child you got is the best parent you got. I can't trade in the parents; I can't trade in the children. What comes through that door is ours so let's get ready."

As an urban principal, Mr. Williams helped the teachers "get ready" to work with Baker students by being supportive of them. His approach to leadership focused upon building a culture of empowerment by treating teachers in a professional manner and fostering a commitment to effective teaching (Peterson & Lezotte, 1991). Mr. Williams explained as follows:

> There are teachers who are good, who have good ethics, but some have problems giving the heart. Commitments have a heart, so teaching should have a heart. When you've got heart, ain't nothing gonna stop you. And many teachers there had heart; I can honestly say that. They were expected to do more with those kids than the average teacher in this district does, and they worked hard to do that. My job was to try to help them find that heart. I had retreats for them; I tried to give them the best. The teachers knew that I'd try to get everything for them that they needed. I cared about them as much as I cared about the kids.

Clearly, Mr. Williams's comments illustrate the primacy of a supportive administrator in urban schools. As principal, he understood that teachers must be valued and respected because they are working directly with students and families. He perceived his administrative role as one that communicated his appreciation of the jobs that they did. However, support was not enough. Mr. Williams soon realized that he could not simply tell the teachers what to do; he had to join them on their journey in developing more effective instructional strategies.

Moreover, Mr. Williams recognized that he was disconnected from what was actually occurring in classrooms. This disconnection caused him to undergo a transition in his role of urban principal. His role was changing from an organizational manager to an instructional leader. Bliss (1991) asserted that urban principals' direct involvement in curriculum and instructional issues in the classroom typically stem from the political and social ramifications of low test scores and poorly educated students.

For Mr. Williams and Baker Elementary School, declining reading scores on the statewide test was the central problem. Mr. Williams commented that literacy was one of his biggest problems: "The kids at this school just don't score well, and sometimes the teachers and I felt that we had no immediate or long-term solution to our literacy woes." In order to improve the test scores, Mr. Williams organized several meetings with his teachers to discuss the situation. In the following section, we provide excerpts from one such faculty meeting. For clarity, we specifically identify Mr. Williams's comments and provide general comments from several teachers:

Mr. Williams: Well, I guess you probably already know why I called this faculty meeting today. Well, it's about our test scores. Believe me, I know that you have worked very hard this year, but our test scores are extremely low again. In some areas, our students scored lower than they did last year. I know it's frustrating. I'm frustrated and I know that you are frustrated, but we are going to have to rectify the situation. I guess you heard the rumors that our school might be taken over by the State Department of Education. I wonder what are we doing wrong? I know we can't be doing everything wrong here at Baker.

Teacher 1: Why are schools judged as "good or bad" simply based on test scores? I don't think it's fair and I'm upset. Every year we hear the same old thing—"your students scored low."

Teacher 2: I mean, we are working as hard as we can with our students. But let's face it, our kids come to school with real problems, and we are, like, expected to work miracles. It's really hard sometimes to get these kids really motivated to learn.

Teacher 3: I mean, realistically, what can we do about the test scores? I'm so tired of hearing the same news year in and year out. I feel like

	quitting and doing something else. [Mr. Williams said that several teachers agreed with this teacher.]
Mr. Williams:	We can't feel sorry for ourselves. I know that we are in a tough spot, but we have to work together to do something about this situation.
Teacher 4:	But, what? I'm at a loss and I'm tired. I mean, they tell us not to teach to the test, and I don't want to teach to the test, but I'm beginning to feel like I should.
Teacher 5:	If we teach to the test, the test will become our curriculum, and I don't think that's the answer.
Teacher 6:	If that's not the answer, then what is the answer? What should we do? How can we help these kids do better? It seems like we are between a rock and a hard place.

The fact that Mr. Williams organized these meetings and tried to talk about these literacy, instructional, and curricular issues represents a more hands-on approach that is critical for urban principals who want to improve their students' academic performance (Bliss, 1991; Seashore Louis & Miles, 1991). Typically, urban principals delegate these issues around curriculum and instruction to grade-level chairpersons or subcommittees. Mr. Williams explained to us why he could not do so.

> As principal, the district and the state held me directly responsible for the low test scores. I expected teachers to help students to do better on [the] test, but I really didn't know how to tell them to do so. It's a very complicated issue. I can't just go into the classroom with the magic cure; we have to all put our heads together and think how we are gonna help these kids do better. So I can't just concentrate on the administrative end; I have to really work on the instructional end as well. Because what's really killing us is low test scores and our kids' failure on literacy-related issues—mainly reading and writing.

In order to help teachers think about curriculum and instructional issues around literacy, Mr. Williams decided to focus upon parent involvement. Edwards and Pleasants (1997) affirmed that students' literacy development can be enhanced when parents are involved in their children's educational lives. After taking time to talk with families, Mr. Williams discovered that parents were not interested in or aware of their children's difficulties in reading and writing because they were caught in financial crises. Often, they were evicted from their homes or left before they had to pay rent. Although some parents were on welfare, others worked two and three legitimate jobs to survive, while others sold drugs. Mr. Williams described the desperate situations that many parents faced.

> We gotta find some way of meeting the basic needs of the kids. Parents were saying, "I can't meet the needs of my kids, so don't tell me about learning and

school." These parents were worried about where they're gonna eat, where they're gonna sleep, if they have to fight.... And the most amazing part of what I saw in this crack cocaine community was that a lot of them didn't use it. They were the sellers and the dealers. I've never seen so many mothers in prison. They were selling drugs because the one thing they wanted for their child was to come to school looking good. They remember how they felt when they didn't look good going to school. But before that would happen, they would pay the neighbor off to make sure that she'd take care of her kids in case anything happened. So we are dealing with basic survival here, survival of the family and of the kids.

These issues were overwhelming to Mr. Williams because he could not find a way to connect students' life experiences in this urban community to literacy curriculum and instruction. He could not count on the parents to be consistently involved in their children's education, and the teachers were slowly losing heart and interest in teaching "these kinds of kids." Mr. Williams was completely overwhelmed; his plate was full with the complexity of issues surrounding the low literacy scores and low academic achievement. When he took this job, Mr. Williams knew that he had a "tough juggling act," but he still had to deal with the bottom line of improving test scores and improving the literacy curriculum. Even more disheartening, Mr. Williams did not receive much support from the school district in his endeavor to transform Baker Elementary. In the end, Mr. Williams resigned because he was tired of fighting with the school board for a new building, better materials, and additional faculty members. The year after he left, an interim principal came to the school. The interim principal had tremendous difficulty at Baker Elementary, and the following year a new principal, Mr. Carter, was hired. It is to Mr. Carter's story that we now turn.

Mr. Carter's Story:
Address the Real Issue—Community Mental Health

When I first came to Baker Elementary, it was a complete mess. We had just been reconstituted...our class size had been reduced, and we had some additional funding for reading programs, like Reading Recovery and our tutoring program. As a result, the district expected major improvement on the reading scores, despite the fact that those scores had been extremely low for several years. I was brought here to make some positive changes because it seemed that the interim principal couldn't handle the job.

Mr. Carter's words convey the challenge of being principal at Baker Elementary School. Although he arrived in September 1998, the issues that the school faced, particularly those around literacy and academic achievement, were similar to those that Mr. Williams faced 10 years earlier. Consequently, Mr. Carter was selected by the district to become principal because, like Mr. Williams, he had an unusual administrative approach. Many urban principals manage their schools as though they were organizational islands with self-contained problems and solutions (Sergiovanni, 1994). In contrast, Mr. Carter viewed his school as part of an intricate ecological system that included family, community, and other social institutions (Enomoto, 1997). Grounded in his former work as an urban planner, Mr. Carter used a "systems" approach to highlight connections between the school and its community.

> The demographics of an area are important, especially for a school. Problems and issues that the school faces are set within a certain geographical context, so the housing, welfare, and mental health issues all become salient to schools. Principals tend to think their students have discipline problems, so many urban schools are getting more police in there to handle the kids. But the problem is not discipline; it's community mental heath. When the community is not healthy, kids will come to schools and act out. We need to define school problems and solutions in terms of mental health.

This "mental health" approach illuminates the interconnectedness of school, family, and community. Mr. Carter's perspective that the mental health of institutions such as families, communities, and schools affect students' educational experiences is well established in the literature on school counseling (Purkey & Schmidt, 1987; Schmidt, 1993). Schmidt (1993) suggested that effective principals and other school administrators should pay attention to the elements that contribute to mentally healthy learning environments, such as parent involvement, caring and supportive school personnel, and high teacher and student morale.

Mr. Carter recognized that social and community-related issues could potentially mitigate educational outcomes. Similarly, Edwards, Pleasants, and Franklin (1999) affirmed that

> schools and teachers must realize that children do not live in a utopia free of problems that plague adults. Children are part of society, and what happens in their family, community, and school affects them and all aspects of their development. (p. xix)

Although these community and social issues are salient, particularly for children from diverse socioeconomic, racial, ethnic, and linguistic backgrounds, they are often dismissed or ignored by school districts that are concerned only about the business of educating children. Mr. Carter explained as follows:

> [In] places where there are people of color, the finger gets pointed, not at the people because that would be a very racist thing...but it gets pointed at the institution where those people go. And they [the district] say, "You haven't done for those people what you ought to be doing." And the issue is that their stories about real-life survival aren't being told.... Any time you try to bring those stories into the discussion to say, "Let's deal with the problems in the community and in society," they get washed off the table by your own school system. It's a shame that people...can't or won't address the real issue—the fundamental issues of what's happening in our community and our society.

Like Mr. Williams, Mr. Carter recognized the importance of supporting parents' involvement by listening to their stories in ways that communicated respect and empathy. Further, administrators and teachers who listen to parents are likely to elicit personal knowledge that can connect students to the literacy curriculum (Anderson & Stokes, 1984; Edwards et al., 1999).

In an effort to create a mentally healthy educational environment, Mr. Carter used an adaptation of what Edwards et al. (1999) called "parent stories." Through a set of open-ended questions, parents are invited to tell a story that provides rich information about their child's traditional and nontraditional literacy experiences in the home. In their book, Edwards and her colleagues included the Edwards-Pleasants Questionnaire as a framework for crafting questions to elicit parent responses that are both complex and insightful. We mention just a few examples from the questionnaire:

- What is a normal weekday routine for you and your child? What is a normal weekend like?
- What does your family enjoy doing together?
- How does your child feel about school?
- Is there something about your child that might not be obvious to the teacher or principal, but might positively or negatively affect his/her performance in school? If so, please explain.
- What kinds of things do you do to help your child be successful in school?

Although Edwards and her colleagues suggested a more formal interview approach for collecting parent stories, administrators like Mr. Carter can gather this valuable information from informal conversations. As Mr. Carter listened to parents and their stories, he gained insights about their hardships and their lives.

I don't have what is perceived as the "typical welfare family," parents sitting home getting drunk all day and sending their kids to school and they're just no-count, no-good. I've got a lot of parents who are struggling to get by working two or three jobs, they even pool their households to combine trying to pay the rent and put enough food on the table. So when I try to reach them and they're not there, it's not because they're at the bar or they're drunk somewhere; they're working. And, when I do get hold of them and reach them, they're exhausted. So I have to be aware of that. But I can also look past that and see the humanness in them, and they begin to see the humanness in me. And we end up with a situation where we can have a good dialogue about what needs to happen, and it's not about blaming somebody.

Clearly, parent stories have given Mr. Carter a different perspective about students, families, and communities. By moving beyond the at-risk label typically designated to low-income and minority parents, Mr. Carter fostered the human side of education, one that emphasizes open communication and collaboration between home and school (Edwards et al., 1999). In doing so, Mr. Carter invited these parents into the school by positioning them as "the more knowledgeable others" in terms of their expertise about culturally diverse home literacy environments and practices.

Consequently, parent stories provided critical information about families and communities that transformed the school's literacy curriculum and instruction. Mr. Carter shared this information with teachers to challenge their negative perceptions of parents as "disadvantaged" or "deficit." Parent stories increased teachers' awareness of and respect for the intangible forms of parent involvement and cultural practices, such as creating a supportive home environment, holding high expectations for their children, and making personal sacrifices to help them (Nieto, 1996). Mr. Carter explained as follows:

Teachers are gonna have opinions...and thoughts about how "those kids are." I want them to be able to say, "Look, everybody has a fresh start here." I show them it's important for them to look at the person, let all those bad thoughts go, and understand this person is human just like they are.... Then, it's not so important to tell parents how bad they are or what they've done with their kids is bad. It becomes a matter of helping parents to help their son or daughter become successful.

Using parent stories, Mr. Carter also had a strategy for helping teachers to connect literacy instruction with the home-based literacy experiences and cultural practices in meaningful and significant ways. While many teachers and school administrators pay lip service to having a child-centered literacy curriculum and pedagogy, very few have understood how to accomplish this goal. Parent stories provided the mechanism for Mr. Carter and his faculty to respond to the needs of culturally diverse students and parents. The idea that urban families have their own cultural capital in educating their children is important, and it is imperative that teachers build upon these literacy foundations in an effort to maximize literacy achievement (Reglin, 1995; Taylor & Dorsey-Gaines, 1988).

Important Insights and Conclusions

We have shared the Williams and Carter stories as a testimonial to the urban principal. Like other administrators working in urban schools around the country, these two men have witnessed the devastation of the community and its effects upon the lives of students and their families. However, Mr. Williams and Mr. Carter have made important inroads to working with and understanding their students and their families. Both stories highlight the caring, the compassion, and the dedication that these two principals had for serving urban families, who are often considered to be America's "throwaway" population (Taylor & Dorsey-Gaines, 1988). Their success in working with parents shows that it is possible for educators to build positive relationships with families and their communities. The lesson learned from both stories is that teachers and administrators must have a strong commitment to giving the maximum so that all children have a chance to learn and to succeed.

More important, the Williams and Carter stories exemplified the changing nature of the urban principalship. Urban principals can no longer narrowly prescribe their role as organizational managers and focus their attention upon administrative duties. In order for urban schools to be effective, today's principals must also serve as strong instructional leaders. This type of leadership emphasizes culture building, in terms of fostering a mentally healthy school environment that empowers teachers, students, and parents. In effect, teachers and administrators who listen to parents invite them to share personal knowledge about their home literacy environment and cultural practices in ways that foster home-school collaborations (Edwards et al., 1999). Further, urban principals and teachers can transform literacy curriculum and instruction by drawing upon these rich sources of information (Taylor & Dorsey-Gaines, 1988).

We believe, as Mr. Williams and Mr. Carter do, that the first step to effective teaching in urban elementary schools is making a personal investment in students, families, and the community. Challenging the negative perceptions and stereotypes about urban families and communities is central to providing literacy instruction that is appropriate and responsive to the needs of cultur-ally diverse students (Edwards et al., 1999). Similarly, Taylor & Dorsey-Gaines (1988) asserted that

> If we are to teach, we must first examine our own assumptions about families and children and we must be alert to the negative images in the literature.... Instead of responding to "pathologies," we must recognize that what we see may actually be healthy adaptations to an uncertain and stressful world. As teachers, researchers, and policymakers, we need to think about the children themselves and try to imagine the contextual worlds of their day-to-day lives. (p. 203)

Both Mr. Williams and Mr. Carter empathized with the families because they were acutely aware of the hard times in the surrounding community. Neither principal blamed families for their problems because many of them were cognizant of the mental health issues in society. However, these urban principals took the initiative to introduce parents to some of the nuances of school-based discourse. By inviting parents to come to visit their children's classrooms, creating a positive learning environment that welcomed parents, and interacting with parents in respectful ways, Mr. Williams and Mr. Carter em-powered families to take more active roles in their children's academic lives.

We feel that it is imperative that urban principals take the next step and use home-school connections in ways that specifically foster students' litera-cy development. Children come to school with a wealth of literacy knowledge from their homes, and it is important for teachers and administrators to build upon those early learning experiences (Anderson & Stokes, 1984; Edwards & Pleasants, 1997). Urban principals like Mr. Williams and Mr. Carter help to build partnerships between school and home. These partnerships can serve as a foundation for urban principals and teachers to collect "parent stories," which provide specific information about the traditional and nontraditional early literacy activities within the home (Edwards et al., 1999). With these parent stories, teachers and administrators have the unique opportunity to gain vital information about students' familial and cultural literacies that can be used to inform curriculum and instruction.

We conclude our article with an insightful comment from Mr. Williams that serves as a reminder to urban educators about the important roles they play in the lives of their students and families:

> Other than drugs, school is the biggest influence on this community. The school is the only hope they have.... That's why I became a principal, so I could have a positive impact on my kids and their families. I like my job. I get to work with great kids who are really, really smart...and I can make these kids winners.

We believe urban administrators and teachers can make a positive impact in the lives of culturally diverse children, families, and communities. By understanding how social, economic, linguistic, and cultural factors mediate schooling, urban principals and teachers can develop more student-centered approaches to literacy curriculum and instruction. In doing so, urban teachers can connect to students' individual learning styles and build upon their prior knowledge and experiences. Like Mr. Williams and Mr. Carter, we acknowledge that for this kind of teaching urban educators must make a transition from business as usual toward a new vision of education that unites administrators, teachers, parents, and communities in ways that enhance the literacy development and academic achievement of urban children.

The authors wish to acknowledge the support of the research reported here from the Center for the Improvement of Early Reading Achievement (CIERA), under the Educational Research and Development Centers Program, PR/Award Number R305R70004, administered by the Office of Educational Research Improvement, U.S. Department of Education, and from the Spencer Foundation Small Grant Program.

REFERENCES

Anderson, A.B., & Stokes, S.J. (1984). Social and institutional influences on the development and practice of literacy. In H. Goelman, A. Oberg, & F. Smith (Eds.), *Awakening to literacy* (pp. 24–37). Exeter, NH: Heinemann.

Anyon, J. (1997). *Ghetto schooling: A political economy of urban educational reform.* New York: Teachers College Press.

Bliss, J.R. (1991). Strategies and holistic images of effective schools. In J.R. Bliss, W.A. Firestone, & C.E. Richards (Eds.), *Rethinking effective schools: Research and practice* (pp. 43–57). Englewood Cliffs, NJ: Prentice Hall.

Bogotch, I.E., & Taylor, D.L. (1993). Discretionary assessment practices: Professional judgements and principals' actions. *The Urban Review, 25,* 289–306.

Corno, L. (1989). What it means to be literate about classrooms. In D. Bloome (Ed.), *Classrooms and literacy* (pp. 29–52). Norwood, NJ: Ablex.

Edwards, P.A., & Pleasants, H.M. (1997). Uncloseting home literacy environments: Issues raised through the telling of parent stories. *Early Child Development and Care, 127/128,* 27–46.

Edwards, P.A., Pleasants, H.M., & Franklin, S.H. (1999). *A path to follow: Learning to listen to parents.* Portsmouth, NH: Heinemann.

Enomoto, E.K. (1997). Schools as nested communities: Sergiovanni's metaphor extended. *Urban Education, 32,* 512–531.

Goodlad, J.I. (1984). *A place called school: Prospects for the future.* New York: McGraw-Hill.

Kozol, J. (1991). *Savage inequalities: Children in America's schools.* New York: Crown.

Michigan School Report. (1998). [Online]. Available: www.state.mi.us/mde/cfdata/msr98/msr_bldg.cfm

National Council of Jewish Women. (1999). *Parents as school partners*. [Online]. Available: eric-web.tc.columbia.edu/families/NCJW_child/principals.html

Neufeld, B. (1997). Responding to the expressed needs of urban middle school principals. *Urban Education, 31*, 490–509.

Nieto, S. (1996). *Affirming diversity: The sociopolitical context of multicultural education* (2nd ed.). White Plains, NY: Longman.

Osterman, K.E., Crow, G.M., & Rosen, J.L. (1997). New urban principals: Role conceptions at the entry level. *Urban Education, 32*, 373–393.

Parsons, T. (1958). Some ingredients of a general theory of formal organization. In A.W. Halpin (Ed.), *Administrative theory in education* (pp. 40–72). New York: Macmillan.

Peterson, K.D., & Lezotte, L.W. (1991). New directions in the effective schools movement. In J.R. Bliss, W.A. Firestone, & C.E. Richards (Eds.), *Rethinking effective schools: Research and practice* (pp. 128–137). Englewood Cliffs, NJ: Prentice Hall.

Polite, V.C., & McClure, R. (1997). Introduction. *Urban Education, 31*, 461–465.

Purkey, W.W., & Schmidt, J.J. (1987). *The inviting relationship: An expanded perspective for professional counseling*. Englewood Cliffs, NJ: Prentice Hall.

Ramirez, R., Webb, F.R., & Guthrie, J.W. (1991). Site-based management: Restructuring decision-making for schools. In J.R. Bliss, W.A. Firestone, & C.E. Richards (Eds.), *Rethinking effective schools: Research and practice* (pp. 169–184). Englewood Cliffs, NJ: Prentice Hall.

Reglin, G.L. (1995). *Achievement for African American students: Strategies for the diverse classroom*. Bloomington, IN: National Educational Service.

Schmidt, J.J. (1993). *Counseling in schools: Essential services and comprehensive programs*. Boston: Allyn & Bacon.

Seashore Louis, K., & Miles, M.B. (1991). Toward effective urban high schools: The importance of planning and coping. In J.R. Bliss, W.A. Firestone, & C.E. Richards (Eds.), *Rethinking effective schools: Research and practice* (pp. 91–111). Englewood Cliffs, NJ: Prentice Hall.

Sergiovanni, T.J. (1994). Organizations or communities? Changing the metaphor changes the theory. *Education Administration Quarterly, 30*, 214–226.

Taylor, D., & Dorsey-Gaines, C. (1988). *Growing up literate: Learning from inner-city families*. Portsmouth, NH: Heinemann.

Stopping the Silence: Hearing Parents' Voices in an Urban First-Grade Family Literacy Program

Robert J. Nistler and Angela Maiers

usso and Cooper (1999) pointed to the beginnings of a parent revolution in urban schools, an end to "disorganization and near silence" (p. 140). They cited evidence demonstrating that the family is no longer the silent partner in urban schools in the United States. They suggest that recent polls and actions indicate a movement toward greater involvement and voice on the part of parents with children in urban schools. The following report of a family literacy program is an example of how parents, long silenced by inability to successfully negotiate the public school system, can establish themselves as valued partners with teachers in the literacy development of their children at home and in school.

Research studies of early readers and investigations of emergent literacy uniformly conclude that parental beliefs, aspirations, and actions critically affect children's literacy growth (Routman, 1996). We (a university professor and a first-grade teacher) established a joint home-school family literacy program to help parents understand how important their role is in their child's literacy growth. We sought to help parents appreciate that they do have important skills to share, but we also wished to empower them with additional skills that would enhance their understanding of literacy development and provide the confidence and support necessary to contribute to their children's literacy development. We believed that it was crucial for the families with whom we interacted to understand (a) that their children's literacy development can be fostered, (b) that this development must be valued in all homes, and (c) that it should be viewed as a *shared* responsibility between home and school.

We built our program on our beliefs that parents are a powerful, underused source of knowledge—a great untapped resource in many schools. Families can provide teachers with a vast reservoir of talent, energy, and insight. Instead, parents often can be made to feel uncomfortable and unwelcome within the school environment; parent insights may be dismissed as unimportant. However, it is just such insight that is needed for informed classroom instruction. Rather than viewing the school and home as separate and distinct, we must honor our common goal to help children become successful learners.

Originally published in *The Reading Teacher* (2000), volume 53, pages 670–680.

Our stance toward the value of home-school connections is consistent with Morrow's (1995) call for studies of family literacy that take a variety of perspectives in order to gain knowledge not only from professionals in the field but from the families and children as well. Elish-Piper (1997) noted that too often family literacy programs do not fully explore or value diverse family backgrounds. This report of our program addresses what occurs when parents and children engage in literate activities *during* the school day with emphasis on combining the strengths of home literacy with school. Information shared from our experiences can provide valuable information to educators to help continue or initiate strong literacy development in children. In addition, it points to the value of regular interactions with parents to better understand their beliefs, attitudes, daily challenges, and perceptions of the roles they play in the literacy development of their children.

The program described in this article represents what Neuman, Caperelli, and Kee (1998) described as "small wins." Drawing from Benjamin and Lord (1996) and Connors (1994), Neuman et al. stated,

> In contrast to a "big bang" effect—the belief that the debilitating effects of illiteracy will be eradicated—gains in family literacy can more aptly be described as "short stacks of small wins" which serve as indicators of improvements that produce visible results. (p. 251)

They concluded that "Richly detailed qualitative analyses may ultimately provide the most tangible, personal, and powerful means of demonstrating the effects of family literacy programs as well as the processes and dynamics of instruction that contribute to them" (p. 251).

Program Setting

This article focuses on two different cohorts of families of Angela Maiers's first-grade students across two academic years. As an intact classroom unit, the students had been randomly assigned to her classroom, and they represented the general first-grade population at their school. This classroom is in an urban elementary school that follows a modified calendar as a type of year-round schedule. The school serves approximately 470 students and 300 families in the inner city of Des Moines, Iowa, USA. In general, class size in this classroom averaged 15 students. During the first year of this study, the mobility rate at this school was 85% (229 exits and 298 entries). Within Angela's classroom during the second year, 6 students were there for the duration. Beyond those,

30 other students entered or departed during the course of the school year. Enrollment of the more mobile students ranged from one week to six months.

A predominance of children in the school qualify for free or reduced-price lunch, resulting in the district providing free meals for all. Of the adult residents in the area from which the school draws its students, 38% have no high school diploma or GED (General Equivalency Diploma). Of the mothers, 33% have less than a high school diploma. According to the state definition, 102 children in the school were considered "homeless" at some time during the first year of this program. Teachers report that a number of parents have difficulty providing basic necessities, such as hats, gloves, warm coats, shoes, and school supplies. Many have had past negative school experiences and are so focused on basic necessities that it becomes difficult for them to meet their children's educational needs.

Within this elementary school environment, it was unknown what literacy experiences children might have had prior to school. Lack of consistent in-depth parent-teacher interactions limited opportunities for learning about literacy activities in the home. What was known was that entering first graders in this urban school lacked the early literacy experiences requisite for future success in the school setting. As educators, we recognize the importance of understanding home literacy experiences and parents' roles in their children's school experiences. We recognize that values placed on literacy, and not on social status, race, or economics, are what make for a home rich in literacy (Morrow, 1995). However, research also points out that the types and forms of literacy practiced in homes can be incongruent with what children encounter in school (Auerbach, 1989). Long-term studies by Au (1981) and Heath (1983), and more recently by Paratore, Melzi, and Krol-Sinclair (1999) and McCarthey (1997), provided detailed accounts of children and families struggling to reconcile the familiar sociocultural patterns of functioning in their homes and communities with the vastly different and often confusing environment of the public school. Collectively, these studies, as well as others not cited, elaborated on the conflicting nature of school and community incongruencies that Auerbach identified. Further, these studies provided clear direction for improved social and academic classroom environments.

Description of the Program

Although this program was initiated by the first-grade teacher, Angela, she had very strong feelings about shared ownership between parents and teacher. In her words,

My intention was not to adopt a school model of literacy, but rather to provide an exchange between home and school to support students' literacy growth. As weeks passed, "my" classroom quickly became "ours." We became a community of learners. The atmosphere was that of cooperation. There was an ambiance of learning with a fine balance of stimulation and nurturing.

During our sessions, families identified problems, shared resources, became supports for one another, and a commitment to family literacy developed. The traditional parent-teacher relationship was turned upside down as parents welcomed me into their world. Emotions shared were honest, strong, and sincere. This project was born out of genuine respect for the parents' role as their child's first and primary educator. From the beginning, they were equal partners in the endeavor. I found they embraced the responsibility, accountability, and freedom of having a voice. When I met with parents, it was important that they knew that it was their program. Decisions were jointly made, from our meeting times and dates to the types of activities planned. Communication was varied and continuous. I learned to listen more and talk less.

With a one-month break when school was not in session during fall and spring semesters and a two-week winter holiday break, 13 sessions and a final picnic were held during the first year, and 15 sessions were held during the second. Parents of children in the first-grade classroom were invited to join their child for directed and informal literacy and related social activities. Parents or others representing students' families visited school from 8:45 a.m. until 11:30 a.m. on designated Fridays. During these times, adult-student pairs were guided through early literacy instructional activities. Angela consistently modeled literacy behaviors that could be repeated and extended at home.

Activities began with normal daily routines including a teacher-generated written message to parents and children (morning message), song, pledge, and sharing. A Poem of the Week consisting of four lines of words, word families, and language familiar to students was read from large chart paper. Participants then broke into four student/parent member cooperative groups where they received a copy of the poem. The poem was also printed on standard sentence strips, and students were guided by parents as they sequenced the strips. After reconstructing the text of the poem, students cut up the sentence strips into individual words. Students then reconstructed the poem. As a final step, students received a printed version of the poem, which they glued and illustrated in their own Poem Book. Poems were later used for familiar rereading and silent reading time by parents and children.

Following the cooperative poem groups, the teacher or a parent/student pair led the group through reading and singing an alphabet song, based upon a poem that focused on specific letter sounds. Food preparation activities were next. These were designed to be simple and provided opportunities for the teacher to model reading the recipe; point out key words; and help adults and students measure, pour, and stir ingredients. Attention was drawn to recognition of numbers and words from the recipes, vocabulary related to cooking, and observations of how ingredients change when they are combined. Children also worked with basic math concepts such as counting, measurement, and part-whole relationships.

Next, families moved to the literacy stations that were always available in the classroom. They participated in a variety of literacy and math activities at these centers, which provided interactive and nonthreatening ways for parents to interact with their child and understand skills and concepts reinforced in the classroom. Sample stations included Dramatic Play Area, Computer, Exploration/Science Theme of Magnets, Tool and Building Station, Math Manipulative Station, Piano and Music Station, Reading Corner, and Publishing and Art Center. As families became accustomed to the routine and make-up of the workstations, they began to contribute ideas and materials to modify them.

In addition to the scheduled activities, the teacher met with individual adults during this time and throughout the week to discuss concerns regarding students' literacy development, and how to promote it, as well as other pertinent family issues (e.g., health, housing, instructional materials, transportation, child care, employment). During year one, a one-hour teacher/parents seminar to discuss such concerns was held after parents and children worked together. During year two, this activity was woven into the morning activities. Angela shared her rationale for this changed approach in the following journal entry.

> I'd like to discuss my reasoning behind changing the schedule. Last year's program had four very distinct blocks. The cooking project, poem groups, the center time, and the parent seminar component (a very vital component for last year). The parents that belonged in the group last year really needed that kind of support and kind of encouragement between themselves and from me. There were several things that were going on that bonded the parents together like a death of a student and a very seriously ill student. Many of the parents had concerns with housing, and it was a very close and consistent group for attendance. They looked forward to coming each week.
>
> This year there were several factors why that component is not working. It is not that it [the parent group] is not important, I just think that it is being done differently this year. We have quite a different group, and the needs of parents are different. There isn't a closeness of parents this year due to the high mobility rate of my classroom. The parents are working more than the parents last year, so we have several different representations (surrogates) from families. We have cousins, aunts, uncles, neighbors, and friends representing students, which is valuable. The family thinks the program is valuable enough that a parent [or

adult] comes, but we see a lot of different people coming. There is not a cohesive group coming to the program; there is no core group. So, what I have been doing in place of the parent group time is to go to the different groups at the centers and talk to the parents about what they can do at home with their children, so I still get that focused teaching moment, only it is happening on an individual basis versus a group basis.

Methods Used for Program Evaluation

This family literacy program began inauspiciously as described by Angela (Maiers & Nistler, 1998).

> This program began in my head when the parent coordinator asked me to "pilot" a program that involved more than the standard two-parent activities and conference required...each year. We felt that if parents came to school on a regular basis that they would want to participate in more school activities.
>
> I'm sure they [parents] all thought I was crazy that very warm day in July when I, their child's first-grade teacher, showed up at their doorstep with a colored box of "stuff." I had no idea what I was getting into and no idea where this road would take me. (p. 223)

Because of the evolving nature of this program, it was critical that Angela develop consistent means for documenting all that occurred in order to inform program development. From the outset, Angela kept a personal journal in which she shared her observations and reflections related to this program and its participants. In addition, she interviewed a family representative for each student at the beginning, midterm, and end of the academic year. Audiotapes of these interviews were transcribed so we could better use this information to learn about our program and our families. The interview information was helpful but inconsistent for families who moved away from school with little or no advance notice to allow for an exit interview. Our semistructured interview guide is included in the Figure.

Information collected by Angela was augmented by my field notes chronicling what I observed during my visits to Friday sessions. During year two of the program, an undergraduate education student joined me in observing and writing down her observations of the Friday sessions. Angela and I, joined by undergraduate student Abby Sims in year two, discussed our observations, impressions, concerns, and suggestions for change nearly every week of the program. These discussions occurred by phone, in triads, or meetings between two of us, and they became an important way to make sense of our experiences in this program. So much was happening that it became very important for each of us to have this outlet to share with the others.

Figure. Interview guide

1. What activities do you find most enjoyable when you come to school?
2. How often are you able to read with your child at home?
3. Have you done anything new or different this year with literacy at home?
4. How often are you able to visit the library with your child?
5. What is your biggest barrier to attending school activities?
   - job conflicts
   - time
   - transportation
   - baby-sitting
   - interest
   - other
6. How do you plan to continue being involved in school activities?
7. Do you feel informed about activities that occur at school?
8. Which of the following do you find most informative about what is happening at school?
   - classroom newsletter
   - parent message board
   - phone calls
   - notes home
   - school newsletters
   - schoolwide notes
   - personal notes to yourself
   - personal notes to your child
   - personal contact
   - other
9. General comments:

Equally important, parents helped us know what to do differently, what worked, and what was needed. Angela was always meeting with parents either at school, outside school, or on the phone to gather feedback about their children and this program.

Levels of Involvement

This program created a structure for involving parents and children in the children's development as readers and writers at school with the hope this would transfer to home practices as well. Families' involvement in this program was uniformly high when viewed in terms of (a) attendance, (b) interactions with others in the classroom community, and (c) participation in literacy activities in school and at home.

Attendance

During year one 96.5% of the students enrolled in Angela's classroom were represented at Friday sessions. During year two 94.5% of her students were represented at program sessions in which she was in the classroom (maternity leave notwithstanding). It should be noted that in year two, 6 of the 14 students enrolled in August were still enrolled at the end of the program. Attrition of families throughout the year was due to their leaving this school rather than a decision not to participate. Turnover of students was prevalent there. As the teacher noted,

> My class list has changed by eight students already only 4 weeks into school. One day I got three new students in less than a 2-hour block. Four of the home visits that I did were no-shows at the beginning of school. There is a possibility of losing three families again over the next couple of weeks. This is life at this school.

Whether physically attending program sessions or not, families of students demonstrated involvement by attending, sending a substitute family member, calling to report absences, or sending supplies to support the morning activities. For example, an early entry in Angela's journal during year two demonstrates the use of family surrogates. (Pseudonyms are used for all students and parents.)

> Grandma came to the first Friday group. From the start she kept telling me she could only stay 15 or 20 minutes. She said this about three or four times and ended up getting really involved in the book boxes and stayed the entire session!

Other entries from Angela's journal demonstrate parental efforts and good intentions to attend and be involved.

> During the first session Lisa was only going to stay a short time because she had worked all night and still came to group without sleep! She stayed almost the entire time! She really interacted well with her daughter.
>
> Tasha's mom stopped in to visit this morning. Tasha's aunt told her how much fun Friday was, and Tasha was disappointed she couldn't come. She is working out a new schedule at work and wants to really try to make it next Friday. She said if not, she would definitely be in on another day to work with her daughter. I got her working with the school success worker to deal with some family issues with housing and her marriage. She has kept all her meetings, and I think it is going well.
>
> Both mom and dad attended and stayed the entire time! They both commented to me personally about how well they felt the morning went and how glad they were they came. Both work outside construction type jobs, and I know scheduling time will be a large barrier to their attendance.

To create and sustain involvement, recruitment needed to be innovative and persistent. To achieve successful participation, it was important for Angela to acknowledge and remove potential barriers that would affect attendance. Obstacles can be either physical or psychological. Parents repeatedly commented on how family circumstances, job issues, or other such obstacles were possible factors for not being involved. Yet, not one family in this program indicated they did not want to be there for their child.

Reducing physical barriers such as transportation and child care was foremost on Angela's agenda. Baby-sitting was offered to parents, and rides were given when needed. These services were offered, but as the parents formed a closer knit community they began to negotiate and share resources to confront these barriers. As parents grew closer to one another, rides were shared and traded, and families began to bring younger siblings to school for the morning activities. Angela had established an atmosphere that was family friendly and conducive to visitors. Families were comfortable bringing younger siblings and infants. It was not unusual to see Angela pick up the classroom telephone and hear her respond to an absent parent, "Get over here now and bring that baby with you!" Many parents commented on how they appreciated being able to participate at school with *all* their children.

Emotional barriers affecting attendance were addressed on a different level from those of a physical nature. Negotiating emotions such as fear of school, low self-esteem, and cultural and familial differences were more subtle and difficult to eliminate. With time spent together at school, under Angela's constant encouragement, family members began to feel more comfortable and confident in the school environment. Near the end of year two, Abby noted the following observation.

> It's 10:10 a.m. Angela hugs three moms as they leave. She's at the front door. [Parents line up like first graders would on their way out the door.] "It means so much to your kids that you're here," she tells them as they leave.

Interactions With Others in the Classroom Community

The promise of helping their child succeed in school may be the initial reason parents became involved in the program, but classroom observations suggest that this interest, combined with a feeling of personal success and accomplishment, promoted continued participation. Friendships were built as parents and teacher learned from one another. The formal and informal parent/teacher interactions gave parents the opportunity to talk about community issues and personal experiences and to express their thoughts and opinions in a nonthreatening and caring environment, as is apparent in the following parent's note to Angela.

> Thank you for all your extra support. I had my daughter when I was 16 years old, so it's nice to have advice from other mothers that are more educated. Sometimes I want to just give up, but I can't—I went through that with my mother. She left me when I was 5, and I never found her 'til I was 12 years old. With the way things are now, at home, it's been really hard. I am open to any options to help with my daughter. Thanks so much.

This program also gave parents the opportunity to learn about their child's school and classroom, and it gave the teacher a chance to learn about the families involved. As one parent offered, "This is a great program. It is fun to see how the classroom works and get to know the other parents and students. We look forward to coming. It is like a family time." Angela was brought into the world of her students and became an equal partner working with families on the shared goal of helping children in this inner-city school develop and grow. These efforts on the part of the adults in their lives were not lost on the students, as the following written statement by a first grader indicates.

> Every Friday my class cooks together. My mom comes and cooks with us. I feel so excited and happy and glad. I sit by my mom, and my mom sits by me. I cook by my mom and my mom cooks by me. We have lots of fun together. I love Fridays.

Abby captured the essence of classroom interactions for students and families when she shared the following observations early in year two of the program.

> Watching 14 eager faces on Friday mornings as they watch for their parents or grandparents to arrive is a sight in itself. Children experience coloring, reading, cutting, pasting, and cooking with their parents, all of which promote literacy.... I see such great things coming from this program. I see an opportunity for parents to get involved in their first grader's life in a way that he or she may never be a part of for the rest of their student's schooling. I also see the effort and care children put into their time with their families, and the pride they take in showing them what they have achieved with Angela. The students feel valued—important. But most of all, they feel like they are a part of something special. They are a part of a singular program that allows who they most value, their parents and family, to be a part of something that is uniquely theirs, Mrs. Maiers's first-grade class.

Participation in Literacy Activities at Home and School

A primary intent of this program was to model behaviors that support literacy at home. Parents were encouraged to use literacy in many ways with their children, including reading, writing, composing letters, journal keeping, and cooking. Adults were also encouraged to engage in these literacy behaviors at home. Parental comments regarding the carryover of school literacy activities to the home indicate that they engaged in activities introduced, modeled, and practiced during the biweekly Friday sessions.

> I have sentences at home that I have him write, like from the reading groups [at school].
>
> I make sentences and Jason helps me put them together, then he writes the sentence just like we do in group.
>
> We've done cut-outs at home [poem group activity].

Parents wanted to help their children succeed in school, but often requested help and guidance about how to do this most effectively. With time in the program, parents' confidence in the value of their interactions with their children increased, as did confidence in their reading ability and their own capacity to help their children with school activities. This was evident as parents assumed greater responsibility for conducting classroom literacy activities. Abby briefly describes one such occurrence.

> Karen's mom was actively engaged in the text as she read it to the class, laughing just as much as they did. She literally had children hanging off her by the end of the story. Students were too absorbed in her reading the book to notice incoming parents and phone calls.

Through participation in the program, parents learned what was expected of their children at school, and they became more aware of what their children were capable of doing with support. Sometimes that support came in the form of carving out individual space at home for a student's school-based belongings.

> We try to help with her homework more. She keeps everything in her box that her and James (father) made [personal storage box for reading materials at home created at first session]. She has a lot of books and papers there.

For others, support was provided as parents modified existing home literacy practices according to what they observed and learned during school-based activities.

> As far as reading, before I used to just read to the kids. Now they sit on my lap, and we point to the words and read a lot more together, and it's to the point now that he'll come to me and say, "You know, it's time for reading." I mean he's actually excited about doing some school stuff now where he wasn't before.

The cooking and singing [in class] is so great. I hate to sing, but I am singing right along with the kids! There is so much learning when we are cooking. My son wants to cook every Saturday. We make it a special thing. He loves making deviled eggs. I'll get the class the recipe.

Elements for Program Success

Neuman et al. (1998) reviewed the files of all the grants that have been funded (52) by the Barbara Bush Foundation for Family Literacy. Analysis of these programs identified successful features of family literacy programs. While not all-inclusive of the body of work available regarding family literacy, these grants do represent the breadth of programs that exist in the field of family literacy. The program features that we identify as critical to the success of our family literacy program are certainly in keeping with the aforementioned findings. We discuss those features next.

Create a Sense of Community

Kambrelis (1995) and Lewis (1995) viewed "community" from a performance perspective in which norms and expectations evolve through negotiation among participants. Lewis stated that

> contexts (including classrooms) are not static social facts or representations but construction zones or performative inventions negotiated by the participants. As such, they are heterogeneous and negotiable. This is crucial because it is within these construction zones that socialization and learning occur and individuals claim particular kinds of social and cultural practices and identities. (p. 150)

Angela's classroom became the type of construction zone alluded to by Kambrelis and Lewis. Parents were interested in supporting their child's literacy learning and in turn felt successes in their own development. Parents talked of the bonds they formed with fellow parents, what they learned from one another, and what Angela learned from them. Individually, Angela talked with parents; they in turn discussed with one another community issues, personal experiences, and other concerns. Every member had something significant to contribute. Families were a rich source of information, both for understanding individual children and for general planning.

Initially, families went individually to Angela to discuss how to address critical needs they had either at home or with their children in school. Over time, families turned to one another for support and information rather than solely relying on Angela.

Role of Teacher

The role of the teacher in this program proved vital. Parents raved about the positive relationship that they had with Angela and that she had with the students. Research suggests that, in general, a teacher's interpersonal skills and professional merit have a significant effect on parental perceptions and willingness to participate (Epstein, 1988). Angela works well with students and adults in a unique manner. However, as we viewed the nature of her interactions we identified elements of them that others can apply in similar programs.

Angela consciously employed a great variety of strategies to ensure that all families believed they were among supportive friends in the classroom community. Simple gestures such as acknowledging all who entered and left the classroom, capturing special family times in the classroom with pictures and distributing these, and providing lists of safety measures for cooking with children established a genuine sense of teacher concern for family members. In addition to these efforts, the individual and group discussions (with Angela and parents as equal participants) contributed to the depth of relationships that were valuable to this program's success.

During a parent discussion group early in the program, Angela asked for advice from those around her. "Since all of you have made it through the terrible 2s with your children, I'd appreciate any advice you could give me for my 2-year-old!" Parents immediately began to share and discuss what it is like having a 2-year-old. This provided an opportunity for parents to share something with Angela rather than feeling that she was always trying to help them. A deeper relationship was beginning as parents shared with one another and with Angela their thoughts, feelings, and most of all their trust.

Further evidence of the nature of the teacher's role in our program was provided when a long-term substitute teacher took over during Angela's eight-week maternity leave at midyear of the second year. In her written observations, Abby noted how Angela and the long-term sub differed in their interactions with families.

> What a difference between Angela's interaction and the substitute teacher. Seeing this for the first time today I made a few observations. First, there was very little personal contact made between the teacher and the students. The entire morning was led with very little parent to parent, student to parent, or teacher to parent interaction. Parents mostly sat at a distance from the group, unless taking disci-

plinary actions, and were minimally involved with the morning's activities. Today exemplified how crucial it is that the teacher have an ongoing relationship with the parents, continually inviting them into the classroom.

The teacher's instructional role was very different as well. Today the teacher was more authoritative than interactive with the students. Although the activities called for the teacher to participate in the activities with the students, there were more disciplinary measures being taken than in previous sessions.

When Angela returned as the regular classroom teacher in February, Abby again noted important differences between the sub's and Angela's roles.

I knew that today would "work." Why? Because of two factors: One, Angela recruited incessantly for today's program. She contacted each child's parent, letting them know that this program is important. Secondly, the parents trust Angela. She is by no means a stranger to them, actively working them into their children's academic lives. Knowing these two things beforehand gave me all the confidence I needed to trust that today's program would soar. And soar it did.

Abby made other observations indicating how the environment changed with Angela's return to the classroom.

Students and parents were sitting in a close-knit group early on in the morning, something that has been lacking in the last two or three sessions. Reviewing the text was thorough. The recipe and directions were initially read and then reread—an important modeling aspect of this program.

Finally, it should be noted that in Angela's absence most families quit attending. Only a core group of three parents maintained involvement.

Maintain Efforts for Ongoing and Varied Communication

A variety of methods were necessary for communicating with all the families in our program. Most parents talked about the positive influence of personal (face-to-face) contacts throughout the week (not only on Fridays) for exchanging a wide range of information. Phone calls were another area of communication that parents appreciated. Calls were used to notify parents of concerns, but conveyed positive messages as well. Rich contacts also occurred during home visits, which helped demonstrate Angela's strong interest in students and families. Over the course of this program, carving out meaningful dialogue took time and patience on the part of the classroom teacher and family representatives, but this investment ultimately contributed to open, trusting relationships.

Consistent Recruitment

Recruitment for participation must be ongoing. Home visits were made before the program began, but due to the mobility rate of the population, recruiting needed to be continuous. Early in the week that a Friday session was scheduled, Angela would send home written fliers reminding parents to participate. In addition, she would list the item or items the family had volunteered to bring for the morning's activities. Most important, Angela would include an envelope containing pictures of each family's participation in the previous session. Finally, as Friday neared Angela would follow up the notes with phone calls to determine each family's intentions to attend.

Participation increased as parents interacted with one another during the sessions and as the word spread among families—and through children's requests for parental involvement as they saw more and more families represented. Yet developing a stable attendance rate takes time. It took several months for families to understand what the program entailed and for other families to join after the initial recruitment. When Angela was absent for eight weeks (four sessions) in December and January of the second year, attendance dwindled and positive engagement in literacy learning activities in the classroom sessions diminished considerably. Average adult attendance during sessions with Angela was 10; this number decreased to 3 when she was out on leave.

Share Program Responsibilities With Parents

Late in year two of our program, Abby recorded discussing with Angela the delicate balance that existed between parent and teacher responsibilities.

> "This is their program, not my program. I may be the facilitator, but it's *their* program. They would not be here if it was just me disseminating information." Later, when Angela and I discussed this last comment, we noted that although Angela acts as the facilitator, it must be *appropriate* facilitation. As we know, without the appropriate guidance, the program is unsuccessful and falls apart. The program is at a point now where the parents feel they are in charge and running the program. It's a fine line. It's like a developmentally appropriate classroom—when does the teacher act as the observer and when must (s)he intervene? Angela guides the group, yet the group acts as a family working together throughout the morning.

There were numerous occasions where observations such as the following demonstrated parents' willingness to do the "work" of the morning.

Jack's dad was jovial and comfortable. He's at a point where he needs very little direction from Angela to "take kids under his wing." He's at a point where he just does it.

To encourage parental involvement Angela made sure that parents were aware of the value of their input, as was the case when she met with a student's mother to plan how to modify her son's behavior in the classroom. Abby noted the following:

> When Angela asked Terrence's mom what advice she might have to help modify Terrence's behavior, Angela sent two messages to Terrence's mom. First, Angela is concerned about Terrence, and secondly, that Angela respects and wants the mom's help.

Engage Participants in a Variety of Literacy Activities

Parents and caregivers engaged in a wide variety of literacy activities with their children. Storybook reading was an integral part of our program. Parents were given access to quality books and also given time to observe and practice interactive storybook reading. Although shared storybook reading has been identified as the most important activity in preparing children for school success, homes where children do not engage in this are not devoid of literacy. As reported by Morrow (1995) and others, families use literacy in many different ways. It was important that families felt these ways were affirmed and valued. The variety of classroom activities parents were exposed to, such as cooking and the many different learning centers, helped parents to see just how much they were contributing to their children's literacy development during their everyday home activities. This proved to be just as important as introducing new uses of literacy.

Teacher Understanding of Family Challenges

The types of literacy activities that parents and caregivers choose are largely dictated by the circumstances in their lives (Paratore, 1995). Despite extensive discussion and modeling, parents still found it difficult to find time to read and write with their children. As reported by parents, outside circumstances and issues played a significant role in whether or not literacy activities occurred at home. Social issues, such as the following incident reported in Angela's journal, indicate the extreme challenges faced in some families.

Robert's mom stole the grandmother's car and money and took off. She has been gone almost 1 week. She left the kids with grandma, but she is in bad health and has no money to raise them. She sent them to live with relatives in Missouri. This is very upsetting.

Whenever possible, Angela worked with parents to find appropriate social services to deal with the events in their lives.

It Was All Worth the Effort

Parents exhibited strong values to help their child succeed, reinforcing the belief that where literacy is valued it is nurtured. One criticism of many programs designed for parents, especially low-income African American parents, is that they "won't come because they are simply not interested in helping their children" (Taylor & Dorsey-Gaines, 1988). We found this to be absolutely untrue. Morrow (1995) noted that even parents who lack knowledge about the school program do not lack interest in their child's school, or learning how to help their children at home. The common thread with all the families we worked with was that they genuinely cared about their children's education.

Never was this more in evidence than in the following incident. Angela was teaching a graduate course on family literacy and parental involvement. She had gathered a panel of "parent experts" to share their opinions regarding parental involvement in children's literacy development. The panel consisted of parents who had participated in our family literacy program with their children. As parents began to address her students Angela's thoughts turned to her initial encounter with Jack and his father, David. She later noted the following in her journal.

> As David sat there today so proud, so confident and strong, my mind drifted back to that summer day in July as I visited his apartment trying to convince a seemingly unconvincible [sic] parent about the benefits of parent involvement. On July 16, 1996, I had made the following entry in my family literacy journal.
>
> Today I visited four families, but it was the last visit of the day that has stayed with me. I met David and his son Jack. They live in a one-bedroom apartment with David's cousin until they can find a place of their own. He had recently moved and has found work with a local construction company. David is raising his son alone. Jack's mother is in jail.
>
> I introduced myself to Jack, and told him that I was going to be his teacher for the coming year. I shared with David some of my hopes for a new program I was implementing in my first-grade classroom involving parents in a new way. He stood there and looked at me with his arms tightly crossed and said in a

matter-of-fact way that he would not be participating in any program. He explained his busy schedule with work and the responsibilities he faces as a single father. He allowed me to continue with details of what I proposed. He politely listened, but there was an invisible wall between us. His guard was up, and he seemed so unresponsive to what I had to say. I continued trying to get him excited about working together, but in the back of my mind I knew that for many possible reasons he may not come. I asked him to meet me at school any time the first week so that I could help Jack make a smooth transition at his new school.

In the short time I was there, David shared with me that his experience in Jack's previous school was frustrating and upsetting to both of them. I wanted so badly for this year to be different. I thanked them for their time and told them that I looked forward to our next meeting. There was no answer as to whether or not he would be meeting me at school to discuss the program farther. I left an open invitation and did not push the issue. The entire time we talked he kept looking to Jack, referring to him. His love and commitment to his son was evident. Our first meeting is in 1 week. I will wait and see.

Angela's thoughts returned to her class discussion, which she also noted in her journal.

October 28, 1998

David sat before the group of graduate education students one of a panel of parents addressing "Creating family-school partnerships." I had asked David to be a guest on the panel, and it took all I had to keep my composure when he talked. I was beaming with pride in awe of how much he had grown in the time we had worked together. He did come that first day for our first meeting and from that point he never stopped being involved. Now, he is sharing his story with others. He points his finger to the audience of graduate students seated eagerly to hear from parents their thoughts and insights about parent involvement.

He begins, "You teachers, parent involvement is the most important thing you can do in our classrooms. It is everything. She got me to come, and you have to get your parents there, too. My parents weren't involved. I was abused. They were not there for me, but I am there for him."

If those powerful words were not enough for my students to hear, across the room sat his son Jack, looking at his father with great admiration and respect. Their eyes were locked on one another. The room went silent as David became emotional. David apologized to the group for breaking down. He paused and continued. "I want to see him graduate. I didn't graduate. My boy (his eyes are filled with tears), he is the most important thing in the world."

I wanted so badly to race up there and give him a hug, but I had to continue the facilitation of the panel. Another parent reached over and gently patted David on the back for support. I commented with a heartfelt "Thank you for sharing." Inside I was bursting. He has given so much to make Jack's life better than his own. My admiration and respect for him is immense. He thanked the panel and myself for giving him the opportunity to share his insights. He repeated several times how important and special it made him feel to be a part of this group and to help teachers work more successfully with the parents in their classrooms. It was me who should be thanking him. My class listened to his words and saw the love in his eyes as he looked at his son.

When he left that day, he told me that he had lost his job, and they were moving on again to find work and a place to live. He had already made plans to go and meet with Jack's new teacher. Won't she be the lucky one. He hugged me and thanked me for all that I had done for him and his son. I gave him my address and asked him to send me an invitation to Jack's graduation. I will wait and expect a special piece of mail in 10 years or so. This will be a day that I will never forget. It made all the extra time and effort worth every minute and more. Thank you, David, for all that you have taught me about being a teacher, parent, and friend. Although I cannot re-create that special day, this journal entry illustrates the powerful and lasting impact working closely with parents can have on students, teachers, and children. It is a small window into understanding the vital role families play in the education of their children.

Interest in and a commitment to family literacy continues to grow. Parental involvement programs such as this one are designed to work with parents for the primary purpose of improving their child's literacy development (Epstein, 1988; Swap, 1993). This article describes what can occur when parents and children engage in literate activities *during* the school day. We found that by working closely with families we can further understand parents' beliefs, attitudes, and perceptions of the roles they play in the literacy development of their children. In turn, parents are able to give voice, through their actions, to the commitment they feel for their children to succeed.

The authors wish to acknowledge the support of the FINE Foundation of Iowa for their financial support for the second year of this program.

REFERENCES

Au, K. (1981). Participation structures in a reading lesson with Hawaiian children: Analysis of a culturally appropriate instructional event. *Anthropology and Education Quarterly, 11,* 91–115.

Auerbach, E.R. (1989). Towards a social-contextual approach to family literacy. *Harvard Educational Review, 59,* 165–181.

Benjamin, L., & Lord, J. (1996). *Family literacy.* Washington, DC: Office of Educational Research and Improvement.

Connors, L. (1994). *Small wins: The promises and challenges of family literacy* (Tech. Rep. No. 22). Baltimore: Center on Families, Communities, School & Children's Learning, Johns Hopkins University.

Elish-Piper, L. (1997, December). *The responsiveness of urban family literacy programs: What's happening and what's not?* Paper presented at the annual meeting of the National Reading Conference, Scottsdale, AZ.

Epstein, J. (1988). How do we improve programs for parental involvement? *Educational Horizons, 66,* 55–59.

Heath, S.B. (1983). *Ways with words: Language, life, and work in communities and classrooms.* New York: Cambridge University Press.

Kambrelis, G. (1995). Performing classroom community: A dramatic palimpsest of answerability. In K. Hinchman, D. Leu, & C. Kinzer (Eds.), *Perspectives on literacy research and practice* (44th yearbook of the National Reading Conference, pp. 148–160). Chicago: National Reading Conference.

Lewis, C. (1995). The idealized classroom community: A critique from a performance perspective. In K. Hinchman, D. Leu, & C. Kinzer (Eds.), *Perspectives on literacy research and practice* (44th yearbook of the National Reading Conference, pp. 161–168). Chicago: National Reading Conference.

Maiers, A., & Nistler, R.J. (1998). Changing parent roles in schools: Effects of a school-based family literacy program in an urban first-grade classroom. In T. Shanahan & F. Rodriguez-Brown (Eds.), *47th yearbook of the National Reading Conference* (pp. 221–231). Chicago: National Reading Conference.

McCarthey, S.J. (1997). Connecting home and school literacy practices in classrooms with diverse populations. *Journal of Literacy Research, 29,* 145–182.

Morrow, L.M. (Ed.). (1995). *Family literacy connections in schools and communities.* Newark, DE: International Reading Association.

Neuman, S., Caperelli, J., & Kee, C. (1998). Literacy learning, a family matter. *The Reading Teacher, 52,* 244–252.

Paratore, J. (1995). Implementing an intergenerational literacy program: Lessons learned. In L.M. Morrow (Ed.), *Family literacy connections in schools and communities* (pp. 37–53). Newark, DE: International Reading Association.

Paratore, J., Melzi, G., & Krol-Sinclair, B. (1999). *What should we expect of family literacy? Experiences of Latino children whose parents participate in an intergenerational literacy project* (Literacy Studies Series). Newark, DE: International Reading Association; Chicago: National Reading Conference.

Routman, R. (1996). *Literacy at the crossroads: Crucial talk about reading, writing, and other teaching dilemmas.* Portsmouth, NH: Heinemann.

Russo, C., & Cooper, B. (1999). Understanding urban education today. *Education and Urban Society, 31*(2), Prologue.

Swap, S.M. (1993). *Developing home-school partnerships: From concepts to practice.* New York: Teachers College Press.

Taylor, D., & Dorsey-Gaines, C. (1988). *Growing up literate: Learning from inner-city families.* Portsmouth, NH: Heinemann.

RIGHT

Children have a right to reading instruction

---

that makes meaningful use

---

of their first language skills.

Introduction

Robert S. Rueda

A visit to almost any urban (and increasingly suburban and rural) classroom will confirm that students are more diverse, especially in terms of language background. Current projections indicate that English language learners will make up about 25% of the entire U.S. school population by 2020 (García, 2000). (Note: The term *English language learners* refers to children who are acquiring English as a second language. A range of other terms also have been used to describe these children, for example, *second-language learners, bilingual students, students who are limited-English proficient or limited-English speaking*. In this context, the term *English language learners* refers to all these students.) Although the biggest part of this group speaks Spanish, there are a multitude of other languages such as Cantonese, Mandarin, Korean, Arabic, and Vietnamese. In some large urban school districts, the number of language groups served can approach 90 to 100. Providing appropriate reading instruction for these students is clearly an important priority. It is encouraging that the International Reading Association, in *Making a Difference Means Making It Different: Honoring Children's Rights to Excellent Reading Instruction*, has explicitly addressed this issue in Right 8—children have a right to reading instruction that makes meaningful use of their first language skills.

The three articles in this section shed light on native language use and its place in literacy acquisition and instruction. The first article, by James Paul Gee, provides a broad view of reading from a sociocognitive perspective. The other two articles, by Lee Gunderson and Donna Mahar respectively, provide insights about the role of language and culture in literacy instruction for adolescent readers. Gunderson's article reports findings of an investigation of over 35,000 immigrant students in Canada. Mahar's case study provides an in-depth look at the literacy and cultural struggles of two seventh-grade students.

Before discussing this right regarding native language use and its place in literacy acquisition and instruction in more detail, it is useful to consider the special role that language in general plays in reading and literacy.

A Note on Language

Language is the universal medium of communication among humans, and is relatively easily acquired before most children enter school. However, the fact that almost all students learn language before formal schooling can be deceptive. In reality, language is highly complex and serves multiple cognitive, social, and other purposes. For example, it is important for establishing and maintaining one's personal identity. It is often used as a social marker and routinely functions as a transmitter and storage device for knowledge and culture. Gee's article in this section points out that perhaps most important, language is used as a tool for mediating interaction with the world and with oneself (in the form of thinking and self-regulation) (see also Vygotsky, 1934/1978). Not surprisingly, language is of great concern to those interested in facilitating children's acquisition of reading and literacy. This is especially true in the case of English language learners, where issues such as choice of language of instruction are critical.

In U.S. society, as in other places in the world, language proficiency is often correlated with other factors and does not exist independently of other factors of importance for reading, literacy, and eventual school achievement. Non–English-speaking status is often related to socioeconomic status, ethnicity and/or race, cultural practices, and other critical variables. Thus language proficiency should not be considered alone, but rather as one of several interrelated factors mediating school success.

The Nature of Reading and Literacy

Before considering the issues involving reading instruction for English language learners, it is useful to first consider the nature of reading and literacy in general. As Gee (2001) points out, reading is more than psycholinguistic processing skills, although they are clearly important. A wider view is necessary if we speak to issues of diversity, in particular those involving culture and language, equity and access. Although psycholinguistic skills may be more universal, the understandings of literacy, cultural practices around literacy, everyday contexts for literacy, motivations for using literacy, access to print, and other factors are far from universal. It is these latter factors in particular that are likely to be highly salient factors for certain subgroups of students, such as English learners. It is important to recognize that English language learners from diverse communities may come to school with background knowledge, discourse conventions, and experiences with and understandings of the functions of print and literacy that may differ from those normally expected in all-English classrooms. These differences are important, because they may impact a student's willingness to engage in literacy and reading unless they are accounted for in terms of reading materials, reading activities, and other aspects of classroom instruction. At a minimum, teachers should ensure that there are a variety of reading materials available that reflect students' backgrounds and lives outside of school.

As Gee reminds us, language is important for other reasons as well. It can be seen as the "glue" that holds together the essence of a particular sociocultural setting. He describes Discourses as social languages embedded in specific communities of practice: "A Discourse integrates ways of talking, listening, writing, reading, acting, interacting, believing, valuing, and feeling (and using various objects, symbols, images, tools, and technologies) in the service of enacting meaningful socially situated identities and activities."

The Acquisition of Reading and Literacy for English Learners

What do we know about how English learners acquire reading and literacy? Generally, the reading development of English learners is similar to that of monolingual English speakers. It appears that all children use their developing knowledge of language, their background knowledge of the world in general, and their understanding of print conventions when they begin reading. It is also known that those who already have some exposure to reading and literacy either at home or school have an easier time becoming literate in English than those who do not. Researchers think that the ability to transfer what one knows about language and literacy in his or her native language to a second language is likely due to the fact that there seems to be an underlying proficiency that is not language specific. Thus, while transfer of this proficiency to the second language is not always automatic, native language instruction can not only make reading a more comprehensible activity, it also can serve as a bridge to later English literacy.

Language and literacy develop in a very similar fashion in both the first language and the second language. As in English, reading, writing, speaking, and listening are very interrelated, but they do not all develop at the same rate. Listening and speaking, for example, develop more quickly than reading and writing skills. Although many English language learners will have developed their listening proficiency in English to about 80% of what is expected of native-English speakers by about grade 3, their reading and writing skills in English will remain below 50% of what is expected for native-English speakers. It is not until after the fifth grade that their different language skills begin to parallel each other.

Although languages may vary in their vocabulary and grammar, there appears to be an underlying language proficiency construct, as noted earlier, that allows bilinguals to transfer conceptual information and strategies from one language to another. As a result, bilinguals do not have to relearn concepts when they shift to a new language. For example, researchers have reported that Spanish-speaking first graders who had developed phonological awareness (sound-symbol correspondence) in Spanish were able to transfer this awareness to the decoding of English words with similar sound-symbol correspondence. Awareness of the phonemic structure of one's native language also is a significant and positive predictor of early reading acquisition in English.

English language learners who acquire literacy in their home language usually have an easier time of acquiring literacy in their second language than children who are not literate in their home language. These children do not have to learn to read in a language that they do not understand. They are able to use the literacy concepts that they have acquired in their home language to approach reading in English. Thus, it is common to see that older immigrant students who have been schooled in their first language, and therefore have a strong first language base, often have better academic outcomes than other students. When English language learners are taught how to read in the language that they know best, then cognitive confusion and learning and language delays are avoided.

As a final point, it has been noted that different languages may differ from English in the areas of language structure, vocabulary, and grammar. These differences may need to be pointed out explicitly rather than assuming that they will be learned naturally, although this may vary for different students. Languages also differ in areas such as text organization that might affect how students comprehend text. For example, English language learners may encounter difficulties in reading unfamiliar English text because of limited access to word meanings and novel rhetorical structures.

Is a Focus on Primary Language All That Is Needed?

While one's native language is a critical tool for mediating learning experiences, especially within the challenging context of formal schooling, few quibble with the idea that English literacy is necessary to succeed in contemporary U.S. society, least of all parents of English learners. As Gunderson's article in this section notes, English has become a world language that dominates business and science. Will use of native language instruction by itself lead to academic success? While it may be an important part of early reading instruction for English learners, it may be seen as one of several related issues needing attention. For example, Gee in his article points out that while phonics has been a focus of intervention because of its relation to early school success, early language abilities are just as critical. They are both related to early phonological awareness as well as to early reading success. Currently, the pendulum falls most heavily on side of phonics, and less so on the side of early oral language development. Consideration to more balance may be useful.

Gee further argues, however, that is it not just general language that is important, because even poor children come to school with impressive language abilities. Gunderson and Mahar note that these out-of-school discourses, even when they are in English, can be appropriated to help scaffold engagement with literacy not only for young students but for older students, as well. However, in terms of conventional literacy as practiced in school, it is specific verbal abilities tied to specific school-based practices and genres (what some researchers have called academic language) that are important. These protoforms are the basis of later school-based language and genres. While native language instruction may be important, it is necessary to link it with practices and genres that will lead to school success.

Why Focus on Primary Language Skills?

There are several solid reasons for focusing on first-language skills in reading and literacy instruction. Among other reasons, the use of first-language skills makes sense because

- ◆ in the early stages of literacy, it makes difficult material, tasks, and concepts comprehensible and thus easier to understand—students can keep up the pace of their English-speaking peers at the same time that they are acquiring English;
- ◆ it can serve as a bridge to later English literacy; and
- ◆ it is closely linked with one's identity, community, and sense of self.

Although some students can acquire literacy when their native language is ignored, it will make the task much more difficult for most, especially when literacy resources and practices outside of school do not map well onto conventional school-like literacy.

Although many teachers may not share the languages of their English learner students, especially in classrooms with multiple language groups, they can support English language learners' literacy development in the home language by asking parents and family members to read to children in their home language. This practice shows students that their home language is valued and provides parents with an opportunity to foster important reading and literacy skills. English language learners also should be allowed to use their home language in the classroom. Researchers have reported that English language learners who used their home language in all-English classrooms to help each other participate in classroom activities and learn instructional content performed higher on academic measures in English compared to English language learners who did not use their home language. An easy way to provide English language learners with a home language resource in the ESL and all-English classroom is to make sure that they have access to bilingual dictionaries and reference materials.

Above all, as Gunderson observes, it should be kept in mind that limited English proficiency does not mean limited intelligence. In the past, diverse languages and cultures have often been treated as dysfunctional limitations to be shed at the earliest opportunity. The alternative, of which there are many good illustrations in the literature, is to recognize language and culture as resources for instruction rather than obstacles. When appropriated in meaningful ways, they can be powerful tools to mediate school success.

REFERENCES

García, G.E. (2000). Bilingual children's reading. In M.L. Kamil, P.B. Mosenthal, P.D. Pearson, & R. Barr (Eds.), *Handbook of reading research* (Vol. 3, pp. 813–834). Mahwah, NJ: Erlbaum.

Gee, J.P. (2001). Reading as situated language: A sociocognitive perspective. *Journal of Adolescent & Adult Literacy, 44,* 714–725.

Gunderson, L. (2000). Voices of the teenage diasporas. *Journal of Adolescent & Adult Literacy, 43,* 692–706.

Mahar, D. (2001). Positioning in a middle school culture: Gender, race, social class, and power. *Journal of Adolescent & Adult Literacy, 45,* 200–209.

Vygotsky, L.S. (1978). *Mind in society: The development of higher psychological processes* (M. Cole, V. John-Steiner, S. Scribner, & E. Souberman, Eds. and Trans.). Cambridge, MA: Harvard University Press. (Original work published 1934)

Reading as Situated Language:
A Sociocognitive Perspective

James Paul Gee

M y main goal here is to situate reading within a broad perspective that integrates work on cognition, language, social interaction, society, and culture. In light of recent reports on reading (National Reading Panel, 2000; Snow, Burns, & Griffin, 1998) that have tended to treat reading quite narrowly in terms of psycholinguistic processing skills, I argue that such a broad perspective on reading is essential if we are to speak to issues of access and equity in schools and workplaces. I also argue that reading and writing cannot be separated from speaking, listening, and interacting, on the one hand, or using language to think about and act on the world, on the other. Thus, it is necessary to start with a viewpoint on language (oral and written) itself, a viewpoint that ties language to embodied action in the material and social world.

I have organized this article into four parts. First, I develop a viewpoint on language that stresses the connections among language, embodied experience, and situated action and interaction in the world. In the second part, I argue that what is relevant to learning literacy is not English in general, but specific varieties of English that I call "social languages." I then go on to discuss notions related to the idea of social languages, specifically Discourses (with a capital D) and their connections to socially situated identities and cultural models. In the third part, I show the relevance of the earlier sections to the development of literacy in early childhood through a specific example. Finally, I close the article with a discussion of the importance of language abilities (construed in a specific way) to learning to read.

A Viewpoint on Language

It is often claimed that the primary function of human language is to convey information, but I believe this is not true. Human languages are used for a wide array of functions, including but by no means limited to conveying information (Halliday, 1994). I will argue here that human language has two primary functions through which it is best studied and analyzed. I would state

Originally published in *Journal of Adolescent & Adult Literacy* (2001), volume 44, pages 714-725.

these functions as follows: to scaffold the performance of action in the world, including social activities and interactions; to scaffold human affiliation in cultures and social groups and institutions through creating and enticing others to take certain perspectives on experience. *Action* is the most important word in the first statement; *perspectives* is the most important word in the second. I will discuss each of these two functions in turn.

Situated Action

Traditional approaches to language have tended to look at it as a closed system (for discussion, see Clancey, 1997). Any piece of language is treated as representation (re-presenting) of some information. On the traditional view, what it means to comprehend a piece of language is to be able to translate it into some equivalent representational system, either other language (one's own words) or some mental language or language of thought that mimics the structure of natural languages (e.g., is couched in terms of logical propositions).

However, there are a variety of perspectives today on language that tie its comprehension much more closely to experience of and action in the world. For example, consider these two remarks from work in cognitive psychology: "comprehension is grounded in perceptual simulations that prepare agents for situated action" (Barsalou, 1999a, p. 77); "to a particular person, the meaning of an object, event, or sentence is what that person can do with the object, event, or sentence" (Glenberg, 1997, p. 3).

These two quotes are from work that is part of a family of related viewpoints. For want of a better name, we might call the family "situated cognition studies" (e.g., Barsalou, 1999a, 1999b; Brown, Collins, & Dugid, 1989; Clancey, 1997; Clark, 1997; Engestrom, Miettinen, raij Punamaki, 1999; Gee, 1992; Glenberg, 1997; Glenberg & Robertson, 1999; Hutchins, 1995; Latour, 1999; Lave, 1996; Lave & Wenger, 1991; Wenger, 1998). While there are differences among the members of the family (alternative theories about situated cognition), they share the viewpoint that meaning in language is not some abstract propositional representation that resembles a verbal language. Rather, meaning in language is tied to people's experiences of situated action in the material and social world. Furthermore, these experiences (perceptions, feelings, actions, and interactions) are stored in the mind or brain, not in terms of propositions or language but in something like dynamic images tied to perception both of the world and of our own bodies, internal states, and feelings: "Increasing evidence suggests that perceptual simulation is indeed central to comprehension" (Barsalou, 1999a, p. 74).

It is almost as if we videotape our experiences as we are having them, create a library of such videotapes, edit them to make some prototypical tapes (or set of typical instances), but stand ever ready to add new tapes to our library. We reedit the tapes based on new experiences or draw out of the library less typical tapes when the need arises. As we face new situations or new texts we run our tapes—perhaps a prototypical one, or a set of typical ones, or a set of contrasting ones, or a less typical one, whatever the case may be. We do this to apply our old experiences to our new experience and to aid us in making, editing, and storing the videotape that will capture this new experience, integrate it into our library, and allow us to make sense of it (both while we are having it and afterward).

These videotapes are what we think with and through. They are what we use to give meaning to our experiences in the world. They are what we use to give meaning to words and sentences. But they are not language or *in* language (not even in propositions). Furthermore, since they are representations of experience (including feelings, attitudes, embodied positions, and various sorts of foregrounds and backgrounds of attention), they are not just information or facts. Rather, they are value-laden, perspective-taking movies in the mind. Of course, talking about videotapes in the mind is a metaphor that, like all metaphors, is incorrect if pushed too far (see Barsalou, 1999b, for how the metaphor can be cashed out and corrected by a consideration of a more neurally realistic framework for "perception in the mind").

On this account, the meanings of words, phrases, and sentences are always situated, that is, customized to our actual contexts (Gee, 1999a). Here context means not just the words, deeds, and things that surround our words or deeds, but also our purposes, values, and intended courses of action and interaction. We bring out of our store of videotapes those that are most relevant to understanding our current context or those that allow us to create and construe that context in a certain way. We can see this in even so trivial an example as the following: If you hear "The coffee spilled, go get the mop," you run a quite different set of images (that is, assemble a quite different situated meaning) than when you hear "The coffee spilled, go get a broom."

On this account, too, the meaning of a word (the way in which we give it meaning in a particular context) is not different than the meaning of an experience, object, or tool in the world (i.e., in terms of the way in which we give the experience, object, or tool meaning):

> The meaning of the glass to you, at that particular moment, is in terms of the actions available. The meaning of the glass changes when different constraints on action are combined. For example, in a noisy room, the glass may become a

mechanism for capturing attention (by tapping it with a spoon), rather than a mechanism for quenching thirst. (Glenberg, 1997, p. 41)

While Glenberg here is talking about the meaning of the glass as an object in one's specific experience of the world at a given time and place, he could just as well be talking about the meaning of the word *glass* in one's specific experience of a piece of talk or written text at a given time and place. The meaning of the word *glass* in a given piece of talk or text would be given by running a simulation (a videotape) of how the glass fits into courses of action being built up in the theater of our minds. These courses of action are based on how we understand all the other words and goings on in the world that surrounds the word *glass* as we read it: "The embodied models constructed to understand language are the same as those that underlie comprehension of the natural environment" (Glenberg, 1997, p. 17).

If embodied action and social activity are crucially connected to the situated meanings oral or written language convey, then reading instruction must move well beyond relations internal to texts. Reading instruction must be rooted in the connections of texts to engagement in and simulations of actions, activities, and interactions—to real and imagined material and social worlds.

Perspective-Taking

Let me now turn to the second function of language already mentioned. Consider, in this regard, the following quote from Tomasello (1999):

> The perspectivial nature of linguistic symbols, and the use of linguistic symbols in discourse interaction in which different perspectives are explicitly contrasted and shared, provide the raw material out of which the children of all cultures construct the flexible and multi-perspectival—perhaps even dialogical—cognitive representations that give human cognition much of its awesome and unique power. (p. 163)

Let's briefly unpack what this means. From the point of view of the model Tomasello was developing, the words and grammar of a human language exist to allow people to take and communicate alternative perspectives on experience (see also Hanks, 1996). That is, words and grammar exist to give people alternative ways to view one and the same state of affairs. Language is not about conveying neutral or objective information; rather, it is about communicating perspectives on experience and action in the world, often in contrast to alternative and competing perspectives: "We may then say that linguistic symbols are social conventions for inducing others to construe, or take a perspective on, some experiential situation" (Tomasello, 1999, p. 118).

Let me give some examples of what it means to say that words and grammar are not primarily about giving and getting information but are, rather, about giving and getting different perspectives on experience. I open Microsoft's website: Is it selling its products, marketing them, or underpricing them against the competition? Are products I can download from the site without paying for them free, or are they being exchanged for having bought other Microsoft products (e.g., Windows), or are there strings attached? Note also how metaphors (like "strings attached") add greatly to, and are a central part of, the perspective-taking we can do. If I use the grammatical construction "Microsoft's new operating system is loaded with bugs" I take a perspective in which Microsoft is less agentive and responsible than if I use the grammatical construction "Microsoft has loaded its new operating system with bugs."

Here is another example: Do I say that a child who is using multiple cues to give meaning to a written text (i.e., using some decoding along with picture and context cues) is reading, or do I say (as some of the pro-phonics people do) that she is not really reading, but engaged in emergent literacy? (For those latter people, the child is only really reading when she is decoding all the words in the text and not using nondecoding cues for word recognition.) In this case, contending camps actually fight over what perspective on experience the term *reading* or *really reading* ought to name. In the end, the point is that no wording is ever neutral or just "the facts." All wordings—given the very nature of language—are perspectives on experience that comport with competing perspectives in the grammar of the language and in actual social interactions.

How do children learn how words and grammar line up to express particular perspectives on experience? Here, interactive, intersubjective dialogue with more advanced peers and adults appears to be crucial. In such dialogue, children come to see, from time to time, that others have taken a different perspective on what is being talked about than they themselves have. At a certain developmental level, children have the capacity to distance themselves from their own perspectives and (internally) simulate the perspectives the other person is taking, thereby coming to see how words and grammar come to express those perspectives (in contrast to the way in which different words and grammatical constructions express competing perspectives).

Later, in other interactions, or when thinking, the child can rerun such simulations and imitate the perspective-taking the more advanced peer or adult has done by using certain sorts of words and grammar. Through such simulations and imitative learning, children learn to use the symbolic means that other persons have used to share attention with them: "In imitatively learning a linguistic symbol from other persons in this way, I internalize not only their communicative intention (their intention to get me to share their attention) but also the specific perspective they have taken" (Tomasello, 1999, p. 128).

Tomasello (1999) also pointed out—in line with my previous discussion that the world and texts are assigned meanings in the same way—that children come to use objects in the world as symbols at the same time (or with just a bit of a time lag) as they come to use linguistic symbols as perspective-taking devices on the world. Furthermore, they learn to use objects as symbols (to assign them different meanings encoding specific perspectives in different contexts) in the same way they learn to use linguistic symbols. In both cases, the child simulates in his head and later imitates in his words and deeds the perspectives his interlocutor must be taking on a given situation by using certain words and certain forms of grammar or by treating certain objects in certain ways. Thus, meaning for words, grammar, and objects comes out of intersubjective dialogue and interaction: "Human symbols [are] inherently social, intersubjective, and perspectival" (Tomasello, 1999, p. 131).

If value-laden perspectives on experience are connected to the situated meanings oral or written language convey, then, once again, we have an argument that reading instruction must move well beyond relations internal to texts. Reading instruction must be rooted in the taking and imagining of diverse perspectives on real and imagined material and social worlds. The moral of both the functions of language that we have discussed is this: Our ways with words (oral or written) are of the same nature as our ways with ways of understanding and acting on the material and social world. In a quite empirical sense, the moral is one Freire (1995) taught us long ago: Reading the word and reading the world are, at a deep level, integrally connected—indeed, at a deep level, they are one and the same process.

Social Languages

The perspective taken thus far on language is misleading in one respect. It misses the core fact that any human language is not one general thing (like English), but composed of a great variety of different styles, registers, or social languages. Different patterns of vocabulary, syntax (sentence structure), and discourse connectors (devices that connect sentences together to make a whole integrated text) constitute different social languages, each of which is connected to specific sorts of social activities and to a specific socially situated identity (Gee, 1999a). We recognize different social languages by recognizing these patterns (in much the way we recognize a face through recognizing a certain characteristic patterning of facial features).

As an example, consider the following, taken from a school science textbook: "1. The destruction of a land surface by the combined effects of abrasion and removal of weathered material by transporting agents is called erosion.... The production of rock waste by mechanical processes and chemical changes is called weathering" (Martin, 1990, p. 93).

A whole bevy of grammatical design features mark these sentences as part of a distinctive social language. Some of these features are heavy subjects (e.g., "The production of rock waste by mechanical processes and chemical changes"); processes and actions named by nouns or nominalizations, rather than verbs (e.g., "production"); passive main verbs ("is called") and passives inside nominalizations (e.g., "production...by mechanical processes"); modifiers that are more "contentful" than the nouns they modify (e.g., "transporting agents"); and complex embedding (e.g., "weathered material by transporting agents" is a nominalization embedded inside "the combined effects of...," and this more complex nominalization is embedded inside a yet larger nominalization, "the destruction of...").

This style of language also incorporates a great many distinctive discourse markers, that is, linguistic features that characterize larger stretches of text and give them unity and coherence as a certain type of text or genre. For example, the genre here is explanatory definition, and it is characterized by classificatory language of a certain sort. Such language leads adept readers to form a classificatory scheme in their heads something like this: There are two kinds of change (erosion and weathering) and two kinds of weathering (mechanical and chemical).

This mapping from elements of vocabulary, syntax, and discourse to a specific style of language used in characteristic social activities is just as much a part of reading and writing as is the phonics (sound-to-letter) mapping. In fact, more people fail to become successful school-based, academic, or work-related readers or writers because of failing to master this sort of mapping than the phonics one.

There are a great many different social languages—for example, the language of medicine, literature, street gangs, sociology, law, rap, or informal dinner-time talk among friends (who belong to distinctive cultures or social groups). To know any specific social language is to know how its characteristic design features are combined to carry out one or more specific social activities. It is to know, as well, how its characteristic lexical and grammatical design features are used to enact a particular socially situated identity, that is, being, at a given time and place, a lawyer, a gang member, a politician, a literary humanist, a "bench chemist," a radical feminist, an everyday person, or whatever. To know a particular social language is either to be able to "do" a particular identity, using that social language, or to be able to recognize such an identity, when we do not want to or cannot actively participate.

Let me give two further examples of social languages at work. First, I'll use an example I've used in this journal before. It's about a young woman telling the same story to her parents and to her boyfriend (*JAAL*, February 2000; Gee, 1996). To her parents at dinner she says, "Well, when I thought about it, I don't know, it seemed to me that Gregory should be considered the most offensive character." But to her boyfriend later she says, "What an ass that guy was, you know, her boyfriend." In the first case, the young woman is taking on the identity of an educated and dutiful daughter engaged in the social activity of reporting to her parents her viewpoints on what she has learned in school. In the second case, she is taking on the identity of a girlfriend engaged in the social activity of bonding with her boyfriend.

Here is a second example from Myers (1990, p. 150): A biologist wrote in a professional science journal, "Experiments show that *Heliconius* butterflies are less likely to oviposit on host plants that possess eggs or egg-like structures." Writing about the same thing in a popular science magazine, the same biologist wrote, "*Heliconius* butterflies lay their eggs on *Passiflora* vines. In defense the vines seem to have evolved fake eggs that make it look to the butterflies as if eggs have already been laid on them." In the first case, the biologist is taking on the identity of professional scientist engaged in the social activity of making experimental and theoretical claims (note, for instance, the subject "Experiments") to professional peers. In the second case, the biologist is taking on the identity of a popularizer or scientific journalist engaged in the social activity of telling the educated public a factual story about plants and animals (note, for instance, the subjects "butterflies" and "vines").

Now here is the bite of social languages and genres: When we talk about social languages and genres, oral and written language are inextricably mixed. Some social languages are written; some are spoken. Some have both spoken and written versions; written and spoken versions are often mixed and integrated within specific social practices. Furthermore, social languages are always integrally connected to the characteristic social activities (embodied action and interaction in the world), value-laden perspectives, and socially situated identities of particular groups of people or communities of practice. If discussions about reading are not about social languages (and thus, too, about embodied action and interaction in the world, value-laden perspectives, and socially situated identities), then they are not, in reality, about reading as a semiotic meaning-making process (and it is hard to know what reading is if it is not this).

Here is another part of the bite of talk about social languages and genres. Both inside and outside school, most social languages and genres are clearly not acquired by direct instruction. While some forms of (appropriately timed) scaffolding, modeling, and instructional guidance by mentors appear to be important, immersion in meaningful practice is essential. Social languages and genres are acquired by processes of socialization, an issue to which I will turn below.

It is inevitable, I would think, that someone at this point is going to object that social languages are really about the later stages of the acquisition of literacy. It will be pointed out that the current reading debates are almost always about small children and the earlier stages of reading. What, it will be asked, has all this talk of social languages got to do with early literacy? My answer is, everything. Social languages (and their connections to action, perspectives, and identities) are no less relevant to the first stages of learning to read than they are to the later ones (and there are not so much stages here as the same things going on over time at ever deeper and more complex levels). However, before I turn to the relevance of social languages to early childhood at the end of this article, I need to develop briefly a few more theoretical notions related to social languages.

Discourses

I said earlier that social languages are acquired by socialization. But now we must ask, socialization into what? When people learn new social languages and genres—at the level of being able to produce them and not just consume them—they are being socialized into what I will call Discourses with a big "D" (I use discourse with a little "d" to mean just language in use, Gee, 1996, 1999a; see also Clark, 1996). Even when people learn a new social language or genre only to consume (interpret), but not produce it, they are learning to recognize a new Discourse. Related but somewhat different terms others have used to capture some of what I am trying to capture with the term *Discourses* are communities of practice (Wenger, 1998), actor-actant networks

(Latour, 1987, 1991), and activity systems (Engestrom, Miettinen, & raij Punamaki, 1999; Leont'ev, 1978).

Discourses always involve language (i.e., they recruit specific social languages), but they always involve more than language as well. Social languages are embedded within Discourses and only have relevance and meaning within them. A Discourse integrates ways of talking, listening, writing, reading, acting, interacting, believing, valuing, and feeling (and using various objects, symbols, images, tools, and technologies) in the service of enacting meaningful socially situated identities and activities. Being-doing a certain sort of physicist, gang member, feminist, first-grade child in Ms. Smith's room, special ed (SPED) student, regular at the local bar, or gifted upper-middle-class child engaged in emergent literacy are all Discourses.

We can think of Discourses as identity kits. It's almost as if you get a tool kit full of specific devices (i.e., ways with words, deeds, thoughts, values, actions, interactions, objects, tools, and technologies) in terms of which you can enact a specific identity and engage in specific activities associated with that identity. For example, think of what devices (e.g., in words, deeds, clothes, objects, attitudes) you would get in a Sherlock Holmes identity kit (e.g., you do not get a "Say No to Drugs" bumper sticker in this kit; you do get both a pipe and lots of logic). The Doctor Watson identity kit is different. And we can think of the Sherlock Holmes identity kit (Discourse) and the Doctor Watson identity kit (Discourse) as themselves parts of a yet larger Discourse, the Holmes-Watson Discourse, because Watson is part of Holmes's identity kit and Holmes is part of Watson's. Discourse can be embedded one inside another.

One Discourse can mix or blend two others. For example, Gallas (1994) created a sharing-time Discourse (a way of being a recognizable sharer in her classroom) that mixed Anglo and African American styles. Discourses can be related to each other in relationships of alignment or tension. For example, Scollon and Scollon (1981) have pointed out that school-based Discourses that incorporate essayist practices and values conflict with the values, attitudes, and ways with words embedded in some Native American home and community-based Discourses (i.e., ways of being a Native American of a certain sort). These latter Discourses value communicating only when the sender knows the receiver of the communication and his or her context and do not value the sorts of fictionalizing (generalizing) of sender and receiver that essayist practices involve.

Cultural Models

Within their socialization into Discourses (and we are all socialized into a great many across our lifetimes), people acquire cultural models (D'Andrade & Strauss, 1992; Gee, 1999a; Holland & Quinn, 1987; Shore, 1996; Strauss & Quinn, 1997). Cultural models are everyday theories (i.e., story lines, images, schemas, metaphors, and models) about the world that people socialized into a given Discourse share. Cultural models tell people what is typical or normal from the perspective of a particular Discourse (or a related or aligned set of them).

For example, certain types of middle-class people in the United States hold a cultural model of child development that goes something like this (Harkness, Super, & Keefer, 1992): A child is born dependent on her parents and grows up by going through (often disruptive) stages toward greater and greater independence (and independence is a high value for this group of people). This cultural model plays a central role in this group's Discourse of parent-child relations (i.e., enacting and recognizing identities as parents and children).

On the other hand, certain sorts of working-class families (Philipsen, 1975) hold a cultural model of child development that goes something like this: A child is born unsocialized and with tendencies to be selfish. The child needs discipline from the home to learn to be a cooperative social member of the family (a high value of this group of people). This cultural model plays a central role in this group's Discourse of parent-child relations.

These different cultural models, connected to different (partially) class-based Discourses of parenting, are not true or false. Rather, they focus on different aspects of childhood and development. Cultural models define for people in a Discourse what counts as normal and natural and what counts as inappropriate and deviant. They are, of course, thereby thoroughly value laden.

Cultural models come out of and, in turn, inform the social practices in which people in a Discourse engage. Cultural models are stored in people's minds (by no means always consciously), though they are supplemented and instantiated in the objects, texts, and practices that are part and parcel of the Discourse. For example, many guidebooks supplement and instantiate the above middle-class cultural model of childhood and stages. On the other hand, many religious materials supplement and instantiate the above working-class model of childhood.

Figure 1 summarizes the discussion so far, defining all the theoretical tools and showing how they are all related to one another.

Figure 1. Summary of tools for understanding language and literacy in sociocultural terms

Discourses: Ways of combining and coordinating words, deeds, thoughts, values, bodies, objects, tools, and technologies, and other people (at the appropriate times and places) so as to enact and recognize specific socially situated identities and activities.

Social languages: Ways with words (oral and written) within Discourses that relate form and meaning so as to express specific socially situated identities and activities.

Genres: Combinations of ways with words (oral and written) and actions that have become more or less routine within a Discourse in order to enact and recognize specific socially situated identities and activities in relatively stable and uniform ways (and, in doing so, we humans reproduce our Discourses and institutions through history).

Cultural models: Often tacit and taken-for-granted schemata, story lines, theories, images, or representations (partially represented inside people's heads and partially represented within their materials and practices) that tell a group of people within a Discourse what is typical or normal from the point of view of that Discourse.

Early Literacy as Socioculturally Situated Practice

I turn now to a specific example involving early literacy from my own research. I do this both to give a more extended example of the perspective I have developed so far and to show the relevance of this perspective to early childhood and the earliest stages of the acquisition of literacy. The event is this: An upper-middle-class, highly educated father approaches his 3-year-old (3:10) son, who is sitting at the kitchen table. The child is using an activity book in which each page contains a picture with a missing piece. A question is printed under the picture. The child uses a "magic pen" to rub the missing piece and "magically" uncovers the rest of the picture. The part of the picture that is uncovered is an image that constitutes the answer to the question at the bottom of the page, though, of course, the child must put this answer into words.

In the specific case I want to discuss here, the overt part of the picture was the top half of the bodies of Donald and Daisy Duck. The question printed at the bottom of the page was "In what are Donald and Daisy riding?"

(Note the social language in which this question is written. It is not the more vernacular form: "What are Donald and Daisy riding in?") The child used his pen to uncover an old-fashioned Model T sort of car with an open top. Donald and Daisy turn out to be sitting in the car.

The father, seeing the child engaged in this activity, asks him, after he has uncovered the car, to read the question printed below the picture. Notice that the father has not asked the child to give the answer to the question, which is a different activity. The father is confident the child can answer the question and has a different purpose here. It is to engage in an indirect reading lesson, though one of a special and specific sort.

The father is aware that the child, while he knows the names of the letters of the alphabet and can recognize many of them in words, cannot decode print. He is also aware that the child has on several previous occasions, in the midst of various literacy-related activities, said that he is "learning to read." However, in yet other activities, at other times, the child has said that he "cannot read" and thereafter seemed more reluctant to engage in his otherwise proactive stance toward texts. This has concerned the father, who values the child's active engagement with texts and the child's belief, expressed in some contexts and not others, that he is not just learning to read, but is in fact "a reader."

We might say that the father is operating with a however tacit theory (cultural model) that a child's assuming a certain identity ("I am a reader") facilitates the acquisition of that identity and its concomitant skills. I believe this sort of model is fairly common in certain sorts of families. Parents co-construct an identity with a child (attribute, and get the child to believe in, a certain competence) before the child can actually fully carry out all the skills associated with this identity (competence before performance).

So, the father has asked the child to read the printed question below the picture of Donald and Daisy Duck sitting in the newly uncovered car. Below, I give the printed version of the question and what the child offered as his "reading" of the question:

Printed version: In what are Donald and Daisy riding?

Child's reading: What is Donald and Daisy riding on?

After the child uttered the above sentence, he said, "See, I told you I was learning to read." He seems to be well aware of the father's purposes. The child, the father, the words, and the book are all here in sync to pull off a specific practice, and this is a form of instruction, but it's a form that is typical of what goes on inside socialization processes.

The father and son have taken an activity that is for the child now a virtual genre—namely, uncovering a piece of a picture and on the basis of it answering a question—and incorporated it into a different *metalevel activity*. That is, the father and son use the original activity not in and for itself but as a platform with which to discuss reading or, perhaps better put, to coconstruct a cultural model of what reading is. The father's question and the son's final response ("See, I told you I was learning to read") clearly indicate that they are seeking to demonstrate to and for each other that the child can read.

Figure 2, which will inform my discussion that follows, (partially) analyzes this event in terms of the theoretical notions we have developed above.

From a developmental point of view, then, what is going on here? Nothing so general as acquiring literacy. Rather, something much more specific is going on. First, the child is acquiring, amid immersion and adult guidance, a piece of a particular type of *social language*. The question he has to form—and he very well knows this—has to be a *classificatory question*. It cannot be, for instance, a narrative-based question (e.g., something like "What are Donald and Daisy doing?" or "Where are Donald and Daisy going?"). Classificatory questions (and related syntactic and discourse resources) are a common part of many school-based (and academic) social languages, especially those associated with nonliterary content areas (e.g., the sciences).

Figure 2. Partial analysis of a literacy event

Text	=	Written:	In what are Donald and Daisy riding?
		Read:	What is Donald and Daisy riding on?
		Remark:	See, I told you I was learning to read.
Social language	=	Classification question	
Genre	=	Uncover the piece of the picture, form a classification question to which the picture is an answer, and give the answer	
Cultural model	=	Reading is the proactive production of appropriate styles of language (e.g., here a classificatory question) and their concomitant meanings in conjunction with print	
Discourse (identity)	=	Emergent reader of a certain type (filtering school-aligned practice into primary Discourse)	

The acquisition of this piece of a social language is, in this case, scaffolded by a genre the child has acquired, namely to uncover the piece of the picture, form a classificatory question to which the picture is an answer (when the parent isn't there to read the question for the child), and give the answer. This genre bears a good deal of similarity to a number of different nonnarrative language and action genres (routines) used in the early years of school.

Finally, in regard to social languages, note that the child's question is uttered in a more vernacular style than the printed question. So syntactically it is, in one sense, in the wrong style. However, from a discourse perspective (in terms of the function its syntax carries out), it is in just the right style (i.e., it is a classificatory question). It is a mainstay of child language development that the acquisition of a function often precedes acquisition of a fully correct form (in the sense of contextually appropriate, not necessarily in the sense of grammatically correct).

In addition to acquiring a specific piece of certain sorts of social languages, the child is also, as part and parcel of the activity, acquiring different cultural models. One of these is a cultural model about what reading is. The model is something like this: Reading is not primarily letter-by-letter decoding but the proactive production of appropriate styles of language (e.g., here a classificatory question) and their concomitant meanings in conjunction with print. This is a model that the father (at some level quite consciously) wants the child to adopt, both to sustain the child's interest in becoming a reader and to counteract the child's claims, in other contexts, that he can't read. Of course, the child's claim that he can't read in those other contexts reflects that, in other activities, he is acquiring a different cultural model of reading, namely one something like this: Reading is primarily the ability to decode letters and words, and one is not a reader if meaning is not primarily driven from decoding print. As his socialization proceeds, the child will acquire yet other cultural models of reading (or extend and deepen ones already acquired).

The genres, social languages, and cultural models present in this interaction between father and son existed, of course, in conjunction with ways of thinking, valuing, feeling, acting, and interacting and in conjunction with various mediating objects (e.g., the book and the "magic pen"), images (the pictures of Donald, Daisy, and the car), sites (kitchen table), and times (morning as father was about to go to work). In and through the social practices that recruit these genres, social language, and cultural models, the 3-year-old is acquiring a Discourse. The father and the child are coconstructing the child as a reader (and, indeed, a person) of a particular type, that is, one who takes reading to be the proactive production of appropriate styles of language and meanings in conjunction with print. This socially situated identity involves a self-orientation as active producer (not just consumer) of appropriate meanings in conjunction with print—meanings that, in this case, turn out to be school and academically related.

However, this Discourse is not unrelated to other Discourses the child is or will be acquiring. I have repeatedly pointed out how the social language, genre, and cultural models involved in this social practice are in full alignment with some of the social languages, genres, cultural models, and social practices the child will confront in the early years of school (here construing schooling in fairly traditional terms).

At the same time, this engagement between father and child, beyond being a moment in the production of the Discourse of a certain type of reader, is also a moment in the child's acquisition of what I call his primary Discourse. The child's primary Discourse is the ways with words, objects, and deeds that are associated with his primary sense of self formed in and through his (most certainly class based) primary socialization within the family (or other culturally relevant primary socializing group) as a "person like us." In this case, the child is learning that "people like us" are "readers like this."

Now consider what it means that the child's acquisition of the reader Discourse (being-doing a certain type of reader) is simultaneously aligned with (traditional) school-based Discourses and part of his acquisition of his primary Discourse. This ties school-related values, attitudes, and ways with words, at a specific and not some general level, to his primary sense of self and belonging. This will almost certainly affect how the child reacts to, and resonates with, school-based ways with words and things.

Reading and Early Language Abilities

Many of the recent reading reports (e.g., see Gee, 1999b; National Reading Panel, 2000; Snow, Burns, & Griffin, 1998) have stressed that there is significant correlation between early phonological awareness and later success in learning to read and, thus, called for early phonemic awareness training in schools and early sustained and overt instruction on phonics. However, some of these reports are aware that a good many other things, besides early phonological awareness, correlate with successfully learning to read in the early years of school. It turns out, for instance, that the correlation between early language abilities and later success in reading is just as large as, if not larger than, the correlation between early phonological awareness and success in reading. Indeed, as one might suspect, early language abilities and early phonological awareness are themselves correlated (Snow, Burns, & Griffin, 1998):

> Performance on phonological awareness tasks by preschoolers was highly correlated with general language ability. Moreover it was measures of semantic and syntactic skills, rather than speech discrimination and articulation, that predicted phonological awareness differences. (p. 53)

> What is most striking about the results of the preceding studies is the power of early preschool language to predict reading three to five years later. (pp. 107–108)

> On average, phonological awareness ($r = .46$) has been about as strong a predictor of future reading as memory for sentences and stories, confrontation naming, and general language measures. (p. 112)

So what are these early language abilities that seem so important for later success in school? According to the National Research Council's report (Snow, Burns, & Griffin, 1998), they are things like vocabulary—receptive vocabulary, but more especially expressive vocabulary—the ability to recall and comprehend sentences and stories, and the ability to engage in verbal interactions. Furthermore, I think that research has made it fairly clear what causes such verbal abilities. What appear to cause enhanced school-based verbal abilities are family, community, and school language environments in which children interact intensively with adults and more advanced peers and experience cognitively challenging talk and texts on sustained topics and in different genres of oral and written language.

However, the correlation between language abilities and success in learning to read (and in school generally) hides an important reality. Almost all children—including poor children—have impressive language abilities. The vast majority of children enter school with large vocabularies, complex grammar, and deep understandings of experiences and stories. It has been decades since anyone believed that poor and minority children entered school with "no language" (Gee, 1996; Labov, 1972).

The verbal abilities that children who fail in school lack are not just some general set of such abilities, but rather specific verbal abilities tied to specific school-based practices and school-based genres of oral and written language of just the sort I looked at in the earlier example of the 3-year-old making up a classificatory question. This 3-year-old will have been exposed to a great number of such specific, but quite diverse, practices, each offering protoforms of later school-based and academic social languages and genres. These protoforms, always embedded in specific social practices connected to specific socially situated identities (and useless when not so embedded), are the stuff from which success in school-based and academic reading flows. These are the sorts of protoforms that must be delivered to all children—amid ample practice within socialization in specific Discourses—if we are to have true access and equity for all children.

REFERENCES

Barsalou, L.W. (1999a). Language comprehension: Archival memory or preparation for situated action. *Discourse Processes, 28,* 61–80.

Barsalou, L.W. (1999b). Perceptual symbol systems. *Behavioral and Brain Sciences, 22,* 577–660.

Brown, A.L., Collins, A., & Dugid, P. (1989). Situated cognition and the culture of learning. *Educational Researcher, 18,* 32–42.

Clancey, W.J. (1997). *Situated cognition: On human knowledge and computer representations.* Cambridge, England: Cambridge University Press.

Clark, A. (1997). *Being there: Putting brain, body, and world together again.* Cambridge, MA: MIT Press.

Clark, H.H. (1996). *Using language.* Cambridge, England: Cambridge University Press.

D'Andrade, R., & Strauss, C. (Eds.). (1992). *Human motives and cultural models.* Cambridge, England: Cambridge University Press.

Engestrom, Y., Miettinen, M., & raij Punamaki. (Eds.). (1999). *Perspectives on activity theory.* Cambridge, England: Cambridge University Press.

Freire, P. (1995). *The pedagogy of the oppressed.* New York: Continuum.

Gallas, K. (1994). *The languages of learning: How children talk, write, dance, draw, and sing their understanding of the world.* New York: Teachers College Press.

Gee, J.P. (1992). *The social mind: Language, ideology, and social practice.* New York: Bergin & Garvey.

Gee, J.P. (1996). *Social linguistics and literacies: Ideology in Discourses* (2nd ed.). London: Taylor & Francis.

Gee, J.P. (1999a). *An introduction to discourse analysis: Theory and method.* London: Routledge.

Gee, J.P. (1999b). Reading and the New Literacy Studies: Reframing the National Academy of Sciences report on reading. *Journal of Literacy Research, 31,* 355–374.

Glenberg, A.M. (1997). What is memory for? *Behavioral and Brain Sciences, 20,* 1–55.

Glenberg, A.M., & Robertson, D.A. (1999). Indexical understanding of instructions. *Discourse Processes, 28,* 1–26.

Halliday, M.A.K. (1994). *Functional grammar* (2nd ed.). London: Edward Arnold.

Hanks, W.F. (1996). *Language and communicative practices.* Boulder, CO: Westview Press.

Harkness, S., Super, C., & Keefer, C.H. (1992). Learning to be an American parent: How cultural models gain directive force. In R. D'Andrade & C. Strauss (Eds.), *Human motives and cultural models* (pp. 163–178). Cambridge, England: Cambridge University Press.

Holland, D., & Quinn, N. (Eds.). (1987). *Cultural models in language and thought.* Cambridge, England: Cambridge University Press.

Hutchins, E. (1995). *Cognition in the wild.* Cambridge, MA: MIT Press.

Labov, W. (1972). *Language in the inner city.* Philadelphia, PA: University of Pennsylvania Press.

Latour, B. (1987). *Science in action.* Cambridge, MA: Harvard University Press.

Latour, B. (1991). *We have never been modern.* Cambridge, MA: Harvard University Press.

Latour, B. (1999). *Pandora's hope: Essays on the reality of science studies.* Cambridge, MA: Harvard University Press.

Lave, J. (1996). Teaching, as learning, in practice. *Mind, Culture, and Activity, 3,* 149–164.

Lave, J., & Wenger, E. (1991). *Situated learning: Legitimate peripheral participation.* New York: Cambridge University Press.

Leont'ev, A.N. (1978). *Activity, consciousness, and personality.* Englewood Cliffs, NJ: Prentice-Hall.

Martin, J.R. (1990). Literacy in science: Learning to handle text as technology. In F. Christie (Ed.), *Literacy for a changing world* (pp. 79–117). Melbourne, NSW, Australia: Australian Council for Educational Research.

Myers, G. (1990). *Writing biology: Texts in the social construction of scientific knowledge.* Madison, WI: University of Wisconsin Press.

National Reading Panel. (2000). *Report of the National Reading Panel: Teaching children to read.* Washington DC: Author. Available online: www.nationalreadingpanel.org.

Philipsen, G. (1975). Speaking "like a man" in Teamsterville: Culture patterns of role enactment in an urban neighborhood. *Quarterly Journal of Speech, 61,* 26–39.

Scollon, R., & Scollon, S.W. (1981). *Narrative, literacy, and face in interethnic communication.* Norwood, NJ: Ablex.

Shore, B. (1996). *Culture in mind: Cognition, culture, and the problem of meaning.* New York: Oxford University Press.

Snow, C.E., Burns, M.S., & Griffin, P. (Eds.). (1998). *Preventing reading difficulties in young children.* Washington, DC: National Academy Press.

Strauss, C., & Quinn, N. (1997). *A cognitive theory of cultural meaning.* Cambridge, England: Cambridge University Press.

Tomasello, M. (1999). *The cultural origins of human cognition.* Cambridge, MA: Harvard University Press.

Wenger, E. (1998). *Communities of practice: Learning, meaning, and identity.* Cambridge, England: Cambridge University Press.

Voices of the Teenage Diasporas

Lee Gunderson

t has been known for some time that secondary teachers do not consider reading and learning to read as issues that are of much importance to them (e.g., Gunderson, 1986; Ratekin, Simpson, Alvermann, & Dishner, 1985). It is particularly unfortunate that they also do not consider it important to restructure their lessons to account for the needs of students for whom English is a second language (ESL students), nor do they attempt to teach the literacy skills these students need to succeed at academic tasks (Gunderson, 1985). It is more than coincidental that "Minority-language students, especially Hispanic and Native groups, have been characterized by high drop-out rates and poor academic achievement" (Cummins, 1981, p. 19). Secondary teachers' views are clear: "The great majority of content teachers reported that English ability should be a prerequisite for their classes." And further, "English ought to be a prerequisite for immigration" (Gunderson, 1985, p. 49). Instead of improving over the last 15 years or so, immigrant students' dropout rates have increased and their achievement has declined (Gunderson & Clarke, 1998).

Secondary Students, Culture, and Learning to Read and Write

It has been argued that learning to read and write is basic to become a contributing, participating member of society. Many in North America view learning to read and write as the prerequisite that allows both native-born and immigrant students' participation in schools, socialization into society, ability to learn, and academic and professional success. Some view the learning of English as a basic requirement of citizenship for immigrants, their democratic responsibility (Crawford, 1989). The role of English proficiency in ESL students' success at school, including reading, has been viewed as pivotal. "Language is the focus of every content-area task, with all meaning and all demonstration of knowledge expressed through oral and written forms of language" (Collier, 1987, p. 618). Delpit (1988; "A Conversation With Lisa Delpit," 1991) argued that school language represents the "power code." Any system that denies students access to the power code denies them access to the dominant society. However, as Harman and Edelsky (1989) noted, "literacy is not necessarily liberating" (p. 393). They caution, further, that "**merely**

Originally published in *Journal of Adolescent & Adult Literacy* (2000), volume 43, pages 692-706.

knowing how to read and write guarantees neither membership in the dominant culture nor the concomitant political, economic, cognitive, or social rewards of that membership" (p. 393, emphasis in original).

Gee (1992) noted, "To read is to respond appropriately to a specific hegemonic or displaced consensus centered on the values of dominant Discourses, a consensus achieved among persons (in dominant groups or not) whose paths through life have [for a time and place] fallen together with the members of these dominant Discourses" (pp. 74–75). As teachers, we tend to forget that our life paths are part of dominant Discourses. We have mostly lost track of the Discourses of our first cultures; we have become acculturated in the worst sense of the word. We fail to recognize the struggles our immigrant students face, struggles that many of us, or our parents, faced and lost. To be successful in school means immigrants must surrender great parts of their language and culture, just as most teachers have. Teachers, particularly those who teach "academic" classes, must know about culture. If not, immigrant students will continue to fail because culture is part of identity, and identity relates to how well a student does in school and in society.

Cultural Loss

I am an immigrant, a Norwegian American Canadian. Like millions of native English-speaking individuals in Australia, Canada, New Zealand, and the United States, my parents' first culture and language, in my case Norwegian, has withered away. The melting pot has worked. That part of me that is of my parents' first culture is not signified by a hyphen; rather, my first culture has dissolved into something more general, more amorphous. Terms like Swedish American, German Canadian and Italian Australian are not transcendent; they signify for a time individuals' status as newly arrived immigrants. They disappear as identities dissolve into the cultural slurries called Australian, Canadian, or American. Hyphenated names are used in conversations to remind individuals of their first cultures, except when they serve as markers to identify "the others." Terms like Mexican American and African American are often used to marginalize individuals, to separate and segregate them physically and socially from the so-called social mainstream.

First- and second-generation immigrants remember their struggles learning a new language and a new culture. Most often, however, they are convinced that their losses were a consequence of their heroic or pioneer-like efforts to forge new lives for themselves and their families. They view their losses as part of the price they have paid to become members of a new society. Their willingness to sacrifice signifies in their minds their dedication to family and to the democratic ideals of their new country. They are members of the most recognizable diasporas, who retain clearly identified artifacts of their first cultures and languages, like my 98-year-old aunt who sounded like she had just stepped off the boat from Norway.

The individuals of the third, fourth, and fifth generations are the lost ones whose first cultures like unsettled spirits haunt their angst-filled reveries. Becoming an American, an Australian, or a Canadian means the surrender of first languages and first cultures. Children and grandchildren have little sense of what has been lost. They occasionally revel in the broken bits of culture that are the dwindling tokens of their lost identities like *lefsa*, *ufta*, *grapo*, *dolmathes*, *May 1*, and *May 5*, while passionately condemning new immigrants for their apparent reticence to lose what they themselves have lost, their languages and cultures. They are the shadow diasporas, consensually self-validated as groups, but only vaguely.

Language and culture are inextricably linked. Unlike the Gordian knot, nothing comes from separating them because they have little or no meaning apart from each other. And English has become a world language, one that dominates business and science. In many respects it is hegemonic. To participate in the world economy and to benefit from the advances of science, it is believed, one must know English (Gunderson, 2000). English, it is said, has "Disneyfied" culture.

> The garden of delights purveyed by Disney, Mattel or Time Warner for the people of the South is a carefully crafted myth, a US ideological artifact. It serves to demobilize the poor in places where they live, where they suffer poverty and insecurity. Hope becomes increasingly concentrated in the distant and exotic. Delight is found, not in celebrating their own lives and achievements, but in admiration of the shadowy celebrities of film and pop videos. (Seabrook, 1998, p. 23)

As Canagarajah (1993) observed of students of English in Sri Lanka, the oppressed themselves become their own oppressors. The Gordian knot made up of English and Western culture is seductive. It beguiles individuals, and it is oppressive. Gunderson (2000) notes that "the use of English and its philosophy concerning what constitutes important knowledge, was imposed on students around the world" (p. 68). Many ask, "how well students have been served by the subjectivities celebrated by the assigned literary classics, the history and geography of Western civilization's relentless advance, and the scientific pursuit of the knowing division and conquest of nature?" (Willinsky, 1998, p. 112).

Teaching and learning in North America are imbued with features of Eurocentric notions and ideas advocated by school boards, superintendents, and teachers. Eisner (1992) concluded, "Knowledge is always constructed relative to a framework, to a form of representation, to a cultural code and to a personal biography" (p. 14). Cummins (1991) believed that "students from 'dominated' societal groups are 'empowered' or 'disabled' as a direct result of their interactions with educators in the schools" (p. 375). Indeed, teachers consciously or unconsciously reproduce the political system of domination. Eurocentric views and beliefs form the core of the educational thought that guides curriculum development and instructional practice. The demographic data indicate that "five out of six people in the world are non-White," the "vast majority of the world's population is non-Christian" (Banks, 1991, p. 28), and while their school populations are growing increasingly multicultural, North American educators continue to view education within a "mainstream" viewpoint, one that focuses on European values and beliefs.

School-age immigrants struggle against the domination of their first languages and cultures, by a language and a culture that have seemingly conquered the world. It is a domination that threatens to destroy the way they view and think about the world. The dominant view, with its generalizations and notions of certainty, has a tendency of "tribalizing and stereotyping the others" (Duff & Uchida, 1997, p. 454). We teachers as a group tend to view immigrant students as inferior because their English is not standard. Indeed, those features of their English we view as immature or primitive, as evidence of imperfect or poorly developed language, are taken to signify lack of intelligence or ability to learn. Teachers who judge students by their English development are trapped in views that are uninformed and destructive. Limited English proficiency does not mean limited intelligence.

The youngest members of the newest and most visible diasporas cling together in litter-strewn secondary school hallways amid lockers filled with the delicious and dangerous tokens of the dominant culture and Discourses. They learn to speak a "first" second language, not the six o'clock news standard, but a patois steeped in MTV, rap, rebellion, and world domination. The stories that follow are those of high school students who struggle with the impossible tasks of becoming adults, being submerged in a dominant second language and culture, learning English and learning in English, and surviving as immigrants. Their chances of surviving in the content-based worlds of English, social studies, and biology are diminished by their teachers' attitudes and beliefs about ESL students and their cultures.

The Students

Participants were part of two large-scale studies involving approximately 35,000 immigrant students who spoke 148 first languages, came from 132 countries, and represented all socioeconomic levels. While there were some common themes occurring across immigration categories, the term *immigrant* is too broad to be particularly useful; it obscures both subgroup and individual differences. This became painfully obvious as the data were analyzed. Three subgroups—refugee, landed immigrant, entrepreneur—form the focuses of this article, each one further divided generally by language and country of origin. However, the use of such categories can be criticized as imposing a reductionist view on the study, one that is Eurocentric.

The Problems With Schools in Canada

The school system in British Columbia is an English-only system in which there are no bilingual or dual-language classrooms, except for French Immersion. There are differing levels of English support provided to immigrants varying from intact ESL classrooms (one group of ESL students in a class for the school day) to visiting ESL support teachers (the teacher visits classrooms for 40 minutes a week). The goal of ESL instruction is immersion in academic classes taught in English at the secondary school level. Students may opt for foreign language instruction (e.g., 40 minutes a day) beginning at grade 5 in one of several approved languages, such as Mandarin, Punjabi, or German.

Across linguistic and cultural groups, expectations for school and schooling cause considerable difficulty for students and, indeed, for teachers. Gunderson and Anderson (2003) note, "Those who encourage students to be curious, interested, critical, communicative, to hold a plurality of points of view, and a desire to question and make sense of it all, need to be acutely aware that they are teaching a value system. Indeed, it represents 'dominant Discourses' (Gee, 1992). Moreover, it is a value system potentially in opposition to that held by the families of many students." Immigrant students generally viewed learning as a task consisting of a large number of discrete skills to be learned in order, through rote memorization. Those who acquire the most skills and can faithfully remember and reproduce them are the ones who are rewarded with the best grades and rankings.

In Hong Kong all we do, memorize, memorize, memorize, day and night, 5 hours homework memorizing every day. In Vancouver all we do is think, think, think, nothing more. It's hard to think when the teacher doesn't tell you what to do. (18-year-old female, Cantonese speaker, Hong Kong)

You get a lot more freedom in Canada's schools and my friends and me think it's a waste of time, 'cuz in Hong Kong they are forcing you to learn. In Hong Kong they give you a letter grade and a number so like you are number 5 out of 120. (14-year-old male, Cantonese speaker, Hong Kong)

Immigrant parents and students view the different focus on teaching and learning as a problem (Gunderson & Anderson, 2003). This was reflected repeatedly in students' comments. Indeed, about 85% responded negatively about the teaching and learning occurring in Canadian schools.

I like Hong Kong better because the teachers tell you everything you have to know. (16-year-old female, Vietnamese speaker, Hong Kong)

In the Philippines you have 10 subjects a day, and in Canada you have 5 subjects. In the Philippines you have to memorize everything, in Canada you don't. (17-year-old female, Tagalog speaker, the Philippines)

A small number of individuals did not view the differences as necessarily negative, but simply as differences.

You don't always learn from the books, you do projects and stuff like that. In India they don't do projects. Here it is free, in India you have to pay a lot of money. (17-year-old female, Punjabi speaker, India)

Schools in Canada are more fun. Well, I don't know. The schools in Hong Kong, the admission is too tense. In school you just listen to the teacher and go home and do your homework. Here they have more programs. You can talk in class. There are more field trips here. (16-year-old female, Hong Kong)

Gunderson and Anderson (2003) found that immigrant parents behaved differently across groups as they encountered school practices that differed from those with which they were familiar. Some parents ignored the differences, while others took their children out of the classrooms and schools that failed to meet their expectations. Some, particularly those who were business people, tried to change the system. A group of Chinese Canadian parents, "unhappy with the work their children are doing in public schools," has developed plans for a traditional school (Sullivan, 1998, p. 15). One of the school districts in this study has faced considerable pressure from a Chinese parents Association to adopt traditional teaching approaches, including uniforms, memorization, workbooks, and a return to the basics ("Richmond Chinese

Parents," 1999). Members of the diaspora have assumed the role of colonizers and have tried to impose their views on the locals.

Racism From Within and Without

Immigrants confront racism in many forms. About half of them reported instances of racism. The source of the racism varied from that which had immigrated with them to that which sprang from their new environments.

> In India the girls and boys have different schools. English is harder here and science is easier here. Canadian students don't like Indians, they call them rag heads and Pakis. I'm not a Sikh, I'm not from Pakistan, and I don't wear a turban. I'm Catholic. Punjabis are violent, they should stay in India, not bring their fights to Canada. (17-year-old male, Konkanee speaker, India)

Russian refugees felt both alienation and stigmatization, feelings that prompted a group of them to complain to school authorities about the negative attitudes they perceived in their school by administrators, teachers, and fellow students. One block from their school the graffiti shown in the photo was observed.

The Russian graffiti (translated by Daria Semenov of the University of British Columbia) is an adaptation of an old Soviet slogan that reads "Let's (we will) demolish (destroy) damned (cursed) capitalism." The verb is in first-person plural and may be interpreted as "let's" or "we will." The Russian, however, is filled with errors that reveal quite dramatically the effects of learning a second language on the first language. There are fascinating sociocultural possibilities suggested by the graffiti. There are clues that suggest it may have been written by someone whose first language was not Russian, possibly an immigrant from the Ukraine or someone who was a Croatian speaker. Ukrainian students most often attended schools in which the language of instruction was Russian. They were Russian as a second language students.

The Russian refugees we interviewed felt unhappy about their circumstances in life in general and in school in particular.

> Everybody thinks we are Russian mafia, they don't talk to us. I live in refugee hotel with [my] family. I cannot to learning so good the English because we are being all Russians in hotel. (18-year-old male, Russian speaker, Russia)

Socioeconomic issues troubled this particular individual. He reported about his first visit to a supermarket in Toronto, his family's port of entry.

Photo by Lee Gunderson

The abundance was overwhelming. Their first stop was the meat display, and their Canadian government subsistence check was about to be spent entirely on chicken and beef, a shopping cart full. "But our family's friend asking why so much meat and we tell her because next week there will being none." Each of us has a view of the world dictated, in part, by our experiences. Children of abundance, those who have never had to consider the possibility of empty supermarket shelves, think differently about life than those, like Russian refugees, who know times of both plenty and scarcity. The transcendence of possibility the Western child assumes does not exist in the minds of many refugee children. They know the good times and the bad, mostly the bad. All of the refugees spoke of their surprise at the availability of the abundance they associated with the privilege of the rich.

Most of the Russian refugee families lived in government-supported housing. A small transient hotel located five blocks from their school was one of the main locations. The secondary school was located in a high-density urban area filled with high-rise buildings. The two major groups living there were retired individuals and gay men. One block from the school was a large apartment complex where retired people lived.

> They put us in this part where dogs are better than Russian are. We poor house, crowded. All around you see people with dogs, walk dogs. Dogs better than Russians. (18-year-old male, Russian speaker, Georgia)

Russian immigrants in this study had one of the highest dropout rates (nearly 85%) in the school district. They had one of the highest records of difficulties both within and outside of school. Achievement and cultural struggles were closely related.

One 16-year-old Cambodian refugee noted that she had been shocked to find that there were stores in Canada that sold exclusively pet food and supplies and that there were hospitals, including emergency hospitals, for pets. Many refugees thought it was bad that they were placed in neighborhoods that were poor and run-down.

Some instances of racism within groups were due to divisions not readily apparent to the teachers involved.

> The Taiwan kids think they are better than the Hong Kong kids. They think their language is better than Cantonese and they make fun of us talking. The two groups don't like each other, and we stay apart at school. (15-year-old female, Cantonese speaker, Hong Kong)

Chinese New Year's celebrations were planned for one of the secondary schools in this study. One of the art teachers, along with parental volunteers, decorated the main entrance hallway to the school with traditional New Year's colors and decorations, and two parent volunteers produced banners written in Chinese. However, a delegation of irate parents visited the principal to complain that the school was showing "communist writing." The calligraphers were, indeed, from the People's Republic of China, and the parents from Taiwan were outraged that their calligraphy was being shown in the school.

Starving in a Smorgasbord

There was an ironic cruelty experienced by the vast majority of students in this study, one that related directly to students' ability to comprehend content or academic material. They understood well and fervently believed in the importance of English as a key to learning and as a key to success in graduating from high school, getting a job, or going on to college or university. Yet, there was little opportunity to learn English or practice the English they knew in the very schools in which the policy was English-only instruction. The reasons varied. There were sociolinguistic reasons for why they found it difficult to interact with native speakers:

> The white kids are big and loud like gorillas. You have to get out of the way because they so big. They think they own school because they are born here. They are so, so loud you can't be a friends with them 'cuz they don't talk, they scream. They are so rude. (15-year-old male, Vietnamese speaker, Vietnam)

When asked what advice they would give new immigrants, students in this study overwhelmingly reported that they thought practicing English with native speakers was essential. However, they also reported on the many reasons they themselves did not:

> There are too many Chinese. (15-year-old male, Cantonese speaker, Hong Kong)

This student's comment appears racist, but it is not. He complained that all he heard in the hallways and on the schoolyard was Cantonese and that this did not allow him to hear and to practice English. He was concerned that he would never learn "proper English" because he was unable to hear it. He also reported that a number of his Cantonese-speaking friends and their families had moved out of the school district so that they might be "expose to more English." Another commented:

> There are too many Chinese students in [this city]. It is hard to practice English. I am happy that I arrived six years ago when there weren't so many Chinese. (18-year-old male, Cantonese speaker, Hong Kong)

Students suggested that after-school activities were vital for immigrants, both to learn English and to become acquainted with Canadian students, although a majority also responded that they did not participate in them.

> I can't play P.E. because I can't wear shorts, it's wrong, girls can't stay after school either 'cuz it's not our beliefs, we have to go home and stay away from boys, Canadian boys specially, and the girls. Girls and boys, teenagers, shouldn't mix;

it's bad. Canadian girls have no morals, they are bad. (16-year-old female, Punjabi speaker, India)

The Canadian guys make fun of Chinese by pretending they speak it and making funny noises. They are really laughing at us and making fun, specially the white girls. (16-year-old female, Shanghainese speaker, People's Republic of China)

One Korean immigrant in a school with a large Cantonese-speaking population had an interesting viewpoint:

I learned English because the only ones who were friendly to me were Canadian students. The Chinese don't talk to me and they don't want to be friends because I am a Korean and I don't speak Chinese and they don't speak English, just Chinese. (17-year-old male, Korean speaker, Korea)

Students' ability to learn language and to learn academic content was limited by differences related to their first cultures and the culture of school. Systems that do not address these cultural differences fail their students. Secondary teachers and administrators must be concerned about cultural differences and how they affect their students' learning.

The Haves and the Have-Nots

There were fascinating and complex differences between schools. Schools in British Columbia differ demographically from one another depending upon the neighborhood or jurisdiction in which they are located, since students generally attend neighborhood schools. This is particularly true for smaller elementary schools; some, for instance, have populations that are 99% Cantonese speaking, while others have incredibly diverse cultural and linguistic populations. Refugee students are generally located in schools in lower socioeconomic neighborhoods. The Spanish-, Russian-, Afghani-, Pushto-, Vietnamese-, Somali-, Kurdish-, and Croation-speaking refugees generally attend schools in areas of the two school districts associated with lower socioeconomic neighborhoods, while entrepreneurs and rich immigrants such as some Cantonese, Mandarin, and Farsi speakers attend schools in more affluent neighborhoods. Their views about school and schooling differed dramatically.

What It Means to Be a Refugee

The difficulty with categories is that they are artificial and fail to represent the diversity that exists within groups. About 80% of the refugees were from countries in which they had suffered through wars and great social difficulties. These families were poorly educated—often as a result of living in poverty or refugee camps—and had very little employment potential. About 20%, however, were professional families. Parents, primarily the fathers, were doctors, lawyers, professors, and military personnel. They valued education and insisted that their children "study hard and get a good education." Indeed, it was their view that education was the vehicle to become a contributing professional. Many suffered serious setbacks as they were told that their training and credentials were not valid, and, as a result, they could not practice their professions in Canada. Although they were high-level professionals and well-respected individuals, they found themselves working in restaurants and enrolling in English classes so that they could "sit for the exams" that would qualify them to practice their professions in Canada. They expected their children to work hard in school.

> My dad professor in Cambodia, in Canada clean tables [name of restaurant]. He study English night school. He say go school, study, study, be good student, get good grades, go university. University make life better. I study 5, 6, 7 hours all days. (14-year-old male, Cambodian speaker, Cambodia)

It is clear that the labels we use to group our students may cloud our perceptions of them. We must begin to recognize the diversity within the categories we use.

What About ESL Classes?

ESL classes are designed to help students acquire enough English to be able to communicate and to succeed academically. We asked students whether or not they were helpful. Responses differed significantly between schools related to socioeconomic status. Generally, students in lower socioeconomic neighborhoods and schools viewed their ESL courses positively. They were enthusiastic about learning English and about the contributions their ESL courses were making to them.

> When I knew I was put in the ESL class, I was very disappointed. In the first week, I was totally upset and was in a very low mood because I didn't have many friends, and all things around me were unfamiliar. Besides, I didn't want to be distinct from others. I wanted to be a regular student. However, after the first day of integration, the master of hell told me where heaven was. As I first stepped in the regular classroom, I could easily feel the coldness and bitterness in the air. Everyone was indifferent to me. I was standing in front of the

classroom like a fool waiting for the teacher to come. I was so embarrassed that I wanted to cry out and run back to the ESL class. As time went by, I made more friends in the ESL class and we studied together like brothers and sisters. We cared for and helped each other. But I remain an unconcerned visitor in the regular class after 6 months. I talk to no one. So now I am travelling between heaven and hell, back and forth. (15-year-old female, Cantonese speaker, Hong Kong) (Also in Levitan, 1998, p. 82)

About 60% of the students in these schools reported that they wished to go on to college or university, while about 30% wished to find good jobs. The following are general categories of responses:

ESL forces students to read.
They are fun.
They help students learn to write.
Friends are in the same classes.
Students are all alike.
The teachers are nice.
ESL courses give extra time to focus on English.
They help you learn.

These students did comment about some negative features of ESL classes. The primary one was that students in ESL classes are often from the same first-language group and tend to rely on speaking the language exclusively during class.

About 95% of the students in high socioeconomic schools reported that they wished to continue on to college or university. Indeed, many specified their academic goals, such as becoming a doctor, an engineer, or a lawyer. Their views of ESL courses were quite negative. Indeed, they viewed them as interfering with their preparation for university.

Students speak their own language instead of English.
Student don't learn anything useful in ESL classes.
Students miss classes while attending ESL.
Students don't speak English.
ESL classes repeat stuff students have learned.
ESL classes don't help you to learn to read.
Too many students in each class.
ESL classes take up too much time.
ESL classes segregate students.
ESL classes make students second class.

Our conversations revealed they viewed ESL classes as places for second-class students, those who had little chance to go on to university. Indeed, there was a persistent view that ESL classes made them feel like they were problem students, "like those who are crippled or blind." Indeed, one 16-year-old male Polish student noted, "People make fun of me because I was in ESL." A 14-year-old Mandarin-speaking male suggested that "ESL classes would be better if there were some Chinese teachers."

Generally, across schools students had some shared views of teaching and learning in Canada. The following are typical observations.

There is freedom to choose whatever subject a student wants.
School is less stressful.
Courses can be upgraded if a student is not satisfied with a grade.
Less stress on homework.
The facilities are good.
It's possible to make new friends from different cultures.
There is more room to study.
Students learn from a variety of activities not just from books.

Negative comments included the following:

Studying environment is bad.
It's hard to make friends.
Too crowded.
Courses are too easy.
Some teachers are not clear.
Some teachers do not explain concepts clearly.
Difficult to make new friends.

In general students felt schools in Canada were easier because there was less focus on memorization.

The school give you too much time to waste. I saw a lot of people don't do homework. In Hong Kong even the worst student does all their homework. (14-year-old male, Cantonese speaker, Hong Kong)

Interestingly, students and parents felt Canadian schools were easier not because the content was easier, but because there was a lack of identified material to be memorized. Indeed, the students generally reported that content in Canadian schools was more difficult, complex, and advanced. Parents were convinced schools were easier because they did not see their children spending time memorizing facts and details (Balcom, 1995). A small number of students felt Canadian schools were better.

I think maybe Canadian schools are better because they have a higher standard. It makes the student reach, you know, go farther than the level of your knowledge, like higher. (14-year-old female, Tagalog speaker, the Philippines)

The schools in Canada are much better than in India. The teachers and the way they teach is much different than in India. In India there's about 40–50 students. Here we move faster than there. (15-year-old female, Punjabi speaker, India)

Well, schools in Canada are easier. Well, I don't know, they give you a little bit of homework and they don't explain it much. And it's more advanced here for some reason. (17-year-old male, Tagalog speaker, the Philippines)

Schools in Canada are better, they give students a wide range of experiences and courses to go through so they can choose and have a firm choice about what they want to become. It's better funded, too. (15-year-old male, Spanish speaker, Guatemala)

School in Canada is different; here it's healthy and it's difficult. (14-year-old female, Spanish speaker, El Salvador)

Students were quick to offer suggestions to improve schools. They suggested, for instance, that "ESL classes are best when they taught academic stuff." Many students were concerned that ESL courses took away from the time they had to study academic content, and for secondary students this was perceived as a serious problem. This notion is in accord with current views of ESL that suggest that the learning of English and content should be simultaneous (e.g., Swain, 1996). Many students were upset that the use of their first language, or L1, was forbidden in classes: "The teachers don't allow people to translate hard material in classes like physics and social studies" even though "students would find it helpful in science classes to have hard words explained to them in their language or were able to look at their bilingual dictionaries."

We inquired about whether or not students believed bilingual classes would have helped them to learn the difficult material they were required to study. To our surprise, the overwhelming response across groups was no; bilingual classes would not help. Students felt that they wanted to learn content in English because it would help them to learn English and to learn the content in the language in which they would be tested. (There are examinations that students take at grade 12 to gain entry into university.) They noted, however, that being able to get help from someone in their first language, especially for those who were the most recent immigrants, would be useful.

It would be good if we can ask for explanations in Chinese, especially the difficult things. (17-year-old female, Mandarin speaker, Taiwan)

About 30% suggested that bilingual teachers would be helpful so that difficult vocabulary and concepts could be explained in the first language.

Some students commented about their schools' focus on "Canadian" or "English" content, particularly in social studies and English. Generally it was believed that courses favored material that was in the teachers' views "classic."

> We study poetry, but it's always English poetry. I try to talk about Spanish poetry, we have beautiful poems in Spanish in Honduras, but the teacher and the students were not interested. Why can't we study poetry in Spanish, because I think it is so much more beautiful than English poetry. We have poetry in Honduras and they should know about it. (16-year-old female, Spanish speaker, Honduras)

The study of literature, the "classics," is viewed as essential to the development of literate human beings. Central to the study is the notion that a particular body of literature is the canon, like Shakespeare and Chaucer, and to be truly "literate" one must study it. This view ignores the substantial oral and written contributions of most of the cultures of the world. It stigmatizes students' backgrounds as being inferior.

> We study Shakespeare, but I don't know why. Teacher says all educated people should know Shakespeare 'cuz, well, stories, they are the best of all time and they talk about the problems of all human beings, all in the world have, like good and evil. But we have older stories in India. All about good and evil, and maybe Canadian people should know them too. When I was in India we studied Shakespeare too, but Indian stories too. (18-year-old male, Hindi speaker, India)

First-language reading was generally limited to comics, newspapers, and magazines, but never in school. There, students reported, English was the only language anyone was interested in, except, of course, for the "foreign language courses," which native speakers were advised against taking. That is, for example, native-speaking Mandarin students were counseled out of taking Mandarin courses, and most opted to study French.

But She Speaks English!

We asked students about their English, their grades, and their aspirations. Overall, two thirds of the 12,000 parents interviewed in a related study indicated they could not communicate with their children in English (Gunderson & Clarke, 1998). However, parents were also convinced that their children were competent in English because they were able to communicate and translate for them in situations involving such activities as telephone inquiries and shopping interactions. Cummins and Swain (1986) referred to this as Basic Interpersonal Communicative Skills (BICS). There is research that suggests such ability develops in two to three years (Collier, 1987; Cummins, 1981) and that the ability to comprehend and produce more complex language, such as that found in formal lectures and academic texts, develops in five to seven years.

Parents were generally convinced that their children were competent English speakers and that their competence was a key to their success in school. Indeed, they were convinced that their children's basic English ability equipped them to succeed academically. This notion appears to have been a determining factor in both students' and parents' strong views that ESL classes slowed students' academic progress. Parents were convinced that basic English ability, which allowed their children to communicate in fairly simple social settings, prepared them to succeed in academic classes. Students, on the other hand, generally agreed that the most significant difficulties they faced in school involved their difficulties with English. A large majority also concluded that their English ability was not as great as their parents believed nor was their classroom achievement.

> The hardest time is with English. The vocabulary is too hard and in socials the sentences are too hard. I could do all right in Spanish, but not English. (17-year-old female, Spanish speaker, El Salvador)

Teachers, particularly academic teachers, discouraged the use of students' first languages. A large majority of students suggested that their learning of academic content in English would have been improved considerably if they were allowed to consult their bilingual dictionaries or bilingual classmates who could explain difficult vocabulary.

> It will being better if we talking each other, hard words. We know hard words, chemistry and physics words, in Polish, but not English. We will learning more knowing hard words. (16-year-old male, Polish speaker, Poland)

A majority thought they were not succeeding in school because of their English ability. They suggested that the easiest courses were those that required multiple-choice examinations (science and math) and the most difficult were those that required short- and long-essay examinations (English and social studies).

L1 Loss

Students reported that their first language (L1) writing skills had decreased since their entry into Canada. They were convinced, however, that their oral skills were about the same (Clarke, 1997; Gunderson & Clarke, 1998). Clarke observed that students' L1 writing skills had, in fact, declined significantly. The Russian graffiti noted previously provides some interesting evidence concerning the negative effects of learning a second language on a student's first language. Whoever wrote the graffiti used an English double-consonant spelling convention in a Russian word where it does not belong—*capitalism*. This appears to be the overgeneralization of an English spelling rule to Russian. A number of researchers have suggested that learning a second language may have serious negative consequences for the first language. Students in this study were convinced that their oral L1 skills were intact, that they could still communicate with family members in their L1s; however, their L1 reading and writing skills, in their opinions, had deteriorated.

Japanese students in the study were concerned that learning a new language and culture, and especially English, would have a significant effect on their acceptance as members of the Japanese community. This was especially true for those whose fathers were on multiple-year contracts to work in Canada.

> When my family go back to Japan I will no longer be Japanese, and my grandmother is worry that I will no be able to talk to her. I will go to high school in Tokyo with other people who have loss what it mean to be Japanese. (17-year-old female, Japanese speaker, Japan)

Radhakrishnan (1996) argued that learning a new language and a new culture changes in fundamental ways the way an individual views and thinks about the world. In essence, a human being is changed by becoming an immigrant.

A Sense of Identity

The foundation of an individual's sense of self-worth is an aggregate of success, acceptance, belonging, acknowledgment, recognition, and encouragement. To have such a sense, however, one must have a fairly clear awareness of self. Human beings define that which is self by those criteria that are culturally appropriate. Norton-Peirce (1997) concluded that "identity relates to desire—the desire for recognition, the desire for affiliation, and the desire for security and safety" (p. 410).

Members of the diasporas in this study were lost in the spaces between various identities: the teenager, the immigrant, the first-language speaker, the individual from the first culture, the individual socializing into a second language and culture, the individual with neither a dominant first or second culture, but one not of either culture. A sense of belonging contributes significantly to one's identity. Members of the shadow diaspora, many of whom are teachers, have dreams and faint memories, while members of the teenage diasporas have angst. The clearest sense of belonging they have is a result of access to their diasporas. They find acceptance, belonging, acknowledgment, recognition, and encouragement as part of a cohesive diaspora, not from their classrooms, their studies, their teachers, their nondiasporic classmates, or their interactions in school activities.

> I go to school, feel lost, real lost. There's no one here who knows me, my trouble, the war, the killing I seen. The Canadians think I selling drugs. No friends. (19-year-old male, Spanish speaker, Honduras)

This individual, a refugee, entered the school district just after he had turned 19 years old. He came to school sporadically, and dropped out after three months. His whereabouts are unknown.

The students from the more affluent families were able to afford tutoring. Indeed, it has become a thriving business. Tutoring helped students, but it also reminded them of their separateness from the mainstream.

> I go to school all day, then Chinese school for 3 hours, then have a tutor twice a week, then do homework for 4, 5 hours until maybe midnight. Canadian students don't work so hard because they know the language. I am a smart student in Taiwan. I get all good grade. In Vancouver I work so hard but my grades are not so good. I can't go to school activities because my language is not so good and I have to study. (14-year-old male, Mandarin speaker, Taiwan)

Members of a diaspora stick together. Others, like teachers and fellow students, perceive their cohesiveness negatively. These students, on the other hand, find support and affirmation, indeed, a sense of identity and self-worth from membership in the group not easily attained outside of the diaspora.

So, What Does This All Mean for Secondary Teachers?

The shadow diaspora, we who have lost our L1s and first cultures, do not know or cannot remember the pain related to their loss. Immigrant students, those at the secondary level, are immersed in the conflict of loss. Some remain members of tightly knit groups, the teenage diasporas, retaining their first languages, their first cultures, and their distance from English and from native English-speaking students. Others find that their first languages are effective barricades to their participation in school activities. Yet to participate, to abandon first language and the safety net provided by a group whose members share the same first language and culture, begins the inevitable process of cultural and language loss, becoming part of the cultural slurry. Many students we observed acquired with great enthusiasm the culture and language of the school and began to reject outright their L1s and cultures. Indeed, a number of students became embarrassed by their parents' English abilities, and some began to refuse to communicate in L1 with their parents. In many ways, the degree of a student's success in school in Canada is a direct measure of the degree of first cultural loss. As teachers, we must begin to value the languages our students speak. There are a number of ways we can try to accomplish this task.

In the past the use of L1 in school was frowned upon and often punished because teachers were convinced such use would interfere with students' learning of English. However, there is evidence that some L1 activities are not, in fact, detrimental to the learning of English (Walters & Gunderson, 1985). There was general agreement from both students and teachers we interviewed that the use of personal bilingual dictionaries would have been valuable and would not have interrupted the teaching and learning going on in academic classes. One chemistry teacher concluded that she found publishing a list of vocabulary words in advance of her lessons allowed students to identify and learn words they did not know. One school in the study involved ESL students in courses designed to teach them how to apply study strategies to their academic tasks, particularly to reading and writing.

As teachers we are convinced that what we teach, like English, math, physics, science, literature, and geography, is purely academic and objective. It is not. Indeed, our choice of what to teach is determined by local or regional political processes. The way we teach, how we view and interact with students, how they view and interact with us as teachers, and how parents view the relationship between home and school are determined by processes informed by beliefs and values that exist within our culture. Immigrant students and parents often have different views and beliefs, those they have assumed are "normal." Their expectations for and about school and schooling are part of their cultural backgrounds. These differences can cause considerable difficulties for students, parents, and teachers.

Indeed, Gunderson and Anderson (2003) describe a situation in which school personnel attempted to explain their grading practices and evaluation procedures through an after-school parent-teacher meeting involving a demonstration that included cookies and milk. Rather than being helpful, the session engendered more negative feelings toward the school's assessment and evaluation procedures than had previously existed because of the parents' reaction to the use of cookies and milk in a session they thought would be "serious." The session turned out to be a classic example of cultural misunderstanding.

While it is easy to recommend increased cultural understanding and knowledge, it is considerably more difficult to accomplish. Being aware of our own cultural biases and beliefs related to teaching and learning will help us to be aware that immigrant students and parents come to school with deeply ingrained beliefs and values that may be antithetical to our own. What to do about the differences is more difficult.

A large majority of immigrant parents and students believe that teaching and learning should be teacher centered, that the teacher is the source of knowledge, and that her or his task is to communicate the knowledge to students so that they can hear it, memorize it, and faithfully reproduce it on an examination. Western teachers generally appear to believe, although there is a great diversity of belief in the teaching community, that teaching and learning should be student centered, that learning should be exploration, and that learning how to learn is more important than acquiring a particular set of facts about an academic discipline. Western teachers appear to believe that developing independent, questioning critical thinkers and learners is a primary goal of teaching and learning. All of the secondary teachers we spoke to maintained that developing critical thinkers was their primary goal. This is antithetical to students in many cultures who are convinced that they must learn the truth that exists independently in teachers' heads and in print and neither of these sources of information should be questioned. Indeed, many immigrant students view student-centered activities as ludicrous, as an abandonment of the basic principles of teaching and learning they hold to be valuable. Many expressed feelings of contempt for the teachers, whom they believed had abrogated their responsibilities. Most parents with whom we spoke were convinced there was something wrong because teachers were not teaching and students, in their opinions, were not learning what they needed. The teachers were not telling students what to do.

Communicating with parents is difficult. Dealing with parents from different cultures is potentially even more difficult. What is abundantly clear is that across cultures, parents, teachers, and other interested adults want desperately, especially for their own sons and daughters, "the best" in education and opportunity. Many view the best as being a product, the accumulation of knowledge that will enable their children to pass a test that will allow them to enter a university and subsequently to graduate and become a member of a profession. This is a politically conservative approach to the values of schooling which aim to maintain an oppressive, stratified society. Both students and parents in the present study believed that the teaching and learning approach they encountered in the schools violated their children's right to learn the knowledge they needed to succeed. One "multicultural worker" at one school told me that she thought it was shameful that the education system had been changed from a focus on product to a focus on process. She saw little logic in changing a system that had clearly worked for teachers and for people like me, a university professor. She wondered whether the system was being changed so new immigrants would not have the same opportunities that Canadians had enjoyed for years.

No teaching is apolitical, and no teacher is culture free. The way we teach, the content we teach, and the biases we communicate through our teaching are culture-specific interpretations of what is good, what is truth, and what is knowledge. Indeed, Pennycook (1998) concluded "that all education is political" (p. 190).

There is a paradox. The postmodern view of knowledge is that it is local, that there are no universals. This view has legitimized the voices of diversity, those that have traditionally been marginalized. Norton-Peirce (1997) argued that "greater attention to the voices of the learners generates unexpected consequences and new understanding" (p. 415). The results of this study suggest there are multiple voices, the teachers', the parents', the students', and the communities', that often are opposing. A difficult task for teachers is to value differing points of view, particularly when they are diametrically opposed to their own and that of the school. Indeed, it may be that some should not be valued, such as using ultrasound to identify female fetuses so they can be aborted ("American Doctor," 1994). Teachers must be critical of their own cultural biases, but they must also make judgments that differentiate "good" from "bad." This is a judgment made from a point of view related to a particular culture. As members of a Western culture, most teachers advocate for the development of independent, critical thinkers and learners. This focus is not necessarily evil, although some parents and students will think so. This is the essential difficulty.

The students in this study, although in an English-speaking school system that by policy featured English-only instruction, found it difficult to get easy access to English. These findings confirm Norton-Peirce's (1995) conclusion that "inequitable relations of power limit the opportunities L2 learners have to practice the target language outside of the classrooms" (p. 12). Findings of this study show that immigrant students themselves identify interactions with native English speakers as the single most important way to improve their English, their learning of Canadian culture, and their integration into Canadian society. They also show conclusively that they did not for various social, sociolinguistic, and cultural reasons, in fact, interact with native English speakers.

Duff and Early (1999) confirmed in their study the students' statements that they do not interact in class. The ESL consultant in one of the school districts in the present study designed a summer school camp to encourage cross-cultural communications. The first camp attracted 68 students, 67 female and 1 male, all immigrant students. Indeed, he has concluded that the notion of *multicultural* has come to mean "nonwhite" and that Canadian-born students, those who appear most in need of learning about multicultural issues, are convinced that the term does not include them (T. Carrigan, personal communication, 1998). It is clear that school personnel must develop programs that allow and encourage immigrant students to meet, communicate with, and interact with native English speakers. It is equally as true that native English speakers are in need of such programs.

Many, if not all, Western teachers belong to shadow diasporas. We should help students preserve what we have lost. Unfortunately, this is no easy task. We can begin by valuing students' backgrounds and by trying to incorporate their voices into a cultural mosaic rather than watching them disappear as they dissolve into a cultural slurry. There is, at the present, no easy way to accomplish this task. The findings of the present study do not provide many answers to the multiple problems that have been described; they have, however, delineated a number of questions to be addressed. However, if secondary teachers do not take an interest in their students' languages and cultures, then students will continue to fail to learn the academic content their teachers value so highly.

REFERENCES

American doctor criticized for providing gender revealing services in British Columbia. (1994, May 5). *The Vancouver Sun*, p. B1.

Balcom, F. (1995, November 7). Immigrant parents believe BC schools too easy. *The Vancouver Sun*, pp. A1, A2.

Banks, J.A. (1991). *Teaching strategies for ethnic studies* (4th ed.). Needham Heights, MA: Allyn & Bacon.

Canagarajah, A.S. (1993). Critical ethnography of a Sri Lankan classroom: Ambiguities in student opposition to reproduction through ESOL. *TESOL Quarterly, 27*, 601–626.

Clarke, D.K. (1997). *The language and academic achievement of immigrant students in English-only schools.* Unpublished master's thesis, University of British Columbia, Vancouver, BC, Canada.

Collier, V.P. (1987). Age and rate of acquisition of second language for academic purposes. *TESOL Quarterly, 21*, 617–641.

A conversation with Lisa Delpit. (1991). *Language Arts, 68*, 541–547.

Crawford, J. (1989). Official English might sound good, but it could translate into school trouble. *American School Board Journal, 176*, 41–44.

Cummins, J. (1981). Age on arrival and immigrant second language learning in Canada: A reassessment. *Applied Linguistics, 2*, 132–149.

Cummins, J. (1991). Empowering minority students: A framework for intervention. In M. Minami & B.P. Kennedy (Eds.), *Language issues in literacy and bilingual/multicultural education* (Reprint Series No. 22, pp. 372–390). Cambridge, MA: Harvard Educational Review.

Cummins, J., & Swain, M. (1986). Linguistic interdependence: A central principle of bilingual education. In *Bilingualism in education* (pp. 80–95). New York: Longman.

Delpit, L.D. (1988). The silenced dialogue: Power and pedagogy in educating other people's children. *Harvard Educational Review, 58*, 280–298.

Duff, P., & Early, M. (1999). *Language socialization in perspective: Classroom discourse in high school humanities courses.* Paper presented at the American Association of Applied Linguistics, Stamford, CT.

Duff, P., & Uchida, Y. (1997). The negotiation of teachers' sociocultural identities and practices in postsecondary EFL classrooms. *TESOL Quarterly, 31*, 451–486.

Eisner, E. (1992). Objectivity in educational research. *Curriculum Inquiry, 22*, 9–15.

Gee, J.P. (1992). Reading. *Journal of Urban and Cultural Studies, 2*, 65–77.

Gunderson, L. (1985). A survey of L2 reading instruction in British Columbia. *Canadian Modern Language Review, 2*(1), 44–55.

Gunderson, L. (1986). Content reading and ESL students. *TESL Canada Journal, 4*, 49–53.

Gunderson, L. (2000). How will literacy be defined in the new millennium? *Reading Research Quarterly, 35*, 68–69.

Gunderson, L., & Anderson, J. (2003). Multicultural views of literacy learning and teaching. In A. Willis, G.E. Garcia, R. Barrera, & V. Harris (Eds.), *Multicultural issues in literacy research and practice.* Mahwah, NJ: Erlbaum.

Gunderson, L., & Clarke, D.K. (1998). An exploration of the relationship between ESL students' backgrounds and their English and academic achievement. In T. Shanahan & F.V. Rodriguez-Brown (Eds.), *National Reading Conference Yearbook 47* (pp. 264–273). Chicago: National Reading Conference.

Harman, S., & Edelsky, C. (1989). The risks of whole language literacy: Alienation and connection. *Language Arts, 66*, 392–406.

Levitan, S. (1998). *I'm not in my homeland anymore: Voices of students in a new land.* Scarborough, ON: Pippin.

Norton-Peirce, B. (1995). Social identity, investment, and language learning. *TESOL Quarterly, 29*, 9–31.

Norton-Peirce, B. (1997). Language, identity, and the ownership of English. *TESOL Quarterly, 31*, 409–429.

Pennycook, A. (1998). *English and the discourses of colonialism.* New York: Routledge.

Radhakrishnan, R. (1996). *Diasporic mediations.* Minneapolis, MN: University of Minnesota Press.

Ratekin, N., Simpson, M.L., Alvermann, D.E., & Dishner, E.K. (1985). Why teachers resist content reading instruction. *Journal of Reading, 28*, 32–43.

Richmond Chinese parents association asks school board for traditional school. (1999, April 3). *The Richmond Press,* p. 1.

Seabrook, J. (1998). The racketeers of illusion. *New Internationalist, 308*, 22–24.

Sullivan, A. (1998). Chinese lead traditional school drive. *The Vancouver Courier, 20*, p. 16.

Swain, M. (1996). Integrating language and content in immersion classrooms: Research perspectives. *Canadian Modern Language Review, 52*, 529–548.

Walters, K., & Gunderson, L. (1985). Using oral reading activities with ESL students in L1 to improve English achievement. *The Reading Teacher, 39*, 118–122.

Willinsky, J. (1998). *Learning to divide the world: Education at empire's end.* Minneapolis, MN: University of Minnesota Press.

Positioning in a Middle School Culture: Gender, Race, Social Class, and Power

Donna Mahar

Mark was suspended from school today. He punched a white boy in the face until the blood spread over the cafeteria floor, and the news seeped through every crevice of the adolescent infrastructure. Three students, friends of the boy who was beaten, pulled Mark back as adult reinforcements were called. A clear-cut case: School policy states that fighting leads to a 5-day suspension. Mark was suspended; the boy who received the physical blows was not. Yet both young men commenced with verbal assaults that were perhaps more damaging than the punches that followed.

The logic behind the decision to suspend one party but not the other opens the door to questions raised by Delpit (1995), Freire and Macedo (1987), Gee and Crawford (1998), and others who see words as powerful tools that maintain a social hegemony where "the rules of the culture of power are a reflection of the rules of the culture of those who have the power" (Delpit, 1995, p. 25). In his middle school Mark is in no way a member of "the culture of power." Mark is one of eight African American students in a total student population of 717. On his seventh-grade team of 125 students, only one other young man is African American. The entire staff of this school is white, and Mark's team teachers are all Caucasian women between the ages of 35 and 43.

What follows is a narrative of two seventh-grade students, Mark and Scott (pseudonyms), both of whom were marginalized by the academic and social aspects of school. Their stories revolve around the issues of language, power, gender, and race. In attempts to find a position of acceptance, both young men used the power of language to establish a dominant stance in the middle school status structure. Mark's weapon was to cast gender taunts at Scott, a tactic that was countered with racial slurs that had a profound impact on both students and the entire school community. My interest in Mark and Scott's literacy beyond the classroom walls stemmed from a teacher research project I was conducting. It was this use of language as a tool of power that helped me define and tighten my qualitative study.

Originally published in *Journal of Adolescent & Adult Literacy* (2001), volume 45, pages 200–209.

Developing a Research Framework

Every year I found I was fascinated, frustrated, and greatly concerned by students who appeared to be marginalized by the academic system. Even my carefully constructed workshop model did not always pave the way for academic success. The questions this group of bright yet disenfranchised students posed ultimately led me back to the university to explore the field of teacher research.

My initial research question was "What role does adolescent literacy have in a middle school classroom, and how is this role affected by the teacher's authoritative voice?" In moving to design a research plan, I found several subquestions emerging:

> What happens when marginalized students with a strong personal commitment to writing are asked to engage in teacher-directed discourse?
>
> How will students view their personal literacies if they become part of the classroom discourse?
>
> Does a student's personal literacy have as much validity for the student as a teacher-directed assignment if the outcome measures the same growth/knowledge?
>
> What aspects of school discourse and curricula are essential for students to integrate so that they will not be marginalized members of mainstream society?

The preceding questions, coupled with the journal I had begun at the start of the academic year, led to a focus on case studies of bright yet marginalized adolescents. For most of these students race, gender, and social class seemed to keep them from accessing the codes necessary to succeed in the dominant social and academic discourse communities of middle school.

Classroom Structure

I began my journal in order to gain some insight to the complexities of adolescent literacies and their impact on the classroom. I started by noting students' reading, writing, and speaking that was not in any way connected to the academic discourse, but was rich with insight and perceptions of the world beyond school.

As I reviewed my notes every night, the students who, although possessing strong personal literacies, lacked the skills to access the codes of power in the traditional middle school environment always seemed to be to the forefront. To understand the role their personal literacies played in the academic setting, it would help to have a bird's-eye view of how our seventh-grade English classroom was structured. When I began teaching middle school in the late 1980s I established a workshop-based, reader response classroom that had Rosenblatt's (1978) transactional theory as its underlying structure. Although these reading and writing workshops allowed students to explore texts of personal interest, the door was closed to the subtextual dynamics (Gallas, 1998) that played a critical role in their lives. In many ways I was still the facilitator of the dominant discourse of power. I was the teacher there to guide, instruct, and nudge students into the domain of literacy as defined by academic standards. As my understanding of adolescent literacies changed during the 1990s, so did my classroom. Although much of the traditional workshop structure remained, I began to seek ways to include issues of race, gender, and social class in the curriculum.

Currently, half of the students' grade is determined by a literary letter submitted to me every three to four weeks. The books the students read are self-selections, although I do try to encourage new genres and authors in my responses. In addition to the literary letters, students also keep personal writing journals. Here they write poems and stories that are of personal interest. Once a week we have a brief publishing workshop during which students are encouraged to send their poems to professional publications. For many marginalized students, this becomes the highlight of the class. More so than the students who are concerned with grades, these students who have not previously experienced any success in school suddenly begin to see their poems in magazines and newspapers. A few of these budding creative writers even begin to take a greater interest in the more teacher-directed aspects of class.

The second half of each student's grade for a 10-week period is determined by his or her work on teacher-designed thematic units. On an average there are two units each marking period. Each unit incorporates a dramatic, artistic, and written component. The drama and art projects are done in cooperative groups, with the written component being a portfolio that offers a variety of writing styles and assignments from which to select.

At the start of the past academic year, all thematic units were redesigned to center around issues of social justice. In previous years when social themes entered the curriculum, the door to classroom discourse opened for students who were usually left at the threshold. For many of the marginalized students the topics led to interesting class discussions, art projects, and poetry; very few, however, would turn in a completed portfolio of written work.

Data Collection and Research Methodology

My journal was an invaluable record as I attempted to explore what had been for me the uncharted territory of adolescents' personal literacies in the classroom. A nightly ritual became "cooking" these journal observations (Hubbard & Power, 1999). Cooking involved looking at the raw data I collected during the day and trying to find a combination of ingredients that would address my research questions. This quest rarely led to a rolling boil of insight; a slow simmer of new questions was usually what I was left with. Some nights the rather cryptic scrawls and mosaic of notes that I used to quickly record "ah ha" moments in the midst of teaching led to some frustrating recipes.

In addition to my journal and notes, my data collection included the following student artifacts: academic journals and reading logs, personal journals that for most students were composed of poetry, literary letters, metacognitive reflections at the end of a unit of study, and artwork. As my research progressed I conducted interviews with students to follow up on ideas presented in their writing and during class discussions. Although most of my questions were for verification, where I asked students to "confirm or disconfirm" hypotheses I had made about their nonacademic literacies (Spradley, 1979, p. 126), other questions took on the aspect of native-language verification where I asked the students to define unfamiliar terms to me in hopes of avoiding a translation into language other than their own (Spradley, 1979). With all interviews I attempted to clarify, and accurately record, nuances of adolescent literacy that were not part of my knowledge base.

Data Analysis

I found that as I began to analyze my data, like any novice I tried all the tools available to me before I found the one that worked. At first I used colored sticky notes to categorize students and code their responses to aspects of personal and academic literacy. I also tried semantic domain analysis, in which I looked at different groups within the marginalized category (Spradley, 1979). I found looking at "folk terms," terminology specific to students' out-of-class discourse, to be helpful; this type of analysis also offered a visual research memo (Hubbard & Power, 1999). Ultimately, though, it was through my writing of a narrative interpretation of five marginalized students that my data began to take on a framework that addressed aspects of my questions. I began to understand what Hynds and Appleman (1997) meant when they wrote the following:

> We learned we had to follow our informants beyond the classroom walls, into their communities, and even well beyond the official time frames of our research in order to discover the complicated process of becoming literate. (p. 290)

Following these five students led to student interviews, discussions with parents, trips to the guidance office to check prior academic records, discussions with counselors and sixth-grade teachers, and discussions with the five students' peers for clarification of "folk terms." As I made myself open to their literacies beyond the requirements of seventh-grade English class, I found these students stopping by before school, after school, and even during lunch to discuss aspects of self-expression that were personally meaningful. These adolescents were beginning to show me what aspects of literacy they engaged in when their schoolwork was done.

A Research Snapshot

In terms of my research questions, the intersection of Mark's and Scott's use of language as a tool of power demonstrated that the role adolescent literacy plays in the classroom is directly affected by what happens outside of the classroom. Also, perhaps the authoritative voice of the teacher is not a dominant force in a classroom when subtexts of gender, race, and power are seeping in from the cafeteria and corridors. These nonacademic settings often appear to be the center stages of adolescent literacies and self-expression.

After the fight discussed at the opening of this article, Mark and Scott became the primary focus of my study. Both of their histories underscore that the subtextual dynamics of home and the hallways can have a direct impact on academic success.

Mark's Story

As a white woman who holds a position of power over students, I can never fully understand what school is like for Mark as one of 8 African American students out of a student population of 717, nor can I fully appreciate the power and pain that a racial slur can inflict. My discussions with counselors and former teachers, review of prior academic records, and interviews with Mark helped me to flesh out a picture of him as an individual, rather than as just another statistic in the school's records or another student in my class. My teacher research helped me to appreciate that the fight in the cafeteria was much more than a schoolboy altercation; it was an intersection of language, power, and social class occurring in what is commonly seen as the level playing field of public education.

Mark has a history of acting impulsively both in the classroom and in the more unstructured areas of the halls, bus, and playground. His classroom comments are usually not offensive, yet he fails to follow the formal protocol of sitting still for 42 minutes and speaking only after being addressed by the teacher. In less formal workshop settings Mark moves around frequently. He will request immediate feedback to questions or concerns, even if this infringes on another student's conference.

Mark takes medication at lunchtime to help this "impulsivity." Bloom's (2000) comment on "Generation Rx" brings Mark to mind: "handing out medications at lunch time is easier than creating classes that keep intelligent and curious kids from squirming, daydreaming and talking back" (p. 24). This medical model is much easier to deal with than confronting the complex issues of social class, cultural power, and the resulting inequalities. It is interesting to note that frequently when Mark has had a difficult time adjusting to the protocols of a class, the question raised is "Did he take his medication?"

Why did Mark begin to pummel his cohort at lunch? As with all situations the answer depended on the perspective of the person you asked. Mark was suspended because the fight was deemed "unprovoked" by administrators after they interviewed the boys who were in the closest proximity to the situation. That these three young men happened to be friends of the boy who was punched did not seem to affect the veracity of their statements in the questioner's eyes. Mark also denied that any offensive term had been said, although other students reported Scott's use of the term in days prior to this event.

Mark's mother readily acquiesced with the administrative decision, while Scott's parents were vocal in their concern over their son's safety. Several of Mark's teachers were concerned about his medication. He had failed to take his dose for two days in a row prior to the incident; this appeared to offer an acceptable rationale for an apparent random act of violence. The immediate response of one of his team teachers after hearing that Mark was suspended was "Yes!" She felt badly about what had happened, but was glad she did not have to have him in class for five days.

The account rendered by the majority of Mark's peers was quite different from those previously described. The word that worked its way from the cafeteria, down the hallways, and into the classes was that the white boy had called Mark a "nigger." The story was told and retold throughout the afternoon, a legend in the making. Was it the truth? As with all legends the truth may not be in the legend itself, but in what it reflects about the culture that creates it. In this adolescent culture, the "n word" sent a chill through the entire community. From the perspective of Mikhail Bakhtin (as cited in Wertsch, 1991), a Russian literary critic and philosopher, this offensive term could be an "authoritative" word. It definitely commanded more authority than most words used by a teacher in a classroom setting.

Although not aware of it, students appeared to be demonstrating Bakhtin's concept of "multivoicedness" (Wertsch, 1991). By stating their outrage at this alleged inimical remark, Mark's cohorts were distancing themselves from any of the social connotations that this remark carries. It was their knowledge of what was socially appropriate that allowed them to speak as if with one voice against even the suggestion that Mark had been maligned in this way. In doing this they were illustrating an understanding of the codes of power; overt racial slurs are not socially acceptable in their white middle-class culture. However, their verbal outrage does not enable Mark to access the codes with which his peers are so facile. He remains an outsider being defended by the ruling class; in a sense this could be seen as noblesse oblige for the 21st century.

In an attempt to understand what may have contributed to Mark's and Scott's use of discourse as a social weapon, I interviewed their seventh-grade guidance counselor, who was also Mark's counselor in sixth grade. He reported that prior to starting seventh grade, Mark's academic history was marked by an inability to sit still, failure to raise his hand to speak, and comments that seemingly did not relate to the teacher-directed topic at hand. Interviews with Mark's sixth-grade teachers corroborated this assessment. Mark did not follow the traditional school script that was second nature to most students in his academic peer group. He appeared resistant to what Freire termed the "banking system of education where students are seen as the depositories" (Gaughan, 1997, p. 95).

The guidance counselor observed a big change in Mark's behavior in seventh grade. He appeared to be less impulsive and antagonistic, and more willing to follow expectations when they were clearly explained to him, not left for him to intuit. My observations of Mark's classroom behavior are consistent with this appraisal. When asked to do something that might be posed as a choice, he would often not participate in any activity. If one specific option was directly explained, Mark would attend to that task. Delpit's insights on veiled power seem to apply to Mark in unstructured classroom situations:

> But those veiled commands are commands nonetheless, representing true power, and with true consequences for disobedience. If veiled commands are ignored, the child will be labeled a behavior problem and possibly officially

classified as behavior disordered. In other words, the attempt by the teacher to reduce an exhibition of power by expressing herself in indirect terms may remove the very explicitness that the child needs to understand the rules of the new classroom culture. (1995, p. 34)

My journal observations reveal a change in Mark's attitude toward writing occurring in late January. Prior to this time, Mark had been very selective in what he would choose to write. Out of class he would read one personal reading selection each month; usually these were books by R.L. Stine. He was conscientious about writing a literary letter and appeared to look forward to the response. The stance that I took in responding to these letters was free from the more authoritative overtones found when responding to more teacher-directed assignments. With regard to the teacher-directed assignments, whether they were selections for a portfolio or parts of a thematic assignment, Mark would often attempt bits and pieces without turning in a finished product. Mark was often productive during group discussions or projects as long as he was given frequent specific directions. As far as the personal journal, Mark had eschewed any part of this. Perhaps the open-ended, independent nature of this class component kept Mark at bay.

The first change in Mark's approach to writing was in regard to the personal journal. Mark began to write poems during the time set aside in class for journal writing. He then became quite persistent in sending his poems to various local publications. He requested teacher feedback in terms of spelling and the correct submission protocol, but he was not open to suggestions that would lead to a rethinking of his text. The poems had a very simple, repetitive rhyme scheme; it seemed much more important to have the poem rhyme than to develop imagery or theme. Three of his poems were published in rapid succession by two local papers. Mark made copies of these and distributed them to his teachers, the guidance counselor, and the vice principal. He received positive accolades from both parents and made sure he always had copies of the published text with him in his notebook.

When I look at the factors that may have contributed to this change, what Gallas (1998) referred to as the "sub textual dynamics of classroom life" (p. 22) seem to have a significant role. Being published brought a degree of extrinsic reward to all students. Awards, candy, posters in the hallway, recognition during the morning announcements, and a profile in the parent newsletter guaranteed positive recognition. In terms of the subtextual dynamics of the classroom culture, the poetry journal had taken on a status outside of the class with a group of marginalized young men with whom Mark associated. Several kept personal journals that they would exchange among themselves. Occasionally they would share poems with the class or me, yet these were not offered with feedback in mind. They were concerned about their message, not the format or use of conventions of Standard English. Mark's poems were quite simplistic in comparison with those written by his friends; nevertheless, they allowed him a stake in their social discourse and social group (Bakhtin, as cited in Wertsch, 1991).

Another notation in my journal during this same period notes that Mark was suddenly appearing in my room every morning prior to the start of school. He would bound in with a "Yo" or "What's up?" and then stand by the window to watch other students enter the school. When asked why he was hanging out in the room he expounded on how he did not like his home-room. After Mark's departure one morning a few boys told me that other students were looking to start a fight, and Mark was trying to avoid it. Mornings were often a time when students dropped by to talk about their personal poetry and publication. By having a stake in this social group, Mark now had a valid reason not to be in the halls.

Being one of the few African American students in the school left Mark open to comments by both faculty and other students that at times showed the degree of oblivion those in the dominant culture have toward those who are not in their cultural niche. One day an Iroquois storyteller was presenting in Mark's class. Prior to telling the creation myth, she asked if anyone knew the various clans. Students began stating bear, turtle, and other animal names. One student yelled out "the Ku Klux Klan." He was sitting at Mark's table when he said that. When I took the student in the hallway and asked if he knew what that meant, he stated, "it is a group that hurts black people." When I asked why he said that, after a few minutes of shoulder shrugs and "I don't knows" he stated that he just thought it was funny. A few minutes after returning to the room, Mark came up to me and asked me not to yell at the boy for "he probably didn't know what the Klan was." Not only did this underscore the ways Mark is excluded from the dominant culture, it showed the lengths he goes to to excuse this culture when it violates his own.

Mark's poetry was not the only way his approach to writing changed in the late winter. In February students were given the assignment to write a story that showed survival and courage. The selection could be either fiction or nonfiction with drafts to be critiqued by peers, literary circle discussion groups, and the instructor. By the end of February Mark had composed two drafts of his story. He even offered to read it aloud to a literature circle. His story was about a trucker who became lost in a blizzard and the lengths he goes to in order to survive. Mark modeled the protagonist after his father who is a truck driver; he even wrote to the manufacturer of his dad's truck to get information regarding the make and model. Mark was open to both teacher and student feedback and did not become defensive when suggestions were offered. Again, this was a big change in behavior from earlier in the year. Mark may not have been part of "the culture of power," but he seemed to be learning some of the codes and was making an attempt to acquire some of this previously elusive currency (Delpit, 1995).

At this point I felt that I needed to know more about why this shift was occurring. I asked Mark if I could interview him about this. He was initially hesitant, but he did offer to write me a note after he had time to think about it. His reflections are as follows:

> I started to send my poems in because I saw another good poet (also one of my good friends) Josh. He would write about things in his life. So I thought if I did what he did, I could get my poems published. So I just started writing poems. At first I didn't want to send them in, but you told me to send them in and see what happens. I started getting published, and I just wrote more poems and sent them in too.

Mark was beginning to identify himself as a writer. He also was finding ways to incorporate his home life into the world of school. He wrote the following passage when asked why he decided to write his story about a trucker:

> I selected my dads truck to base my story on because that is mostly the only thing I know about. I grew up around trucks. There was only 3 people in my whole family that didn't drive a truck, and that is what I want to be when I grow up.

Three school days after the successful literature circle discussion about his truck text, Mark was suspended. After the suspension, the truck story was never completed. Mark also stopped sharing his poetry. My journal notes reflect a feeling like "a heavy load" hanging over the students. This line from Langston Hughes's "A Dream Deferred" (1994) seemed to permeate the entire team. No one wanted to discuss the "n word" incident, yet it remained a palpable entity.

Scott's Story

Scott, the young man who was the object of Mark's physical blows, was a new student, entering a sixth- through eighth-grade middle school during seventh grade. Scott was entering a domain of highly structured social groups that did not readily welcome an outsider. When I reflected on his struggle to find a voice in the realm of adolescent literacies, the following passage from *Speak* by Laurie Halse Anderson came to mind:

> We fall into clans: Jocks, Country Clubbers, Idiot Savants, Cheerleaders, Human Waste, Eurotrash, Future Fascists of America, Big Hair Chix, the Marthas, Suffering Artists, Thespians, Goths, Shredders. I am clanless.... I have entered high school with the wrong hair, the wrong clothes, the wrong attitude. And I don't have anyone to sit with. (Anderson, 1999, p. 5)

The quest to be accepted by a "cool" group was a primary focus of Scott's first month of seventh grade.

I met Scott several days before school started as he toured the building with his mother. She was extremely supportive and nurturing and voiced concern regarding Scott's transition to a new school. Scott presented with an eager, friendly demeanor that seemed to belie any real need to worry. Early in September Scott brought in his favorite book of poetry to share with the class. He seemed eager to please teachers in class and was very comfortable with the academic script, although his out-of-class work ethics did not reflect careful attention to detail or to the required aspects of thematic assignments.

By the five-week interim report his grades were in the 80s in all subjects, and his parents requested a meeting with his teachers. Both parents are professionals who place emphasis on education and school success. Scott has an older sister who found academic and social success easy to come by. Her success made Scott's struggle to achieve A's appear to be a bit of an anomaly for his parents. It was agreed that Scott would move from an accelerated math class to a regular seventh-grade math class so that he could concentrate his efforts on all subjects. Although this was a sound move educationally, in terms of the adolescent culture this was a major demotion in status and a rough blow to a person struggling to find social acceptance.

Throughout the fall Scott struggled to find a group with which to align himself. Early in the year he began to eat lunch in my room with about 20 other students who for a variety of reasons did not want to enter the school cafeteria. This is by no means a cohesive group; although a few students may sit together and talk, on most days they resemble toddlers who are engaged in parallel play. New people may drift in and out depending on changing group dynamics, but for three weeks Scott was a regular. On one occasion I left the room for about five minutes to speak with a colleague. When I returned the vice principal was standing at the door with Scott beside her. Apparently a milk carton had been thrown across the room by a young woman who was aiming for Scott's head. This was not characteristic of the young woman or the group. When I asked what precipitated it, the students said Scott had been teasing her. In an effort to fit in Scott was trying on the wise guy stance with little luck. As with many wise guys, once he turned stoolie his fate was sealed, at least with that social group.

By January Scott did find a group to align himself with, the swim team. He was quite proud of this and even wrote a poem about the team to send for publication and to hang on the classroom wall. Many of the boys on this team were highly marginalized both socially and academically. Throughout January and February jokes about Speedos seemed to be the chosen form of adolescent levity. These continual comments began to breed a less than subtle undercurrent of animosity.

In "Resisting Gender-Binding in the Middle School," McCracken (1996) wrote the following:

> Boys and girls who don't fit the stereotypical gender-role expectations are also profoundly disadvantaged in the classrooms and schools where gender stereotypes go unchallenged. The AAUW-sponsored survey of sexual harassment, *Hostile Hallways* (1993), found that one of the more frequently mentioned forms of sexual harassment in schools is calling a student a homosexual. Eighty-six percent of 1,600 public school students surveyed in grades 8–11, said they would be "very upset" if they were called gay or lesbian.... No other type of harassment—including actual physical abuse—provoked a reaction this strong among boys. (p. 20)

For two months Scott had been greeted in the hallways with "gay," "fag," and "homo," terms that seemed to elicit a humorous response from the ever-present crowd of adolescent spectators. Often it appeared that Mark was offering the first offensive salutation.

Supervisors in the cafeteria had heard Scott call Mark the racial slur on several occasions prior to the day of the fight, just as they had heard Mark cast gender taunts at Scott. What makes this more than a schoolboy scuffle is that both young men used semantics to establish a social code of power. The suspension resulted from the physical blows Mark delivered, yet perhaps the more powerful beating came from the words both young men deliberately cast. Bakhtin (cited in Wertsch, 1991) felt that meaning comes into existence only when two or more voices come into contact, when the voice of the listener responds to the voice of the speaker. Mark and Scott obviously sent each other a personal message regarding what is unacceptable social language in their specific stratum of society.

It is unfortunate that the power that discourse played in this event was initially side-stepped in favor of the more comfortable, and socially expedient, discussions of medication, anger management, and appropriateness of this academic setting for Mark. Dillon and Moje's (1998) comments on how adolescents' exploration of different subjective positions affects those around them could shed some light on the response of school personnel:

> As adolescents explore different subject positions, and as they are positioned by others around them—whether parents, peers, or teachers—they project various subjectivities to their teachers. If an adolescent takes on a "resistant" student subjectivity, then are his or her options limited because we, as teachers, researchers, and parents, position him or her as uncaring, unmotivated, or unteachable? If we listen carefully to this adolescent's talk, then might we be able to understand and even respect the reasons for his or her resistance? (p. 195)

It appeared that listening to Mark and Scott's "talk" might lead to broader issues that a school suspension or conflict mediation might not be able to address.

Implications for Teacher Researchers

When I began this foray into teacher research, I perceived that my study would be contained within the classroom walls and focus on adolescent literacies as they pertained to academic discourse. For Mark and Scott, becoming literate was not just a matter of academic success. Each young man needed to become literate in the adolescent social codes of behavior, as well as socially appropriate modes of self-expression, before the classroom could become a comfortable place to experiment with personal literacies and power.

Mark needed to become familiar with the codes of power that operated in both the social discourse of peers and the dominant academic discourse of the school. After the cafeteria incident, a series of copycat baitings occurred. It became great sport for a group of young men to see who could set Mark off by saying the offensive term. Mark did not resort to a physical response; however, his display of rage did result in several visits to the in-school suspension room. His reactions also resulted in several discussions with the school counselor, the vice principal, and team teachers. The approach taken by these adults was an explicit discussion of power and language. Although not planned, the approach used was similar to the aspects of power discussed by Delpit (1995). In particular, Delpit's fourth code of power, "if you are not already a participant in the culture of power, being told explicitly the rules of that culture makes acquiring power easier" (p. 25) applies to the discussions between Mark and the adults attempting to help him navigate difficult terrain.

Mark ended the year by successfully completing two classes he had been failing as well as remaining out of the in-school suspension room. His stance in class reflected a new value for academic coinage; he participated appropriately in group work and began to complete assignments that were teacher directed. By acknowledging his world, educators opened the door a bit wider for Mark to value their discourse.

Scott also ended the year in a position of greater comfort. The gender taunts abated once the swim season was over, and Scott began to appear more relaxed in both the classroom and hallways. Rather than try to impress the teacher during class, an approach that did not bring acceptance with his peers, he began to become more social during group work. His group was always productive in terms of the class assignment, but much of their discourse centered on social events outside of school. Laughing, note passing, and inside jokes allowed Scott to become part of a social group where he was accepted and comfortable. By the end of the year he was "going out" with a very popular female member of this group as well as sustaining a solid B average in his classes. By allowing adolescent literacies a place in the classroom, time to negotiate social scripts was given an additional venue outside the strict social strata of the cafeteria and hallways. Both Scott and Mark appeared to benefit academically when the subtextual dynamics of adolescents' literacies were brought to the forefront rather than being swept under the curricular rug.

Fecho (2000) wrote of how teacher research conducted in one's own classroom is perhaps both an asset and liability. He stated that it is difficult being both a reader of data and an actor in the events being recorded: "At times data collection fell by the wayside if the teacher in me was too consumed by the immediacy of the moment" (p. 377). Because I was not present at the fight, this gave me an opportunity to review my data as it may pertain to an incident outside of the classroom. It also gave me the opportunity to interview other staff members regarding their perceptions of Mark, Scott, and the circumstances of the fight. Perhaps most important, this intersection of two marginalized students gave me the opportunity to add a new dimension to my classroom observations. Adolescents have discourse patterns that are often established outside of the classroom that can illuminate the stance they take toward academic and social activities occurring during the school day. The literacies they bring to school will have a definite impact on how students respond to teachers and other students.

Although I aligned myself with reader-response theory rather than New Criticism in my reading and writing instruction, in many ways I took a New Critical stance in terms of classroom hegemony. In regard to classroom control and discipline, I was the dominant force. This was definitely the stance taken by the majority of adults after the fight. I am not advocating classroom chaos, but perhaps it is worth taking the time to look beyond an adolescent's immediate reaction to a situation, person, text, or discussion to see what underlying factors may be contributing to this social posturing. By focusing on an event outside of my classroom domain, I was able to look at Scott's and Mark's words as they applied to their respective worlds (Freire & Macedo, 1987). In order to understand, and appreciate, the role of adolescent literacy in the classroom, teachers may at times have to set aside their authoritative voice and learn to read both the world and words of the diverse group of adolescents who make up the classroom mosaics.

REFERENCES

Anderson, L.H. (1999). *Speak.* New York: Farrar, Straus & Giroux.

Bloom, A. (2000, March 12). Generation Rx. *The New York Times Magazine,* pp. 23–24.

Delpit, L. (1995). *Other people's children: Cultural conflict in the classroom.* New York: The New Press.

Dillon, D.R., & Moje, E. (1998). Listening to the talk of adolescent girls: Lessons about literacy, school and life. In D. Alvermann, K. Hinchman, D. Moore, S. Phelps, & D. Waff (Eds.), *Reconceptualizing the literacies in adolescents' lives* (pp. 193–222). Mahwah, NJ: Erlbaum.

Fecho, B. (2000). Critical inquiries into language in an urban classroom. *Research in the Teaching of English, 34,* 368–395.

Freire, P., & Macedo, D. (1987). *Reading the word and the world.* Westport, CT: Bergin & Garvey.

Gallas, K. (1998). *"Sometimes I can be anything." Power, gender, and identity in a primary classroom.* New York: Teachers College Press.

Gaughan, J. (1997). *Cultural reflections: Critical teaching and learning in the English classroom.* Portsmouth, NH: Boynton/Cook.

Gee, J.P., & Crawford, V.M. (1998). Two kinds of teenagers: Language, identity, and social class. In D. Alvermann, K. Hinchman, D. Moore, S. Phelps, & D. Waff (Eds.), *Reconceptualizing the literacies in adolescents' lives* (pp. 225–245). Mahwah, NJ: Erlbaum.

Hubbard, R.S., & Power, B.M. (1999). *Living the questions. A guide for teacher-researchers.* York, ME: Stenhouse.

Hughes, L. (1994). Harlem(2). In A. Rampersad (Ed.), *The collected poems of Langston Hughes* (p. 426). New York: Alfred A. Knopf.

Hynds, S., & Appleman, D. (1997). Walking our talk: Between response and responsibility in the literature classroom. *English Education, 29,* 272–294.

McCracken, N. (1996). Resisting gender-binding in the middle school. *Voices From the Middle, 3*, 4–10.

Rosenblatt, L. (1978). *The reader, the text, the poem: The transactional theory of the literary work.* Carbondale, IL: Southern Illinois University Press.

Spradley, J. (1979). *The ethnographic interview.* New York: Harcourt Brace Jovanovich.

Wertsch, J.V. (1991). *Voices of the mind: A sociocultural approach to mediated action.* Cambridge, MA: Harvard University Press.

RIGHT

Children have the right to equal access

---

to the technology used for the improvement

---

of reading instruction.

Introduction

Paola Pilonieta and William E. Blanton

The "information superhighway" was heralded in the 1990s as the mechanism that would connect all citizens to a vast array of telecommunication opportunities. Unfortunately, not all citizens are partaking of these opportunities. According to the fourth report of the U.S. National Telecommunications and Information Administration (NTIA) (2000), only 42% of U.S. households have Internet access; furthermore, U.S. households with incomes of more than $75,000 are six times more likely to be connected to the Internet than households with the lowest income levels. The NTIA report indicates that there is unequal ownership of computers and Internet access based on income, race, and ethnicity. These technological inequities are also found in schools.

Page (1998) outlines how race and students' socioeconomic status (SES) determine the abundance of computers and Internet connections in schools. Schools that service students from higher SES and from nonminority backgrounds are more likely to have better student-computer and computer-Internet ratios than schools with predominantly low-SES or minority students. In addition, there is also inequitable use of computers in schools. When computers are used in economically disadvantaged schools, they are used for drill-and-practice activities. In contrast, in affluent schools, computers are used for activities that require critical thinking. Because of the inequitable access to technology, a digital divide has emerged consisting of the technology "haves" and "have-nots." This divide is not merely about computers or Internet access; it includes disparities in access to information, computer literacy, and literacy in general.

Limited computer and Internet access in schools exacerbated by the same limitations in the home has serious implications for individuals of low-SES and minority backgrounds, especially in today's technology-driven job market. Today's students will become members of a complex work environment in which the ability to utilize technology will be a prerequisite to successful entry into almost any profession. Individuals with restricted access to technology will lack the basic skills necessary to ensure success in the workplace and will be at an immediate disadvantage when entering the job market. The International Reading Association recognized the relevance of these issues and how reading instruction can ameliorate the situation in *Making a Difference*

Means Making It Different: Honoring Children's Rights to Excellent Reading Instruction in Right 9—children have the right to equal access to the technology used for the improvement of reading instruction.

In the future, locating, accessing, reading, analyzing and evaluating, and using information of all kinds will require increasing knowledge of microcomputers, telecommunications, and computer-retrieval systems for documents and other media. Writing will rely on computer and multimedia systems as well as one's ability to compose and edit. In addition, mathematical and science literacies and related problem solving will require knowledge of computer-based tools and the ability to comprehend and manipulate databases and representational systems. Just as important, most every form of collaborative work activity will be mediated through technologies, and workers must be able to work in relation with one another. It is no longer acceptable for schools to remain separate from the larger society with respect to computer-based technologies. Schools must gradually transform their organizational structures, curriculum, and teaching tools to reflect the way development, thinking, learning, information management, communicating, and problem solving are done beyond their walls.

Schools have been teaching a certain kind of literacy—mastery of basic skills through explicit instruction—that is not embedded in goal-oriented activity. They also have been teaching other forms of literacy such as mathematics literacy, science literacy, and social studies literacy in ways that are outmoded, for example, literal recall of isolated facts that are painfully tedious. It is inappropriate to continue this kind of traditional instruction in skill areas and subject matter using technologies. The goal must be to change, to integrate, to differentiate, and to complement literacy instruction and learning activities with technologies, enabling students to master and appropriate knowledge, skills, and literate ways of thinking, and transforming their identities through participation in technologically mediated literacy practices.

We recognize that making technologies available will not by itself transform literacy education. However, access to and participation in technologically mediated literacy activities can support a beginning. Schools need to embrace new and imaginative ways of thinking about the presentation of curriculum, new kinds of teacher and student roles, new tools for measuring and evaluating literacy performance, and new ways of organizing literacy instruction, all based on a clear understanding of what and how students ought to be learning, including, but not limited to, opportunities made possible by microcomputers, multimedia, and telecommunications.

How Does Technology Affect Reading Instruction?

We have progressed past the industrial age into the information age in which accessing the most appropriate information in the least amount of time and communicating it in the most effective and efficient manner are of utmost importance. The Internet is the catalyst for all this change. As a result, the definition of literacy has evolved as well. Instead of reading the static text on a page, children need to learn how to navigate through the dynamic format of hypertext. Leu (1997) describes three ways in which the definition of literacy has expanded. First, being literate now means knowing how to surf the Web, or finding the information necessary to complete a task. When faced with a vast amount of websites on any given topic, it is important that children know how to choose the appropriate source of information. Second, children need to acquire the tools to keep up with the ever-changing world of technology. Instead of *being literate, becoming literate* is the more appropriate term, because it describes how literacy is a developmental process that is never completely achieved as long as technology continues to transform itself (Leu, 1997). Finally, using the Internet entails teaching students to analyze the information they find with a critical eye. Whereas books have a certain degree of authority and often present information in an objective manner, information on the Internet is more susceptible to represent a particular agenda or viewpoint. Children need to be taught how to judge the validity of the information found on websites.

Why Should Teachers Use Technology in Their Classrooms?

By infusing technology into their curriculum and allowing all students to have equal access to computers, regardless of race or achievement levels, teachers are providing opportunities that bridge the digital divide. In addition, students will benefit as they gain the skills that will be required of them as they enter the job market.

Despite the ubiquitous nature of the computer in today's society, there is still a need for systematic research regarding its effectiveness. However, there is evidence of the many benefits that computers can offer. In its investigation of computer technology and reading instruction, the National Reading Panel (National Institute of Child Health and Human Development, 2000) maintains that there is a general agreement in the literature that computer technology can be used to successfully deliver various types of reading instruction. The panel also notes that there are exciting learning possibilities in exploring the use of hypertext in reading instruction and in pairing word-processing programs with reading instruction as reading develops in conjunction with writing.

How Can Teachers Use Technology in Their Reading Program?

The article by Jay Blanchard, John Behrens, and Gary Anderson in this section describes the Lightspan Project, which is helping to ameliorate the digital divide and connect homes with schools. The goal of the project is to enhance school achievement through game-like educational CDs. The program uses more than 100 CDs that are correlated with the school curricula in reading, language arts, and mathematics. Because the software operates on both computers and Sony PlayStations, it allows families who cannot afford computers to use the software with the less expensive PlayStations; low-SES children can reap the benefits of this software as well. Evaluations of the Lightspan Project indicate that it provides an equitable instructional network that positively affects student achievement.

In the second article, Donald J. Leu describes an instructional framework that integrates the Internet with all areas of the curriculum. He provides websites for each subject area and outlines how to plan a research activity that uses the Internet. He also provides examples of Internet workshops that he has developed and explains how such an activity can be incorporated into a teacher's schedule.

The third article, by Donald J. Leu, Rachel A. Karchmer, and Deborah Diadiun Leu, discusses the parallels of Miss Rumphius and learning communities or envisionments that are being created on the Internet. The authors also explain the changing nature of literacy and provide websites where teachers can seek advice and ideas on using the Internet in their classrooms.

How Will This Affect My Class?

The articles in this section provide several examples of how computers and the Internet can be incorporated into any classroom. All teachers, especially those working with students whose social and financial resources are limited, share the responsibility of adequately preparing students for the future. Without question, this future will involve computers in most work and everyday activity. Teachers need to take advantage of every opportunity to integrate technology into their curriculum and instruction so that students will possess the knowledge and skill necessary for engaging in activities mediated through computers and telecommunications.

REFERENCES

Blanchard, J., Behrens, J., & Anderson, G. (1998). The effects of concurrent classroom and home instructional video-game use on student achievement: A preliminary study. *Computers in the Schools, 14*(3/4), 65–78.

Leu, D.J., Jr. (1997). Caity's question: Literacy as deixis on the Internet. *The Reading Teacher, 51,* 62–67. Available: http://www.readingonline.org/electronic/RT/caity.html

Leu, D.J., Jr. (2002). Internet workshop: Making time for literacy. *The Reading Teacher, 55,* 466–472.

Leu, D.J., Jr., Karchmer, R.A., & Leu, D.D. (1999). The Miss Rumphius effect: Envisionments for literacy and learning that transform the Internet. *The Reading Teacher, 52,* 636–642.

National Institute of Child Health and Human Development. (2000). Computer technology and reading instruction. In *Report of the National Reading Panel. Teaching children to read: Reports of the subgroups.* [Online]. Available: http://www.nichd.nih.gov/publications/nrp/ch6.pdf

National Telecommunications and Information Administration (NTIA). (2000). *Falling through the net: Toward digital inclusion* [Online executive summary]. Washington DC: Author. Available: www.ntia.doc.gov/ntiahome/digitaldivide/execsumfttn00.htm

Page, M. (1998). Conflicts of equity: Educational technology in America. *Computers in Schools, 14*(3/4), 137–153.

The Effects of Concurrent Classroom and Home Instructional Video-Game Use on Student Achievement: A Preliminary Study

Jay Blanchard, John Behrens, and Gary Anderson

Technology has come to dominate American life and is an eternal part of daily life. As a result, modern technology is seen by many as a new Prometheus: the creator of a modernistic order. But this tendency to attribute mythical powers to technology should not be confused with the monumental tasks technology is expected to accomplish under a variety of dazzlingly difficult and almost impossible conditions. One of these tasks is nurturing the moral, social, and educational development of American children. To accomplish this task technology must deal with the challenge of connecting the two major institutions of learning for children: families and schools. Nothing could be more difficult.

The Importance of Connecting Families and Schools

Connecting families and schools means that characteristics, beliefs, and practices of everyone from these institutions have effects on the moral, social, and educational development of children. Simply put, the family-school connection means that homes and schools are connected and linked through students—and these connections and links have effects which are important for children (Benton Foundation, 1997; Birman, Kirshstein, Levin, Matheson, & Stephens, 1997; Booth & Dunn, 1996; Bronfenbrenner, 1979, 1986; Epstein, 1996; Featherstone, 1976; Hoover-Dempsey & Sandler, 1995; Lareau, 1989; Lightfoot, 1978; Ryan, Adams, Gullotta, Weissberg, & Hampton, 1995; Scott-Jones, 1995; Steinburg, 1996; Swap, 1993; U.S Department of Education, 1994, 1996).

The family-school connection is a field of study that did not exist before the 1960s and can claim two founders: (a) The Elementary and Secondary Education Act of 1965 (ESEA) which specified that parents were expected to assume a more direct role in their children's formal education, and (b) The Civil Rights Act of 1964, Section 402, and the resulting research by James S.

Originally published in *Computers in the Schools* (1998), volume 14, number 3/4, pages 65–78. Reprinted with permission of The Haworth Press, Inc., Binghamton, NY.

Coleman on the importance of family in the education of disadvantaged children (i.e., Equality of Educational Opportunity, Coleman et al., 1966). Since that time, researchers have struggled to map the family-school connection and understand how all the relationships fit together. Of course, the commonsense assumption is that positive family-school connections help ameliorate a lot of negative factors that impact student outcomes. The American public seems to agree with this assumption. The 29th Annual Phi Delta Kappa/Gallup Poll (Rose, Gallup, & Elam, 1997) found that 86% of the public believe that parental support is the most important factor in determining a school's success. In addition, review of data from the largest survey undertaken in American education, namely, the National Education Longitudinal Study of 1988, clearly pointed to one factor that promoted educational success: the degree to which parents are actively involved in their children's education.[1] Spurred on by interest in the importance of families, the U.S. Department of Education published *Strong Families, Strong Schools* (1994) and the National Committee for Citizens in Education published *The Family Is Critical to Student Achievement* (Henderson & Berla, 1994). These documents provided the research base necessary to support claims about the importance of the family-school connection in student outcomes—and the opportunities for technology.

Connecting Families and Schools With Technology

Today most families of school-age children spend a large portion of their lives using technologies, whether looking at screens, listening to music, or talking on telephones. While families and schools have had almost universal access to a variety of technologies, unfortunately they have not been used to connect and link for instructional purposes to any degree that would suggest widespread impact (Cuban, 1986, 1993; Educational Testing Service, 1997; Glennan & Melmed, 1996). However, that may be changing!

If you are an American child, or for that matter a child from any other industrialized country, chances are very good you have a video-game computer attached to a TV in your home. Judging from consumer product estimates and U.S. Census data, there are more video-game computers of the 16-, 32-, and 64-bit variety from Sega, Nintendo, and Sony in America than there are families with school-age children (50 million versus 35 million respectively[2]). These video-game computers have been used for gaming and not for education. There is a reason for this! Until very recently (January 1997), instructional programs for TV video-games did not exist. However, beginning in 1997, Sony (i.e., PlayStation) and Lightspan Partnership introduced the first 32-bit CD-ROM video-game computer with CD programs that featured K–8 instructional content.[3]

The First Preliminary Study

This is the first study to examine the effects of video-game computers and CD instructional programs on student achievement. This study is important, not only because it is the first, but because it investigates technologies that allow families and schools to have equivalent technology. Put another way, it is the first study of family-school connection networks that focuses on instruction. Never before in the history of educational technology have families and schools had reliable, affordable, entertaining, and equitable family-school connection network opportunities (Blanchard, 1998). What this means is that the family-school connection can be an instructional network that functions anytime and anywhere—not just at school during school hours.

Family-School Connection and Technology Research

As mentioned earlier and for obvious reasons, no studies exist that have used video-game computers. However, in the last few years several studies have used equivalent technologies in homes and schools: Those technologies have generally been personal computers (with modems and printers). While these studies are not specifically about video-gaming technology, nonetheless they provide a means to consider some of the issues in this study (*Project TELL*, Birenbaum, Hochwald, & Kornblum, 1994; *Lightspan Project*, Godin, 1996[4]).

Project TELL (1990–1993, New York City) placed computers (with modems and printers) along with voice-messaging in the classrooms and homes of elementary students. According to an evaluation of Project TELL (Birenbaum, Hochwald, & Kornblum, 1994), the technologies were welcomed by the students, families, and teachers—and the technologies had a powerful influence on student achievement because of enhanced learning opportunities at home. It is noteworthy that, during the project, damage, theft, or loss of the equipment was nil.

The Lightspan Project placed equivalent technologies (computers and printers) in homes and classrooms at several sites across the United States. The instruction in the project focused on K–6, reading, language arts, and mathematics. Godin (1996) completed a survey evaluation of the project (81 teachers in grades K–6 along with 445 families) and found that (a) most teachers used the technologies with students each day, (b) most students used the technologies at home each school day, (c) most parents used the technologies with their children at home, and (d) about half of the parents used the technologies *without* their children on some occasions. As a result of the project, parents claimed that they learned more about their children and what their children were doing in school. They also claimed that their children's interest and motivation toward school increased as a result of the family-school connection technologies.

Method

Participants

Eighty-seven students began the study (46 male, 41 female) and 71 students completed all phases of the study (37 male, 34 female). The students were all fifth graders and no students were involved in special education classes. The students came from two multi-ethnic urban schools in a large southwestern city (US). The schools' attendance boundaries were adjacent to each other and both are Title 1 schools.

Three intact classrooms of fifth graders were used in the study: (a) an experimental group (N = 30), (b) an affiliate group (N = 27), and (c) a control group (N = 30). The experimental and affiliate groups were in one school and the control group in the neighboring school.[5] The experimental group had equivalent video-game technology in the classroom and homes. The affiliate group had no technology in the classroom or homes but were next door to the experimental classroom—and with indirect access to the technologies through visits to the classroom and homes. The control group had no technologies or access to technologies except that which would normally be available.

Procedures and Materials

The study lasted 10 weeks (February to May 1997; one-week spring break). Student achievement was measured with the Stanford Achievement Test (9th Edition) Form S, Intermediate 2 (Harcourt Brace, 1996). Pre- and post-tests were administered across the same two days for all groups. Three subtests of the Stanford were used: vocabulary (20 minutes, 30 questions), reading comprehension (30 minutes, 54 questions), and mathematics procedures (30 minutes, 30 questions). The mathematics procedures subtest was used as a measure of internal validity. Tests were administered by the teachers, in their classrooms. Tests were collected and returned to the researchers and the tests were then scored by clerical help unfamiliar with the study.

Once the study began, the researchers had no contact with the students and teachers with the exception of picking up usage logs from the experimental classroom.

Experimental Group Procedures

Classroom use. A Sony PlayStation and two multimedia personal computers were available in the classroom along with instructional CDs that worked with both types of computers.[6] Students were trained on the use of the Sony PlayStations and the multimedia computers by their classroom teacher. Students were allowed to use any of the computers and CDs during "free-time." They usually worked in groups of two or three. The teacher made no special efforts to focus activities on computer use or on the instructional content of the CDs.[7] Students completed classroom usage logs every time they used the classroom computers. Students estimated the time of use and which of the eight CDs were used. The usage logs were collected and tabulated for each student every week. On average, students used the PlayStation at school for one hour each week. (Usage ranged from 10 minutes to almost two hours a week.)

Home use. The teacher rotated 10 PlayStations and CDs among the students every two weeks. Thus, a majority of the students had access to the PlayStations at home for a total of 4 weeks during the 10 weeks of the study. To check out a PlayStation for home use, one of the student's parents had to attend a short training session conducted at school on PlayStation and CD operations.[8]

Students and their families kept weekly usage logs estimating the time each day that the students used the technology. The logs were returned with the Sony PlayStation and CDs at the end of each two week period. On average, students used the PlayStation at home for 5 hours for each two-week period. (Usage ranged from 1 hour to over 10 hours.)

Affiliate Group Procedures

The teacher and students completed their normal activities for the 10 weeks of the study and were unaware of the purposes of the research. However, these students were often in the experimental classroom and were observed using (or watching) the technologies either on the PlayStations or the multimedia computers—usually as part of a group between class sessions, at lunch time, or before school. It was also noted that some affiliate students worked with the technologies while at the homes of experimental group students. No attempts were made to interfere with serendipitous use of the technologies by the affiliate group.

Control Group Procedures

The teacher and students completed their normal activities for the 10 weeks of the study and were unaware of the purposes of the research.

Instructional Content

Eight CD-ROMs were used in the study—both at school and at home. The CDs contained biographies and commentary about 203 historical figures from 19th- and 20th-century America. Each biography was organized around text, video and audio about the historical figure and featured audio, MPEG-2 quality video, animation, and graphics. Students could also access art, music, and literature related to the historical figure. Three multimedia games accompanied each biography. The games focused on testing students' reading comprehension skills using a variety of clues.

The instructional objectives, in addition to historical knowledge of the character and culture, focused on (a) vocabulary comprehension, (b) reading and reviewing comprehension, (c) critical thinking and study skills, and (d) communicating.[9]

Results

Three one-way Analyses of Variance (ANOVA) were computed on changes in pre/post tests across the experimental, affiliate, and control groups for reading comprehension, vocabulary, and mathematics procedures scores (dependent measures). In addition, an Analysis of Covariance (ANCOVA) was computed on the post-test scores using the pre-test scores as the covariate to determine if there were differences between ANOVA and ANCOVA analyses.[10]

One ANOVA was statistically significant. The ANOVA for Groups X Reading Comprehension: $F(2,68) = 7.08$, MSE = 49.6, $p = .002$ was statistically significant. The difference means on the reading comprehension subtest, pre > post, were +2.9 (N = 26) for the experimental group, –.5 for the affili-ate group (N = 20) and –4.4 (N = 25) for the control group (see Table 1). Concerning the ANCOVA analysis, conclusions regarding the significance at the .05 level were identical to the ANOVA.

To assess the differences between particular groups, post-hoc compar-isons were used (Scheffe Post Hoc Tests). The results indicated that neither the control nor the affiliate groups were different enough from each other to consider the effects to be significantly different. This was also the case for

Table 1. Pre/post test means and standard deviations for reading comprehension

Group	N	Pre	Post
Experimental	26	29.8 (11.1)	32.7 (10.6)
Affiliate	20	30.7 (10.1)	31.2 (11.6)
Control	25	34.0 (8.8)	29.6 (9.4)

Table 2. Pre/post test means and standard deviations for mathematics procedures

Group	N	Pre	Post
Experimental	27	19.2 (7.3)	20.4 (6.0)
Affiliate	20	17.7 (7.5)	21.7 (5.8)
Control	24	19.9 (6.6)	23.1 (5.4)

Table 3. Pre/post test means and standard deviations for vocabulary

Group	N	Pre	Post
Experimental	27	18.1 (6.0)	20.1 (6.7)
Affiliate	21	19.1 (5.9)	20.8 (4.8)
Control	25	21.4 (3.5)	22.3 (4.7)

the experimental versus affiliate groups. However, the experimental group showed change that was significantly higher than that of the control group (p = .002). This may be an artifact of the decrease in scores in the control group. To assess whether the experimental group showed an average change greater than expected by chance from their own original scores, a one-group dependent t-test was computed. The t-test was approximately significant at p = .0507 with $t(25)$ = 2.05. The effect size for this difference was .41, which is considered a moderately large effect.

The two ANOVAs for testing for group differences in Mathematics Procedures ($F(2,68)$ = 1.91, MSE = 23.5, p = .155) and Vocabulary ($F(2,70)$ = .384, MSE = 7.34, p = .969) were not significant (see Tables 2 and 3).

Discussion

Comprehension

In the study, experimental students outperformed all other students on the comprehension subtest (see Table 1). Why? It would appear that there are at least two possible reasons. First, the Stanford Comprehension subtest focuses on students reading passages and answering various types of comprehension questions. This is similar to the Lightspan instructional activities. Clearly the students had several hours of practice reading (and listening) to text followed by opportunities to answer comprehension questions. In essence, students had lots of opportunities to practice test-taking skills (reading passages and answering questions). Second, the Lightspan instructional activities featured opportunities for students to practice a number of comprehension strategies (e.g., compare and contrast, critical thinking, main idea, supporting details). These strategies could then have transferred to tasks on the Stanford Comprehension subtest. While both of these reasons (singularly or in combination) may account for results, it is unclear at this time which or for that matter if other reasons are possible. Future research would do well to get more accurate records of what instructional activities were used and for how long.

Vocabulary

In the study, experimental students outperformed the other groups but not to a significant degree. What can be made of these results? As can be seen in Table 3, experimental students increased their scores by about two questions while the other groups increased their scores by about one question. While this result is in need of replication, nevertheless, it suggests that the vocabulary identification knowledge as well as vocabulary acquisition strategies in the CDs helped but only the vocabulary acquisition strategies transferred to test performance because the word knowledge (vocabulary) questions in Stratus did not match the questions about vocabulary on the Stanford.

Mathematics

There were no significant differences between pre/post gain scores on the mathematics subtest for experimental, affiliate, and control students as would be expected since the experimental procedures did not include mathematics instruction (see Table 2). However, the purpose of the mathematics subtest was not to measure mathematics performance but instead was a measure of internal validity. In any study involving experimental groups with new technologies and control groups without new technologies, teachers and researchers may be inclined to the Hawthorn Effect or bias. To ensure these were not at work in the present study, the mathematics subtest was included (teachers were not aware of the purpose for the mathematics subtest). If experimental students outperformed affiliate and control students, perhaps the Hawthorne Effect or bias might be at work. As can be seen in Table 2, there were no significant differences between pre/post test gains of experimental, affiliate, and control groups on the mathematics subtest.

Affiliate Group

An important aspect of this study was the use of an affiliate group; that is, students that had access to the technology, but not in their classrooms or as a part of other instructional activities. For these students the possible benefits of technology would come through indirect or incidental means (before and after school, during recesses, at home, etc.). In this study, there were no statistically significant differences between pre/post test gain scores for all subtests involving the affiliate and control groups students. So, the indirect or incidental impact of technology on achievement was nil. But that does not mean more research is not needed on the incidental impact of technology on classrooms, that is, classrooms without technology but in schools where technology is available—and this includes the incidental use of technologies in family-school connection (students visiting other students that have technology in their homes).

In Conclusion

This preliminary study is important because it is the first to examine the family-school connection with video-game technology. The study seems to indicate that through video-game technologies, families and schools have access to reliable, affordable, entertaining, and equitable instructional networks that might positively affect student achievement. And, these networks can potentially function anytime and anywhere.

The interoperability provided by video-game technology can develop and enhance the reciprocal influence of schools and homes on student outcomes. This means that when homes and schools are connected and linked through technology, these connections will have effects which are important for everyone. While this is only a preliminary study, nevertheless, it suggests that video-game technology presents an almost endless supply of fascinating opportunities for all stakeholders in student outcomes—including students—to help the family-school connection. But, finding ways to enhance student outcomes presents a set of stubborn and bedraggling problems that, so far, we have not been able to solve without technology. Add to this the fact that enhancing student outcomes takes place on rapidly changing social, economic, educational, and political landscapes—and video-game technology has its hands full.

NOTES

1. *The NELS:88 survey was a national random sample of about 25,000 eighth graders, parents, teachers, and school administrators in 1,000 public and private schools. The follow-up studies of 1990 and 1992 looked at a subsample of the original participants when the students were in 10th and 12th grades respectively.*

   Also, analyses of data are beginning (September 1997) from the National Longitudinal Study of Adolescent Health (a survey of 90,000 children and adolescents from 12–18). Initial analyses indicate that teenagers with close ties to family members report less at-risk behaviors.

2. *For additional information see (a)* Nintendo: At the top of its game, Business Week, *June 9, 1997, pp. 72–73; (b)* Nintendo trade-in threatens price war, Marketing Week, *May 8, 1997, pp. 23–24; (c)* Off-computer: CD-ROM and the game machines, EMedia-Professional, *March 1997, pp. 66–68; (d)* U.S. Census Bureau, Current Population Reports: Household and Family Characteristics: *March 1995 (Released October 1996; pp. 20–488).*

3. *SEGA also offers a 32-bit CD-based video-game computer named "Saturn."*
4. *Two other studies may have implications from family-school connection research.* ThinkLink *(Cline, Omanson & Sisung, 1994) used a video-on-demand service in Michigan for several years.* The Buddy System Project *(Rockman & Mayer, 1994) in Indiana is a popular, on-going, statewide program that equips schools and families to use technology. Updated specific achievement data were not available.*
5. *The school population (N = 1,200) for experimental and affiliate groups was identified as 46% white, 9% black, 40% Hispanic, 4% Native American, 1% other; 45% two-parent families; 72% free-reduced lunch; 23% limited-English proficiency). The school population of the control group was similar. Unequal Ns in Tables 1, 2, and 3 are due to data on students that transferred out of the school, transferred into the school, or subjects who were absent on post-testing days.*
6. *The system requirements for the multimedia computer were MPEG 2 video support and for the PlayStation only a TV and game controller (no keyboard needed).*
7. *It seems noteworthy that students and teacher often had impromptu discussions about the historical figures and their cultures as a result of the CDs. This seemed particularly the case after students watched and listened to many of the live-action video monologues.*
8. *No attempt was made to survey the views of parents about the use of technology in the home or the family-school connection. Also, no attempt was made to survey parent use.* Unlike Project TELL *(Birenbaum, Hochwald, & Kornblum, 1994), one PlayStation was stolen from a home and one PlayStation was returned damaged beyond use. Both were replaced at a cost of $150.00 each. No CDs were lost or damaged during home use.*
9. *The Lightspan CDs (Stratus) feature a story line with four high school students—Tony, Jessica, Max, and Sara—who are working on a class assignment with Ms. Stafford. She introduces them to a futuristic Web application that enables the students to access anyone, anywhere, at any time in the past, present, or future.*

   The CDs provide students with an opportunity to read biographies and commentary about 203 historical figures from the 1800s and 1900s as well as important themes such as social reform, literature, art, and the westward expansion. Students can also view live-action video monologues of the historical figures.
10. *Pretest-posttest treatment design can be computed using either a repeated measures ANOVA of gain scores or ANCOVA on the post-test scores with the*

pre-test scores used as the covariate. When subjects are randomly assigned to treatments as individuals the additional statistical power of the ANCOVA leads to preference for this approach. However, when intact groups (e.g., classrooms) are randomly assigned to treatment conditions, the repeated measures ANOVA is generally preferred (Maxwell & Delaney, 1990, pp. 392–395).

REFERENCES

Benton Foundation. (1997). *What's going on. The learning connection.* Washington, DC: Benton Foundation. (Benton Foundation available at www.benton.org or benton@benton.org)

Birenbaum, H., Hochwald, E., & Kornblum, W. (1994). *Project TELL: Telecommunications for learning* (Third Year Report to NYNEX). New York, Stanton/Heiskell Center for Public Policy in Telecommunications and Information Systems, City University of New York (33 West 42nd Street, Room 400N, NY 10036).

Birman, B., Kirshstein, R., Levin, D., Matheson, N., & Stephens, M. (1997). *The effectiveness of using technology in K–12 education: A preliminary framework and review.* Washington, DC: U.S. Department of Education, Office of Educational Research and Improvement.

Blanchard, J. (1998). The family-school connection and technology. In A. Robertson (Ed.), *Proceedings of the Families, Technology, and Education Conference* [Online]. Champaign, IL: ERIC Clearinghouse on Elementary and Early Childhood Education. Available: http://ericps.crc.uiuc.edu/fte/ftehome.html

Booth, A., & Dunn, J. (1996). (Eds.). *Family-links: How do they affect educational outcomes.* Mahwah, NJ: LEA.

Bronfenbrenner, U. (1979). *The ecology of human development: Experiments by nature and design.* Cambridge, MA: Harvard University Press.

Bronfenbrenner, U. (1986). Ecology of the family as a context for human development: Research perspectives. *Development Psychology, 22,* 723–742.

Cline, J., Omanson, R., & Sisung, N. (1994). *Evaluation of ThinkLink: September 1, 1993–August 31, 1996.* Warren, MI: Warren Consolidated Schools.

Coleman, J., Campbell, E., Hobson, C., McPartlan, J., Modd, A., Winfield, F., et al. (1966). *Equality of educational opportunity* Washington, DC: U.S. Government Printing Office.

Cuban, L. (1986). *Teachers and machines: The classroom use of technology since 1920.* New York: Teachers College Press.

Cuban, L. (1993). *How teachers taught: Constancy and change in American classrooms (1880–1990).* New York: Teachers College Press.

Educational Testing Service. (1997). *Computers and classrooms: The status of technology in U.S. schools.* Princeton, NJ: Author.

Epstein, J. (1996). Perspectives and previews on research and policy for school, family, and community partnerships. In A. Booth & J. Dunn (Eds.), *Family-Links: How do they affect educational outcomes* (pp. 209–246). Mahwah, NJ: LEA.

Featherstone, J. (1978). *What schools can do.* New York: Liveright.

Glennan, T., & Melmed, A. (1996). *Fostering the use of educational technology.* Santa Monica, CA: RAND Corporation.

Godin, K. (1996). *Lightspan evaluation research: Final report.* Portsmouth, NH: RMC Research Corporation (1000 Markey Street, Portsmouth, NH 03801).

Harcourt, Brace. (1996). *Stanford Achievement Test* (9th Ed.). San Antonio, TX: Harcourt Brace Educational Measurement.

Henderson, A., & Berla, N. (1994). *A new generation of evidence: The family is critical to student achievement.* Washington, DC: National Committee for Citizens in Education. (Available from the Center for Law and Education, 1875 Connecticut Avenue, NW, Suite 510, Washington, DC 20009)

Hoover-Dempsey, K., & Sandler, H. (1995). Parental involvement in children's education: Why does it make a difference? *Teachers College Record, 97*(2), 310–331.

Lareau, A. (1989). *Home advantage: Social class and parent involvement in elementary education.* New York: Falmer Press.

Lightfoot, S. (1978). *Worlds apart: Relationships between families and schools.* New York: Basic Books.

Maxwell, S., & Delaney, H. (1990). *Designing experiments and analyzing data: A model comparison approach.* Pacific Grove, CA: Brooks/Cole.

Rockman, S., & Mayer, K. (1994). *The Buddy system, 1988–1993: A synthesis of research findings and recommendations for future research and action.* Indianapolis, IN: Corporation for Educational Technology (17 West Market Street, Suite 960, Indianapolis, IN 46204).

Rose, L., Gallup, A., & Elam, S. (1997). The 29th Annual Phi Delta Kappa/Gallup Poll. *Phi Delta Kappan, 79*(1), 41–59.

Ryan, B., Adams, G., Gullotta, R., Weissberg, R., & Hampton, R. (1995). (Eds.). *The family school connection.* Thousand Oaks, CA: Sage.

Scott-Jones, D. (1995). Parent-child interactions and school achievement. In B. Ryan, G. Adams, T. Gullotta, R. Weissberg, & R. Hampton (Eds.), *The family school connection* (pp. 75–107). Thousand Oaks, CA: Sage.

Steinberg, L. (1996). *Beyond the classroom.* New York: Simon & Schuster.

Swap, S. (1993). *Developing family-school partnerships.* New York: Teachers College Press.

U.S. Department of Education. (1994). *Strong families, strong schools.* Washington, DC: Author.

U.S. Department of Education. (1996). *Parents and schools: Partners in student learning, survey on family and school partnerships.* Washington, DC: National Center for Education Statistics, Office of Educational Research and Improvement (NCES 96-913).

Internet Workshop: Making Time for Literacy

Donald J. Leu, Jr.

"I just don't have the time." Whenever literacy educators tell me they have not integrated the Internet with their literacy curriculum, this is almost always the explanation they provide. When I ask what they mean, I hear two different explanations. Some teachers say they don't have time in their schedule; other teachers say they don't have time to learn new instructional strategies for using a complex tool like the Internet.

I understand. The demands on us today, especially in the world of reading and writing, are enormous. Where do you find the time to fit another period into an already crowded schedule? You can't. How do you find the time to learn complicated new instructional strategies? Impossible! There is never enough time in any day to do all that needs to be done. Extras have to rest on the back burner while priorities are met first.

And yet, I *don't* understand. To me, preparing children for their future is not an extra, it is central to our role as literacy educators. Clearly we require an instructional framework that takes little time to learn and does not require us to sacrifice another element of the curriculum. It should also be consistent with what we know about the new literacies of the Internet.

In Search of a Theoretical Framework

For several years, a number of us in the literacy community (Karchmer, 2001; Kinzer & Leander, 2003; Labbo & Reinking, 1999; Leu, 2000; Reinking, McKenna, Labbo, & Kieffer, 1998; and many others) have been exploring the changing nature of reading and writing. We believe that the Internet and other information and communication technologies (ICTs) are changing the nature of literacy and literacy learning as they become an increasingly important part of our lives. This work is leading toward a theoretical framework in which to understand the changes to literacy that are taking place today.

We have argued that global economic changes have generated new information technologies that generate new literacies. In this new world, what becomes critical to our students' literacy future is the ability to identify important problems, gather and critically evaluate relevant information from information networks, use this information to resolve central issues, and then clearly

Originally published in *The Reading Teacher* (2002), volume 55, pages 466–472.

communicate the solution to others. In short, a global economy and the changes to ICT that accompany it change the nature of work (Mikulecky & Kirkley, 1998) and change the nature of literacy (Leu, 2000; Luke, 2000; Warschauer, 2000).

At least three themes emerge from this exploration, each of which is essential to understanding the new literacies of our future. First, literacy is deictic; new literacies emerge from new technologies, regularly changing what it means to read and write (Leu, 2000). Second, literacy learning becomes increasingly social as multiple literacies emerge from rapidly changing technologies (Leu & Kinzer, 1999). No individual can be expected to be literate in all of the new technologies for reading and writing. Instead, what becomes important is knowing how to acquire a new literacy from others when we need it as we share and exchange strategies useful in the new literacies of reading and writing. Finally, learning how to learn continuously new literacies becomes just as important as becoming proficient in a current definition of literacy (Leu, 2002); learning to learn is at the core of the new literacies. It is not just that we want students to know how to read and write; we want them to know how to continuously learn new skills and strategies required by the new technologies of literacy that will regularly emerge.

There is much to add and to revise as we build this theoretical framework. As we do, we must also seek instructional practices consistent with what we know about the changes taking place in literacy as the Internet and other ICTs become increasingly important to our literacy lives.

Internet Workshop

This column describes a new instructional framework, Internet Workshop, one designed around the three themes identified in this emerging framework of how literacy is changing. Because Internet Workshop fits easily into the instructional schedule of any classroom, it can be used without sacrificing another element of the curriculum. In the time it takes to read this article you could learn how to use Internet Workshop in your classroom, preparing students for the literacy future they deserve. Give me 10 minutes of your time, and I'll show you how to integrate the Internet with your literacy program.

Internet Workshop (Leu & Leu, 2000) consists of an independent reading of information on the Internet around a topic and a location initially designated by the teacher; it concludes with a short workshop session where students can share and exchange the ideas and strategies they discovered during their work on the Internet. Internet Workshop permits students to learn from one another about content information, critical literacy skills, and the new literacies of Internet technologies. It is one of the easiest approaches to use with the Internet, being familiar to anyone who is already using a workshop approach for reading or writing instruction.

Internet Workshop has many variations. It may be used as a directed learning experience, a simulation, a center activity, or with many other instructional practices you already use. Generally, though, it contains these procedures:

1. Locate a site on the Internet with content related to a classroom unit of instruction and set a bookmark for the location.

2. Design an activity, inviting students to use the site as they accomplish content, critical literacy, or strategic knowledge goals in your curriculum. (As children progress, you may also invite them to develop independent inquiry projects.)

3. Complete the research activity.

4. Have students share their work, questions, and new insights at the end of the week during a workshop session. You may also use this time to prepare students for the upcoming workshop experience.

Locate a Site

Prepare for the Internet Workshop by locating an Internet site containing information at an appropriate level for your students and related to your classroom unit. Once you have found the site, set a bookmark for your students. This limits random surfing and exploration of sites unrelated to your unit, an important child safety issue, especially in the younger grade levels.

How do you quickly find a site on the Internet containing useful information related to your classroom unit and at an appropriate grade level? One strategy is to simply use a search engine or a directory organized for teachers and children, one that also screens out inappropriate sites for children. You might begin with one of these locations:

◆ Yahooligans (http://www.yahooligans.com/) is a directory and a Web guide designed for children. Sites are appropriate for ages 7 to 12.

◆ Ask Jeeves for Kids (http://www.ajkids.com/) is a directory and a search engine based on natural language. You simply type in a question, and it finds the best site with the answer. Sites are appropriate for use by children.

- Searchopolis (http://www.searchopolis.com/) is a directory and search engine organized for students in the elementary grades, middle grades, and high school.
- KidsClick! (http://sunsite.berkely.edu/KidsClick!/) is a directory and search engine developed for kids by the Ramapo Catskill Library System.

A second strategy is to select one of several central sites for each subject area and explore the resources for use during Internet Workshop. A central site is one that contains an extensive and well-organized set of links to resources in a content area. In a sense, it is like a directory for a content area: reading, math, science, social studies, or another topic. Most are located at stable sites that will not quickly change. As you explore the Internet, you will discover these well-organized treasure troves of information. They will become homes to which you will often return, and you will develop your own favorites. (Table 1 lists some of the better central sites within content areas common to schools.)

Table 1. Central sites for major content areas

Content area	Website	
Science	Eisenhower National Clearinghouse	http://www.enc.org:80
	Science Learning Network	http://www.sln.org/index.html
Math	Eisenhower National Clearinghouse	http://www.enc.org:80
	The Math Forum	http://mathforum.com
Social studies	History/Social Studies for K–12 Teachers	http://www.execpc.com~dboals/boals.html
Reading/literature	SCORE Cyberguides to Literature	http://www.sdcoe.k12.ca.us/SCORE/cyberguide.html
	The Children's Literature Web Guide	http://www.ucalgary.ca/~dkbrown/index.html
	The Literacy Web	http://www.literacy.uconn.edu

Design an Activity

The second step is to design an activity related to the learning goals of your unit, using the site you have bookmarked. The activity may be designed for several purposes:

- ◆ to introduce students to a site that you will use in your instructional unit;
- ◆ to develop important background knowledge for an upcoming unit;
- ◆ to develop navigation strategies; or
- ◆ to develop the critical literacies so important to effective Internet use.

It is important during this step to provide an open-ended activity for students, one where they have some choice about the information they will bring back to the workshop session. If everyone brings back identical information, there will be little to share and discuss during the workshop session. You may wish to prepare an activity page for students to complete and bring to the Internet Workshop session, or you may simply write the assignment in a visible location in your classroom. An example of an activity page appears in Figure 1.

The activity page in Figure 1 was created by two sixth-grade teachers to develop background knowledge about Japan and to help students think more critically about information they find on the Internet. The teachers located Kids Web Japan (http://www.jinjapan.org/kidsweb/), a site developed by the Japanese Information Ministry for students in other countries who want to learn more about Japan. They set a bookmark to this central site on the classroom computers.

Notice how the tasks on the activity page are open ended, inviting students to make their own discoveries at this location and bring these to Internet Workshop to share at the beginning of the unit. For example, each student is invited to read different news articles about events in Japan. This is an essential aspect of any assignment prepared for Internet activity. Open-ended questions invite students to bring many different types of information to Internet Workshop for discussion. Little discussion will take place if you have students search only for facts like "How high is Mt. Fuji?" Discussion is at the heart of Internet Workshop.

Notice also how critical thinking is supported by asking students to think about who created the website and how the stance of the authors might shape the information they place there. Critical literacy skills are essential to develop as you use the Internet.

Figure 1. An activity page developed for Internet Workshop to introduce a unit on Japan

Exploring Japan

Internet researcher: _____ Date:_____

Objectives

This Internet Workshop will introduce you to our unit on Japan. You will have an opportunity to explore an important resource on the Internet for our unit. You will also learn about recent news events from Japan and learn to think more critically about what you read on the Internet. Take notes in your Internet journal and share them at our workshop session.

News about Japan

1. Go to the bookmark I have set for Kids Web Japan (http://jinjapan.org/kidsweb/) and scroll down to the bottom of this page. Now click on the button Monthly News (http://jinjapan.org/kidsweb/news.html) and read several recent news stories from Japan. Choose ones of interest to you. Find out what is happening in Japan, take notes, and be ready to share them during Internet Workshop.

_____
_____
_____

Critical thinking

2. Be a detective. What clues can you find at Kids Web Japan (http://jinjapan.org/kidsweb/) to indicate that the information at this site comes from the government of Japan? Write them down and bring these clues to Internet Workshop. How did you find them? Write down the strategies you used.

_____
_____
_____

3. If the information at this location comes from the government of Japan, how might this shape the news stories presented in Monthly News (http://www.jinjapan.org/kidsweb/news.html)? Write down your ideas and bring them to Internet Workshop.

_____
_____
_____

Your choice

4. Visit at least one of the many other locations at Kids Web Japan. You decide where to go! Write down notes of what you discovered and share your special discoveries with all of us during Internet Workshop.

_____
_____
_____

Evaluation rubric

    8 points—You recorded important information for each item (4 × 2 = 8 points).
    2 points—You effectively shared important information with us during our workshop session, helping each of us to learn about Japan.

_____

10 points—Total

Complete the Research Activity

The third step is to complete the research activity during the week. If you have access to a computer lab at your school you may wish to schedule a period to complete the activity in that facility. This is essential if you have a departmentalized program in the upper grades and see your students for only one or two periods each day.

In self-contained classrooms with one or two Internet computers, you may wish to assign students to a schedule such as the one in Table 2. This provides each student with one hour of Internet access each week—30 minutes by themselves and 30 minutes with a partner. This is usually sufficient time to complete the research activity for Internet Workshop.

A schedule, such as the one in Table 2, is possible only when you control your time. It will also require one or two students to be working on their Internet Workshop research activity while other lessons take place in your classroom. Students quickly catch up on these experiences, but you should regularly change your schedule so that no student misses the same lesson each week. In addition, you should never schedule your weakest student in any subject area to miss that subject during the day. Having 30 minutes with a partner every week can effectively help students learn from each other and lets them try out new skills independently.

Have Students Share Their Work

The concluding experience each week is a short workshop session where students share and compare the information they discovered, discuss their developing skills in critical analysis, and raise new questions to be explored in upcoming weeks. In the example on Japan, students brought notes from the news articles they read to the workshop session. The discussion of current events proved useful in introducing the unit on Japan because it developed background knowledge for future reading experiences. At the same time, the unit introduced the resources at this Internet site, one the class would use many more times in upcoming Internet Workshop activities.

The most exciting parts of this workshop session, however, were the second and third activities. Students reported finding many different clues that led them to believe that the site was developed by the Japanese government. This prompted a discussion of how important it is to look for a link that explains who developed any website you discover. These links are often labeled "About this site." Students learned that information at this location helps them

Table 2. A weekly computer schedule posted for Internet Workshop

Time	Monday	Tuesday	Wednesday	Thursday	Friday
8:30–9:00 a.m.	Michelle	Michelle/Becky	Chris/Emily	Shannon/Cara	Cynthia/Alana
9:00–9:30 a.m.	Chris	Julio/Miguel	Jeremy/Tyna	Kati	Patti
9:30–10:00 a.m.	**Internet Workshop**	Ben	Aaron	Lisa	Julia
10:00–10:30 a.m.	Shannon	**Physical education**	Paul	**Physical education**	Andy
10:30–11:00 a.m.	**Library**	Mike	Scott	Faith	Melissa
11:00–11:30 a.m.	Cynthia	Eric	James	Linda	Sara
11:30 a.m.–12:30 p.m.	**Lunch**	**Lunch**	**Lunch**	**Lunch**	**Lunch**
12:30–1:00 p.m.	Alana	Tyna	Miguel	Cara	Emily
1:00–1:30 p.m.	Becky	Jeremy	Ben/Sara	Mike/Linda	Julio
1:30–2:00 p.m.	Eric/James	Aaron/Melissa	**Music**	Paul/Scott	**Class meeting**
2:00–2:30 p.m.	Kati/Lisa		Faith/Andy	Patti/Julia	

to understand who created the information on a website. It also helps them to think carefully about how this determines the author's stance toward the information presented. The students also learned how an author's stance shapes the information provided to readers. Each weekly workshop session will provide many opportunities to learn critical literacy skills and strategies like this as you work with your students.

Internet Workshop can be concluded with ideas to explore in the next research activity, and the Internet Workshop cycle continues. Over time, as students become familiar with the purpose and practices of Internet Workshop, they may begin inquiry projects as groups or individuals and bring the information they discover back to the next workshop session.

Internet Workshop: Variations on a Theme

Internet Workshop may take a variety of forms. As I worked to develop this instructional framework, I invited teachers from around the world to share their instructional needs with me and allow me to design lessons based on this model. The process has helped me better understand the potentials of Internet Workshop and expand my thinking about its use.

A Simulation

A particularly challenging assignment came from a reading and language arts teacher in Wisconsin, USA. Her class was reading about the sinking of the *Titanic*, and she wanted to conduct a simulation of the U.S. Senate hearings on that disaster. She also wanted four students to take the roles of U.S. senators and listen to testimony from survivors, ask questions, and write a final report with recommendations to steamship lines. The other students were to each take the role of a survivor or newspaper reporter and research the story of a survivor, then compose a written presentation with testimony about that passenger's experience aboard the fateful ship. The teacher planned to use the simulation experience to conclude her unit on this topic in an engaging fashion as she helped students develop research and writing skills.

In half an hour of searching, I found all of the resources needed for the simulation and quickly put up a webpage for her class to use. You may view the Internet Workshop we developed at Ms. Fields's Internet Workshop on the Titanic (http://sp.uconn.edu/~djleu/titanic.html). An especially important central site for this activity was The Encyclopedia Titanica (http://www.encyclo

pediatitanica.org/index.html), an extensive collection of links to resources about the disaster, including a database of the passengers, with links to information on the Internet about many of them.

Letter Names in Kindergarten

Internet Workshop is not limited to the upper elementary grades; it may be used at every grade level, even as low as kindergarten. Another teacher who was interested in trying Internet Workshop with his students had been told that they were too young to use the Internet. We developed an Internet Workshop activity for his writing center to help students develop letter-name knowledge and the ability to form letters.

First, we found a multimedia resource to help children learn letter names, ABC Gulp (http://www.brainconnection.com/teasers/?main=bc/gulp), and quickly developed an age-appropriate Internet Workshop activity. At ABC Gulp (see Figure 2) you click on the frog's belly to hear the name of one of the letters displayed on the right side of the screen. Then you select the letter to match the name you hear and click on it. If you select the correct letter, the frog's tongue whips out and eats it. If you select the incorrect letter, a fly appears in one of the boxes at the top. At the end of a session you can see how many letters you correctly identified. Young children enjoy watching the frog eat the various letters.

I suggested that we place ABC Gulp on this teacher's Internet computer before students arrived in the morning and provide them with a simple assignment when it was their turn to visit the reading and writing center. Each child was to play the game with the frog, attempting to identify each letter correctly. When he or she completed the experience, each child was to write his or her favorite letter on a large piece of paper with a crayon and bring it to the Internet Workshop session. At the end of the week, each did so and shared the letter name with everyone else. The children engaged in several quick activities around the names of all the letters they had selected. One was to name as many letters as they could. Another was to stand up with other students and use their letters to spell a child's name.

It was a great workshop session and showed how the Internet can be used effectively with children at the kindergarten level. In addition to learning letter names, the children developed several new literacies of the Internet as they showed one another various strategies. These included how to use the Reload button on the browser software to call up the site again when it didn't completely download to their computer. Some students also learned how to

Figure 2. An activity on the Internet designed to help students practice letter-name knowledge

ABC Gulp (http://www.brainconnection.com/teasers/?main=bc/gulp)

Used with permission of Brainconnection.com and Scientific Learning Corporation

use the mouse to navigate on the screen and how to use the clicker to select an item. These new literacy skills were important for many children and were used by them frequently during the rest of the year.

Children's Literature

Another variation, suitable for any grade, is to develop independent Internet Workshop activities around the works of exceptional literature children read in class. In this model, students read a work of literature and then complete an activity from the Internet related to the work they have read. Afterward, they share their experience with the rest of the class during the weekly Internet Workshop session. An exceptional central site for Internet Workshop literature experiences is Cyberguides (http://www.sdcoe.k12.ca.us/SCORE/cyberguide.html), organized around standards developed in California, USA. Linda Taggart-Fregoso and her colleagues in San Diego have done an exceptional job of developing Internet activities around major works of children's and adolescents' literature for grades K–12. Each cyberguide has four different activities for each book, with links to resources on the Internet needed to complete each activity. Students choose at least one of these activities to complete each week and then share their work and the book they read, prompting others to consider the book for their next reading experience.

Author Studies

Is your class reading the works of an important author (or illustrator) in the world of children's literature? You can easily have an Internet Workshop session on that person. Locate the author's homepage on the Internet and invite students to search for two or three important ideas about the person's life to share at the workshop session. I like to use the extensive collection located at Authors and Illustrators on the Web (http://www.acs.ucalgary.ca/~dkbrown/authors.html).

Mathematics

Internet Workshop may also be used in a content area such as mathematics. Here, you might assign students a challenging math problem of the week. You can use locations such as the following, which provide a different weekly math challenge for students to solve.

- ◆ Math Forum Problems (http://mathforum.com/library/problems/)
- ◆ Brain Teasers (http://www.eduplace.com/math/brain/)
- ◆ Problem of the Week Homepage (http://www.sits.ac.za/ssproule/pow.html)

When Internet Workshop is used in math, students can bring back to the workshop session the strategies they used to solve a problem, as well as the answer to it. In this way Internet Workshop may be used to develop new insights and problem-solving strategies in mathematics while introducing important new resources to your math program.

Internet Workshop can have as many variations as a creative teacher can have good ideas. We have seen how it may be used to introduce a unit in a content area, conduct a simulation, teach letter-name knowledge, develop critical literacy skills, integrate the Internet with a literature program, conduct author studies, and develop problem-solving skills in math. Internet Workshop is a very flexible tool, designed to assist you in your important work.

Developing the New Literacies With Internet Workshop

Another important aspect of Internet Workshop is that it permits you to discover the new literacies emerging from Internet technologies with your students. These new literacies emerge as rapidly as new technologies and new websites develop. It is hard to keep up, but Internet Workshop will provide a vehicle for you to do so.

Some of the new literacies you can uncover during Internet Workshop might include skills and strategies such as how to do the following:

- ◆ use all of the features effectively on a new search engine,
- ◆ find out who developed a webpage and how this developer might shape the information presented,
- ◆ determine when a webpage was last updated,
- ◆ find an online expert to assist with an important classroom project and how to do this safely,
- ◆ discover more information about an author you have read,
- ◆ use the URL for a site to uncover clues about who created it and why, and
- ◆ find out what other classrooms around the world are doing in your area of study.

All of these tasks reveal new literacies important for our students to develop. Many of them will be discoveries your students will make and then teach you. Discovering the new literacies and learning together with your students is one of the important aspects of Internet Workshop; it models for students how they will need to learn from others the continuously emerging new literacies of Internet technologies.

Using Internet Workshop as an action forum for discovering and exchanging the new skills, strategies, and insights demanded by the new literacies of the Internet will help you to prepare students in important ways for their future. In addition, Internet Workshop is consistent with what we are discovering about the new literacies of Internet technologies including these observations: Literacy is increasingly deictic, literacy learning is increasingly social, and the new literacies require you to learn how to learn continuously emerging new literacies from new technologies. Used in this way, Internet Workshop may become an important new tool for you to begin using in your classroom. And because it's so similar to other workshop approaches that may already be familiar to you, it requires little additional time to integrate the Internet with your reading and writing curriculum.

Today we all face many new challenges and responsibilities in our work. We can begin using the Internet in our reading and writing classrooms quickly with Internet Workshop; we can learn new lessons together as we begin our Internet journeys. The Internet can become a regular part of our classroom literacy program, allowing us to prepare students for the futures they deserve.

Now, be honest. Did that take much more than 10 minutes of your time?

REFERENCES

Karchmer, R.A. (2001). Teachers on a journey: Thirteen teachers report how the Internet influences literacy and literacy instruction in their K–12 classrooms. *Reading Research Quarterly, 36,* 442–466.

Kinzer, C.K., & Leander, K.M. (2003). Technology and the language arts: Implications of an expanded definition of literacy. In J. Flood, D. Lapp, J.M. Jensen, & J.R. Squire (Eds.), *Handbook of research on teaching the English language arts* (2nd ed., pp. 546–565). Mahwah, NJ: Erlbaum.

Labbo, L.D., & Reinking, D. (1999). Negotiating the multiple realities of technology in literacy research and instruction. *Reading Research Quarterly, 34,* 478–492.

Leu, D.J., Jr. (2000). Literacy and technology: Deictic consequences for literacy education in an information age. In M.L. Kamil, P.B. Mosenthal, P.D. Pearson, & R. Barr (Eds.), *Handbook of reading research* (Vol. 3, pp. 743–770). Mahwah, NJ: Erlbaum.

Leu, D.J., Jr. (2002). The new literacies: Research on reading instruction with the Internet. In A.E. Farstrup & S.J. Samuels (Eds.), *What research has to say about reading instruction* (3rd ed., pp. 310–336). Newark, DE: International Reading Association.

Leu, D.J., Jr., & Kinzer, C.K. (1999). *Effective literacy instruction* (4th ed.). Upper Saddle River, NJ: Prentice Hall.

Leu, D.J., Jr., & Leu, D.D. (2000). *Teaching with the Internet: Lessons from the classroom* (3rd ed.). Norwood, MA: Christopher-Gordon.

Luke, C. (2000). Cyber-schooling and technological change: Multiliteracies for new times. In B. Cope & M. Kalantzis (Eds.), *Multiliteracies: Literacy learning and the design of social futures* (pp. 69–91). London: Routledge.

Mikulecky, L., & Kirkley, J.R. (1998). Changing workplaces, changing classes: The new role of technology in workplace literacy. In D. Reinking, M. McKenna, L.D. Labbo, & R. Kieffer (Eds.), *Handbook of literacy and technology: Transformations in a post-typographic world* (pp. 303–320). Mahwah, NJ: Erlbaum.

Reinking, D., McKenna, M., Labbo, L., & Kieffer, R. (Eds.). (1998). *Handbook of literacy and technology: Transformations in a post-typographic world.* Mahwah, NJ: Erlbaum.

Warschauer, M. (2000). The changing global economy and the future of English teaching. *TESOL Quarterly, 34,* 511–535.

The Miss Rumphius Effect: Envisionments for Literacy and Learning That Transform the Internet

Donald J. Leu, Jr., Rachel A. Karchmer, and Deborah Diadiun Leu

Many of us have enjoyed the story of *Miss Rumphius* (Cooney, 1982). In this delightful book, Barbara Cooney describes how the title character travels the world, accumulating many adventures. Eventually, however, she returns to her home by the sea and discovers a way to make the world a better place by planting lupines, beautiful wildflowers, wherever she goes. The story illustrates how a committed individual can envision a better world and then act on that envisionment, transforming all of our lives. It is an important lesson for each of us.

The story is also a useful metaphor for a revolutionary development taking place in literacy education. Just as Miss Rumphius made the world a better place by planting lupines wherever she went, teachers and children are enriching our instructional worlds by planting new visions for literacy and learning on the Internet, transforming the nature of this new technology. These instructional resources are then used by other classrooms, making our students' worlds richer and more meaningful.

Recently, we have been studying how teachers and their students create new envisionments for literacy and learning with Internet technologies. Stories of these events are so common and have such profound impact that we have been looking for an appropriate label to capture this phenomenon. Since Miss Rumphius also sought to make the world a better place, we refer to this as the Miss Rumphius Effect. The Miss Rumphius Effect has the potential to change our instructional lives, providing us with many new and exciting resources for teaching. At the same time, it will also change the nature of literacy as new forms of information and communication appear.

Envisionments for Literacy and Learning on the Internet

What is an envisionment? Envisionments take place when teachers and children imagine new possibilities for literacy and learning, transform existing technologies to construct this vision, and then share their work with others. By sharing effective resources and strategies on the Internet, we are quickly

Originally published in *The Reading Teacher* (1999), volume 52, pages 636–642.

developing rich curriculum networks that transcend materials previously available for instruction. It is an exciting and potentially powerful development in the field of literacy education.

One example has been developed by Mark Ahlness, a third-grade teacher at Arbor Heights Elementary School in Seattle, Washington, USA. Mark developed Earth Day Groceries Project at http://www.halcyon.com/arborhts/earthday.html. Each year, Mark and his students run this project to encourage other classrooms to decorate paper grocery bags with environmental messages and distribute these to stores for Earth Day. The project increases environmental awareness, making our world a more beautiful place. In 1998, over 484 schools participated in this important project, distributing more than 162,000 grocery bags with environmental messages (see Figure 1). Visit Mark's website and explore the potential of this wonderful resource for your curriculum.

Or consider several international projects that took place recently on the Internet. For example, Peter Lelong and his year 4 students at the Fahan School in Hobart, Tasmania, conducted extensive research about the cultures

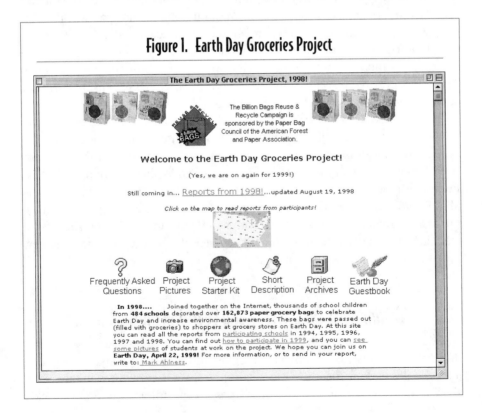

Figure 1. Earth Day Groceries Project

of Indonesia. As part of their study, Peter's students developed a beautiful version of the traditional Indonesian folk tale *The Blooming Flower of Flores* and posted this on the Internet to share with others at http://www.fahan.tas.edu.au//Compute/Flores/pgone.html. Since then, many classrooms have visited this site to read their work.

This activity led to a second envisionment for literacy and learning in Peter's class—an extensive e-mail project with Indonesian students in Malang, East Java. During the project, students in both countries learned about one another's culture through their studies and correspondence. Check out the Hobart-Malang Electronic Mail Project at http://www.fahan.tas.edu.au//Compute/indo.html. Since posting the results of their collaborative study, teachers and children from around the world have visited this site. It is an outstanding resource, providing important information about the cultural contexts in these two countries. It also establishes a wonderful model for collaborative learning between students in different cultural contexts. As teachers and children explore this location, using it as part of their curricula, many see related projects for their own classrooms.

This is what happened in Ms. Hos-McGrane's grade 6 social studies class at the International School in Amsterdam, The Netherlands. After reading about the experiences at the Fahan School, students in Amsterdam integrated the story "The Blooming Flower of Flores" into their own envisionment for literacy and learning, Creation Stories and Myths at http://www.best.com/~swanson/creation/cstorymenu.html. This is a growing collection of creation stories and myths from around the world. It is yet another outstanding curriculum resource developed by a teacher and her students, available for all of us to use.

And the Miss Rumphius Effect does not end here. Other classrooms studying creation tales have visited. Ms. Hos-McGrane's classroom page, exploring the extensive collection of multicultural folk tales and using them in their own study. As they do so, teachers and children around the world envision new possibilities for their own classroom homepages from the wonderful models established by these exemplary educators.

The Miss Rumphius Effect

Every day, teachers and children just like the ones we've mentioned are constructing new visions for literacy and learning with Internet technologies, making their work available to other classrooms. Figure 2 describes a few of the many new resources created by these talented people. We encourage you to visit these fine locations.

Figure 2. Examples of exceptional envisionments for literacy and learning on the Internet

SCORE Cyberguides at http://www.sdcoe.k12.ca.us/score/cyberguide.html is the best site available on the Internet for immediate classroom integration of literature experiences with Internet resources. Pay a visit and see the wonderful work being directed by Don Mayfield and Linda Taggart-Fregoso from the San Diego schools in California, USA. The genius of this site is that any teacher may contribute an envisionment for books and activities with Internet resources that have worked in his or her classroom. All units contain objectives, activity procedures, teacher-selected websites, and a rubric for evaluation. Each unit is aligned with California's Academic Content Standards. It's a wonderful resource!

The Read In! at http://www.readin.org/TheReadIn/ReadIn.html is a daylong celebration of reading and literature that takes place each year during April. First initiated by Jan Brown's third-grade class in Turlock, California, and Delores Willoughby's third-grade class in Chickasha, Oklahoma, USA, it has grown to include over 250,000 children, teachers, and children's authors around the world. Children discuss books they are reading and participate in classroom activities and live chat session with children's authors. Pay a visit and prepare your students for this year's special day when The Read In! takes place.

Research at http://www.nueva.pvt.k12.ca.us/~debbie/library/research/research.html was developed by Debbie Abilock and Marilyn Kimura at the Nueva School in Hillsborough, California, USA, and is an exceptional resource to assist students and teachers doing research on the Internet. Especially useful is their table showing which search engines are most useful for finding different types of information. If you wish to help your students learn how to search the Internet more effectively, pay a visit.

The Looney Lobsters at http://bps.boston.K12.ma.us/rc328sb/D4.html is the site of the Looney Lobsters, a travel buddy project organized by teacher Marjorie Duby and her fifth-grade students at the Joseph Lee School in Boston, Massachusetts, USA. Marjorie is one of the most accomplished developers of travel buddy projects, collaborative Internet projects based on stuffed animals that travel from classroom to classroom sparking Internet communication and collaboration. Children in the visiting classroom share regional literature experiences, the activities of their travel buddies, and other information with participating classrooms. Read about Marjorie's many exciting Internet projects with other classrooms. If you are lucky, you will be able to join one!

Book Rap at http://rite.ed.qut.edu.au/oz-teachernet/projects/book-rap/br.html is managed by Cherrol McGhee, a teacher at the Hillview State Primary School in Queensland, Australia. Book raps are literature discussion groups that take place between classrooms around the world via e-mail. Visit this outstanding location and join a scheduled discussion about a book your class is reading. Better yet, sign up to coordinate a discussion for a book your class will read, so your students can exchange responses with students around the globe.

(continued)

Figure 2 (continued). Examples of exceptional envisionments for literacy and learning on the Internet

Loogootee Elementary West Home Page at http://www.siec.k12.in.us/~west/ was created by Tammy Payton, a first-grade teacher and Web editor at Loogootee Elementary West in Loogootee, Indiana, USA. This award-winning site is a wonderful model for all elementary schools. It consists of a variety of resources such as educational links, instructions for creating a webpage, lesson plans, Internet projects, student work, and tips on how to evaluate other websites and chat rooms. The site also includes several Power Point slide shows, which offer step-by-step instructions on how to integrate technology in the elementary classroom. This is the perfect resource for new Internet users!

Mrs. Silverman's Second Grade Class at http://kids-learn.org/ is a colorful website that provides a glimpse into Susan Silverman's second-grade classroom. The site is divided into a number of sections including pages about the teacher, the students, their classroom projects, their school, and their favorite educational links. Susan also gives a detailed description of the Internet projects her class completed during previous years. One project, Stellaluna's Friends, gave students around the world the opportunity to conduct research on bats and share their new knowledge with others via the Internet.

Room 100, Buckman Elementary School at http://buckman/pps.k12.or.us/room100./room100.html developed by Tim Lauer and Beth Rohloff, K–2 teachers in Portland, Oregon, USA. Work by their students provides an exceptional resource for other young children around the world. Listen to children read their Space Alphabet Book, listen to Beth and her students being interviewed about their work studying monarch butterflies, view images in the classroom microscope cam, study the time line children created of Dr. Martin Luther King, Jr.'s life and accomplishments, enjoy poems children have written about the wind, learn from children's research about famous women, or study the bus safety rules this class has developed. Besides being an exceptional model for a classroom homepage, these curriculum resources are being used by primary classrooms around the world.

Journey Exchange at http://www.win4edu.com/minds-eye/journey was developed by a former third-grade teacher in New York. This project location provides a wonderful way to integrate the language arts and social studies. Students research and develop a five-city journey around the world. Then they exchange clues to the locations with their Internet partners. Each student attempts to discover the cities and the travel itinerary of the other.

The Miss Rumphius Effect is producing fundamental change in the nature of classroom literacy instruction. It has profound consequences for all of us as new curricular materials are developed in classrooms and become available to others. A unique aspect of the Miss Rumphius Effect is that classrooms around the world are exchanging their envisionments. While teachers and children have always constructed envisionments for literacy and learning within their individual classrooms using earlier technologies, doing so on the Internet is fundamentally different. The Internet breaks down traditional classroom walls, making each envisionment immediately accessible to other classrooms. This access allows each of us to benefit from other classrooms' envisionments and to include them in our curriculum. We see an example of this in the story of how the wonderful resources developed by teachers and children at the Fahan School in Tasmania led to connections with schools in Malang, East Java, the International School in the Netherlands, and many others.

The Miss Rumphius Effect has both theoretical and practical implications. From a theoretical perspective, evidence for a Miss Rumphius Effect supports Bruce's suggestion (1997) that literacy, and the cultural context in which it exists, transforms technology. It is clear that new technologies transform the nature of literacy (Reinking, 1998). We are quickly becoming aware, however, that this is not a one-way street. Just as new technologies change literacy, literacy also changes new technologies within a transactional relationship. Teachers and children are transforming the Internet by constructing curriculum that reflects the needs and realities of the classroom—an exciting prospect.

Another important consequence is that the Miss Rumphius Effect contributes to the continually changing nature of literacy (Leu, 1997, 2000). As new envisionments for literacy are regularly developed and exchanged, new definitions of literacy appear, requiring new forms of knowledge and new strategies for successfully exploiting these information resources. The Miss Rumphius Effect speeds up the already rapid pace of change in the forms and functions of literacy we are beginning to see on the Internet.

In terms of practice, the Miss Rumphius Effect provides important support for all of us as we seek to keep pace with the continuously changing landscape of literacy it creates. By exploring other teachers' classrooms we learn new ways to support our own students. We have much to learn from one another as we discover the importance of exchanging envisionments and building upon the successful models of others.

How do teachers exchange envisionments for literacy, supporting one another in providing better literacy and learning experiences for children? Teachers share information in many informal ways as they begin to encounter one another during their journeys on the Internet. They are also discovering several types of locations that support these exchanges: central sites for Internet project descriptions, central sites for stories of teachers' journeys, and mailing lists (listservs).

Central Sites for Internet Project Descriptions

Increasing numbers of teachers are taking a project approach to Internet use in their classroom, using an instructional framework sometimes called Internet Project (Leu & Kinzer, 1999; Leu & Leu, 1999). Internet Project is a collaborative instructional strategy in which learning experiences are developed and exchanged between two or more classrooms over the Internet. One example of Internet Project, "Passage to Hiroshima," took place recently between a classroom in Nagoya, Japan, and classrooms in several other countries around the world. In this envisionment for literacy and learning, a classroom in Nagoya sought collaborating classrooms interested in studying the importance of peace and international cooperation. The class proposed to exchange useful sites on the World Wide Web related to world peace. They also asked participating classrooms to develop interview and research questions that the Nagoya class could use during their upcoming trip to Hiroshima. They volunteered to interview citizens of Hiroshima and then share the results, including photos, upon their return. Thousands of projects similar to this one take place each day on the Internet between collaborating classrooms.

Each of these projects is another example of how teachers and children are transforming the Internet through new envisionments for literacy and learning. If you are interested in exploring these envisionments, visit a location where teachers describe upcoming projects and seek other classrooms to join them. You could do this at a number of central sites where teachers post their project descriptions to find collaborative partners. One of the best locations is Global SchoolNet's Internet Projects Registry at http://www.gsn.org/pr/index.html. Here you will find a search engine to permit you to search a rich set of upcoming projects for your class. Permanent, ongoing projects may be found at Global Schoolhouse Projects and Programs Main Page http://www.gsn.org/project/index.html. If you are looking for collaborative projects with schools in other countries, pay a visit to Intercultural E-mail Classroom Connection at http://www.stolaf.edu/network/iecc/, a wonderful resource provided by St. Olaf College in Northfield, Minnesota, USA. Additional information about a project-based approach to using the Internet in your classroom may be found at NickNacks Telecollaborate! http://www1.minn.net:80/~schubert/NickNacks.html.

Stories of Teachers' Journeys

One of the best ways to get acquainted with Internet use in the K–12 classroom is to learn from teachers who have been using this technology with their students. A few locations are devoted to sharing these teachers' envisionments. They post stories by teachers describing the new worlds that begin to open when Internet technologies are integrated into their classroom lessons. These stories are excellent models if you are just beginning your journey into classroom Internet use.

Several websites are specifically created to give classroom teachers a chance to share their Internet stories, as well as to offer advice on the best sites, projects, and collaborations available. You can find stories about these envisionments for literacy and learning with Internet technologies at sites such as the following:

EDs Spotlight on Effective Practice at http://www.EDsOasis.org/Spotlight/Spotlight.html includes articles written by elementary through postsecondary and adult educators about lessons they have learned with Internet and other technologies. Current topics include the purpose of the Internet, how to create Power Point presentations, the changing role of the teacher with the integration of technology, and inservice technology workshops for teachers. Visitors to the site can nominate an exemplary classroom teacher or technology coordinator, who will be given a chance to share his or her Internet expertise.

Teacher Testimony at http://www.4teachers.org/testimony/ consists of several in-depth articles focusing on topics such as technology use with special-needs children and stories of how teachers become comfortable with new technologies in their classrooms. There is also a link to the Teacher Testimony Archives so you can read through past articles of interest.

The Global Schoolhouse: Articles at http://www.gsh.org/wce/articles.htm contains a collection of over 50 articles on a wide range of technology-related topics. Most contain stories written by educators describing their envisionments for literacy and learning. Current topics at the time of writing include software use, distance learning, website construction, steps to take when first integrating technology, and community collaboration over the Internet. Elementary, junior high, and high school level educators are all represented.

Mailing Lists as Gathering Places for Exchanging Envisionments

Many teachers also discover new envisionments through mailing lists or listservs. A mailing list, often referred to as a *listserv*, is a discussion group for e-mail subscribers. A message sent to the posting address is distributed to everyone who has subscribed to that list. This enables subscribers to participate in conversations among a wide circle of colleagues who share similar interests. By "listening" to the discussions, you will quickly discover many new envisionments for literacy that can be used in your classroom. Subscribing to the right mailing list(s) will provide you with many new instructional ideas as you discover how other teachers respond to common challenges.

How do you subscribe to a mailing list? There are slightly different procedures, depending upon which software a list uses. Listserv is the most common software used for mailing lists, but other popular programs include Listproc and Majordomo. You will find directions for using all types of mailing list software at the following locations.

- ◆ EdWeb E-Mail Discussion Lists and Electronic Journals at http://sunsite. unc.edu/edweb/lists.html
- ◆ Liszt Select at http://www.liszt.com
- ◆ TileNet at http://www.tile.net/tile/listserv/index.html
- ◆ Pitsco's Launch to Lists at http://www.pitsco.com/p/listservs.html

Each location contains extensive lists of mailing lists organized by topic. Each also contains a search engine. These are useful locations to begin your search for the mailing list that matches your precise interests.

To subscribe to a mailing list using Listserv, the most common software, send a subscription message via e-mail to the list's administrative address. Figure 3 indicates the administrative addresses for several mailing lists popular among literacy educators. Type the administrative address in the "To:" box of your e-mail window. Leave the "Subject" box blank. Then, type a subscription message in the first line of the "Message" box. Your subscription message should contain only the following information:

subscribe [list name] [your first name] [your last name]

Be certain to disable your signature, if you use one with your e-mail software; any other information in your subscription message will confuse the mailing list software.

For example, to subscribe to RTEACHER (the mailing list run in conjunction with this column that discusses instructional practices related to traditional as well as Internet literacies), you would address your message to the administrative address for this mailing list at listserv@listserv.syr.edu. Rachel's subscription message would look like this:

subscribe RTEACHER Rachel Karchmer

Figure 3. Important mailing lists for the literacy education community

Name	Administrative address	Posting address	Participants and content
RTEACHER	listserv@listerv.syr.edu	rteacher@listserv.syr.edu	A mailing list devoted to conversations about all forms of literacy education, including the use of the Internet for literacy and learning. The educators on the list are very supportive of others new to the Internet. Currently, there are approximately 400 subscribers.
TAWL	listserv@listserv.arizona.edu	tawl@listserv.arizona.edu	A discussion group on teaching from a whole language perspective. Archives are located at http://listserv.arizona.edu/lsv/www/tawl.html. Currently, there are approximately 400 subscribers.
NCTE-talk	For subscription directions, visit http://www.ncte.org/chat	For posting directions, visit http://www.ncte.org/chat/	This is the main mailing list for the National Council of Teachers of English. It is a high traffic list. At the NCTE website (http://www.ncte.org/chat) you can subscribe to a number of different listservs/mailing lists devoted to English education, K–12.
KIDLIT-L	listserv@bingvmb.cc.binghamton.edu	kidlit-l@bingymb.cc.binghamton.edu	This is a list for people interested in children's literature. Many librarians subscribe, so it is a perfect place to find titles in areas that interest you. This is also a very supportive list. Currently, there are approximately 3,000 subscribers.

(continued)

Figure 3 (continued). Important mailing lists for the literacy education community

Name	Administrative address	Posting address	Participants and content
MULTC-ED	listserv@umdd.umd.edu	multc-ed@umdd.umd.edu	This mailing list offers a forum to discuss diversity issues. Topics include gender, disability, race, religion, ethnicity, and sexual orientation. A useful list to better understand issues of multicultural education. Currently, there are approximately 500 subscribers.
K-12ADMIN	listserv@listserv.syr.edu	k12admin@listserv.syr.edu	Participants on this list include teachers and K–12 administrators. Topics covered include core curriculum instruction, implementation of media technologies in the classroom, and staff development. This is a useful listserv for all educators interested in school-related issues. Currently, there are approximately 1,200 subscribers.
Web66	listserv@tc.umn.edu	web66@tc.umn.edu	This list offers educators an opportunity to discuss how the World Wide Web affects the K–12 curriculum. Teachers also exchange information about how to effectively integrate the Web into the classroom. Currently, there are approximately 1,100 subscribers.

Shortly, you will receive a "Welcome" message. Save this message! It usually gives you directions for how to post a message to the mailing list as well as directions for leaving the list.

To "unsubscribe," or leave a list, you usually send an "unsubscribe" message to the administrative address. The message should read as follows:

unsubscribe [listname]

To unsubscribe from the RTEACHER list, for example, you would address your message to the administrative address for this mailing list at listserv@listserv.syr.edu and then send the following message:

unsubscribe RTEACHER

Many educators find mailing lists to be a useful way to discover new envisionments for literacy and to share their own envisionments with others. They are a wonderful way to sustain your professional development, meet new colleagues, and make new friends. You may wish to join at least one of the mailing lists in Figure 3 and explore its potential to support your needs.

The Shifting Epistemology of Effective Instructional Practice

Increasingly, technology is changing faster than our ability to evaluate its utility for literacy by using traditional approaches (Kamil & Lane, 1998; Leu, in press). In literacy research, for example, it has become difficult, if not impossible, to develop a consistent body of published research within traditional forums before the technology on which a study is based is replaced by an even newer technology. Unless this situation changes, it is likely that traditional research will play a much less important role in defining our understanding of new technologies and new literacies. We believe this potential may result in a fundamental change in the epistemology of effective literacy instruction. Teachers' envisionments, tested in the realities of actual classroom practice, are likely to become more important in defining effective literacy instruction. In the future, the Miss Rumphius Effect may exert an even more powerful influence in determining effective classroom strategies for teaching and learning.

Increasingly, classroom teachers, not researchers, may define the most effective instructional strategies for literacy and learning. Teachers can evaluate instructional effectiveness and quickly spread word about an especially useful strategy on the Internet faster than researchers who currently require substantial time before results are published, often in journals with limited circulation. Our understanding of effective literacy instruction may be informed more often by teachers who use continuously changing technologies on a daily basis and less often by traditional forms of research.

Perhaps, as Broudy (1986) suggested, we will have to depend more on the credibility of advocates for different claims than on verifying the truth of their claims. This would be an important development in our field. Increasingly, teachers who develop highly effective and widely recognized envisionments for literacy may serve as central informants for effective instructional practice. There would be a pleasant irony to this development, for, like Miss Rumphius, we would return home to the place where the most important part of our work takes place—the classroom.

REFERENCES

Broudy, H.S. (1986). Technology and citizenship. In J. Culbertson & L.L. Cunningham (Eds.), *Microcomputers in education* (85th yearbook of the National Society for the Study of Education, pp. 234–253). Chicago: University of Chicago Press.

Bruce, B.C. (1997). Literacy technologies: What stance should we take? *Journal of Literacy Research, 29,* 289–309.

Kamil, M.L., & Lane, D.M. (1998). Researching the relationship between technology and literacy: An agenda for the 21st century. In D. Reinking, M. McKenna, L.D. Labbo, & R. Kieffer (Eds.), *Handbook of literacy and technology: Transformations in a post-typographic world* (pp. 323–342). Mahwah, NJ: Erlbaum.

Leu, D.J., Jr. (1997). Caity's question: Literacy as deixis on the Internet. *The Reading Teacher, 51,* 62–67.

Leu, D.J., Jr. (2000). Literacy and technology: Deictic consequences for literacy education in an information age. In R. Barr, M.L. Kamil, P.B. Mosenthal, & P.D. Pearson (Eds.), *Handbook of reading research* (Vol. 3, pp. 743–770). Mahwah, NJ: Erlbaum.

Leu, D.J., Jr., & Kinzer, C.K. (1999). *Effective literacy instruction* (4th ed.). Upper Saddle River, NJ: Prentice-Hall.

Leu, D.J., Jr., & Leu, D.D. (1999). *Teaching with the Internet: Lessons from the classroom* (2nd ed.). Norwood, MA: Christopher-Gordon.

Reinking, D. (1998). Synthesizing technological transformations of literacy in a post-typographic world. In D. Reinking, M. McKenna, L.D. Labbo, & R. Kieffer, (Eds.), *Handbook of literacy and technology: Transformations in a post-typographic world* (pp. xi–xxx). Mahwah, NJ: Erlbaum.

LITERATURE CITED

Cooney, B. (1982). *Miss Rumphius.* New York: Viking.

RIGHT

Children have a right to classrooms

that optimize learning opportunities.

Introduction

Jeanne R. Paratore

To optimize the likelihood that all students will achieve high levels of reading achievement, the 10th and final right in *Making a Difference Means Making It Different: Honoring Children's Rights to Excellent Reading Instruction*—children have a right to classrooms that optimize learning opportunities—urges educators and policymakers to look beyond the particulars of the reading lesson to other factors that evidence tells us influence students' opportunities to learn. To honor this right, five factors have been identified as especially important: class size, high-quality and ample instructional materials, well-prepared teachers, family and community involvement, and well-maintained buildings. In preparation for reading the articles supporting this right, a brief review of the evidence that links each of these factors to student achievement is provided.

Class Size

After many years of conflicting evidence regarding the effects of various teacher-student ratios on student achievement, the Tennessee legislature funded an experiment, Project STAR (Student-Teacher Achievement Ratio), that helped sort out the issues related to class size and student outcomes. This series of rigorously designed experimental studies yielded findings that are widely regarded as trustworthy and definitive. The details of the investigations are reported in full in several publications (for example, Finn & Achilles, 1990; Finn, Gerber, Achilles, & Boyd-Zaharias, 2001). In sum, the data indicate that, at every grade level studied (kindergarten to grade 3), students in small classes (13–17 students) significantly outperformed their peers in regular classes (22–26 students) and in regular classes with a full-time teacher aide. Further, the researchers report that the effects were greatest for minority students and students attending inner-city schools. No achievement differences were found for students in either regular classes or regular classes with a full-time teacher aide. A full and rigorous review of the longitudinal data led the researchers to three conclusions that are important to teachers, administrators, and policymakers:

1. Continuous attendance in small classes is important; results indicate that academic effects increase with each additional year.

2. Introducing small classes in the earliest years of schooling is important. Results were greatest for students who attended small classes beginning in kindergarten.

3. Small class size has a lasting impact, with students maintaining statistically significant academic gains in grades 4, 6, and 8.

Instructional Materials

Studies of the effectiveness of instructional programs or materials have failed to yield any consistent or conclusive results regarding the superior nature of any particular instructional material or program in comparison with any other (Bond & Dykstra, 1967/1997; National Clearinghouse for Comprehensive School Reform, 2001). However, studies of classrooms where children achieve higher than expected gains in reading have found that such classrooms have a large supply of books across a wide range of difficulty levels (Allington & Johnston, 2002). In addition, evidence suggests that instructional materials are congruent across the variety of instructional settings in which students learn. That is, in settings where children receive additional instructional support, the instruction is designed to extend the classroom program through additional lessons or practice opportunities that address the same skills or strategies within the same or similar content.

Well-Prepared Teachers

Among the most recent contributions to our understanding of the relationship between preparedness of teachers and student achievement is the work of Linda Darling-Hammond (1999). Using multiple data sources, including surveys from all 50 states, case studies, and results from the National Assessment of Educational Progress, Darling-Hammond found that "teacher quality characteristics such as certification status and degree in the field to be taught are very significantly and positively correlated with student outcomes" (p. 29). Further, Darling-Hammond reported that the effects of teacher quality are more consequential than the effects of class size, poverty, and English language proficiency. These findings are consistent with earlier studies (e.g., Ferguson, 1991; Sanders & Rivers, 1996) and strengthen the evidence that teacher effectiveness is a critical factor in differential student performance.

Family and Community Involvement

The role of parents, and in particular the effects of parental discipline, on children's school success has long been a concern of teachers and administrators. Although related studies are few in number and correlational in nature, there is evidence to suggest that ineffective and inconsistent parental discipline has a negative effect on school achievement (DeBaryshe, 1993; Switzer, 1990; Toussaint, 1998). Among the most influential work in helping teachers and administrators respond to the need to involve parents in children's learning has been that of Joyce Epstein (2001). Based on her own work and on a review of related studies, Epstein argues that "although parents' educational backgrounds differ, both more and less-educated parents have similar goals to those of the school for their children's education" (p. 36). The challenging task facing administrators and teachers is to identify and implement effective ways to share with parents the types of support and activities that are most likely to make a difference in their children's school achievement.

School Buildings in Sound, Physical Condition

In 1996, the General Accounting Office (GAO) reported that three out of every five schools in the United States required extensive repair or replacement of at least one major structural feature, and that as many as 14 million U.S. students presently attend school in buildings that are regarded as below standard or even dangerous. Although Duke (1998) argues that "research-based justification for school construction is hardly necessary when the safety and welfare of young people are at stake" (p. 11), he also notes that such evidence does exist. A review of seven related studies indicated that students in newer, "modernized" schools are likely to have higher test scores than their peers in older, nonmodernized schools. Modernized schools were defined as those that offered students "planned learning environments" (p. 8) identified as spaces which have been created for the primary purpose of learning. Duke notes that many and varied factors are considered in assessing the quality of the learning environment, among them "building age, ventilation, visual factors, color of interior of facilities, amount of space, design of space, lighting, site size, building utilization, building maintenance, special instructional facilities, and school size" (p. 7). Similar results were reported by Earthman (1998), whose review of the literature led him to conclude that the condition of school buildings may account for as much as 5 to 17 percentile rank points in student achievement scores.

Optimizing Learning Opportunities

What is striking when one reads the literature related to these "noninstructional" factors that influence students' opportunities to learn is the extent to which the negative impact of each factor is more likely to be present in high-poverty, urban schools than in higher income school communities. The evidence that each factor individually introduces greater risk for school failure, and that together the factors combine to compound risk for failure, underscores the magnitude of the challenge that urban school administrators and teachers face in providing effective learning opportunities for each and every child. In the articles presented in this section, authors suggest actions teachers and administrators may take in relation to these noninstructional factors and, by so doing, increase students' opportunities to learn.

In the first article, university professor and teacher James F. Baumann and a parent, Deborah Thomas, offer their suggestions for how teachers can work with parents in low-income, minority families to support literacy learning at home and at school. They confront the stereotypes that are often held about parents who are economically poor and undereducated. Through a written record of their yearlong interactions, they describe the ways they worked together to overcome the barriers to school success for Natasha, Deborah's daughter and Jim's student. The dialogue they share with us is genuine, unvarnished, and compelling. Although their work represents a single case study, it provides a road map for others who wish to help children start on the path toward academic success.

In the second article, the importance of family and community support is again addressed. Consistent with Right 10, Robert B. Cooter, Earlene Mills-House, Peggy Marrin, Barbara A. Mathews, Sylvia Campbell, and Tina Baker argue that if children are to attain the grade-level achievement goals mandated by their board of education, all stakeholders in the community must actively support children's school success. They describe the steps they have taken at the district level to involve family members and other stakeholders. In addition to detailed suggestions for implementing each initiative, they provide a list of references and materials that are available to support replication of their ideas.

In the third article, Joseph Sanacore addresses the "sources of support" teachers need if they are to accommodate the needs of all students. He suggests ways to reduce class size, improve teacher preparedness through high-quality professional development, and choose appropriate instructional materials. He provides explicit and practical ways to provide such support within typical schools and classrooms. Although the contexts for his suggestions are a secondary school setting, each can be easily and effectively applied at any level of schooling.

The issues addressed in Right 10 are both numerous and far-reaching, and the selected articles touch on only some of them. In so doing, they remind us that achieving high-quality education for every child is a complex task and one that must be a community affair—no single teacher, administrator, parent, or school board member can "go it alone." Rather, to achieve the learning goals we have for every child, combined efforts of all stakeholders are necessary. It is likely that the articles will answer some questions and raise others. For example, how can limited resources be used to address the range of important issues, how should limited resources be allocated across grade levels and types of schools, what types of professional development are likely to be most effective in a particular school or district, who should take responsibility to develop and lead home-school partnership efforts? These articles may serve as a way to start conversations that will help educators and policymakers to plan and implement changes that will truly provide children the schools they deserve.

REFERENCES

Allington, R.L., & Johnston, P.H. (2002). *Reading to learn: Lessons from exemplary fourth-grade classrooms.* New York: The Guilford Press.

Baumann, J.F., & Thomas, D. (1997). "If you can pass Momma's tests, then she knows you're getting your education": A case study of support for literacy learning within an African American family. *The Reading Teacher, 51*, 108–120.

Bond, G.L., & Dykstra, R. (1997). The cooperative research program in first-grade reading instruction. *Reading Research Quarterly, 32*, 348–427. (Original work published 1967)

Cooter, R.B., Jr., Mills-House, E., Marrin, P., Mathews, B.A., Campbell, S., & Baker, T. (1999). Family and community involvement: The bedrock of reading success. *The Reading Teacher, 52*, 891–896.

Darling-Hammond, L. (1999). *Teacher quality and student achievement: A review of state policy evidence.* Seattle: University of Washington Center for the Study of Teaching and Policy.

Debaryshe, B.D. (1993). A performance model for academic achievement in adolescent boys. *Developmental Psychology, 29*, 795–804.

Duke, D.L. (1998). *Does it matter where our children learn?* Washington, DC: National Research Council of the National Academy of Sciences and the National Academy of Engineering.

Earthman, G.I. (1998). *The impact of school building condition and student achievement, and behavior.* Paper presented at the European Investment Bank/Organization for Economic Coordination and Development International Conference, Luxembourg,

November 16–17, 1998. (ERIC Document Reproduction Service No. ED441329)

Epstein, J. (2001). *School, family, and community partnerships: Preparing educators and improving schools.* Boulder, CO: Westview Press.

Ferguson, R.F. (1991). Paying for public education: New evidence on how and why money matters. *Harvard Journal on Legislation, 28,* 45–498.

Finn, J.D., & Achilles, C.M. (1990). Answers and questions about class size: A statewide experiment. *American Educational Research Journal, 27*(3), 557–577.

Finn, J.D., Gerber, S.B., Achilles, C.M., & Boyd-Zaharias, J. (2001). The enduring effects of small classes. *Teachers College Record, 103*(2), 145–183.

General Accounting Office. (1996). *School facilities: America's schools report differing conditions.* Washington, DC: Government Printing Office.

National Clearinghouse for Comprehensive School Reform. (2001). Taking stock: Lessons on comprehensive school reform from policy, practice, and research. *Benchmarks, 2,* 1–11.

Sanacore, J. (1997). Reaching out to a diversity of learners: Innovative educators need substantial support. *Journal of Adolescent & Adult Literacy, 41,* 224–229.

Sanders, W.L., & Rivers, J.C. (1996). *Cumulative and residual effects of teachers on future student academic achievement.* Knoxville: University of Tennessee Value-Added Research and Assessment Center.

Switzer, L.S. (1990). Family factors associated with academic progress for children with learning disabilities. *Elementary School Guidance and Counseling, 24,* 200–206.

Toussaint, N. (1998). A community that values learning. *Thrust for Educational Leadership, 28,* 26–28, 35.

"If You Can Pass Momma's Tests, Then She Knows You're Getting Your Education": A Case Study of Support for Literacy Learning Within an African American Family

James F. Baumann and Deborah Thomas

By the time I got to the fifth grade, we moved, and my brother and sister went to Pine Forest Elementary, and the teachers did not care over there. They would just pass them on anyway, whether they was getting it or not. Until Momma put a stop to it. She said, "If my children don't got it, don't you pass my kids." I mean Momma would give us tests at home, you know, to make sure that we could pass.... If we could pass Momma's test, then it was good enough for us to go on to the sixth grade. If we couldn't pass Momma's test, we couldn't go to the sixth grade. That's how Momma was.... If you can pass Momma's tests, then she knows you're getting your education.

Through these words, Deborah conveys the source of the value for and commitment to education that persists in the Thomas household, in which Deborah is raising three young daughters. Like her mother, Deborah expects that her children will learn; demands excellence from her children's teachers and schools; and provides her children the love, structure, and academic support to ensure their literacy learning. In this article, we tell the story of how Deborah and her family are striving to obtain and use literacy to defeat the racism and poverty that have shadowed them all their lives. As part of this story, we address how teachers can work with parents and caregivers of low-income, minority families to support literacy learning at school and at home.

We tell this story as a case study, a shared inquiry that has spanned several years. But we speak from different perspectives and experiences: Deborah from her role as parent and Jim from the role of teacher. Jim took a leave from his university position and taught second grade full time for an entire school year at Oak Street Elementary School, which is located in a medium-sized southern U.S. community (Baumann, 1995a). Deborah's daughter, Natasha, was in Jim's class. During the year, Deborah and Jim came to know each other through their mutual concern for Natasha and her learning.

Originally published in *The Reading Teacher* (1997), volume 51, pages 108–120.

As trust grew through experience and knowledge, Deborah and Jim worked as a team to support Natasha's learning at school and home.

Because of the personal and sensitive nature of events we describe, Deborah has chosen pseudonyms for her first and last names. Natasha and her two younger sisters, Adrienne and Katrina, are also pseudonyms, as are names of schools, communities, and other persons mentioned in this article. We describe all events exactly as they happened, however, trying neither to romanticize nor to sensationalize them. We have not sugar-coated the hardships and frustrations that Deborah and her family have faced as African Americans living in the U.S. South. All is not rosy and bright, and Deborah and her daughters continue to deal with racial discrimination, economic hardships, and family sadness.

Jim learned much during his year teaching second grade (Baumann, 1996a, 1996b). As a racial, cultural, and economic outsider to the Oak Street School community, Jim had to first recognize and then confront various preconceived beliefs he held about low-income, minority children and families. Our purpose in writing is to convey that just because a family may have little

Natasha, lost in a book in Jim's second-grade classroom. Photo by James F. Baumann.

money, be of a minority cultural group, or be headed by a single parent does not mean that there is not care and support for literacy learning in the home. Rather, contrary to social stereotypes and general beliefs, families like Deborah's are likely to hold a strong commitment to literacy and learning upon which teachers can build and develop powerful home/school literacy connections. There is much promise in Deborah's future and that of her daughters, and she and the families of other students in Jim's class taught him that income and color are poor predictors of educational values and academic achievement. We hope that the courage and candor with which Deborah shares her story challenges other teachers to look for, find, value, nurture, and build upon the support for literacy learning that is there within the families of children they teach.

We begin by exploring the myths and realities concerning relationships among culture, income, and educational achievement. Then we present Deborah's story of struggles and successes. Next we address how other teachers might seek out and build upon the values and support within families of students in their classrooms. We conclude with some thoughts about growth in awareness and understanding as teachers of diverse children.

Myths, Realities, and Insidious Biases

The data are unequivocal regarding minority children, poverty, and educational opportunity. Whereas 21% of all U.S. children under 18 live in poverty, the percentages jump to 43% and 41%, respectively, for African American and Hispanic youth (*Youth Indicators 1996*, 1996). In homes headed by single mothers, the child poverty rate soars to 53% overall and to 63% and 68% for African American and Hispanic youngsters. Factor in the reality that school funding varies dramatically by socioeconomic status (Wise, 1967), and it comes as no surprise that minority children are likely to attend less privileged schools (Bartoli, 1995; Kozol, 1991) and often live in unhealthy, unsafe environments (Kozol, 1995).

Given the inequities culturally or linguistically diverse children experience, it may not be surprising that they have been referred to variously as educationally "at risk" (Cuban, 1989), "likely to fail" (Hidalgo, Siu, Bright, Swap, & Epstein, 1995), and "disorganized" or "pathological" (Moynihan, 1965). The "at risk" perspective is compatible with a deficit view (Flores, Cousin, & Diaz, 1991), which suggests that low-income, minority, or linguistically diverse children are "socially disadvantaged" (Hidalgo et al., 1995) and therefore not likely to be cared for physically or psychologically at home nor supported by family members in their schooling (Fine, 1990).

The reality, however, is that cultural orientation, ethnic identity, or first language predicts little about family support for literacy and schooling. Clark's (1983) study of high- and low-achieving high school seniors from low-income, urban, African American families revealed that it was "the family members' *beliefs*, *activities*, and overall *cultural style*" (pp. 1–2) that were associated with student achievement. The "leadership behavior and the sheer will" (p. 61) of single mothers of high-achieving students and factors such as parents making frequent school contacts and expecting to play a major role in their child's schooling were critical in the students' academic success.

Taylor and Dorsey-Gaines's (1988) case studies of the literacy development of young, urban, African American children living in poverty also fight the stereotype. These researchers found rich, literate home environments in the Shay Avenue families they came to know. The Shay families demonstrated "a quiet determination" and "optimism about the future" to "keep them going, struggling and surviving" (p. 192) as they found ways to support and develop their children's literacy at home and in school.

Much additional research exploring African American (e.g., Heath, 1983; Shockley, Michalove, & Allen, 1995) and Hispanic and Latino/a (e.g., Cummins, 1989; Trueba & Delgado-Gaitan, 1989) families and communities supports the notion that parents of minority children have an intense concern for their children's education and learning. Moll's (1992) research paints a rich portrait of the culturally diverse family with parents and other caregivers at the center who are "funds of knowledge" (p. 21) from which teachers can draw in educating children in school. Similarly, Heath and Mangiola (1991) recommend that teachers of culturally and linguistically diverse children replace a deficit mentality with a positive expectation viewpoint, substituting the notion of "children of promise" for "children at risk."

But the myths involving diverse children, their ability, and their achievement live on (Delpit, 1995; Ladson-Billings, 1995). Good-intentioned teachers (Massey, Scott, & Dornbusch, 1975) and minority children themselves (Elrich, 1994) may believe that children of color or those speaking languages other than English may not be quite as academically capable as their mainstream classmates. Like Vivian Paley (1979), who realized that "my luggage had 'liberal' ostentatiously plastered all over it, and I thought it unnecessary to see what was locked inside" (p. xiv), Jim gradually became aware of residual biases he harbored regarding diverse children and their families as the school year progressed:

In spite of growing up in a home without any overt prejudices expressed; in spite of prior experience teaching and working in a multicultural setting in the 1970s; in spite of possessing a politically and intellectually liberal attitude—when I faced myself honestly, I realized that I carried deep down an expectation that parents and caregivers of poor or minority children would not value and support their children's learning at a level commensurate with my middle-class experience and expectations. Oh, how wrong I was.... (Baumann, 1995b, p. 4)

Given this context, we share our unplanned inquiry: Deborah's story of determination and success and Jim's learning along with Natasha and his other students. We relate our experience in the hope that other teachers might examine their beliefs and open their eyes, minds, and hearts as well.

Deborah's Story

Deborah's story demonstrates the myths associated with stereotyping family values and practices on the basis of race, gender, marital status, income, or education. We tell this story through a case record of talk and writings, all in our own unedited words. We include many excerpts from audiotaped conversations of Jim, Deborah, and her family; we also include a few sections from Jim's research/teaching journal, which he kept daily throughout his year in second grade.

Racism, Poverty, and Unequal Opportunity

Deborah grew up in a rural area of the U.S. South in the 1970s and 1980s. The Civil Rights movement, War on Poverty, and Great Society of the 1960s had little impact in Deborah's community; economic and civil justice did not prevail. For example, Deborah faced overt racism while in high school:

Deborah: When I was in my last year in high school, we had the Ku Klux Klan visit the school. Literally. They stood out there with their little signs and stuff.

Jim: You mean like during the school day?

Deborah: During the school day! They would even stop our school buses, get up on the school bus, passing out fliers. All this happened in '87.... They had sheets over their face, their little hats....

Jim: In broad daylight?

Deborah: In broad daylight. They stood around the big court house in Pineville.... Man, it was just a trip back in them days.

Deborah also faced prejudice inside school, as in middle school when she had a racist teacher:

Deborah: They had prejudiced teachers. I had this reading teacher, and it was my seventh-grade year. She kept being hard on me, I guess because I was the only black in the room.

Jim: Really.

Deborah: I was very smart. Everything that she threw at me, I could transform. It didn't matter. She just used to stay on me for some odd reason. I see some girls going to the bathroom one day, and I said, "Ms. Wilson, could I go to the bathroom?" She said, "No you can't." I said, "Why can't I go?" She said, "You know why? Because I'm so prejudiced, that's why."

Jim: She admitted that?

Deborah: Yes, she said it straight to my face.... So, after that, me and her, we didn't have a good understanding. She would give me my work and that be it. She wouldn't try to explain it to me. She was trying to like make it hard for me.

White students also harassed and taunted Deborah and other black children:

This little guy that was in the room [in middle school].... He came up to me one day and said "nigger nigger nigger" and like that. He was just playing in my face. And at that time, it made me kind of upset for him to say that. So I told him, come up in my face and say it. So he got all up in my face saying "nigger nigger nigger." And the next thing I know I had hit him. And the teacher, she run in the room and yanks me. She said, "Deborah, you going to the office." I said, "You don't even know what happened, and you all ready to send me to the office."

The racial situation in Deborah's high school resulted in high dropout rates for African American youth.

Deborah: There were a lot of black males that quit—quit school because they was more like talking to white girls. And in Pine County, they do not play that; regardless of what, they don't play that.... They would get suspended for a little old something, I mean, 10 days at a time. You know, if you get like 20 days unexcused...

Jim: Then you're out.

Deborah: Yeah.

Jim: So they'd force them out is what you're saying?

Deborah: Yeah. That's what they were doing, forcing them out. They wouldn't end up graduating, you can bet on that.

Racism affected not only Deborah's education but that of her mother and father.

Deborah: My mom didn't finish school. She had me when she was 14. And back then, once you get pregnant, they kick you out of school.

Jim: You were out.

Deborah: You couldn't finish high school. They also kicked my dad out of school.

Deborah finished high school but was unable to continue her education: "When I came out of high school, I was pregnant with Tasha [Natasha], so that kind of threw me for a loop. So I ended up going to work after I had her." Deborah is currently raising her three daughters alone. Natasha's father is in prison for a capital offense, the father of Deborah's second daughter was recently released from prison and lives in another part of the state, and the father of her youngest daughter, although residing locally, is not in the Thomas household.

Being a black, single parent in the South presents struggles for Deborah and her children today. The trailer park several miles from Oak Street Elementary where Deborah and her daughters lived throughout Natasha's second-grade year was not a safe environment:

Where we stay now, there's a lot of people that are on drugs out there. And like my baby, she's 3 years old, and she can say, "Momma, that man right there, he's on drugs." And you can look at him and tell.

The violence in their neighborhood kept them prisoners in their own household:

Deborah: My kids don't want to be outside. And I can't blame them because there's so much happening out here. Like last year, we had problem with folks getting killed out here, getting stabbed and shot out here with the drugs.... We just don't go outside. We always in the house.

Jim: It must be frightening.

Deborah: It is. It really is. I even walk them to the bus stop. I be out there when they get off the bus.

But economics make it difficult for Deborah to find a suitable place to live and raise her children:

We've been looking for somewhere else to move. We really don't want to move to a project because the same stuff is happening there. We're just really trying to find us somewhere else to move to.... But with the money situation.... It's our only problem, the money situation.

Overcoming the Barriers

The preceding narrative would seem to fuel the stereotype: an unemployed, African American single parent living on public assistance. The stereotype suggests that children living in such a situation would be likely to experience difficulties in school and perhaps be behavior problems. Further, the common prediction would be that the cycle of poverty would continue in yet another generation. But that is not so. In spite of a hostile educational environment, Deborah valued learning and persisted in her education:

> I worked hard all the way up to the 12th grade. I worked hard to try to get out of school. I mean my 11th-grade year, I wanted to quit school [laughs]. I really did; I wanted to quit school. But I finished on to the 12th grade, and it was hard to finish the 12th grade with all that going on. It was really hard.

Deborah has found better living conditions for herself and her children. After Natasha's second-grade year, the family moved from the trailer park to live temporarily with Deborah's sister. They later moved to their own rental house. "I have my own bedroom, now," said Natasha, beaming with pride.

Deborah has also fulfilled a pledge to herself to continue her education:

Jim: I don't mean to pry, but have you looked into educational opportunities for yourself? You went to high school, but you said you didn't have a chance....

Deborah: See, that's the thing of it, I'm going back to school this year.

Jim: Are you?

Deborah: That's why I'm getting her [Katrina] in Head Start. I'm going to cosmetology school.

Jim: Are you. That's great. Because it's never too late....

Deborah: I know it's not. I always said once I get all of them in school, I was going back. And this is such a perfect opportunity for me to go back. I really got it just the way I want it.

Jim: Well, congratulations.

Deborah: It's just something that I always wanted to do. I always thought of it, but I never could get to finish because I had the kids. Now I don't see nothing that can stop me now.

Supporting Learning at School and Home

Deborah refutes the low-income, minority, single-parent stereotype in many ways, but none more profoundly than the manner in which she supports her children's schooling and learning. Deborah was always wanting to know what was happening at school and what she could do to support Natasha's learning and that of her sisters. Deborah took advantage of Parent-Teacher Organization (PTO) meetings and other programs to help her learn more about the school program.

> I go to all [PTO] Parenting Fairs.... Yes, we normally go to all of them because I be wanting to know everything. I want to know what's available to me as far as helping their education. You know, I try to stay in contact with the teachers, see what they [Deborah's daughters] need, help them as far as making their reading strong and math. I try to stay in touch with all of the teachers.

Deborah always kept in touch with Jim, telephoning him at school or home, asking him questions about how Natasha was doing, what was going on at school, and how she could help at home. For example, in October Jim sent home a progress report and invited parents to phone him or to come in for conferences. Within minutes of when Natasha stepped off the bus that day after school, Deborah was on the phone to Jim, who later commented about the conversation in his journal:

> I had one call already at school, right afterwards from Natasha's mom, who has been very good about calling other times when she has had questions or concerns. That is really nice. She wondered what "word attack skills" meant because there was a "U," an unsatisfactory, in that area. And she wondered what she could do to support Natasha at home. I explained what word attack meant and said that she could help best by just taking time to read books to her and with her and share books with her. And I suggested two or three times a week at least that she set aside some time to do some reading. And I said I would be happy, too, if Natasha would let me know what those nights are to help Natasha select some books that she could be reading to and with her mom. So that is real exciting....

Deborah followed through, and reading at home became habitual throughout the school year and beyond. In the summer after second grade, Deborah noted, "We really had a good time with the reading. We want to keep that reading up; we've been doing a lot of reading."

Deborah visited school regularly. For example, for several consecutive days Deborah sat in on Jim's reading strategies period, joining Natasha in her reading and writing and entering the discussions of the literature the students were reading. Deborah never offered an explanation for her visit, so the following summer, Jim inquired:

Jim:	I've got a question.... Sometime—maybe in the winter or early spring—you came in about two or three days in a row and sat in on our reading class.
Deborah:	Uh huh.
Jim:	That was great. At first I thought it had something to do with the school choice thing [the local school district's response to court-ordered desegregation]. I thought it had to do with that....
Deborah:	No, I just dropped in. Mostly I started with Adrienne. I was going to her class because she was having a little problem paying attention to her class. So, I would drop by her class and sit in there for a little while. And then I would just drop in Natasha's class. There wasn't nothing to it; I just dropped in the class.

Deborah sees high ability in her daughters. For example, she recognizes their inquisitiveness as intelligence:

> They [her daughters] ask me about AIDS and stuff like that. And I try to give them all the answers I can. Anything when it comes to sex and stuff like that. They're so smart. I didn't know they were so smart until they asked me all kinds of questions.

Deborah views her daughters as academically capable and has high academic expectations for them. Whether her daughters will succeed is not a question. It might take them a little more time, it might take more effort than that required of other children, it might take lots of support and encouragement, but they will achieve and succeed:

Jim:	How far do you think your kids will go or should go in school?
Deborah:	They *better* finish! [laughs]
Jim:	Finish what?
Deborah:	They better finish school, as far as going all the way to 12th.... They say they going to go to college, but I don't want to pressure them into it. I *want* them to go, but I don't want to pressure them into going.
Jim:	Think they can do it?
Deborah:	I *know* they can do it.
Jim:	Good.
Deborah:	Yeah, they can do it. They can do it....

Support for school came from other family members also. Deborah's mother and sister visited Oak Street often, picking the girls up for activities, filling in at a conference when Deborah could not be there, attending the hot dog and chili supper, coming to see Natasha perform in the class play, and so forth.

As she did for Deborah and her brothers and sisters, grandmother continues to create tests for Deborah's daughters:

Deborah: That's how she [grandmother] know that Tasha and Adrienne are doing real good in school.

Jim: Because they can pass Momma's tests [laughs].

Deborah: If they pass Momma's tests, they can pass anything [laughs]. She has the best formula. She has a test like a level higher than what they are, so that's how I know that they are doing real good in school if they can pass her tests. She's not been letting them slide; she's on it. In other words, she is *on* it.

Natasha's father also supports her schooling and learning, although it must be from afar through correspondence:

Deborah: She likes to write to her dad.... He keeps telling her, "Natasha, whatever you're going to do, your daddy is behind you all the way. I might can't be there, but I'm behind you all the way." And he writes like three or four times a week.

Jim: That's wonderful.

Deborah: So they are doing real good. I think that's one reason for her being so serious cause he didn't finish school. He tell her, "Natasha, I didn't finish school; I want my girl to finish." That's his baby.

For Natasha and her sisters, family literacy is a powerful reality. In addition to the support from their mother, fathers, aunt, and grandmother, the girls support one another. For example, Jim brought some gift books for the girls when he visited Deborah's family at their trailer one day. During the entire time Jim and Deborah spoke, Natasha sat on the sofa and read aloud the new books to her younger sisters. Deborah also finds her daughters reading to one another, teaching one another, and playing school:

She [Natasha] likes reading to them [points to Adrienne and Katrina]. They more like think of her as a teacher, in other words.... Like Tasha, she taught her [Katrina] to count to 25, and she's only 3. And like Adrienne, she taught her to how to count in Spanish to 10.... Tasha taught her [Katrina] how to spell her name now. They just surprise me that they're learning all this stuff.

Academic Dividends

All the support, work, and effort paid off (Baumann & Ivey, 1997). At the beginning of second grade, Natasha's instructional level on an informal reading inventory (IRI) was primer. In May, however, when Jim conducted end-of-year IRIs, her instructional level was third grade. As part of his IRI analysis and record keeping, Jim wrote the following about Natasha's growth at that time:

> Natasha has made exceptional progress this year. She has moved from being a very tentative, reluctant reader to a confident, fairly fluent one. She is a solid beginning third-grade-level reader at this point and is on the verge of independence in word identification and comprehension. Her work effort has paid off, and the support she has received from home has been substantial and significant. I am extremely proud of Natasha's progress, and she and her mom should be likewise pleased and proud.

Natasha herself recognized that hard work resulted in growth in reading. During a home visit the summer after second grade, Jim had the following conversation with Natasha:

Jim: What kind of reader are you now?

Natasha: I'm a good reader.

Jim: Why are you good? What makes you good?

Natasha: 'Cause I practice.

Deborah likewise saw how her support and Natasha's hard work paid dividends. In this same conversation, Jim turned to Deborah and inquired:

Jim: How about you, from a mom's perspective?

Deborah: I think she got real good at reading. She know words I didn't think that she knew. It was more like you helped her get those big words that she wasn't getting before then. At the beginning [of second grade], she was struggling with those words, but now she's real good at big words. Even teaching her little sister them words.

Sharon, Natasha's reading buddy from the fifth-grade room next door to Jim's classroom, also saw Natasha develop in reading maturity. One day during late winter, she wrote in Natasha's reading journal, "I read *The Cat Sat.* I read it with Natasha. She is a very nice person to read with. She is a very good reader and her reading is improving a lot."

Natasha continues to make fine progress in school. Jim visits her regularly at Oak Street, talking, reading, and writing with her. Her family continues to provide the rich environment she needs to thrive academically. Literacy growth for Natasha is no accident. It is happening because there is good communication between school and home and because of the support that Deborah and her extended family provides Natasha.

The Foundation of Value and Support

Why does Deborah value education, literacy, and learning in spite of the in-equities and indignities she faced in her own schooling? One undeniable factor is Deborah's mother.

Jim: Did some of that value [for education] come from your mother?

Deborah: Yes, all of it, really, narrows down to Momma.... She's always pushed us. She always told us that we can do anything we set our minds to. And I'm living proof of that. I finished high school and am starting another school, and I know I'm going to finish this school.

Deborah's mother demanded that her children apply themselves and devoted time to helping them:

When we got home from school, she wanted to know if we had any work we had got from school and work we had to do. And she went over it. She never give us the answers, but she would always help out with the first two or three. After that, we had to do it on our own.... Momma was always strict on all of us as far as school work. School work was our first priority.

For instance, in third grade when Deborah's grades began to slide, her mother turned off the TV and conducted a home study hall to get her back on track:

She took the TV from me. Every day I got home, I had to sit at that table and do my work.... She didn't have to spite me; she just took what I loved the most.... And after that, I know that she meant business and I wanted to get my education. So it was good, you know.

Momma's values for literacy remain evident today as she too is continuing her education: "My mom only went to the ninth grade. Now she's going back to school to get her GED" [Test of General Educational Development; equivalent to high school diploma].

The family members in the Thomas household continue to provide support for education and learning. Just as Deborah's mother supported her as a youngster, she continues to provide Deborah encouragement for her adult education program:

She stayed on us about school. She wanted us to be way better than she was. I could always count on her to push me. And that's like with [cosmetology] school now. She pushes me.... Like if I say, "Well, Momma, I really don't feel like going today," she'll say something like, "Well, you need to go on and finish this so we can start on making all this money...." She see me succeeding.

The support is mutual. Deborah encourages her mother in her GED program: "I keep pushing her like she push me. I push her. We push one another." And Deborah sees it as her responsibility to continue this value for literacy and education for successive generations: "I just hope that when they [her daughters] do get kids, I hope they can pass it on—staying on their kids' education because they can never get enough of it. I mean, *I* don't never get enough of it."

Creating a School-Home Collaboration

Given Deborah's story, Jim's experience, and the research on literacy education for diverse children, how might teachers and parents work together to help children achieve their academic potential? We offer ideas for developing school and home structures that mutually support children's learning. Some of these principles and suggestions address teachers more than parents; others speak more to parents than teachers. In all instances, however, we believe the ideas we put forth will enable teachers and parents jointly to support low-income, minority children's literacy development at school and home.

Recognizing and Celebrating Differences

Educators supporting multicultural curricula consistently acknowledge that appropriate, successful teaching involves the recognition and appreciation of how people differ ethnically, culturally, and racially (e.g., Ladson-Billings, 1994; Strickland, 1994). Rather than pretending to be "color blind" (Delpit, 1995; Paley, 1979), culturally responsive teachers are "color conscious" (Baldwin, 1988) and appreciate individual differences. Jim used multicultural literature as one means to recognize cultural diversity. For example, per class tradition, on his birthday Terrence received a gift book, in this case, *Teammates* (Golenbock, 1990), the story of Jackie Robinson's breaking of the "color barrier" in professional baseball and how Pee Wee Reese, a white Brooklyn Dodger teammate, befriended Robinson. Terrence asked Jim to read the book aloud to the class, which led to an extended discussion of racism in the United States historically and in contemporary times. Jim and his students compared Robinson's story to information from other books they had read that dealt with racism against blacks (e.g., *A Picture Book of Jesse Owens*, Adler, 1992; *"Wanted: Dead or Alive": The True Story of Harriet Tubman*, McGovern, 1965; *If You Lived at the Time of Martin Luther King*, Levine, 1994).

Jim's class discussed multiculturalism through other literature as well. For example, they all learned about Jewish American culture and the interface with African American culture by reading, enjoying, and discussing Patricia Polacco's wonderful books *Mrs. Katz and Tush* (1992b) and *Chicken Sunday* (1992a). Similarly, reading and discussing *Angel Child, Dragon Child* (Surat, 1983) enabled students to confront stereotypes they had about Asian cultures, and everyone's thinking about cross-cultural issues was provoked after reading Allen Say's (1993) *Grandfather's Journey*. On occasion, racial tensions surfaced in the classroom or playground, and Jim and students had candid discussions about them. These conversations were sometimes troubling or uncomfortable, and those in the class community neither pretended to be all alike nor always got along perfectly. But taking the time to celebrate cultural differences, trying to understand our prejudices and misunderstandings, and learning from one another created a closer, more respectful classroom family.

When Natasha was in third grade, Jim and Deborah talked about an operetta on famous black Americans Natasha's class had just performed, and Deborah recalled her own schooling: "We didn't get a Black History Month in Pine County. We got Martin Luther King holiday, but we didn't really get it as a holiday. We got it as a teacher work day." Jim inquired, "They didn't respect the day to give teachers off?" to which Deborah responded, "No." This led to a discussion about the place of black history in the elementary curriculum and Deborah's comment: "One thing that I dislike about school—I think they ought to be able to learn about African Americans all through the year, the school year, instead of just in February. 'Cause there's a lot that I didn't know about African Americans until I went to Tasha's play."

Our point in sharing this episode is the importance of teachers not only being color conscious and taking the time to acknowledge multiculturalism but also making it an integrated part of the curriculum, not an add-on (Eldridge, 1996) component to a social studies unit or something that is addressed in a single month. Strickland (1994) recommended that teachers "take special care to see to it that African American children are familiar with literature by and about African Americans" (p. 333), and Delpit (1995) stated, "Our children of color need to see the brilliance of their legacy" (p. 177). Recognizing, learning about, and celebrating cultural richness and differences are critical elements in constructing a supportive home-school relationship among teachers and parents.

Great Expectations

Parents' beliefs in their children and their abilities predicts student learning and growth (e.g., Clark, 1983), and Deborah has great confidence in her children's abilities: "Both of them [her daughters in school] are real smart and serious about school.... They are capable. All my kids are capable. They come home now learning *me* stuff." Deborah also has high academic expectations for her daughters. For example, with regard to their reading, she both challenges and supports her children: "I want them to be a strong reader. I don't want them to be no borderline or under the line. I want them to be way above the line. So I try to make them read just about all the time [laughs].... We read. We read all the time [laughs]. We read."

Deborah appreciated high expectations for her daughters at school. When Natasha was struggling with school work, Deborah said she "just kept studying" and commented on how Natasha responded to encouragement: "Tasha said, 'Mr. Baumann said I can do this,' so she believed she could do it." In a conversation about teachers' beliefs and expectations at the end of the school year, Jim commented to Deborah: "The real important thing is that you care and that you expect a lot from them [Deborah's daughters]. And that's important because I expected a lot from them [Tasha and his other students] because they *can* do it. And if they believe that, then the sky's the limit." Deborah replied, "That's right, the sky *is* the limit."

The implication for teachers is to believe in and expect diverse children—all children—to learn. Ladson-Billings's (1994) research revealed that successful teachers of African American children were those who "believe that all of their students can succeed rather than that failure is inevitable for some" (p. 25). For these teachers, "Students were not permitted to choose failure in their classrooms. They cajoled, nagged, pestered, and bribed the students to work at high intellectual levels" (Ladson-Billings, 1995, p. 479). Delpit (1995) wrote, "We say we believe that all children can learn, but few of us really believe it" (p. 172). As educators and parents, we must fight the deficit mentality and learn to truly believe in the abilities within all children of all colors.

Challenging, Gently Pushing, and Nurturing

Scholars who research and write about educating minority or low-income children (e.g., Rueda, 1991; Strickland, 1994) maintain that one way to counteract the deficit fallacy is to provide diverse children a demanding, culturally responsive curriculum. Deborah wants her children to be challenged at school;

she commented one day that she appreciated Jim expecting much from Natasha: "You didn't give her no slack." Deborah wants teachers to provide her daughters a rigorous curriculum: "Give them harder words for spelling and reading. Give them homework. I want them to work hard for everything!" Just as Delpit (1988) talks about providing minority children access to the culture of power through instruction in power code literacy, so too Deborah wants her daughters to have the tools to compete in our society: "Don't just pass them on. They need to learn what it takes to make it in the world."

But Deborah also considers it her responsibility to provide her children the encouragement to succeed:

> Tasha, she's got the ability to learn, but her thing is she's more like...she's more like scared of failure. She got to where she don't want to try. So I'm kind of push-ing her on that because I know she can do it. 'Cause...look at *me*, I finished school, and I know my kids can finish.... And that's why I'm there to push her, to make her go on with it.

Just as Deborah was motivated and encouraged by Momma, she views it as her role to motivate her own daughters in their schooling:

> I'm there to push them when they don't want to...when they feel like they can't do it. I let them know that it don't matter what it is, that they can accomplish *any-thing*. It doesn't matter what it is. It might take some time, but you can accom-plish anything.

But this does not mean that teachers of diverse children should employ a sink-or-swim approach or confuse academic rigor with their responsibility to individualize and teach students, not just academic subjects. Strickland (1994) cautions teachers about adopting a "one-size-fits-all curriculum." Instead, she encourages teachers to recognize the "great differences among the children we teach," acknowledging that "respecting and building on these differences is an important part of what good teachers do" (p. 334). Jim viewed his role as that of a lovingly demanding teacher. So while Deborah was glad that Jim did not "give slack," she also appreciated engaging and interesting instruction: "You [to Jim] made it more fun for her to learn. In other words, she was real-ly enthusiastic about learning."

Deborah also appreciates teachers who share decision making with stu-dents and teach them responsibility: "Let the kids decide some things.... Give them choices, responsibilities." Deborah cited specific examples such as let-ting the students select words for spelling, choosing which books to read, or deciding how an assignment might be done. Deborah noted that the combination of high expectations and opportunity for choice had a positive impact on Natasha: "Natasha, she being more responsible because of it now."

Overall, Deborah asks for concern and respect from teachers: "I like for all my kids to have teachers who really care about them and their learning.... And I want them [her children] to know that if someone respects them, I want them also to be respectful to them." Deborah also asks for patience and understanding from teachers: "I say, just bear with them [Deborah's daughters]; take a little time with them. Just bear with them." In sum, Deborah shows love, structure, expectation, and care with regard to her daughters' schooling (Taylor & Dorsey-Gaines, 1988), and she looks for and expects teachers to challenge, instruct, persist, and motivate her children in the school environment (Ladson-Billings, 1994).

Making Time, Communicating, and Doing Homework

Jim asked Deborah what she would recommend to other parents to help their children achieve in school, and she talked about committing time and taking an interest in school work: "I suggest that they spend a lot of time with their kids. A lot of people I know of now, their kids are pretty much on their own as far as homework." Deborah emphasized the importance of time for single parents like herself: "I would say to single mothers, there's nothing too hard for you to do to help your kids. I mean, I have a busy schedule, and I try to manipulate my schedule so I can help them.... I always make a little time slot for my kids."

Deborah and her daughters follow a daily routine when they all get home from school:

> The first thing I do is relax. I take like 30 minutes for that. Then after that, I get Tasha and I help Tasha with her homework. And I guess it will take from 30 to 45 minutes. And Adrienne, she don't have as much homework as Tasha because she's under there [first grade], so it might be 10 or 15 minutes for her. And Katrina [preschooler], we just go over her ABCs and 123s and stuff like that. But we all make time. We commit time to just taking time out to do homework.

But it's not all homework and tutoring. Deborah understands that children have interesting, complicated lives, and she wants to know about what they do and how they feel:

> Like when I call Tasha to help her with her homework, we don't start immediately with her homework. We start with "How was your day? What did you do in school today?" You know, we *talk* about stuff, and I ask about what problems she had and, I even ask her about her little friends and be interested in what

she's doing. And see, that's a better way to go about helping them with their homework, especially when they got something difficult that they're working on.

Bartoli (1995) found that parents in low-income, inner-city neighborhoods appreciated good school-home communication: "Parents were quite concerned about the school progress and behavior of their children.... Parents were particularly appreciative of teachers who had taken an interest in their child, sent notes and newsletters home, and otherwise kept them informed about what was happening in school" (p. 81). So, too, Deborah appreciated direct communication: "I was glad when you sent those [notes] home 'cause we didn't know what to work on before.... I want to know *everything*. And with both of them in school, it's kind of hard sometimes."

Deborah and Jim wrote notes to each other, phoned each other, and visited at school. "You [Jim] as a teacher, I could talk to you, like when she [Natasha] was going through a struggling time with her math, reading, anything. You know, I could more like talk to you, and you could suggest things." For example, after Jim had suggested that Natasha, her mom, and sisters practice reading at home, Deborah followed through. The zippered plastic bags filled with paperback trade books and "Leo, the Read-With-Me Lion" stuffed animal went home with Natasha, came back to school, and went home again:

> Well, I liked the idea that she needed some books to come home for some practice reading. That was real good because I think that mostly strengthened her reading better than she was. Because we really read the stories that you sent home.... We read a lot now. And that really took a good turn for us. That reading idea really strengthened her.

In conclusion, at the end of a long conversation about schools and teachers, Jim asked Deborah, "What kind of teachers would you like your daughters to have?" Deborah replied, "I guess I'm looking for a teacher to be like my Momma was to me." This simple, direct answer summed up what the research and theoretical literature tells us and what Deborah knew in her heart from experience—that a good teacher cares about children, expects them to learn, challenges and actually teaches them, makes learning enjoyable and relevant, communicates well, and respects children and is respected by them.

The Exception Is the Rule

As the school year progressed, Jim learned that what he saw in Deborah and her family was not unique. He saw firsthand that to be economically poor or of a minority culture did not mean that families were "disadvantaged" or that families did not value education. He saw this not only in Deborah's family but in the families of other children in his class. For example, after an afternoon and evening of parent-teacher conferences in November, Jim made the following journal entry:

> I am feeling good about the relationships that I'm developing and maintaining with the families. Some of them have marvelous support at home, for example, the last conference I had, Alexis's mom and dad, both very caring and concerned parents. Really wishing for her to get good schooling and a good education. Such a sweet kid. You know, I think they are economically really rough off, but boy do they have wealth in lots of other ways. And it is really refreshing to see that. That is true of some of the other conferences, and really most of the situations in their own way.... Mara's mom and dad were both there, and have some concerns about her learning and behavior, but they are certainly interested and willing to work and receptive to good suggestions, and boy what more can you ask for. Shenika's mom was there, a single parent with two younger children and Shenika. Well behaved kids and a mother who is very concerned and interested in her child's growth and clearly supports and cares, and it shows. Shenika is a marvelous student. Does excellent work at school. It is not coincidental, I believe, that her mom is so tuned in and aware and so concerned. Vanessa's mom was there with her little brother in tow, and another instance of where the mom is trying to go to school herself and care for two children and, you know, improve her situation and wants only the best for her. Quaris's grandmother, marvelous lady, wonderful lady, was there this afternoon. She is caring for him and two other siblings, and, you know, Quaris is fortunate to have her, to be able to look after him and to study with him. Quaris has got much to do and much to learn, but it is encouraging.... I have seen some children who are economically very disadvantaged but very rich in other ways. So it still boils down to people loving and caring and wishing for and putting forth the effort to get the most out of life for their children.

Indeed, love and care are what Deborah provided and continues to provide her children. Deborah and parents of other students in Jim's class taught him to recognize the power and richness that was there when he opened his eyes and ears. But the real lesson goes beyond seeing and hearing to opening one's heart and examining one's beliefs, as Lisa Delpit (1995) expressed in *Other People's Children*:

> We do not really see through our eyes or hear through our ears, but through our beliefs. To put our beliefs on hold is to cease to exist as ourselves for a moment—and that is not easy. It is painful as well, because it means turning yourself inside out, giving up your own sense of who you are, and being willing to see yourself in the unflattering light of another's angry gaze. It is not easy,

but it is the only way to learn what it might feel like to be someone else and the only way to start the dialogue. (pp. 46–47)

Deborah and Jim started the dialogue, and it continues to the present. And they hope that their experience working together to promote the literacy development of Natasha and her sisters might be useful to others—other parents who might follow Deborah's example in supporting their children's literacy learning, and other teachers who might examine their beliefs, look for the support and richness that is there in their students' families, and build on it to teach the "other people's children" they have in their classrooms.

Jim's year teaching second grade, his work as a teacher researcher, and the case study inquiry Deborah and Jim present in this article were supported in part by the National Reading Research Center of the University of Georgia and the University of Maryland under the Educational Research and Development Centers Program (PR/AWARD NO. 117A20007) as administered by the Office of Educational Research and Improvement, U.S. Department of Education. The findings and opinions expressed here do not necessarily reflect the position or policies of the National Reading Research Center, the Office of Educational Research and Improvement, or the U.S. Department of Education. We wish to thank the following persons for their thoughtful comments on drafts of this article: JoBeth Allen, who has conducted action research in Oak Street classrooms for many years; Donna E. Alvermann, codirector of the National Reading Research Center; Patricia Brown, principal of Oak Street Elementary School; Veda McClain, an Oak Street parent and former PTO president; and Betty Shockley-Bisplinghoff, a former Oak Street teacher researcher.

REFERENCES

Baldwin, J. (1988). A talk to teachers. In R. Simonson & S. Walker (Eds.), *The Graywolf annual five: Multicultural literature* (pp. 3–12). St. Paul, MN: Graywolf Press.

Bartoli, J.S. (1995). *Unequal opportunity: Learning to read in the U.S.A.* New York: Teachers College Press.

Baumann, J.F. (1995a). Sabbatical in second-grade: Reflecting on the lived experience. In K. Hinchman, D.J. Leu, & C.K. Kinzer, (Eds.), *Perspectives in literacy research and practice* (44th Yearbook of the National Reading Conference, pp. 390–399). Chicago: National Reading Conference.

Baumann, J.F. (1995b, December). *"At risk" in second grade: Can we all learn when the teacher is in the racial, cultural, economic, linguistic, and gender minority?* Paper presented at the meeting of the National Reading Conference, New Orleans, LA.

Baumann, J.F. (1996a). Conflict or compatibility in classroom inquiry? One teacher's struggle to balance teaching and research. *Educational Researcher, 25*(7), 29–36.

Baumann, J.F. (1996b). The inside and outside of teacher research: Reflections on having one foot in both worlds. In C.K. Kinzer, D.J. Leu, & K. Hinchman (Eds.), *Literacies for the 21st century: Research and practice* (45th Yearbook of the National Reading Conference, pp. 500–511). Chicago: National Reading Conference.

Baumann, J.F., & Ivey, G. (1997). Delicate balances: Striving for curricular and instructional equilibrium in a second-grade, literature/strategy-based classroom. *Reading Research Quarterly, 32,* 244–275.

Clark, R. (1983). *Family life and school achievement: Why poor black children succeed or fail.* Chicago: University of Chicago Press.

Cuban, L. (1989). The "at risk" label and the problem of urban school reform. *Phi Delta Kappan, 70,* 780–801.

Cummins, J. (1989). *Empowering minority students.* Sacramento, CA: California Association of Bilingual Educators.

Delpit, L. (1988). The silenced dialogue: Power and pedagogy in educating other people's children. *Harvard Educational Review, 58,* 280–298.

Delpit, L. (1995). *Other people's children: Cultural conflict in the classroom.* New York: New Press.

Eldridge, D. (1996). When the shoe won't fit: Sizing up teachers' concerns about and responses to diversity in the language arts classroom. *Language Arts, 73,* 298–304.

Elrich, M. (1994). The stereotype within. *Educational Leadership, 51*(8), 12–15.

Fine, M. (1990). Making controversy: Who's "at risk?" *Journal of Urban and Cultural Studies, 1,* 55–68.

Flores, B., Cousin, P.T., & Diaz, E. (1991). Transforming deficit myths about learning, language, and culture. *Language Arts, 68,* 369–379.

Heath, S.B. (1983). *Ways with words: Language, life, and work in communities and classrooms.* Cambridge, England: Cambridge University Press.

Heath, S.B., & Mangiola, L. (1991). *Children of promise: Literacy activity in linguistically and culturally diverse classrooms.* Washington, DC: National Education Association.

Hidalgo, N.M., Siu, S., Bright, J.A., Swap, S., & Epstein, J.L. (1995). Research on families, schools, and communities: A multicultural perspective. In J.A. Banks & C.A.M. Banks (Eds), *Handbook of research on multicultural education* (pp. 498–524). New York: Macmillan.

Kozol, J. (1991). *Savage inequalities: Children in America's schools.* New York: Crown.

Kozol, J. (1995). *Amazing grace: The lives of children and the conscience of a nation.* New York: Crown.

Ladson-Billings, G. (1994). *The dreamkeepers: Successful teachers of African American children.* San Francisco: Jossey-Bass.

Ladson-Billings, G. (1995). Toward a theory of culturally relevant teaching. *American Educational Research Journal, 32,* 465–491.

Massey, G.C., Scott, M.V., & Dornbusch, S.M. (1975). Racism without racists: Institutional racism in urban schools. *The Black Scholar, 7*(3), 2–11.

Moll, L. (1992). Bilingual classroom studies and community analysis: Some recent trends. *Educational Researcher, 21*(2), 20–24.

Moynihan, D. (1965). *The Negro family: The case for national action.* Washington, DC: U.S. Department of Labor.

Paley, V.G. (1979). *White teacher.* Cambridge, MA: Harvard University Press.

Rueda, R. (1991). Characteristics of literacy programs for language-minority students. In E.H. Hiebert (Ed.), *Literacy for a diverse society: Perspectives, practices, and policies* (pp. 93–107). New York: Teachers College Press.

Shockley, B., Michalove, B., & Allen, J. (1995). *Engaging families: Connecting home and school literacy communities.* Portsmouth, NH: Heinemann.

Strickland, D.S. (1994). Educating African American learners at risk: Finding a better way. *Language Arts, 71,* 328–336.

Taylor, D., & Dorsey-Gaines, C. (1988). *Growing up literate: Learning from inner-city families.* Portsmouth, NH: Heinemann.

Trueba, H., & Delgado-Gaitan, C. (1989). *School and society: Learning content through culture.* New York: Praeger.

Wise, A.E. (1967). *Rich schools, poor schools.* Chicago: University of Chicago Press.

Youth Indicators 1996: Trends in the well-being of American youth. (1996). Washington, DC: U.S. Department of Education, National Center for Education Statistics.

LITERATURE CITED

Adler, D.A. (1992). *A picture book of Jesse Owens.* New York: Scholastic.

Golenbock, P. (1990). *Teammates.* San Diego: Harcourt Brace Jovanovich.

Levine, E. (1994). *If you lived at the time of Martin Luther King.* New York: Scholastic.

McGovern, A. (1965). *"Wanted dead or alive": The true story of Harriet Tubman.* New York: Scholastic.

Polacco, P. (1992a). *Chicken Sunday.* New York: Philomel.

Polacco, P. (1992b). *Mrs. Katz and Tush.* New York: Dell.

Say, A. (1993). *Grandfather's journey.* Boston: Houghton Mifflin.

Surat, M.M. (1983). *Angel child, dragon child.* New York: Scholastic.

Family and Community Involvement: The Bedrock of Reading Success

Robert B. Cooter, Jr., Earlene Mills-House, Peggy Marrin, Barbara A. Mathews, Sylvia Campbell, and Tina Baker

allas Public Schools (Texas, USA), much like other large urban school districts throughout the United States, has experienced serious literacy challenges in recent decades. Several years ago achievement test data indicated that only about one in four children were reading at grade level by the end of third grade (on average students read about six months below level). This third-grade benchmark has proven to be a meaningful indicator of progress, or lack thereof, nationally. In the case of Dallas, by the time students reach ninth grade their average reading level is some 2½ years below grade placement. It is not difficult to see the correlation between low literacy levels and such social problems as a rise in juvenile crime, an attraction for many youngsters to gangs, and a general sense of hopelessness among so many children.

In 1997 Dallas Public Schools launched a new balanced literacy initiative aimed at ensuring that all students attain an appropriate level of reading fluency by the end of third grade. Mandated by the board of education, the Dallas Reading Plan is a kindergarten through third-grade initiative calling for such reforms as the identification of research-documented "benchmark" skills and concomitant assessment procedures for emergent and early readers, a Reading Academy for some 3,000 teachers patterned after staff development programs used in highly successful corporations, targeted programs for children having special learning needs, and family and community outreach programs (see Figure 1). The goal of this latter category, *family and community outreach*, is to create a literacy education support system with primary caregivers in the homes as well as other stakeholders in the community as a critical adjunct to the balanced literacy program in the local schools.

In this article we describe several steps we have taken at the school district level that build upon the natural bedrock of support for children in Dallas— family members and other stakeholders concerned about improving literacy. In addition to ideas that could be adapted by other teachers, school districts, and their neighborhood communities, we provide a short list of references and materials we have generated that are available for replication efforts.

Originally published in *The Reading Teacher* (1999), volume 52, pages 891–896.

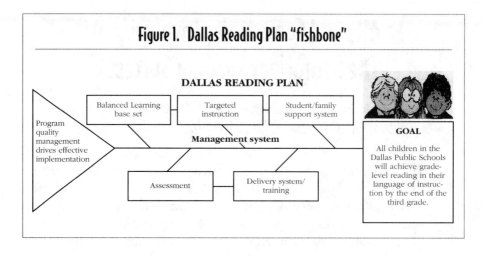

Figure 1. Dallas Reading Plan "fishbone"

DALLAS READING PLAN

Program quality management drives effective implementation

Balanced Learning base set

Targeted instruction

Student/family support system

Management system

Assessment

Delivery system/ training

GOAL

All children in the Dallas Public Schools will achieve grade-level reading in their language of instruction by the end of the third grade.

DEAR Dallas

Research indicates that young children read on average about seven to eight minutes during the school day (Anderson, Hiebert, Scott, & Wilkinson, 1985). Yet we know that the development of fluent reading requires massive amounts of practice in order to satisfy student interest, build fluency, increase vocabulary, and improve comprehension. Research data on the status of reading in Dallas revealed that many students had significant fluency and comprehension problems, and that most teachers were not providing sufficient independent reading time as a regular part of the daily routine. Clearly, some sort of sustained silent reading on a daily basis was needed. It was from this documented need that DEAR Dallas was born.

The goal of DEAR Dallas (modeled after the *D*rop *E*verything *A*nd *R*ead classroom strategy) was to get the entire city to join Dallas Public Schools in making a dramatic statement in support of reading. Our vision was that all citizens, children and adults, would stop whatever they were doing for 10 minutes at an assigned time (10:00 to 10:10 a.m. on March 6) and read a book, newspaper, or magazine just for fun. Publicity was arranged in cooperation with local newspapers, television, and radio stations, and with the city buses that traveled about the city brandishing large advertising banners (see Figure 2) to help spread the word.

Who joined the DEAR Dallas citywide effort? Nearly everyone. The mayor proclaimed March 6 as "DEAR Dallas Day" and joined in by reading with all teachers and children of Dallas in grades K–12. The police chief, also a strong supporter of children and education in Dallas, joined in along with downtown businesses and corporate offices. Governor George W. Bush, seeing DEAR Dallas as concordant with his statewide reading initiative, issued a statement praising the effort and explaining that we must all encourage our children to read every day for fun and to strengthen their literacy skills for improved life choices. Other prominent community leaders were asked to share with us the title of the book they planned to read during the event, which led to the publication of the first ever "Superintendent's Adult Reading List."

Getting DEAR time started at the classroom or school level has been quite simple. It begins with an understanding that time set aside for pleasure reading is not a frill, but a necessity in a balanced reading program. Teachers should set aside at least 20 minutes per day for students to self-select and read books. We teach students to self-select books using the "Rule of Thumb"

Figure 2. DEAR Dallas poster

method (Reutzel & Cooter, 1996): After choosing a book of interest, open the book to any page with a lot of words and count the number of words you don't know. If you use all five fingers to count unknown words on one page the book is too difficult; put it back and choose another you like just as well. For children in grades K–1 we have found it necessary to have DEAR time for about 10 minutes twice a day due to their shorter attention spans. Schoolwide DEAR time can be achieved with the principal's support. Simply set aside a time daily when everyone reads. It is a truly powerful tool that can have magnificent results when everyone participates.

To get our districtwide DEAR campaign off the ground we formed a committee headed up by an energetic and charismatic lead teacher. Because of her rather infectious enthusiasm she was able to enlist the support of central office administrators, principals, corporate sponsors, and the local media. DEAR is a wonderful common sense strategy that virtually sells itself, but to get it going on a districtwide basis requires an inspirational and vivacious teacher-leader. Fortunately, such people are common to our profession.

DEAR Dallas will continue now as a yearly event in the city and is being adopted by many neighboring school districts. We are also working with all Dallas schools to make the first Thursday of each month DEAR time. One thing is certain: Many children are now engaging in independent reading activities daily in school and at home as part of their teacher's normal literacy education routine.

Reading With Wishbone: Videotapes for Parent Outreach

DEAR Dallas was just the beginning of our campaign to encourage reading at home. As the Dallas Reading Plan teachers and other team members scanned the horizon for opportunities, we discovered a fabulous resource in our own backyard—a dog named Wishbone (see Figure 3). The creation of Lyrick Studios, Wishbone is a popular character on Public Broadcast System (PBS) stations in the United States who is a remarkable promoter of great books. We thought he might be able to help us encourage many children, parents, and caregivers to use our public libraries more often.

Wishbone is the lovable Jack Russell terrier who each week reenacts a famous classic novel for viewers. Fully costumed in period clothing appropriate to the highlighted book, Wishbone draws youngsters and adult viewers alike into the wonderful world of books. Our colleagues at Lyrick Studios agreed to join our balanced literacy effort and offered Wishbone's services as our Ambassador of Reading.

Figure 3. Wishbone promotional drawing

©1995 Big Feats! Entertainment. All rights reserved. Used with permission. WISHBONE is a trademark and service mark of Big Feats! Entertainment.

Two great products have arisen from this exciting collaboration that is of benefit not only to Dallas children, but to interested teachers across the United States. The primary product is a high-quality videotape coproduced by the Dallas Reading Plan and Big Feats! Entertainment. Titled *DEAR Families: Paws to Read...With Wishbone*, this film features Wishbone in captivating vignettes extolling the virtues of recreational reading through DEAR time. In essence, it features Wishbone acting out a series of book talks and offering advice to children and adults for choosing books for family DEAR time. This humorous tale is appropriate for children, Parent-Teacher Association and civic groups, and especially for families. We have included a copy of the videocassette tape in the Reading Backpacks (see next section) for all our K–3 classrooms so that every family is sure to be exposed to the helpful information about libraries and the DEAR concepts presented by Wishbone.

Teachers everywhere who are interested in motivating parents to read with their children can take advantage of this Wishbone video, too.

Arrangements have been made so that teachers can order the Wishbone video at a very minimal cost (about US$3) for their classroom or school (see our Internet homepage for ordering information at the end of this article). It's a great way to "unleash" the power of reading!

Reading Backpacks

One of the challenges we face in Dallas is getting high-quality books written in English and Spanish into the hands of children at home. Many of our families are economically disadvantaged and simply do not have books for their children to read. Beginning in the fall of 1998, we implemented a Reading Backpacks strategy to get books of appropriate interest and reading levels into each child's home at least once per week.

Based on the Traveling Tales Backpacks concept (Reutzel & Cooter, 1996; Reutzel & Fawson, 1990) for promoting writing, the Dallas Reading Plan provided each and every K–3 classroom teacher in the district with five Reading Backpacks, a large supply of trade books on varying topics and readability levels in both English and Spanish, easy activities for parents to do with their children on printed card stock adapted from Mooney's (1990) Reading To, With, and By strategies, a copy of the Wishbone video, and some materials for written responses (markers, colored paper, scissors, etc.). We also included a simple Family Report Form for adults to note which books were read by their child and to whom, as well as any reader response activities they were able to do at home. In this way teachers are able to track student interests and, to a degree, outside reading habits.

Reading Backpacks are regarded as a wonderful success in our schools and are treasured by our young readers. We include our Internet homepage address later in this article for teachers interested in obtaining a list of Reading Backpack contents and the books we selected.

Summer Food and Reading Program: Volunteer Training

One of the great concerns in urban communities is the welfare of children during the summer months. When schools are out many children regress in their literacy development. Another worry is that some of the children may not have access to the nutritious meals available to them during the school year. To respond to both of these needs, the Greater Dallas Community of Churches

(GDCC) developed a Summer Food and Reading Program. They discovered that a city with numerous restless 5–12-year-olds, comfortable space at local churches, a pool of enthusiastic volunteers, and 20,000 gently used donated books can provide all the ingredients needed for a successful summer "reading and feeding" program.

A one-to-one reading program offered by GDCC during the summer of 1997 successfully reached a number of the children who originally dropped in just for a meal, but some children were less than enthusiastic about the reading portion of the day. In an effort to reach all of the children at some 50 sites in the 1998 Summer Food and Reading Program, GDCC planners asked the Dallas Reading Plan leadership for help in improving their reading program activities. We selected the Reading To, With, and By model (Mooney, 1990) to involve some of the more reluctant readers. Several of the Dallas Reading Plan's Lead Reading Teachers set about designing interactive training for the volunteers in effective balanced reading instruction.

Making reading fun was one of the basic tenets of the training model for the more than 200 volunteer tutors from Building Blocks (a church group) and Americorp (America Reads Challenge Act of 1997). Volunteers were taught ways to read aloud favorite poems and stories, encourage buddy reading using big books, make big books, and encourage children's oral reading through support strategies. Volunteers were also taught how to establish a print-rich environment using the children's own work.

The success of the training sessions was apparent as judged by the reactions of the children, volunteers, and organizers. Children citywide reported to family members that reading was their favorite part of the day. Building Blocks volunteers, many of whom were teens from local churches, expressed a sense of empowerment because of the training. This potent connection to the community is one that we plan to expand as we seek to develop a new literacy ecology for many children during summer months.

To start your own summer reading and nutrition program, we suggest contacting local church leaders, social support agencies, and youth organizations (boys and girls clubs, the local YMCA, etc.). Urban centers have a number of such agencies that are looking to leverage their resources through partnering. Business-oriented clubs, such as Rotary International and Kiwanis, can also be helpful in recruiting volunteers and securing funding. Our efforts have been boosted by the generous support of several foundations that are interested in literacy. Gifts from US$500 to six figures are not unheard of for a well-designed plan.

The Reading Channel

One of the tools many large urban school districts have at their disposal is one or more "public access" cable television channels from local providers. Dallas Public Schools has five such channels. As a direct result of the DEAR Dallas campaign and the Wishbone partnership, the Dallas Reading Plan was offered its own public access channel by the school district. While production arrangements and offerings are still emerging, the new Reading Channel has much to offer in our family outreach efforts.

During the fall of 1998 we launched the Reading Channel as a support for families in raising literate children. One way this is accomplished is to air each evening during prime time (6:00–9:00 p.m.) alternative television offerings oriented toward positive literacy habits. We learned that, as part of the Public Broadcasting System (PBS) and cable television charters, school districts having a public access channel could rerun at no charge any PBS program from the prior year. Thus, such programs as *Reading Rainbow, Mr. Rogers' Neighborhood, Sesame Street*, and, of course, our friend *Wishbone* could be aired on our new Reading Channel. A regular slate of offerings is planned so that the Reading Channel can become a welcomed friend to families in our district and region.

School districts interested in taking advantage of public access channels should do several things. First, check with the central office administrator responsible for communications and distance learning initiatives in your school district. This person is a valuable resource who will know the details of public access initiatives in your district and the procedures to get things started. If your district is new to this kind of enterprise, then contact the cable television provider(s) in your area directly and inquire as to the public access provisions in their charter. Finally, if you are interested in rebroadcasting PBS television programs like the ones mentioned above, get in touch with your area Public Broadcasting affiliate to learn about how you can partner with them to make your plan a reality.

Refrigerator Reading

Whether engaging in a major reading initiative in a large urban center or in a single classroom, communication with families is critical. Many times adults will say to our teachers, "I would love to help my child become a better reader...I just don't know what to do. Can you help me?" We have found that monthly newsletters for families are a great vehicle for communicating easy-to-do activities to primary caregivers.

We call our newsletter *Refrigerator Reading*, a reference to the age-old practice of putting important school papers on the refrigerator for everyone to see. It is a simple one-page document we send to all 3,000 kindergarten through grade 3 teachers for them to disseminate each quarter. Included are ideas for parents (available in Spanish or English) pertaining to such topics as helping your child self-select high-interest books, read-alouds, how to encourage recreational writing, being a good listener when your child reads, retellings, questions after reading, study tips, and ways to become involved in your child's classroom as a volunteer. We also like to highlight special activities in the community that relate to our reading mission and include humorous tales about school life (like one principal's "No whining" rule).

Reports that some parents collect our newsletters and mail copies to others have confirmed the usefulness of this friendly medium.

The Dallas Reading Plan Internet Homepage

As computers in homes, public libraries, workplaces, and schools have become increasingly commonplace, many organizations are establishing an Internet homepage. We persuaded a talented "Web master" (a "techie" already on the district payroll) to help us design a new homepage (see Figure 4) for our initiative as a distance learning tool for parents, teachers, college researchers, foundations, business leaders, and others frequently asking for more information on reading. The webpage enables people from around the world to access at any time information on the Dallas Reading Plan, upcoming learning events, how to contact Dallas's "reading czar" or other program leaders and teacher-coaches, support materials for assisting children in becoming literate in the home, ways of establishing literacy materials centers in schools, links to other related Internet websites, and many other options.

The homepage is a living document that is constantly under construction and revision and is a terrific tool for serving all stakeholders in the balanced literacy reform effort. We invite readers to "surf the Net" and look us up at http://www.dallas.isd.tenet.edu/depts/reading/index.html.

Figure 4. Dallas Reading Plan homepage

http://www.dallas.isd.tenet.edu/depts/reading/index.html

Family Literacy as the Bedrock of Improvement

Urban centers around the globe often struggle with the question of how to improve the literacy learning of their students. Considering the increasing literacy demands placed on society in the Information Age, we cannot justify anything less than a global call to arms in the war against illiteracy (Wertheimer & Drew, 1998).

For any reading initiative to succeed one must enlist the support of family and community members. We have learned that when parents and other caregivers are provided with helpful information and concomitant reading materials they nearly always respond in ways that help their children succeed. The efforts outlined in this article represent our first steps along a path leading to greater literacy for our children. They are strategies that seem to be helpful for native speakers of English as well as for children who initially are speakers of other languages.

When one launches a major literacy initiative for urban children it is somewhat tempting to believe that part of the struggle will be getting families to join the effort. This is not so. When families send their children to our schools each day, they send to us the best and most precious gift they have. When we are able to offer them quality suggestions for helping their children succeed they deeply appreciate the assistance. They are the bedrock of literacy support for their children. We need to build our literacy efforts and programs upon this bedrock.

REFERENCES

Anderson, R.C., Hiebert, E.F., Scott, J.A., & Wilkinson, I.A.G. (1985). *Becoming a nation of readers: The report of the commission on reading.* Washington, DC: The National Institute of Education.

Reutzel, D.R., & Cooter, R.B. (1996). *Teaching children to read: From basals to books.* Columbus, OH: Merrill/Prentice-Hall.

Reutzel, D.R., & Fawson, P.C. (1990). Traveling tales: Connecting parents and children in writing. *The Reading Teacher, 44,* 222–227.

Mooney, M.E. (1990). *Reading to, with, and by children.* Katonah, NY: Richard C. Owen.

Wertheimer, L., & Drew, D. (1998, May 31). The enemy: Illiteracy. *Dallas Morning News,* p. 1.

Dallas Reading Plan Information
Internet homepage http://www.dallas.isd.tenet.edu/depts/reading/index.html
E-mail rcooter@pigeon.dallas.isd.tenet.edu

Reaching Out to a Diversity of Learners: Innovative Educators Need Substantial Support

Joseph Sanacore

During the past several decades, educators have been experimenting with a variety of humanistic innovations to enrich students' academic, social, and emotional growth. These innovations include mainstreaming, inclusion, and detracking, and their intent is to reach out to all students, especially at-risk learners.

While responding to a diversity of learning needs, educators are simultaneously being asked to raise standards for their students. For example, in New York State, high school students are now required to complete several Regents courses. During the next several years, more Regents courses across the curriculum will be required. The goal of the New York State Education Department is to phase in the all-Regents curriculum so that students are exposed to more challenging standards and therefore are better prepared to enter college or the workplace. This direction concerning innovative efforts and higher standards is taking place throughout the United States.

Since teachers and administrators believe in the value of this direction, they undoubtedly will do their best to accommodate the needs of all students, including those at risk of failing. To successfully reach out to diverse learners, however, teachers require substantial support. Although budget-minded critics will argue that such support is costly, they need to be reminded that an investment in prevention today will eliminate or lessen the expense of remediation tomorrow. Preventive efforts are also sensitive to the emotional frustrations and self-esteem problems associated with remedial instruction. Furthermore, support that is aimed at prevention is well matched with society's thrust to erase illiteracy and aliteracy.

Not surprisingly, educators who receive substantial help are more effective when carrying out worthwhile innovations that increase all students' potential for success. This notion of support is vitally important because students' "at riskness" will not disappear and because the United States government and educational community continue to believe in the efficacy of raising academic standards. The following sources of support are therefore intended as a complement to and a scaffold for teachers and administrators who experiment with different ways of meeting a diversity of learning needs.

Originally published in *Journal of Adolescent & Adult Literacy* (1997), volume 41, pages 224–229.

Curricular Congruence

At-risk learners benefit from instructional activities that are carefully planned and mutually supported by classroom teachers and learning center staff. Unfortunately, many schools provide separate instruction in both settings. For example, in the English classroom, students may explore the theme of good and evil by reading and discussing William Golding's *Lord of the Flies*, whereas in the learning center, at-risk students may complete workbook exercises and other fragmented activities that are unrelated to the instructional theme. Clearly, at-risk learners are more likely to be successful when classroom and learning center teachers provide them with congruent goals, resources, strategies, and skills.

In the October 1988 issue of *The Clearing House*, I discussed the importance of connecting the classroom and the learning center, and I suggested a model that can be adapted to both push-in and pull-out efforts. This model represents an ambitious approach, and it can be a major source of support for at-risk learners. Specifically, these learners receive language arts instruction seven periods a week. Twice a week, the majority of students experience a double period of instruction, while the at-risk learners are enriched with activities that support the language arts program. For example, if *Lord of the Flies* is being highlighted, the classroom teacher might immerse students in interactive activities concerning important themes, concepts, and vocabulary of the novel. Meanwhile, the learning center teacher might engage individuals in a similar instructional focus, while providing support through a prereading plan, structured overview, semantic mapping, or semantic feature analysis.

An important part of this classroom/learning center connection is cooperative planning time that is built into the teaching assignments of the English staff. These professionals are scheduled weekly for 24 periods of teaching and for 1 period of mutual planning with the learning center staff (see Figure). During the planning session, the key players discuss their community of learners and organize congruent activities that support effective learning.

Creating a closer link between the classroom and the learning center makes sense. This approach increases transfer of learning and simultaneously lessens the incidence of fragmented, reductionistic teaching. Thus, at-risk learners have more opportunities to engage in cohesive instruction directly related to their learning strengths and needs. Although curricular congruence is not a cure-all, it is a serious source of support for helping at-risk learners to be successful and independent.

Figure. An English teacher's schedule representing mutual planning with learning center staff

	1	2	3	Period 4	5	6	7	8
M	Eng 9	Eng 9 double period	Eng 9	Prep	Lunch	Speech Arts	Other Voices	Duty
T		Prep		Eng 9 double period				
W		Eng 9 double period		Prep				
Th		Prep		Eng 9 double period				
F		Classroom teacher and learning center staff meet for mutual planning		Prep				

Adapted from Sanacore (1988)

Special Education Teacher as Team Teacher

Similar to the intent of curricular congruence is the changing role of the special education teacher serving as a team teacher. This inclusionary perspective helps learners with mild, moderate, and severe disabilities to be successful in the heterogeneous classroom and, thus, to be genuine members of the learning community. In a chapter of Richard Villa and Jacqueline Thousand's *Creating an Inclusive School* (Alexandria, VA: Association for Supervision and Curriculum Development, 1995), middle-grades science teacher Nancy Keller and special educator Lia Cravedi-Cheng describe their bonding as team teachers, which led to the social and academic growth of both themselves and their students.

Initially, the key players decided to meet at least one period each week for mutual planning. During this time, they focused on building a trusting relationship as they defined and redefined professional roles, discussed content to be covered, planned related instructional activities, and assessed student outcomes. These and other planning agendas set the stage for continued growth with a variety of joint responsibilities, such as having conferences with parents, managing student behavior, and covering the logistics (e.g., setting up labs).

While reflecting on their professional growth, Keller and Cravedi-Cheng realized that successful inclusion occurs when both teachers and students receive support. Especially important for the team teachers were continuous opportunities to plan cooperatively, develop goals, consider flexible roles, maintain personal accountability, and engage in reflection. These experiences helped the teachers to merge their talents, to reaffirm their commitment to all students, and to reach their audience academically and socially. As was expected, both special needs students and their nondisabled peers became contributing members of the learning community.

Similar sources of support are presented in the December 1994/January 1995 issue of *Educational Leadership*, which focuses on the theme of the inclusive school. In her article "Essential Questions—Inclusive Answers," Cheryl Jorgensen describes an interdisciplinary program at Souhegan High School (Amherst, New Hampshire, USA). The learning environment for grades 9 and 10 involves two teams for each grade level, with approximately 85 students in each team. Social studies, science, English, and special education teachers share daily blocks of time—2½ hours in the morning and 1 hour in the afternoon—and these professionals may organize instruction in a variety of ways to accommodate students' learning needs. An important part of these efforts is collaborative planning time for content area teachers and special educators.

Interestingly, special needs students at Souhegan High do not usually require instructional modifications in their heterogeneously grouped classes; however, when support is needed for nurturing full participation, it may be provided by peers, adults, adapted resources, or assistive technology. Individuals also benefit from modified expectations; for example, a physically disabled learner may have his or her lines in a theatrical performance tape recorded by a classmate. When the lines are to be read aloud, the disabled learner leans on a pressure switch, which then activates the lines.

These kinds of positive experiences benefit the entire learning community. When school administrators, classroom teachers, and special educators support these efforts, they enrich learners with opportunities for growth that will last a lifetime.

Volunteers and Paraprofessionals

Another source of help for students and teachers in a heterogeneous learning environment is an "extra set of hands." In *The Reading Resource Handbook for School Leaders* (Norwood, MA: Christopher-Gordon, 1996), Del Patty, Janet Maschoff, and Peggy Ransom provide useful insights about parent volunteers and teacher aides supporting the language arts program. Specifically, these individuals may nurture learning by functioning as effective role models. They can read to students, listen to them read, listen to their retellings after silent reading, ask challenging questions on their reading, coach their efforts, share and monitor reading and writing, develop instructional materials, administer interest and attitude inventories, organize a class newspaper, assist with bulletin boards and classroom displays that encourage reading and writing, and help out on field trips.

Volunteers and aides can make valuable contributions to the classroom context, and their support is vital to accommodate the diversity of learning needs that have increased markedly in recent years.

Patty, Maschoff, and Ransom suggest that administrators, coordinators, or reading advisory boards administer questionnaires to obtain pertinent information for eliciting, managing, and developing effective volunteers and aides. Thus, in responding to a questionnaire that invites community participation, potential support people have opportunities to reflect on such items as "I would be able to read to students" and "I could work on bulletin boards to encourage reading." When formulating a management plan, a major consideration is matching the "right" volunteers or aides with the "right" teachers.

One way of attaining this goal is to have teachers complete a questionnaire related to potential assignments for aides. For example, in responding to assignments like "Administer reading attitude and reading interest inventories to small groups of students," teachers may indicate whether the assignments are extremely important, fairly important, or not important in the classroom. Since support people need to grow and develop, they should be given opportunities to complete items that represent potential workshop topics. These topics include "Conduct activities to help students' reading comprehension" and "Know the characteristics of children with learning problems." Next to the topics, respondents may indicate if they have a great need, moderate need, or little need to learn about the topics.

Well-constructed questionnaires and surveys provide useful information that can lead to a functional plan of action for eliciting, managing, and developing effective volunteers and aides.

Supporting students and teachers with an "extra set of hands" increases their chances of success. This support is especially needed in heterogeneous learning environments, which are enriched and challenged daily by a diversity of strengths and needs.

Instructional Resources

Students' journey toward success also involves natural immersion in authentic resources. All learners, including those at risk of failing, benefit from literacy-rich classrooms cluttered with paperbacks, anthologies, fiction and nonfiction works, dramas and comedies, poetry, illustrated books, "how-to" manuals, bibliotherapeutic stories, talking books, large-print books, dictionaries, magazines, newspapers, and pamphlets. Students are more apt to respond positively to these materials when they are permitted to choose from a wide variety of options, when they observe teachers respecting their choices, and when they are encouraged to read at their own comfortable pace in the classroom.

Being sensitive to students' interests and strengths will also help them to meet content area expectations, especially if teaching and learning are organized around important themes and concepts. For example, if the instructional unit concerns the U.S. Civil War, an individual may demonstrate his or her preferred learning style by reading illustrated materials and by creating a flowchart showing important battles. Others may respond to thematic and conceptual aspects of the study unit in ways that represent their unique styles, as the teacher guides them to focus on instructional outcomes that fulfill curricular expectations. These flexible considerations not only provide immediate learning benefits, but also promote the lifelong love of learning.

Not surprisingly, this flexibility also applies to technological resources, which play a major role in helping students to be successful. Disabled learners, in particular, may benefit from adaptive hardware, such as seating devices, switches, electronic communication aids with voice synthesizers, and computers that scan printed materials and read the text aloud. While these and other hardware adaptations are necessary for individuals to learn effectively, certain software products are needed to meet a broad range of special needs.

In the October 1995 issue of *Technology & Learning*, a panel of experts suggests software for special needs students but acknowledges that much of the software will benefit all learners as well. Among these resources are *Write: OutLoud* (Don Johnston), which is a talking word processor, and *Language Experience Recorder* (Teacher Support Software), which is another talking word processor that reads back learners' writing by a nonjudgmental source. In addition, *Storybook Weaver* (MECC), a multimedia product, stimulates creative writing and can be used across the curriculum. Also worth mentioning is *Student Writing Center* (The Learning Company) which provides opportunities for making choices, incorporating graphics, and producing reports, newspapers, and other documents.

Although appropriate instructional resources can facilitate learning in heterogeneous classrooms, a problematic economy has caused school administrators to allocate budgets for the basic curricula. Thus, textbooks, workbooks, software, and hardware related to basic skills are given top priority status, while resources supporting lifetime literacy efforts are considered a frill. Certainly, this "small-picture" perspective is detrimental to students' immediate and long-term growth because its reductionistic emphasis will dissuade students from wanting to learn and therefore will lessen their intrinsic motivation for developing the habit of learning.

Even with a difficult economy, effective administrators and teachers can secure appropriate resources (both qualitatively and quantitatively) by working cooperatively with the Parent-Teacher-Student Association to sponsor a resource drive. Through coffee klatches, newsletters, and other communication outlets, the PTSA can motivate the community to donate usable print and nonprint materials, software, and hardware. Afterward, a committee of teachers can organize these materials and designate them for content areas and grade levels. Another way of securing resources is to pursue financial support from the school budget, PTSA, teacher and administrative associations, local industry, and material and equipment grants.

A wide variety of resources in heterogeneous classrooms is a major source of support for students and teachers. This effort increases the chances that special needs students and their nondisabled classmates will respond positively to literacy learning and will use it throughout their lives.

Class Size

As learners progress through the grades, they experience a number of transitions, including larger school buildings, seven or eight teachers and instructional periods each day, and larger classes. James Ysseldyke and Bob Algozzine (*Special Education: A Practical Approach for Teachers*, Boston: Houghton Mifflin, 1995) believe that students without disabilities probably make these transitions more easily than learners with special needs. Educators should therefore work cooperatively to provide smooth passages for all students, especially those with disabilities.

An important consideration in attaining this goal is the creation of smaller classes so that teachers can accommodate the strengths and needs of a diversity of learners. As early as the 1950s, the National Council of Teachers of English recommended that class loads for English teachers should not exceed 100. In a section of *Handbook of Research on Teaching the English Language Arts* (New York: Macmillan, 1991), Allan Glatthorn reviews research concerning class size and suggests implications for instruction.

For example, in smaller classes, achievement seems to increase; discipline appears to improve because teachers better manage disruptive behavior, learners exhibit greater self-control, and students are more apt to focus on learning; participation tends to increase because potentially aggressive individuals are enabled to "gain the floor"; teachers' feedback is more likely to improve; and students' motivation and self-esteem seem to improve, while their anxiety appears to decrease.

Surprisingly, smaller classes do not necessarily lead to significant variations in teaching methods (i.e., placing greater emphasis on individualized instruction), probably because teachers do not receive related staff development. Glatthorn concludes "If English teachers are expected to respond to student writing and to involve students in discussion, then the argument about the need for smaller English classes would seem to be ended" (p. 444).

Glatthorn's review of the research has schoolwide implications. As educators across the curriculum continue to reach out to a diversity of students, they need a variety of support. Lowering class size is an important way of helping members of the learning community to contribute their best.

Staff Development

Whether educators are experimenting with curricular congruence, connections between special education and team teaching, volunteers and paraprofessionals, instructional resources, or smaller classes, they need the support of staff development. My experiences in public education and my review of professional literature inform me that teachers and administrators who carry out innovations benefit from staff development options. These options include the following.

- ◆ Full-day sessions. With release time provided by substitute teachers, the professional staff is able to focus on important issues during full-day workshops. These sessions are especially effective when they are teacher led, focus on pertinent needs, are spaced throughout the year, and encourage the application of new ideas to the classroom context.

◆ Study groups. Educators enjoy being equitable members of study groups that highlight collaboration, reflection, and growth. In successful study groups, a number of ingredients are evident, such as purpose, flexible logistics, professional materials, transfer of learning, electronic networking, and broad-based assessment. (For more on this approach to staff development, see this column, September 1993 *Journal of Reading.*)

◆ Peer coaching. Teachers who are interested in using new strategies that benefit their students consider peer coaching to be an important part of staff development efforts that drive the change process. According to Beverly Showers and Bruce Joyce (*Educational Leadership*, March 1996), peer coaching is effective when the entire faculty is involved, when critical feedback is omitted and collaborative activity is emphasized, when the teacher being observed is the "coach" and the teacher doing the observation is the "coached," and when professionals learn from one another by engaging in a variety of cooperative activities that have an impact on students' learning.

◆ School/university partnerships. For more than a decade, the University of Southern Maine in Portland and a group of school districts have effectively merged the worlds of theory, research, and practice. This partnership has progressed through different phases, including having initial conversations, reflecting on the conversations, taking steps to restructure schools, and making changes in teacher education. Ann Lieberman elaborates on this process as well as other teacher development practices in the April 1995 *Phi Delta Kappan.*

◆ Time for collaboration. Busy teachers need time to collaborate. In the September 1993 issue of *Educational Leadership*, Mary Anne Raywid summarized the results of her research concerning how schools provide time for shared reflection. For example, in one school where educators were involved with a new cultural literacy curriculum, the building administrator offered to reduce the school day by 45 minutes on Mondays, Wednesdays, and Fridays if the teachers would contribute another 45 minutes of their own time.

Complementing Raywid's research are Mike Schmoker's findings, which are presented in his recent monograph *Results: The Key to Continuous School*

Improvement (Alexandria, VA: Association for Supervision and Curriculum Development, 1996). Schmoker believes that teamwork is an effective form of staff development and that this kind of collaboration is especially powerful when it is connected with clear goals, data analysis, and time for reflection. This results-oriented context has benefited schools throughout the United States, including the Adlai E. Stevenson High School in Lincolnshire, Illinois. At Stevenson High School, students enter the building at 10:30 a.m. nine times a year so that teachers have time to collaborate.

Providing a variety of staff development options is a tangible way of recognizing, appreciating, and supporting innovative efforts. When schools respond flexibly to their professional needs, educators are more likely to experiment with new strategies that benefit students.

Support Is Vital

Humanistic innovations, such as mainstreaming, inclusion, and detracking, are intended to reach a diversity of learners and are useful for helping these learners achieve success with higher standards. As teachers and administrators carry out such innovations, they need substantial support. The six suggestions described in this month's column provide some of the tools for responding effectively to students' strengths and needs in heterogeneous classrooms.

Because of space limitations, other considerations have not been covered. For example, students need opportunities to gain insights about potential careers. Fortunately, the May 1995 issue of *Educational Leadership* focuses on the theme of connecting with the community and the world of work, and the April 1996 issue of *Phi Delta Kappan* provides a special section concerning the school-to-work transition. These and similar considerations enrich students with both immediate and lasting benefits.

Innovative teachers and administrators need serious support as they reach out to all learners, including those at risk of failing. Unless schools accommodate this need, educators will be unable to help all members of the learning community achieve their best.

Afterword

Jennifer D. Turner and Youb Kim

Despite decades of educational reform, effective and equitable literacy instruction for urban students remains an elusive goal (Anyon, 1997; Delpit, 1995). To truly effect change, we must come to the realization that the challenges that administrators, teachers, students, and parents face in urban schools are not theirs alone; we have a moral obligation to respond to these challenges by rolling up our collective sleeves and digging into the task of transforming inadequate literacy curricula and pedagogies. Indeed, Bill Hammond, cochair of the International Reading Association (IRA) Urban Diversity Initiatives Commission, declares that "There is no more important work of the Association than to ensure that urban youth receive thoughtful and effective reading instruction" (IRA, 2002). We commend IRA and the Urban Diversity Initiatives Commission for their unwavering commitment to urban education, and we believe that *Promising Practices for Urban Reading Instruction* is an important first step in creating a new vision of literacy education for urban students.

Throughout this unique collection, we noticed a recurring theme woven within and across the successful practices and strategies that the authors so compellingly describe. We believe that *ownership* is at the center of effective reading instruction for urban students (Au, Mason, & Scheu, 1995; P.D. Pearson, personal communication, 2003). As scholars from culturally diverse backgrounds, the concept of ownership resonates deeply with our own experiences of acquiring school literacy. As an African American child growing up in Philadelphia, Pennsylvania, USA, Jennifer encountered many teachers who perceived her to be "at risk" simply because she was a minority student living in an impoverished urban community. Similarly, as an ESL student and parent, Youb succeeded despite low expectations of teachers who thought she was "inferior" because her linguistic and cultural capital differed from mainstream America. For us, the process of learning the school-based codes and practices associated with the "culture of power" (Delpit, 1995, p. 282) has been difficult, even painful, at times, and we suspect that other culturally and linguistically diverse urban students have also struggled to become literate in classrooms and schools that seemed unfriendly and alienating.

What made the difference in our academic lives was the presence of a few dedicated teachers who strongly supported our intellectual endeavors and saw our "differences" as resources rather than as deficits. Put simply, these teachers fostered our ownership of school literacy because they believed we were intelligent and competent readers and, more important, that we *deserved* to have the kind of instruction that would maximize our potential. Consequently, it was encouraging for us to read *Promising Practices for Urban Reading Instruction* because we see ownership of school literacy for urban students as a fundamental goal of this work, and as an overarching ideal developed through the 10 children's literacy rights that serve as the framework for this volume.

But how do urban teachers and administrators foster ownership of school literacy for their students? Given the economic, social, cultural, and instructional complexities of urban schooling, how do educators design curriculum and pedagogy that will help students to value school literacy as an integral part of their lives? In what follows, we explore connections between ownership and effective reading instruction for urban students based on the work in this book. Specifically, we illuminate issues of ownership of school-based literacies concerning three groups involved in the process of urban schooling: urban students, urban parents, and urban teachers. Finally, we close with suggestions for future directions.

Ownership of School Literacy for Urban Students

The key to ownership of school literacy for urban students is high-quality reading instruction. Many students in urban schools are subjected to "the pedagogy of poverty" (Haberman, 1996, p. 118), characterized by skill-and-drill instruction, low-level questioning, and an emphasis on remediation. Despite their good intentions, urban teachers may employ these instructional techniques simply because they do not know "what works" with the culturally and linguistically diverse children in their classrooms.

Promising Practices for Urban Reading Instruction offers innovative strategies that teachers at any educational level can use to transform their literacy practice. One of the most critical strategies is balanced literacy. As Schmidt aptly notes in her introduction to Right 2, a balanced approach to literacy instruction can provide urban students with the necessary tools for proficient reading and can enhance their motivation to read. Because a balanced approach promotes skill development within the context of meaningful and authentic literacy activities and facilitates student understanding of themselves as readers and writers, it provides "learner ownership" (Dahl & Freppon, this volume). This same type of student ownership is apparent as a result of the balanced approach to literacy that Tatum (this volume) crafted for his low-achieving African American readers. By explicitly teaching decoding and other skills within the context of culturally relevant literature, Tatum's students made significant gains on the citywide test, dramatically changed their attitudes toward reading, and were well on their way to owning school literacy.

In addition to taking a balanced pedagogical approach, urban teachers who promote ownership of school literacy also craft appropriate reading instruction based on students' individual needs (Right 1). To do so, urban teachers must identify the strengths and needs of their students through alternative assessment procedures (Right 5). Traditional forms of assessment, such as IQ tests; high-stakes tests; and large-scale, norm-referenced standardized tests may have inherent cultural and linguistic biases and may not provide information that is helpful in making day-to-day curricular and instructional decisions (Gunderson & Siegel, this volume; Klingner, this volume). Thus, Serafini (this volume) suggests that teachers use inquiry-based assessments that support reflection on teaching and learning and involve students in meaningful ways.

Beyond employing alternative forms of assessment, crafting individualized instruction also requires teachers to acknowledge, understand, and build on the strengths of urban students. Although urban students may have complex social, economic, and educational needs, they are resilient children with a wealth of cultural and linguistic knowledge. Teachers who facilitate ownership of school literacy design instructional activities that highlight the strengths in these students' lives rather than the weaknesses (Mahar, this volume). For example, many urban communities offer print-rich environments for students, and by taking literacy walks teachers could develop literacy lessons that draw from the forms of print (e.g., graffiti, posters, billboards, street signs) that are personally meaningful to them (Orellana & Hernandez, this volume).

Parental support is another strength that many urban students have; even when parents are in extremely difficult situations, such as living in impoverished, drug-infested neighborhoods and working long hours at minimum-wage jobs, most are still concerned about their children's learning at school and respond positively when asked to support literacy learning through activities at home (Yaden et al., this volume).

Finally, linguistically diverse students also possess strength in their primary language skills (Right 8). English learners who are literate in their first language may acquire ownership of school (or English-based) literacy more easily, because they can draw from their developing knowledge of language, their understanding of print conventions, and their discursive knowledge (e.g., social and cultural conventions, norms, and values) when they begin reading in school (Gee, this volume; Gunderson, this volume; Rueda, this volume). Thus, primary language skills can serve as a "conceptual bridge" to English literacy for urban English language learners when these skills are incorporated into and linked with reading instruction (Gunderson, this volume; Rueda, this volume).

Urban teachers can also foster ownership of school literacy by exposing students to a wide variety of books and other reading materials in classroom, school, and community libraries (Right 4). Urban students cannot take full ownership of school literacy when they do not have access to multiple textual genres. In lower SES urban classrooms, where informational texts were almost nonexistent, providing more substantive experiences with informational texts to lower SES children may enhance their achievement in informational reading and writing and may make these activities more attractive and inspirational (Duke, this volume). Similarly, there is a scarcity of African American literature of high literary and artistic quality in most early elementary classrooms, and all students, not only African American students, need to have access to this type of literature, because it validates the importance of African American people in society (Hefflin & Barksdale-Ladd, this volume). Teachers who select and use more African American literature in their instructional practices affirm positive self-images for African American students, and not surprisingly this affirmation is an essential component of ownership, because it makes reader-text connections more meaningful and fosters a love of reading (Edwards, Danridge, McMillon, & Pleasants, 2001).

Finally, urban students need to have greater access to technology in order to close the digital divide (Right 9). In many urban schools, technology is considered an "extra" that requires considerable time and money to implement into classrooms, but the authors who address this right through their work describe practical strategies for making technology affordable, accessible, and "ownable" for urban students. Instructional materials that are compatible with personal computers and video-game equipment (e.g., Sony PlayStations) could be a viable option for making technology more equitable and, consequently, may enhance the reciprocal influence of school and homes on urban student achievement (Blanchard, Behrens, & Anderson, this volume). Urban teachers can also make technology more accessible to students by incorporating it into literacy curriculum and instruction, and to that end Leu (this volume) and Leu, Karchmer, and Leu (this volume) provide useful websites and other information about Internet workshops that support literacy learning in classrooms. By drawing from technology as an instructional resource, teachers and children can envision new possibilities that will greatly enhance classroom instruction and may foster ownership of school literacy for urban students.

Ownership of School Literacy for Urban Parents

In order for urban children to take ownership of school literacy, their parents and communities must be actively involved in their academic lives (Right 7). This means that it is important for urban parents to also have a sense of ownership of school literacy, because, as Edwards (this volume) observes, parents are their children's first teachers and thus profoundly influence the quality and quantity of their children's literacy experiences. Research suggests that urban parents may acquire ownership of literacy when they collaborate with schools and teachers in ways that meaningfully connect to literacy curriculum and instruction (Edwards & Danridge, 2001; Yaden et al., this volume). Urban principals can play an integral role in establishing these home-school partnerships by taking responsibility as instructional leaders and creating a school culture that is invitational toward urban parents. It is not enough for teachers and administrators to simply open schoolhouse doors for urban parents; they must take the time to listen carefully and thoughtfully to parents' stories about their families, their jobs, and their hopes and dreams for their children in order to make literacy instruction more relevant to students' lives (Danridge, Edwards, & Pleasants, this volume).

Although there are multiple avenues that urban schools can pursue to connect with parents, Nistler and Maiers (this volume) illustrate how family literacy programs can develop strong home-school relationships. Interestingly, these collaborative parent-teacher efforts not only positively affected students' literacy learning, they also fostered a sense of ownership of school literacy for urban parents who had previously felt unwelcomed and disempowered in school. Importantly, the time working with the teacher and their children in the classroom helped urban parents to become more comfortable and confident in the school environment and taught them school-based literacy behaviors for themselves and their children that could be supported through activities at home (e.g., reading, letter writing, cooking).

Ownership of School Literacy for Urban Teachers

Finally, it is imperative for urban teachers to take ownership of school literacy if they expect to be successful with their students. In many urban schools, with their deteriorating buildings, overcrowded conditions, and limited resources, teachers may feel as disempowered by existing reading curricula and instructional techniques as the students (Anyon, 1997; Ayers & Ford, 1996;

Kozol, 1991). Consequently, many urban teachers may believe that they have very limited ownership of school literacy and thus need guidance and support as they begin to develop and enact new professional knowledge about diverse students, pedagogy, and literacy.

Successful urban teachers acknowledge that children have a right to a well-prepared teacher who keeps his or her skills up to date through effective professional development (Right 3), and we believe that this is the key to teacher ownership. In order to develop culturally sensitive pedagogies and improve cultural communication with students and families, urban teachers must first learn more about their own cultural identities by examining the personal beliefs, attitudes, and perceptions that they hold about different groups of people (Schmidt, this volume). Through a deeper awareness of their own cultural values, urban teachers may develop an understanding of how culture shapes diverse students' cognitive activities, social styles, and attitudes toward reading, and expand their cultural knowledge through (a) conducting investigations about students' perceptions of reading, (b) learning more about students' home environments through parent interviews and/or home visits, and (c) developing a flexible interpretation of culturally based reading behavior (Field & Aebersold, this volume). Thus, by "owning" cultural knowledge of self and others, urban teachers will be more likely to educate culturally and linguistically diverse children in a responsive manner.

Although cultural knowledge is an essential component of teacher ownership of school literacy, it is equally important for urban teachers to challenge their assumptions about educating diverse students if they intend to design classroom environments that optimize learning opportunities (Right 10). One way for urban teachers to uncover negative perceptions of low-income minority students and families, and to subsequently change those beliefs, is to work closely with them (Baumann & Thomas, this volume). Often, urban educators mistakenly assume that diverse parents do not have the time, energy, or desire to be involved in their children's academic lives. However, when urban teachers develop collaborative relationships with parents that are respectful and provide useful information and suggestions for promoting literacy development and academic achievement, they begin to realize that there are many culturally and linguistically diverse families who deeply value education and are willing to support their children's learning and literacy development (Cooter, Mills-House, Marrin, Mathews, Campbell, & Baker, this volume).

Another assumption that urban educators need to challenge is the myth that they can fight the battle for effective and equitable schooling alone. Teachers seeking to reform their curriculum and instruction need substantial support from multiple sources, including (a) assistance from special education teachers, volunteers, and paraprofessionals; (b) instructional resources (e.g., smaller class size, substantial reading materials); and (c) staff development opportunities (Sanacore, this volume). Teachers who take ownership of school literacy do not teach in isolation; rather, these teachers recognize that "it takes a village to educate a child," and thus they initiate and sustain cooperative relationships with other educators as a means of promoting literacy achievement. In so doing, these urban teachers acknowledge that children have a right to supplemental instruction from professionals specifically prepared to teach reading (Right 6), and they are willing to develop cooperative partnerships with reading specialists and other educators with special training. Rather than feeling threatened, urban teachers should see reading specialists and Reading Recovery teachers as collaborative consultants who share ownership for each child's success in reading. By listening to one another, coordinating instruction, and pooling their expertise, urban teachers, in conjunction with specialized reading professionals, could provide the intensive literacy instruction and individualized attention necessary for helping struggling readers to own school literacy (Babbitt & Byrne, this volume; Hedrick & Pearish, this volume; Quatroche, Bean, & Hamilton, this volume).

Final Thoughts and Reflections

We have been very inspired by reading *Promising Practices for Urban Reading Instruction*. Not only does this collection of work place urban children at the center of critical conversations concerning educational equity and literacy achievement, it does so in an optimistic and heartfelt way. What we found most refreshing was the emphasis on the affective dimensions of urban literacy education; contributing authors openly and honestly describe a wide range of emotions, perceptions, and thoughts that urban educators may experience as they attempt to successfully educate children within the complicated reality of urban schooling. This suggests to us that ownership of school literacy is an intellectual and emotional enterprise for urban teachers as well as students, and in order to design thoughtful reading curriculum and instruction, teachers must be willing to meaningfully engage with students in ways that touch their hearts and minds.

We believe that creating a new vision of urban literacy education will be one of the most important tasks of the new millennium. *Promising Practices for Urban Reading Instruction* is an excellent starting point, but we must go

further. Two areas that warrant further attention are (1) successful literacy instruction in urban settings and (2) preservice teacher education. We have gained a great deal of insights from studies of exemplary practices; however, we need to understand more specifically how teachers creatively invent pedagogy that meets the needs of culturally and linguistically diverse students. In light of growing diverse student populations, we also need to understand how to better prepare preservice teachers to work in urban schools. As we embark on a journey toward this vision of educational equity, we know that the road will be difficult, but the difference that will be made in the lives of urban children will be worthwhile.

REFERENCES

Anyon, J. (1997). *Ghetto schooling: A political economy of urban educational reform.* New York: Teachers College Press.

Au, K.H., Mason, J.M., & Scheu, J.A. (1995). *Literacy instruction for today.* New York: Pearson.

Ayers, W., & Ford, P. (Eds.). (1996). *City kids, city teachers: Reports from the front row.* New York: The New Press.

Delpit, L. (1995). *Other people's children: Cultural conflict in the classroom.* New York: The New Press.

Edwards, P.A., & Danridge, J.C. (2001). Developing collaboration with culturally diverse parents. In V.J. Risko & K. Bromley (Eds.), *Collaboration for diverse learners: Viewpoints and practices* (pp. 251–272). Newark, DE: International Reading Association.

Edwards, P.A., Danridge, J.C., McMillon, G., & Pleasants, H.M. (2001). Taking ownership of literacy: Who has the power? In P. Mosenthal & P.R. Schmidt (Eds.), *Reconceptualizing literacy in the new age of multiculturalism and pluralism* (pp. 111–136). Greenwich, CT: Information Age Publishing.

Haberman, M. (1996). The pedagogy of poverty versus good teaching. In W. Ayers & P. Ford (Eds.), *City kids, city teachers: Reports from the front row* (pp. 118–130). New York: The New Press.

International Reading Association (IRA). (2002, January 7). *International Reading Association names Bill Hammond as Urban Diversity Initiatives Commission cochair: Commission to help urban youth receive effective reading instruction* [Online press release]. Available: www.reading.org/media/press/press020107.html

Kozol, J. (1991). *Savage inequalities: Children in America's schools.* New York: Crown.

Appendix A: The International Reading Association's Commitment to Urban Education

Carmelita Kimber Williams and Richard Long

To meet the challenges of helping children in urban areas to become effective readers, the International Reading Association (IRA) is committed to helping teachers, schools, and communities address the needs of urban educators. High poverty rates, a highly diverse student population, and a high turnover rate among classroom teachers all contribute to the unique set of challenges facing U.S. urban schools. Children in urban areas need teachers who are skilled in language and literacy instruction, and who possess extensive knowledge about cultural differences, socioeconomic matters, and other issues that affect learning. To support these educators, the Association publishes a wide range of articles and books that are of interest to those working in urban settings (see the annotated bibliography in Appendix B).

In the spring of 2000, the Association established the Urban Diversity Initiatives Commission. The commission was charged with recommending ways to increase the number of high-quality teachers in U.S. inner cities and to improve urban education by

◆ expanding IRA resources directly related to urban schools,

◆ enhancing teacher education to include instruction on the unique literacy needs of urban children, and

◆ expanding the understanding of research on urban education and making it directly applicable to improving urban literacy.

Other goals of the commission included making recommendations for preservice and inservice teacher development, setting a research agenda for urban education, developing teacher education policies, and developing policies for alternative certification programs.

The Association has furthered the work of the commission by sponsoring leadership academies on urban diversity, creating an urban deans' network to focus on the structure of preservice teacher education, conducting research symposia to synthesize what we know and what we need to know about reading in urban settings, having sessions at IRA-sponsored conferences, and forming a partnership with the National Urban Alliance to support the Urban Partnership (UP) for Literacy. The mission of UP for Literacy is to mobilize communities of citizens, educators, and scholars committed to having all pre-K to grade 12 students—especially children of color and those in disadvantaged circumstances—achieve high levels of literacy.

IRA strongly believes that to honor the 10 children's literacy rights outlined in *Making a Difference Means Making It Different: Honoring Children's Rights to Excellent Reading Instruction* and presented in this book, classrooms must be restructured, sufficient monetary investments must be made, and communities must wholeheartedly support reading reform efforts.

Appendix B: Annotated Bibliography of IRA Resources Related to Urban Literacy

Lina Lopez Chiappone

Right 1—Children have a right to appropriate early reading instruction based on their individual needs.

Barone, D.M. (1999). *Resilient children: Stories of poverty, drug exposure, and literacy development.* Newark, DE: International Reading Association; Chicago: National Reading Conference.

> The author defines and examines assumptions about children who were prenatally exposed to crack/cocaine and who have other risk factors that may negatively affect their literacy development. By displacing the existing myths about "crack babies," teachers and parents are able to support learning and see these children as successful learners.

Christie, J., & Perriconi, G. (1998). El juego y sus implicancias educativas en el aprendizaje de la alfabetización. *Lectura y Vida, 19*(1), 39.

> The authors develop the notion of creating classroom learning centers where students learn to read and write through dramatic play.

Duke, N.K. (2000). Print environments and experiences offered to first-grade students in very low- and very high-SES school districts. *Reading Research Quarterly, 35*, 456–457.

> A study investigated whether there are any differences in the print environments and experiences that are offered to children in different socioeconomic status (SES) school settings. The print environments and experiences offered to grade 1 children in 10 very low-SES school districts and in 10 very high-SES school districts were examined. The results revealed that markedly different print environments and experiences were offered to children in low-SES classrooms than their high-SES counterparts. Four conclusions are drawn from the findings.

Mathes, P.G., Howard, J.K., Allen, S.H., & Fuchs, D. (1998). Peer-assisted learning strategies for first-grade readers: Responding to the needs of diverse learners. *Reading Research Quarterly, 33*, 62–94.

> This article reports findings pertaining to the effectiveness of Peer-Assisted Learning Strategies for First-Grade Readers (First-Grade PALS) as a tool for enhancing the reading achievement of different learner types, particularly low-achieving students, representing the range of academic diversity typically present in primary-grade classrooms. Results indicate that all learner types were positively affected by participation in First-Grade PALS, with the greatest gains indicated for low-achieving students.

Neuman, S.B., Celano, D.C., Greco, A.N., & Shue, P. (2001). *Access for all: Closing the book gap for children in early education.* Newark, DE: International Reading Association. The authors detail a study that found a serious lack of quality books in many child-care centers, and that many states do not have clear guidelines for using books to create literacy exposure in child-care settings and prekindergarten classrooms. The chapters highlight trends in children's publishing and the children's book market, detail the authors' study and its results, describe a state that has made excellent progress in early education standards, and give possible solutions for closing the book gap for young children.

Right 2—Children have a right to reading instruction that builds both the skill and the desire to read increasingly complex materials.

Baker, L., & Wigfield, A. (1999). Dimensions of children's motivation for reading and their relations to reading activity and reading achievement. *Reading Research Quarterly, 34,* 452–477.
This study was designed to assess dimensions of reading motivation of fifth- and sixth-grade students and examine how these dimensions related to students' reading activity and achievement. The study demonstrates that reading motivation is multidimensional and should be regarded as such in research and in practice.

Gaskins, I.W. (1998). There's more to teaching at-risk and delayed readers than good reading instruction (Distinguished Educator series). *The Reading Teacher, 51,* 534–547.
This article discusses the evolution of programs at the Benchmark School where, for almost 30 years, children with severe reading difficulties have learned to read. The author addresses students' difficulties reading narrative text, expressing ideas in writing, content area reading, learning sight words and decoding, understanding how to learn, applying strategies across the curriculum, and taking charge of personal style and motivation.

Hadaway, N.L., Vardell, S.M., & Young, T.A. (2001). Scaffolding oral language development through poetry for students learning English. *The Reading Teacher, 54,* 796–806.
This article discusses the importance of providing opportunities for ongoing oral language development for all students, the particular needs of children learning English as a second language, and the unique appropriateness of poetry as a vehicle for providing practice and pleasure in oral language skill development. The authors note that poetry provides a relaxed and pleasant way for students to practice oral language skills.

Ivey, G., & Broaddus, K. (2001). "Just Plain Reading": A survey of what makes students want to read in middle school classrooms. *Reading Research Quarterly, 36,* 350–377.
This article uses students as primary informants about what motivates them to read in their middle school classrooms. The survey indicates that students valued independent reading and the teacher reading aloud, and they emphasized quality and diversity of reading materials rather than classroom setting or other

people. The article considers the access to reading materials in the classroom and lack of diverse reading materials at school.

Lee, C.D. (1995). A culturally based cognitive apprenticeship: Teaching African American high school students skills in literary interpretation. *Reading Research Quarterly, 30*, 608–630.

This study investigated the implications of signifying, a form of social discourse in the African American community, as a scaffold for teaching skills in literary interpretation. This investigation is related to the larger question of the efficacy of culturally sensitive instruction. This approach is offered as a model of cognitive apprenticing based on cultural foundations.

Moje, E.B. (2000). *"All the stories that we have": Adolescents' insights about literacy and learning in secondary schools.* Newark, DE: International Reading Association.

The author emphasizes the importance of building strong relationships with adolescent students and integrating their out-of-school experiences into a curriculum that will engage their learning and help them see a larger purpose to their education. This book draws from the extensive knowledge base and experience of teachers with whom the author has worked, and summarizes related literacy research.

Rex, L.A. (2001). The remaking of a high school reader. *Reading Research Quarterly, 36*, 288–314.

There is ample evidence that students frequently move unsuccessfully from a lower to a higher academic track, but little research into how students successfully make that transition. This ethnographic investigation builds on scholarship in literacy and teaching and learning suggesting that, to be successful, students' identities as readers, writers, and speakers need to be remade within classrooms whose practices are conducive to integration.

Roller, C.M. (1996). *Variability not disability: Struggling readers in a workshop classroom.* Newark, DE: International Reading Association.

Shifting the focus to ability rather than disability, this book offers a fresh perspective and new ideas on the challenging, often frustrating task of finding an instructional approach flexible enough to accommodate the wide variance in students' abilities. The author lays out an instructional framework for working with struggling readers in a workshop setting.

Scala, M.C. (2001). *Working together: Reading and writing in inclusive classrooms.* Newark, DE: International Reading Association.

The author describes how students with disabilities benefit from reading and writing in general education classrooms where literacy is a personal, academic, and social event in which children are immersed all day. The author advocates using a balanced approach that structures these activities in a variety of formats to ensure that children are continually challenged and successful.

Worthy, M.J., Moorman, M., & Turner, M. (1999). What Johnny likes to read is hard to find in school. *Reading Research Quarterly, 34*, 12–27.

Research about the importance of interest in learning suggests that students who have access to materials of interest are more likely to read and thus to improve their reading achievement and attitudes. This study examined the reading preferences and access to reading materials of sixth-grade students from three middle schools in a large ethnically and economically diverse southwestern U.S. school district. Interviews with teachers and librarians along with classroom visits showed that the availability of the most popular materials was limited across schools and classrooms.

Right 3—Children have a right to well-prepared teachers who keep their skills up to date through effective professional development.

Allington, R.L., & McGill-Franzen, A. (2000). Looking back, looking forward: A conversation about teaching reading in the 21st century. *Reading Research Quarterly, 35,* 136–153.

> This article presents a conversation between two researchers and frequent collaborators on studies of policy for at-risk children. The authors share what they learned about teaching reading from studies conducted during the past century and identify themes significant at various points in time that have surfaced again. Here they discuss their views on school choice, teacher development, and mandated instructional materials.

Braunger, J., & Lewis, J.P. (2000). *Using the knowledge base in reading: Teachers at work.* Newark, DE: International Reading Association; Portland, OR: Northwest Regional Educational Laboratory.

> This collection of vignettes, a companion to *Building a Knowledge Base in Reading,* features several teachers in grades K–6 whose work illustrates research-based principles of how children learn to read and write, and the environments that support literacy learning. The vignettes reflect the 13 core understandings about learning to read that are introduced in the companion volume.

Broaddus, K., & Bloodgood, J.W. (1999). "We're supposed to already know how to teach reading": Teacher change to support struggling readers. *Reading Research Quarterly, 34,* 426–451.

> Focusing on the first three years of Reading Partners, this article explores the evolving perspectives of six school members who served as tutors (three first-grade teachers, two Title I teachers, and the school principal) on professional development, classroom language arts instruction, and schoolwide literacy curriculum. This qualitative study was conceived as an examination of a community-based literacy intervention program through teachers' eyes; however, the focus of the inquiry gradually shifted to teacher development and curriculum reform as school personnel became personally involved as tutors.

De Pauw, C., Quiroz, G., & Torres, R.M. (1997). Las matrices de aprendizaje: un texto desde donde construir nuevas prácticas docentes. *Lectura y Vida, 18*(4), 25.

> The authors argue that there is a need to closely examine how preservice teacher education is structured and taught as a basic step toward establishing new and meaningful practices in education.

Farstrup, A.E., & Samuels, S.J. (2002). *What research has to say about reading instruction* (3rd ed.). Newark, DE: International Reading Association.

> The third edition of this respected volume provides current research along with instructional implications that reflect the rapidly evolving professional context in which the research is used. Educators will find information on how to teach students to read based on evidence from a broad base of effective, well-designed research. Topics have been updated and added to better reflect current thinking in the field and address issues that have come to national and international attention for a number of reasons, including the recently released U.S. National Reading Panel report.

Jiménez, R.T., Moll, L.C., Rodríguez-Brown, F.V., & Barrera, R.B. (1999). Latina and Latino researchers interact on issues related to literacy learning. *Reading Research Quarterly, 34,* 217–230.

> The authors present a conversation between four Latino/a researchers and professors dealing with the literacy learning and instruction of linguistically diverse students. The article considers professional development and identity, representation in academe, assessment of linguistically diverse students, current movements in literacy instruction, teaching style/process of instruction, content of instruction, field of literacy, and teacher training.

Stewart, M.T. (2002). *Best practice? Insights on literacy instruction from an elementary classroom* (Literacy Studies series). Newark, DE: International Reading Association.

> Stewart suggests examining real classrooms—teachers and students actively involved in literacy learning—to determine what works in practice. The author encourages preservice and inservice teachers to undertake practitioner research and incorporate reflective practice in the classroom.

Right 4–Children have a right to access a wide variety of books and other reading material in classroom, school, and community libraries.

Brozo, W.G. (2002). *To be a boy, to be a reader: Engaging teen and preteen boys in active literacy.* Newark, DE: International Reading Association.

> When it comes to reading, teen and preteen boys are your toughest students. Solutions are at hand in this one-of-a-kind book that offers ideas for using literature with positive male archetypes to motivate boys to read and capture their unique imaginations. The author demonstrates how to work with adults in the community to positively influence boys' literacy behavior and create conditions that encourage them to read. He also points out that the strategies presented may also benefit girls by exposing them to positive male images that are unlike the stereotypes of masculinity they are exposed to every day.

Condemarín, M. (1997). Tratamiento de la familia en la literatura infantil y juvenil contemporánea. *Lectura y Vida, 18*(3), 23.

> This article presents a critical analysis of the transformation of the concept of family that is reflected in modern children's and adolescent literature.

Cresta de Leguizamón, M.L. (1997). De bibliotecas móviles a bibliotecas escolares. *Lectura y Vida, 18*(4), 37.

> The author describes a library program that helps low-income areas have access to library materials required for school as well as materials for pleasure reading.

Donovan, C.A., & Smolkin, L.B. (2001). Genre and other factors influencing teachers' book selections for science instruction. *Reading Research Quarterly, 36*, 412–440.

> This descriptive study examined the use of trade books as part of the science curriculum, including factors such as genre and teachers' assumptions that influence decisions about the books that they choose to use. Issues addressed include access to reading materials in the classroom, the lack of diverse reading materials at school, and the place and purpose of student independent reading.

Espinosa, C. (1998). La identidad latinoamericana en la literatura infantil del Caribe. *Lectura y Vida, 19*(2), 31.

> The article offers a retrospective on Caribbean children's literature and how it has helped define the Latin American identity through historical texts and narrative folklore.

Leseman, P.M., & de Jong, P.F. (1998). Home literacy: Opportunity, instruction, cooperation and social-emotional quality predicting early reading achievement. *Reading Research Quarterly, 33*, 292–318.

> In this study home literacy is considered a multifaceted phenomenon consisting of a frequency or exposure facet (opportunity), an instruction quality facet, a parent-child cooperation facet, and a social-emotional quality facet. The study looked at a multiethnic, partly bilingual sample of 89 families with 4-year-old children living in inner-city areas in the Netherlands. A variety of measures are used to determine if reading achievement in school was mediated by home literacy. Literacy opportunities in the home, instruction quality, and cooperation quality were found to be significant factors.

Neuman, S.B. (1999). Books make a difference: A study of access to literacy. *Reading Research Quarterly, 34*, 286–311.

> This study examines the impact of an intervention targeting economically disadvantaged children in child-care centers. The program was designed to flood over 330 child-care centers with high-quality children's books, at a ratio of five books per child, and provide 10 hours of training to child-care staff. Process measures indicated enhanced physical access to books, greater verbal interaction around literacy, and more time spent reading and relating to books as a result of the intervention.

Neuman, S.B., & Celano, D. (2001). Access to print in low-income and middle-income communities: An ecological study of four neighborhoods. *Reading Research Quarterly, 36*, 8–26.

> This study examines access to print in two low-income and two middle-income neighborhood communities in a large industrial city. It documents the availability of print in these communities, focusing on resources considered to be influential in a child's beginning development as a writer and reader. It describes the

likelihood that children will find books and other resources in local preschools, school libraries, and public library branches, as well as the likelihood that they will see signs, labels, and logos in public places (spaces) conducive to reading. Results of the yearlong analysis indicated striking differences between neighborhoods of differing income in access to print at all levels of analyses.

Tiedt, I.M. (2000). *Teaching with picture books in the middle school.* Newark, DE: International Reading Association.

Discover how picture books can be used to engage sixth, seventh, and eighth graders in meaningful learning activities. Many of these so-called "little" books are rich with diverse subject matter that offers engaging models for writing. Older students enjoy sharing picture books with younger children and can polish their oral language skills as they practice reading aloud, dramatizing, or storytelling as ways of engaging beginning readers.

Right 5—Children have a right to reading assessment that identifies their strengths as well as their needs and involves them in making decisions about their own learning.

Au, K. (2000). Assessment and accountability. *The Reading Teacher, 54,* 394–396.

This article discusses six books that give a range of perspectives on the issues of assessment and accountability, from the use of standardized reading tests to creating student and professional portfolios. The author states that these books will provide teachers with the knowledge to make sound assessment decisions and with practical suggestions to document student and personal performance and learning.

Miras, M., Castells, N., & Jolibert, J. (2000). La evaluación de la lectura y la escritura mediante pruebas escritas en las etapas de educación primaria (6–12) y secundaria (12–16). *Lectura y Vida, 21*(3), 6.

This piece provides a critical analysis of assessment practices using a variety of data sources for the assessment of reading and writing at the secondary and college level.

Shiel, J., & Cosgrove, J. (2002). International assessments of reading literacy. *The Reading Teacher, 55,* 690–692.

The authors look at why countries participate in international literacy assessments, how reading literacy is measured, what such assessments have revealed to date, and what the future might hold. They note that a particular advantage of international studies is that associations between variables such as gender or socioeconomic status and reading literacy can vary across countries, prompting individual countries to examine their situations.

Solé, I., Castells, N., & Borzone de Manrique, A.M. (2000). Evaluación en el área de lengua: pruebas escritas y opiniones de los profesores (primera parte). *Lectura y Vida, 21*(2), 6.

This article presents data from a research project on assessment practices in reading and writing, including teacher opinions on assessments, analyses of assessment instruments, and the conclusions that were drawn from the results.

Strickland, D.S., Ganske, K., & Monroe, J.K. (2001). *Supporting struggling readers and writers: Strategies for classroom intervention 3–6.* Portland, ME: Stenhouse; Newark, DE: International Reading Association.

This book provides teachers, administrators, and staff developers with research-based practices on the literacy learning and teaching of low-achieving intermediate students. The authors explore the factors that contribute to success and failure in literacy and provide systematic and ongoing approaches for helping students who are most at risk, including low-achieving students and English language learners.

Valencia, S., & Wixson, K.K. (2001). Inside English/language arts standards: What's in a grade? *Reading Research Quarterly, 36,* 202–217.

The writers contend that standards-based reform is a worthwhile endeavor that offers a way to address inequities of the past and to raise the ceiling for all. They maintain that standards-based evaluations are nonpartisan, that such evaluation activities are unlikely to move the quest for standards-based reform forward, and that educators must become a force in standards-based reform. The article examines the reports on standards produced by the American Federation of Teachers, the Fordham Foundation, the Council for Basic Education, and Achieve.

Right 6—Children who are struggling with reading have a right to receive intensive instruction from professionals specifically prepared to teach reading.

Dillon, D.R. (2000). *Kids InSight: Reconsidering how to meet the literacy needs of all students.* Newark, DE: International Reading Association.

The author encourages teachers to view students' actions in light of new data and renew their teaching efforts so that they can meet the needs of all learners. This foundational book of the Kids InSight series details the different requirements of being an insightful teacher at all grade levels, reports the author's experiences conducting research in two classrooms, and describes the interactions of teachers and students in these classrooms.

Fitzgerald, J. (2001). Can minimally trained college student volunteers help young at-risk children to read better? *Reading Research Quarterly, 36,* 28–46.

The study addresses at-risk first- and second-grade students' reading growth as they were tutored by volunteer college students participating in the recent national America Reads initiative. On average, children made statistically significant gains in instructional reading level that could be attributed to the tutoring.

Gaskin, I.W. (1996). Procedures about word-learning: Making discoveries about words. *The Reading Teacher, 50,* 312–327.

This article describes how elementary educators (a principal, a reading supervisor, and two first-grade teachers) collaborated to develop research-based procedures to help at-risk first graders to become "word detectives."

International Reading Association. (2002). *Evidence-based reading instruction: Putting the National Reading Panel report into practice.* Newark, DE: Author.

In 2000, the National Reading Panel completed the most comprehensive review of existing reading research to be undertaken in U.S. education and found that for children to become good readers they must be taught phonemic awareness skills, phonics skills, reading fluency, vocabulary development, and comprehension strategies. In order to aid educators in implementing these components in the early grades, the International Reading Association has assembled a compilation of articles from its journal *The Reading Teacher* that address best practices related to the five essential components.

Leslie, L., & Allen, L. (1999). Factors that predict success in an early literacy intervention project. *Reading Research Quarterly, 34,* 404–424.

The reported studies were conducted over two years to examine the effectiveness of an early literacy intervention project for inner-city children in grades 1–4. Children who were either nonreaders or were one or more years below grade level in reading received small-group literacy instruction from preservice teachers after school for 10 weeks each semester until they achieved grade-level reading. Parents were involved by attending literacy events and reading with their child at home. Children enrolled in the project made more progress after one semester than a group of untutored children. The results and implications are discussed in relation to other early intervention projects.

Vivas, E., & Wolman, I.S. (1997). Prevalencia de desempeño en lectura en escolares venezolanos según tipo de texto. *Lectura y Vida, 18*(1), 17.

The authors present results of a study on the reading comprehension difficulties of fourth-grade Venezuelan students reading a variety of texts, including narrative and expository. The article includes a discussion of how to implement strategies for intervention.

Right 7–Children have a right to reading instruction that involves parents and communities in their academic lives.

Britto, P.R. (2001). Family literacy environments and young children's emerging literacy skills. *Reading Research Quarterly, 36,* 346–347.

A study examined the link between family literacy environments and young children's emerging literacy skills. Participants were 126 African American, welfare-eligible, predominantly single mothers and their preschool and school-aged children.

Jordan, G.E., Snow, C.E., & Porche, M.V. (2000). Project EASE: The effect of a family literacy project on kindergarten students' early literacy skills. *Reading Research Quarterly, 35,* 524–546.

> The article investigates effectiveness of Project Early Access to Success in Education, which includes parent education sessions on assisting their children's developing literacy abilities, at-school parent/child activities, and at-home book-mediated activities. The authors found improvement in language skills, with a strong impact on the children who scored low at the pretest, as well as high levels of participation in the project and high levels of satisfaction.

Meoli, P.L. (2001). Family stories night: Celebrating culture and community. *The Reading Teacher, 54,* 746–747.

> This article describes a program in which each family shares a story in its native language and the children then provide an English translation when the original was a language other than English. The author concludes with the hope that through fostering relationships with students and their families, all can benefit from the merging of the school and home cultures.

Morales, A. (1997). Fronteras socioculturales: usos y prácticas de lectura y escritura de alumnos de la comunidad boliviana en la escuela pública argentina y en el hogar. *Lectura y Vida, 18*(3), 5.

> The author presents a study of the sociocultural discontinuities observed between the Bolivian community and teachers in a public school in Buenos Aires, Argentina. Effects on student achievement are discussed from several perspectives.

Paratore, J.R., Melzi, G., & Krol-Sinclair, B. (1999). *What should we expect of family literacy? Experiences of Latino children whose parents participate in an intergenerational literacy project* (Literacy Studies series). Newark, DE: International Reading Association.

> The book explores in detail the effects of parental involvement in a literacy project on Latino children's academic performance. The authors investigate the ways that parents who participate in an intergenerational literacy project support their children's academic achievement, the ways these children use literacy at home alone and with their parents, and the nature of these children's school experiences.

Rasinski, T.V., Padak, N.D., Church, B.W., Fawcett, G., Hendershot, J., Henry, J.M., et al. (Eds.). (2000). *Motivating recreational reading and promoting home-school connections: Strategies from* The Reading Teacher. Newark, DE: International Reading Association.

> The book addresses classroom-tested ideas, resources, and activities to create motivational tools and home-school partnerships for making literacy learning more effective and engaging. Topics include poetry, cooperative groups, classroom libraries, multiculturalism, reading workshops, peer tutoring, reading buddies and coaches, supporting parents and families, linking home and school, and community involvement.

Rosenberg, C.R., & Condemarin, M. (2000). Culturas orales y alfabetización: un desafío para la escuela. *Lectura y Vida, 21*(2), 18.

> The article analyzes interactions within oral cultures in northeast Argentina, with an emphasis on the cultural discontinuity between home and school literacy practices and how to best address the differences.

Speilman, J. (2001). The family photography project: "We will just read what the pictures tell us." *The Reading Teacher, 54,* 762–770.

> The purpose of the family photo project was to collect evidence about learning in the "life school" of families. The article describes the second session in which people brought in artifacts to tell family stories about learning in their homes. Findings were that families and teachers involved in this project become more aware of home experiences as part of literacy education.

Right 8–Children have a right to reading instruction that makes meaningful use of their first language skills.

Blake, M.E., & Sickle, M.V. (2001). Helping linguistically diverse students share what they know. *Journal of Adolescent & Adult Literacy, 44,* 468–475.

> This article suggests that when students improve their ability to code-switch from the local dialect (African American English) to Standard English, they improved their academic achievement, particularly in science and math. Indications are that future teachers need to be exposed to many different cultures and dialects in terms of teacher preparation.

Cresta de Leguizamón, M.L. (1999). Ciclos temáticos: una alternativa para el desarrollo de la lectoescritura bilingüe. *Lectura y Vida, 20*(4), 26.

> Students in a fourth-grade bilingual school work on developing oral and written language skills within a whole language framework using thematic units. Student-centered lessons incorporated the use of authentic oral and written language and reading, as well as cooperative groupings.

Jiménez, R.T. (1997). The strategic reading abilities and potential of five low-literacy Latina/o readers in middle school. *Reading Research Quarterly, 32,* 224–243.

> Jiménez investigated the strategic literacy knowledge, abilities, and potential of five low-literacy Latina/o students in middle school. Three of the students were bilingual in Spanish and English, and they received the majority of their instruction in a special education classroom. The remaining two students were selected from a bilingual at-risk classroom and were Spanish dominant. Implications of this research include rethinking instructional design and expectations concerning the learning of low-literacy Latina/o students in middle school.

Jiménez, R.T., Moll, L.C., & Rodríguez Brown, F.V. (1999). Latina and Latino researchers interact on issues related to literacy learning. *Reading Research Quarterly, 34,* 217–230.

> A group of Latino/Latina educators discusses various topics relating to the literacy learning and instruction of linguistically diverse students. They discuss pro-

fessional development and identity, the representation of Latinos/Latinas in acad-
eme, the assessment of linguistically diverse students, current movements in literacy instruction, teaching styles/processes of instruction, content of instruction,
the field of literacy, and teacher training.

Kreuger, E., & Townshen, N. (1997). Reading clubs boost second-language first
graders' reading achievement. *The Reading Teacher, 51*, 122–127.
  The authors describe "Reading Clubs," a program designed and carried out by
  two first-grade teachers in which small groups of students (primarily second-
  language learners) thought to be at risk for failure were coached daily. Nineteen
  of the targeted 23 students were successful enough to move with their peers to
  second grade.

Rodríguez, T.A. (2001). From the known to the unknown: Using cognates to teach
English to Spanish-speaking literates. *The Reading Teacher, 54*, 744–746.
  This article considers how if educators view students' first language as a problem that needs to be eradicated, perhaps they make learning English more difficult. The author describes an approach focusing on cognates used with 20 middle
  school students in their first year of a transitional program in south Florida.

Schon, I., & Corona Berkin, S. (1996). *Introducción a la literatura infantil y juvenil.*
Newark, DE: International Reading Association.
  The authors explain why children's literature is significant and explore the many
  different types of Spanish-language books available to young people. Each chapter contains a comprehensive bibliography of books listed at the appropriate
  reading level for beginning, intermediate, and young adult readers.

William, J.A. (2001). Classroom conversations: Opportunities to learn for ESL students
in mainstream classrooms. *The Reading Teacher, 54*, 750–757.
  The article notes that educators should examine the theoretical backgrounds of
  their beliefs to determine how mainstream values affect educational opportunities
  for linguistically and culturally diverse students. The author suggests that educators must carefully combine theory and practice within broader social, cultural,
  and historical contexts to produce reasoned decisions as they guide the academic progress of English language learners in mainstream classrooms.

Right 9–Children have the right to equal access to the technology used for the improvement of reading instruction.

Burniske, R.W. (2000). *Literacy in the cyberage: Composing ourselves online.* Arlington
Heights, IL: Skylight Professional Development.
  This book available from IRA shows how to expand instruction so that electronic literacy becomes an essential component of classroom instruction as students
  learn how to interpret and process volumes of information critically and
  reflectively. The author explains nine interrelated literacies that each focus on a
  particular online communication skill. Included are case studies, teacher tips,

samples of students' writings, definitions, examples of website screens, and lists of Web addresses.

Cresta de Leguizamón, M.L. (2000). De lo analógico a lo digital: el futuro de la enseñanza de la composición. *Lectura y Vida, 21*(4), 4.

The author discusses the impact of digital technology on society and teaching, emphasizing the digital support of language arts through the use of computers and the Internet, particularly in developing writing skills.

Karchmer, R.A. (2001). The journey ahead: Thirteen teachers report how the Internet influences literacy and literacy instruction in their K–12 classrooms. *Reading Research Quarterly, 36,* 442–466.

This article indicates that the teachers viewed the Internet's influence on reading as an extension of traditional literacy skills. The author notes that the elementary teachers noticed an increase in their students' motivation to write when their work was published on the Internet for a greater audience, but the secondary teachers did not find that was the case.

Labbo, L.D., & Reinking, D. (1999). Negotiating the multiple realities of technology in literacy research and instruction. *Reading Research Quarterly, 34,* 478–492.

The writers discuss how the perspective of multiple realities might generate frameworks for guiding and interpreting literacy research in relation to practice. Having suggested why this perspective may be useful, they consider the five goals for integrating technology with literacy instruction that make up their framework. These goals include that new technologies should be used to prepare students for the literacy of the future and new technologies should be used to empower students.

Lunsford, K.J., & Bruce, B.C. (2001). Collaboratories: Working together on the Web. *Journal of Adolescent & Adult Literacy, 45,* 52–58.

Lunsford and Bruce studied how scientists, writers, teachers, and students come together to share their expertise, to construct something more than they might have alone, and to learn from one another in the process. The article notes the powerful collaboration tools being developed and explored in a "virtual workspace" and lists websites where educators can get involved.

Owen, R.F., Hester, J.L., & Teale, W.H. (2002). Where do you want to go today? Inquiry-based learning and technology integration. *The Reading Teacher, 55,* 616–625.

Owen and colleagues describe two projects that incorporated inquiry into urban educational settings. The article offers practical considerations for employing technology-enhanced inquiry in the classroom and discusses broader theoretical issues related to the contribution of technology to literacy learning and motivation when students ask their own significant learning questions, which, in the long run, lead to more questions.

Wepner, S.B., Valmont, W.J., & Thurlow, R. (Eds.). (2000). *Linking literacy and technology: A guide for K–8 classrooms.* Newark, DE: International Reading Association.

This book explores the changes taking place in today's literacy classrooms as new technologies create new opportunities for the teaching of language. This book shows educators and curriculum specialists how to use technology to foster literacy development in K–8 classrooms and how to help prepare students for their literacy futures.

Right 10–Children have a right to classrooms that optimize learning opportunities.

Baker, S., Gersten, R., & Keating, T. (2000). When less may be more: A two-year longitudinal evaluation of a volunteer tutoring program requiring minimal training. *Reading Research Quarterly, 35*, 494–519.

This article describes "Start Making a Reader Today" (SMART), a volunteer tutoring program that helps K–2 students at risk of reading difficulties. The authors found that the program improved students' word reading, reading fluency, and word comprehension, though level of performance at the end of second grade was still much lower than that of average-achieving students. The article discusses issues regarding volunteer training and involvement.

Brozo, W.G., Walter, P., & Placker, T. (2002). "I know the difference between a real man and a TV man": A critical exploration of violence and masculinity through literature in a junior high school in the "hood." *Journal of Adolescent & Adult Literacy, 45*, 530–538.

The article explores ways to help students think critically about violence and masculinity in order to point out options for life beyond their urban neighborhood. The authors build activities around events and characters from classroom literature, striving to bring the seventh graders to a broader awareness of the prevalence of violent masculinities.

Daisey, P., & Jose Kampfner, C. (2002). The power of story to expand possible selves for Latina middle school students. *Journal of Adolescent & Adult Literacy, 45*, 578–587.

The authors describe how middle school language arts and mathematics teachers integrated biographical storytelling about successful Latinas and reflective and affirmative writing with their instruction. The article notes that Latinas face special social and cultural pressures that prompt many girls to leave school without a diploma.

Diaz, C. (1998). La construcción de la mirada individual: experiencia de un taller de lectura y escritura en el Gran Buenos Aires. *Lectura y Vida, 19*(2), 38.

Diaz describes the process of making a storybook written by students from low socioeconomic backgrounds in Buenos Aires, Argentina, as part of a reader and writer's workshop.

Key, D. (1998). *Literacy shutdown: Stories of six American women* (Literacy Studies series). Newark, DE: International Reading Association.

This book explores the way that cultural arrogance and assumptions affect women's lives and their literacy development. The author tells the stories of women from different life circumstances to show the importance of literacy learning in all areas of life and the ways that educators, often unconsciously, shut out students from different cultural or economic backgrounds.

McCarthey, S.J. (2002). *Students' identities and literacy learning* (Literacy Studies series). Newark, DE: International Reading Association.

The chapters highlight the influences of school and, to some extent, home contexts on students' identities as readers and writers, and give numerous implications for practice. McCarthey collected data from three sites in which teachers implemented writing workshop and literature-based instruction in grades 3–6. This book focuses on the students in these sites, who were from diverse cultural and social backgrounds. The author demonstrates the power of the teacher-student relationship, the importance of the classroom curriculum, and the influence of parents and peers on students.

Morrow, L.M. (1997). The effect of a literature-based program integrated into literacy and science instruction with children from diverse backgrounds. *Reading Research Quarterly, 32*, 54–76.

This study determines the impact of a literature-based program integrated into literacy and science instruction on achievement, use of literature, and attitudes toward the literacy and science program. The author finds that literature/science group children scored better on all literacy measures than literature-only group children, who scored better on all measures (except on standardized tests) than control group children.

Risko, V.J., & Bromley, K. (Eds.). (2000). *Collaboration for diverse learners: Viewpoints and practices.* Newark, DE: International Reading Association.

This book brings together several expert perspectives on achieving effective collaboration to accelerate the literacy development of diverse learners. It includes resources for decision making and program planning, including in-depth analyses of collaborative efforts, multiple ways to think about collaboration and its implementation, and examples of collaborative projects that are successfully in place in schools throughout the United States.

Wolf, S.A. (1998). The flight of reading: Shifts in instruction, orchestration, and attitudes through classroom theatre. *Reading Research Quarterly, 33*, 382–415.

The author follows an ethnically diverse third- and fourth-grade urban classroom of school-labeled remedial readers as they moved from round robin reading to the construction of a classroom theatre in which they interpreted and performed literary text. The study finds that children began to see themselves not only as characters and actors but also as readers.

Appendix C: Selected Urban Education Websites

William T. Hammond

Africana.com: Gateway to the Black World
http://www.africana.com
> Africana.com promotes the understanding of black history and culture. This comprehensive site covers African American lifestyle, heritage, worldview, and art. Africana.com also provides original articles written by Africana.com staff writers; top news headlines; commentaries on books, movies, and music; and an online discussion group, TalkBack.

Alonzo A. Crim Center for Urban Educational Excellence
http://education.gsu.edu/CUEE
> The Alonzo A. Crim Center promotes educational excellence in urban schools and cities by creating a "Community of Believers" who will increase life opportunities for children and their families. The center's mission is to develop, implement, replicate, and lead research-based programs that are successful in creating partnerships between schools and the community. The center sponsors a variety of programs and initiatives related to urban education, including a master's degree program specifically for teachers in urban school settings.

Asian American Net
http://www.asianamerican.net
> This website is meant to promote and strengthen cultural, educational, and commercial ties between Asia and North America. Asian American Net encourages high school, college, and university students and teachers to learn more about Asia and encourages Asian Americans to embrace their national and cultural origins. The site provides links to Asian American organizations, U.S. schools that have Asian American studies programs, who's who of Asian Americans, up-to-date news stories regarding Asia, and much more.

Asian American Resources (AAR)
http://www.ai.mit.edu/people/irie/aar
> This site includes links to Asian American organizations; cultural media, such as music, art, and literature; and personal homepages. Users also can sign up for the AAR Forum, which provides a relaxed, polite atmosphere to discuss Asian American related issues with others.

Center for Multilingual, Multicultural Research
http://www-rcf.usc.edu/~cmmr/
> This center, located in the Rossier School of Education at the University of Southern California, provides a base for those interested in instruction related to

multilingualism, English as a second language, foreign language, multiculturalism, and related areas and the opportunity to come together for research and program collaboration. The website covers a wide range of topics, including language acquisition, bilingualism and biliteracy, language proficiency testing, and integrating language and content instruction.

Center for Research on Education, Diversity & Excellence
http://www.crede.ucsc.edu

The Center for Research on Education, Diversity & Excellence (CREDE) is a program focused on improving the education of students whose abilities are challenged by language or cultural barriers, race, geographic location, or poverty. The site offers a wealth of resources—including the center's research findings, products, and tools—and links to urban education resources and topics.

Center for Urban Education
http://www-gse.berkeley.edu/research/urbaned/Center_urban_ed.html

The center supports school-based research and reform efforts that focus on problems and issues confronting urban schools. The website lists the Center for Urban Education activities and contact personnel and provides information on two innovative programs aimed to prepare teachers and principals to succeed in urban schools. In the future, the site will offer an archive of published and unpublished papers and books on urban education.

Council of Great City Schools
http://www.cgcs.org

The Council of the Great City Schools (CGCS) is a coalition of 60 of the largest urban public school systems in the United States that works to promote urban education through legislation, research, instruction, and other special projects designed to improve the quality of urban education. Included on the website are links to other urban education resources; full-text issues of *Urban Educator*, the publication of CGCS; research reports and data; and other special features.

DiversityWeb: An Interactive Resource Hub for Higher Education
http://www.diversityweb.org

DiversityWeb is designed to serve practitioners seeking to place diversity at the center of their schools' educational and societal mission. The site is a comprehensive index of multicultural and cultural diversity resources, including full-text issues of the newsletter *Diversity Digest* and conference papers, ideas for staff and student development, and research and trends in the field.

ERIC Clearinghouse on Urban Education
http://eric-web.tc.columbia.edu

This online archive provides a comprehensive and significant collection of school-based research and links to research on urban education. The site also has a section focusing on education issues in the news.

Index of Native American Resources on the Internet
http://www.hanksville.org/NAresources
>This site provides thousands of links to websites dealing with almost every aspect of Native American life and culture. Current news articles related to Native American issues also are provided.

The Institute for Urban and Minority Education
http://iume.tc.columbia.edu
>The Institute for Urban and Minority Education (IUME) conducts research to better understand the experiences of diverse urban and minority group populations. The site provides information on IUME program areas, IUME-related announcements and news, and a listing of publications written by IUME staff.

Latino American History: A Guide to Resources & Research on the Web
http://web.uccs.edu/~history/index/latino.html
>This site, created by the University of Colorado's department of history, offers links to resources on Latin American history, popular culture, and religion and links to online discussion groups centered on Hispanic American study topics. Latin World and Latino Link are just two of the great resources that provide contemporary cultural information.

Leading for Diversity Research Project
http://www.arcassociates.org/leading/index.html
>Leading for Diversity is a federally funded project whose purpose is to improve the preparation of future school leaders so they can encourage interethnic relations. The site includes resources for educators, reports and publications, and an overview and bibliography of the research project.

The Mid-Atlantic Regional Educational Laboratory: Laboratory for Student Success
http://www.temple.edu/department/LSS
>The Laboratory for Student Success (LSS) is 1 of 10 Regional Educational Laboratories funded by the Institute of Education Sciences of the U.S. Department of Education to revitalize and reform educational practices. The primary mission of the LSS is to bring about lasting improvements in the learning of the mid-Atlantic region's increasingly diverse student population. The LSS site contains briefs about urban education topics and urban education links.

Multicultural Pavilion: Resources and Dialogues for Equity in Education
http://www.edchange.org/multicultural
>The Multicultural Pavilion offers educators, students, and activists many resources on multicultural education and opportunities for interaction and collaboration. Features of the site include a teacher's corner, a research room, and community forums.

National Association for Chicana and Chicano Studies
http://clnet.ucr.edu/research/NACCS
>The purpose of the National Association for Chicana and Chicano Studies (NACCS) is to advance the interest and needs of the Chicana and Chicano community through critical, rigorous research. The website provides listings of

research publications on the Chicana and Chicano community and upcoming NACCS events.

National Clearinghouse for English Language Acquisition and Language Instruction Educational Programs (NCELA)
http://www.ncela.gwu.edu

This site collects, analyzes, and disseminates information relating to the effective education of linguistically and culturally diverse learners in the United States. Resource databases, language and education links, and weekly NCELA news are just a few of the resources that the site offers.

National Council of La Raza: Making a Difference for Hispanic Americans
http://www.nclr.org

The National Council of La Raza (NCLR) strives to reduce poverty and discrimination and improve life opportunities for Hispanic Americans. The NCLR website provides capacity-building assistance to support and strengthen Hispanic community-based organizations as well as applied research, policy analysis, and advocacy.

National Institute for Urban School Improvement
http://www.edc.org/urban/index.htm

The institute supports inclusive urban communities, schools, and families to build their capacity for sustainable successful urban education. The site offers a listing of products, links to websites and listservs of related organizations, an electronic newsletter, and an online database of research and information related to urban education and inclusive schooling.

Native Americans—Internet Resources
http://falcon.jmu.edu/~ramseyil/native.htm

The Internet School Library Media Center's Native American page provides teachers, librarians, students, and parents with access to bibliographies, directories to pages of individual tribes, history and historical documents, periodicals, and general links.

NativeWeb: Resources for Indigenous Cultures Around the World
http://www.nativeweb.org

NativeWeb is an educational organization that disseminates information from and about indigenous nations, peoples, and organizations around the world and that fosters communication between native and nonnative peoples. Teacher resources and other information about indigenous peoples are available on the website.

North Central Regional Educational Laboratory
http://www.ncrel.org

The North Central Regional Educational Laboratory (NCREL) is an organization that provides research-based resources and professional development opportunities to educators and policymakers. Resources NCREL offers for urban educators include the Urban Education Monograph series, CITYSCHOOLS, and Pathways to School Improvement.

Race and Ethnicity Online
http://www.apsanet.org/~rep

> This site is the online home of the Section on Race, Ethnicity and Politics, one of the largest subfields in the American Political Science Association (APSA). The section represents more than 500 political science professors, graduate students, authors, and editors who specialize in the politics of Native, African, Latino, and/or Asian Pacific Americans. The site includes information on the annual conference as well as access to a listserv, resources, and publishers.

Tolerance.org: A Web Project of the Southern Poverty Law Center
http://www.tolerance.org

> The online resources and ideas provided on Tolerance.org promote and support antibias activism, tolerance, and diversity. The resources include daily news related to the cause, resources for parents and teachers, and educational games for children.

Urban Education (Electronic Journal)
http://www.sagepub.com/journal.aspx?pid=213

> This online journal, available by subscription only, analyzes critical issues facing inner-city schools. Annual special issues provide in-depth examinations of the most timely topics in urban education.

Valuing Our Differences: Celebrating Diversity
http://www3.kumc.edu/diversity

> This site provides a calendar of the major ethnic celebrations worldwide.

LC 5128.5 .P76 2003
Mason, Pamela A.
Promising practices for ur